EDWARD ELGAR AND HIS WORLD

Edward Elgar
and His World

EDITED BY BYRON ADAMS

PRINCETON UNIVERSITY PRESS
PRINCETON AND OXFORD

Published by Princeton University Press, 41 William Street,
Princeton, New Jersey 08540
In the United Kingdom: Princeton University Press,
3 Market Place, Woodstock, Oxfordshire OX20 1SY

Library of Congress Control Number 2007924749

ISBN-13: 978-0-691-13445-1 (cloth)
ISBN-13: 978-0-691-13446-8 (paperback)

British Library Cataloging-in-Publication Data is available

This publication has been produced by the Bard College Publications Office:

Ginger Shore, Director

Mary Smith, Cover design

Natalie Kelly, Design

Text edited by Paul De Angelis and Erin Clermont

Music typeset by Don Giller

This publication has been underwritten in part by a grant from
Furthermore: a program of the J. M. Kaplan Fund.

To the memory of William W. Austin
Scholar, Musician, and Teacher

> This, then, is the message, which, knowing no more as I unfolded
> the scroll of it, what next would be written there, than a blade of
> grass knows what the form of its fruit shall be, I have been led on
> year by year to speak, even to this its end.
>
> —John Ruskin, *Fors Clavigera*, June 1877

Contents

PART IV
SUMMATION

Acknowledgments

First and foremost, I must thank Leon Botstein, whose leadership of the Bard Music Festival is masterful; indeed, this series is the direct result of his vision. I am grateful for the support of Irene Zedlacher and indebted to the encouragement proffered by Christopher H. Gibbs. As with all the volumes in this series, the production schedule for *Edward Elgar and His World* came with inviolable deadlines, and so I must express my gratitude to the fine scholars who have contributed to this volume. All the contributors have been cooperative, alert, erudite, and much to my relief, good-humored. I commend my editorial assistant, Eric N. Peterson, for his alacrity, meticulousness, and willingness to work through the night if necessary. I offer thanks to my student Brennon Bortz, who patiently initiated me into the mysteries of editing at the computer. I am grateful to Lauren Cowdery for her tactful but expert advice. I owe a debt of gratitude to Gary Mick, Brett Banducci, and, especially, Marcus Desmond Harmon, all of whom helped me to correct the proofs. It has been a privilege to work with Paul De Angelis and Natalie Kelly, and with Ginger Shore of the Bard Publications Office, as well as with that paragon of copy editors, Erin Clermont.

Among the many archives consulted by the contributors to this volume, I want especially to acknowledge the British Library, the Bodleian Library at Oxford, The Worcester County Records Office, the Faculty of Music Library at Oxford, and the Elgar Birthplace Museum; thanks to other such institutions are scattered throughout. I thank the Academic Senate of the University of California, Riverside, for their practical support of this project, as well as my colleagues and students in the Department of Music who have assisted me in innumerable ways.

Permissions and Credits

Novello & Co. has graciously given permission to reprint musical excerpts from the following works by Edward Elgar: Cello Concerto in E Minor, op. 85; "Chanson de nuit"; *The Crown of India*, op. 66; *The Dream of Gerontius; Falstaff*, op. 68; *The Music Makers; Nursery Suite; The Sanguine Fan*, op. 8; *The Spirit of England;* Symphony no. 1 in A-flat Major, op. 55; Symphony no. 2 in E-flat Major, op. 63; Variations on an Original Theme, op. 36 (the *Enigma* Variations).

The following copyright holders have graciously granted permission to reprint or reproduce the following copyrighted material. Acknowledgments for other works may also appear under some of the figures or in the notes.

Ascension. Stained glass window (1887), St. Philip's Cathedral, Birmingham, Sir Edward Burne-Jones. Photo: Jonathan Berg / www.bplphoto.co.uk

The Golden Stairs. 1880, Edward Burne-Jones, © Tate Gallery, London 2007.

Christ in the Wilderness. 1873 (oil on canvas), Ivan Nikoleevich Kramskoy (1837–87). Tretyakov Gallery, Moscow, Russia, RIA Novostl / The Bridgeman Art Library.

Christ in the House of His Parents. 1849–50, Sir John Everett Millais. Photo credit: Tate Gallery, London / AA Resource, NY.

The Elgar Window and the Elgar memorial plaque, Worcester Cathedral, by permission from Worcester Cathedral.

Isabella, Sir John Everett Millais (1829–96) / © Guildhall Art Gallery, city of London / The Bridgeman Art Library.

"The Murder of Nurse Cavell," from *The War Illustrated: A Picture Record of Events by Land, Sea and Air.* Reproduced by permission of the British Library.

The P. S. Wings in the O.P. Mirror, Walter Sickert, by permission of the Musée des Beaux Arts, Rouen.

Portrait of Cardinal Newman (1801–90), oil on canvas, Sir John Everett Millais (1829–96) / Private collection / The Bridgeman Art Library.

Vesta Victoria at the Bedford, Walter Sickert, Richard Burrows Collection.

Grateful acknowledgment is also made to Furthermore, a program of the J. M. Kaplan Fund, for a grant underwriting the publication of this volume

Of Worcester and London:

An Introduction

BYRON ADAMS

> We begin now to see clearly the Elgar dichotomy: the Worcestershire
> Elgar and the London Elgar, the private Elgar and the public Elgar.
> The division is apparent in the music. The great works of 1899 and
> 1900 belong to Worcestershire and to the private Elgar, accordingly
> they have an authentic ring of truth.
> —Percy M. Young, *Elgar O.M.: A Study of a Musician*, 1955

By all rights, 1912 should have been the crowning year of Edward Elgar's
career, his long progress from provincial obscurity to fame and riches
consummated at last. In this year Elgar and his wife, Alice, whose faith in
her husband's genius had been vindicated so spectacularly, moved into
Severn House, an elegantly appointed home in London designed by the
fashionable architect Norman Shaw. As they took possession on New Year's
Day, Sir Edward and Lady Alice Elgar may have reflected on how far
they had come since 1890, when an earlier attempt to gain a foothold in
the metropolis met with discouragement. During this uncertain and disappointing period in Kensington, Alice Elgar, who was forty-one and
pregnant with her first and only child, had been forced to sell her pearls
to make ends meet.[1] In the autumn of that unhappy year, Elgar and his
family abandoned London, retiring once again into the dull routines of
provincial Worcestershire. Some twenty-two years later, their situation
took the sting from memories of earlier struggles: the Elgars had arrived,
and in a style befitting Britain's leading composer. As their daughter,
Carice, later reminisced, Severn House, grand as it might be, was "by no
means everybody's house as it would only accommodate a small family
such as ours, as everything was sacrificed to the long stately corridor and
the large music room and annexe, a large dining room and large basement,

two large bedrooms and three quite small ones, and two even smaller for the staff."[2]

Here a proud Lady Elgar held "at homes" on Saturday afternoons, attracting eminent guests such as Henry James, George Bernard Shaw, and Arthur Nikisch.[3] Sir Edward was less sanguine than his wife about the move to London, however. When flighty Dora Penny, portrayed as "Dorabella" in the tenth of the *Enigma* Variations, first entered Severn House, she enthused to the composer, "You *are* in clover here." Elgar replied darkly, "I don't know about clover—I've left that behind at Hereford—but Hereford is too far from London; that's the trouble."[4]

Elgar's forebodings proved, alas, all too prescient. Severn House, furnished in part through the generosity of wealthy friends such as Edward Speyer and Frank Schuster, was expensive—ruinously so. Projects such as *The Crown of India*, op. 66 (1912), a sumptuous masque composed by Elgar for Oswald Stoll's lavish music hall, the Coliseum Theatre, were undertaken in part to provide much needed cash.[5] Elgar, who had become accustomed to ecstatic receptions for his compositions, such as occurred with both the First Symphony in 1908 and the Violin Concerto in 1910, was dismayed that his Second Symphony had garnered a much more restrained response from audiences and critics. At the 1911 premiere, he exclaimed in dismay to his friend W. H. Reed, "What is the matter with them, Billy? They sit there like a lot of stuffed pigs."[6]

Under the strain, Elgar's health, never very robust, began to fray. On May 28, Alice Elgar wrote in her diary, "E. very uneasy about noise in the ear."[7] Elgar was diagnosed with Ménière's disease, a mysterious illness of the inner ear that often particularly affects middle-aged men. The composer's case of this chronic illness seems to have been confined to episodes of vertigo and tinnitus without significant loss of hearing, although hearing loss can, and often does, manifest itself in some sufferers. As Ménière's disease is made worse by adrenalin release, it is not surprising that Elgar suffered with particular intensity during this worrisome time, and the trauma of the diagnosis itself may have exacerbated matters.[8]

But all of these problems—finances, illness, changes of musical fashion—paled into insignificance in August of 1914, when the familiar world came crashing down around his and everyone else's ears. From the windows of the frigid Severn House (virtually impossible to heat due to wartime fuel shortages), the Elgars watched the war intrude into the night skies over London: in her diary entry for September 8, 1915, Alice Elgar noted that she "ran to the window and then fled out to look through other windows . . . The sky was lit by flying searchlights—part of Zeppelin visible like a gilt box, and star-like shells bursting more or less near it, and the boom of guns sounding!"[9] Worn out from composing music to support the war effort, and battered by fluctuating war news as well as by the disruptions to concert life that inevitably brought financial disruptions in their wake, the composer continued to suffer from ill health. Elgar may have experienced a severe episode of vertigo related to Ménière's disease during a train journey in April 1916, and in March 1918 he had a tonsillectomy, at that time an acutely painful operation for a man of sixty-one.[10] In uncertain health and upset by the war, Elgar sought refuge in the countryside, in 1918 renting a very modest cottage in Sussex, "Brinkwells," literally in the middle of nowhere. Here his creative faculties were renewed, and he completed the Cello Concerto as well as what William W. Austin called "the astonishing trilogy of chamber music."[11]

Elgar's retreat from London to rural Sussex in the face of wartime anguish might at first seem evidence for Percy Young's construction, expressed in the headnote, which divides the composer into the public poet who lived in metropolitan splendor at Severn House and the private artist alone with his deepest, most authentic thoughts amidst the Malvern Hills. Young's vision of a bifurcated Elgar remains popular, and similar rhetoric shows up in analyses by commentators such as Frank Howes, who divides the composer into "the Elgar who writes for strings and the Elgar who writes for brass."[12] The work of this protean composer cannot be parsed neatly, however. Elgar was deeply torn about his roots in Worcestershire: between his first unsuccessful 1890 sojourn in London and the success in 1899 of the Variations on an Original Theme, op. 36—the *Enigma* Variations—he spent a great deal of time in the West Midlands bemoaning his fate as an obscure provincial musician hampered by his status as a tradesman's son and a Roman Catholic.[13] Elgar's friend and employer Rosa Burley recalled that "he had at this time, and indeed never lost, a marked Worcestershire accent and was not then a young man of any particular distinction, yet he had the habit of speaking of Malvern in the condescending manner of a country gentleman condemned to live in a suburb."[14] In fact, the young Elgar ached to get to London. As an aspiring youth he scrimped and saved enough money to take violin lessons in London from Adolphe Pollitzer, and once in the capital would attend concerts avidly. Until the mid-1920s, he continued to do so whenever he was in London. Without the varied musical venues of the metropolis, from concert halls to the soirees held in the London salons of influential patrons such as Frank Schuster, Elgar could hardly have attained either fame or honors so rapidly after 1899.

More to the point, Elgar's music simply cannot be divided up neatly into the extroverted urban and the introspective—and thereby somehow more authentically "English"—rural. Simple geography belies a conven-ient division into the pastoral or vulgarly imperial, for Elgar wrote his lively, brassy musical love letter to the capital, the *Cockaigne* Overture, op. 40 (1901, and suggestively subtitled "In London Town") while residing in Malvern. Indeed, nearly all of Elgar's public and populist composi-tions, including all five of the *Pomp and Circumstance* marches, were composed in the West Midlands, and his anguished and, in spite of the large orchestral and choral forces employed, intimate reaction to the war, *The Spirit of England*, op. 80 (1915–17), was mainly composed in London. Interestingly, the most nakedly autobiographical and most private of his scores, *The Music Makers*, op. 69 (1912), was finished in the city. The day that Elgar completed this score, the self-dramatizing composer wrote to his friend Alice Stuart-Wortley: "I sent the last page to the printer . . . I wandered alone onto the [Hampstead] heath—it was bitterly cold—I wrapped myself in a thick overcoat & sat for two minutes, tears streaming out of my cold eyes and loathed the world."[15]

After Elgar's death in 1934, Vaughan Williams, Howes, and others sought to remold his history closer to their own ideological desires, co-opting Elgar's posthumous reputation for their own brand of English musical nationalism. In an obituary tribute penned in 1935 for a special memorial issue of *Music and Letters*, Vaughan Williams eulogized Elgar to suit his own agenda: "He has that peculiar kind of beauty which gives us, his fel-low countrymen, a sense of something familiar—the intimate and personal beauty of our own fields and lanes." Later in the same tribute, Vaughan Williams asserted that Elgar achieved a "bond of unity" with English lis-teners "not when he is being deliberately 'popular,' as in *Land of Hope and Glory* or *Cockaigne*, but at those moments when he seems to have retired into the solitude of his own sanctuary."[16] In the same issue of *Music and Letters*, Howes divided the composer's oeuvre into private "strings" and public "brass." Such critics as Howes, faintly embarrassed by Elgarian exu-berance, tended to prefer the introspective, pastoral music for "strings," especially the Introduction and Allegro, op. 47 (1904–5), a work in which the composer comes tantalizingly close to quoting a Welsh folk tune.[17] Such efforts to recruit Elgar posthumously into their ranks of the "English Musical Renaissance" were doomed to fail, especially in the face of Elgar's quite public lack of interest in all of the signifiers that marked (to a greater or lesser degree) renaissance composers such as Vaughan Williams. As Elgar's friend W. H. Reed has testified, the composer "had no great affec-tion for the Elizabethan composers . . . He liked Purcell, but would not join in the furore about Tudor music that arose amongst a certain set of young composers . . . He would not rave about folk-tunes . . . he held that the business of a composer is to compose, not to copy."[18] Indeed, Elgar once exclaimed forthrightly, "I write the folk songs of this country."[19]

Rather than espousing an overt ideology, many biographers have preferred to concentrate on the composer's fascinating, contradictory, and infuriating personality. For some authors, Elgar has served as a pretext for indulging in an ill-advised nostalgia about the Edwardian era—actually a time of rapid scientific change and political upheaval—as if the entire period was a luxuriant perpetual summer before the carnage of the First World War. Of the reign of the grossly self-indulgent Edward VII, one distinguished Elgarian scholar once wrote that "life was more leisurely then, the countryside less spoilt, birds and butterflies more numerous, gardens more scented, most human beings less sophisticated and cynical. . . . There was *style* [author's emphasis] in that era and most of all a degree of innocence and charm which was to blasted away for ever [*sic*] by the First World War."[20] All of this expensive loveliness was enjoyed by a tiny percentage of the British population, however; the scented gardens and unspoiled countryside would have been an alien environment to industrial laborers working six days a week in "dark satanic mills" that spewed out pollution on an unprecedented scale.[21] Upward mobility was much less common than in today's Britain, and the process was extremely painful, as the diaries and letters of those working-class men and women who did better their lot (including Elgar himself) eloquently attest.

Recently, however, musicologists studying Elgar have begun to plot a course to avoid the seductions of nostalgia. Building on a foundation laid by Robert Anderson, Diana McVeagh, Jerrold Northrop Moore, James Hepokoski, Julian Rushton, and others, these scholars have started to examine Elgar using tools provided by critical theory, colonialist studies, and revisionist history, as well as intriguing multivalent approaches in music theory. A number of monographs and essay collections on Elgar have been published in recent years, encouraged in part by such distinguished journals as *Music and Letters*, *The Musical Times*, and, above all, *19th-Century Music*, in whose pages a series of searching articles on this British composer, some quite provocative, have appeared over the past few years. The essays that constitute *Edward Elgar and His World* advance this re-evaluation of the composer and his music by studying him in a series of different contexts—his worlds, so to speak. While the essays in this book are grouped by their relation to either Worcester or London, the essays themselves often suggest how porous such boundaries were for him (and are for us), as Elgar frequently seems to have a foot planted in each, unsure exactly to which world, if any, he really belonged.

Elgar's ambivalent vacillations between town and country, faith and doubt, high and low, set off resonances that chime from essay to essay in ways both revealing and unexpected. Charles Edward McGuire, in the first chapter of the "Worcester" section of this book, investigates Elgar's cultural Catholicism; Rachel Cowgill, in the final chapter of the "London" section, illuminates the ways in which Elgar's Catholicism pervaded his reactions to the First World War and affected the creation of his "war requiem," *The Spirit of England*. Matthew Riley also touches upon Elgar's early Catholicism in the context of the composer's boyhood in Worcester and explores ways that this and other factors may have contributed to the view of Elgar as an "escapist" composer; both Riley and Cowgill use books by Elgar's contemporary H. G. Wells to explicate aspects of the composer's personality and work. In a counterpoint to McGuire's research on Elgar's Catholic education, I explore how the composer's self-tutelage, manifested in childhood and encouraged by his mother, acted both to tie him to and to liberate him from the modest class position into which he was born. Nalini Ghuman and Deborah Heckert organize their essays around Elgar's masque, *The Crown of India*, but while Ghuman uses the score to elucidate the fraught question of Elgar's possible collusions with imperialism, Heckert provides a portrait of the composer as a "public poet" who embraced modernity by entering into the vital popular culture of the Edwardian music halls. Daniel M. Grimley's essay on Elgar's musical populism, and the attendant charges of "vulgarity" leveled against the composer, might be read profitably alongside Aidan J. Thomson's lively investigation of those contemporary critics who were less than enamored of Elgar's music. While Thomson, Heckert, and Ghuman place Elgar in the context of his public life, especially in urban settings, Sophie Fuller demonstrates how a web of private social and musical connections served Elgar's career and molded his music. The world revealed by Fuller stands in contrast to the private spaces that the composer inhabited as a boy in Worcester, especially the uneasy intimacy of his family circle. It is to be hoped that readers will make many such connections throughout this volume, enriching their understanding of Elgar's music and character. By design, the two "documents" chapters are placed in the center of *Edward Elgar and His World*, functioning as a bridge between the two worlds: Aidan J. Thomson's reception history of Elgar's oratorio, *The Apostles*, looks back toward Worcester, the Three Choirs Festival, and the choral tradition of the West Midlands; Alison I. Shiel's documentation of the Violin Concerto looks ahead toward one of the composer's greatest triumphs in the concert halls of London.

As is customary with this series, Leon Botstein provides a summation that brings together many of the issues discussed throughout the volume.

Botstein connects Elgar's aesthetics and ambitions to the work of Arnold, Longfellow, and Ruskin, as well as to the canvases of the Pre-Raphaelite painters Millais and Burne-Jones. Furthermore, Botstein aptly views Elgar's life and work though the lens provided by the writings of Cardinal Newman, whose poem "The Dream of Gerontius" provided the libretto for the composer's great oratorio. By providing a broad context that engages specifically with Elgar's cultural Catholicism, Botstein's thoughtful peroration suggests paths for future research.

Did Elgar ever decide between the life represented by London and that of Worcester? By 1919, he realized that he could not maintain Severn House, and tried to sell it; he did succeed in finding a buyer—who paid a disappointingly low sum—a year after his wife's death in 1920.[22] Thus Elgar's second experiment at living in London came to an end more melancholy than the first. For the last fourteen years of his life, Elgar lived mostly in comfortable country houses, enduring fluctuations in musical fashion that often relegated his music to an earlier, pre-war age. Although his output as a composer slowed drastically after his wife's death, it is an exaggeration to say that he did not continue to compose: who among admirers of Elgar's music would choose to renounce such exquisite occasional works as *The Nursery Suite* (1931)? The aging composer showed a certain enterprise by embracing new technologies such as radio broadcasting and the phonograph recording. In the years after Lady Elgar's death, he set about creating a performing tradition for his music based on his own recordings, surely one of the first composers to do so.

Near the end of his life, riddled with the cancer that would kill him, Elgar asked to be cremated and have his ashes scattered at the confluence of the Severn and Teme rivers.[23] Unfortunately, this touching and wholly appropriate wish, along with his urgent request that his desultory sketches for a Third Symphony be burned, was shown no respect by his daughter and by his supposedly loyal friends. In the end, he was buried with his wife in the dreary churchyard of St. Wulstan's Catholic Church in Little Malvern, and the Third Symphony was completed later by other hands, dishonoring his memory.[24]

To what world did Elgar finally give his allegiance? He was happy neither in the West Country, where he yearned for the plaudits of London, nor in the great city, where he cast a nostalgic halo of prelapsarian innocence around his childhood in Worcester. Instead he internalized both places, importing aspects of London and Worcester into his true homeland, that of his imagination. While Elgar was composing his major works in the first decades of the twentieth century, Marcel Proust—with whom the English composer shared at least one acquaintance, Gabriel Fauré—was gradually discovering within himself the vast landscape of his *roman fleuve, À la recherche du temps perdu*. Describing a septet created by his fictional composer Vinteuil, Proust writes eloquently of the mysterious imaginary world inhabited by composers. His words may offer a key to understanding Elgar's tormented life and appreciating his enduring work: "Each artist seems thus to be the native of an unknown country, which he himself has forgotten, and which is different from that whence another great artist, setting sail for the earth, will eventually emerge. . . . Composers do not actually remember this lost fatherland, but each of them remains all his life unconsciously attuned to it; he is delirious with joy when he sings in harmony with his native land, betrays it at times in his thirst for fame, but then, in seeking fame, turns his back on it, and it is only by scorning fame that he finds it when he breaks out into that distinctive strain the sameness of which—for whatever its subject it remains identical with itself—proves the permanence of the elements that compose his soul."[25]

NOTES

1. Michael De-La-Noy, *Elgar the Man* (London: Allen Lane, 1983), 55.

2. Percy M. Young, *Alice Elgar: Enigma of a Victorian Lady* (London: Dennis Dobson, 1978), 167.

3. Jerrold Northrop Moore, *Edward Elgar: A Creative Life* (Oxford: Oxford University Press, 1984), 631, 646.

4. Mrs. Richard Powell (Dora Penny), *Edward Elgar; Memories of a Variation*, 4th ed., rev. and ed. Claud Powell (Aldershot: Scolar Press, 1993), 119.

5. Felix Barker, *The House that Stoll Built: The Story of the Coliseum Theatre* (London: Frederick Muller Ltd., 1957), 179.

6. Quoted in Robert Anderson, *Elgar* (New York: Schirmer Books, 1993), 102.

7. Moore, *Elgar: A Creative Life* (Oxford: Oxford University Press, 1984), 630.

8. Both Jerrold Northrop Moore and Michael Kennedy have cast doubt whether or not Elgar really was suffering from Ménière's disease. Moore opines that the composer's giddiness might have been "only the symptom of a deep desire to escape," while Kennedy declares that a tonsillectomy that Elgar had in 1917 effected a cure, as the composer "was not afflicted by deafness during the remaining sixteen years of his life." See Moore, *Elgar: A Creative Life*, 630 and Michael Kennedy, *The Life of Elgar* (Cambridge: Cambridge University Press, 2004), 153. Both writers ignore the complaints Elgar voiced throughout his later life, of distracting noises in his ear and debilitating episodes of giddiness, which are just as much symptoms of Ménière's as progressive deafness. One such instance is recorded in a letter from Carice Elgar to Alice Stuart-Wortley posted on 2 June 1920: "It was arranged that [Elgar] should go to his sister yesterday, but he had another giddy attack in the morning . . . The Dr. says he *is* better today, but wants to keep him

quiet a little longer . . . It is so distressing this giddiness again—& depresses him so." Jerrold Northrop Moore, ed., *Edward Elgar: The Windflower Letters. Correspondence with Alice Caroline Stuart Wortley and Her Family* (Oxford: Clarendon, 1989), 241.

9. Andrew Neill, "Elgar's War: From the Diaries of Lady Elgar, 1914–1918," in *Oh, My Horses! Elgar and the Great War,* ed. Lewis Foreman (Rickmansworth: Elgar Editions, 2001), 29.

10. According to Alice Elgar's diary of 8 April 1916, before catching the train, her husband had said "he felt giddy & was not sure he would go." Elgar was befriended in his distress by a concerned army officer, Captain Dillon, and spent time in a nursing home. See Moore, *Elgar: A Creative Life*, 695.

11. William W. Austin, *Music in the 20th Century: From Debussy through Stravinsky* (New York: W. W. Norton, 1966), 87.

12. Frank Howes, "The Two Elgars," *Music and Letters* 16, no. 1 (January 1935): 26–29, reprinted in *An Elgar Companion,* ed. Christopher Redwood (Ashbourne: Sequoia Publishing, 1982), 259.

13. See Rosa Burley (and Frank Carruthers), *Edward Elgar: The Record of a Friendship,* (London: Barrie & Jenkins, 1971), 27–28, 38.

14. Ibid., 25–26.

15. Letter of 19 July 1912 in Jerrold Northrop Moore, *Windflower Letters*, 103.

16. Ralph Vaughan Williams, "What Have We Learnt from Elgar?" *Music and Letters* 16, no. 1 (January 1935): 13–19, reprinted in Ralph Vaughan Williams, *National Music and Other Essays*, 2nd ed., ed. Michael Kennedy (Oxford: Oxford University Press, 1987), 248–55.

17. Howes, "The Two Elgars" in Redwood, *Elgar Companion*, 259.

18. W. H. Reed, *Elgar as I Knew Him* (Oxford: Oxford University Press, 1989), 86–87.

19. Quoted in Michael Kennedy, *Portrait of Elgar* (Oxford: Oxford University Press, 1968), 74.

20. Michael Kennedy, *The Life of Elgar* (Cambridge: Cambridge University Press, 2004), 2.

21. At Renishaw, the stately home of the Sitwell family, the lawns and gardens were covered with thick black coal dust from neighboring iron foundries for most of the Edwardian and Georgian periods; see Philip Ziegler, *Osbert Sitwell* (New York: Alfred A. Knopf, 1999), 15.

22. Moore, *Elgar: A Creative Life*, 745–46, 760.

23. Ibid., 823.

24. This rage for "completing" unfinished scores by Elgar, unleashed by the completion of the Third Symphony, now includes a sixth *Pomp and Circumstance* march and a piano concerto, both based on the most slender of sketch materials.

25. Marcel Proust, *Remembrance of Things Past: The Captive*, trans. C. K. Scott Moncrieff and Terence Kilmartin (New York: Random House, 1982), 258–59.

PART I
WORCESTER

Measure of a Man:

Catechizing Elgar's Catholic Avatars

CHARLES EDWARD McGUIRE

In Memoriam (I): The Pan-Christian Avatar, or "What Is the Meaning of Prayers for the Dead?"

In the back of the nave of Worcester Cathedral is the Elgar Window, a memorial to the composer Edward Elgar. This window is an adornment the cathedral holds with pride: besides the requisite postcards, pamphlets, and Pitkin guides for sale in the gift shop, signs pointing the way to the window are attached to the walls of the cathedral itself, greeting visitors as they enter from the north door. The window, designed by Archibald Nicholson, was the result of an appeal by Ivor Atkins (friend of Elgar's and longtime organist of Worcester Cathedral) and the dean of the cathedral, William Moore-Ede. Its construction proceeded rapidly in the ancient building, and the dedication occurred on September 3, 1935 at the Worcester meeting of the Three Choirs Festival, a little over a year after Elgar's death. As was fitting for a fallen cultural hero, Viscount Cobham, then Lord Lieutenant of Worcester, unveiled the memorial.[1]

The Elgar window is an idealized representation of several scenes from *The Dream of Gerontius*. It is constructed of three panels, capped by six smaller arched windows (figure 1). In the center, Gerontius appears in two manifestations. In the lowest panel, he is the sick, dying old man from Part I of the oratorio. His attendants pray for him, underscored by the text "Go forth upon thy journey, Christian Soul" (Part I, rehearsal number 69). This prayer sends the viewer into the second segment of the window above, where Gerontius, transformed into the Soul, is borne aloft toward the throne of Christ by an obviously masculine Angel.[2] Surrounding the throne, right, left, and above, are other angels hovering around a rainbow; they sing a hymn (from Part II of *Gerontius*, rehearsal number 60), "Praise to the

Figure 1. The Elgar Window, Worcester Cathedral.

Holiest in the height, and in the depths be praise." The window's side panels feature holy figures, including local saints with nationalistic connotations—Dunstan, Oswald, and Wulstan—the musical figures Saint Cecilia and Gregory the Great, plus a number of the persons mentioned in the Part I prayers of *Gerontius,* which are labeled for those not familiar with popular hagiographic iconography.[3] Close by the window is a more specific memorial plaque (figure 2), with the inscription "Edward Elgar O.M.,

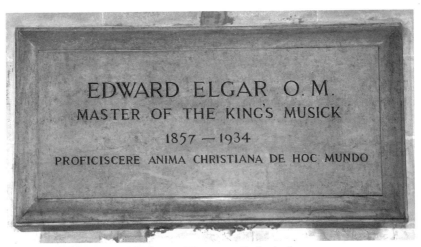

Figure 2. Elgar memorial plaque, Worcester Cathedral.

Master of the King's Musick, 1857–1934, Proficiscere Anima Christiana De Hoc Mundo." This Latin phrase, drawn from the liturgy, is sung by the Priest at the end of the first part of *Gerontius* (Part I, rehearsal number 68).

For the window's dedication, "Nimrod" from the Variations on an Original Theme, op. 36 (the *Enigma* Variations) followed Ludwig van Beethoven's *Drei Equale* for trombones. An afternoon performance of *The Dream of Gerontius* (in the time slot traditionally reserved at the Three Choirs Festival for Felix Mendelssohn's *Elijah*) completed the day's events.[4]

That these memorials were appropriate to Elgar is not in question. After all, at the time of his death on February 23, 1934, he was Britain's "official composer," a status publicly acknowledged by his being made a baronet and awarded the Order of Merit, and in his position as Master of the King's Musick. Even if his music was not at the time as revolutionary or relevant as that of a younger generation of British composers, the program to proclaim him as "essentially English" or even "quintessentially English"—and therefore a totem of nationalism—had already begun.[5] Worcester was proud of its native son, and there was no place more appropriate to begin memorializing him than within the walls of its most famous building.

Yet both Elgar's memorial window and plaque would not have been deemed appropriate in Worcester Cathedral at the time of the premiere of *Gerontius* in 1900. After the English Reformation, the cathedral had become an Anglican building. Elgar at his own death was at least nominally a practicing Catholic and the texts chosen for both memorials were from "The Dream of Gerontius," a poem by the notorious nineteenth-century Catholic convert, Cardinal John Henry Newman. Although Elgar softened some of the doctrinal edges of the poem, his oratorio remained a celebration of mystical, even fervent Catholicism—so much so that its performance was banned for nearly a decade in Gloucester Cathedral as "inappropriate," and performances in the Anglican cathedrals at Worcester and Hereford took place only after large segments of the text were bowdlerized, removing the more objectionable Catholic elements.[6] In the space of three decadès, then, Elgar's religion was deemphasized and defused enough by his fame that he could be seen not as Catholic but as a sort of pan-Christian.

The risk of such an interpretation of Elgar is that it both oversimplifies and undervalues his Catholic influences. To have been memorialized so easily within a church of a different faith calls into question the strength and importance of his faith. One conclusion could be that Elgar's faith was weak. Through numerous anecdotal examples, Jerrold Northrop Moore offers this opinion in his biography *Edward Elgar: A Creative Life*. Discussing the confirmation of Elgar's daughter, Carice, Moore presents Elgar as having a lack of regard for both religion and his daughter. Moore states that neither Edward nor Alice Elgar attended Carice's confirmation—the sacrament in which a Catholic publicly proclaims his or her religion. Instead, Moore maintains, the Elgars deputized Rosa Burley—not herself a Catholic—to take care of the effort on June 11, 1903, while Elgar stayed at home to work on *The Apostles*.[7] The anecdote is an interesting one, and it does a great deal to solidify Moore's case; however, it is not true. Carice Elgar was confirmed on May 19, 1907 (Pentecost), long after Moore's date of 1903, as is made clear in Carice's letter of 24 May 1907 to the Leicester family and by the confirmation register at Belmont Abbey (figure 3).[8] Rosa Burley had nothing to do with the matter. May Grafton, Elgar's niece who *was* a Catholic, acted as Carice's sponsor, and both Edward and Alice Elgar attended, along with Alfred Kalisch and Julia "Pippa" Worthington; according to Alice's diary, they had tea with the bishop after the ceremony.[9]

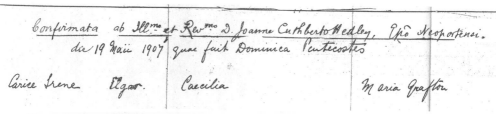

Figure 3. The confirmation register at Belmont Abbey.

Such anecdotes make for lasting impressions, however, and Moore and others use them continually to press an interpretation of Elgar's faith as weak. This has become the position of the popular Elgar press, maintained at the time of this writing on the Web site of the Elgar Society:

> It is therefore perhaps inevitable that, when he produced *The Dream of Gerontius*, a setting of a poem by a Roman Catholic Cardinal which explores various tenets of the Catholic faith, people should jump to the conclusion that his Catholicism underlay his whole life. But his faith was never that strong.[10]

Faith, of course (or lack of it), is not the point. Even if Elgar's faith was "never that strong" the experiences he had as a Catholic youth and a composer rising to fame affected his compositional output, his relationships with others, and, in short, his whole life. No matter what the state of his faith, Elgar was—and remained—culturally Catholic. His early Catholic roots influenced his view of the world around him and conditioned Britain's view of him. The popular presentation of faith "never that strong" is an anachronism. It takes a view from the late twentieth century, when ritual secularism largely replaced religion in Great Britain, and ascribes it to an age when all Christian religions, including Elgar's Catholicism, were steeped in ritualistic practices that were both spiritual and cultural.

The popular negating of Elgar's Catholicism both at his death and today serves an obvious end: it makes Elgar's music safer, more palatable for a British audience. In essence, it creates an avatar for Elgar as the "essentially English composer" beyond the reach of any of the complicating factors of partisan religion. An avatar is the embodiment of an archetype. As a manifestation of a symbol or a motif, it is akin to both an interpretation (when applied to an individual from an external person or source) and a disguise (when applied to an individual by him- or herself). The avatar might be built from certain elements of the individual, refracted and interpreted to point toward a specific meaning, or it might be an honest representation of that individual. The Elgar memorialized in Worcester Cathedral in 1935 was interpreted by those around him as "Pan-Christian," just as many today interpret a lack of faith in Elgar as another avatar, "Weak Faith." It is not surprising that both academic and popular scholars would attempt to transform Elgar in such a way. Doing so sheds responsibility for some of the more problematic compositions Elgar created, including *The Apostles* and *The Kingdom*, and allows us to concentrate more on his secular instrumental compositions.[11] Creating a newer avatar for Elgar also seems wholly rational and reasonable, given that Elgar himself devised so many over the course of his own life, from the itinerant Victorian-era inventor to the English gentleman, uninterested in music.[12] Contriving the Weak Faith and the Pan-Christian avatars satisfies the need to safely negate his Catholicism—what John Butt presciently called the "most 'foreign'" aspect of Elgar's background—while making the composer safely "English."[13] Further, this strategy serves to validate the often banal and even boorish statements Elgar made to interviewers, anecdote-publishing friends, and the like.

The purpose of this essay is to trace Elgar's history of, and responses to, Catholicism against the backdrop of Catholic history in Great Britain throughout his life, from 1857 until 1934. This era witnessed profound changes for Catholicism in England, including an increased civil role for English Catholics within society as a whole, the growth to greater numbers through both conversion and Irish immigration, fundamental shifts in English-Catholic doctrine, and the struggles of Catholicism—like all religions of the time—against Liberalism and the application of scientific evidence and reasoning to questions of faith and perceived wisdom. Continual prejudice against Catholics and Catholicism was a simple fact within Elgar's world, and the composer's perception of this prejudice, along with such prejudice itself, colored his moods, reactions, and judgments.[14] All of these elements were in flux throughout Elgar's lifetime, and their impact on his beliefs and his approach to Catholic culture and English culture were profound. His beliefs were fluid throughout his life, and thus he created a set of multiple avatars to facilitate self-representation. Criticism and biography, in turn, have accepted the later, more cynical Weak Faith avatar at face value without questioning the truth of it or its earlier manifestations. Consequently, throughout this investigation, I will catechize Elgar's Catholic avatars, those he created for himself and the varied embodiments he projected to his friends, family, and the public at three stages in his life.

The catechism is the Catholic profession of faith: a set of ritualistic questions posed to children during religion classes and sometimes within certain masses. When you "catechize" an individual, you probe his or her beliefs. Although the avatars to be examined include the posthumous one (Pan-Christian), already briefly examined, the bulk of this study will test the avatar present during Elgar's youth, the "Faithful Child." This will include a detailed examination of Catholic education during the era to locate the sources of Elgar's childhood systems of belief. Shorter discussions of avatars present during his marriage and the early years of his success (the "Publicly Faithful" avatar), as well as from 1905 until his death (the "Weak Faith" avatar) will be examined to ascertain his relationship to the religion of his birth and how cultural Catholic elements affected his life and compositions. Catechizing these avatars will show that despite making light of

Catholicism and all religions throughout the last decades of his life, and even moving toward elements of a nature-loving secularism, Catholic tenets retained a strong hold upon Elgar.[15]

English Catholicism in the Mid-Nineteenth Century, or "How Do You Prove That the Pope or Bishop of Rome Is the Successor of St. Peter?"

Elgar, who was born in 1857, was alive during one of the most tumultuous times in English Catholic history. Until 1791, Catholicism was outlawed as a religion in England, with exceptions made for embassy chapels of foreign governments; prior to this Catholics often had to worship in secret, and a permanent Catholic infrastructure in England was impossible. The right to worship freely was given in 1791 and basic rights of franchise and political office were granted to Catholics under the Emancipation Act of 1829.[16] After centuries of prohibition, the reestablishment of the Catholic hierarchy in England in 1850 turned what had been a "mission church" in England into a permanent one, with dioceses, parishes, and typical church organizational structures, including the presence of permanent bishops and cardinals. This event, along with the 1869–1870 doctrines of papal infallibility (the belief that when the Pope spoke *ex cathedra* he could not err on matters of Church doctrine) and the immaculate conception (the belief that the Virgin Mary was born free of the taint of original sin) caused a great deal of Protestant protest and even riots against Catholics, and remained a constant problem within England until the mid-1870s.[17] But such factors, though engaging and damaging, paled in comparison to the attention given to internal questions that arose within nineteenth-century English Catholicism. During Elgar's life, the three major groups of English Catholics—the Old Catholics, including the family of his boyhood friend Hubert Leicester; the converts to Catholicism, including his first teacher, Caroline Walsh, and his own mother, Ann Elgar; and Irish-immigrant Catholics—held a constant, often rancorous conversation about the direction the English Catholic Church should take. Elgar experienced directly the first two of these three groups.

Each of these Catholic constituencies had different intellectual, political, and class bearings, and each has been studied in independent ways, often at odds with the other. Questions of doctrine and subsequent change have been examined but often focus solely on a perceived shift from the culture of Old English Catholicism to Ultramontanism.[18] The Old English Catholics were mapped as reserved, intellectually naive, inclined to yield diplomatically to the Protestant majority in most things, and class-stratified. Most of the Old English Catholics were landed gentry, farmers, and agricultural laborers.[19] Rather than agitating directly for political equality, as the immigrant Irish Catholics and converts did, the Old English Catholics were generally moderate if not conservative in their demands regarding political power and their place within English society. For much of the nineteenth century, the Old English Catholics had great difficulty responding to the needs of either the immigrant Irish or the converts because they had spent much of their lives isolated from other classes.[20] Even aspects of aesthetics differed. The Old English Catholics favored Gothic designs. Immigrant Irish Catholics in general thought such neo-Gothic buildings were too expensive, particularly in new urban Catholic enclaves. Catholic converts, who tended to be Ultramontanists, feared that a Catholic Gothic revival would lead English Catholics to emphasize a national character of Catholicism instead of an international one.[21]

Ultramontanism has been defined frequently over the last century. The term literally means "beyond the mountains" (similar to the Italian *oltremontano*). From 1829 forward, English-language sources used it to mean strong support of papal authority. A mid-nineteenth-century definition comes close to the contemporary, almost militant spirit of the movement:

> The essence, then, of Ultramontanism of English Catholics we take to be this; that by divine institution no branch of the Church has any rights whatsoever against the supreme authority of the Pope, and that the "national" principle of action, on which all human affairs must be conducted in the secular order, is totally inapplicable to the affairs of religion. As a practical corollary to this doctrine, we hold that it is of primary importance to the well-being of Catholicism in any country that no hindrance whatsoever should exist between the See of Rome and the clergy and laity of that country, or to the direct action of the Pope upon his spiritual subjects in all spiritual things.[22]

With their fervent belief in the supremacy of the Pope in all things spiritual, Ultramontane Catholics were in direct conflict with the English Protestant majority, who saw this at least partially as an issue of national sovereignty. They feared that English Catholics would be loyal to the Pope instead of being loyal to the Crown. Most of the nineteenth-century Catholic converts fell into the Ultramontane camp, as this was the most public face of nineteenth-century English Catholicism. With the publication of Newman's sermon "The Second Spring," Ultramontane Catholics considered themselves part of a renewal of English Catholicism, and "Second

Springers" considered themselves to be more intellectually inclined and more in league with the primary aspects of the Catholic faith than their Old English Catholic brethren.[23] In other words, to the Ultramontanes, "its own brand of Catholicism was Catholicism itself, and any deviation an inadequate rather than an alternate expression of the same essential faith."[24]

Ultramontanism won the historiographical war. The discussions of nineteenth-century English Catholicism describe triumphant Second Springers imposing a mystical, Rome-loving doctrine throughout England, and the Old English Catholics disappearing.[25] Yet as Mary Heimann noted in 1995, Old English Catholic ideals and traditions survived long into the nineteenth century. Indeed, many of the factors traditionally associated with Ultramontanism, including the popularization of extraliturgical devotions and the increase in personal devotional books had their roots in pre-nineteenth-century English practices, especially the Old English Catholic's extraliturgical prayer book of choice, *The Garden of the Soul*.[26] Moreover, while Ultramontane ideals were gradually accepted as the public face of English Catholicism, Old English Catholic practices still existed throughout the entire century, and many Catholics resisted change. The impact of Ultramontane elements was limited by timing and geography. In Yorkshire English-Catholic parishes, syllabi from the 1860s still held to eighteenth-century Garden-of-the-Soul English-Catholic tenets; the first Ultramontane "knottier points of dogma" were not introduced in Yorkshire parish schools until 1868 and were not fully integrated into the religious syllabi until 1876.[27]

Thus, for the Catholics living in these tumultuous times, everything was new, and everything was up for debate. Throughout the century a series of journals argued over the elements of the reconstituted religion: its physical fabric, how it should present itself publicly to the larger Protestant majority around it, what elements of new rituals it should accept, and how to promote such elements within its systems of education.

The "Faithful Child" Avatar: 1857–1889, or
"In What Manner Must Baptism Be Administered, So As To Be Valid?"

The "Faithful Child" avatar has two facets: Elgar's religious education against the backdrop of events in Catholic history and how biographers discuss his religious education. From Elgar's birth in 1857 until he left Worcester for London in 1889, Catholicism was the major spiritual and cultural fact of his life: he attended a Catholic church and three Catholic schools, had Catholic friends, and received his first major musical employment as an organist at a Catholic church. Whether or not Elgar had a strong faith during this period is inconsequential, because the ritual identifiers that marked him as Catholic were always present and easily apparent to those around him.

Readers of the many Elgar biographies will find Catholic education mentioned, even placed prominently within the context of the composer's early life. Percy Young's *Elgar, Newman, and* The Dream of Gerontius: *In the Tradition of English Catholicism* provides a typical example of how scholars use Elgar's education. Note that in the following passage, Young employs Elgar's Catholic education as an example illustrating the composer's life-long sense of alienation from the rest of society:

> There is no reason to believe that the education provided for Edward Elgar here was in any way inferior to that of any other school in Worcester. He was at school altogether ten years, benefiting from a longer period of education than many of his contemporaries. Attendance at a Catholic School in England, however, could lead to a sense of alienation. As was the case within living memory in the early years of this century, boys at such schools were regarded by their contemporaries—under parental influence—with a degree of suspicion. Elgar—not only in youth—was sensitive, subject to moods of withdrawal, and often misunderstood.[28]

In this and other passages, Young views English Catholicism from one lens only, that of a unified, monolithic religion. But such presentation of Catholicism is really just lip service, because the same Catholic facts are mentioned in passing and then easily forgotten for the more compelling narrative of Elgar's personal and complicated history. Every biographer who dwells at any length on Elgar's youth mentions at least one of the three Catholic schools he attended: a Dame school run by Miss Caroline Walsh at 11 Britannia Square, Worcester; St. Anne's School at Spetchley

Park; and Francis Reeve's school at Littleton House in Lower Wick.[29] Most of the biographers mention these institutions only in combination with something from Elgar's future rather than dwelling for any length of time on Elgar's childhood. Within the narratives of their examinations, Walsh's school is where Elgar received his first formal piano lessons; the woods surrounding St. Anne's supposedly gave Elgar one of his inspirations for *The Dream of Gerontius;* and a stray comment by Reeve may have inspired part or all of *The Apostles* and *The Kingdom.*[30]

But a Catholic school in 1860s England was more than just a place to receive inspiration for the musical future. During Elgar's years in these three schools he was trained in Catholic theology above all other subjects, which a series of articles in the Catholic journal *The Rambler* makes clear. Besides being theologically desirable, some saw teaching Catholic religion as a political necessity, since outside the confines of the church or the classroom Catholics would still have to live within a larger Protestant world:

> Mixed up as all classes of Catholics are with Protestants, it is the height of cruelty not to arm them with fit weapons to fight the battle of faith against its enemies. We must recollect that religious controversy is not confined to the pulpit, the platform, and the periodical. It is not the especial privilege of the noble and the wealthy. Its sounds are heard as loudly in the workshop, the kitchen, and the field, as in the halls of a university. Boys and girls begin the intellectual struggle.[31]

Catholic education, then, was an integral part of the struggle. And that battle extended beyond merely preserving elements of pride. The articles in *The Rambler* divide Catholic education from that of their Protestant counterparts, viewing it as elemental to the preservation of the soul

> because Protestantism, though it may instruct the mind, yet is utterly powerless to train the soul; it may store the memory with knowledge, and even enforce a certain outward decency of conduct in morals, but it cannot penetrate man's nature in the inmost recesses of his heart; and without this, education is but a dream.[32]

Consequently, education that "armed" Catholics with a generous religious and theological underpinning was viewed as necessary to the moral, cultural, and political survival of English Catholics. Other subjects were possible, but anything for the young Catholic had to be grounded in religion first and religion foremost.[33]

Elgar began his education in 1863 and over the course of the next few years attended three distinctly different types of schools: a Dame school primarily for girls; a mixed school at Spetchley Park; and, from about 1869 to 1872, a school for young gentlemen at Littleton House. All three schools were Catholic, and all three emphasized elements of religion over all other subjects—at least according to the evidence that has survived.

Caroline Walsh, who ran the Dame school, was, like Elgar's mother, a convert to Catholicism.[34] Her calling to the Church stretched into the more fervent "Second Spring" variety and her conversion around 1846 was only a first step. She quickly joined the Daughters of the Heart of Mary (taking their threefold vows of chastity, poverty, and obedience) and attended their Charing Cross school for about four months in 1851 as preparation for religious education work in Worcester. When not teaching the students, she ministered to Worcester's spiritual welfare by walking "round among the poor Catholics of the town. She obliged the sluggards to leave their beds and prevented them from missing Mass."[35] Her rooms at Britannia Square were in what was evidently considered a convent by the Catholic hierarchy since she was given the title of Superior in 1852. The school was supported by the small tuition payments made by students like Elgar and his sisters, as well as a grant of £245 made by Henry Foley.[36]

St. Anne's, the school at Spetchley Park, is a bit more difficult to pin down. A charity school, it existed from 1842 until 1986. Initially, the Berkeley family, members of the local Catholic gentry, created the school for all children of the community—Catholic or Protestant.[37] It is likely (though currently not known) that by the time Elgar attended St. Anne's in the mid-1860s, it was entirely a Catholic foundation. Between 1857 and 1863 (before Elgar arrived at the school), the Sisters of St. Paul ran the institution.[38] As an order, they were influenced by their continental roots (the Sisters of St. Paul were founded in the eighteenth century in Chartres and arrived in England from France in 1847; the order did not become independent in England until 1864) and by their growing numbers, who were both Old English Catholics and converts. According to the Berkeley family, Elgar attended the school for two terms, so it is likely he arrived in 1867 or 1868, because he began attending his next school in 1869.[39]

Littleton House, Francis Reeve's school, unlike Walsh's or St. Anne's, was a for-profit enterprise. It tailored "Young gentlemen . . . for Commercial pursuits" and was a fixture of the Worcester Roman Catholic world.[40] Reeve, according to Jerrold Northrop Moore, initially wanted to be a priest, but after a childhood fall he was banned from that ambition since nineteenth-century Catholicism required the purported guise of both spiritual and material perfection: any bodily injury or chronic ailment destroyed the opportunity for a young man or woman to take holy orders.[41] Instead, Reeve followed a different path: he married, had a number of children, and taught Catholic boys. According to the Census of 1871 (the year Elgar and his friend Hubert Leicester neared the completion of their attendance of Reeve's school), Reeve and his wife, Lucy (listed as "Assistant to Schoolmaster"), maintained twenty-two boarding students aged six to sixteen (four of them their oldest sons) in addition to their four other children younger than age six.[42] Reeve also took day students from the town, such as Elgar and Leicester. Basil Maine stated that when Elgar attended Reeve's school there were about thirty students there.[43]

Advertisements for Reeve's school note that besides engaging in subject studies, "students attend Mass daily."[44] This agrees with the general discussions of midcentury English-Catholic education. Perhaps the most striking element of such descriptions is how much time was spent conforming to ideas of Catholic ritual and prayer:

> The pattern of the school was fitted to the Church year. On Holidays of Obligation the children attended Mass in the morning and then had the afternoon off. This happened for the Feasts of the Ascension, Whitsun, Corpus Christi, Saints Peter and Paul and All Saints; also Epiphany and the Assumption if they fell during term. This was of course in addition to attendances at Sunday Mass, Benediction, and catechism, which were also the responsibility of the schools. Children were questioned on Monday morning and those who had not been to Mass were punished. . . . The regular [school] routine included daily prayers each morning and hymn singing.[45]

The round of required mass attendance, continual professions of faith, and submission to the Catholic calendar would have created a further sense of community for Catholic children and held them apart from their Protestant neighbors.

Part of the Faithful Child avatar intersects with Elgar's attempt to mythologize his past, to create a serviceable and romantic history for himself. His schooling was part of this, and when later recalling it for biographers and friends he used Reeve as a touchstone for his religious oratorios. Elgar gave Reeve credit for planting the seed of the plot and purpose of *The Apostles* in a well-known anecdote which was published in most Elgar biographies after it appeared in 1905 in Robert J. Buckley's early interview-based study:

> The idea of the work originated in this way. Mr. Reeve, addressing his pupils, once remarked: "The Apostles were poor men, young men,

at the time of their calling; perhaps before the descent of the Holy Ghost not cleverer than some of you here." This set me thinking, and the oratorio of 1903 is the result.[46]

The mythological genesis of the work lent Elgar a sense of purpose for *The Apostles* beyond the merely musical: it fastened the composition to Christian education.

Central to the progression of Elgar's early faith and education was his relationship to the Worcester parish of St. George's. Though a student at Walsh's Dame school and Littleton House, typical religious instruction for Catholics at midcentury was handled by the parish priest, who might visit the school several times a week to teach and catechize the students.[47] During most of Elgar's school years, there were two priests at St. George's, the most permanent being Father William Waterworth, S.J.[48] Waterworth arrived in Worcester during 1857 and left in 1878.[49] He had an impressive pedigree for a parish priest posted to a sleepy provincial town: education at a Jesuit grammar school in London followed by seminary at Stonyhurst, the most celebrated Catholic public school in England, where students were taught at a level comparable to Cambridge or Oxford; rector of the Jesuit Church of St. James's, Spanish Place, one of the most important Catholic churches in London; and confessor to Henry Edward (later Cardinal) Manning.[50] Fr. Waterworth certainly encouraged Ultramontane theology when he gave an eleven-year-old Elgar a votive picture of St. Joseph, with a simple French text, and likely would have instructed Elgar to pray to such an image.[51] Two prayers to St. Joseph were commonly available to Catholics in *The Garden of the Soul;* each asks for intercession from Joseph.[52]

Most sources, be they Worcestershire history or Elgar biography, present Fr. Waterworth as an erudite, affable individual loved by his Catholic parishioners and local Protestants alike. Fr. Brian Doolan's brief history *St. George's, Worcester: 1590–1999* is typical of the Waterworth hagiography, noting that the priest was

> described by his Jesuit obituarist as "a model of Rectors." . . . He was a considerable scholar who had been destined for an academic career but this was impeded by delicate health. He lectured regularly to the "Worcester Cathedral Institute," contributed articles to *The Rambler* and *The Dublin Review* and was a notable preacher. He was on the warmest personal terms with the Dean and Canons of the Cathedral and other Protestant divines in the city.[53]

If this is the case, Waterworth must also have been charming and disarming, for his writings are militantly pro-Catholic, almost to the point of anti-Protestant condescension. Elgar's primary religious teacher and leader wrote a number of books that take the rhetorical stance that the English Reformation was at best a tragic mistake and at worst a hideous crime against humanity.

Some of Waterworth's attacks on Anglicanism were so cogent and radical that they were reprinted in cheap pamphlets for wider distribution to agitate the Catholic populace. Such was the case with his "The Popes and the English Church," originally published in the October 1870 issue of *The Month* and quickly reprinted by the Catholic Truth Society, a popular Ultramontane organization.[54] Waterworth's words are those of an impassioned partisan as he denies the legitimacy of the Anglican Church:

> Anglicanism is, as at present constituted, hopelessly anti-Catholic. It is a sheer nationalism, and such a nationalism is destructive of one of the great marks of the Church, distinctly indicated in the Creed of the Apostles and the Creed of Nicea, namely, Catholicism—"I believe in the Holy Catholic Church": "I believe in One, Holy, Catholic and Apostolic Church."[55]

The major thrust of the article begins at this point: there is only one Church, and it has always been (and still was in Waterworth's time) under the spiritual and temporal leadership of the Pontiff, and any attempts to remove elements of the Church from the control of the Pontiff are morally bankrupt and illegitimate. No figure is safe from Waterworth's harsh and unyielding criticism; he calls Oliver Cromwell "unprincipled."[56]

Waterworth's entire corpus of writings presents all elements of Anglicanism, including the infrastructure it confiscated during the Reformation and created afterward, as illegitimate. His writings from the 1850s are if anything even more absolutist in tone, especially regarding the veracity of other denominations and the absolute spiritual power and the necessity of the Pope. To Waterworth, any Englishman who recognized a "Protestant establishment" was flawed and a pretender because Protestant establishments were temporal and not divine—to him, the only church was the Catholic Church and, as he repeatedly stated, "all others are false."[57] Waterworth would even take historical events and place a distinctly Catholic spin on them, such as when he conflated the English love of freedom and independence with Catholicism:

> The introduction of the Liturgy of Edward VI into this country, in the year 1549, was the signal of insurrection: after a lapse of more than 300 years, that Liturgy is still the fruitful source of discontent

and religious and civil agitation. When it was first of all forced upon the nation, seventeen counties rose up nearly simultaneously, sword in hand, to defend their religious liberties. In the words of the first Article of the great Charter of English freedom, they declared that "the Church of England shall be free, and enjoy her rights and liberties inviolate." These words of Magna Charta signify that Sovereigns shall not meddle with the Church; that the Pope shall direct the spiritual authorities to the exclusion of other influences; and that the appointment of Prelates shall not be interfered with by the temporal power. Catholics, jealous of the tyranny and assumptions of a bad king, extorted our glorious Charter from King John.[58]

Such was Fr. Waterworth, the man "esteemed by the Catholics and the Protestants." Waterworth's anti-Anglican view of history differs greatly from the dominant discourse espoused by pro-Anglican historians such as George Macaulay Trevelyan, who asserted that the English nation gained its essential character only through the Reformation.[59] In contradistinction to the dominant Anglican ideology, Waterworth's aggressive Catholic revision of English history—echoed today by such revisionist historians as Eamon Duffy—was the basis of the primary religious education of the young Elgar and, indeed, of all the other Catholics in Worcester.[60]

Indeed, Waterworth's effects on Catholics around Elgar were profound. Elgar's own sister, Ellen Agnes (also referred to as "Helen Agnes" and nicknamed "Dot" or "Dott"), became a Dominican nun in 1902 and eventually a prioress.[61] Elgar's schoolmate Hubert Leicester, who hailed from an old Catholic family, embraced the Catholic history of Worcester with relish, using it as an arena for Ultramontane polemical writings. In 1932, he published a short pamphlet about the history of Catholicism in Worcester, from Henry VIII's Protestant Reformation through the penal times. A good deal of Leicester's language in this publication mirrors the militant tone Waterworth used in his own writings. Leicester refers to "the so-called Reformation" and terms Henry VIII's confiscation of Church lands and property "stealing." Indeed, Leicester maps the entire history of the English Reformation as an exercise in theft, stating that those who turned away from Catholicism did so for love of money, not religion, claiming, "When the first Bills were introduced into Parliament for the establishment of an English Protestant Church, the measures were passed principally by the votes of the holders of ill-gotten wealth."[62] Like the polemics of Waterworth, there was no room for compromise within Leicester's rhetoric—yet his writings appeared decades after the establishment of basic civil rights for Catholics in England and after his long and illustrious political career.[63]

While Leicester presented a wholly Ultramontane face, Elgar associated himself with the Ultramontane faction on at least two occasions, either voluntarily or because he was required to do so for professional advancement. The first instance was when he began as organist at St. George's. In the second instance, Elgar placed an advertisement in the Catholic magazine *The Tablet* in 1878, advertising his services as combined secretary and music teacher. *The Tablet* was one of the most important organs of Ultramontane Catholic news and opinion throughout the nineteenth century.[64] Elgar's advertisement spoke diligently to that world:

> To Musical Catholic Noblemen, Gentlemen, Priests, Heads of Colleges, & c., or Professors of Music—A friend of a young man, possessed of great musical talent, is anxious to obtain partial employment of him as Organist or Teacher of Piano, Organ, or Violin, to young boys, sons of gentlemen, or as Musical Amanuensis to Composers or Professors of Music, being a quick and ready copyist. Could combine Organist and Teacher of Choir, with Musical Tutor to sons of noblemen, & c. Has had several years experience as Organist. The advertiser's object is to obtain musical employment for him, with proportionate time for study. Age 21, of quiet, studious habits, and gentlemanly bearing. Been used to good society. Would have unexceptional references. Neighbourhood of London preferred; the Continent not objected to. Disengaged in September.[65]

The advertisement presents Elgar as flexible in his abilities and eager to apply himself to almost anything for the sake of employment. Had it proved successful, such a position would have kept him in the insulated doctrinal world of Ultramontane Catholicism, and the advertisement shows Elgar's willingness to live and work within that world. But young Elgar's notice did not evince the most savvy business strategy because advertising in *The Tablet* meant the readers would be primarily Ultramontane Catholics—converts—and not the Old English Catholics, who might have had the money and resources to hire Elgar for such a desirable position.

Elgar found no suitable employment from his advertisement; however, St. George's soon gave him a modest professional position. He deputized there as organist for his father in 1872, was appointed assistant organist in 1873, and eventually became titular organist in 1885, serving until he departed for London in 1889.[66] Consequently, Elgar had ample opportunity to compose Catholic music and partake in Catholic ceremonies.[67] One nonliturgical devotional ceremony during these years, on October 7, 1888, inaugurated the "Apostleship of Prayer" and the blessing of a Sacred Heart statue which still exists in St. George's today. Sacred Heart statues were icons used for extraliturgical devotions in the nineteenth century in churches or at home; *The Garden of the Soul* shows seven pages of prayers for this ritual.[68] As the *Catholic Encyclopedia,* published between 1907 and 1914, noted, "Devotion to the Sacred Heart may be defined as the devotion to the adorable Heart of Jesus Christ insofar as this Heart represents and recalls His love; or what amounts to the same thing: devotion to the love of Jesus Christ insofar as this love is recalled and symbolically represented to us by his heart of flesh."[69] The importance of this event is reflected by the presence of the visiting Bishop Edward Ilsley, who officiated at the service; traditionally, bishops visited parishes for the sacraments of confirmation and ordinations, as well as installing a new priest in the parish. The Litany of the Sacred Heart, which began to appear in Catholic devotional prayer books after 1875, is a brief ritual that includes responses to prayers said by a celebrant.[70] Its form is close to the "Agnus Dei" prayer, since after addressing Christ's heart with numerous blandishments (including "Heart of Jesus, burning furnace of charity, /Heart of Jesus, abode of justice and love") it simply asks for Christ's mercy.[71] For this ceremony, Elgar composed his last composition for St. George's, the *Ecce Sacerdos.* The composition is quite concise (only fifty-three measures long) and Elgar dedicated it to Hubert Leicester.[72]

Leicester's fervent Ultramontane prose clearly reflected Waterworth's early influence as a religious teacher. Elgar, too, might have traveled this path, but the only tangible manifestation of fervor before 1889 was the completion of *Ecce Sacerdos.* In his Faithful Child years, Elgar's experiences with Catholicism were steady but various. From the time of his education until he left Worcester for London, he was never conscious of a life without aspects of the Catholic Church, either because he was learning about it through the offices of Walsh, Reeve, the teachers at Spetchley Park, and Fr. Waterworth, or because he was employed as a musician at St. George's. It cannot be known if he shared Hubert Leicester's religious fervor at this time, as nothing within the extant anecdotal or historical record, outside of his Catholic religious music, suggests an intense devotion to Catholicism save the ineffectual advertisement to be a musician for Catholic families or organizations. It is only in his next incarnation, as the "Publicly Faithful" avatar, that Elgar seeks to project an overtly Catholic image.

The "Publicly Faithful" Avatar: 1889–1905, or "What Is the Meaning of This Frequent Use of the Sign of the Cross?"

In the period between 1889 and 1905, Elgar manifested the "Publicly Faithful" avatar in three ways: by attending mass, by publicly proclaiming himself a Catholic in interviews and compositions, and by complaining to friends and intimates about the anti-Catholic prejudice that he experienced repeatedly. Once he arrived in London in 1889, it is easy to detect signs of a sort of religious fervency that developed during the early years of his marriage. Elgar attended church no less than fifty times in 1890,despite frequent illness and bad weather frustrating his attendance.[73] Elgar's only child, Carice, also became a public manifestation of the family's religious faith: as a schoolgirl she was made to wear a prominent gold cross tied with a black ribbon around her neck.[74] Public proclamations of his creed appeared on the scores of his oratorios *The Dream of Gerontius*, *The Apostles*, and *The Kingdom*, which he dedicated "A.M.D.G." (*Ad majorem dei gloriam*—"To the greater glory of God"). While not unheard of at the beginning of the twentieth century, Elgar's dedications of his oratorios to the Almighty was certainly unusual among British composers.[75] The publicity for all three of these oratorios, leading up to their premieres in 1900, 1903, and 1906, respectively, included discussion in both the musical press and the English Catholic press.[76] Elgar arranged for a public expression of belief to be published with Canon Charles Vincent Gorton's libretto interpretations of the last two oratorios; Gorton's interpretations were sold at performances.[77] At the first performance of *The Apostles* Elgar presented the singers with postcard copies of Ivan Kramskoi's mystical painting *Christ in the Wilderness* (its subject looking realistically human and upset) and let it be known publicly that he composed *The Apostles* with a print of the painting in his study.[78] He also allowed *Gerontius* to be used as a fund-raising piece for the building of the Catholic cathedral in Westminster on June 6, 1903.

Besides proactive presentations of his Catholicism, Elgar also exhibited some reactive ones, such as when he complained to the unsympathetic Rosa Burley about his perception of prejudice against Catholics:

> [Elgar] replied that I little knew how seriously his career had been hampered by his Catholicism. He told me of post after post which would have been open to him but for the prejudice against his religion, of golden opportunities snatched from his grasp by inferior men of more acceptable views. It was a subject on which he evidently felt very bitter for he embroidered it at great length.[79]

Again, the question here is not necessarily one of faith: in this period, Elgar complained to Burley that he had suffered because those in power around him identified him as *Catholic,* which was a negative public definition instead of the positive one Elgar strove to present to the world during this time.

Other signs of the Publicly Faithful avatar are external to Elgar. Even though his Catholic faith may have been "never that strong," English Catholicism's faith in Elgar remained steadfast. The *Catholic Directory,* an organizational compendium of Catholic parishes within England, proudly named Elgar in a list of "Catholic Knights."[80] The *Catholic Encyclopedia* gushingly noted the fame of *Gerontius.*[81] But his Catholicism could and did often expose Elgar to various sorts of criticism, even after he became famous. The prominent critic Edward Algernon Baughan stated in 1906, when *Gerontius*'s fame was assured by many successful performances, that it "is almost groveling in its anguish of remorse, and it has the peculiar sentimentality that is characteristic of the later Roman Catholic Church."[82]

Even during this era, though, cracks in the Publicly Faithful avatar are apparent. Elgar's marriage to Alice Roberts is a good example. When the two were married, on May 8, 1889, Alice was still a Protestant and practicing Anglican, thus making the union to a Catholic a "mixed marriage." Such a marriage would have seemed eminently reasonable to the young Elgar; his parents maintained a "mixed" liaison from the time of Ann Elgar's conversion to Catholicism in 1856 until William Henry Elgar's deathbed conversion in the first decade of the twentieth century. Yet by 1884 Ultramontane doctrine, taught to all English Catholics through the process of catechism, said that "mixed marriages" were forbidden in the Catholic Church except "for very grave reasons and under special conditions."[83] This prohibition may have caused Elgar and Alice Roberts some difficulty, since they chose not to marry in Malvern or Worcester, where Elgar's Catholic roots were strongest, but at the London Oratory on Brompton Road.[84] That Alice Roberts converted to Catholicism after her marriage to Edward Elgar is immaterial, and it would not have mitigated the delicacy of the situation; under the proscribed rubrics of the time, had Elgar's Catholicism been the conservative Ultramontane variety expected of a midcentury convert's child, Alice would have had to become a Catholic convert herself, before the marriage.

Long after the end of the Publicly Faithful period, professions of Elgar's faith were continued by others on his behalf, but in the years after he completed *The Kingdom,* the composer's testimonies to his religious beliefs decreased steadily. Geoffrey Hodgkins notes that at this time "Elgar abandoned what we may call orthodox religious belief . . . and turned to a more humanistic outlook, which gradually became embittered and sceptical."[85]

The culprit, besides Elgar's general depression and hypersensitivity, may well have been his growing fame: the acclaim garnered by the *Enigma* Variations and *Gerontius* placed him firmly in the spotlight as a public figure and musician with many more conducting opportunities and a brief, tumultuous professorship at the University of Birmingham. Such recognition came at the expense of lost time for composing, and both *The Apostles* and *The Kingdom* were much smaller works than originally planned.[86] Once complete, they did not become the obvious successors to *Gerontius*, and the difficulty of composing them to his own satisfaction turned Elgar away from completing another oratorio—the composition with which he would publicly proclaim his faith—for the rest of his life. Although incandescent during its duration, Elgar's Publicly Faithful phase lasted only a few years of his life.

The "Weak Faith" Avatar: 1905–1934, or "What Is the Faith of the Catholic Church Concerning the Eucharist?"

In the last period of Elgar's religious development, from 1905 while he composed *The Kingdom* to the end of his life, Elgar's faith seemed only to falter. As Hodgkins notes, he did keep up appearances, attending a succession of churches in Hereford (until 1910), London and Sussex (from 1910 to 1923), and Worcester (from 1923 until his death in 1934). Certain biographers tell us that Elgar attended these churches because Alice wished him to do so—even ordering him a regular Sunday morning cab in Hereford for this purpose—or because he particularly admired a priest in one parish or another.[87] In this period he also indulged in hobbies as an amateur scientist, perhaps as a countermove against religion, first with chemistry and later with microscopes.[88] During these years, in public and semipublic pronouncements, the composer began to project aspects of the "Weak Faith" avatar. He allowed himself to be modern and skeptical regarding religion in the face of new scientific discoveries and tied himself more closely to elements of the land and nature.

Elgar's skepticism came out most clearly when describing his young life in Worcester. When he received the Freedom of the City of Worcester from then-mayor Hubert Leicester in 1905, Elgar reminisced about his days working at St. George's as an organist, when Leicester was his choirmaster. At the time they were both in a wind quintet, and in the process of his own mythmaking, implied that composing music for the quintet took precedence over religion: "We met on Sunday afternoons, and it was an understood thing that we should have a new piece every week. The sermons in our church used to take at least half an hour, and I spent the time composing the thing for the afternoon."[89]

Further skepticism occurred in letters to Leicester, criticizing the material elements of Catholicism in Rome following a trip there in 1908:

> If you have any religious feeling whatever, don't go to Rome—everything money—clergy gorgeous & grasping. . . . "Special music" (bombardon & side drum & Gounod's Ave Maria). Present Pope a good holy simple man but knows nothing . . . should be replaced by permanent Commission with secretary who could be dismissed.[90]

Through such observations and actions, Elgar began to distance himself from elements of Catholicism both in private and public communication for the last three decades of his life. Further, he publicly presented himself as someone who, though Catholic, could appreciate the art and cultural offerings of Protestants, as was the case in an interview with Rudolph de Cordova:

> I attended as many of the [Anglican] Cathedral services as I could. . . . The putting of the fine organ into the Cathedral at Worcester [1874] was a great event, and brought many organists to play there at various times. I went to hear them all. The services at the Cathedral were over later on Sunday than those at the Catholic church, and as soon as the voluntary there was finished at the church I used to rush over to the Cathedral to hear the concluding voluntary.[91]

The quotation still locates Elgar as a practicing Catholic (ever important for the composer of semisacred oratorios in the first decade of the twentieth century) and gives him an innocent reason to go to the cathedral (to hear music), but places him in a category of valuing art over dogma—thus helping him appear more universal.

Aside from doubt of Rome and publicly valuing music over Catholicism, Elgar made a self-conscious attempt to link himself with nature and thus create a sort of proto-naturalistic spirituality. This is what Elgar would be remembered for, as others have noted, since the historiography of the composer is largely one of associating him with the pastoral impulse.[92] In a preface he wrote in 1930 for Hubert Leicester's *Forgotten Worcester*, Elgar romanticized his life as a child in the small city by transforming all that was important into the glorious image of a country sunrise:

> It is pleasant to date these lines from an eminence distantly overlooking the way to school; our walk was always to the brightly-lit west.

Before starting, our finances were rigidly inspected—naturally not for me, being, as I am, in nothing rigid, but quite naturally, by my companion, who tackled the situation with prophetic skill and with the gravity now bestowed on the affairs of great corporations whose accounts are harrowed by him to this day. The report being favourable, two pence were "allowed" for the ferry. Descending the steps, past the door behind which the figure of the mythical salmon is incised, we embarked; at our backs "the unthrift sun shot vital gold," filling Payne's meadows with glory and illuminating for two small boys a world to conquer and to love. In our old age, with our undimmed affection, the sun still seems to show us a golden "beyond."[93]

The "golden beyond" was the neighborhood of Worcester where Reeve's Littleton House was located, separated from the main section of the city by an easily traversed river.

Elgar's compositions became part of the nostalgic enterprise that eventually valued nature over faith. *Gerontius* is a case in point, and many scholars have been so captivated by Elgar's imagery that they ignore the larger ramifications of the transference from works of faith to works of nature. Michael Kennedy is a case in point:

From 1866 to 1868, young Edward attended a Roman Catholic school at Spetchley. This was under the patronage of the Lord of the Manor, Robert Berkeley. Many years later Elgar told Ernest Newman that "as a boy he used to gaze from the school windows in rapt wonder at the great trees swaying in the wind; and he pointed out to me a passage in *Gerontius* in which he had recorded in music his subconscious memories of them." Although Newman did not enlarge upon this, it is fairly reasonable to suppose that the passage concerned is in Part II, rehearsal cue [68] at "the summer wind among the lofty pines."[94]

Belief in the divinity of nature was easily transferred into doubts about the veracity of the afterlife, as can be seen from Kennedy's collection of anecdotes about the composer's latest articulated beliefs:

[In his last years Elgar] expressed a wish that he should be buried at the confluence of Severn and Teme, without religious ceremony. He had for many years avoided going to church and while dying and still lucid he refused to see a priest, none other than the son of Gervase Elwes. He objected to the church's "mumbo jumbo," he said. His consultant, Arthur Thomson, was impressed by his "magnificent courage." Elgar told him he had "no faith whatever in an afterlife. I believe there is nothing but complete oblivion."[95]

Such private admissions were entirely in keeping with his skeptical nature and, private as they were, suited the image of Weak Faith well. Yet just before he died, the legacy of Elgar's cultural Catholicism reaffirmed itself strongly. On his deathbed, Elgar received last rites from Fr. Reginald Gibb of St. George's parish, probably at the instigation of Carice and Philip Leicester (Hubert Leicester's son), since Elgar was almost certainly unconscious from doses of morphine. Moore notes that Gibb later claimed in newspaper reports he had obtained a confession of faith from Elgar, but this testimony may have been exaggerated.[96]

In Memoriam (II): The Old English Catholic Avatar, or "What Do You Mean by Extreme Unction?"

Elgar always identified himself with the country, preferring it to life in London. Even before he was knighted, he dressed like a member of the gentry and took up aristocratic sports such as golf (and later games like billiards). He showed a predilection for chivalry and things Gothic; he was a political conservative. With the exception of *Gerontius,* most of his sacred works were compositions of appeasement, easily sung by either Catholic or Anglican congregations.[97] He composed a number of pieces for the Three Choirs festivals that were quickly taken up by Anglican choirs throughout England and have remained a part of the Anglican choral tradition. In short, Elgar became the embodiment of an Old English Catholic: with a set of beliefs more reserved than mystical; a readiness to appease the dominant Protestant majority; and a readiness to act his part as a gentleman when needed. Indeed, if this was the case, it makes Elgar's lack of a permanent memorial at St. George's understandable. For a church whose tradition within English Catholicism was to stress the public propagation of the Ultramontane tenets proclaimed by Waterworth and other like-minded parish priests, Elgar's distinctly non-Ultramontane pronouncements may well have discouraged his boyhood parish from celebrating or memorializing him.

St. George's may never have had the opportunity. Elgar was buried in a grave beside his wife at St. Wulstan's Catholic Church in Little Malvern; at his request, the requiem was said as a Low Mass, so no music was performed. Doolan notes, however, that St. George's celebrated a High Mass (sung) in his honor around this time, performing an early version of

Elgar's 1902 *Ave Verum Corpus* with its original "Pie Jesu" requiem mass text. This is an interesting substitution, since it associates a hymn that celebrated Christ's suffering (identified in the nineteenth century with the Ultramontanes) with the traditional Lacrymosa text.

St. George's modest commemoration to Elgar paled in comparison to the elaborate expressions of mourning offered to his memory at the Anglican Worcester Cathedral. Indeed, the Elgar Window presents only one facet of such memorials. On March 2, 1934, a week after Elgar's death, the cathedral organized a "national memorial service" using members of the Three Choirs Festival Chorus and included selections from his last three oratorios: Prelude to Part II of *The Apostles;* Prelude to *Gerontius,* concluding solo and chorus from Part I ("Proficisere Anima Christiana"), selections from Part II popularly known as "Angel's Song" and "Angel's Farewell"; and parts of *The Kingdom,* including the Virgin Mary's meditation ("The Sun Goeth Down") and "The Lord's Prayer."[98] The prayer intoned by Dean Moore-Ede at this occasion was conspicuously ecumenical:

> We give thee humble and hearty thanks that it pleased Thee to endow our fellow citizen Edward Elgar with that singular mastery of music, and the will to use it in Thy service, whereby he being dead yet speaketh: now filling our minds with visions of the mystery and beauty of Nature; now by the concert of sweet and solemn sounds telling our hearts secrets of life and death that lie too deep for words; now soaring with Angels and archangels and with all the company of Heaven in an ecstacy of praise; now holding us bowed with the broken and contrite heart before the throne of judgment. We thank Thee for the great place he holds in the glorious roll of England's Masters of Music. We thank Thee for the love and loyalty which ever bound this her son to the Faithful City.[99]

Aside from being demonstrative about "Nature," the prayer commends Elgar's music for its power to affirm both a Christian faith and solemn comfort.[100] Again, this Elgar is "Pan-Christian" and proudly celebrated in the Anglican cathedral as Worcester's "native son." Yet the musical selections listed above also came from the fertile period of Elgar's full flower into fame, namely, 1899–1906. As a manifestation of Elgar's pan-Christian avatar as well as the changing nature of the times, these works—with their intense yet evanescent Catholic overtones—were wholly welcome in the Worcester Cathedral. In essence, they foreshadowed the presentation of both the memorial plaque with its mystical Latin declaration and the memorial window with its safer English version.[101]

The semisacred oratorio selections were not the only items on the program for the memorial concert. Also featured were three movements from Elgar's first major compositional success, the *Enigma* Variations: I—C.A.E., a musical portrait of Alice Elgar, the composer's wife; IX—Nimrod, characterizing Elgar's friend August Jaeger; and XIII—***, Elgar's noble friend and patron Lady Mary Lygon. By luck or by design, Ivor Atkins and W. H. Reed, close friends throughout Elgar's life, chose works that spoke to Elgar's long-standing ideals of domesticity, erotic friendship, and unrequited love.[102] Their choices pointed the way beyond public proclamations of Elgar's religion to the increasingly secular world he would inhabit in the years after 1905. The Weak Faith avatar, denuded of Elgar's spiritual beliefs, became dependent on his friendships, not his childhood beliefs, and consequently became safe for consumption by all.

Elgar in his lifetime saw English Catholics move from a marginalized community into the mainstream of society. The composer's successful and honored career was a certain sign of this shift. Yet even so, a backlash of prejudice against Catholics was a pungent memory for Elgar's Catholic friends and contemporaries. Some, like Leicester, chose to delve deeper into their own faith for any public presentation, and Elgar certainly adopted this stance in the early years of his career. Old prejudices die hard within a culture, however, and today's biographers must reexamine Elgar in the light of his Catholic upbringing. Was he a man whose faith was "never that strong," or did he embody the avatar of an "Old English Catholic" in order to present a publicly acceptable religious facade? Elgar's mixed religious background, inherited from his parents, his own mixed marriage, and his work within a predominantly Anglican profession made being able to speak to both faiths not just convenient, but a necessity for his survival. In such a world, it is no wonder the man did not feel at ease.

NOTES

I would like to thank the staffs of the Elgar Birthplace Museum, Heywood College Library, Worcestershire Local History Center, Worcestershire County Records Office, and British Library, as well as David Morrison, archivist of the Worcester Cathedral, Abbot Paul Stoneham of Belmont Abbey, Steven Plank, and Ari Sammartino for their gracious assistance in my research for this article. Sarah Jean Clemens, Alexandra Monchick Reale, Rebecca Riding, and Christopher White provided additional research; without their kind and timely aid, the final version of this article would not have been possible. All subhead quotations are from Richard Challoner's English-language catechism, *The Catholick Christian Instructed in the Sacraments, Sacrifice, Ceremonies, and Observances of the Church: By Way of Question and Answer* (Philadelphia: C. Talbot, 1786).

1. Anthony Boden, *Three Choirs: A History of the Festivals* (Phoenix Mill, Eng.: Alan Sutton, 1992), 183.

2. It is clear the figure is Christ and not God from the cross that forms part of the halo, the right hand making the sign of benediction, and the left hand holding an orb, which is the symbol of Christ's kingdom on earth. The point is further clarified in a description of the window published in the London *Times,* 5 January 1935: "Dominating the design is the figure of Christ wearing royal and sacerdotal vestments. His right hand is raised in blessing and in His left He holds the starred orb symbolical of universal rule over heaven and earth. Round the throne is the rainbow symbolical of God's covenant with Man." The masculine gender of the Angel echoes the pronouns used by Elgar in *Gerontius* and by Cardinal John Henry Newman in the original text. See "his ample palm," Part II, rehearsal number 9; and "I will address him. Mighty one, my Lord, my Guardian Spirit, all hail!" Part II, rehearsal number 17.

3. *Times* (London), 4 September 1935.

4. Ibid.

5. A critical reaction was already building in the 1920s, but manifestations of it abound in the obituaries and appreciations of Elgar in the April 1934 issue of *The Musical Times.*

6. See Charles Edward McGuire, "Vaughan Williams and the English Music Festival: 1910," in *Vaughan Williams Essays,* ed. Byron Adams and Robin Wells (Aldershot: Ashgate Press, 2003), 260; and Jerrold Northrop Moore, ed., *Elgar and His Publishers: Letters of a Creative Life* (Oxford: Oxford University Press, 1987), 1:351–52; 371–75.

7. "Alice wrote on June 11: 'E. very badsley [*sic*] & dreadfully worried &c.' Carice's confirmation took place that day but neither parent attended, leaving all the arrangements to Miss Burley." Jerrold Northrop Moore, *Edward Elgar: A Creative Life* (Oxford: Oxford University Press, 1984; repr. 1999), 407.

8. Carice's letter to the Leicester family is dated "Empire Day, [19]07." Letter of Carice Elgar to Hubert Leicester, [24 May] 1907, Worcestershire County Records Office, 705:185 BA 8185/1. The confirmation record from Belmont Abbey notes that Carice Irene Elgar "took the Confirmation name Caecilia and her Godmother was Maria Grafton. She was confirmed by Bishop Cuthbert Hedley O.S.B. . . . on the Feast of Pentecost, 19th May 1907." A copy of the confirmation register confirms the spelling of her name as "Caecilia." Letter to author from Abbot Paul Stoneham of Belmont Abbey, 28 April 2006.

9. Elgar Birthplace Museum photostat of Alice Elgar's diary, 19 May 1907. The full entry reads: "E. & A. C. May, Pippa & Mr. Kalisch to Belmont at 10–15. Lovely there & finer. big car—Connelly—Lovely drive afterwards by Callow & Aconbury & Green Crize—most lovely. Saw Plover on road & little ones, E. picked one up & showed us—most darling. To Belmont in car again at 4. Carice confirmed. Very quiet & beautiful ceremony. All to tea with the Bishop Abbot afterwards."

10. "Elgar—The Man Behind the Music," http://www.elgar.org/2theman.htm (accessed July 11, 2006).

11. See, for instance, the preface to Robert Anderson's *Elgar:* "I came later to *The Apostles* and have never much admired it. Perhaps my strictures about this work and others will seem harsh. Now and again I have been unable to conceal my disappointment when Elgar is obviously below his best." Robert Anderson, *Elgar* (New York: Schirmer Books, 1993), xii.

12. See Byron Adams, "The 'Dark Saying' of the Enigma: Homoeroticism and the Elgarian Paradox," in *Queer Episodes in Music and Modern Identity,* ed. Sophie Fuller and Lloyd Whitesell (Urbana: University of Illinois Press, 2002), 225–26; and Meirion Hughes, "The Duc D'Elgar: Making a Composer Gentleman," in *Music and the Politics of Culture,* ed. Christopher Norris (New York: St. Martin's Press, 1989), 41–68.

13. John Butt, "Roman Catholicism and Being Musically English: Elgar's Church and Organ Music," in *The Cambridge Companion to Elgar,* ed. Daniel M. Grimley and Julian Rushton (Cambridge: Cambridge University Press, 2004), 108.

14. For discussions of Catholic prejudice in the era, see Edward R. Norman, *Anti-Catholicism in Victorian England* (New York: Barnes & Noble, 1968); Walter L. Arnstein, *Protestant Versus Catholic in Mid-Victorian England* (Columbia: University of Missouri Press, 1982); and D. G. Paz, *Popular Catholicism in Mid-Victorian England* (Stanford, Calif.: Stanford University Press, 1992). Michael Wheeler's *The Old Enemies: Catholic and Protestant in Nineteenth-Century English Culture* (Oxford: Oxford University Press, 2006) was in press at the time of writing.

15. Few attempts have been made to reach beyond the surface of Elgar's Catholicism and see it for what it was: a religious, but more important, a cultural heritage that created a parallel world often in sharp relief to the dominant Protestant world around him. Pertinent studies include Geoffrey Hodgkins's pamphlet "Providence and Art: A Study in Elgar's Religious Beliefs" (Rickmansworth: Elgar Editions, 1979, repr. 2002); John Butt, "Roman Catholicism and Being Musically English: Elgar's Church and Organ Music"; and Byron Adams, "Elgar's Later Oratorios: Roman Catholicism, Decadence and the Wagnerian Dialectic of Shame and Grace,"both in *Cambridge Companion to Elgar,* esp. 81–105. See also Charles Edward McGuire, "One Story, Two Visions: Textual Difference Between Elgar's and Newman's *The Dream of Gerontius,*" in *The Best of Me: A Gerontius Centenary Companion,* ed. Geoffrey Hodgkins (Rickmansworth: Elgar Editions, 1999), 84–101; as well as McGuire, "Elgar, Judas, and the Theology of Betrayal," in *19th-Century Music* 13, no. 3 (2000): 236–72; and McGuire, *Elgar's Oratorios* (Aldershot: Ashgate Press, 2002).

16. The Emancipation Act of 1829 was passed to enable checks on English Catholics' potential power that today seem rather paranoid: "The Emancipation Act [of 1829] as passed prescribed a new parliamentary oath which denied papal deposing powers and any 'temporal or civil jurisdiction' of the Pope in England. Catholics were also obliged to swear that they would not subvert the Establishment of the Church of England. No Catholic priest was to sit in the House of Commons. Nearly all of the offices were opened to Catholics—only those of Lord Chancellor, Keeper of the Great Seal, Lord Lieutenant of Ireland, and High Commissioner of the Church of Scotland being still reserved to Protestants. Catholics could become members of corporations. No Catholic bishop was to assume a territorial title traditionally attached to the State Church. The Catholic clergy were not allowed to

officiate outside their own places of worship. A clause banning religious orders from the realm—aimed at the Jesuits, whose formal reconstitution in England came in a papal decree which arrived just as the Bill was being formulated in the Cabinet—was never put into effect." See Edward Norman, *Roman Catholicism in England from the Elizabethan Settlement to the Second Vatican Council* (Oxford and New York: Oxford University Press, 1985), 63–64. Clauses like these were written into the Emancipation Act because of the great fear that English Catholics would be beholden to Rome—a sadly typical prejudice in the nineteenth century that lingered into the twentieth.

17. Ibid., 69: "The period between 1850 and Gladstone's controversy over the Vatican Decrees of 1874, in fact, was one marked by a rigorous and literate anti-Catholicism in English public life, with periodic petty rioting got up by popular Protestant speakers."

18. Ultramontanist triumphal histories largely ignore the growing Irish-Catholic population by barely noting the Irish existed, deeming them ineffective except at the extremely local level. See Edward R. Norman, *The English Catholic Church in the Nineteenth Century* (Oxford: Clarendon Press, 1984); John Bossy, *The English Catholic Community, 1570–1850* (New York and Oxford: Oxford University Press, 1976); and Derek J. Holmes, *More Roman than Rome: English Catholicism in the Nineteenth Century* (London: Burns & Oates; Shepherdstown, Eng.: Patmos Press, 1978).

19. Holmes, *More Roman than Rome,* 22.

20. Ibid., 46.

21. Ibid., 70.

22. "Ultramontanism for England," in *The Rambler* 3, no. 43 (July 1857), ed. John Moore Capes: [1]–2. See also definitions A1b and B1b in the *Oxford English Dictionary,* 2nd ed., s.v. "Ultramontanism."

23. The sermon was initially preached in 1852 at the First Provincial Synod at Westminster (St. Mary's, Oscott) and published in 1856 as part of *Sermons Preached on Various Occasions.* A later edition commonly available is John Henry Newman, "Sermon X: The Second Spring," in *Sermons Preached on Various Occasions* (London: Longmans, Green, 1904), 163–82.

24. Mary Heimann, *Catholic Devotion in Victorian England* (Oxford: Clarendon Press, 1995), 10.

25. The typical brief description of Ultramontanism in England focuses on the sweeping power of this "Second Spring": "Devotional practice was also undergoing a change at this time. The eighteenth-century Catholic tradition had been contemplative and restrained, but as a group the 'Old Catholics' were being superseded by ultramontanes who wished to establish new devotional styles and approaches to the faith. The focus of ultramontanism was the Church in Rome. It emphasized the centrality of Papal authority and the Pope as head of the Church worldwide. The hierarchical structure gave priests and bishops greater control over their congregations. Although this was necessary in large urban parishes, it limited the influence of the laity. The taste for continental Catholicism was also expressed in devotional styles and outward fittings. Where the Old Catholics were reserved, the ultramontanes were extrovert. They favoured churches filled with statues, holy pictures, candles and incense; priests wearing vestments; elaborate processions; and devotions to the Blessed Sacrament and the Sacred Heart. Religion for Old Catholics was a personal and meditative experience; for ultramontanes it was colorful and emotional, and emphasized a group identity that was part of the Universal Church." Suzanne Roberts, *Catholic Childhoods: Catholic Elementary Education in York, 1850–1914* (York: Borthwick Publications, 2001), 13–14.

26. Heimann, *Catholic Devotion,* 68. *The Garden of the Soul: A Manual of Spiritual Exercises and Instructions for Christians Who, Living in the World, Aspire to Devotion* by Bishop Richard Challoner was first published in 1740 and reprinted frequently until the twentieth century. Heimann notes that its popularity was so great it became a shorthand language—"Garden-

of-the-Soul Catholics" meant the Old English Catholics, as opposed to the recent converts or Irish-Catholic immigrants (72)—and that attempts to "convert" them to Ultramontane purposes by the English-Catholic hierarchy failed (81).

27. Roberts, *Catholic Childhoods*, 18.

28. Percy Young, *Elgar, Newman, and* The Dream of Gerontius: *In the Tradition of English Catholicism* (Aldershot: Scolar Press, 1995), 84.

29. "Dame school" is a generic description for any working-class school. See Jonathan Rose, *The Intellectual Life of the British Working Classes* (New Haven and London: Yale University Press, 2002), 151.

30. Basil Maine identifies Polly Ryler as Elgar's piano teacher. See *Elgar: His Life and Works* (London: G. Bell & Sons, 1933), 1:9; and Michael Kennedy, *Portrait of Elgar,* 3rd ed. (Oxford: Clarendon Press, 1987; repr. 1995), 19.

31. "Popular Education," *The Rambler* 6, no. 32 (August 1850): 101–2.

32. "Popular Education," *The Rambler* 10, no. 55 (July 1852): 8.

33. As Suzanne Roberts notes, "Education was *the* Catholic issue par excellence. . . . Together, church and school provided a distinct Catholic culture and identity to protect the Catholic population from Protestantism and instill in them Catholic values. The schools, while delivering the rudiments of an elementary education, primarily existed, as far as the Church was concerned, to teach the Catholic Faith." See Roberts, *Catholic Childhoods*, 9.

34. Moore, *Elgar: A Creative Life,* 17.

35. Daughters of the Heart of Mary archives, Wimbledon, quoted in Fr. Brian Doolan, *St. George's, Worcester: 1590–1999* (Birmingham: Archdiocese of Birmingham Historical Commission, 1999), 11. The information in this paragraph is largely from this source, 10–11; Doolan had access to archives that were unavailable at the time of writing.

36. Ibid., 16.

37. Eileen Hodgson, "The Berkeley Family of Spetchley Park (Part 2)," in *The Worcestershire Recusant: The Journal of the Worcestershire Catholic History Society* 16 (December 1970): 28.

38. Letter of Sister Anne Cunningham, archivist of the Sisters of St. Paul, Birmingham, 8 January 2006. It is usually stated in the biographical literature that when Elgar attended the school, it was still being run by the Sisters of St. Paul; see, for instance, Young's *Elgar, Newman, and* Gerontius, 83; and Moore, *Elgar: A Creative Life,* 35, n. 4. Moore's footnote states: "The sisters [*sic*] of St. Paul taught there until 1870–1, when they went out to nurse the wounded in the Franco-Russian War. . . . After that date teaching at Spetchley was in the hands of seculars." A source that might shed light on this discrepancy, a manuscript history titled "Records of Spetchley Parish," by Fr. A. L. Delerue, written before he left the area in 1876 and still held in the Berkeley Family Archives, was unavailable at the time of writing.

39. Letter from David H. J. Smith, archivist to the Berkeley family, 25 February 2006.

40. Moore, *Elgar: A Creative Life,* 37.

41. Ibid., 37–38.

42. Census records, Parish of St. John's, Schedule 82, 1871. Littleton House seems to have been used as a school for some time before Reeve's arrival. The transcript of the 1851 census housed at the Worcestershire History Centre lists a school run by Walter Caton (Curate of Powick and Schoolmaster), five servants, twenty students aged eight to fifteen, an assistant schoolmaster, a wife, a son, and a sister-in-law. Census records, Parish of St. John's, f. 46–47 (transcript), 1851.

43. Maine, *Elgar,* 1:11.

44. *The Catholic Directory, Ecclesiastical Register, and Almanac* (London: Burns and Oates, 1861), 249. Similar advertisements may be found in the issues of 1862 (228) and 1863 (224). By the time of Elgar's attendance, Reeve's advertisement was considerably shortened. These advertisements refer less to the instruction at the school, concentrating instead on the "large and airy rooms and extensive grounds for recreation." *Catholic Directory,* 1869, 329.

45. Roberts, *Catholic Childhoods*, 20.

46. Robert J. Buckley, *Sir Edward Elgar* (New York: J. Lane, 1905), 8. Most biographers mention this anecdote either when discussing *The Apostles* or Elgar's education at the hands of Reeve. See, for instance, Diana McVeagh, *Edward Elgar: His Life and Music* (London: M. M. Dent & Sons, 1955), 5; and Percy Young's *Elgar, O.M.: The Study of a Musician* (London: Purnell Book Services, 1973), 34–35.

47. Roberts, *Catholic Childhoods*, 17. See also *The Tablet*, 21 August 1869, 369: "The priest of necessity is the real master of the school, and the teacher is valuable in proportion as he knows how to play second fiddle and exercise his own powers in harmony with his superior's will."

48. According to Moore, Waterworth was a great intellect kept from leaving Worcester because of delicate health; see Moore, *Elgar: A Creative Life*, 15. A number of priests filled the other position at St. George's during Elgar's school years, changing frequently. Positively identifying these priests is difficult because the *Catholic Directory* often supplies more than one first name: the 1862 issue notes the presence of Fr. James Lomax as the second priest at the parish (96) and the 1863 directory names a Fr. Walter Lomax (85).

49. Thompson Cooper and Leo Gooch, "Waterworth, William," in the *Oxford Dictionary of National Biography* (Oxford: Oxford University Press, 2004).

50. Until 1871, Catholics, Dissenters, and Jews were not permitted to matriculate from Oxford or Cambridge universities. Some attended as students during the nineteenth century, but they were not allowed to take degrees. Nineteenth-century Catholics could receive higher education at St. Mary's, Oscott and University College, London. On Waterworth as confessor to Manning, see Young, *Elgar, Newman, and* Gerontius, 83.

51. Moore, *Elgar: A Creative Life*, 37. Elgar cared enough about this votive picture to save it, and it can be seen at the Elgar Birthplace Museum. An enlarged copy of it is in Jerrold Northrop Moore, *Spirit of England: Edward Elgar in His World* (London: Heinemann, 1984), 54.

52. Challoner, *The Garden of the Soul* (London: Burns, Oates, and Washbourne, 1945), 188–89.

53. Doolan, *St. George's, Worcester,* 17. Moore, using quotations from a Jesuit obituary in the magazine *Letters & Notices* 16 (1883): 150–53, states that "on account of his learning and his kindness and zeal, [Waterworth] was much esteemed by the Catholics and Protestants." See Moore, *Elgar: A Creative Life*, 15.

54. Initially organized by Fr. Herbert Vaughan (consecrated as bishop of Salford in 1872; made cardinal by Leo XIII in 1893), the Catholic Truth Society was reorganized in 1872 by the convert James Britten, who continued Vaughan's mission of publishing cheap pamphlets to inform the poor of Britain about elements of the "truth" of Catholicism in the nineteenth century. The organization still exists today, and on its website, http://www.cts-online.org.uk/CTS_history.htm (accessed April 21, 2006), a largely celebratory history section does not mention the high propaganda value of articles like those written by Waterworth.

55. William Waterworth, S.J., *The Popes and the English Church* (London: Catholic Truth Society, [1870]), 1.

56. Ibid., 19.

57. William J. Waterworth, S.J., *England and Rome: Or, The History of the Religious Connection Between England and the Holy See, from the year 179 to the Commencement of the Anglican Reformation in 1534. With Observations on the General Question of the Supremacy of the Roman Pontiffs* (London: Burns & Lambert, 1854), 121, 377–78, 380–81; and *Origin and Developments of Anglicanism: Or, A History of the Liturgies, Homilies, Articles, Bibles, Principles and Governmental System of the Church of England* (London: Burns and Lambert, 1854), v–vi, 388. See also Waterworth, *The Jesuits: Or, An Examination of the Origin, Progress, Principles, and Practices of the Society of Jesus;*

With Observations on the Leading Accusations of the Enemies of the Order (London: Charles Dolman; Hereford: W. Phillips; Liverpool: P. Hogan, 1852), 51–52.

58. William Waterworth, S.J., *Queen Elizabeth v. The Lord Chancellor; Or, A History of the Prayer Book of the Church of England. In Relation to the Purchas Judgment* (London: Burns, Oates and Company, 1871), 3.

59. See, for instance, George Macaulay Trevelyan, *History of England* (London and New York: Longmans, Green, 1926).

60. An example of revisionist history that echoes Leicester's views is Eamon Duffy, *The Stripping of the Altars: Traditional Religion in England 1400–1580* (New Haven and London: Yale University Press, 1992).

61. See Richard Smith, "Elgar, Dot and the Stroud Connection—Part One," *Elgar Society Journal* 14, no. 5 (July 2006): 14–20. Although most biographical sources give Elgar's sister's name as "Helen Agnes," the baptismal register shows her name as "Ellen Agnes."

62. Hubert Leicester, "How the Faith Was Preserved in Worcestershire: A Paper Read by Alderman Leicester, K.C.S.G., at the Eucharistic Congress at Droitwich, 2nd of August, 1932" (Worcester and London: Ebenezer Bayliss & Son, [1932]), 4.

63. Leicester's own avatar was that of a paternal "Gentleman Catholic." He gave Carice Elgar a missal upon her confirmation in 1907; letter of Carice Elgar to Hubert Leicester, 24 May 1907. Leicester also mounted and displayed a letter from Bishop W. B. Ullathorne, sent to his father, 28 December 1886. Worcestershire County Records Office, 705:185 BA 8185/1.

64. Initially a journal owned by the Catholic laity, *The Tablet* was bought in 1868 by Fr. Herbert Vaughan, later Cardinal Manning's replacement as head of the English Catholic Church. Under his editorial policies *The Tablet* became a primary voice in the discussion regarding Ultramontanist topics such as papal infallibility and the immaculate conception. See Norman, *English Catholic Church in the Nineteenth Century,* 360–61.

65. *The Tablet,* 1 June 1878, 698. See also Young, *Elgar, O.M.,* 42. Young believes that the advertisement might have been placed through the auspices of Fr. Waterworth or the Leicester family.

66. Hubert Leicester, *Notes on Catholic Worcester, Compiled . . . for the Centenary of the Opening of St. George's Church, Sansome Place* (Worcester: Trinity Press, [c. 1929]), 30.

67. A general discussion of Elgar's sacred music, both Catholic and Protestant, may be found in John Allison, *Edward Elgar: Sacred Music* (Bridgend: Seren, 1994); and in Butt, "Roman Catholicism," 106–19.

68. Challoner, *Garden of the Soul,* 128–35.

69. "Devotion to the Sacred Heart of Jesus," in *Catholic Encyclopedia* (New York: Appleton, 1907–1914).

70. Heimann, *Catholic Devotion,* 44.

71. "Devotions to the Sacred Heart," in Challoner, *Garden of the Soul,* 131–32. In a way, this service reads much like the litanies Elgar presented in his redaction of Part 1 of *Gerontius* (rehearsal number 64).

72. Allison, *Sacred Music,* 52–54.

73. Hodgkins, "Providence and Art," 6. Since Elgar was new to London, he might have attended church fifty times in order to "try out" the priests at each institution and decide which clerics best suited his idea of doctrine.

74. Moore, *Elgar: A Creative Life,* 352.

75. See McGuire, "Elgar, Judas, and the Theology of Betrayal," 271 n. 109.

76. Reports on all three oratorios preserved at the Elgar Birthplace Museum include discussions of them in the Catholic periodicals *The Tablet, Truth, The Catholic News, The Catholic Columbian,* and others. Elgar Birthplace Museum, cuttings files, vols. 5–9.

77. C. V. Gorton, *The Apostles, Sacred Oratorio by Edward Elgar: An Interpretation of the Libretto* (London: Novello and Company, [1903]); and *The Kingdom, Sacred Oratorio by Edward Elgar: An Interpretation of the Libretto* (London: Novello and Company, [1906]).

78. Elgar's use of Kramskoi's painting is an interesting case study of cross-cultural reinterpretation of a religious object. The painting is one of several by this late-nineteenth-century Russian Orthodox painter that depicts aspects of great men engaged in the public good, often at odds with their own desires. *Grove Art* notes that Kramskoi stated that "he wanted to convey to the viewer a sense of Christ's moral choice as an example applicable to their own lives when torn between serving an ideal or adhering to private concerns." (Elizabeth K. Valkenier, "Kramskoy, Ivan," *Grove Art Online*, Oxford University Press, http://www.groveart.com, accessed June 30, 2006). Elgar originally acquired a photographic reproduction of the painting from the Anglican canon C. V. Gorton (he compiled the libretto for Elgar's 1896 oratorio *The Light of Life*). Gorton may have been attracted to the human-looking Christ making a moral choice, but Elgar, in a letter to the singer David Ffrangçon Davies noted that it was "my ideal picture of the lonely Christ." Geoffrey Hodgkins, *Somewhere Further North: Elgar and the Morecombe Festival* (Rickmansworth: Poneke Press, 2003, 36). Thus Elgar equated the painting with similar devotional images of Christ used contemporaneously by Catholics in Great Britain.

79. Rosa Burley and Frank C. Carruthers, *Edward Elgar: The Record of a Friendship* (London: Barrie & Jenkins, 1972), 26.

80. See, for instance, *Catholic Directory, Ecclesiastical Register and Almanac* (London: Burns and Oates and Washbourne, Limited, 1932), 65.

81. *Catholic Encyclopedia*, s.v. "Oratorio." In a telling remark, the entry names Elgar's contemporary Edgar Tinel "the most gifted of composers who have reclaimed the oratorio from non-Catholic supremacy." Tinel, a Belgian composer, included a great deal of Gregorian chant and Palestrinian counterpoint in his oratorio *St. Francis* (1886–88). Elgar may have used Gregorian chant as a basis for his music in *The Apostles*, but he did not write a book on the subject, as Tinel did in 1890, and his counterpoint is certainly not touched by Palestrina. External and obvious reference to things Gregorian were a particular sign of Ultramontanism. John Butt theorizes that Elgar's "essentially English" musical style might have come from his work with Gregorian chant while organist at St. George's. Butt, "Roman Catholicism," 107–8.

82. Edward Algernon Baughan, "'The Apostles' and Elgar's Future," in *Music and Musicians* (London: Lane, 1906), 202.

83. *One Hundred Ninetieth Thousand: The Explanatory Catechism of Christian Doctrine, Chiefly Intended for the Use of Children in Catholic Schools* (London: 1884), 57; quoted in Heimann, *Catholic Devotion*, 114.

84. The London marriage of Elgar and Alice Roberts might also have been for reasons of family tradition and lore. The composer's father, Henry, although he lived in Worcester at the time, married Ann Greening in 1848 in London as well. See Young, *Elgar, Newman, and* Gerontius, 82; Moore, *Elgar: A Creative Life*, 5. The liberal nature of the London Oratory on Brompton Road may have been preserved because at its 1884 dedication, Pope Leo XII proclaimed it to be "*the* Oratory" in England, much to the chagrin of Cardinal John Henry Newman. The oratory was richly appointed and garnered impressive donations from wealthy Catholics. In contrast, Newman's oratory in Birmingham was a "patchwork . . . with its factory roof, painted walls and worn benches." See Meriol Trevor, *Newman: The Pillar of the Cloud* (London: Macmillan, 1962), 2: 611. Newman, feeling slighted, did not attend the dedication of the London Oratory in 1884, using old age as his excuse. He did, however, dispatch a gift and several priests of the Birmingham Oratory on his behalf, and attended a funeral at the London Oratory for the Dowager Duchess of Norfolk in 1886.

85. Hodgkins, "Providence and Art," 16, 18.

86. See McGuire, *Elgar's Oratorios,* 178–83, for a discussion of the genesis of the compositions from the original grand design to shorter works.

87. Hodgkins, "Providence and Art," 20.

88. Moore, *Elgar: A Creative Life,* 479.

89. Quoted in Doolan, *St. George's, Worcester,* 20.

90. Conversation between Elgar and the Leicester family, 17 June 1908, noted by Philip Leicester and quoted in Moore, *Elgar: A Creative Life,* 527.

91. Rudolph de Cordova, "Interview with Dr. Elgar," in *The Strand Magazine,* May 1904, 538–39, quoted in Michael Kennedy, *Portrait of Elgar,* 3rd ed. (Oxford: Clarendon Press, 1987; repr. 1995), 23.

92. See Matthew Riley, "Rustling Reeds and Loft Pines: Elgar and the Music of Nature," *19th-Century Music* 26, no. 2 (Fall 2002): 155–77.

93. Edward Elgar, foreword to Hubert Leicester's *Forgotten Worcester* (Worcester: Ebenezer Bayliss/Trinity Press, 1930), 10–11.

94. Kennedy, *Portrait of Elgar,* 20–21. The interior quote is from an article by Ernest Newman in the *Sunday Times* (London), 23 October 1955.

95. Kennedy, *Portrait of Elgar,* 328–29.

96. Moore, *Elgar: A Creative Life,* 823. The squabbling over where the dying Elgar should be buried, with Granville Bantock and John Reith attempting to maneuver the composer's Catholic corpse into the Anglican necropolis of Westminster Abbey, makes for sorry reading; see Michael De-la-Noy, *Elgar the Man* (London: Allen Lane, 1983), 228–29.

97. If not sung by both congregations during Elgar's time, they certainly are today. See *Elgar's Cathedral Music* (dir. Donald Hunt; Hyperion: CDA66313, 1988), a compact disc that presents a mixture of Elgar's Catholic church music composed in Latin for St. George's along with some of the Three Choirs Festival psalm settings with English texts, sung by the choir of Worcester Cathedral and conducted by Donald Hunt, who was for many years their organist.

98. Boden, *Three Choirs,* 179–80. Boden's description is likely taken from "The Memorial Service in Worcester Cathedral," in *The Musical Times* 75, no. 1094 (April 1934): 313.

99. Ibid.

100. The capitalization in this passage is a direct transcription. *Nature* is a telling word in this case, especially since the obituary that precedes it conflates the natural Elgar with the modernists, speaking of a new love for Elgar by the "younger generation" who "are taking to Elgar's music, amid the dark ways of modernism, as they do to a burst of sunshine in cloudy weather." "Edward Elgar," *The Musical Times* 75, no. 1094 (April 1934): 313.

101. A similar avatar, bridging Elgar to Anglicanism, appeared with the unveiling in the early 1980s of the Elgar statue, "midway between the High Street site of the Elgar family music shop and the cathedral, scene of so many performances of [Elgar's] music." John C. Phillips, "The Elgar Statue," *The Musical Times* 121, no. 1649 (July 1980): 440. The statue faces the cathedral, its back to St. George's Catholic Church. While the popular view of Elgar might acknowledge his Catholicism, the acknowledgment is not important enough to stand in the way of a good metaphor.

102. In his essay "The 'Dark Saying' of the Enigma," found in *Queer Episodes in Music and Modern Identity,* Byron Adams broadly asserts that the Lygon family was Roman Catholic, noting that Evelyn Waugh based the Catholic Marchmain family of *Brideshead Revisited* largely on the Lygons (220). Although individual members of family may have partaken of Catholic rituals (Lady Sybil, for instance, was married in the London Oratory on Brompton Road) or even converted to Catholicism (a rumor based on Lord Beauchamp's repeated attendance at solemn masses), evidence for the family's supposed Catholicism is ambiguous at best. Generations of Lygons matriculated at Christ Church Oxford; several, including

Frederick Lygon (B.A., 1852; M.A., 1856), John Lygon (B.A., 1806; M.A., 1808), and William Beauchamp Lygon (B.A., 1804; M.A., 1808) took degrees at that institution long before Catholics were allowed to do so in 1871. See Joseph Foster, *Alumni Oxionienses: The Members of the University of Oxford, 1715–1886: Their Parentage, Birthplace, and Year of Birth, with a Record of Their Degrees* (Oxford and London: Parker and Col., 1888), 3: 885. According to the *Oxford Dictionary of National Biography*, Frederick Lygon was known for both his composition of an Anglican hymnal used at the family's private chapel at Madresfield Court and his Anglican High Church views, which his son William (the seventh Earl Beauchamp) thought were bigoted. William Lygon's opinion of his father leaves room to speculate about the later Lygons' Catholic sympathies.

Elgar the Escapist?

MATTHEW RILEY

One of the more serious charges that can be brought against Elgar is that his art is escapist. This criticism can be targeted in several ways. Most obviously, Elgar was committed to a late-Romantic expressive idiom, to overall monotonality (his works usually begin and end in the same key), and to diatonicism as a basic point of tonal reference. These factors meant that during the first two decades of the twentieth century Elgar's music began to lag behind "progressive" developments in European music. More specifically, some of the literary themes that interested Elgar point to a desire to forget the reality of the present. He embraced the Victorian cult of chivalry and peopled his works with brave knights and heroic kings. As he reached middle age, he wrote music for and about children that echoes a well-known vein of late Victorian and Edwardian literary whimsy (Frances Hodgson Burnett, Kenneth Grahame, J. M. Barrie).[1] Finally, in his symphonic works there are moments when Elgar abandons the "musical present" to dwell on thematic reminiscences of earlier movements. At such points the past seems to take on an enchanted quality that the present can never match.

Since Freud, it is common to associate the notion of escape with regression. In this view, to be an escapist means not just to evade adult responsibilities but to suffer from a psychological disorder in which libido is arrested at an infantile stage of development (the "oral" phase). Furthermore, on a cultural level it could be alleged that escapist impulses are easily manipulated (and perhaps originally induced) by commercial or political forces that seek to cement their power and to dilute popular resistance.

But there is another possible perspective. A long tradition of English radicalism links dream, escape, and protest. Victorian medievalists such as A. W. N. Pugin, Thomas Carlyle, Charles Kingsley, and John Ruskin invoked a distant, alluring past in order to focus their passionate concern for the reform of contemporary society. William Morris's visual designs took inspiration from a medieval world where, he believed, the division of labor was unknown, the worker free. His utopian *News from Nowhere* (1890) imagined a future, post-revolutionary England steeped in beauty and innocent of money. These escapists wanted to change the world; they held up their dreams and visions as stimuli to action.[2] Perhaps the most eloquent plea for the value of escapism was made in the late 1930s by Elgar's fellow West Midlands Catholic, J. R. R. Tolkien (a direct literary descendant of Morris). In defending his attraction to "fairy stories," Tolkien warned against confusing the escape of the prisoner with the flight of the deserter: "Just so a Party-spokesman might have labeled departure from the misery of the Führer's or any other Reich and even criticism of it as treachery." The companions of "escape," he explained, are "disgust," "anger," "condemnation," and "revolt."[3]

In this light, a reexamination of Elgar's escapist impulses seems feasible. The present essay sketches an approach to the task. The problem is too large to tackle systematically here: there are too many compositions that could be cited, too many aspects of the late Victorian and Edwardian worlds that are relevant to Elgar's outlook. Instead, this investigation takes several novel, and perhaps provocative, perspectives on Elgar. The first half examines his personality and attitudes by means of two comparisons. Fiction by Elgar's contemporary H. G. Wells and historical writings by his friend Hubert Leicester provide lenses through which to view his personal circumstances. They bring into play some sociological issues relevant to Elgar's escapism concerning class and religion, respectively. The second half of the essay turns to Elgar's compositions, focusing on his characteristic treatment of sudden tonal shifts and evaluating the specifically musical escapism that becomes possible in his works.

Mr. Polly

H. G. Wells, born nine years after Elgar, was another shopkeeper's son. His father's business failed, and he worked his way to national recognition through self-help and hard work. During the first decade of the twentieth century—when Elgar enjoyed his greatest public esteem—Wells wrote three semiautobiographical novels that featured young, lower-middle-class men: *Love and Mr. Lewisham* (1900), *Kipps* (1905), and *The History of Mr. Polly* (1909). In each case the main character is innocent and aspiring but ill educated and trapped in unpromising employment: all the ingredients for escapist behavior are in place.

The character most akin to Elgar is Mr. Polly, whose father owns a music and bicycle shop. Mr. Polly is imprisoned first in the routine of a dull job in a drapery emporium and then in marriage and a High Street shop in Fishbourne in which he foolishly invests some unexpectedly inherited capital. Mr. Polly receives an inferior education and constantly struggles against straightened financial circumstances and meager opportunities for self-improvement. Before his fortunate windfall, he alternates between the shop floor and the employment office. However, he never fully loses his sparks of imagination and wonder. Deep inside him there lurks the conviction that "there was beauty, there was delight; that somewhere—magically inaccessible perhaps, but still somewhere—were pure and easy and joyous states of body and mind."[4] Mr. Polly therefore lives out a dual existence. He avidly collects books, and he prefers to lose himself in them than look after his shop properly. He is a keen cyclist, and at weekends goes on long rides to explore the countryside. His reading is totally unsystematic (and in this respect probably more like Elgar's than the latter would have admitted), mixing classics (Shakespeare, Boccaccio, Rabelais) with modern adventure stories and thrillers.[5] He falls in love in courtly fashion, after the manner of a character in a chivalric romance. As an autodidact, Mr. Polly is uncertain of the pronunciation of words he has seen only in print, but is enthusiastic in devising ringing phrases and sometimes ridiculous neologisms. He has a tendency to verbal pretence, but is also vulnerable to the conversational faux pas.

Mr. Polly suffers from chronic indigestion—of mind as well as body—and thus frequent bouts of bad temper. These afflictions are the result of the impossible conditions that English society imposes on him. The novel begins with Mr. Polly sitting on a stile in a field, with an aching stomach. After fifteen years of unrewarding shopkeeping, he finds his business on the verge of bankruptcy. He is in his mid- or late thirties (the age at which Elgar was still a frustrated provincial violin teacher, seemingly destined for permanent obscurity). Mr. Polly decides to burn the shop and kill himself, allowing his wife to live off the insurance payment. He goes through with the arson, but somehow forgets to execute the suicide. So he pockets a share of the money and abandons his former existence to become a cheerful vagabond, wandering the woods and lanes of southern England. By the end of the novel he is fortunate enough to settle into a job at a country inn, where he enjoys an idyllic existence as a ferryman on a river and works for the comfortable fat woman who owns the establishment. Here he feels "mellowish and warmish." His existence is "as safe and enclosed and fearless as a child that has still to be born."[6] So Mr. Polly, who was all along an "artless child of nature," escapes to a womblike refuge.

Elgar, living in the real world, never achieved such a decisive and successful escape. His indigestion of the mind—and tendency to dyspeptic outbursts and theatrical displays of self-pity—remained to the end of his life. Many of the illnesses he suffered during his thirties and forties may well have been at least partly psychosomatic. The early scars left by the Victorian class system made him ashamed of his origins and profession, resentful of establishment "insiders," but also, conversely, left him afflicted by an unattractive snobbery, overvaluing material possessions, and affecting the behavior of a leisured amateur. His father's music shop was not especially profitable, nor were Elgar's teaching rounds, which in any case he loathed. Even in later years, when he had secured a national reputation, he constantly feared having to fall back on teaching or worse. He frequently contemplated suicide—or claimed to—but never attempted the deed. Like Mr. Polly, Elgar had a small slice of financial luck—in his case it was his wife's (relatively modest) income—but his attempt to develop a career in London between 1889 and 1891 failed, and he was forced to return to his provincial origins and renew his old connections. During the 1890s, his prospects often seemed bleak. One day early in that decade, when he was in his mid-thirties, Elgar, in "a pitifully overwrought state," explained his troubles to his friend Rosa Burley, the headmistress of the school where he taught the violin. She described his account as "an outpouring of misery that was positively heartrending."[7] The theme was Elgar's high artistic ambitions, which, he maintained, were constantly thwarted by poverty and the drudgery of his daily job.

Clearly Mr. Polly lags some way behind Elgar both in creative imagination and in artistic, social, and sartorial pretension. But in other respects the two appear rather disconcertingly alike. Elgar was largely self-taught and always carried with him the anxieties of the autodidact. As a young man he immersed himself in books and acquired a taste for chivalry and romance. Later he became a book collector and dabbled on the fringes of literary scholarship.[8] His letters display an enduring delight in wordplay. He claimed to have preserved into adulthood a childlike sense of wonder and imagination within himself. Above all he was devoted to the countryside and to cycling, and took every opportunity to lose himself far from civilization.

Nevertheless, despite these parallels in their characters, the differences between the respective destinies of Elgar and Mr. Polly are stark. Mr. Polly discovers that "if the world does not please you *you can change it*."[9] Wells's novel thus describes the successful transformation of Mr. Polly's life. Like Wells, whose portrait of Mr. Polly drew upon his own life experience, Elgar transgressed the hidebound class divisions of the time to become a famous and honored artist. Thus for Elgar the rural idyll remains a temporary refuge; he must always return to society to find a home, make a living, and, of course, make music. Elgar never conducted an incendiary experiment to match Mr. Polly's burning of his shop, for Elgar harbored ambitions for self-advancement more like those of Wells himself than the quietist solution embraced by Mr. Polly.[10] Aside from Elgar's obvious responsibilities as a father and husband, there was probably too much conservativism in his character, both politically and personally, for him to make a sharp break and abandon his aspirations to respectability and public approval. Guided by his wife, in the 1890s Elgar attempted to escape his difficulties through the alternative methods of hard work, social climbing, and eventually the cultivation of royal patronage, but this deepened his entanglement in English society and, in the end, did not cure his mental indigestion. In this light Elgar's escapism is a paradoxical impulse. Like Mr. Polly's, it is deeply embittered, but it coexists with an outward tendency not only to accept but even to strengthen the original entrapment. The next section suggests a model for this uncomfortable condition, finding it—literally—just down Elgar's street.

Worcester Forgotten and Remembered

> How often in years gone by, while pacing the lonely cloisters of our venerable cathedral, have I endeavored in imagination to refill the void with its former occupants—to note their appearance, dress, and employment—to enquire of these shadowy unrealities their history, thoughts, hopes, and aspirations, and to restore for a few moments the gorgeous pomp and circumstance of a wondrous institution now gone for ever.
> —John Noake, *The Monastery and Cathedral of Worcester* (1866)

Toward the end of his life, Hubert Leicester, Elgar's childhood companion, fellow Catholic, Worcester stalwart, and five times mayor of the city, penned a series of contributions to its history: *Notes on Catholic Worcester* (1928), *Forgotten Worcester* (1930), *How the Faith Was Preserved in Worcestershire* (1932), and *Worcester Remembered* (1935).[11] Although Elgar's foreword to *Forgotten Worcester* implies that the pair were chalk and cheese in terms of personality, their social origins were similar (class, religion, upbringing on High Street), both enjoyed upward career trajectories (Leicester became a successful accountant), and both held their hometown in high esteem and relished its traditions of civic ceremony. Leicester's books echo some of Elgar's basic beliefs and attitudes and flesh them out in a way that Elgar himself never did. Leicester emerges from them as an ambivalent figure, filled with civic pride but deeply dissatisfied with the present and yearning for the return of a distant past that was swept away long ago in what he regards as a violent catastrophe.

Leicester's introduction to *Forgotten Worcester* strikes a note of solemn local patriotism. He has written the book solely to satisfy a request from the mayor. He hopes that the work will confirm the importance of the city and inspire the native.[12] He then lays out a personal interpretation of "History" in the large—not just the history of Worcester, but that of England as a whole over two millennia. The first era (1–669 C.E.) was pagan, and he passes over it swiftly. For Worcester, the second (669–1155) started at the time of the conversion of the kingdom of Mercia to Christianity. Society was now shaped by the teachings of the Church, which upheld a duty to administer to the needs of the less fortunate. To this end abbeys, friaries, priories, convents, churches, and cathedrals were established, which provided relief to the poor, sick, and orphaned, and education to those who needed it. This regime maintained direct links between the community, the spiritual values of its people, and the dispensation of local charity. "Rates [local taxes], as we know them to-day, were things unheard of."[13] The third era (1155–1540) witnessed the development of trade and commerce and the awakening of "the general desire to acquire money"; it thus contained the first seeds of modern decline. The activities of the Church were now ably supplemented by guilds and corporations, which regulated the behavior of tradesmen, arranged public entertainments, and provided insurance for the citizens against misfortune, criminal damage, or loss. The era ended with society's definitive fall from grace: "This dual management, for satisfying the new wants of the community, continued till the sixteenth century, when the religious houses were dissolved, the guilds banned, and the lands and possessions of both bodies (which were really the property of the people) seized by the Crown."[14] Leicester's characterization of the fourth era (1540–1930) is terse and devastating: "After the religious houses were abolished, the financial, or mercenary age commenced, and brought with it the extension of the rent system, the introduction of rates, taxes, and ground rents, and the reduction of most of our institutions to a mercantile basis. And in this state we are today."[15]

Leicester's books periodically return to aspects of this narrative and expand upon the details. Mention of the English Reformation is usually scornful, with the word placed within quotation marks: "the fateful 'Reformation'"; "what is known as the 'Reformation.'"[16] Leicester regards its immediate outcomes as sacrilege and rapine, and its long-term impact as far-reaching social alienation. *Worcester Remembered* tenderly records a catalogue of "outrages" committed against the religion of the city: the prohibition of the Mass, the abolition of altars and crucifixes, the despoiling of "sacred images," the reuse of consecrated altar stones as paving, and the plunder of the shrines of Saint Oswald and Saint Wulstan. Heavy fines imposed by the Crown on recusants enriched the exchequer and coerced the English people into accepting Protestantism against their true wishes.[17] Leicester takes similar pains in documenting the damage inflicted on Worcester Cathedral by Cromwell's troops during the English Civil War: the destruction of "sacred statues," the smashing of stained glass, the use of the building as a stable, and "other atrocities too vile to be mentioned."[18] The long-term consequences of the Reformation were no less dire. The chapter in *Forgotten Worcester* on "Ancient Guilds as They Affected Worcester" praises the pre-Reformation guild system for its reliance on local beneficence, pride, and solidarity, and aims several barbs at the modern system of state welfare provision. "All these services were performed by the Guilds in days when men were prepared to pay for what they received, and did not expect, as so many do to-day, to receive these benefits as their right. . . . In the trade Societies of to-day, the main objects are to force up wages and obtain for the worker constant increase of pay, while those of the masters have it as their object to so manage matters that the price of commodities may be put up to the advantage of the producer." Similarly, in modern times insurance is provided by "commercial companies run for the sake of profit." These developments owe their existence ultimately to the expansion of the state in the sixteenth century, when poor laws and workhouses had to be established to substitute for the work of the monasteries and guilds, and taxes levied to pay for them.[19]

Leicester's views appear to rest on a combination of staunch local patriotism and middle-class resentment of taxation and state bureaucracy. Welfare is best administered between and among fellow citizens; when the state steps between those who fund and receive welfare, both suffer. His tone of disillusion in this regard may owe something to the industrial strife of the 1920s and the economic depression of the 1930s. What is distinctive about his writings, however, is the combination of these politically Conservative themes with a strong emotional attachment to a lost culture of Catholicism, which casts an air of mystery and romance over the whole account. He rejects the prevailing view of the English Reformation as a heroic phase of national self-definition. His condemnation of central government's "crimes" against the English people is reminiscent of early-nineteenth-century radical texts such as William Cobbett's *History of the Protestant Reformation* (1824–27) and *Rural Rides* (1830). His devotion to medieval Catholicism and its social mission echoes the opinions of the Victorian architect and medievalist A. W. N. Pugin, whose writings compared the society of the Middle Ages favorably with that of the present. (Pugin regarded the modern city as filthy, cramped, violently policed, and brutal in its effect on the poor.)[20] These themes became commonplaces of Victorian medievalism, articulated by Thomas Carlyle and the "Young England" circle, and then by John Ruskin and the Christian Socialists. Later they were taken up by William Morris and the Guild Socialist movement.[21] Leicester thus writes within a tradition that challenges the basic narrative about English identity and history made by British governments and the Church of England for several centuries.

The connections between Leicester and Elgar are oblique yet intriguing, given the men's common origins. In 1905, during Leicester's first stint as mayor of Worcester, he arranged for Elgar to be awarded the freedom of the city. At the ceremony Elgar (wearing his Yale University robes) processed solemnly through the streets alongside the civic dignitaries.[22] In 1930, possibly influenced directly by Leicester's writings, Elgar composed his *Severn Suite,* whose movements evoke Worcester's medieval past ("Worcester Castle," "Tournament," "Cathedral," "Commandery").

Elgar's letters contain an abundance of references to the distant past of his own life, many of them associated with his childhood and early adulthood in Worcester, and, especially in later years, infused with passionate regret and longing for a lost idyll.[23] Leicester's books, too, have their warm domestic aspects: they blend personal and family memories, legend and hearsay, and genuine historical findings, merging personal and collective memory. To be sure, aside from the decision to set Cardinal Newman's "The Dream of Gerontius"—at the time a controversial move—Elgar seldom advertised his attachment to the mystery and majesty of Catholic worship, and he certainly did not utter public polemics on the subject: he was a cultural Catholic rather than a militant believer.[24] Still, in 1931 he could write about the College Hall in Worcester: "The College Hall is a favorite subject for meditation with me, carrying, as it does, the happiest memories of great music, with a halo of the middle ages combined with an odour of sanctity which even the sacrilege of the reformers has not wholly destroyed."[25] (This sensual description resonates with Elgar's more general attachment to display and ceremonial, his liking for "colorful" music, and his impatience with the English taste for the plain.)

But Leicester's most significant parallels with Elgar are found at the levels of tone and rhetoric. Leicester's books are marked by an undercurrent of loss and anger and a sense of belatedness. The distant past is characterized by perfect unity; this was the time of "what had always been the 'one faith' of Christendom."[26] Past and present worlds are separated by a definitive break at 1540, a break violently imposed by external forces against which the inhabitants of England, and Worcester in particular, are helpless.

Although Leicester looks forward to the future unification of the Anglican and Catholic churches, his remarks in that regard sound as much like pious formulae as real hopes. When he lets down the guard of the respectable citizen and diligent antiquarian, Leicester emerges, like Elgar, as a man of contradictions: an accountant who hates commercialism and a Catholic with a sense of disinheritance within the city to which he professes devotion. As with Elgar, there is in practice no easy way out of this predicament. For the present, a better world can be glimpsed only through memory and imagination.

Some Musical Escape Routes

Rather than presenting a comforting illusion, Elgar's best music occasionally stumbles across the intuition of a happy existence that for the most part remains out of reach. It is escapist in this sense, and numerous passages and techniques could be cited in illustration. The pastoral interludes in the choral and symphonic works (*Caractacus, In the South, Falstaff,* the symphonies) could be viewed as isomorphic to Mr. Polly's weekend excursions: they are wonderfully idyllic, but they do not last. Thematic reminiscence in Elgar's works—the recollection of material from an earlier movement in a later movement—is often as sensual as his memory of College Hall in Worcester: the recollections are prepared portentously, presented mysteriously, and cloaked in a hazy atmosphere. The cadenza of the Violin Concerto and the slow movement of the Second Symphony contain well-known examples. (By contrast, the musical "present" of the later movement is usually far more prosaic.) There is a common process in Elgar's symphonic works whereby a grandiose climax swiftly recedes and gives way to intimate, introspective music—a process known in the literature as "withdrawal."[27] During the 1910s, Elgar developed a tendency to conclude his major compositions with bitter irony or with palpable, unresolved duality. His last two substantial symphonic works, *Falstaff* (1913) and the Cello Concerto (1919), along with *The Music Makers* (1912), endure painful ruptures in their final bars, which push dream and reality, memory and present consciousness into stark oppositions. In all these examples, escape is characterized by displacement: digression from the main "argument" or "frame" of a piece. Such displacement is almost always corrected in the end. Interludes recede, reminiscences fade, and movements end with the reiteration of their "proper" frame and close in the "home" key. It is very unusual for a movement in one of Elgar's scores to be permanently disrupted by an escapist digression and its overall course altered. Just as in Elgar's life, there is no equivalent to Mr. Polly's successful act of resistance. Despite their shared determination to succeed in a caste-bound society, Elgar possessed little of Wells's resilience or enterprise, traits the author drew upon and transmuted to create the character of Mr. Polly. This is not to say the displacements leave no mark on Elgar's music. Reality prevails, but at a price: it is diminished and discredited. In the final bars of Elgar's later symphonic works, closure is achieved, but resolution is absent.

A related form of escape by displacement is illustrated by Elgar's characteristic use of abrupt tonal shifts or slippages. In many cases these shifts are soon reversed, allowing the music to resume in its original tonal sphere. They are parenthetical utterances, indicating moments of distraction or fleeting reverie. A late but charming example is found in a piece titled "Dreaming," from the 1931 *Nursery Suite* (Example 1). Drowsiness turns briefly to deeper slumber six bars after rehearsal number 57, as a 6–4–2 chord on D♭ enters, the parts marked lento, espressivo, pianissimo, and the double basses entering briefly to darken the color. But the music soon finds its way back to the tonic E♭ and continues on its way. The examples could be multiplied. For instance, the songs from Elgar's incidental music to the stage play *The Starlight Express*—given to a character known as the Organ Grinder— contain three such digressions—again flatward—each of which coincides with a call for a return to the dreams and enchantment of childhood. The reassertion of the mundane adult world is effected briskly, and sometimes brutally. The opposition between dream and reality is starkly underlined.[28]

In the symphonic works, tonal displacement occasionally receives more complex treatment. Although in the final analysis an uncomfortable duality is upheld, the effect of the displacement is felt longer. In Example 2, for instance, from the Adagio of the First Symphony, a movement cast in D major, a sequence in A major underpins a rising diatonic linear pattern in the upper voice, beginning C♯–D–E–F♯ (Examples 2a and 2b). The sequence stops when the progression turns to G♮ instead of G♯. This turns out to be a chromatic passing note that merely delays the appearance of dominant harmony (with G♯s) and then tonic harmony, completing an implicit progression of a sixth in the upper voice: C♯–A. The sequence then begins again. But in the meantime the G♮ is expanded by means of a G major chord and its applied dominant. During that expansion, the regular progress of the sequence is halted; the pulse is less marked; the texture broadens; musical time slows. This example does not present an absolute duality: the music of the sequence already possesses an idyllic tone, and the G major harmony is well integrated into the musical paragraph by virtue of the underlying voice-leading. Indeed, the broadening of the textual and rhythmic dimensions impels the music onward and allows, as

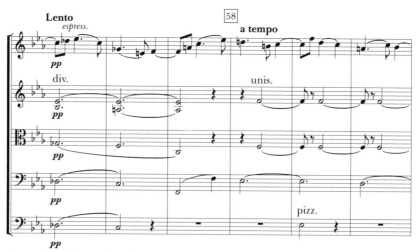

Example 1. "Dreaming," *Nursery* Suite, rehearsal nos. 57–58.

it were, the sequence to unfold all the more expansively on its repetition. In this view the G major music stores up a kind of potential energy, which is released on the return to A major, the overall key of this passage.

In Example 3, from the Larghetto of the Second Symphony, the mustering of forces for a grand climax is interrupted and partially reversed by a shift from a B-flat major/G minor sphere to D major, combined with a slowing of tempo, a sudden reduction in dynamics, and a fleck of color from the clarinets. Here the sense of purpose and drive of the preceding bars is sapped—not altogether, but the gradual buildup taking place during this section has to begin all over again in the new key, D major. The

Example 2a. Adagio, Symphony no. 1 in A-flat Major, op. 55.

Example 2b. Adagio, Symphony no. 1 in A-flat Major, op. 55, voice-leading reduction.

music finds its way back to the tonal center of this section of the movement—F major—although much more gradually than in the excerpt from the Adagio from the First Symphony cited in Example 2a. Still, F major is asserted unambiguously at the climax of the Larghetto (see full score, rehearsal number 76) and is stabilized thereafter, so the section overall is tonally closed.

The Adagio of the Cello Concerto is perhaps the closest Elgar ever comes, from the perspective of tonality, to a wholly "escapist" movement.

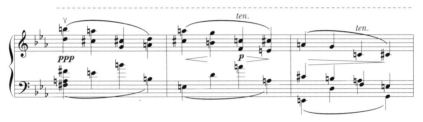

Example 3. Larghetto, Symphony no. 2 in E-flat Major, op. 63.

The piece is framed by an eight-bar period in B-flat at its beginning and end, but otherwise the tonality is fluid. A few ideas are repeated in irregular sequences, moving swiftly through distant modulations with no apparent rationale for the choice of keys that are briefly established. In Example 4, where the harmonic progressions are based around chromatic motions in parallel sixths, the abrupt tonal shifts are coordinated with changes of instrumental color (woodwind replacing strings) and, for the soloist, upward leaps to 9–8 appoggiaturas. The movement as a whole amounts to a reverie, which acquires a kind of coherence only through the consistency of its waywardness. Its melancholy quality arises not just from its obsessive dwelling on a handful of ideas but from its determination to be always distracted by them.[29] Still, this attitude is sustained for only sixty bars; the opening of the finale reasserts conventional rhetoric and function and gets the concerto back on course.

The techniques illustrated by these examples have long been admired by commentators on Elgar. They are usually understood—surely correctly—as evidence of some kind of musical-cum-psychological dualism. According to Diana McVeagh:

> The half-shy, half-impulsive moments in Elgar's music often come from a chord escaping from the prevailing tonality either to double back at once . . . or to turn right aside . . . [here she cites part of Example 3]. This was from the first a personal fingerprint . . . Always

Example 4. Adagio, Cello Concerto in E Minor, op. 85.

the unexplained chord is itself simple; its aloofness comes from its alien context, it is lingered over in a sudden hush, and its effect is of a withdrawal, a shrinking for an instant into a secret self, that is the essence of Elgar the dreamer.[30]

And Wilfred Mellers puts it thus:

In music such as this [part of Example 4] the rhetorician is silenced; in the free rubato of the lyricism an intimate human voice speaks directly to you and me, while an unexpected chord or modulation reveals the private heart beneath the public manner.[31]

The idea of a "secret self" or "private heart" into which Elgar "withdraws" is a commonplace of the critical literature. Although occasionally pushed to injudicious extremes, it is undoubtedly invited both by his behavior and by his music.[32]

But one might venture a further, less familiar observation, for there is a striking feature common to all these examples of tonal displacement. In each case the moment of "withdrawal" or "shrinking" coincides with an alteration in what might be termed the musical dynamic (referring now to an analogy with forces in mechanics, not loudness). On the one hand, there is a certain relaxation; on the other, suspense, like a holding of the breath. The relaxation is partly rhythmic—the effect of slowing, pausing, or the nonarticulation of pulse—and partly the result of the harmonic shift. Since the new chord has no conventional function in the old key, the harmonic logic that might otherwise link the music's past and present and point on to its future is suspended. For a moment, as it were, things seem easy: a weight is lifted; the pressure of directed motion is released. In Examples 2 and 4, the upward leaps at the moments of tonal shift, followed by unhurried descents, accelerating only gradually, present unmistakable images of floating. These metaphors of weight and motion clarify the character of the escape under discussion here: it is an escape of the body. The music articulates the first half of Mr. Polly's conviction: somewhere, however inaccessible, exist "pure and easy and joyous states of body and mind."

The notion of bodily escape in Elgar is striking because so many aspects of his mature style—style in both the sense of his personal behavior and the idiom of his music—can be linked to the Victorian disciplining of the male body. Elgar did not attend one of the great public schools, such as Eton or Rugby, but something of the ethos of those institutions—the value of strenuous physical exercise and its relation to virtue and chivalry ("fair play") and to British imperialism—nevertheless seeped into his consciousness and into his music, too. His liking for a regular, clearly marked pulse, usually in march time; his use of florid, "courtly" gestures in his melodic lines; the many broad, serene tunes that sit precisely in the register of a male tenor voice—whether or not they are sung—could all be cited. By the same token, the emphasis on chivalry and medieval romance in Elgar's choice of texts, his attraction to grand ceremonial, his call for English music to adopt "an out-of-door sort of spirit," and his description of the motto theme of the First Symphony as a "sort of *ideal* call" resonate strongly in their various ways with the constructions of masculinity by Thomas Carlyle, Charles Kingsley, and others.[33] In many cases those constructions centered on the regulation and control of masculine "energy." On these terms, Elgar's sudden tonal shifts represent the rare moments when the regulating practices break down and the energy is released in some new form. The results are not, as the Victorians might have feared, chaotic, but marvelously easeful.

Part of Elgar believed in the self-disciplines and even embraced them; he probably never wholly lost his tendency to high-minded Victorian idealism, however diluted or overwritten by other attitudes it may have become in later years.[34] It is of crucial importance, however, to recognize that Elgar himself did not live up to the ideals of physical masculinity sketched out here. Indeed, his mental indigestion appears to have manifested itself rather clearly in the movements of his body. Contemporary accounts described Elgar as nervous, twitchy, and ill at ease in formal company; caricatures of him conducting portrayed him as hunched, bony, and jerky. If anything, Elgar's body fitted more closely the category of the neurasthenic in the late Victorian discourse on "decadence" and social "degeneration."[35] In this light, Elgar's carefully posed photographs and his bristling moustache—and indeed the supposed "self-portrait" of the final *Enigma* variation—must be understood as compensatory strategies. The famous photograph taken by William Eller in August 1900 as Elgar was finishing *Gerontius* shows us, as David Cannadine puts it, "Elgar as he wanted to be seen, yet giving away more than he knew: the tradesman's son trying too hard to conceal the fact that he was."[36] Accordingly, many of Elgar's sudden tonal shifts—along with some of his interludes, recollections, and "withdrawals"—could be said to acquire a ring of truth. This is not a truth along the lines of "here is the true Elgar—the poet, the dreamer, not the Edwardian gentleman," for the assiduously cultivated image of the Edwardian gentleman was also the true Elgar. Rather, it is the displacement that matters, and the overall pattern of psychological fault lines that result.

In conclusion, it seems appropriate to distinguish two phases of Elgarian escape. In the first, Elgar attempts to escape his predicament through self-improvement, but in so doing entraps himself further. Evidence for this compulsion can be discerned in his behavior, appearance, and music. But its effects reach even beyond Elgar's own lifetime. For decades after his death, Elgar's image was tarnished by his associations with nationalism, conservatism (artistic and political), and imperialism. These factors have helped confine him to the fringes of music history textbooks and of concert programs (at least, outside the United Kingdom), and until recently made academics wary of him as an object of study.[37] Despite books like this one, Elgar may never wholly escape that marginalization. But the self-defeating first phase of escape is a precondition for the second, emphatically musical phase. At this point the opportunity arises for Elgar to develop some of the most affecting and powerful qualities of his music and to create a good deal of what we now value highly in his work. It was, in a way, part of Elgar's genius to entrap himself so tightly; perhaps only a shopkeeper's son could have brought it off with such conviction.

NOTES

1. On the topic of Elgar and childhood, see Michael Allis, "Elgar and the Art of Retrospective Narrative," *Journal of Musicological Research* 19 (2000): 289–328; and Matthew Riley, "Childhood," in *Edward Elgar and the Nostalgic Imagination* (Cambridge: Cambridge University Press, 2006), chap. 5.

2. Elgar's *The Dream of Gerontius* and *The Apostles* carry epigraphs from Ruskin and Morris, respectively. Elgar quoted Kingsley in his lecture "English Composers" as professor of music at the University of Birmingham, and may have tacitly invoked him during an interview with Gerald Cumberland in 1905. Elgar probably identified with the idealistic aims of these writers, although the extent to which he endorsed their specific political agendas is unclear. See Brian Trowell, "Elgar's Use of Literature," in *Edward Elgar: Music and Literature,* ed. Raymond Monk (Aldershot: Scolar Press, 1993), 197, 228–39; Edward Elgar, *A Future for English Music and Other Lectures,* ed. Percy M. Young (London: Dennis Dobson), 91.

3. J. R. R. Tolkien, *Tree and Leaf: Including the Poem "Mythopoeia"* (London: HarperCollins, 2001), 61. Tolkien's observation that critics have made the confusion "not always by sincere error" may even hint at the connections between modernist aesthetics and authoritarian politics in the 1930s.

4. H. G. Wells, *The History of Mr. Polly* (London: Penguin, 2005), 14.

5. See Trowell, "Elgar's Use of Literature," 182–326.

6. Wells, *Mr. Polly,* 206.

7. Rosa Burley and Frank C. Carruthers, *Edward Elgar: The Record of a Friendship* (London: Barrie and Jenkins, 1972), 38.

8. As witnessed by his letters to the *Times Literary Supplement* between 1919 and 1923, discussed (disparagingly) by Trowell, "Elgar's Use of Literature," 201–3.

9. Wells, *Mr. Polly,* 159.

10. A possible exception to this rule is the explosion that took place after one of Elgar's chemical experiments in his garden shed in Hereford. But this was apparently accidental. W. H. Reed, *Elgar as I Knew Him* (London: Victor Gollancz, 1936), 39.

11. Hubert A. Leicester, *Notes on Catholic Worcester* (Worcester: Ebenezer Bayliss, 1928); *Forgotten Worcester* (Worcester: Trinity Press, 1930); *How the Faith Was Preserved in Worcestershire* (Worcester: Ebenezer Bayliss, 1932); *Worcester Remembered* (Worcester: Ebenezer Bayliss, 1935; repr. East Ardsley: S. R. Publishers Ltd., 1970). See also Leicester's *Notes on the History of Freemen* (Worcester; printed for private circulation, 1925).

12. Leicester, *Forgotten Worcester,* 15, 19.

13. Ibid., 17.

14. Ibid., 18.

15. Ibid.

16. Ibid., 64; Leicester, *Worcester Remembered,* 49.

17. Leicester, *Worcester Remembered,* 50–52.

18. Leicester, *Forgotten Worcester,* 65; *Notes on Catholic Worcester,* 16.

19. Leicester, *Forgotten Worcester,* 92, 104, 113, 112.

20. Leicester would have approved of Pugin's drawing of "contrasted residences for the poor" from *Contrasts* (1836). As the historian of religion Nigel Yates has observed, "The noble monastic buildings are replaced by a utilitarian workhouse; a diet of beef, mutton, bread and ale by one of bread and gruel; the poor person in his quasi-monastic habit by a beggar in rags; the master dispensing charity by a master wielding whips and chains; decent Christian burial by the dispatch of the corpse for dissection by medical student; and the discipline of an edifying sermon by that of a public flogging." A. W. N. Pugin, *Contrasts* and *The True Principles of Pointed or Christian Architecture* (Reading: Spire Books Ltd., 2003), app., fig. 14; Nigel Yates, "Pugin and the Medieval Dream," in *Victorian Values: Personalities and Perspectives in Nineteenth-Century Society,* ed. Gordon Marsden (London and New York: Longman, 1990), 60–70, esp. 65.

21. See William Stafford, "'This Once Happy Country': Nostalgia for Pre-Modern Society," in *The Imagined Past: History and Nostalgia,* ed. Christopher Shaw and Malcolm Chase (Manchester and New York: Manchester University Press, 1989), 33–46; and Frances Hutchinson, *The Political Economy of Social Credit and Guild Socialism* (London: Routledge, 1997), 14–15.

22. See Jerrold Northrop Moore, *Edward Elgar: A Creative Life* (Oxford: Oxford University Press, 1984), 465.

23. Allis speaks of a "surfeit of references to past events" in "Retrospective Narrative," 291; see also 328 for some examples.

24. See Charles McGuire's essay in this volume for a detailed discussion of Elgar's Catholicism.

25. 3 June 1931 in Jerrold Northrop Moore, ed., *Edward Elgar: Letters of a Lifetime* (Oxford: Clarendon Press, 1990), 438. Cited also in Allis, "Retrospective Narrative," 322.

26. Leicester, *Notes on Catholic Worcester,* 16.

27. For a discussion of the history of this idea, see Riley, "Identity," chap. 6 in *Nostalgic Imagination.*

28. Two of Elgar's letters refer to his liking for flatward modulation: to A. J. Jaeger, 19 September 1908, and to Ernest Newman, 27 October 1908. See Jerrold Northrop Moore, ed., *Elgar and his Publishers: Letters of a Creative Life* (Oxford: Clarendon Press, 1987), 2:710; and Moore, *Letters of a Lifetime,* 199. For a discussion of the modulations in the Organ Grinder's songs, see Riley, *Nostalgic Imagination,* chap. 5. Numerous antecedents for Elgar's flatward shifts can be found in nineteenth-century music, most notably in Schubert. For a discussion that links these phenomena with modern philosophical dualism, see Karol Berger, "Beethoven and the Aesthetic State," *Beethoven Forum* 7, ed. Mark Evan Bonds (Lincoln and London: University of Nebraska Press, 1999), 17–44.

29. For further discussion of melancholy in the Cello Concerto, see Christopher Mark, "The Later Orchestral Music," in *The Cambridge Companion to Elgar,* ed. Daniel M. Grimley and Julian Rushton (Cambridge: Cambridge University Press, 2004), 166–69.

30. Diana McVeagh, *Edward Elgar: His Life and Music* (London: J. M. Dent, 1955), 200–201.

31. Alec Harman, Anthony Milner, and Wilfred Mellers, *Man and his Music* (London: Barrie & Rockliffe, 1962), 970.

32. See Riley, *Nostalgic Imagination,* chap. 6.

33. Elgar, *A Future for English Music,* 57; letter to Ernest Newman, 4 November 1908, cited in Moore, *Letters of a Lifetime,* 200.

34. Elgar's biographer Basil Maine referred to "the growing scepticism of Elgar's attitude to life," but added that "it is one of the many contradictions that are to be discerned in his character, that this scepticism exists in him together with an intense and noble idealism. The problem is to discover which of the two is the more deeply rooted." Basil Maine, *Elgar, His Life and Works* (London: G. Bell & Sons, 1933), 1:197.

35. See for instance, the caricature of Elgar conducting (1905), reproduced without attribution in Elgar, *A Future for English Music*, 44–45; and the two Edmond Kapp drawings of Elgar conducting held by the Barber Institute of Fine Arts, University of Birmingham. See also the extract from Gerald Cumberland's *Set Down in Malice: A Book of Reminiscences* (London: Grant Richards, 1919), reproduced in *An Elgar Companion*, ed., Christopher Redwood (Ashbourne: Sequoia/Moorland, 1982), 130–36; and the commentary on this passage by Byron Adams, "The 'Dark Saying' of the Enigma: Homoeroticism and the Elgarian Paradox," in *Queer Episodes in Music and Modern Identity*, ed. Sophie Fuller and Lloyd Whitsell (Urbana: University of Illinois Press, 2002), 223–24.

36. David Cannadine, "Sir Edward Elgar," in *The Pleasure of the Past* (London: Collins, 1989), 121.

37. This tradition is maintained in Richard Taruskin's *The Oxford History of Western Music* (Oxford: Oxford University Press, 2005), which ignores Elgar entirely.

Elgar and the Persistence of Memory

BYRON ADAMS

The attribute of intelligence is not to contemplate but transform.
— Jean Piaget, *Psychology and Epistemology,* 1972

"I am self-taught in the matter of harmony, counterpoint, form, and, in short in the whole of the 'mystery' of music," declared Edward Elgar in a 1904 interview published in *The Strand Magazine*. The composer then laid the necessity for self-tutelage at the feet of his humble birth: "When I resolved to become a composer and found that the exigencies of life would prevent me from getting any tuition, the only thing to do was to teach myself. . . . I read everything, played everything, and heard everything I possibly could."[1] Elgar's claim is characteristically flamboyant and self-dramatizing, but it is essentially accurate. All of Elgar's biographers have traced the stages of Elgar's learning, demonstrating that the composer was indeed essentially self-taught in music theory and that he amassed his formidable technique largely through his own initiative.[2]

As the interview suggests, Elgar was clear concerning his unconventional education, the facts of which were well-known within his profession as well as in academia. When the composer was awarded an honorary doctorate from Cambridge in 1900, the Public Orator pointedly lauded Elgar as an "autodidactus."[3] But if, like Schoenberg, Elgar was one of the stunningly successful autodidacts of music history, the question arises how his self-education shaped his later habits and choices. What exactly does it mean to be an autodidact, that is, one who undertakes to educate oneself?

Applied to Edward Elgar, this question proves to be of great import, especially as several possible answers can illuminate aspects of both the man and his music. Recent investigations of autodidacts in the fields of social history and educational psychology provide a lens through which to view the experience of this ardent autodidact from Worcester. A clearer outline of Elgar's personality and creative process emerges when he is placed among contemporary British working-class people striving to better themselves. New work in educational psychology may help reveal the effect that his early learning experiences may have had on several mature compositions. Definitive conclusions cannot be reached in an essay of this size: with a subject as complex as learning—especially when applied to Elgar's multifaceted and contradictory personality—it will only be possible to provide a starting point for a much longer scholarly journey.

The Voracious Reader

Print is the technology of individualism.
—Marshall McLuhan, *Gutenberg Galaxy:
The Making of Typographic Man*, 1962

To comprehend better Elgar's keen need for self-education, the true nature of his class background must first be described without sentimentality. Although many writers on Elgar speak of his family as lower-middle-class tradesmen, this designation became appropriate only several years after Elgar's birth in 1857. Elgar was born into a working-class family that later rose in the world to a marginally higher station. During the course of a conversation recorded by Siegfried Sassoon, Elgar's patron Frank Schuster summed up the social status of the composer's parents: "E[lgar]'s mother [was a] barmaid at a little pub. E[lgar]'s father used to ride around the country on a cob and tune pianos for the local gentry."[4] (Elgar himself gave a similar description of his father, with the telling addition that "he never did a stroke of work in his life.")[5] Born in 1822, William Elgar came to Worcestershire from Dover with some practical musical skills, the ability to tune a piano, and a very modest education; at least one of his son's biographers has called William "semi-literate."[6] Despite his thoroughbred mare and cultivated air of gentility, William Elgar's modest financial status, lack of education, and manner of labor left him poised between the lowest rungs of the lower-middle class and the upper echelons of the unvarnished working class. When William took his son along on his professional visits to Madresfield Court, palatial home of the noble Lygon family, young Edward was dispatched to play with his social equals, the children of the head gardener.[7]

If the class status of his father was ambiguous, the origins of Elgar's mother, Ann (née Greening), were frankly working class.[8] Born in the same year as her husband, Ann came from a family of poor and largely illiterate farm laborers; for a very few years she attended the local parish school at Weston-under-Penyard.[9] Ann learned to read during her abbreviated formal education and evinced an early love of learning. As a teenager, she left her native Herefordshire to settle in Worcester, working at a tavern called The Shades.[10] Here she met her future husband, with whom, after their marriage in 1848, she had seven (or possibly eight) children.[11] At first the couple lived simply, as befitted their modest social status and income. Shortly after settling in Worcestershire, William Elgar became a fixture on the local musical scene, playing among the second violins in various ensembles and, unusual for an Anglican, accepting the post of organist of St. George's Roman Catholic Church in 1846.[12] These musical odd jobs provided a welcome supplement to his income as an itinerant piano tuner. In 1860 William Elgar, who was luckily assisted by his hardworking brother Henry, opened a music shop at 10 High Street in Worcester. Due to Henry Elgar's diligence, and in spite of William's indolence, the shop was moderately prosperous.[13] With the opening of this shop, young Edward's family made its modest ascent into the ranks of lower-middle-class tradesmen.

The more censorious among their small-town neighbors may well have considered the Elgar family to be less than perfectly respectable. William used his pay to imbibe more than a pint or two, an expensive habit that was the source of continuing friction at home. Worse yet, in 1852 Ann Elgar converted to Roman Catholicism, the result of having followed her husband to St. George's when he played organ for Sunday mass. Ann's conversion, made in the face of her husband's exasperated disapproval, was audacious indeed for the daughter of Protestant farm laborers in a rural town.[14] Not only was she seeking religious consolation but self-assertion in rigid little Worcester.

Ann Elgar's desire for individual choice, joined with a lifelong habit of reading, puts her squarely within the tradition of the autodidacts whose testimonies are collected in Jonathan Rose's *The Intellectual Life of the British Working Classes*.[15] Beginning in the late eighteenth century and concluding in the latter decades of the twentieth century, Rose's book, though filled with statistics regarding the education, reading, and cultural preferences of its subjects, is most valuable for its testimonies. In a manner as admirable as it is unusual, working-class voices rise from Rose's pages, their words often eloquent. Rose's procedure of interlacing testimony with fact and sociological analysis produces a landscape teeming with earnest self-educators, which challenges received opinion on the nature of the working class during the Victorian, Edwardian, and Georgian eras.

If placed in the company of the working-class learners who populate Rose's history, Ann Elgar is unusual only in that, given the rigid gender boundaries of the time, fewer women are found in their ranks than men.[16] Given the obstacles, she must have been extraordinarily determined to gain control over her own lot and improve the lives of her children. The seed of Ann's ambitions bore fruit with two of her five surviving children: Ellen Agnes, who took the vows of a nun after her mother's death and eventually was appointed prioress of the Convent of St. Rose of Lima at Stoke; and her oldest surviving son, Edward, who became successful beyond his mother's wildest hopes.[17]

Nowhere is Ann Elgar's strength of character demonstrated more plainly than in her struggle to obtain the best education possible for Edward. He was born thirteen years before the 1870 Education Act (also known as the Forster Act), which, as Rose notes, "supplemented the church schools (which had never served the entire population) with state schools governed by elected school boards."[18] Before this reform, working-class children generally received a scant few years of instruction. Before 1870, practically no educational opportunities were open to the working classes; those that existed were private and often affiliated with religious organizations. For working-class Roman Catholics, the situation was often dire.

Elgar was first sent to a Dame school, a charity establishment primarily intended for girls. This school was run by Miss Caroline Walsh, whom Charles Edward McGuire accurately characterizes as a fervent "Catholic convert."[19] On the basis of the available evidence, Miss Walsh's Dame school—a designation that does not refer to the gender of the instructors but, as Rose writes, is "a generic term applied to any working-class private school"—seems to have been at least competently organized, serious, and decorous.[20]

The quality of Elgar's next school, St. Anne's, is open to question based on the composer's own memories. This school was established by the venerable and Catholic Berkeley family at their estate, Spetchley Park, as a charitable institution intended chiefly for those children whose parents worked on the estate itself.[21] In a letter of 1912 to Ernest Newman, who was visiting Spetchley Park at the time, the composer reminisced that "S[petchley] is the village where I spent so much of my early childhood—at the Catholic School house: my spirit haunts it still."[22] Perhaps the general context of this letter to Newman, which mostly concerned Elgar's *The Music Makers*, a deeply autobiographical score, prompted Elgar to exaggerate Spetchley's significance, as he spent just two terms there.[23] The more so that this recollection was confided to none other than Ernest Newman, who related in 1955, quite late in his own life: "Elgar told me that as a boy he used to gaze from the school windows in rapt wonder at the great trees in the park swaying in the wind."[24] It is disconcerting, however, that the adult composer's chief memory of St. Anne's was looking out the schoolroom window—rather than anything he might have learned there.

The last few years of Elgar's formal education, from 1869 to 1872, were spent at Francis Reeve's school, Littleton House, which was situated across the Severn River from Worcester Cathedral. Elsewhere in this volume, McGuire paints a vivid portrait of this institution, and the young Elgar was lucky indeed to attend what was, in essence, a modest Catholic "public" school run by a professional schoolmaster, for profit.[25] How Ann Elgar managed to pay for Edward's schooling there is a wonder, given the slender household budget. Reeve must have been an effective teacher, since the adult Elgar once wrote him a brief encomium that declared, "Some of your boys try to follow out your good advice & training, although I can answer for one who falls only too far short of your ideal."[26] That Elgar remained in school until fifteen is a testament to his mother's steely determination in the face of both fluctuating income and the easygoing indifference of her husband.[27]

Through her love of reading, her own writing, and her taste in authors, Ann Elgar neatly fits the profile of a working-class autodidact of nineteenth-century Britain. To her granddaughter Carice, Ann wrote in 1897, "When I was a very young girl I used to think I should read all the books I ever met with."[28] (Recall Elgar's own testimony, quoted previously, that "I read everything, played everything, and heard everything I possibly could.") Like many others of her class, Ann knew instinctively that learning would give her a greater measure of agency over her inner life. One working-class autodidact testified: "Life only becomes conscious of itself when it is translated into word, for only in the word is reality discovered." Of this observation, Rose notes: "That was the autodidacts' mission statement: to be more than passive consumers of literature, to be active thinkers and writers."[29]

A striking aspect of many working-class readers was a marked devotion to poetry. Furthermore, many of these working-class readers were not merely "passive consumers" of poetry, but wrote verse themselves. Ann Elgar was one such amateur poet; though lacking technical polish, her poetry is often touching in its sincerity and infinitely more readable than the technically accomplished verse, sadly marred by a simpering gentility, written by Edward's cultivated wife, Alice.

One of Ann Elgar's favorite poets was the American Henry Wadsworth Longfellow, an enthusiasm she passed on to Edward.[30] Longfellow's mellifluous verse struck a resonant and sustained chord in the hearts of British readers.[31] That he was fêted by the great reflected this: on an 1868 visit to England the American poet was granted degrees by both Cambridge and Oxford; was received at Windsor by Queen Victoria; and was handsomely entertained by the likes of Gladstone, Dickens, Ruskin, and

Tennyson.[32] As Newton Arvin remarks, "The most familiar of his poems—it will by no means do to say always his best—had entered, as it might seem ineradicably, into the popular consciousness."[33] An additional inducement for working-class British readers was that along with other American authors, Longfellow was published in inexpensive editions, for, as Rose observes, the "United States failed to sign an international copyright agreement until 1891. . . . Thanks to this availability, the literary conservatism so common among the working classes was reversed in the case of American authors, who were enjoyed by common readers long before they acquired respectability in critical circles."[34]

Longfellow's poetry appealed to nineteenth-century readers such as Ann Elgar for several reasons: its suave, easy-to-memorize verse patterns; a surface propriety overlaying an intense and at times vaguely erotic romanticism; its vivid descriptions and lucid narrative flow; and its unashamed appeal to the emotions. Like many, Ann Elgar may have modeled her own verse after the American's more domestic lyrics.[35] Ann's touching couplet evoking her daughter Ellen—"Slender, thoughtful tender maid, / Like a young fawn in the shade"—is reminiscent of Longfellow's "The Children's Hour," with its touching description of his own daughters: "Grave Alice, and laughing Allegra, / And Edith with golden hair."[36] In addition, chivalric romances enthralled Ann Elgar; her daughter Lucy once wrote that her mother's youth had "been peopled from noble books, and it was in their pages she had met her friends and companions—men romantically honourable and loyal, women faithful in love even unto death; both alike doing nobly with this life because they held it as a gauge of life eternal."[37]

Ann's musical son was particularly drawn to Longfellow throughout the 1890s, setting the American poet's verse in two large choral scores, *The Black Knight,* op. 25 (1889–92) and *Scenes from the Saga of King Olaf,* op. 30 (1895). Elgar also used Longfellow's translation of Froissart for one of his finest songs, "Rondel," op. 16, no. 3. (1894). Like his mother, Elgar was inspired by figures such as King Olaf; the dynamic passages extracted directly from Longfellow for *Scenes from the Saga of King Olaf* inspired some of the composer's most dashing music. Furthermore, Elgar modeled the third tableau of Part I of his oratorio *The Apostles,* op. 49 (1902–3), "In the Tower of Magdala," on Longfellow's portrait of Mary Magdalene as found in the epic poem *The Divine Tragedy.* Although the composer's verses are drawn from holy writ, the dramatic progression of this tableau is indebted to Longfellow's portrayal of the penitent Magdalene.[38]

The book by Longfellow that held the most intense fascination for both mother and son was *Hyperion* (1839). In 1899 Elgar sent a copy of this volume to one of his great champions, the German conductor Hans

Richter, along with a letter that confided, "I send you the little book about which we conversed & from which I, as a child, received my first idea of the great German nations."[39] One wonders what, if anything, Richter made of this sentimental gift, for Longfellow's book is an odd hybrid production that might have puzzled any native German. Cast in four volumes, *Hyperion* is a *Wanderroman* clearly modeled upon Goethe's *Wilhelm Meisters Lehrjahre* (1796). Longfellow retails the experiences of a young American, Paul Flemming, who, as he attempts to forget the death of the "friend of his youth," journeys through early nineteenth-century Germany.[40] Flemming's travels are drenched in German literature and culture; indeed, the American author has his protagonist "improvise" remarkably polished translations of contemporary German poets such as Salis and Uhland. This selection of verse tastefully decorates a travelogue through the Teutonic landmarks favored by American and English tourists during the nineteenth century—such as Edward and Alice Elgar, who took several holidays to Bavaria in the 1890s. Arvin shrewdly observes that *Hyperion* gave such travelers "an agreeable sense of moving among the *Sehenswürdigkeiten* of the Rhine valley, the Alps, the Tyrol—the Rhine itself, the Rhone glacier, Mont Blanc at sunrise, the Jungfrau as seen from the Furca Pass, the ancient castle at Heidelberg, or the Franciscan church at Innsbruck."[41]

Longfellow cheerfully uses his characters as mouthpieces for the expression of his own earnest aesthetic beliefs. A great many serious discussions ensue between the protagonist and a variety of interlocutors, often culminating in proclamations about the meaning of "Art" and the role of "the Artist." Flemming and his friends are given to spouting aphorisms such as "The artist shows his character in the choice of his subject" and "Nature is a revelation of God; Art is revelation of man. . . . It is the creative power by which the soul of man makes itself known through some external manifestation or outward sign."[42] Although the dialogue of *Hyperion* is so stilted as to be virtually unreadable today, it made a deep impression upon Elgar. The young Elgar may have seen himself in Longfellow's protagonist, whom Arvin describes as "serious, intense, high-minded, a little humorless and prudish, but sensitive and imaginative."[43] Influenced early in life by the pronouncements that passed for conversation in *Hyperion*, the adult composer rose to such heights himself, as when he dismisses an opinion of Roger Fry: "Music is written upon the skies for you to note down. . . . And you compare that to a DAMNED imitation."[44]

Elgar drew from *Hyperion* the text for his cantata *The Black Knight*—in particular Uhland's uncanny "Der Schwarze Ritter," one of the hero's spontaneous translations that tend to pour forth at crucial junctures of the narrative. Although the surface of Longfellow's "romance" is genteel to the point of obliquity, the subject is German Romanticism, after all, and undercurrents of eroticism pervade the book. Newton Arvin comments that when *Hyperion* was published it "enjoyed at first a mild success of scandal"; perhaps American readers of 1839 knew just how to interpret obliquity.[45] In any case, the protagonist's improvised translation of Uhland's grim poem comes at the most erotically charged moment in the novel: Flemming is alone with a comely young Englishwoman, Mary Ashburton, and is in the process of courting her. This poem describes how the Black Knight, a figure of supreme potency who combines both Eros and Thanatos, unseats the king's son in a joust and then dances with the king's daughter, causing the "flowerets" in her hair to fade and drop to the ground. She is thus deflowered as her partner "coldly clasped her limbs around." Both son and daughter then wither and die before their father's eyes, poisoned by their shame as they drink "golden wine," as the grim knight exults in the final line: "'Roses in the spring I gather!'" After commenting that the "knight in black mail, and the waving in of the mighty shadow in the dance and the dropping of the faded flowers, are all strikingly presented," Longfellow's hero remarks that Uhland's poem "tells its own story and needs no explanation."[46]

Elgar's choice of this poem, which as Aidan J. Thomson has insightfully observed is the obverse of the narrative of Wagner's *Parsifal*, speaks to a darker inheritance that the young Edward may have received from his mother.[47] Elgar constantly reenacted in his own life moments of tension between repression and disclosure such as those that figure in the Mary Ashburton chapters in *Hyperion* with some intensity. As Jerrold Northrop Moore points out, when Ann Elgar chose excerpts from Longfellow's volume for her scrapbook, "she copied out several passages from *Hyperion* bearing directly on the artist and his problems. . . . The first was from a scene in which the young hero contemplates the ruins of a high old castle above the Rhine, and seems to hear it say: 'Beware of dreams! Beware of illusions of fancy! Beware of the solemn deceivings of thy vast desires.'"[48]

In its brevity and simplicity, Ann Elgar's couplet describing her son Edward evinces an acute psychological penetration: "Nervous, sensitive and kind, / Displays no vulgar frame of mind." But most children are vulgar at times, and it is healthy for them to be so. Did Ann instinctively use *Hyperion* as an instrument for asserting her influence over her disconcertingly emotional and, even at an early age, obsessive son? Was this her very effective way of teaching him to police his own emotions, of keeping him from slipping into a "vulgar frame of mind"? If so, what, exactly, did she fear for him? That he might slip into some kind of "vulgarity" if not warned of the "solemn deceivings" of his "vast desires"?

The effect of their shared devotion to Longfellow's *Hyperion* on her son's psychological development cannot, perhaps, be gauged fully. It is certain, however, that Ann Elgar's taste in literature exercised a deep and lasting effect on the sort of poetry that her son set to music over the course of his career. When Elgar was moved to write poetry himself, such as for "The River," op. 60, no. 2 (1909), his verse is reminiscent of Longfellow's in both mood and scansion, but such was the vogue: other writers, including Tennyson and A. C. Benson, provide the same patterns. Nevertheless, a great deal of the poetry set by Elgar features the smooth stress patterns and chiming rhymes favored by Longfellow and reflects his mother's taste for such lyric effusions. Elgar was rarely tempted to set poetry outside the canon of his own early tastes; although he knew Walt Whitman's poetry, he was, with Parry, one of the few British composers of the time to find no musical potential in this American's expansive verse.[49]

In his loyalty to the literary idioms of his youth, including classic authors, Elgar demonstrated a trait common to many working-class autodidacts: a tenacious and detailed persistence of memory. Elgar held fast to early aesthetic and literary experiences and returned to them repeatedly over the course of his adult life. In this process, acquiring used books played a large part. Like many penurious readers, Elgar soon became expert in the collection of old editions purchased at bargain prices. In Robert J. Buckley's early biography of Elgar, published in 1904, the author testifies: "The composer revealed himself as a book enthusiast, a haunter of the remoter shelves of second-hand bookshops, with a leaning to the rich and rare."[50] Intimidated by the ever-snobbish Alice Elgar, who sent him a detailed commentary on the interview before it appeared, Buckley turns Elgar's "haunting of second-hand bookshops" into evidence of the composer's connoisseurship—a "leaning to the rich and rare."[51] Elgar may in fact have developed this habit in his youth because new books were expensive. Such constraints meant that working-class readers often favored literature of earlier periods, including the eighteenth century, which could be obtained in inexpensive popular editions, in secondhand bookstalls, in cheap reprints, or, as in Elgar's case, by happenstance.

Certain of the composer's biographers have seen Elgar's interest in earlier literature as a mark of extraordinary intellectual curiosity, but a fascination with such authors was common among working-class autodidacts in the mid-nineteenth century.[52] In the interview with *The Strand Magazine* in 1904 Elgar explains how he began to "read everything":

I had the good fortune to be thrown among an unsorted collection of old books. There were books of all kinds, and all distinguished by the characteristic that they were for the most part incomplete. I busied myself for days and weeks arranging them. I picked out the theological books, of which there were a great many, and put them on one side. Then I made a place for the Elizabethan dramatists, the chronicles including Barker's and Hollinshed's, besides a tolerable collection of old poets and translations of Voltaire and all sorts of things up to the eighteenth century. Then I began to read. I used to get up at four or five o'clock in the summer and read—every available opportunity found me reading. I read till dark. I finished reading every one of those books—including the theology. The result of that reading has been that people tell me that I know more of life up to the eighteenth century than I do of my own time, and it is probably true.[53]

In an earlier interview with F. G. Edwards, Elgar relayed this story in a less vivid fashion but named titles: "In this way, he made the acquaintance of Sir Philip Sydney's *Arcadia,* Baker's *Chronicles,* Drayton's *Polyolbion,* etc."[54] In "Elgar's Use of Literature," Brian Trowell wrote, "Edwards originally mentioned only Sir Philip Sydney" but Elgar added the rest of the list to the proof. Trowell opines that "these are indeed extraordinarily unlikely books for a fifteen-year-old to read, more a test of endurance than a literary experience."[55] Trowell misses a vital point, however, for an impecunious but voracious reader starved for material virtually any book will suffice, especially if nothing else is available. As Rose relates in his history, the self-educated Marxist author T. A. Jackson (1879–1955) testified that as an adolescent he read "Pope, old volumes from the *Spectator, Robinson Crusoe,* Pope's translations of Homer, and a copy of *Paradise Lost*" for "the simple reason that there was nothing else to read." Jackson later commented, in terms surprisingly close to those of Elgar, that "mentally speaking" he dated "from the early 18th century."[56] Rose further cites the memories of C. H. Rolph, who recalled that his father, a London policeman, read such books as "Aristotle's *Ethics, The Koran,* Xenophon's *Memorabilia,* the *Nibelungenlied*" as well as "Schiller's *William Tell.*" After considering the effect of Xenophon on a London policeman of the Edwardian era, it is perhaps less difficult to imagine a young Edward Elgar devouring Sydney, Voltaire, and other authors more abstruse.

Ann Elgar's reading may have included easily acquired classics, such as Alexander Pope's translation of the *Iliad,* a volume that remained popular with working-class readers throughout the nineteenth century.[57] Such an interest in these classic authors may account for Frank Schuster's curious belief, told to Sassoon, that Elgar's mother "used to sit up half the night reading Greek and Latin with him when a boy."[58] Whereas it is certainly true that some working-class readers did teach themselves Greek and Latin, it seems unlikely that a woman with a wayward husband and five children to feed, clothe, and educate had time to acquire the linguistic skills required to read Homer or Virgil in the original. In December 1874, Ann expounded upon the challenges of her situation: "It is no joke to have men and women to rule, and keep peace between, and to keep *home* in something [of] order and comfort."[59] Michael De-la-Noy is tartly dismissive of Schuster's remark, implying that it was the result of a typically Elgarian exaggeration, but it is quite possible that Schuster was laboring under a misapprehension, since it seems unlikely that Elgar, even in his most self-mythologizing moods, would have concocted such an improbable tale. But it is entirely plausible that Elgar related to Schuster how his mother used to read *translations* of the Greek and Latin classics to him.[60] Reading aloud was a major form of entertainment and edification in all kinds of households throughout the nineteenth century and, indeed, until the advent of radio broadcasting.[61]

However he may have found the literature of earlier eras, including the Greek and Latin classics, Elgar's youthful interest in writers of earlier centuries—especially that of the previous one—resonated throughout his work. Has any other English composer since the death of Arne written so many minuets? These minuets, along with a light sprinkling of gavottes, appear throughout his career. Aside from the dedicated Minuet for Piano (1897; later orchestrated as op. 21), they appear in such disparate works as the Harmony Music no. 5 (1878), containing a minuet that Elgar reworked fifty-two years later for the *Severn Suite,* op. 87 (1930); the first *Wand of Youth* Suite, op. 1A (despite the fanciful opus number, this score dates from 1907); *The Crown of India* Suite, op. 66 (1912); and the incidental music to *Beau Brummell* (1928). Evocations of the eighteenth century occur in the Variations on an Original Theme, op. 36 (*Enigma* Variations, 1898–99)—Elgar once implied that the eighth variation, "W.N.," was in part "suggested by an eighteenth-century house"—and consistently throughout his ballet, *The Sanguine Fan,* op. 81 (1917), the action of which unfolds in a rococo setting. Jerrold Northrop Moore writes: "*The Sanguine Fan* score opened with an '18th century theme' (as the diary described it)—a courtly minuet elaborately descending."[62] (This four-measure minuet theme, usually

Example 1. "Minuet" Theme, *The Sanguine Fan,* op.8, starting three measures after the opening.

presented as an antecedent phrase in search of a balancing consequent, permeates the entire work; it is treated almost like a ritornello throughout a substantial part of the score and is the source from which most of the thematic material is derived.) None of these minuets give off even the merest whiff of either irony or pastiche: Elgar's musical antiquarianism was spontaneous, sincere, and informed by childhood memories.

One result of his unsupervised early reading may have been Elgar's compulsion toward mystification.[63] As part of this inner game, and to throw pursuers off his track, Elgar often sprinkled his manuscripts with epigraph "hints" from seemingly obscure sources such as Virgil, Tasso, Lesage, and others. It is not always apparent, however, that the composer was familiar with the entire book from which he quotes—or indeed where he may have found the epigraph in the first place. For example, the notoriously ambiguous line that Elgar affixed to the score of his Violin Concerto was drawn from Alain-René Lesage's eighteenth-century picaresque novel, *L'Histoire de Gil Blas de Santillane* (1715–35; translated into English by Tobias Smollett in 1748 as *The Adventures of Gil Blas of Santillane*). Given its eighteenth-century provenance, and its translation by a noted English novelist of that period, *Gil Blas* would seem to fall firmly within the ken of Elgar's literary enthusiasms; Brian Trowell has observed that this novel "was much better known in Elgar's time than it is today," an assertion that may well be true, but for which the author declines to offer even anecdotal evidence. Moore has pointed out, however, that this epigraph may have come to Elgar through the mediation of a contemporary poet, W. E. Henley, who quoted the same phrase—"*Aquí está encerrada el alma de . . .*"—at the beginning of a volume titled *Echoes*.[64] Did Elgar seek to appear more learned than he was, or was the temptation to expropriate a good mystifying quotation just too strong for him to resist?

The epigraph drawn from Ruskin's *Sesame and Lilies* (1865) that Elgar inscribed on the full score manuscript of *The Dream of Gerontius* is another matter altogether, and points up the composer's contradictory allegiances regarding his working-class origins. This epigraph is drawn from the first of the lectures that constitute *Sesame and Lilies*, "Of Kings' Treasuries," section 9: "This is the best of me; for the rest, I ate, and drank, and slept, loved, hated, like another: my life was as the vapor, and is not: but this I saw and knew: this, if anything of mine, is worth your memory."[65] Unlike the ambiguity surrounding *Gil Blas*, Elgar had clearly read *Sesame and Lilies*: he had received this volume, along with Ruskin's *The Seven Lamps of Architecture*, *The Crown of Wild Olive*, and others, as a gift from E. W. Whinfield in 1889.[66] Induced by Charles F. Kenyon, a journalist who wrote under the pseudonym Gerald Cumberland, into recommending models of pure literary style, Elgar innocently cited Shakespeare, Ruskin, and Cardinal Newman.[67] Elgar's response to Cumberland thus places Ruskin in a triumvirate at the top of his pantheon.

Brian Trowell remarks that today it seems "not only odd, but disappointing" that Elgar declined to evoke Ruskin's name during the course of the Peyton Lectures he gave at the University of Birmingham in 1905–6.[68] But Elgar may have had cogent reasons for not quoting Ruskin directly, for as Trowell astutely observes, "Few people read Ruskin today, and it is curious how superficial our notions of 'Ruskinian aestheticism' have become. . . . In his own time, Ruskin was considered by many to be an unsettling and dangerous writer, or at best an impractical visionary."[69] Although Ruskin was admired by nearly all for his art criticism, his radical theories on political economy, including his comments on the need for a fixed wage for workingmen, were pilloried in the British press. *The Saturday Review,* for example, excoriated Ruskin's political writings as "eruptions of windy hysterics . . . utter imbecility."[70] Ruskin's plea in *Sesame and Lilies* for educational reforms designed to benefit workingmen and women, including for the establishment of "great libraries that will be accessible to all clean and orderly persons at all times of the day and evening" are far less startling than his suggestion that "maximum limits should be assigned to incomes, according to classes."[71] For voicing such progressive and compassionate sentiments, Ruskin, who put his educational beliefs into practice by teaching at the Working Men's College, was revered by working-class readers.[72]

As Percy M. Young has noted, the public lecture itself was a tradition rooted in an ethic of Victorian adult education that had its roots in the working-class Mechanic's Institutes—and Ruskin was widely considered the preeminent master of the public lecture. Even though Ruskin is not cited, Elgar's Peyton Lectures are in essence a Ruskinian project. Young writes: "Elgar, the beneficiary of Victorian education and non-education, did not attempt to disguise a moral purpose, as is shown particularly by his loaded adjectives and his inspirational quotations from other writers. . . . Nor did he fail to draw attention to the responsibility that should be borne by those who controlled the nation's wealth."[73] Elgar's retentive memory allowed him to echo certain passages from *Sesame and Lilies* in both style and substance. Even the controversy engendered by Elgar's lectures is reminiscent of how certain Ruskinian ideas were received by the popular press.

Although Elgar did not go so far as to suggest fixed incomes for the British populace—the very idea would have been abhorrent to him—some of the recommendations he made in the Peyton Lectures are like Ruskin's in *Sesame and Lilies.* In the second lecture, "English Composers," Elgar makes a number of sensible and enlightened suggestions, including his declaration, "*I would like to see in every town*—a large hall capable of accommodating a large *sixpenny audience*." Reporting on this lecture, the *Birmingham Post* amplified Elgar's remarks: "Sir Edward wished to see in every town a large hall capable of accommodating a large sixpenny audience, for the working classes, with their education, should be provided for as they were in Germany."[74] In a later lecture, Elgar declared forthrightly, "*English working-men are intelligent: they do not want treating sentimentally, we* must give them the real *thing, we* must give them of the best because we want them to have it, not from mere curiosity to see HOW they will accept it. *What we do* in literature and art, we might do in music."[75] Not only does this passage reflect the covert resentment of a man who had tasted the bitter cup of condescension based on class inequity, but it also represents Elgar's internalization of the progressive educational reforms posited by Ruskin and other Victorian social reformers. Elgar's call for inexpensive but dignified concert venues for working-class listeners is strikingly reminiscent of Ruskin's utopian desire, articulated in *Sesame and Lilies* ("Of King's Treasuries," section 49) that "royal or national libraries will be founded in every considerable city, with a royal series of books in them . . . their text printed all on leaves of equal size, broad of margin, and divided into pleasant volumes, light in the hand, beautiful and strong."[76]

Several reasons may account for the absence of references to Ruskin in the Peyton Lectures, the most obvious of which is that they have survived only as a series of fragmentary drafts: given the often incomplete and at times inchoate form of his lecture notes, it is impossible to assert that Elgar did not spontaneously invoke Ruskin at some point, as he did when speaking with Gerald Cumberland. (However, Ruskin's name does not appear in any of the detailed accounts published in the *Birmingham Post* or any of the other reports included in Young's painstaking, indeed heroic, edition of the Peyton Lectures.) But there may have been another reason why Elgar would have not felt altogether comfortable quoting Ruskin. By 1905, Ruskin may have been too obviously associated with the aspirations of workingmen and women and even too politically radical for Elgar, the former piano tuner's son, to quote without suffering a queasy twinge of unsought self-revelation; in other words, Elgar may have suspected that citing Ruskin directly might recall to some minds the modest circumstances of his own birth and thus a declaration of literary and political allegiances to a lower class.[77]

Elgar was a consistent and devoted Tory in his political affiliations, and he strongly identified with the ruling classes whose ranks he sought to join, but a closer inspection of the seemingly impermeable facade of his conservatism reveals it to be riddled with small, almost reflexive, caveats. Elgar's political sympathies were not unusual for a working-class autodidact of the Victorian and Edwardian periods: many members of the British working class during Elgar's youth were conservative in their mores, cultural preferences, and often in their political views as well. Rose quotes Robert Roberts, who described British industrial laborers of this period as "Tory, royalist and patriotic."[78] Of those workingmen and women who leaned leftward in their political convictions at the beginning of the twentieth century, most might well have been described as Ruskinian socialists—only a highly vocal minority described themselves as communists.[79]

Elgar was hardly adverse to upward mobility, profiting as he had from the tenacious ambitions of his mother. Robert Anderson has noted that Ann "illustrated her teachings with an extract on 'Vulgar People': 'Being poor is not of itself a disqualification for being a gentleman. To be a gentleman is to be elevated above others in sentiment rather than situation.'"[80] This extract voices a conviction held by many working-class autodidacts: the elevated sentiment often achieved by a refinement of the intellect was not just a monopoly of the upper classes but could be cultivated by any questing mind, regardless of birth.[81] To succeed among the wealthy, however, it was best to combine elevated sentiment with either dim perception or unlimited generous forgiveness, neither of which attributes Elgar possessed in any degree. His incessant social climbing, often unfairly laid at the feet of his wife, who was born into a markedly higher class than her husband, may have been an attempt to mitigate feelings lacerated by a thousand small but precisely remembered indignities. Despite his bent for self-pity and exaggeration, Elgar's vexation at perceived cuts and insults may often have had a tangible basis, as such social checks were the main machinery that kept the Victorian and Edwardian hierarchy in working order, besieged as it was by newcomers.[82] Elgar was a prime candidate for expulsion on at least three counts: his working-class origins, his circumscribed formal education, and his Roman Catholicism. Any of these factors might have barred him from assuming the prerogatives that were jealously guarded by the Victorian and Edwardian upper classes, but Elgar had a card up his sleeve to trump the social game so evidently stacked against him: his prodigious talent. And though Elgar's talent did in fact help him into a higher class status, its magnitude could never entirely allay the composer's insecurity about his new social standing—especially among those so entirely devoid of talent themselves.

From early years, Elgar was possessed by a longing for reassurance that could never be assuaged fully, even by his patient wife. No honor was ever enough to mitigate his feelings of exclusion from the upper classes—

even when, to all appearances, he had joined them. Elgar's simmering class-based anger was always on the verge of boiling over. Asked in 1922 to contribute toward a frivolous project—a dollhouse for Queen Mary—Elgar responded with a tirade. As Sassoon recorded in his diary:

> The subject provoked an outburst from Elgar; he delivered himself of a petulant tirade that culminated in a crescendo climax of rudeness aimed at Lady M[aud Warrender] (who is a fashionably-attired Amazon with a talent for singing and archery; quite a noble creature, and extremely amusing). "I started with nothing, and I've made a position for myself!" ejaculated the Order of Merited composer who masquerades as a retired army officer of the conservative club type. "We all know that the King and Queen are incapable of appreciating anything artistic; they've never asked for the full score of my Second Symphony to be added to the Library at Windsor. But as the crown of my career I'm asked to contribute to—a DOLL'S HOUSE for the QUEEN!! I've been a monkey-on-a-stick for you people long enough. *Now I'm getting off the stick.*"[83]

Though this outburst makes for sorry reading, it contains a distant echo of Ann Elgar's wholly admirable resistance to discrimination based on rank, contained in her opinion, similar to that of Cardinal Newman, that the status of "gentleman" is independent of birth or wealth and can be acquired through self-improvement. Sassoon, an outsider himself in British society due to his Jewish father and homosexuality, but nevertheless born to privilege, snickered at the idea of a famous composer who "masquerades as a retired army officer" making such a fuss over a dollhouse. But Sassoon missed the tension that lay beneath Elgar's truculence: an insult to his honor, his talent—the reason for the composer's almost Ruskinian contempt of the inartistic hereditary aristocracy and his impassioned cry, "I started with nothing, and I've made a position for myself!"

Brian Trowell has described Elgar as "a progressive" Conservative whose "politics were instinctive and emotional, not intellectual, and appear to have sprung from a romantic and escapist identification with the great Tory families of Queen Anne's reign, many of whom were Catholic and even Jacobite in their sympathies."[84] Trowell neatly encapsulates the paradox of Elgar's political convictions by modifying his characterization of the composer's Tory allegiances with the appellation "progressive." While surely most political convictions are "instinctive and emotional, not intellectual," to suggest that Elgar's political beliefs had their origins solely in an "identification with the great Tory families of Queen Anne's reign" is to court oversimplification. Elgar was far from "progressive" on occasion, as when he shamefully resigned from the Athenaeum to protest the election to that select establishment of Ramsey MacDonald, a working-class autodidact much like himself and the first Labour prime minister.[85] Elgar was capable of behaving in a patronizing manner to members of the working class, but he is hardly the only man who—having struggled past the doorman—has to turn and defend the door by which he has just entered. Despite his penchant for weaving a potent mythology about his origins, Elgar was never so deluded as to deny his past, however much he may have embroidered it. Even when he assumed the borrowed plumage of an "English gentleman," which for a piano tuner's son from Worcester may have ineluctably led to Tory convictions, Elgar never tried to efface the basic outlines of his youth, which he retailed often, in detail and publicly. Elgar sought to eat his cake and have it: not only did his natural gifts allow for spectacular upward mobility from his working-class origins ("I've made a position for myself"), but his internalization of his mother's definition of a "gentleman" may have convinced him that he was entitled to that exalted position by right, thus transcending the otherwise intractable barriers of birth and formal education. Elgar's Ruskinian progressivism, which doubtless assumes poignancy when viewed in light of his own history, had little to do with the Tory politics worn like an expensive tweed suit by this English gentleman. Rather, Elgar's politics testified to his status as an autodidact whose origins were firmly rooted in working-class soil.

On the Beautiful in Music

> Every object that emerges into the focus of attention has meaning
> beyond the "fact" which it figures.
> —Suzanne Langer, *Philosophy in a New Key,* 1942

Viewing Elgar's literary taste and political affiliations from the perspective provided by the traditions of working-class autodidacts illumines both his psychological development and his choice of texts. In addition, a study of Elgar's instrumental music and aesthetics benefits from an investigation of the peculiar ways in which memory functions for self-learners. Cognitive scientists have conducted surprisingly little research into autodidacticism. However, a recent book edited by the British educational researcher Joan Solomon, *A Passion to Learn: An Inquiry into Autodidacticism,* sheds some light on this unaccountably neglected subject. Consisting of fourteen case studies of self-learners, Solomon's book touches upon such topics as the effect of emotion upon learning, the importance of self-motivation, and, crucially, the sense of a life mission that often is manifested early in life. Solomon eloquently describes autodidacts as "frequently emotional, strongly autonomous, passionate, and future-orientated"—traits that were conspicuous facets of Elgar's personality as well.[86]

As Solomon carefully documents, learning acquired by autodidacts early in life exercises a peculiarly strong influence throughout their later lives; ways of remembering are thus of paramount importance to later success. Citing the research of the Canadian psychologist Endel Tulving, Solomon writes: "The present understanding of memory defines it in three quite different modes of operation." She later summarizes the three modes of memory:

> The *semantic memory* relies on remembered abstract conceptual words that need to be applied in a new context. *Procedural memory* is remembered non-verbally in our bodies where it was first practiced. Tulving's special new contribution was *episodic memory*. This is the familiar way in which we recall a whole incident complete with perceptions (including smells), cognition (if we were learning or experiencing) and emotional reactions which make up motivation (horror, delight, curiosity, etc.). . . Looked at in another way we may see that emotion and cognition are, after all, not so very different.[87]

All of these ways of remembering might be relevant to a study of Elgar's musical life. Procedural memory—lodged in the somatic memory—allowed Elgar to learn to play the violin and become a celebrated conductor. Episodic memory is exemplified by the way in which the young violinist in Worcester who played Hérold's *Zampa* Overture fastened it in his memory well enough so that hearing a passage from Brahms's Third Symphony enabled him to recall Hérold's score and thus make a telling connection between overture and symphony in the third Peyton lecture delivered in Birmingham.[88] The mode that will be the primary focus of this line of investigation, semantic memory, permitted Elgar to remember in minute detail certain abstract concepts learned early in life that he would transform over the course of his career: an abstract concept such as a system of key symbolism, for example, may well have become a building block for his formal procedures as well as a stylistic trait. In semantic memory, an abstract concept once learned may be reinterpreted, but retains something of the integrity of the first encounter.

As is clear from Rose's study and Elgar's biography, autodidacts are voracious readers whose exceptional memories retain an astounding amount of what they have read in remarkable specificity. Equally evident from Elgar's Peyton Lectures is that he shared an unfortunate characteristic common to many autodidacts, a problem that surfaces frequently throughout their lives. Because autodidacts teach themselves without outside guidance, the knowledge they amass often contains odd lacunae even within an otherwise detailed body of information about a subject that interests them passionately. Misconceptions that could have been corrected easily by more systematic pedagogy can persist well into middle or even old age. Elgar became an expert violinist due in part to his lessons with the noted virtuoso and pedagogue Adolphe Pollitzer. In contrast, after a few lessons in childhood, his exploration of the piano was essentially unguided. Violinists praise his expert writing for strings, but many pianists who have performed Elgar's music remark that his writing for the instrument is often idiosyncratic and cannot be characterized as "pianistic."

Although Elgar expressed a healthy skepticism concerning the texts he used to educate himself as a boy—and he dismissed the textbooks of Charles-Simon Catel and Luigi Cherubini as "repellant"—the influence of the books in his youthful library cannot be overestimated.[89] As previously noted, indigent autodidacts read and remembered the driest of texts if those books were the only ones available; Rose quotes working-class readers who testified that they read avidly such unappetizing tomes as algebra treatises, "back numbers of the *Christian World*," and, in one dire instance, "a Post Office Directory for 1867, which volume I read from cover to cover."[90] Next to these, textbooks by Cherubini, John Stainer, and Catel seem alluring, if not downright racy. These volumes, which the composer kept over the course of his life and which are now housed in the collection at the Elgar Birthplace Museum, are the pillars upon which rests the edifice of Elgar's musical self-education: he devoured them, read them critically, annotated them, and tenaciously stored them in his memory.

The adolescent Elgar must have turned with relief from the strictures of Cherubini and Stainer to Berlioz's enthralling *Treatise on Modern Instrumentation and Orchestration* as well as to the invitingly poetical books by Ernst Pauer. Pauer was an Austrian composer, pianist, and pedagogue who settled in England in 1870, teaching piano first at the Royal Academy and then, in 1876, at the National Training School for Music, the precursor of the Royal College of Music. Noted for presenting a series of historical recitals that spanned keyboard music from 1600 to the present—he used a harpsichord for the earlier items—Pauer was a respected presence on the British musical scene until his retirement to Germany in 1896.[91] Elgar possessed two of Pauer's little books, which are primers rather than textbooks, both published by Novello. Pauer's *Musical Forms* (author's preface dated 1878) is a brief general survey of basic formal designs such as the sonata and the variation; *The Elements of the Beautiful in Music* (author's preface dated 1877) is an exuberantly Romantic exegesis of music aesthetics.

The Elements of the Beautiful in Music is the sole treatise on aesthetics that has survived from the young composer's library and may well have had an even greater impact on his compositional development than Pauer's admirably lucid explanation of musical form. The title page is stamped "Elgar Brothers Music Sellers, Worcester," so it was in Elgar's hands early. That the adolescent Elgar, who signed the title page with his customary bold script, attentively read *The Elements of the Beautiful in Music* is evident in two instances of penciled underlining.[92] Pauer's book would have been attractive to Elgar for several reasons, not the least of which is its exalted tone, strongly reminiscent of Ruskin in passages—not to mention of Longfellow's Paul Flemming. Pauer shares with Ruskin a philosophical viewpoint that might be termed "Romantic Platonism," an aesthetic whose emphasis on striving for the ideal and espousing high moral values chimed with the young Elgar's musical and literary predilections. Ruskin writes in *The Queen of the Air* (section 42) that music is "the teacher of perfect order and is the voice of the obedience of angels and the companion of the course of the spheres of heaven."[93] He surely would have agreed with Pauer's assertion that "it is evident that religion and art are closely connected," not to mention the Austrian's belief that "art has to exhibit to humanity the ideal picture of what perfect human beauty can be."[94]

Despite the similarity of their titles, Pauer's book has little in common with Eduard Hanslick's 1854 volume, *Vom Musikalisch-Schönen* (*On the Beautiful in Music*). Sharing only a broad debt to German philosophy, Pauer is closer to the critical writings of Schumann than the austere Hegelianism of Hanslick.[95] Indeed, Hanslick poured scorn on the very writers, such as Schumann, who served Pauer as exemplars; the Viennese music critic castigated such authors—and doubtless would have included Pauer in this company—as deluded Romantics who wrapped discussions of music "in a cloud of high-flown sentimentality."[96] Judging by an excursus found in the fifth Peyton lecture, titled "Critics," Elgar had read at least some Hanslick with care and, as Trowell has observed, shared with the Viennese music critic an unease, common to certain other composers of the period, about music's "'poetical-pictorial' associations."[97] But Elgar shrewdly deconstructs Hanslick's seemingly uncompromising aesthetic stance by pointing out an inconsistency. Elgar quotes the critic's assertion, embedded in a review of Brahms's Third Symphony—"Spoken language is not so much a poorer language as no language at all, with regard to music, for it cannot render the latter"—but then remarks, "Hanslick allows himself to call the opening theme of the last movement 'a sultry figure' foreboding a storm."[98]

Unlike Hanslick, however, Pauer was perfectly at ease making sweeping generalizations about such high-toned but vague concepts as "tone-painting," "ideal beauty," "truth," and the "infinite." Pauer's frequent evocations of the "ideal" put him squarely in the tradition of German Romantics; he quotes from both Schelling and Schiller and cites Plato, Aristotle, Pythagoras, Kant, Ferdinand Hand, and Hegel in his preface. Such vocabulary would have set Hanslick's teeth on edge and seems quaint today. But some of Pauer's statements—such as "uneducated intellects will never reach the pure heights of perfection"—may have deeply resonated in a boy with aspirations, trapped in modest circumstances with few obvious prospects, who was doggedly reading Pauer in pursuit of the "mystery" of music.[99]

Pauer does not stop at exhortation: in detailed affective descriptions of each of the major and minor keys he posits a theory of keys. By so doing, Pauer is part of a long tradition that includes Kirnberger and other eighteenth-century German theorists who speculated on the relationship of keys and temperament within the context of *Affektenlehre*.[100] Berlioz compiled a description of keys in his *Treatise on Modern Instrumentation and Orchestration*, a text well-known to Elgar, but Berlioz is exclusively concerned with the intersection of keys with instrumental technique. Rimsky-Korsakov's unsystematic association of key areas with color would seem at first to be close to Pauer's characterizations, but there is a crucial difference between the two: Pauer uses an affective vocabulary while the Russian composer veers into the realm of synesthesia. Rimsky-Korsakov's disciple V. V. Yastrebtsev recorded in his diary that "the various keys suggest various colors, or rather shades of color, to Rimsky-Korsakov. . . for example, E major seems tinged with a dark blue, sapphire-like color."[101] The point is not whether Kirnberger's theory, or Rimsky-Korsakov's system, or Pauer's associations for key centers are objectively "correct," or that they may contradict other such systems, but that Pauer's theories may have meant something to Elgar and may have influenced, consciously or unconsciously, his choice of keys in certain of his scores. If Pauer's designations for keys did influence Elgar—and there is reason to suggest they did—then surely this is a powerful instance of semantic memory, as the English composer would have constantly returned to a set of abstract ideas throughout his life, reinterpreting them while still retaining something of their original import.

Through Pauer's descriptions, the various keys evoke certain moods and mental states such as innocence (C major), sadness (C minor), and dreamy melancholy (G minor).[102] Pauer's hypotheses are presented with a peculiarly Teutonic mixture of thoroughness and sentiment as he asserts: "In music, the innermost feelings of the composer are displayed; and in so far as the characteristic is founded on the individual or personal feeling, an original composition must in itself be characteristic. . . . The characteristic shows itself by means of the tones and intervals, and finds expression through the minor and major keys, through the time and movement, through the accent, the rest, the figures, and passages and last, but not least, through the melody." Pauer declares that "the proper choice of key is of the utmost importance for the success of a musical work; and we find that our great composers acted in this matter with consummate prudence and with careful circumspection." Pauer is careful to offer a caveat to his characterizations of the different tonalities by noting: "It cannot be denied that one composer detects in a certain key qualities which have remained entirely hidden from another. . . . We lay down a rule which admits many exceptions. . . . All we can safely do is to name the characteristic qualities of the keys as we deduce their characteristic expression from universally admired and accepted masterpieces: and thus we need not fear to misstate or to misapprehend the bearing of the subject." Further, he takes the precaution of recommending variety through modulation: "When the composer has chosen his key, he will be careful to handle it in such a manner that it does not attain too great a prominence, which would result in monotony, and cause fatigue and lack of interest in the listener; but he will manage to suffuse his work with the special characteristics of the key, which is thus made to glimmer or shine through the piece without asserting itself with undue strength."[103]

Pauer's assertions, including his descriptions of each key, might seem a charming but inconsequential byway of Romantic aesthetics were it not for the autodidact from Worcester with the fantastically retentive memory. For those who have even a glancing acquaintance with Elgar's music, Pauer's descriptions are suggestive. According to Pauer, "D major expresses majesty, grandeur, and pomp, and adapts itself well to triumphant processions, festival marches and pieces in which stateliness is the prevailing feature."[104] After the first *Pomp and Circumstance* March—famously in D major—ceases to ring in the reader's ears, the question naturally arises: How often do Pauer's discussions of keys tally with Elgar's music? Such a study would be informative if one bore in mind that not even a slavish dedication to Pauer and his ideas would result in a complete match between Elgar's key selection and Pauer's characterizations, since Pauer left room for inventiveness and creativity—and that the ambitious young Elgar would have felt he possessed both. The point is not whether Elgar consciously planned out his works to conform to Pauer's descriptions—an improbable hypothesis at best, as there are instances where Elgar's music contradicts the Austrian's characterizations—but rather how his tenacious memory may have colored certain musical decisions as a result of his early reading.

So, though it is certainly too fanciful to suggest that Elgar designed the complex key relationships of *The Dream of Gerontius* so that the supernal opening of the second part would conform to Pauer's description of F major as a key full of "peace and joy . . . but also express[ing] effectively a light, passing regret . . . [and], moreover, available for the expression of religious sentiment," it is, however, worth remarking that this is the only extended passage in F major in the entire score.[105] Was Elgar's reading of Pauer a seminal factor in the composer's choice of key? Nothing in the elaborate key structure of *Gerontius,* which, Elgar's sketches show, was planned early in the score's genesis, required that this particular crucial moment be cast in F major. In other words, tonal logic alone cannot explain why Elgar selects keys for certain expressive contexts.

A striking instance of a key that seems to act as a particularly potent signifier for Elgar is that of E-flat major, which Pauer describes as a "key which boasts the greatest variety of expression." Pauer continues, remarking, "At once serious and solemn, it is the exponent of courage and determination, and gives to a piece a brilliant, firm and dignified character. It may be designated as eminently a masculine key." Pauer often draws his examples from Beethoven, whom he praises as "the composer whose works may be taken pre-eminently as a type of ideal beauty."[106] That Beethoven's *Eroica* Symphony in E-flat Major looms large behind Pauer's characterization of this key cannot be doubted, although as a pianist, Pauer may have also had in mind the *Emperor* Concerto, cast in the same key as the symphony.

To follow Elgar's use of E-flat throughout his mature music would be a revealing exercise, but discussion here will be restricted to five major works composed over thirteen years: the *Enigma* Variations; the concert overture *In the South (Alassio)* (1903–4); the Second Symphony (1911); *The Music Makers* (1912); and, finally, his "symphonic study," *Falstaff* (1913). Of these scores, *In the South* and the Second Symphony share E-flat major as the dominant tonality; the "Nimrod" variation from the *Enigma* Variations is cast solely in that key; the fifth stanza of *The Music Makers* begins in E-flat; and a single theme from *Falstaff* cast in E-flat will be discussed. All of these scores have masculine associations; four of these works specifically evoke two of Elgar's closest male friends.

The "Nimrod" variation, the climactic ninth of thirteen, is the emotional and structural climax of the *Enigma* Variations, and portrays Elgar's loyal friend August Jaeger.[107] One of the curiosities of Pauer's book that could be related to the use of E-flat major for this heartfelt music is that the Austrian author does not merely characterize key centers, but time signatures as well. Pauer thus declares triple time to be expressive of "longing, of supplication, of sincere hope, and of love. . . . It possesses a singular tenderness and a remarkable fund of romantic expression."[108] Inquiry into a composer's creative process can only be speculative, but it is striking that Pauer's descriptions of key and time signature constitute a virtual recipe for the "Nimrod" variation, surely one of the most moving evocations of the intense tenderness that can lie at the heart of male friendship.

Example 2. Opening Measures, "Nimrod" variation, Variation IX of the *Enigma Variations*, op. 36, starting at rehearsal number 33.

Example 3. Recall of the "Nimrod" variation from the fifth stanza of *The Music Makers*, op. 69, starting at rehearsal number 51.

Elgar explicitly connected both his concert overture *In the South* and the Second Symphony to his friend and faithful patron Frank Schuster, the homosexual son of a wealthy banker. Siegfried Sassoon, in an otherwise venomously penned portrait of Schuster, noted that his erstwhile friend's "hero-worship of Elgar was (justifiably) the most important achievement of his career, because he really did help Elgar toward success and recognition."[109] Schuster tirelessly promoted Elgar's music in aristocratic and artistic circles, and, as Sophie Fuller discusses elsewhere in this volume, Schuster's elegant home in London and his country house, The Hut, in Bray-on-Thames, were important sites for Elgar, who occasionally used the estate as a refuge when composing. Elgar trusted Schuster so explicitly that he designated his patron as one of his daughter's guardians when the composer and his wife left for America in 1905.[110] Even death did not fully curtail Schuster's generosity, for he left Elgar the considerable sum of £7,000, writing in the bequest that the composer had "saved my country from the reproach of having produced no composer worthy to rank with the German masters."[111] Elgar was deeply saddened by his patron's death, writing to Schuster's sister, Adela, "By my own sorrow—which is more than I can bear to think of at this moment (a telegram [announcing Schuster's death] has just come) I may realize some measure of what this overwhelming loss must be to you."[112]

Elgar dedicated *In the South* to Schuster. The composer wrote that his friend would find the overture filled with "light-hearted gaiety mixed up in an orchestral dish [in] which [,] with my ordinary orchestral flavouring, cunningly blent, I have put in a warm cordial spice of love for you." *In the South,* inspired, as the title attests, by a journey to Italy, was completed barely in time for the premiere, which took place on the third evening of a festival devoted to Elgar's music.[113] In a remarkable show of devotion, Schuster offered practical proof of his admiration by underwriting this ambitious undertaking, in effect assuming responsibility for any financial loss that might have occurred.

Elgar wrote to Percy Pitt that the opening of *In the South* portrayed "the joy of living" and had an "exhilarating *out-of-doors* feeling." The overture's initial theme was originally jotted down as a musical depiction of the "moods of Dan" in 1899—Dan was a boisterous dog belonging to Elgar's friend George Robertson Sinclair—and was cast originally in E major.[114] Robert Anderson aptly observes that the example of Strauss's *Ein Heldenleben* may have induced Elgar to transpose this theme to E-flat major, but, as we shall see, there may well have been another reason for this change. The broader questions of why Elgar projected human emotions onto a dog and how this anthropomorphic projection called forth such varied and expressive ideas are unanswerable, though the surprisingly varied "moods of Dan" themes are suited perfectly to the scores in which they appear.[115]

Shortly after Schuster's death in 1928, Elgar wrote to Adela Schuster, who had requested of the composer an epitaph for her brother: "I want something radiant, bright & uplifting for dear Frankie's memorial stone & I cannot find it: forgive me I have failed. I have said in music, as well as I was permitted, what I felt long ago,—in F[rank]'s own Overture 'In the South' & again in the final section of the Second Symphony—both in the key that he loved most I believe (E flat)—warm & joyous, with a grave and radiating serenity: this was my feeling when the Overture was dedicated to him 24 years ago & is only intensified now."[116] Did Elgar transpose the opening theme of *In the South* from its original E major to E-flat major in part because he knew that Schuster "loved" the lower key? As Elgar designed the overture as a special gift to Schuster, a friend who relished all manner of male company, one can only speculate whether or not, lurking in back of his mind, there might have been a persistent wraith of memory of Pauer's description of E-flat major as "masculine." By far the most interesting aspect of Elgar's letter to Adela Schuster, however, is that as late as 1928 his characterization of E-flat major is reminiscent in style of Pauer's affective vocabulary—"the exponent of courage and determination, and gives to a piece a brilliant, firm and dignified character."

Elgar's Second Symphony has been associated with any number of the composer's friends and acquaintances. Often mentioned is Edward VII, to whose memory the work is dedicated.[117] Lady Elgar invoked Alfred Rodewald, whose death in 1903 deeply agitated her husband, as an inspiration for the harrowing slow movement.[118] Elgar himself declared that a theme in the last movement was a portrait of Hans Richter: "Hans himself!"[119] Alice Stuart-Wortley has been construed as a muse for the symphony through readings—of variable insight depending on the interpreter—of the composer's letters to her.[120] Frank Schuster is rarely mentioned, however, despite Elgar's clear statement that the symphony's poetic coda, cast in E-flat major, was inspired by him. One wonders if Elgar ever mentioned his intention to Schuster, who was very much alive in 1911 when this symphony in his favorite key was premiered. Once again, Elgar provided a motto for the symphony that has given rise to much speculation, the first line from one of Shelley's poems: "Rarely, rarely comest thou, / Spirit of Delight!"[121] Describing this score, throughout which E-flat major glimmers and shines, Elgar wrote to his publisher in terms that conjoin his 1928 letter to Adela Schuster with Pauer's characterization of E-flat major, for, he confided, "The spirit of the whole work is intended to be high & pure joy: there are retrospective passages of sadness but the whole of the sorrow is smoothed out & ennobled in the last movement, which ends in a calm & *I hope & intend,* elevated mood."[122]

The Music Makers, a setting of an ode by the poet Arthur O'Shaughnessy (1844–81) for mezzo-soprano, chorus, and orchestra, was finished a year

Example 4. Excerpt from the coda of the Finale, Symphony no. 2 in E-flat major, op. 63, five measures after rehearsal number 170.

after the first performance of the Second Symphony. The poem expresses an earnest, striving ideology reminiscent of Longfellow's more exhortatory poetry, as well as a high vision of the artist's calling that recalls the American author's *Hyperion*. Here, however, as Aidan J. Thomson has observed, Elgar deconstructed O'Shaughnessy's poem by using quotations from his own scores, creating an agonistic relationship between the text's optimism and the music's repeated tendency toward pessimistic dissolution. Semantic memory thus assumed a crucial role in the creation of *The Music Makers:* Elgar treated themes from previously composed works as abstract entities thrust into a wholly new context, yet still retaining something of their original import. *The Music Makers* is surely the most self-referential of Elgar's autobiographical scores; of this work, he wrote to Ernest Newman, "I am glad that you like the idea of the quotations: after all art must be the man, & all true art is, to a great extent egotism & I have written several things which are still alive."[123]

The Music Makers may furnish further evidence of Schuster's connection to the Second Symphony. In the most protracted allusion in the score, Elgar uses the "Nimrod" variation to illustrate lines in O'Shaughnessy's fifth stanza, which reads in part: "But on one man's heart it hath broken, / A light that doth not depart; / And his look, or a word he hath spoken, / Wrought flame in another man's heart."[124] Of this passage Elgar testified, "Here I quoted the 'Nimrod' Variation as a tribute to the memory of my friend, A. J. Jaeger: by this I did not mean to convey that his was the only soul on which light had broken or that his was the only word, or look, that wrought flame in another man's heart."[125] For this tribute to Jaeger, Elgar not only quotes the "Nimrod" variation, but begins this stanza in the variation's key of E-flat major as well, making this the only quotation in *The Music Makers* that appears in its original key.[126] (After the initial statement of the "Nimrod" theme, this section vacillates between E-flat major and A-flat major—Pauer describes this key as "full of feeling and replete with a dreamy expression"—before finally settling into the latter.)[127] Since the key scheme in *The Music Makers* is as intricate as any other of Elgar's major works, the composer may well have designed the tonal plan to accommodate this excursion in E-flat major. As Moore notes, the recall of the

Example 5. Quotation from the coda of the Finale, Symphony no. 2, in *The Music Makers*, starting at rehearsal number 53.

"Nimrod" variation "dwarfed all the short surrounding *Music Makers* figures—especially when 'Nimrod' found a wonderful coupling with the final descending figure from the Second Symphony in the same key."[128]

As mentioned earlier, Elgar told Adela Schuster that he had portrayed her brother in the coda of the Second Symphony, the pervading theme of which is Moore's "descending figure." Was Schuster one of the men, along with Jaeger, whose word or look "wrought flame in another's man's heart"? And did Schuster, whose favorite key of E-flat is common to all this music, have an inkling of Elgar's tribute in the symphony's coda and, thus, in *The Music Makers?* As Diana McVeagh once exclaimed, "If [Elgar] genuinely disliked people wondering about his private life, why had he not learned his lesson from 'enigma'? To cap it all, he composed *The Music Makers,* with its allusions and references, many of which could not be fully understood by anyone who know nothing of his past life."[129]

But not all of Elgar's self-revelations were made consciously. In his "symphonic study" *Falstaff,* the theme that, according to the composer's own description, portrays Prince Hal in "his most courtly and genial mood" is cast in E-flat major. Unlike the "Nimrod" variation, the Second Symphony,

Example 6. Prince Hal as "courtly and genial," *Falstaff,* op. 68, starting at rehearsal number 5.

or *The Music Makers,* a fictional character is portrayed in Pauer's "eminently" masculine key in *Falstaff.* Although a full analysis of *Falstaff* is beyond the scope of this essay, it can be pointed out that this first Prince Hal theme undergoes a development both psychological and musical, since its apotheosis (rehearsal number 127) represents the royal progress of Prince Hal, just crowned as Henry V, and occurs just before his ruthless repudiation of Falstaff: "How ill white hairs become a fool and jester!" (*2 Henry IV,* 5.5.41, 46).[130]

Whereas some Shakespearean scholars have discerned a homoerotic bond between Prince Hal and Falstaff—one that the new king must break decisively to assume full authority—others, such as Stephen Greenblatt, have viewed this relationship as one between a failed surrogate father and a son who must repudiate his "false father" to reach maturity. (Given the seemingly limitless levels of meaning in Shakespeare, both may be equally valid.) Greenblatt writes that Shakespeare may have had his own father, John, in mind when he created Falstaff, whose "fantasies about the limitless future" invariably "come to nothing, withering away in an adult son's contempt."[131] Given Elgar's uncanny ability to project his imagination into the souls of others, whether actual or fictional, is it possible that while he re-created Shakespeare's Falstaff in his own image, he also secretly identified with Prince Hal, who, despite unpromising beginnings, achieves majesty?[132] Did not Elgar reject his own father, who, according to his scornful son, "never did a stroke of work in his life"? Schooled by his mother to discipline—or repress—his emotions through voracious reading and incessant self-learning, Elgar assumed the mantle of a man of "stern reality" who in 1885 displaced his father as organist at St. George's, and then progressed royally to fame, an honorary doctorate at Cambridge, knighthood, the Order of Merit, and other coveted honors.[133]

Any composer's creative process is shrouded in an impenetrable mystery, and the last thing that can be expected of any artist is a foolish consistency. It is clear that Elgar's early reading, encouraged by his mother, made him into a lifelong autodidact; her literary tastes informed his own, and those tastes influenced his choice of texts. More mysterious are the ways in which Elgar's retentive memory enabled him both to reflect and to transform the humdrum realities of his youth into imperishable works of art, and thereby transcend the unpromising circumstances of his birth. Elgar certainly took full advantage of the creative freedom evinced by Pauer's "great composers" and never espoused a systematic approach to any part of the "mystery" of music. However much the autodidact from Worcester may have retained and transformed Pauer's theories in the vast storehouse of his memory, certain of that author's observations, when read in light of Elgar's achievement, assume the force of prophecy: "He who aims at the greatest, the highest, must summon all his strength. . . . Art has to exhibit to humanity the ideal picture of what perfect human beauty can be."[134]

NOTES

The author wishes to thank Charles Edward McGuire, John Lowerson, Lauren Cowdery, Eric N. Peterson, Paul De Angelis, Howard Meltzer, Conrad Susa, and Chris Bennett for their help in the completion of this essay, which is dedicated to Diana McVeagh.

1. Rudolf de Cordova, "Illustrated Interviews: LXXXI—Dr. Edward Elgar," *The Strand Magazine* 25 (May 1904): 539. Reprinted under the title "Elgar at 'Craeg Lea,'" in Christopher Redwood, ed., *An Elgar Companion* (Ashbourne: Sequoia Publishing, 1982), 117–18.

2. Jerrold Northrop Moore's history of Elgar's early educational experiences is particularly detailed; see Jerrold Northrop Moore, *Edward Elgar: A Creative Life* (Oxford: Oxford University Press, 1984), chaps. 2–4, 14–63.

3. Ibid., 1.

4. Siegfried Sassoon, *Diaries 1920–1922*, ed. Rupert Hart-Davis (London and Boston: Faber and Faber, 1981), 223.

5. Conversation with Mr. and Mrs. Alan Webb, 13 January 1931, recorded by Alan Webb immediately afterward and quoted in Jerrold Northrop Moore, *Elgar: A Creative Life*, 4.

6. Michael De-la-Noy, *Elgar: The Man* (London: Allan Lane, 1983), 18.

7. Dorothy E. Williams, *The Lygons of Madresfield Court* (Logaston: Logaston Press, 2001), 96. This passage sheds an interesting light on Elgar's relationship with the Lygon family, and especially Lady Mary Lygon, who is portrayed in the penultimate movement of the *Enigma* Variations: "Edward Elgar was only on the periphery of Lady Mary's circle. She was aware that as a boy he had sometimes accompanied his father on his piano-tuning visits, during which the young lad was dispatched usually to play with the family of the Head Gardener." Although Lady Mary Lygon encouraged the composer by attending his premieres whenever possible and invited him to participate in local musical events she sponsored, she retained a lively sense of the class differences between Elgar, the Roman Catholic son of a piano tuner, and her own family, ancient in lineage and predominantly— but not exclusively—High Church in religion. Oddly, Michael De-la-Noy describes William Elgar in old age as having the face of a "head gardener"; De-la-Noy, *Elgar: The Man*, 19. Interestingly, Frank Schuster told Sassoon that Elgar's father was "always asked to lunch, of course," but did not specify upon which table—servant's or master's—this meal was spread. See Sassoon, *Diaries 1920–1922*, 223.

8. Although many biographers spell her name with an *e* as "Anne," she signed herself "Ann." See Michael Trott, "Elgar's Remarkable Mother," *Elgar Society Journal* 13, no. 4 (March 2004): 25.

9. Ibid., 25. Trott describes Ann Elgar as "a voracious reader" who "acquired a love of poetry and the countryside." Michael De-la-Noy, on the other hand, describes her as "only just literate in English." The truth, as usual, may reside between these two extremes. See De-la-Noy, *Elgar: The Man*, 28.

10. Although some writers have preferred euphemisms such as "commercial inn," William Elgar himself referred to The Shades as a "tavern" in an 1845 letter sent to his family in Dover, quoted in De-la-Noy, *Elgar: The Man*, 19.

11. For the uncertainty arising about the number of children born to William and Ann Elgar, see Robert Anderson, *Elgar* (New York: Schirmer Books, 1993), 3–4. Five of the Elgars' children reached adulthood.

12. De-la-Noy, *Elgar: The Man*, 20, 22.

13. Moore, *Elgar: A Creative Life*, 17.

14. Ibid., 6, 17–18. William Elgar even wrote to his family castigating "the absurd superstition and play-house mummery of the Papist" (15), but seems to have had little regard for the Church of England or the Wesleyans.

15. Jonathan Rose, *The Intellectual Life of the British Working Classes* (New Haven and London: Yale University Press, 2002), 1–11.

16. Ibid., 2, 20, 73, 76–77.

17. The confusion over the spelling of Ann Elgar's Christian name was passed down to the next generation through her youngest child, who, though baptized Ellen Agnes was consistently called "Helen Agnes" by her siblings. This confusion over nomenclature extended to her nickname, which is spelled variously as "Dot" or "Dott." See Richard Smith, "Elgar, Dot and the Stroud Connection—Part One," *Elgar Society Journal* 14, no. 5 (July 2006): 14–20. All ambiguities in this regard were resolved once and for all in 1903, when Dot (or Dott, or Ellen, or Helen) took vows in the Dominican Order and assumed the name Sister Mary Reginald. Her vocation was marked by ill health but steady promotion until 1919, when she was elected Mother General of the five linked convents of St. Rose of Lima. See Richard Smith, "Elgar, Dot and the Stroud Connection—Part Two," *Elgar Society Journal* 14, no. 6 (November 2006).

18. Rose, *Intellectual Life of the British Working Classes*, 148.

19. Charles Edward McGuire's research concerning the fierce nature of Miss Walsh's beliefs, and the uncompromising way these beliefs were put into practice, further suggest that her Dame school was run in an orderly—and probably highly disciplined—fashion. See McGuire's essay in this volume.

20. Rose, *Intellectual Life of the British Working Classes*, 151. The order that reigned at Miss Walsh's establishment was unusual, as many Catholic Dame schools of the time were slovenly and ineffective. In general, Catholic education for working-class children before 1870 was a shambles. As Rose reports, "Working-class Catholics stand out as more critical of their schooling than Anglicans or Dissenters. . . . They gave their schools and teachers a much lower positive rating, were much more likely to complain about corporeal punishment, reported lower parental interest in education, were less likely to see any benefit in their education, were far more prone to regret the quality of their schooling, and were much happier to leave school" (184).

21. Moore, *Elgar: A Creative Life*, 35–36. For more information on St. Anne's, see Charles Edward McGuire's essay in this volume.

22. Jerrold Northrop Moore, ed., *Edward Elgar: Letters of a Lifetime* (Oxford: Clarendon Press, 1990), 248.

23. For more information concerning Elgar's attendance at St. Anne's, see Charles Edward McGuire's essay in this volume, note 38.

24. Moore, *Elgar: A Creative Life*, 40–41.

25. Though certainly not one of the great public schools like Eton or Charterhouse, Littleton House can be characterized as a "public" school due to its "private" exclusivity: in other words, fees were assessed.

26. Anderson, *Elgar*, 5.

27. Elgar's boyhood friend Hubert Leicester recalled: "E.'s mother always worried as to where the money was coming from; his father taking life very easily, enjoying his rides into the country for piano-tuning, and the proceeds of each visit more than likely swallowed up by the unnecessary expense incurred in getting there." Quoted in Moore, *Elgar: A Creative Life*, 17. William Elgar's indifference, even contempt, for his son's ambitions can be inferred from Hubert Leicester's testimony that Elgar's "mother was always ready to help and encourage him, but his father and uncle were merely amused and scoffed at these childish efforts [at composition]—an attitude in which they persisted until E[lgar]

really had made his way in the world. . . . They failed to see, not only that they had an exceptionally gifted boy in the family, but even that he was moderately clever at music." Quoted in Moore, *Elgar: A Creative Life*, 28. After quoting Leicester's memory, Moore makes the apt if chilling observation, "Perhaps they did not want to see it."

28. Anderson, *Elgar*, 2.

29. Rose, *Intellectual Life of the British Working Classes*, 57.

30. Moore, *Elgar: A Creative Life*, 64.

31. For Longfellow's popularity among working-class British readers, see Rose, *Intellectual Life of the British Working Classes*, 54, 85, 371, 374, 375.

32. Newton Arvin, *Longfellow: His Life and Work* (Boston and Toronto: Little, Brown, 1962), 148.

33. Ibid., 318.

34. Rose, *Intellectual Life of the British Working Classes*, 354.

35. Ann Elgar kept a scrapbook filled with quotations from various authors, with Longfellow the most often represented; see Anderson, *Elgar*, 2.

36. Ann's couplet is quoted in De-la-Noy, *Elgar: The Man*, 26. "The Children's Hour" in Henry Wadsworth Longfellow, *The Complete Poetical Works of Henry Wadsworth Longfellow* (Boston and New York: Houghton, Mifflin and Company, 1894), 225–26.

37. Quoted in Moore, *Elgar: A Creative Life*, 5.

38. See Byron Adams, "Elgar's Later Oratorios: Roman Catholicism, Decadence and the Wagnerian Dialectic of Shame and Grace," in *The Cambridge Companion to Elgar*, ed. Daniel M. Grimley and Julian Rushton (Cambridge: Cambridge University Press, 2004), 97. Elgar was hardly the only composer of the late nineteenth century to be inspired by Longfellow: Samuel Coleridge-Taylor and Antonin Dvořák both found inspiration in *Hiawatha*. For a searching investigation of Dvořák's interest in *Hiawatha*, see Michael Beckermann, *New Worlds of Dvořák: Searching in America for the Composer's Inner Life* (New York: W. W. Norton, 2003), 25–66.

39. Moore, *Letters of a Lifetime*, 81.

40. Henry Wadsworth Longfellow, *Hyperion: A Romance* (Philadelphia: David McKay Publisher, 1893), 8. The gender of this dead friend, who is recalled several times in the course of *Hyperion*, is never identified. In an uncharacteristic lapse, Moore writes that the protagonist of Longfellow's book "travels through Germany and Switzerland to forget an unhappy love affair," but the only unhappy love affair alluded to in *Hyperion* occurs at the climax, some two-thirds of the way through the narrative (book 3, chap. 6). See Moore, *Elgar: A Creative Life*, 64.

41. Arvin, *Longfellow*, 118.

42. Longfellow, *Hyperion*, 163, 235.

43. Arvin, *Longfellow*, 117. For Elgar's uncanny ability to project himself into the personalities of others, including literary characters, see Byron Adams, "The 'Dark Saying' of the Enigma: Homoeroticism and the Elgarian Paradox," in *Queer Episodes in Music and Modern Identity*, ed. Sophie Fuller and Lloyd Whitsell (Urbana and Chicago: University of Illinois Press, 2002), 230–31, 235, 237.

44. Letter of George Bernard Shaw to Virginia Woolf, 10 May 1940; quoted in Moore, *Elgar: A Creative Life*, 738. This incident occurred at a luncheon in March 1919.

45. Newton, *Longfellow*, 55.

46. Shortly after this incident, Mary Ashburton jilts the hero. Longfellow, *Hyperion*, 249–52.

47. Aidan J. Thomson, "Re-reading Elgar: Hermeneutics, Criticism and Reception in England and Germany, 1900–1914," Ph.D. diss., Oxford University, 2002, 114f.

48. Moore, *Elgar: A Creative Life*, 69; the quotation from Longfellow is in book 1, chap. 3. See Longfellow, *Hyperion*, 25.

49. Late in life Elgar sent a Christmas card that featured a quotation from *Leaves of Grass;* see Moore, *Elgar: A Creative Life*, 782–83.

50. Robert J. Buckley, "Elgar at 'Forli'" in Redwood, *An Elgar Companion,* 113.

51. Brian Trowell, "Elgar's Use of Literature," in *Edward Elgar: Music and Literature,* ed. Raymond Monk, (Aldershot: Scolar Press, 1993), 193.

52. Rose, *Intellectual Life of the British Working Classes,* 4–5, 38–39, 126, 187.

53. De Cordova, "Elgar at 'Craeg Lea,'" 118–19. Robert Anderson's convincing version of the mysterious appearance of the tattered old books is that "there was a bookseller who stored his stock in an Elgar loft." Anderson, *Elgar,* 9.

54. F. G. Edwards, "Edward Elgar," *The Musical Times* (October 1900), reprinted in Redwood, *An Elgar Companion,* 38.

55. Trowell, "Elgar's Use of Literature," 192.

56. Rose, *Intellectual Life of the British Working Classes,* 129–30, 128.

57. Ibid., 95, 130, 374. Of particular interest in light of Ann Elgar's poetical ambitions was the beneficent effect that Pope's translations of Homer had upon working-class women poets of the eighteenth century, an influence that may well have persisted into the nineteenth century (18).

58. Sassoon, *Diaries 1920–1922,* 223.

59. Quoted in Moore, *Elgar: A Creative Life,* 68–69.

60. Elgar told Buckley that his mother "read translations of the Latin classics, of the Greek tragedians and talked in the home of what she read." Robert J. Buckley, *Sir Edward Elgar* (London: John Lane, The Bodley Head, 1904), 5–6. Brian Trowell has sensibly observed: "The fact that Anne [*sic*] Elgar read classical authors in translation evidently became garbled by double hearsay when Sassoon reported Schuster in 1922 as saying that 'she used to sit up half the night reading Greek and Latin with him [Elgar] when a boy.'" Trowell, *Elgar's Use of Literature,* 300, n. 69.

61. See, for example, Rose, *Intellectual Life of the British Working Classes,* 110, 374–75. For Ann Elgar's practice of reading poetry to her children, see Moore, *Elgar: A Creative Life,* 9.

62. Concerning "W.N.," Anderson, *Elgar,* 315. The diary that Moore alludes to parenthetically is presumably that of Alice Elgar. Moore, *Elgar: A Creative Life,* 702.

63. There is so much literature on this aspect of Elgar's character that one particularly fine essay must suffice as an introduction: see Diana McVeagh, "A Man's Attitude to Life," in Monk, *Edward Elgar: Music and Literature.*

64. Moore, *Elgar: A Creative Life,* 586, n. 170. For further discussion of the Lesage quotation that Elgar affixed to the Violin Concerto, see the documents about the concerto presented by Alison I. Shiel in Part II of this volume.

65. John Ruskin, *Sesame and Lilies,* in *The Complete Works of John Ruskin,* ed. E. T. Cook and Alexander Wedderburn (London: George Allen, 1905), 18:61.

66. Anderson, *Elgar,* 8. See also letter of E. W. Whinfield to Edward Elgar, 25 November 1886, in Moore, *Letters of a Lifetime,* 17. In his letter to Elgar, Whinfield writes that it "was a real pleasure to me to find out, accidentally, that you cared for Ruskin's books and had not got any: and I instantly made up my mind that I would set that last deficiency, right." According to Moore, however, the edition of *Sesame and Lilies* owned by Elgar was the fourth edition, published by Smith, Elder and Company in 1867. See Moore, *Elgar: A Creative Life,* 323, n. 89. Ruskin delivered "Of King's Treasuries" on December 6, 1864, in the Town Hall, Rusholme. John D. Rosenberg, ed., *The Genius of John Ruskin: Selections from His Writings* (Charlottesville and London: University of Virginia Press, 1998), 296.

67. Charles F. Kenyon [Gerald Cumberland], *Set Down in Malice: A Book of Reminiscences* (London: Grant Richards, 1919), 86.

68. Trowell, "Elgar's Use of Literature," 230.

69. Ibid., 229.

70. John Dixon Hunt, *The Wider Sea: A Life of John Ruskin* (J. M. Dent & Sons Ltd., 1982), 275.

71. Ruskin, *Sesame and Lilies*, 104, 106.

72. Ruskin taught art at the Working Men's College founded by F. D. Maurice in 1854. Hunt, *The Wider Sea*, 212. As for Ruskin being revered by the working class, see Rose, *Intellectual Life of the British Working Classes*, 49, 119, 191–92, 418.

73. Edward Elgar, *A Future for English Music and Other Lectures*, ed. Percy M. Young (London: Dennis Dobson, 1968), 1–8.

74. Ibid., 86–87.

75. Ibid., 213. Of his editorial policy in regard to the use of italics, Young writes that "in the alternative versions of passages shown in the textual commentary all insertions, whether marginal or interlinear are italicized." As for words given entirely in capital letters, Young writes that where "Elgar himself used underlinings such words or passages are in small capitals."

76. Ruskin, *Sesame and Lilies*, 104.

77. The representation of Elgar's literary taste, and the implications of his taste as revealing of class status, was one of Alice Elgar's particular concerns. She bullied F. G. Edwards, for example, into dropping a mention of her husband's devotion to Dickens in an article written in 1900, because Dickens was perceived as a vulgar enthusiasm—that is, working-class. Trowell, "Elgar's Use of Literature," 192–93. For the devotion of working-class readers to Dickens, see Rose, *Intellectual Life of the British Working Classes*, 111–15. There is yet another possible reason for Elgar eschewing references to Ruskin: to spare the feelings of his friend Alice Stuart-Wortley, who was the daughter of Effie Gray, Ruskin's unhappy young wife who escaped him to marry the painter John Everett Millais. As the scandal—one of the truly spectacular ones of the Victorian era—still resonated in 1905, Elgar may have been reluctant to have Stuart-Wortley learn he was making approving citations of Ruskin's work.

78. Rose, *Intellectual Life of the British Working Classes*, 338.

79. When exposed to Marx, many working-class autodidacts—like many sensible people, then and now—found *Das Kapital* opaque and dull; few ever made it beyond the first few chapters. Ibid., 305–7.

80. Anderson, *Elgar*, 2.

81. Elgar echoes his mother's convictions when he states: "The commonplace mind can never be anything but commonplace—& no amount of education no amount of the polish of a university, can eradicate the stain from the low type of mind we call commonplace." Elgar, *A Future for English Music*, 155.

82. A case in point is Edward Dent's seemingly class-based denigration of Elgar's lack of formal education, as well as Francis Toye's gibes at the composer's supposed "velgarity." See Moore, *Elgar: A Creative Life*, 594, 789–90.

83. Sassoon, *Diaries 1920–1922*, 169 (author's italics). What Sassoon may not have realized is that Elgar's Second Symphony was dedicated to the memory of the then reigning monarch's father, Edward VII; thus the composer's seemingly absurd anger over George V's putative negligence in requesting the manuscript of that work for the Royal Library at Windsor. Lady Maud Warrender (1870–1945), who, after the death of her husband lived in a lesbian relationship with the singer Marcia van Dresser (occasioning Sassoon's use of the transparent code word *Amazon*), was the daughter of the eighth Earl of Shaftesbury and one of Elgar's loyal patrons and friends. See also Diane Souhami, *The Trials of Radclyffe Hall* (New York: Doubleday, 1999), 266.

84. Trowell, "Elgar's Use of Literature," 198, 230.

85. Anderson, *Elgar*, 157.

86. Joan Solomon, *The Passion to Learn: An Inquiry into Autodidacticism* (London: Routledge, 2003), 182.

87. Ibid., 65, 170.

88. Elgar, *A Future for English Music*, 103. At least one working-class family cited by Rose owned an piano arrangement of the *Zampa* Overture; such popular works appealed to the musical tastes of working-class performers and listeners. See Rose, *Intellectual Life of the British Working Classes*, 197.

89. Moore, *Elgar: A Creative Life*, 41. Brian Newbould has thoroughly investigated the impact upon Elgar's musical development of both Catel's harmony treatise (1802) and Cherubini's *Counterpoint and Fugue* (English translation by Hamilton and Clark, 1854). See Brian Newbould, "Elgar and Academicism 1: The Untutored Genius," *The Musical Times* 146, no. 1891 (Summer 2005): 72; and Brian Newbould, "Elgar and Academicism 3: Devices and Contrivances," *The Musical Times* 146, no. 1893 (Winter 2005): 31–33.

90. Rose, *Intellectual Life of the British Working Classes*, 376, 372.

91. "Ernst Pauer," in *Grove's Dictionary of Music and Musicians*, ed. Eric Blom, 5th ed. (New York: St. Martin's Press, 1955), 7:595.

92. Elgar has underlined the words *heights* and *depths* in the penultimate paragraph on page 38. I am grateful to Chris Bennett of the Elgar Birthplace Museum for confirming this information.

93. John Ruskin, *The Queen of the Air* in *The Complete Works of John Ruskin*, ed. E. T. Cook and Alexander Wedderburn (London: George Allen, 1905), 19:344.

94. Ernst Pauer, *The Beautiful in Music* (London: Novello, Ewer & Co., 1877), 47.

95. See especially Robert Schumann, "Charakteristik der Tonleitern und Tonarten," *Neue Zeitschrift für Musik* 2 (1835): 43–44.

96. Eduard Hanslick, *The Beautiful in Music*, trans. Gustav Cohen (New York: Liberal Arts Press, 1957), 8.

97. For example, Rimsky-Korsakov tried to distance himself from the program he supplied for *Scheherazade* as being too pictorial; see V. V. Yastrebtsev, *Reminiscences of Rimsky-Korsakov*, trans. Florence Jonas (New York: Columbia University Press, 1985), 13; Trowell, "Elgar's Use of Literature," 231.

98. Elgar, *A Future for English Music*, 171, 173. Percy M. Young, the editor, reprints the English translation of Hanslick's review of the premiere of Brahms' Third Symphony to which Elgar refers, see 154. Elgar was once taken to task by Ernest Newman for exactly the same kind of aesthetic waffling that the composer locates in Hanslick. In an article that appeared in *Manchester Guardian* on 9 November 1905, the day after Elgar's Peyton lecture on Brahms's Third Symphony, Newman indignantly writes: "Some of us may well sit up and rub our eyes in astonishment at [Elgar's] championship of 'absolute music.'" Later on, Newman goes in for the kill: "If Sir EDWARD ELGAR'S thesis is rickety here, what are we to say when we apply it to his own case? How many pages has he written that are frankly descriptive? What is the prelude to 'Gerontius,' for example, or the 'Cockaigne' Overture or 'In the South' but a series of musical 'descriptions'? If he really believes now that music is at its height only when it concerns itself with nothing but purely tonal pattern-weaving, he is condemning all his own best work *en masse*." See 105–6.

99. Pauer, *The Beautiful in Music*, 3–4, 46.

100. Johann Philipp Kirnberger, *The Art of Strict Musical Composition*, trans. David Beach (New Haven: Yale University Press, 1982), 338.

101. Yastrebtsev, *Reminiscences of Rimsky-Korsakov*, 31.

102. Pauer, *The Beautiful in Music*, 23–24.

103. Ibid., 19, 21, 22.

104. Ibid., 24.

105. Ibid., 25.

106. Ibid., 25, 43.

107. For an extended discussion of Jaeger's place within the *Enigma* Variations and the *Dream of Gerontius*, see Adams, "The 'Dark Saying' of the Enigma," 229–31, 233–35. Even the usually unperceptive Dora Penny (the "Dorabella" of the tenth *Enigma* variation), wrote that "in the sudden *piano* [at the conclusion of the "Nimrod" variation], may one not see the composer's love for his friend?" See Mrs. Richard Powell (Dora Penny), *Edward Elgar: Memories of a Variation*, 4th ed., rev. and ed. Claud Powell (Aldershot: Scolar Press, 1993), 130–32.

108. Pauer, *The Beautiful in Music*, 29.

109. Sassoon, *Diaries 1920–1922*, 293.

110. Richard Smith, *Elgar in America: Elgar's American Connections Between 1895 and 1934* (Rickmansworth: Elgar Editions, 2005), 27.

111. Anderson, *Elgar*, 160.

112. Moore, *Letters of a Lifetime*, 404. Moore mentions here that, according to his daughter's diary, Elgar was "very upset" by Schuster's passing. As Carice Elgar's diary is uncommunicative about her father—her diary is mostly a bland record of quotidian events—this comment assumes an unusual expressivity in its context. Elgar acted thoughtlessly toward Schuster at times, as he did to virtually everybody around him; see Adams, "The 'Dark Saying' of the Enigma," 227.

113. Anderson, *Elgar*, 306.

114. Elgar's notes to Pitt are quoted in Anderson, *Elgar*, 306; for the key to the "moods of Dan," see Aidan J. Thomson, review of *Music as a Bridge: Musikalische Beziehungen zwischen England und Deutschland 1920–1950*, ed. Christa Brüstle and Guido Heldt, *Elgar Society Journal* 14, no. 6 (November 2006): 46.

115. For a commonsensical commentary on the "moods of Dan," see McVeagh, "A Man's Attitude to Life," 1.

116. Moore, *Elgar: Letters of a Lifetime*, 414.

117. Elgar, who sentimentalized Edward VII, later felt that the royal family did not value this dedication sufficiently; see note 83 above.

118. See Adams, "The 'Dark Saying' of the Enigma," 218–19.

119. Anderson, *Elgar*, 332, 338.

120. For an insightful comment, see James Hepokoski, "Elgar," in *The Nineteenth-Century Symphony*, ed. D. Kern Holoman, (New York: Schirmer, 1997), 336.

121. Brian Trowell has commented extensively on this motto drawn from Shelley, but his conclusions are less than fully persuasive in toto. Trowell does convincingly connect the symphony to an adaptation of lines from Shelley's poem "Julian and Maddalo: A Conversation" that Elgar used in a letter to Frances Colvin, dated 1 February 1911. Trowell ignores the transparently homoerotic nature of Shelley's poem in favor of promoting his own *idée fixe* concerning Elgar's putative obsession with Helen Weaver. See Trowell, "Elgar's Use of Literature," 256–57, 264–66.

122. Letter to Alfred Littleton, 13 April 1911, in Jerrold Northrop Moore, ed., *Elgar and His Publishers: Letters of a Creative Life* (Oxford: Clarendon Press, 1987), 2:741.

123. Moore, *Letters of a Lifetime*, 248, and Aidan J. Thomson, "Unmaking *The Music Makers*," in *Elgar Studies*, ed. J. P. E. Harper-Scott and Julian Rushton (Cambridge: Cambridge University Press, 2007).

124. The complete fifth stanza of O'Shaughnessy's poem reads: "They had no vision amazing/Of the goodly house they are raising:/They had no divine foreshowing/Of the land to which they are going:/But on one man's soul it hath broken,/A light that doth not depart;/And his look, or a word he hath spoken,/Wrought flame in another man's heart."

125. Moore, *Letters of a Lifetime*, 249–50.

126. Thomson, "Unmaking *The Music Makers*."

127. Pauer, *The Beautiful in Music*, 25.

128. Moore, *Elgar: A Creative Life*, 646.

129. McVeagh, "A Man's Attitude to Life," 2.

130. There are a plethora of detailed analyses of *Falstaff,* including a remarkably detailed exegesis of the score by J. P. E. Harper-Scott in *Edward Elgar, Modernist* (Cambridge: Cambridge University Press, 2006), 107–53.

131. Stephen Greenblatt, *Will in the World: How Shakespeare Became Shakespeare* (New York and London: W.W. Norton, 2004), 70–71.

132. For Elgar's paradoxical strategy of projection, see Adams, "The 'Dark Saying' of the Enigma," 231.

133. In a letter to Charles Buck, 29 October 1885, Elgar wrote: "The old man does not take quite kindly to the Organ biz: but I hope 'twill be all right before I commence my 'labours.'" Quoted in Moore, *Elgar: A Creative Life,* 113.

134. Pauer, *The Beautiful in Music*, 46–47.

"The Spirit-Stirring Drum":

Elgar and Populism

DANIEL M. GRIMLEY

Cultural tourists in the South Midlands, tired perhaps of trawling for edification around the well-trodden circuit of Shakespearean sites in and around Stratford-upon-Avon, are now invited to follow a similar but less familiar itinerary. The Elgar Route, devised and promoted by Worcester City and Malvern Hills District Councils, links together forty-eight different locations with various Elgarian associations along a tour signposted throughout southwest Worcestershire. Bounded on the western side by the Malvern Hills, on the eastern by the River Severn, and radiating outward from Worcester cathedral in the northeast corner, the route offers a condensed historical geography of Elgar's life and musical career. The tour is designed, the brochure suggests, so that motorists "may join it at any convenient point," and though it begins at the Elgar Birthplace Museum in Lower Broadheath, the official numbering of sites along the way cuts across a simple chronological sequence of events in Elgar's biography. Hence, the second location after leaving Lower Broadheath is Birchwood Lodge (the summer cottage Elgar rented between 1898 and 1903, and where he scored *The Dream of Gerontius*), followed by his previous residence, Forli, in Malvern Link (1891–99), where he composed *King Olaf* and *The Black Knight*. The Elgars' somber final resting place, the grave at St. Wulstan's Church, is then passed (site 10), after which motorists double back on themselves disconcertingly and head toward a more cheerful location, Craeg Lea (Elgar's home between 1899 and 1904, while he rented Birchwood Lodge), where he wrote the Variations on an Original Theme, op. 36 (*Enigma* Variations). The route therefore pursues a spatial, rather than linear-temporal, logic. Other sites visited include the Worcester County Cricket Ground at New Road, where "it is *thought* that Elgar was a regular supporter," and an oddly placed, rather uncanny final destination which lies awkwardly away from the official circuit, the site of the Powick asylum, now "demolished," where the young composer devised and conducted light music designed to cheer the troubled inmates.[1]

Evocatively billed as "a journey through Elgar's beloved countryside," the Elgar Route presumably is intended primarily as a means of boosting tourism in the region. It therefore represents a form of commodification, an attempt to package and present Elgar's life so as to generate income from his cultural capital. But it also serves inadvertently to promote an aesthetic ideology that has long lain at the heart of Elgar's historical reception: his music's pastoral associations with western England and with Worcestershire in particular, which in turn can be understood as the iconic representation of a certain kind of idealized Englishness.[2] In this sense, the Elgar Route is highly selective. The brochure tactfully declines to note that many of Elgar's major works, including the symphonies, the concertos, and the "late" chamber music, lie "off route," composed in Hereford, London, and Sussex. The tour furthermore reinforces the programmatic association of place with Elgar's music. The implication is that by visiting sites such as Longdon Marsh, Birchwood Lodge, or Herefordshire Beacon in the Malvern Hills, listeners can gain privileged access into the meaning and significance of Elgar's music. His work's potentially awkward abstraction, its intellectual or aesthetic content, is sublated within an amenable discourse of picturesque associations that are more immediately containable than absolute music.[3] The Elgar Route thus embodies a kind of historical revisionism. The brochure confidently asserts that "Elgar is universally regarded as a composer of the very first rank," a retrospective summation which, until recently if at all, has not been reflected by Elgar's relative status in the critical musicological canon. Significantly, there are no comparably elaborate routes for other British composers such as Ralph Vaughan Williams or Benjamin Britten, whose music has similarly evocative geographical associations.

The Elgar Route simultaneously represents a form of popularization, an attempt to market Elgar's music to a wider audience. And in spite of its uncritical adoption of an ideological context that limits, rather than broadens, the meaning of Elgar's work, such popularization is not necessarily a bad thing. Though it is difficult, from a scholarly perspective, to avoid reinforcing the pejorative connotations that such efforts at commodification evoke, it is surely better to resist objecting to attempts to extend the appeal of Elgar's work. After all, if Elgar's music is to survive in the concert hall, it needs to be able to present itself to such continual reinterpretation and appropriation by new listeners and scholars alike. But more important, this process of popularization is also part of a deeper historical pattern, one that can already be discerned in Elgar's complex relationship with his contemporary audiences, and it can be traced through the ways in which his music invites different levels of interpretation and response. Elgar himself was not a neutral figure in this process. As Tim Barringer has recently explained, the association of place and music subsequently promoted by the Elgar Route was an aspect of the composer's reception from an early stage of his career, and built on Malvern's existing reputation as a spa resort and tourist destination.[4] The vision described in 1900 by F. G. Edwards in *The Musical Times*, for instance, is no less ideologically conceived than that subsequently promoted by the Elgar Route itself:

> The Malvern uplands are to be seen, not described. No appreciative mind can fail to be impressed with the bold outline, the imposing abruptness, and the verdant loveliness of these everlasting hills. Nature has left the impress of her smile on this favored region. It is a steep climb to the hilltop above Malvern Wells, but it more than repays the wayfarer who has eyes to behold and a soul to satisfy. The enjoyment of a quiet stroll along these grassy heights is greatly enhanced by the companionship of one who habitually thinks his thoughts and draws his inspirations from these elevated surroundings.[5]

Barringer argues that Edwards's description, presumably endorsed by Elgar, can be read partly as a statement of class aspiration, in which the sense of physical elevation upon the hills reflected Elgar's desire to escape his essentially urban bourgeois tradesman's origins and ascend ("a steep climb"!) to his wife's upper-middle-class status. It also represents the adoption of a familiar Romantic subject position (that of the "wayfarer" or wanderer), in which the position of survey (from the "grassy heights") marked both control over a lower dominion and proximity to an ethereal realm of divine creative genius. This sense of elevation furthermore suggests an exaltation of artistic value or a heightened aesthetic experience—the domain of high art.

But elsewhere Elgar was no less eager to descend to the valley (both literally and figuratively) in order to ensure the broad popular appeal of his music, either to safeguard revenue (Elgar's correspondence with his publishers illustrate his constant awareness of the need to maximize the commercial value of his work where possible) or perhaps to gain professional esteem in order to justify or validate his occupation as a creative practitioner in a commercial marketplace. The contemporary state of the music profession in Edwardian Britain, as Cyril Ehrlich has observed, was sufficiently precarious for such preoccupation with financial income to be virtually unavoidable, especially for musicians from Elgar's socioeconomic background. As Ehrlich suggests, "A pervasive glut—an excess of supply over any conceivable level of demand—was the prevailing condition of musical life."[6] Indeed, both the early and, arguably, the latter half of Elgar's career attest to some of the difficulties encountered by musicians without a significant independent source of income. "For the majority without such resources," Ehrlich writes, "ceaseless teaching was the common lot, at home and in institutions which attached images of excellence to mediocre realities," a fate that Elgar narrowly avoided. But Elgar experienced firsthand the extent to which, as Ehrlich notes, "the cultural environment of London did not nurture musicianship."[7] Each of the composer's attempts to establish a permanent base in the capital proved unsuccessful.

Elgar's creative response to this professional situation, in spite of the lofty image portrayed by Edwards's piece in *The Musical Times,* was to write music that appealed to different kinds of listeners. Hence, popular elements can be found even in his most "serious" high-art compositions (as discussion of *Falstaff* below will suggest). Indeed, such popular gestures do not represent a capitulation to the commercial forces of the marketplace, but an authentic mode of Elgar's compositional voice. The various sites of production and consumption historically associated with Elgar's work (not necessarily the same as those visited along the Elgar Route) point to his desire to address multiple levels of audience. And the need to communicate with his listeners in diverse contexts accounts for the different voices or musics that can be heard within Elgar's work. Understood from this perspective, the popular emerges as a central category in Elgar's music, but it is one that has not hitherto received extensive critical scrutiny. The popular can also be heard as a contested voice. It is represented most directly by a particular mode of civic music, inspired by the sounds of Elgar's contemporary urban environments and opposed to the lone Romantic discourse of high art music that is prevalent elsewhere in Elgar's work (and which in turn is no less prone to commercial appropriation). The remainder of this essay considers how Elgar's music mediates such tensions in a number of brief case studies that exemplify different kinds of popular music in his work.

Problems of defining the popular in music have been extensively discussed in the critical literature and need not be reiterated here.[8] At least three distinct categories of popular music can be tentatively identified in Elgar's work, each of which represents a different musical style or genre: salon music, music for civic occasions, and music expressive of an Arcadian nostalgia or lost innocence. The first category, salon music, consists of works such as *Chanson de nuit* (discussed in greater detail below) or the earlier hit *Salut d'amour,* pieces of moderate or "graded" difficulty suitable for performance by nonprofessional players in a range of informal contexts or venues. Elgar composed this music partly for his own use: works such as *Very Easy Melodious Exercises in the First Position,* op. 22 for violin and piano were generated initially as teaching material, though it is striking how the hymnic texture of these pieces resembles later works, such as the famous trio from the *Pomp and Circumstance* March no. 1. The category of salon music also includes the various dances (polkas, waltzes, and quadrilles) and chamber pieces composed for performance by members of Elgar's own semiprofessional circle. Here, some of the links with Worcester promoted by the Elgar Route can be justified: such works were part of the staple repertory of the Glee Club to which Elgar belonged as a young man. Likewise, the larger-scale *Harmoniemusik,* or "Sheds," that Elgar wrote for domestic use by a group of amateur wind players link the composer with Worcester.[9]

Salon music represents a musical equivalent of the early-nineteenth-century category of *Trivialliteratur* identified by Peter Bürger—an early Romantic genre of mass-market literature of supposedly lesser aesthetic value directed toward a broad "popular" (meaning urban middle class) readership. As a species of *Trivialmusik,* salon music is problematic for the music historian because its very availability threatens to undermine the autonomous status of the artwork and its associated figure of creative genius. As Carl Dahlhaus has suggested, the mode of reception that such music engenders, which he terms "trivialized listening,"

> ignores or violates one of the major theoretical premises of classical-romantic art: the principle of self-absorption in the work as an aesthetic object. It does this by side-stepping the dialectic of form and content in music, extracting from it a topic or subject matter (mistaken for the work's "contents") and withdrawing from the acoustic phenomenon into the listener's own frame of mind. In this way, the music, instead of constituting an aesthetic object, degenerates into a vehicle for associations and for edifying or melancholy self-indulgence.[10]

Much of Elgar's salon music works in this way, and the manner in which it conforms to these strictures has important implications for the critical reception of his work. As for Sibelius, another late-nineteenth-century composer who wrote many salon pieces, including hit tunes such as *Valse Triste* from his incidental music to Arvid Järnefelt's play *Kuolema* (*Death,* 1903), the aesthetic value of works such as *Salut d'amour* has often been regarded as being in inverse proportion to their mass-market appeal.[11]

This was a view that Elgar partly held himself. In a letter addressed to his publishers at Novello & Co., dated 27 October 1897, Elgar articulated his concerns over the publication of the *Chanson de nuit*, recalling his recent experience with *Salut d'amour:* "I *wish* you could arrange terms for it which would leave me some interest in it: the last Violin piece I wrote [*Salut d'amour*], which unfortunately I sold some years ago for a nominal sum, now sells well—I understand 3,000 copies were sold in the month of January alone."[12] Barely a year later, when Elgar was still struggling to establish himself as a freelance composer, he wrote to August Jaeger at Novello about his aborted plans for a symphony based on the life of General Gordon: "I like this idée but my dear man *why* should I try?? I can't see—I have to earn money somehow & it's *no good* trying this sort of thing even for a 'living wage' & your firm wouldn't give 5£ for it—I tell you I am sick of it all: why can't I be encouraged to do decent stuff & not hounded into triviality."[13]

For Elgar, in his less optimistic moments, salon music did become merely a means to an end: a potential source of income (sadly unrealized in the case of *Salut d'amour*) that detracted from his supposed "higher calling," the composition of large-scale instrumental works such as symphonies. Yet Elgar cannot have maintained this view unequivocally, since he continued to compose similar salon pieces even after achieving a measure of financial security in the early 1900s, and such works evidently provided a certain amount of creative, as well as economic, satisfaction. In this sense alone, Elgar's populism is an ambivalent category.

This ambivalence can be explained partly by tensions within the genre itself. Dahlhaus argues that *Trivialmusik* in the nineteenth century played on the dialectic between autonomy and mass production. Hence, works such as Louis Lefébure-Wély's *Les cloches du monastère*, directly comparable in tone and content to many of Elgar's salon pieces,

> emerged as a paradoxical cross between sentimentality and mechanization, this being the aesthetic reflection of a sociohistorical clash between a philanthropical tradition and a drive toward commercialization and industrialization. It is deliberately bland, but with the pretense of being emotional. It wishes to be direct and intelligible to all, and for this reason remains within the narrowest confines of convention at the same time that it tries to appear as a spontaneous outpouring of feeling. It is banality masquerading as poetry, if only in the form of its title, for the simple reason that the nineteenth century discovered the effect of the poetical in a world that was becoming more and more prosaic.[14]

At first reading, Dahlhaus's analysis appears overly negative, reinforcing the boundaries between high and low art that much recent scholarship has sought to dismantle. It is hard to attach positive value to the suggestion that such works are "banality masquerading as poetry," or that *Trivialmusik* is "deliberately bland" (the implication being that high art—meaning absolute music—is not). But underpinning Dahlhaus's point is a more subtle one, which concerns aspects of musical process as well as reception. Here, salon music is of more intrinsic interest because it occupies a precarious aesthetic position:

> The mechanics behind its power to "touch," though half-submerged, are nevertheless half-visible. The listener is permitted at once to enjoy and despise it. He is spared the exertions of immersing himself in the work, as required of him by great art. The cynicism of the popular-music industry, which converts sentimentality into capital, is answered by a sentimentality which threatens at any moment to turn into cynicism and is not about to stand any nonsense.[15]

This balancing point, at which the music's sensibility just resists the commercial cynicism Dahlhaus associates with the "popular-music industry" in late-nineteenth-century musical culture, accounts for the work's poignancy and freshness. Elgar's salon music is not simply trivial, therefore, but belongs partly within the high-art category of the Romantic miniature. This is a generic divide bridged also by many of Grieg's *Lyric Pieces,* another significant body of work whose salon associations have perhaps prevented substantial critical appreciation.[16] The hybrid genre to which both Grieg's and Elgar's works belong contains pieces whose structural brevity hints at hidden depth or obscurity of meaning.

Chanson de nuit belongs in exactly this category. Its outer sections articulate a hymnic melody of the kind that provides the basis for Elgar's most obviously "popular" tune, the trio from the *Pomp and Circumstance* March no. 1. Musical signs of this hymnic discourse include the subdued dynamic level, the melody's carefully graded profile and registral range (gradually unfolding over an octave and a half while avoiding successive angular leaps), the predominantly diatonic harmonic treatment, and the direction *espress. e sostenuto* over the violin's initial entry. The piano's organ- or harmonium-like accompanying chords suggest that the piece can be heard as a march or a solemn ritualized processional, similar to those in the *Vesper Voluntaries* for organ, op. 14 (1890), which Elgar may have modeled on César Franck's pieces for harmonium (many titled "Offertoire"), music likewise intended for either chapel or domestic consumption. As John Butt observes, the *Vesper Voluntaries* owe their origins to Elgar's employment at the Roman Catholic St. George's church in Worcester, and the individual numbers "doubtlessly reflect something of the experimentation that service accompaniment fostered. [Elgar] clearly followed continental models rather than the traditional Anglican organ style."[17] Though it is not obviously a religious piece, *Chanson de nuit,* which was originally titled "Evensong," shares this sense of liturgical context.[18] The idea of communion suggested by the more urgent and impassioned middle section of the piece is arguably a spiritualized rather than an eroticized one. In that sense, the piece crosses the sacred-secular divide in a manner typical of the genre. As Dahlhaus remarks of Lefébure-Wély's *Les cloches du monastère:*

> If the piece is sufficiently "characteristic" to be perceived at all (and selected from the vast oversupply of "musical commodities"), its harmony, rhythm, and melody nevertheless remain so simple that it poses not the slightest obstacle to a mode of listening that glides across the musical structure and loses itself in an imaginary vision of monastic quietude, or in melancholy self-indulgence in the listener's own need for repose.[19]

It is precisely this sense of quietude—of the convent rather than the monastery, perhaps, given the character piece's conventionally feminine-gendered associations in the nineteenth century—which *Chanson de nuit* evokes.[20] But this spirit of pious kitsch (a designation intended here without pejorative connotations) does not prevent the employment of musical figures that imply a greater degree of abstract musical thinking than the work's title might otherwise suggest. The unstable harmonic progress of the middle section, for instance, is prefigured by the descending chromatic contour of the bass in the opening phrase (mm. 1–8, Example 1a), and the central climax in E-flat major from letter B (mm. 26ff., Example 1b) is anticipated by the first chromatic intrusion in the work, at measure 2. Elements of this motivic chromaticism influence the coda (marked *più lento,* mm. 46ff.), particularly the music's emphasis on A♯, an enharmonic transformation of the pivotal B♭s that had launched the earlier climax from letter B. In *Chanson de nuit,* Elgar succeeds, therefore, in applying the most up-to-date sophisticated harmonic techniques without compromising the genre's essential directness and accessibility of expression. The companion piece of *Chanson de nuit,* the *Chanson de matin,* composed slightly later (1899), achieves a similar state of balance.[21] The melodic design of the outer sections again suggests a chaste innocence characteristic of the genre, but the coda here leads to a sudden moment of inwardness (mm. 93–97) in which Elgar dwells

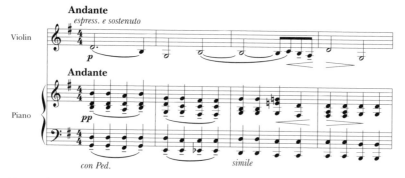

Example 1a. Elgar, *Chanson de nuit,* opening, mm. 1–4.

Example 1b. Elgar, *Chanson de nuit,* central climax, mm. 25–33.

on the juxtaposition of two diatonic seventh chords in first inversion, vi⁷ and vii⁷/V, in a manner that temporarily suspends any firm sense of modality.

If *Chanson de matin* and *Chanson de nuit* point to the use of Continental, rather than English, musical models, as comparison with the *Vesper Voluntaries* and Franck's work suggests, then they also illustrate Elgar's indebtedness to a musical genre with which he has not readily been associated in the critical imagination: French and Italian opera. The mood of innocence and contemplation captured in both works is derived from similar representations of meditative devotion which were common in Romantic opera. The vocal character of the melodic writing in *Chanson de nuit* in particular reinforces the comparison. Elgar had gained firsthand knowledge of the repertoire through membership in the Worcester Glee Club, whose playing list included favorite items from early-nineteenth-century operas, and his correspondence suggests that he was a keen operagoer during his early visits to London in the 1880s and '90s.[22] Reference to opera is also significant because it helps to collapse the tension between popular and high-brow musical styles identified by Dahlhaus. Opera was among the most readily accessible musical forms in nineteenth-century musical culture, even in England, and as a genre it thrived on precisely the "paradoxical cross between sentimentality and mechanization" that Dahlhaus identifies as a characteristic of *Trivialmusik*. As with other salon works of their type, therefore, *Chanson de matin* and *Chanson de nuit* can be imagined as miniature operatic *scenas,* transposed from the public sphere of the opera house into the domestic space of the drawing room. And despite his subsequent historical reputation as a national symphonist in the Austro-German mold, such pieces suggest that Elgar's creative roots lie in an alternative musical milieu.

The second category of popular music that can be identified in Elgar's work consists of pieces written for civic occasions: symphonic marches and commissioned works intended to celebrate large-scale public events such as *Coronation Ode* and the "Imperial Masque," *The Crown of India*.[23] These pieces were often enthusiastically received at their premiere. Henry Wood recalled that, following the London premiere of the *Pomp and Circumstance* March no. 1 in October 1901,

> the people simply rose and yelled. I had to play it again—with the same result; in fact, they refused to let me go on with the program. After considerable delay, while the audience roared its applause, I went off and fetched Harry Dearth who was to sing *Hiawatha's Vision* (Coleridge-Taylor); but they would not listen. Merely to restore order, I played the march a third time. And that, I may say, was the one and

only time in the history of the Promenade concerts that an orchestral item was accorded a double encore.[24]

It is hard at first glance to reconcile the sheer physicality of this audience response with the description of the elevated artistic genius in Edwards's article in *The Musical Times* and its images of pastoral contemplation and meditative companionship. Yet Elgar does not appear to have been uneasy with the prospect of such popular critical appreciation, famously remarking with lip-smacking anticipation to Dora Penny that he had composed "a tune that will knock 'em—knock 'em flat."[25] Earlier, in a letter to Joseph Bennett dated 17 March 1898, he had declared his ambition to compose "a great work—a sort of national thing that my fellow Englishmen might take to themselves and love."[26] Arthur Johnstone observed in the *Manchester Guardian* after a performance of *Coronation Ode* that Elgar appeared to have achieved precisely this ambition:

> It is popular music of a kind that has not been made for a long time in this country—scarcely at all since Dibdin's time. At least one may say so of the best parts, such as the bass solo and chorus "Britain, Ask of Thyself," and the contralto song and chorus "Land of Hope and Glory." The former is ringing martial music, the latter a sort of church parade song having the breadth of a national hymn. It is the melody which occurs as the second principal theme of the longer Pomp & Circumstance march, which I beg to suggest is as broad as *God Save the King, Rule Britannia* and *See the Conquering Hero*, and is perhaps the broadest open-air tune since Beethoven's *Freude Schöner Götterfunken* [*sic*]. Moreover, it is distinctively British—at once breezy and beefy.[27]

Generally, such works have suffered—rather than benefited—from their association with a particular time and location: the sense of place and occasion captured in pieces like the *Ode,* for example, has promoted their subsequent critical neglect. Perhaps the assumption is that after they have served their immediate utilitarian purpose such works are not worthy of admittance to the canon of absolute music. But not all of Elgar's civic or ceremonial music has followed this trajectory: the first and fourth *Pomp and Circumstance* marches in particular have assumed a canonic position in British (and American) musical life that easily perpetuates their high historical profile.

The *Pomp and Circumstance* marches focus attention on a central issue in any critical discussion of Elgar and populism: his music's perceived relationship with broader notions of nationalism and empire. For some writers, this presents an unavoidable stumbling block to full appreciation of Elgar's work. As early as 1924, the polemical critic Cecil Gray explicitly made the link by suggesting that it was "necessary to distinguish clearly between the composer of the symphonies and the self-appointed Musician Laureate of the British Empire, always ready to hymn rapturously the glories of our blood and state on the slightest provocation."[28] Gray's observation embodies in acute form a wider critical turning against imperial modes of thought and expression following the First World War.[29] For Gray "the immortal 'Land of Hope and Glory'" tune from the first march, supposedly Elgar's most extreme expression of colonial expansionism, "may at some time or other have aroused such patriotic enthusiasm in the breast of a rubber planter in the tropics so as to have led him to kick his negro servant slightly harder than he would have done if he had never heard it."[30] Such overtly politicized readings of Elgar's music may not necessarily be endorsed by many scholars today, but a sense of unease nevertheless remains. Brian Trowell, for example, has cautioned:

> We are so used to Elgar's marches that we regard their nationalistic idiom as equivalent to that of Dvořák's Slavonic dances, but they are not so innocent. If we put their glittering orchestral equipage and sheer catchiness to one side for the moment, we realize that they are really a kind of recruitment propaganda, showy street-processions like the example in *Cockaigne*.[31]

Other scholars have proposed radical reinterpretations of Elgar's attitude to empire in such works, either suggesting that his music somehow foreshadows the Empire's decline, or that his commitment to an imperialist cultural project was skin deep at best. Prominent among such revisionists is Bernard Porter, whose broader attitude to the historical status of imperialism is one of skepticism. Porter argues that "there can be no presumption that Britain—the Britain that stayed at home—was an essentially 'imperialist' nation in the nineteenth and twentieth centuries," stressing the contingent or anachronistic nature of unified concepts such as "British society" (which Porter regards as a diverse, complex phenomenon stratified by class, religion, and other factors). Rather, "imperialism can be regarded as ubiquitous, if it is defined broadly and loosely; but the more broadly and loosely it is defined, the less useful it becomes as a descriptive and analytical tool."[32] The principal thrust of Porter's argument is twofold: on the one hand, a need to deconstruct imperialism as a historical phenomenon in nineteenth-century British culture, and on the other, the desire to rescue Elgar's historical reputation from the image of the "jingoistic tub-thumper, a manifestation of the worst aspects of late Victorian and Edwardian bombast." In an essay specifically on Elgar and empire, Porter therefore concludes:

> We have not discussed—because the present writer is not equipped to do so—the question of whether "imperial traits" can be inferred from his abstract works. (Is there such a thing as a "jingo" cadence or key?) Judged by his representational pieces, however, Elgar comes over as a pretty toothless sort of imperialist, as these things went; more dolphin, really, than shark.[33]

The strength of Porter's call for a reevaluation of imperialism based on a close scrutiny of the historical evidence is difficult to resist, but his reading of Elgar's music appears to rest on two assumptions. The first is that Elgar's attitude to the Empire was either an anomaly—an enthusiasm only briefly embraced in the heady years (following his marriage) when Elgar's national career first took off, between the premiere of the *Enigma* Variations (1899) and the First Symphony (1908)—or a charade, to some extent play-acting in the role of imperial artist. The second assumption is that there is somehow a fundamental qualitative distinction between Elgar's "representational pieces" and his pure absolute music. Porter maintains: "There are no peculiarly imperialist intervals, keys, or even orchestrations. We need words to be sure: either libretti, or the titles of orchestral works."[34] But though this latter assumption certainly reflects trends in late-nineteenth-century musical politics, the actual boundaries between different musical genres, as we have seen, were more permeable than this reading would suggest.

It is especially difficult to listen to the *Pomp and Circumstance* marches with neutral ears given this highly polarized reception history. And it would be an all too easy interpretative strategy to "rescue" such music, seeking to problematize the works by suggesting that their apparently blithe tunefulness hides deeper and more uncomfortable musical truths. But Elgar's attitude toward the marches appears to have reflected some sense of this ambivalence. The works' title is taken from a passage in Shakespeare's *Othello* (3.3.347–54):

> [Othello:] O, now for ever
> Farewell the tranquil mind! Farewell content!
> Farewell the plumed troop, and big wars,
> That make ambition virtue! O, farewell!
> Farewell the neighing steed, and the shrill trump,
> The spirit-stirring drum, the ear piercing fife,

> The royal banner, and all quality,
> Pride, pomp and circumstance of glorious war!

More than one writer has commented on the incongruity of these lines in the context of the music's superficially upbeat character. Moore, for instance, notes Elgar's plans (later abandoned) to set Rudyard Kipling's end-of-empire poem "Recessional" around the time of the composition of the first two *Pomp and Circumstance* marches, and draws a parallel between the poem's sense of ceremonial retreat, withdrawal, or decay, and the reflective character of the trio tune from the first march. For Moore, both poem and melody suggest noble defeat rather than triumphant victory, a mood appropriate perhaps for the end of the Boer War.[35] But the Shakespeare reference is even more poignant than this parallel implies, and represents a moving inward or away from public service, accompanied by a sense of outward betrayal. The speech comes from a crucial turning point in the play when Iago has finally persuaded Othello of Desdemona's supposed unfaithfulness, and it represents the apex of the play's argument—the shift from celebration to tragedy. In this sense, it presents a dialogue between civic duty or obligation and personal feeling or expression that lies at the heart of much of Elgar's music, not simply his "populist" works.

The marches also rest upon a tension between archaic and modern elements. In part, this can be explained through reference to Elgar's interest in chivalry. In an interview with Rudolph de Cordova in *The Strand Magazine* in 1904, for example, Elgar is recorded as saying:

> I like to look on the composer's vocation as the old troubadours or bards did. In those days it was no disgrace to a man to be turned on to step in front of an army and inspire the people with a song. For my own part, I know that there are a lot of people who like to celebrate events with music. To these people I have given tunes. Is that wrong? Why should I write a fugue or something which won't appeal to anyone, when the people yearn for things which can stir them—?[36]

As Aidan J. Thomson and others have shown, chivalry is a prominent feature of Elgar's earlier music, from the concert overture *Froissart* to cantatas such as *The Black Knight,* and it represented at least in part an attempt to imagine the modern world according to a sense of renewed moral and aesthetic order.[37] But it also embodied Elgar's notion of music as a form of spectacle or display. In an obituary in the *Sunday Times*, Ernest Newman remarked that Elgar "saw the outer world as a magnificent pageant, every line and colour of which thrilled him," an interpretation that reinforces the sense in much of Elgar's work of ceremony as both entertainment and ritual.[38] Elgar's interview in *The Strand Magazine,* however, also suggests that the marches assumed an anti-institutional quality, Elgar juxtaposing popular appeal (a good tune) against more conventionalized academic standards (fugue). Elgar thus draws attention to his own sense of isolation from formal centers of musical practice while simultaneously pointing to his wider public acclaim. The idea of a chivalric mode of musical discourse, or of Elgar portraying himself as an ancient bard in modern dress, may have been one means of addressing this potential imbalance between popular success and academic critical esteem.

The formal layout of the marches reflects these tensions and dualisms. Even the dedication of the first march, to Elgar's close friend Alfred Rodewald "and the members of the Liverpool Orchestral Society," suggests a bringing together of private and public spheres.[39] The introduction begins with hard-edged modernist linear counterpoint in contrary motion— one of the most famous Neapolitan openings in the repertoire. The initial emphasis on E♭ is enharmonically reinterpreted by the chromatic rise in measure 7 so as to lead *upward* to the dominant A. The main section of the march proper is characterized by a motoric energy: it is modern urban music that evokes the sounds of commerce or manufacturing industry as much as military activity. If, as James Hepokoski and others have suggested, the driving rhythms in the second half of Sibelius's tone poem *Finlandia* can be heard as a representation of a steam engine, thrusting into the future, it is possible to imagine a similar machine-like momentum with the sounds of pistons and valve gear in the outer sections of Elgar's march.[40] The heavy pesante tread of the poco allargando measures therefore becomes a sudden application of the brakes that attempts to bring the rolling musical locomotive under control. In contrast, the largamente first appearance of the trio is presented as an idealized tune or processional, a "national hymn" according to Arthur Johnstone's review of *Coronation Ode* in the *Manchester Guardian,* which suggests a ritualized space or mood of civic dignity even without the references to national pride and territorial expansion later supplied by A. C. Benson's text. If the emphasis in the main sections of the march is on a forward vector, constantly pushing onward in a spirit of modernist progress, the emphasis in the trio (even in its transformed molto maestoso apotheosis) is on circularity and repetition, and the tune ultimately avoids closure.[41] As a whole, therefore, the march combines two fundamentally opposed musical impulses, one forward-looking and progressive, and the other circular and retrospective.

If not universally acclaimed by critics, the first *Pomp and Circumstance* march can reasonably lay claim to being Elgar's most popular work. But, as the above analysis suggests, its populism is contingent and contested.

Though for many commentators, such as Michael Kennedy, the march represents the elevation of empire and a particular (for some, problematic) vision of Englishness, it can equally be heard as a vivid illustration of contemporary urban life. This allusion to processes of mass production and industrialization foreshadowed the work's early reception history: Elgar recorded the complete march on gramophone no less than four times, and "Land of Hope and Glory" three times, and in these forms the piece reached its widest possible audience, most poignantly during the First World War.[42] The catalogue entry for Elgar's first wartime recording, of a truncated version of the march, proclaimed:

> That thrilling broad march melody, now known to every British ear, "Land of Hope and Glory," is played with unspeakable breadth of tone and majesty by these fine players directed by Elgar. No one can listen without experiencing feelings of noble patriotism, such is the nature of its immediate appeal. Every Britisher should possess this unique record.[43]

Though we are now able to listen to Elgar's recording on CD transfer, it is hard to imagine exactly how the piece would have originally sounded played on a gramophone in the trenches or on the home front. Surely at no other time would the music's tensions between its different modes of expression, active and static, modern and retrospective, have seemed quite so stark and polarized: the "spirit-stirring drum" must have beaten hollow indeed.[44]

The third and final category of popular music in Elgar's work relies on a similar tension between modern and retrospective modes of musical discourse. But the works in this category construct the popular in a manner diametrically opposed to the contemporary urban sounds of the first *Pomp and Circumstance* march. In these pieces, the popular is heard as a lost voice, the image of an idealized Arcadian past that is fleetingly recaptured or momentarily regained as though from a considerable musical or historical distance. It therefore becomes the trace of a vanished presence or loss, rather than an affirmation (as in the outer sections of the march) of a modern civic identity. Paradigmatic examples of works in this category include the "canto popolare" (literally, "popular song") in the concert overture *In the South*, and the so-called Welsh tune in Introduction and Allegro. In both cases, the popular melodies have the character of folk songs, and are symbolic of a preindustrialized pastoral idyll or former natural wholeness.[45] This symbolic content is foregrounded through sharp juxtaposition of these "popular" melodies with music of a more overtly modernist character. As Matthew Riley has observed, such gestures are motivated by "a sense that 'reality'—determined by the conventional frame and form of a movement—gives way, in a sudden moment of transformation, to a magical 'inner' world of pastoral simplicity, childlike innocence, or imaginative vision."[46] Therefore the impression that the tunes are musically unprepared or unmotivated by their context lends them their sense of enchantment or bewitchment. In other words, they act as Proustian gateways: moments of intense sensory awareness (heightened musical expressivity) that give way to fragmentary glimpses of lost time.

Elgar's symphonic study *Falstaff* is a challenging final case study in this third category of popular music expressive of lost innocence or Arcadian nostalgia. Elgar himself suggested, "I have, I think, enjoyed writing [*Falstaff*] more than any other music I have ever composed, and perhaps, for that reason, it may prove to be among my best efforts."[47] Despite his estimation, however, *Falstaff* remains among the most problematic of Elgar's major works. Contemporary reviews of early performances dwelled on the work's complex formal layout, the relationship between the music and its literary program, and the music's perceived academicism: the general impression was that the music was "clever" rather than intrinsically beautiful. The *Pall Mall Gazette* complained after the London premiere on November 3, 1913, for example:

> Perhaps it is because there is a need for a good deal of pictorial delineation and incident that "Falstaff" strikes one as being aesthetically unsatisfactory. Putting aside the question of the construction of the work, a lengthy composition without a measure of sensuous charm, of intrinsic beauty of theme, can hardly fail to give the impression of something lacking. "Falstaff" truly is rather forbidding in this respect, and the amazing cleverness is but a poor substitute. One feels, indeed, that, however closely the subject-matter may be said to represent the intended idea, not enough is gained when music's greatest power, its emotional appeal, is so seldom called into play.[48]

Such critical misgivings may have reflected a deeper disquiet concerning the work's complex and at times contradictory response to its Shakespearian source. Elgar's preliminary generic designation of "character study" is significant, since the piece is structurally and gesturally defined by its critical engagement with the character of Falstaff himself. Elgar's music is *interpretative*, in the sense that it presents a number of different and often conflicting aspects of Falstaff's stage character: chivalrous, pompous, fat, recalcitrant, comic, and, above all, populist. Falstaff, more than any other Shakespearean character, craves an audience and plays to the crowd. It is the closing bars of Elgar's work that are therefore the most problematic. The manner in which Elgar responds to the dramatic denouement of Shakespeare's plays, the rejection of Falstaff by the new king, Henry V, at the end of *Henry IV Part 2*, suggests an anxiety about the state of social order or civic authority that adds a new dimension to Elgar's relationship with the popular in music.

The complex formal structure of *Falstaff*, with its multiple disjunctions and layers of meaning, has recently been analyzed in depth by J. P. E. Harper-Scott, and little further needs to be added to this reading.[49] Elgar's own account of the work, published in an analytical note to accompany the premiere, suggests an opening section that functions as an exposition with varied restatement.[50] The second section includes musical textures associated with a conventional developmental space such as fugal passages and points of thematic transformation and liquidation. This development section includes two virtually self-contained movements: a scherzo, based on the Eastcheap tavern material, which includes a full trio and scherzo reprise; and the dream interlude, where Falstaff imagines himself as a young boy (and "page to Thomas Mowbray, Duke of Norfolk"). The reentry of the full orchestra at the Straussian upbeat in measure 743 (rehearsal number 81) has the character of a thematic reprise, but the restatement is swiftly aborted and the music leads into a second developmental episode based on the Shrewsbury battle sequence (*Henry IV Part 1*, Act 5). This new developmental episode parallels the first in that it also includes a self-contained interlude or dream sequence, one of Elgar's most magical and luminous passages, as Falstaff lingers in Judge Shallow's orchard in pastoral Gloucestershire while en route back to London. The fourth and final section, titled "King Henry's Progress," serves as a structural reprise or recapitulation, and includes an apotheosis of the "Prince Hal Theme," a broad martial tune superficially similar to the *Pomp and Circumstance* marches in Elgar's favorite E-flat major.[51] The regular pattern of this recapitulation is interrupted, however, by a series of harmonic and thematic crises, a decisive thematic collapse following Falstaff's rejection, and an extended postlude with wistful reminiscences of earlier material.

Elgar's sketches reveal that he remained unsure about the ending until virtually the final stage of composition. As originally conceived, the work finished in measure 1392 (nine measures after rehearsal number 146), following the statement of what Elgar described to Ernest Newman as a theme that expressed "the undercurrent of our failings and sorrows."[52] Diana McVeagh has drawn attention to the significance of the placement of this theme: it is first heard as a countersubject during the Eastcheap roistering

Example 2. Elgar, *Falstaff*, conclusion.

at rehearsal number 64, but by its final appearance the theme is transformed so that, according to McVeagh, "it is no longer a counterpoint, but at the last a prime, expressive melody, serenely accepted."[53] Regarding gesture, this "failings and sorrows" theme corresponds to the third category of popular music in Elgar's work. It assumes the character of a lost voice or folk song, distantly heard, whose effect is uncanny rather than serene. Like the "canto popolare" from *In the South,* or the Mendelssohn quotation from the Lygon movement in the *Enigma* Variations (variation XIII), the music inspires thoughts of melancholy, loss, and nostalgia. Such moments, according to Carolyn Abbate, assume a special narrative significance: the clarinet melody is one of those "rare gestures in music" associated with the act of enunciation, which "seem like voices from elsewhere, speaking (singing) in a fashion we recognize precisely because it is idiosyncratic."[54] Set off from the main body of the work, and isolated within its own otherworldly context, the tune could be heard as a graphic representation of the moment of Falstaff's death, an event that is only cursorily reported by Shakespeare in the first act of *Henry V.*[55]

Elgar's decision to extend the ending of *Falstaff* beyond this point, however, was motivated by a radical reading of Shakespeare's plays. In the copy of the miniature score of the work that Elgar presented to Alice Stuart-Wortley following the premiere, he marked the flyleaf "*Falstaff* (Tragedy)." Elgar's designation is important because it is not clear that Shakespeare's *Henry IV* plays are, in fact, tragic. Rather, these history plays are characterized by what William Empson calls a deliberate sense of *dramatic ambiguity.*[56] This ambiguity centers on Falstaff's moral role within the work, and his fate at the end of *Henry IV Part 2.* Summoned to London for the coronation of the new king, Falstaff waits in attendance, only to be dismissed with the words "How ill white hairs become a fool and jester! . . . I banish thee, on pain of death," (5.5.48 and 63). Almost as an afterthought, the King summons the Lord Chief Justice, and Falstaff is remanded to Fleet Prison. For some critics, such as George Bernard Shaw, the tone and content of Shakespeare's play were inherently problematic. In a review of a production at the Haymarket Theatre in London, Shaw remarked:

> Everything that charm of style, and vivid natural characterization can do for a play are badly wanted by *Henry IV,* which has neither the romantic beauty of Shakespeare's earlier plays, nor the tragic greatness of the later ones. One can hardly forgive Shakespeare quite for the worldly phase in which he tried to thrust such a Jingo hero as Harry V down our throats. The combination of conventional propriety and brute masterfulness in [Hal's] private tastes is not a pleasant one.[57]

Following Shaw, later critics have noted that the *Henry IV* plays reflect the "real world" of Tudor politics all too closely. Though Shaw was to concede that Falstaff appeared as "the most human person in the play," he was nonetheless of dubious moral character, a "besotted and disgusted old wretch." His populism was therefore a negative moral force: an appeal to the lowest common denominator. Furthermore, for Shaw, Shakespeare's work promoted a grim nationalist agenda, an essentially violent and militaristic view of England, and was therefore unacceptable. But for J. Dover Wilson, writing in 1943 at a time of national crisis, the *Henry IV* plays embodied an urgent political truth or allegory. Falstaff represented a conglomeration of conventional dramatic types: the Devil of the miracle play, the Vice of the morality, and the Riot of the interlude. "As heir to the Vice," Dover Wilson suggests, "Falstaff inherits by reversion the functions and attributes of the Lord of Misrule, the Fool, the Buffoon, and the Jester, antic figures the origins of which are lost in the dark backward and abysm of folk-custom."[58] Falstaff therefore becomes a manifestation of the irrational, the primitive, and the uncontrolled. For Dover Wilson and other writers, Shakespeare's scheme at the end of *Henry IV Part 2* admitted no element of doubt or ambiguity. The rejection of Falstaff was both a necessary and preordained act, in keeping with the mythic role of Prince Hal as prodigal son and, more pressingly, the new king of England. The rule of the Carnival King, as represented by Falstaff, must be brought to an end for the nation's moral and political survival. Falstaff's rejection therefore represented the triumph of a new civic order.

Other critics, from Dryden and Maurice Morgann onward, have interpreted Falstaff as an essentially positive moral presence. A particularly relevant discussion is A. C. Bradley's "The Rejection of Falstaff."[59] Bradley maintains that "Falstaff's dismissal to the Fleet, and his subsequent death, prove beyond doubt that his rejection was meant by Shakespeare to be a catastrophe which not even his humor could enable him to maintain." For Bradley, Falstaff's rejection was tragic, since "the bliss of freedom gained in humor is the essence of Falstaff."[60] Falstaff is therefore seen as a worldly, liberating presence, both for his comic ability to entertain, and, as Empson argues more forcefully, for his critique of the English class system. Falstaff represents precisely the anti-institutional populism that Elgar himself had advocated in his interview for *The Strand Magazine* in 1904. Hence the rejection of Falstaff assumes a sinister quality, since, as Empson suggests, "the real case for rejecting Falstaff at the end of Part II is that he was dangerously strong, indeed almost a rebel leader."[61] Empson's final point, that Dover Wilson's interpretation "is due to a distaste for homosexuality, which is regarded nowadays in rather more practical terms than the Victorian [critics']; the idea of Falstaff making love to the Prince, they feel, really has to be resisted," ultimately reinforces his argument.[62] Falstaff's rejection is more concerned with the imposition of a repressive social order and convention than dramatic necessity.

The closing measures of Elgar's *Falstaff* engage, in some sense, with all of these interpretations. The retrospective character of the "failings and sorrows" theme suggests a sense of loss occasioned by Falstaff's death. In context, this melody seems all the more poignant: the passage opens with a slow playing of the complete Prince Hal theme, with its minor-mode shift, and seems to prepare a simple final cadence in E-flat major. The entry of the woodwind and horns, however, turns the music toward C major, and the cadence is brightened by the addition of trumpets and trombones playing muted and pianississimo. Falstaff's death, in Elgar's interpretation, has an almost visionary quality of transfiguration and a quiet, inward peace. The final eight measures, however, are more ambiguous. Elgar's commentary, in his analytical note, offers little by way of definitive explanation: "The King's stern theme is curtly thrown across the picture, the shrill drum roll again asserts itself momentarily, and with one pizzicato chord the work ends; *the man of harsh reality has triumphed.*"[63] The function of Elgar's late addition to the score is to undermine the retrospective effect of the preceding passage. The music denies any sense of transfiguration, or of Falstaff's narrative presence. Rather, the coda turns toward an objective, hard-sounding E minor and the impersonal military rhythm of the king's theme. The effect of the final pizzicato string chord is deadening, in sharp contrast to the warm glow of Falstaff's death. Elgar's characterization of the new king is therefore surprisingly uncompromising and gritty. The accession to the throne, in *Falstaff,* ultimately has none of the positive, optimistic hope for the future which we might have expected from the composer of *Coronation Ode* or the closing bars of the *Enigma* Variations. It represents a crisis of civic identity, or the brutal silencing of the popular voice.

The central critical question remains whether Elgar's revised ending of his symphonic study presents the rejection of Falstaff as a positive or negative event. Elgar's suggestion, to Alice Stuart-Wortley, that the work was essentially tragic underlines the sense of loss and hollowness in the final measures. His analytical note, however, seems closest to Bradley's reading of the play: that Falstaff's demise was a necessarily ruthless act by the new king, whose career path, in *Henry V,* was to lead to greater violence and bloodshed on the French battlefield rather than a period of political and social stability. There is also a sense, perhaps, that Elgar anticipated the cool reception his work would initially receive, especially following the relatively muted premiere of the Second Symphony. *Falstaff* is Elgar's first large-scale work to turn decisively away from the spirit of positive faith or reconciliation that characterizes so much of his earlier music. The music's "message" is therefore hard to process, and this is possibly the most compelling reason why it has never received the unqualified popular acclaim that has met Elgar's other works, such as the *Pomp and Circumstance* marches. However closely Elgar may have associated himself with the character of Falstaff, his last-minute alteration of the ending completely undermines any sense of idealization. The reassertion of moral order at the end of *Falstaff* hardly has the feeling of triumph, and the final attainment of narrative closure has a distinctly modern edge. Elgar appears to have sensed as much. In the final paragraph of his analytical note, he gave the last word to Prince Hal, and not to Falstaff: "We play fools with the time, and the spirits of the wise sit in the clouds and mock us."[64]

The dramatic ambiguity of the final measures of *Falstaff* suggest that Elgar's approach to the idea of a popular audience, at least as embodied in his musical representation of the Shakespearean character, was a deeply ambivalent one. Falstaff, according to Elgar, represents a powerfully deconstructive, anti-institutional force, and as such is an irresistibly attractive figure. But there is also a sense that such popular appeal is somehow dangerous, or needs to be contained. The poignancy of the conclusion concerns the sense of loss that such containment inevitably creates. This in turn suggests a broader interpretative model for understanding Elgar's popular music. Peter Bürger suggests that "the problems of mass-market literature and the elite consciousness of the artist arise as a result of these contradictory demands confronting art—to be both guardian of a humanity that can no longer be found in life-praxis and yet be available to all."[65] It is for this reason that the doctrine of aesthetic autonomy exists at all, "to act as guardian of human emancipation in a society whose actual life processes do not allow its realization."[66] Elgar's music adopts a number of strategies in order to try to resolve this contradiction. In his salon music, which builds upon a rich preexistent nineteenth-century genre, the illusion of autonomy is maintained by the innovative employment of a range of conventionalized gestures associated with acts of meditation or contemplation. In *Pomp and Circumstance* March no. 1, Elgar articulates a thrilling dualism between opposed modes of musical expression: a modern, progressive, machine-like music inspired by the sounds of the contemporary urban world and a more circular, repetitive music that suggests a sense of civic ritual or ennoblement. In *Falstaff*, however, the tensions between the transformative function of art as autonomous object and the processes of mass production associated with art's commodification are projected through a deep interpretative reading of

Shakespeare's play, in which the spirit of the popular imagination, Falstaff, is ultimately crushed by a sense of "harsh reality."

These case studies offer an experience disconcertingly similar to that provided by the Elgar Route in Worcestershire. They trace a strangely discontinuous and idiosyncratic narrative that ranges across much of Elgar's creative life, charting his relationships with his audiences in a diverse number of venues, arriving ultimately (but fittingly perhaps?) at the ghostly revenant of a madhouse.

NOTES

I would like to thank Byron Adams and J. P. E. Harper-Scott, whose generous and insightful comments on earlier drafts of this essay resulted in numerous improvements.

1. The quotations are from the route guide published by Worcester City and Malvern Hills District Councils (anonymous, undated). The emphasis in the penultimate quotation is mine.

2. For a critical analysis of Elgar's associations with Worcestershire, see Jeremy Crump, "The Identity of English Music: The Reception of Elgar, 1898–1935," in *Englishness: Politics and Culture 1880–1920*, ed. Robert Colls and Philip Dodd (London: Croom Helm, 1986), 164–90; and Jeffrey Richards, *Imperialism and Music: Britain 1876–1953* (Manchester: Manchester University Press, 2001), 44–46.

3. Similar mythologies also operate for aspects of Elgar's biography, where associations with people, and childhood, similarly serve to deflect attention away from his music's abstract quality.

4. Tim Barringer, "'In the Air All Around Us': Elgar's Aesthetics of Landscape," inaugural lecture, AHRC Framework Seminar: "Land, Air, and Water," University of Nottingham, 2 July 2005.

5. F. G. Edwards, "Edward Elgar," *The Musical Times* (1 October 1900), repr. in *An Elgar Companion*, ed. Christopher Redwood (Ashbourne: Sequoia, 1982), 35–36.

6. Cyril Ehrlich, "The Marketplace," in *The Blackwell History of Music in Britain: The Twentieth Century*, ed. Stephen Banfield (Oxford: Blackwell, 1995), 41.

7. Ibid., 44.

8. On difficulties of categorization with particular reference to British music, see Richard Middleton, "The 'Problem' of Popular Music," in *The Blackwell History of Music in Britain*, 27–38, esp. 27–29; and "Locating the People: Music and the Popular," in *The Cultural Study of Music*, ed. Martin Clayton, Trevor Herbert, and Richard Middleton (London and New York: Routledge, 2003), 251–62.

9. See Robert Anderson, *Elgar in Manuscript* (London: British Library, 1990), 8–9, for a summary of the compositions known as "sheds," so named after the building at the back of the Elgars' garden where the wind band used to rehearse.

10. Carl Dahlhaus, *Nineteenth-Century Music*, trans. J. Bradford Robinson (Berkeley: University of California Press, 1989), 314–15.

11. For a discussion of problems in the reception of Sibelius's miniatures, with an attempt to redress the critical balance, see Veijo Murtomäki, "Sibelius and the Miniature,"

in *The Cambridge Companion to Sibelius*, ed. Daniel M. Grimley (Cambridge: Cambridge University Press, 2004), 137–53, esp. 137–42.

12. Jerrold Northrop Moore, *Edward Elgar: A Creative Life* (Oxford: Oxford University Press, 1984), 227.

13. Letter dated 20 October 1898, in Moore, *Elgar: A Creative Life*, 247.

14. Dahlhaus, *Nineteenth-Century Music*, 317.

15. Ibid.

16. On the reception of Grieg's music, see Daniel M. Grimley, *Grieg: Music, Landscape and Norwegian Identity* (Woodbridge: Boydell, 2006), introduction.

17. John Butt, "Roman Catholicism and Being Musically English: Elgar's Church and Organ Music," in *The Cambridge Companion to Elgar*, ed. Daniel M. Grimley and Julian Rushton (Cambridge: Cambridge University Press, 2004), 114.

18. Moore, *Elgar: A Creative Life*, 227.

19. Dahlhaus, *Nineteenth-Century Music*, 315.

20. In this context, it is significant that Elgar's youngest sister, Ellen Agnes (known as "Dot" or "Dott"), took vows and became sacristan, organist, and music mistress, and later prioress, in the Dominican Order. See Percy M. Young, *Elgar, O.M.: A Study of a Musician* (London: Collins, 1955), 36–37, and Richard Smith, "Elgar, Dot and the Stroud Connection—Part One," *Elgar Society Journal* 14, no. 5 (July 2006): 14–20.

21. Moore, *Elgar: A Creative Life*, 266.

22. Based on programs held at the Elgar Birthplace Museum, Moore lists the repertoire of the Worcester Glee Club between 1870 and 1872 as including "the Overtures to *Zampa* (Hérold), *Norma* (Bellini), *Masaniello* (Auber), and *Maritana* (Wallace) . . . and occasionally a big selection from one of the operas—*Norma* or *Il Trovatore*." *Elgar: A Creative Life*, 45. In an interview with Rudolph de Cordova in *The Strand Magazine*, May 1904 (repr. in Redwood, *Elgar Companion*, 115–24), Elgar recalled having played in the orchestra when visiting opera companies performed at the Worcester Theatre, whose repertoire included *Norma*, *La Traviata*, *Il Trovatore*, and *Don Giovanni*.

23. For further discussion of *The Crown of India*, see Corissa Gould, "Edward Elgar, The Crown of India, and the Image of Empire," *Elgar Society Journal* 13, no. 1 (2003): 25–35; J. P. E. Harper-Scott, "Elgar's Unwumbling: The Theatre Music," in *Cambridge Companion to Elgar*, 172–73; and Deborah Heckert, "Contemplating History: National Identity and the Uses of the Past in the English Masque," Ph.D. diss., SUNY at Stony Brook, N.Y., 2003. See also the chapters in this volume by Nalini Ghuman and Deborah Heckert.

24. Quoted in Moore, *Elgar: A Creative Life*, 154.

25. Dora M. Powell, *Edward Elgar: Memories of a Variation* (Oxford: Oxford University Press, 1937), 35–36.

26. Quoted in Moore, *Elgar: A Creative Life*, 234.

27. Quoted in Richards, *Imperialism and Music*, 64.

28. Gray, *A Survey of Contemporary Music* (Oxford: Oxford University Press, 1924), 78.

29. Arnold Bax's opinion of the work is similar, and motivated by similar feelings following the cataclysm of the First World War: "Difficult as it may be to reconcile these contradictions, the fact remains that the impulse to turn out such things as 'Land of Hope and Glory,' the *Imperial March*, the *Coronation Ode* and the regrettable final chorus of *Caractacus* was an integral part of the makeup of this man, a representative, even an archetypal Briton of the last years of Queen Victoria's reign." *Farewell My Youth and Other Writings*, ed. Lewis Foreman (Aldershot: Scolar Press, 1992), 125.

30. Gray, *Ssurvey of Contemporary Music*, 79–80.

31. Brian Trowell, "The Road to Brinkwells: The Late Chamber Music" in *"Oh, My Horses!": Elgar and the Great War*, ed. Lewis Foreman (Rickmansworth: Elgar Editions, 2001), 351.

32. Bernard Porter, *The Absent-Minded Imperialists: Empire, Society and Culture in Britain* (Oxford: Oxford University Press, 2004), 24.

33. Bernard Porter, "Elgar and Empire: Music, Nationalism and the War" in Foreman, *Elgar and the Great War,* 156.

34. Porter, *Absent-Minded Imperialists,* 144.

35. Moore, *Elgar: A Creative Life,* 338–40. Moore also links the melody to Elgar's work on a symphony based on the life of General Gordon, for which the representation of a "noble defeat" would have seemed equally apt.

36. Rudolph de Cordova, "Elgar at Forli," *The Strand Magazine* (May 1904), repr. in *Elgar Companion,* 123.

37. Aidan Thomson, "Elgar and Chivalry," *19th-Century Music* 28 (2005): 254–75; see also Robert Anderson, *Elgar and Chivalry* (Rickmansworth: Elgar Editions, 2002).

38. *Sunday Times,* 25 February 1934, repr. in Redwood, *Elgar Companion,* 155.

39. On Elgar's devastated reaction to Rodewald's sudden early death, see Byron Adams, "The 'Dark Saying' of the Enigma: Homoeroticism and the Elgarian Paradox," in *Queer Episodes in Music and Modern Identity,* ed. Sophie Fuller and Lloyd Whitesell (Urbana: University of Illinois Press, 2002), 218–19.

40. James Hepokoski, "Finlandia Awakens," in Grimley, *Cambridge Companion to Sibelius,* 90–91.

41. The final measure of the third climactic statement of the tune is elided with the reprise of the march (*tempo primo,* rehearsal letter T), so that, strictly speaking, the melody never actually achieves full cadential closure.

42. The complete march recordings took place on June 26, 1914; April 27, 1926; November 12, 1931 (trio alone); and October 7, 1932. "Land of Hope and Glory" recordings made in 1924 and 1931 were never commercially released, but a recording from 1928 with the Philharmonic Choir was issued.

43. Quoted in Foreman, "The Winnowing Fan: British Music in Wartime," *Elgar and the Great War,* 121.

44. On Elgar's creative response to the First World War, in particular his attempts to create a popular ritualistic musical representation of intense grief and collective and personal loss, see my "'Music in the Midst of Desolation': Structures of Mourning in Elgar's *The Spirit of England,*" in *Elgar Studies,* ed. J. P. E. Harper-Scott and Julian Rushton (Cambridge: Cambridge University Press, 2007). Such works occupy a separate Elgarian category of popular music, principally because of their particular historical context.

45. There is no evidence that Elgar ever quoted an actual folk song in any of his works, even though the composition of the Introduction and Allegro coincided with the sudden explosion of interest in folklore in Britain among musicians such as Vaughan Williams, who trained at the Royal College of Music under Stanford and Parry. Elgar seems to have been aesthetically opposed to this kind of activity, and once remarked, "I write the folk songs of this country," an attitude that could perhaps be regarded as further evidence of his desire to appeal to popular appreciation over and above membership of formal academic musical institutions. Quoted in Michael Kennedy, *Portrait of Elgar* (Oxford: Oxford University Press, 1968), 74. For a rich contextual analysis of this passage, see James Hepokoski in Harper-Scott and Rushton, *Elgar Studies.*

46. Matthew Riley, "Rustling Reeds and Lofty Pines: Elgar and the Music of Nature," *19th-Century Music* 26, no. 2 (2002): 177.

47. Interview with Gerald Cumberland [Charles Kenyon], *The Daily Citizen,* 18 July 1913, quoted in Christopher Kent, "Falstaff: Elgar's Symphonic Study," in *Edward Elgar: Music and Literature,* ed. Raymond Monk (Aldershot: Scolar Press, 1993), 105.

48. Anonymous review, *Pall Mall Gazette,* 4 November 1913, Elgar Birthplace Museum, EB Box 1332 (June 1911–June 1914).

49. J. P. E. Harper-Scott, "Elgar's Invention of the Human: *Falstaff,* op. 68," *19th-Century Music,* 28, no. 3 (2005): 230–53; see esp. his formal summary of the work, 240.

50. Edward Elgar, "Falstaff," *The Musical Times* 54 (1913): 575–79.

51. Significant differences, however, given the programmatic context, are the "Prince Hal" tune's modal instability (its second strophe shifts toward E minor) and the fact that Elgar never marks it *nobilmente,* a direction that occurs frequently throughout the *Pomp and Circumstance* marches. These details suggest that musically, from the outset, Elgar's representation of "gracious" Prince Hal is at least tonally ambivalent.

52. Letter dated 26 September 1913, quoted in Anderson, *Elgar in Manuscript,* 127.

53. Diana McVeagh, "Elgar and Falstaff," in *Elgar Studies,* ed. Raymond Monk (Aldershot: Scolar Press, 1990), 141.

54. Carolyn Abbate, *Unsung Voices: Opera and Narrative in the Nineteenth Century* (Princeton, N.J.: Princeton University Press, 1991), 29.

55. This narrative silencing of Falstaff is all the more savage for its betrayal of Shakespeare's promise at the end of the final act of *Henry IV Part 2,* that Falstaff's story would be resumed in the succeeding play. In Laurence Olivier's wartime film version of *Henry V,* Falstaff's death becomes an extended moment of wistful reflection, accompanied in Walton's score by a Purcellian chaconne with descending bass line.

56. William Empson, *Essays on Shakespeare* (Cambridge: Cambridge University Press, 1986), 37.

57. George Bernard Shaw, *Shaw's Dramatic Criticism, 1895–98,* ed. John F. Matthews (Westport, Conn.: Greenwood, 1971), 165.

58. J. Dover Wilson, *The Fortunes of Falstaff* (Cambridge: Cambridge University Press, 1943, repr. 1953), 20.

59. Elgar does not appear to have been aware of Bradley's work, but the essay was an important source for Tovey's analysis, which Elgar certainly read. He made no attempt to correct where Tovey had relied on Bradley's reading of the play, although he had more general reservations about Tovey's approach.

60. A. C. Bradley, "The Rejection of Falstaff" (1909), repr. in *Shakespeare, Henry IV Parts 1 & 2: A Casebook,* ed. G. K. Hunter (London: Macmillan, 1966), 69.

61. Empson, *Essays on Shakespeare,* 67–68.

62. Ibid. This reading, of course, conceals another more common prejudice, namely that homosexual behavior can be dismissed as youthful experimentation, something to be abandoned and rejected in adulthood.

63. Elgar, "Falstaff," *The Musical Times* 54 (September 1913): 579.

64. Ibid. The quotation is from *Henry IV Part 2,* 2.2.134–35; also quoted by McVeagh, "Elgar and Falstaff," 137.

65. Peter Bürger and Christa Bürger, *The Institutions of Art,* trans. Loren Kruger, introduction by Russell A. Berman (Lincoln, Neb., and London: University of Nebraska Press, 1992), 10.

66. Ibid., 11.

PART II
DOCUMENTS

Early Reviews of *The Apostles*

in British Periodicals

SELECTED, INTRODUCED, AND ANNOTATED
BY AIDAN J. THOMSON

The success of *The Dream of Gerontius* in Germany in December 1901 and May 1902 propelled Elgar into Britain's national consciousness on a scale that would have seemed unimaginable just two years earlier. *Gerontius* soon became a favorite with audiences at the larger English provincial choral festivals, ranking alongside *Messiah* and *Elijah* in popularity. Consequently, when it was reported in the musical press in 1903 that Elgar was composing an oratorio for the Birmingham Festival on the life of the apostles, public interest in the project was considerable. The composer, characteristically, played his part in generating publicity. An exchange of letters that took place in late February and early March of 1903 between Elgar and Alfred Littleton, the chairman of his publishers, Novello, reveals the composer's concerns about when the print media should be informed about *The Apostles;* Littleton suggested that *The Musical Times,* Novello's house journal, should be given the right to make the first official announcement of the new work. Elgar responded by meeting the editor, F. G. Edwards, on March 14, 1903, the result of which was two articles: one concerning the libretto of the oratorio, which appeared in the April issue of the periodical; and one about the work's music, which was published in July.[1] These pieces were supplemented in the October issue of the periodical by an essay about the plot and theological implications of *The Apostles* by Canon Charles Vincent Gorton (who had recently founded the Morecambe Festival and through that had befriended Elgar) and complemented by a series of interviews Elgar gave to *The Sketch* (September 16, published on October 7) and to R. J. Buckley of the *Daily Dispatch* (September 24). The *Pall Mall Gazette,* meanwhile, published a piece about the composer on the day of the premiere, October 14.[2] Most importantly, at the composer's suggestion,

Novello brought out two guides to the work in time for the premiere: an interpretation of the text by Gorton and an analysis of the music by August Jaeger.[3] In short, Elgar had done as much as he could to ensure that the audience at the premiere would be as well informed about his new work as possible, in the hope of a favorable reception.

With its premiere, *The Apostles* passed from the domain of its composer—who to some extent could dictate how the piece should be perceived—to that of its audiences, whose views, though mostly positive, were certainly more varied. This fact has been obscured by the existing Elgar literature, which has concentrated on critiques of the work at its premiere but not at subsequent performances. Such neglect is unfortunate, for the early reception history of *The Apostles* suggests that though most critics generally admired the piece, their admiration was often tempered with reservations—about Elgar's use of leitmotif, his style of word setting, the subject matter of the oratorio, and possible shortcomings compared with other similar works. These reservations are an uncomfortable reminder that Elgar's music did not meet with universal approval, even in Britain, but as part of the early "post-history" of the work they should not be ignored.

The articles below attempt to remedy this state of affairs. These documents are a series of reviews of particular performances of *The Apostles* between 1903 and 1905: the Birmingham premiere, the performance in Manchester shortly before the Elgar Festival at Covent Garden in March 1904, the Elgar Festival presentation, the performance at the Three Choirs Festival in Gloucester in September 1904, and the London Choral Society's rendition at Queen's Hall in February 1905. (These were by no means the only performances of the work in the sixteen months that followed its premiere; for reasons of space, reviews of concerts in such venues as Leeds and York have been omitted, along with performances that took place later in 1905, notably at Worcester and Norwich.) The reviews appear in four British music periodicals: *Monthly Musical Record, Musical News, Musical Opinion and Musical Trades Review* (hereafter *Musical Opinion*), and *The Musical Standard*. These journals are less widely available to scholars than *The Musical Times*, thus the reviews below serve a practical purpose. A more important reason for their inclusion, however, is that all four periodicals could claim to be genuinely disinterested about Elgar: unlike *The Musical Times*, none were published by Novello, who, as publisher of *The Apostles*, had a vested interest in promoting the oratorio.

The oldest of the four, *The Musical Standard*, was founded in 1862 as the "only independent representative of music in the London weekly press"—an allusion to the contemporary power not only of Novello's *The Musical Times* but of the Davison publishing house's journal, *The Musical World*.[4]

Originally appearing twice monthly (though by the period of *The Apostles* it ran weekly), the *Standard* specialized particularly in "applying itself to church music and musical literature in some degree . . . [because] there is little or no musical literature, and none of a kind at all adapted for the churchman or the advanced amateur." This emphasis on religious music manifested itself in, for instance, regular columns on organ building or correspondence about organists' positions, but the periodical also offered reviews of new music, concerts, and operas (in London, the provinces, and, from 1868 onward, abroad), news of particular artists and events, and occasional humorous numbers.[5] A new series of the *Standard* began in 1871 and was replaced in turn by an illustrated series in 1894, which ran until 1912. The focus of the periodical changed somewhat over the years, but interest in church music was never entirely eradicated. It is perhaps no coincidence that the first biographical sketch of Elgar appeared in the *Standard* in 1896, shortly after the premiere of his early oratorio, *Lux Christi* (premiered as *The Light of Life*), op. 29.[6]

The year 1871 saw not only the new series of the *Standard* but the first volume of *Monthly Musical Record,* a periodical published by Augener that survived until 1960 under the editorship of such figures as Ebenezer Prout, J. S. Shedlock, Richard Capell, Sir Jack Westrup, and, later, Gerald Abraham. The raison d'être of the *Record* was aesthetic, not commercial. As Prout explained in his opening editorial, it was aimed

> solely at the advancement of the science to which they are specially devoted, [by those who] strongly desire that it should be understood by the public, and particularly by those more immediately interested in the publication of music, that works issued by any other house will be reviewed with the same independent appreciation and impartiality as those issued by themselves. It is their earnest desire that this Journal shall not degenerate into a mere trade advertisement.[7]

Within this aesthetic sphere, Prout explained, the *Record* existed "in the first place to furnish ample intelligence on musical matters, both British and Foreign," through reviews, scholarly writing on historical, analytical, and critical matters, and translations of leading French and German scholars. This interest in Continental music making and criticism may reflect the inferiority complex felt by musical figures in mid-Victorian Britain and the perceived need to improve the level of public discourse on music. Certainly, the prevailing tone of the *Record* is scholarly, in the reviews of new music as much as in the historical essays.

The third music periodical founded during this period was *Musical Opinion,* whose first issue appeared in October 1877. A monthly publication until as recently as 1994, the *Opinion* was in some ways the opposite of *Monthly Musical Record.* A typical issue would consist largely of current musical news, including perhaps an article on a featured composer and concert reviews. A regular feature was "Musical Gossip of the Month," a column by the pseudonymous "Common Time" (it is unclear whether "Common Time" was one author or many, although the consistency of the writer's views would suggest the former). This column took an overview of a particular issue (such as the state and perception of music in Britain), often in a manner that was far more nuanced than its somewhat frivolous title might suggest. Despite this perceptive columnist, *Musical Opinion* was noted primarily not for its weighty musicological scholarship but for its coverage of church music—like *The Musical Standard,* a feature of the magazine was coverage of organists' vacancies and other organ-related matters—and, above all, the quotidian concerns of the music business. Around a third of the periodical was concerned with the sale of musical instruments and music publishing: a practical antidote to the more esoteric aesthetic concerns covered in the *Record.*

The youngest of the four periodicals was *Musical News,* a weekly founded in 1891 in response to the "distinct call for a new journal which shall, at the popular newspaper price of 'One Penny,' furnish news from all parts of the civilised world and supply original articles, not only upon current topics but upon those subjects of permanent interest upon which new light may be thrown from time to time."[8] Indeed, when necessary it became a campaigning newspaper, notably (according to the critic Charles Maclean) under its first editor, T. L. Southgate, who "led some excellent crusades against charlatanries in the teaching world."[9] The format of the periodical followed the pattern established in *Musical Opinion* and *The Musical Standard* of editorial comment, reviews of concerts in London and the provinces, "Foreign Intelligence," correspondence, and miscellaneous items of interest—again with an emphasis on church music, for the syndicate-owned *Musical News* was the organ of the Royal College of Organists.[10] Its style was consciously journalistic rather than academic, and this populist tone was reflected in a price that, its editors hoped, would "interest not only the few, but the many."[11] It also aimed to fill the gap in the market caused by the demise, in 1891, of *The Musical World,* one of whose former journalists, F. Gilbert Webb, became sub-editor of the new periodical.

The articles that follow are divided into four parts: the Birmingham premiere, the Manchester and Covent Garden concerts, the Gloucester performance, and the London Choral Society concert. They have been transcribed directly from the printed sources, and so reflect the usage of each publication, including an inconsistent use of small capitals that was common practice during this period. Within each section the articles appear in chronological order of publication.

Part I: The Premiere
(October 14, 1903)

One of the most important musical events in Britain outside London, the Birmingham Musical Festival was held triennially from 1784 until 1829 and then from 1834 to 1912. The repertoire of the festival was predominantly choral; notable commissions included Mendelssohn's Elijah *(1846), Gounod's* Redemption *(1882), Dvořák's* Requiem *(1891), and all four of Elgar's mature choral works:* The Dream of Gerontius *(1900),* The Apostles *(1903),* The Kingdom *(1906), and* The Music Makers *(1912). The 1903 festival, which took place in Birmingham Town Hall from October 13 to 16, consisted of eight concerts, among which were performances of* Elijah, Handel's Messiah, *and Bach's B-Minor Mass. Most of these concerts were conducted by Hans Richter, who since 1885 had been the principal conductor at the festival, though Elgar directed* The Apostles—*the only new work presented in 1903—himself.[12]*

As the reviews below indicate, the critics' views of the piece were mixed, but the performance itself was a success (unlike the disastrous premiere of Gerontius *under Richter three years earlier). Contributing to this success was the singing of the six soloists, all of whom were highly regarded in oratorio and all of whom would perform the work at least once more during the course of the following year. Emma Albani sang the Blessed Virgin and the Angel Gabriel;[13] Muriel Foster (who had already impressed Düsseldorf audiences as the Angel in* Gerontius*) sang Mary Magdalene;[14] John Coates sang St. John;[15] Kennerley Rumford sang St. Peter;[16] David Ffrangçon Davies sang Jesus;[17] and Andrew Black sang Judas.[18]*

The Birmingham Festival.

Musical News 25, no. 659 (17 October 1903): 316–17

The author of this article, "O. I.," has not been identified.

WEDNESDAY.—The much-anticipated production of "The Apostles" has at length taken place, before one of the most attentive audiences the writer has ever seen. It will be impossible to give more than a mere outline of its general effect in this brief account. We may, however, at once premise that its success as a rare and lofty work of art is assured, and that in most respects it is at least on an equal plane of merit with its predecessor, "The Dream of Gerontius," and, in several, even an advance on that remarkable work. The same strongly-marked characteristics are prevalent in both works, mysticism and deep piety combined with strong dramatic suggestiveness, striking originality of orchestration and subtle use of the *leit-motif* system. These qualities may be said to typify Elgar at his best, and they suffice to produce from his pen a species of music like that of no one else. It is individual to the highest degree, and perhaps this is its greatest strength to-day, when originality in the musical art becomes more and more difficult.

In conformity with a custom which is seemingly becoming general, the composer has himself selected and arranged his libretto. This is mainly from Biblical sources, and is illustrative of the calling of the Apostles, culminating with the Passion, Ascension, and prophecy of the future work of the disciples. The whole libretto is most cunningly chosen for the purpose of displaying a series of vivid and dramatic pictures suggestive to the Christian mind of the most moving and important incidents in the history of the world. At the same time the sacred subject is treated with the utmost reverence, so that not the slightest shock can be produced in the religious feelings of the most sensitive listener. Rather must the reverse happen in the majority of instances, and the hearer comes away with a sense that he has assisted at an elevating act of worship. The whole work may be taken as the most modern representative of the old-time "Passion music" as typified by Bach in his St. John and St. Matthew's Passion [*sic*]. Whilst, however, the design of these earlier works was confined to certain recognised and clearly defined limits, here it is extended so as to embrace other ideas and incidents, all elaborated with the most modern methods of composition. As the composer tells us that the present work is only a portion of his projected design, it is evident that he sees the possibilities of great expansion in this particular form of creative art.

The note of mysticism is at once struck, in the Prologue of which the vocal portions are allotted to a chorus. In it a number of the most important leit-motives are announced, and later on these with many others are woven together with all the composer's inimitable subtlety. The methods prevalent in "Gerontius" are here again constantly in evidence. There are the same frequent subdivisions of muted strings, the same characteristic use of brass, especially of horns, the same large orchestra, and strong contrasts of light and shade, all compelling attention by their mystery. In the later work, however, there is more chromaticism, and in this respect a nearer approach to the continental schools. The motives named in the analytical programme, "Christ's Loneliness" and "Sin," are both instances of this tendency.[19] Indeed, the former phrase is somewhat reminiscent of Wagner's "Parsifal." Such a resemblance, however, is sufficiently rare in Elgar's case. The wonder is that, dealing with such a subject, and coming after such a dominating genius as the Bayreuth master, he is not drawn much more under his sway. Perhaps the most striking motif in its significance and simplicity is that of Christ. This consists merely of a melody of three notes moving by conjunct degrees, but it is harmonised in such a manner as to produce an acute dissonance, at once suggestive of the sufferings of our Lord.[20] The dramatic suggestiveness of the work never flags, and herein perhaps lies its greatest strength. It is often all-absorbing in this respect, as for instance in Christ's delivery of the "Beatitudes," with the running commentary of Mary, the disciples and a chorus, in Mary Magdalene's anguish as she looks out of a Tower by the Sea of Galilee, whilst a chorus suggests worldly pleasures to her, and afterwards when Peter is in danger of being drowned. Again, in the Betrayal of Christ, Judas' repentance is dramatically accentuated by the chorus of priests and singers in the Temple. Their words, by chance apparently, are strangely applicable to Judas' mood. It is in such passages as these that the composer suggests to the mind of the listener a scene, a living picture, without the aid of stage accessories, and certainly no one has hitherto displayed greater skill than he in this direction. His profound mastery of the technicalities of composition all heighten the effect. We have scarcely space here to dilate on Elgar's skill in this respect. If any example were needed, one need only turn to the closing section of this work, some portions of which are scored for two choruses, one semi-chorus, and four solo voices, all more or less simultaneous, and provided with an independent and significant orchestral accompaniment. The work could not have been launched under better auspices. The orchestra was superb, the chorus sang with great intelligence and verve, whilst the solo vocalists, Madame Albani, Miss Muriel Foster, Mr. John Coates, Mr. Ffrangçon Davies, Mr. Kennerley Rumford, and Mr. Andrew Black all showed most satisfactory mastery over the various difficulties they had to contend with.   —O.I.

The Press on "The Apostles."

Musical News 25, no. 660 (24 October 1903): 352–53

This article is a selection of reviews of the premiere from the Times, *the* Standard, *the* Daily News, *and the* Morning Leader. *I have omitted the article in the* Daily News *by E. A. Baughan, as his rather negative views on the piece—that it lacked a central idea, that it mixed realism and mysticism rather too readily, and that its leitmotifs were not always musically interesting enough—are reiterated at greater length in his articles in* Monthly Musical Record *(see below).*

The two parts of "The Apostles" are subdivided into seven parts, called, after the prologue, (1) The Calling of the Apostles; (2) By the Wayside; (3)

By the Sea of Galilee; (4) The Betrayal; (5) Golgotha; (6) At the Sepulchre; (7) The Ascension. These again are subdivided into what may be called scenes for want of a better expression. Canon Gorton aptly sums up the prologue in the sentence—"as is fitting, in the prologue we behold the end from the beginning."[21] It would take far too long to go *seriatim* in one notice through each of the parts and its subdivisions. In the beginning "Jesus went out into a mountain to pray." There follow beautiful scenes of the dawn; of the Temple first shrouded in a dim light, then the dawn flooding the courts as the morning light appears, when Christ calls the disciples and chooses the Twelve. In the second scene, "By the Wayside," occurs one of the most touching and appealing movements in the oratorio—the utterance of the Beatitudes by Christ to the Apostles; in the next, a magnificent scene for Mary Magdalene, followed by an interlude in which the Mater Misericordiae exhorts her to "Come, for there is peace for thee," and a finale, "Turn you to the stronghold, ye prisoners of hope."

The second part begins, after a brief orchestral introduction, with "The Betrayal," in which Judas plays so prominent a part. Dr. Elgar here takes apparently the view of Archbishop Whately and others that Judas had no intention of betraying Christ to death, "but to have been as confident of the will of Jesus to deliver Himself from His enemies by miracle as he must have been certain of His power to do so, and accordingly to have designed to force Him to make such a display of His superhuman powers as would have induced all the Jews . . . to acknowledge Him King."[22] Judas, in a word, was a "misguided zealot, who would substitute his own plan for Christ's will."[23] After "Gethsemane," St. Peter's Denial, the scene without the Temple, we come to Calvary—a scene reverentially conceived and most impressively presented—to Easter Morn, and to the Ascension, where, for the time, the work stops.

In one sense the book, or rather its arrangement, is a little disappointing, as matters at present stand, since it presents rather a series of more or less detached pictures or scenes which are intended ultimately to lead to a definite end. But so far as he has at present progressed Dr. Elgar has treated his subject with a fitting sense of dignity and awe, and everywhere his reverence, sincerity, and conviction are clearly manifested. Much of his writing is in the best manner of genuine Church music, much of it is in the right sense mysterious, as it should be. And precisely because it is the direct outcome of conviction so it carries conviction with it. In spite of the slightly detached nature of the work, of which mention has already been made, one is immensely impressed by such scenes as those referred to; by the whole scene of the lonely Christ upon the Mountain; that "in Cæsarea Philippi," with the splendid climax beginning at the phrase, "Thou art

Peter"; "in Capernaum"; "the Temple"; the awe-inspiring "Golgotha"; the quiet, dignified "scene" of the Ascension; and, in perhaps a slightly different manner, by the storm. Dr. Elgar, as well as his subject, takes us through every kind of emotion; from the beginning to end one is moved—and the result, it must be confessed, is no little physical strain; but it is a strain one willingly submits to. As to the actual writing of the oratorio, there is shown a full mastery over the means of expression; and, though it might be possible to point to one or two small passages that hardly seemed to "come off," they were few enough to be easily ignored, more especially in view of the many that succeeded, and of the general tone of dignity and power of the work; for Dr. Elgar has succeeded in a huge task before which most composers might have quailed.

—*The Times*.[24]

Whatever the verdict of the future may be on Dr. Edward Elgar's oratorio, "The Apostles," there can be no question concerning the lofty purpose of the composer and his consummate mastery of the resources of his art. The work is the product of fervid imagination controlled and guided by keen intellectual perception, a masterful expression in music of spiritual convictions, and in its essence a sacred music drama permeated with the spirit of the preacher. In a brief preface, Dr. Elgar writes:—"It has long been my wish to compose an oratorio which should embody the calling of the Apostles, their teaching (schooling), and their mission, culminating in the establishment of the Church among the Gentiles. The present work carries out the first portion of this scheme: the second portion remains for production on some future occasion."

The composer has written his own libretto, which consists almost entirely of scriptural passages, making liberal use of the Revised Version and the Apocrypha, and placing such passages in the mouths of the characters as indicate their temperament or give dramatic realism to the situation. The general scheme is a series of scenes setting forth incidents in the lives of the Apostles during Christ's sojourn on earth, and Parts One and Two, produced this morning, cover the period from the calling of the Apostles to the Ascension. The music is based on what is technically known as *leitmotifs*, of which ninety-two are specified by Mr. A. J. Jaeger in his exhaustive analytical and descriptive notes.[25] The composition is, indeed, laid out after the same manner as Wagner's "Parsifal," but here its indebtedness ends, for Dr. Elgar's conception and style are distinct from that of the great German master. The keynote of Dr. Elgar's work is lofty mysticism, suggesting the spiritual in a peculiar and often strangely beautiful manner.

The means employed are most elaborate with regard to the instrumentation, but comparatively simple vocally. In addition to the usual orchestra there are parts for base [*sic*] clarionet [*sic*], double bassoon, small E flat gong, large gong, antique cymbals, glockenspiel, keyboard glockenspiel, tambourine, small bells, harps, and organ, and a shofar, the last-named a Jewish instrument used in the Hebrew services. The full score presents a most fascinating study to the musician, and the harmonic scheme challenges all the formulated laws of theorists.

—*The Standard*.

[. . .]

The music is fuller of *liet motifs* [*sic*] even than that of "The Dream of Gerontius," and the polyphony is in many places even more elaborate. The subtleties of orchestration are still more remarkable and triumphantly skilful, but still there is a greater simplicity and directness of speech in critical moments, though there is much brilliant realism—as, for instance, in the themes which represent the people, or those which stand for the scenes of revelry identified with Mary Magdalen [*sic* and *passim*], or the accurate reproduction of the calls of the shofar at the opening of the doors of the Temple at dawn.

Yet the chief note of the music is one of devoted mysticism which we have come to regard as characteristically Elgarish. It is an obvious remark to say that the atmosphere is akin to that of "Gerontius," and in places suggestive of that of "Parsifal," and I mention this rather as a possible help to those who did not hear the work, towards realising its nature, than with any desire to hint that it is not purely distinctive. The mysticism of "The Apostles" has a character of its own. It suggests a stronger, healthier, manlier nature than either of the two works I have suggested a comparison with, and a serener confidence.

It is impossible to describe the work in detail, but one must mention the noble opening chorus, with its note of assured triumph, the splendidly-vigorous scene of the dawn, the massive Psalm, "It is a good thing to give thanks," the impressive majesty of the chorus, "He has chosen them," the dramatic solo of Mary Magdalen, the loftily-inspired music in which Jesus promises to Peter the keys of heaven, and the noble chorus which closes the first part.

In the second part the number of things which seem to call for special mention is even larger, but from them I can only select the wonderfully dramatic scene in which the drama of Judas's repentance enacts itself, while the worship is going on within the Temple. The exquisitely tender scene between the Virgin and St. John at the sepulchre (where a great effect is made by a return of the dawn music from Part I.), the elevated inspiration of the chorus, "Why seek ye the Living?" and the concluding chorus, which is not only a worthy crown of the whole, but is undoubtedly, both in imagination and in execution, the strongest and most moving thing Dr. Elgar has written. In spite of its extreme complexity, it makes an impression of complete unity and of moving inevitably to an appointed end.

—*Morning Leader.*

The Birmingham Musical Festival
by Our Special Correspondent.

The Musical Standard 65, no. 2047 (full series) (24 October 1903): 261

The author of this article, "A. H. S," has not been identified.

Dr. Elgar's "The Apostles"

LONG before the time of performance of Dr. Elgar's new oratorio the Town Hall was thronged, and the appearance of the composer on the platform evoked a storm of applause. "The Apostles" is not a work which can be discussed fully after a single hearing, although perusals of the work previous to the performance had naturally helped one to form a somewhat conclusive opinion. The work, though not yet complete, is so full of detail that one needs several performances before pronouncing judgment. The text had been arranged by Dr. Elgar, and he must be congratulated upon the success achieved in this direction.

A roll of the drum opens the Prologue, and then enter the strings and wood-wind. The chorus enter at the sixteenth bar with "The Spirit of the Lord is upon me." During the chorus various *motiven* are heard from the orchestra, suggestive of "Christ," "The Man of Sorrows" and "Gospel."[26] These practically dominate the whole oratorio. Towards the end of the Prologue, we have a repetition of the words "The Spirit of the Lord is upon me," dying away *ppp,* and the movement ends with a last presentation of the "Gospel" *motif.*

The first part opens with "The Calling of the Apostles," a recitative for tenor, "Jesus went out unto a mountain to pray." The *motif* in the voice part of the "Angel Gabriel" recalls somewhat that in "Gerontius," but it is only in passing. During this solo the chief *motif* of the work is heard and its recurrence assumes majestic proportions. The Dawn Scene, with the sound of the Shofar introduced, and the Morning Psalm are beautiful. The next scene, "By the Wayside," is also beautiful and most impressive; the Beatitudes being pronounced by Jesus, while Mary, John, Peter and Judas utter their comments. The scene by the Sea of Galilee, with Mary Magdalene as the principal character, is also striking, especially the riotous chorus which precedes "The Mirth of the tabrets ceaseth." [*sic*] The storm music, although somewhat original, reminded one too forcibly of a theatrical effect, but in "In Cæsarea Phillippi" we come back once more to greatness and loftiness of conception. The "Consolation" theme, with its beautiful melody, is assigned to Mary.[27] The first part ends with a movement for soli and chorus, "Turn you to the stronghold."

The second part opens with the "Betrayal," the orchestral introduction being made up of themes mentioned before. The orchestral work here is wonderful in its richness of colouring. Shortly after this Judas becomes the central figure, and here we have the Apostles' declaration of willingness to die with Jesus and the determination of Judas to deliver Jesus into the hands of his enemies. Upon Jesus electing to die, Judas discovers he is the betrayer, and following upon his repentance is despair and death. This is possibly the most powerful scene in the whole work, the denial of Peter being an especially dramatic episode. The chorus also, "And he went out and wept bitterly," is fine in conception. The repentance of Judas is a truly marvellous piece of writing, while I was very much impressed with the manner in which the cry of the people, "Crucify him," is brought in.

The next scene, "Golgotha," is introduced by the lighter strings giving the cry, "Eli, Eli," followed by a chorus, "Truly this was the Son of God." A beautifully tender scene between the Mother and the Apostle St. John follows, and with the chorus asking, "Why seek ye the living among the dead?" the final scene, "The Ascension," is reached. The story of the Ascension is told simply but directly, and the second part of the oratorio ends with another somewhat elaborate choral movement, "In Heaven," a semi-chorus of sopranos and contraltos sing the "Heavenly Allelujahs"; whilst on earth Mary, John, Peter and the Apostles have the prayer, "Give us one heart and one way." "Holy Father," the prayer of Christ, is majestic; but the work ends softly and quietly.

As regards the performance, Dr. Elgar took everything very slowly. The principals were: Mme. Albani (the Angel Gabriel and Mary), Miss Muriel Foster (Mary Magdalene), Mr. John Coates (St. John), Mr. Kennerley Rumford (St. Peter), Mr. Ffrangçon Davies (Jesus), all of whom did well.[28] Miss Foster was tenderly pathetic as Mary Magdalene, and exceptional praise must be awarded to Messrs. Davies and Black. The chorus did their work excellently, while the playing of the band was well-nigh faultless. Mr. C. W. Perkins at the organ lent exceptional aid.[29] At the end, Dr. Elgar had a magnificent ovation, being recalled three times. Judging from a first hearing, I should say "The Apostles" is an advance on "Gerontius," and the audience evidently was of the same opinion.

—A. H. S.

The Birmingham Festival.
Elgar's "The Apostles."

Monthly Musical Record 33 (November 1903): 201–2

This article, signed "E. A. Baughan," was written by Edward Algernon Baughan. Baughan was the music critic of the Daily News *until 1912, in which year he was replaced by Alfred Kalisch, and instead became the paper's drama critic.[30] This was perhaps an appropriate move for someone who, Elgar told Gerald Cumberland, could not "hum a melody correctly in tune. He looks at music from the point of view of a man of letters." For an alleged non-musician, however, Baughan's influence in British musical discourse in this period was considerable: besides the* Daily News, *he wrote for the* Westminster Gazette, *the* Morning Leader, *and was editor of the* Musical Standard *between 1892 and 1902. Baughan's view of Elgar's music was mixed: in addition to his reservations about* The Apostles *he felt that* Caractacus *lacked sufficiently dramatic musical themes, and his praise for* Gerontius *was presumably tempered, as Byron Adams has noted, by his reservations about Wagner. Elgar was on sufficiently good terms with Baughan to adopt his suggestion of "In London Town" as a subtitle for* Cockaigne, *but Meirion Hughes's statement that Baughan was a "friend" of the composer is surely an exaggeration: more likely, Elgar was aware that Baughan was too important a figure to be alienated.[31]*

MOST of us went to the Birmingham Town Hall on October 14th expecting much. "The Dream of Gerontius" had marked so great an advance on "Caractacus" that it was only reasonable to suppose that "The Apostles" would hold the same position with regard to "The Dream of Gerontius." And was the advance not continuous? Well, it is very difficult to give a definite opinion after the mere study of a vocal score and after hearing a full performance once, and most of us left the Town Hall in some perplexity of mind. It is the usual thing to say that great works of art are not easily understandable. I agree in so far that no man, however great a critic he may be, ever grasps the full import of a new work at once; but though he may not be able to see all its beauties in the proper perspective, he is not blind to them. I can remember many great compositions of music which I heard for the first time and did not thoroughly understand, and only really loved after close knowledge of them. But even at first they have always left a definite impression of liking or not liking; something in them has appealed strongly, even at a first hearing. Elgar's new oratorio did not do that; it left me finally cold and unmoved. I hasten to add that on some others it had precisely the opposite effect. I think there are reasons why the work did not impress me, quite apart from specifically musical reasons.

To begin with, Dr. Elgar, who has to a certain extent formed his own libretto, which is made up of extracts from the Scriptures and the Apocrypha, has not been very clear in his intentions. In the note which prefaces the score he tells us that it has long been his wish to compose an oratorio which should embody the calling of the apostles, their teaching, and their mission, culminating in the establishment of the Church among the Gentiles. Whether that is a subject which calls for musical treatment or not, it is a clear aim clearly expressed. But in the libretto of "The Apostles" the aim is not kept steadily in view. We have a long scene in which Mary Magdalene expresses her strivings after better things, and another, much longer, in which Judas is fully penitent. The crucifixion itself is passed by as not being within the scope of a work which is entitled "The Apostles," but there is a short scene at Golgotha which does not carry forward the idea of the work as expressed by the composer. Dr. Elgar's book suffers from containing too much. The story of Mary Magdalene would fill a whole cantata or oratorio, so would the character of Judas. Apparently it has been the composer's intention to treat his subject in a series of more or less related pictures, but from this very shifting of the view-point arises much of the inconclusiveness of the oratorio. The composer is reported to have said that he has always been struck with the idea that the apostles were men, and that he has always wished so to treat them in oratorio. But we get so little of the apostles themselves, and so much of extraneous matter, that they are far from being anything but the faintest of shadows. Only Judas and Mary Magdalene are alive, and they were not apostles at all.[32] Perhaps the third part of the oratorio, which was not produced, may bring the apostles into more prominence.

Then, again, Dr. Elgar has so wavered between the outside or picturesque view of his subject and the psychological and spiritual that the one cancels the other out to some extent. Much space in the score is given to the musical description of what may be called the background of the picture, and the more abstract parts of the oratorio which deal with the teaching or schooling of the apostles are hardly extended enough. One feels that the ideas might have been more fully illustrated in music, and the oratorio as a whole thus given a more complete spiritual cohesion. The composer's idea, no doubt, has been to get away from accepted ideas of oratorio. Why not a mixture of realism and spiritualism, or, rather, why not set a spiritual subject in a realistic background? This question, I fancy, Dr. Elgar has asked himself, and I can quite see that its answer would have considerable fascination for a modern composer. He could point to Bach's "Passion" music and to the mixture of the concrete and abstract in Handel's oratorios. Moreover, is there not the more modern example of Dr. Wolfrum's "Weihnachtsmysterium," in which the mixture of realism and abstract ideas has a certain fascination on paper?[33] I think Dr. Elgar has been largely influenced by that work, or, at any rate, the German composer has anticipated Dr. Elgar, who may have seen in that oratorio some kind of realization of the ideas he has long held as to the treatment of this particular subject. Dr. Wolfrum's composition is not very successful, but though I rank Dr. Elgar's work far above it in originality and inspiration, the two have many features in common, and one of these is a certain scrappiness in appeal to the emotions. One heard "The Apostles" and was conscious of much fervent admiration for separate sections of the work—the simple and telling setting of the Beatitudes, for instance—but the whole made no deep and abiding impression.

To come more to details, Dr. Elgar has made much use of the *leit-motif* system, and the enthusiastic analyst of the Birmingham programme book has been almost inarticulate in his admiration for the composer's ingenuity. All musicians must have the deepest respect for Dr. Elgar's clever use of representative themes, but though he employs them with apt poetic significance, he does not seem able, or he is unwilling, to develop them. Nor are they all themes in the ordinary sense, but rather figures, and occasionally appropriate harmonies. Then, again, I am not sure that the composer is not one of those who love complexities for the sake of complexities— just as *l'art nouveau* designers are fanatics in meaningless curves. Many musical conceits, which look interesting on paper and can be logically defended as the natural outcome of the subject musically illustrated, do not tell in performance, except as the unrecognisable woof and web of the whole tapestry. Sometimes that effect is desirable, but often Dr. Elgar gives one the impression that his picture is all background. This is a good deal due to the uninteresting shape of his vocal melody. The design is undistinctive and does not stand out. The finest vocal music in the oratorio is that assigned to Judas, which certainly shows a freer use of the human voice than Dr. Elgar had before exhibited. On the other hand, Mary Magdalene's outburst of penitence, so fine a subject for the musical artist, is weak and unmoving. The choral fantasy which accompanies it is in the composer's most original vein, but from the uninteresting character of the solo music it becomes of too much importance. To return to Dr. Elgar's love of complexity, I must confess that some of his pages in which the chorus and soloists are woven into a whole are only interesting on paper. The music does not come out clearly, and the mind becomes confused by the hurly-burly rather than impressed by a gradually growing climax. To pretend to criticize the work fully from a first performance would be absurd and unfair, of course. On a closer acquaintance much that seems a comparative failure may become justified, and the different parts of the work homogeneous; but my first impressions were that, in spite of the advance which the composer has shown in his technique, and in spite of the many touches of imagination and fancy with which the score abounds, "The Apostles" is not the masterpiece for which we were waiting. It has not the peculiar note of individuality which makes "The Dream of Gerontius" (a much less ambitious work) so sincere and genuine, and in general Dr. Elgar has given me the idea that there is a limit to his creative inspiration. More than ever he has shown that his abilities are equal to any task, but in "The Apostles," brilliant example as it is of modern technique and, better than that, of modern imagination as a factor in the moulding of musical form, I have not yet heard the clear voice of one who is inspired.

—E. A. BAUGHAN

Musical Gossip of the Month
BY 'COMMON TIME'

Musical Opinion 27 (November 1903): 111–12

Musical terms like "Common Time" were not uncommon for journalistic pseudonyms, particularly in less academic, more informal writing (such as the series of leisurely articles about English churches, cathedrals, and the music therein written between 1903 and 1909 by "Dotted Crotchet" of the Musical Times*) or in polemic columns about current musical events. They were also sometimes adopted by correspondents to the letters pages of music periodicals.*

As to Elgar's "The Apostles," what is one to say after a first hearing? To praise certain strikingly ingenious pages in the score would be no praise at all, for everyone knows that Elgar is a very clever musician. Indeed, I think that we may take his cleverness for granted. He is a modern musician who knows how to write in the idiom of his day, and has the courage to write for a chorus as if it were as capable in musicianship as a modern orchestra. This trait of Elgar has done much, and will do more, for the education of choral societies. "The Dream of Gerontius," after its first performance, was generally voted too difficult for our choirs; and, until after its enthusiastic reception in Germany, it looked as if the work would never become popular. Birmingham had failed to do justice to the choral writing of Elgar; and, if Birmingham failed, why should other cities, not so remarkable for their choral abilities, expect to succeed? Yet now I notice that "The Dream of Gerontius" is performed over and over again by the chief choral societies in the kingdom. Either the difficulties were few or our choral singers have been educated up to the point of being able to triumph over them. This courage of Dr. Elgar has also had another effect. It has set the younger men thinking if there was much in the cuckoo cry that oratorio is a played-out branch of art. The old type of choral composition certainly had no great attractions for a modern musician. It was generally assumed that a composer must write down to the choral societies and make his work as simple as possible, or employ an idiom well known to the majority of amateurs, who look on the oratorio and cantata as the chief glory of the musical art.

ALL these considerations make one look on Dr. Elgar as a man who has done more than any other for native art. One need have no fanatical belief in modern music because it is modern to grasp the fact that any branch of art which is conditioned by peculiar and parochial limitations cannot have much life in it. I do not think it will be seriously denied that British oratorio had become a strangely parochial affair, wonderful to the foreigner as an index to the state of municipal taste in the United Kingdom. Of late a movement has been made towards bringing choral singing more in line with modern ideas of variety of expression. Practically, the choir is going through the same process of education which has made the modern orchestra what it is to-day. Not many years ago such orchestral performances as Nikisch[34] and Weingartner[35] can now obtain from a band not accustomed to their methods would not only have been impossible but would not even have been dreamt of. In choral singing there have always been ideals of virtuoso finish; but they have been very crude ideals of violent and unexpected contrasts, no better and no worse than the champion brass band playing of a few years ago. I say "of a few years ago," because now the conductors of the best brass bands have quite other ideals. Indeed, in the higher standard which we now see in choral singing and brass band playing we have the clearest evidence of a musical *renaissance*. The popular forms of our national music making are coming into line with the music which has hitherto been appreciated by only a small class of specially educated or specially gifted men. This could not, of course, be the work of one man, and I do not for a moment claim that honour for Elgar;

but I think that he is the man who has come at the right moment, the man who was wanted, and who has helped to give choral singers a new standard of execution.

THIS introduction may seem discursive, but it is really germane to my criticism of "The Apostles." I wish to recognise to the full the splendid work done by Dr. Elgar and what it means for British art; and yet the work, I frankly confess, seems to me to be a comparative failure. Its mixture of modern orchestral realism and spiritual mysticism is not blended. It is possible that this very mixture may fully express the composer's cast of mind, but it makes an impression of vagueness, of a want of central grip. The music follows the libretto so closely that one cannot be criticised without taking into account the other. Viewed from a purely literary standpoint, the short quotations from the Scriptures and from the Apocrypha which make up the subject of "The Apostles" suffer from a want of proportion and natural sequence. Each section of the book is separate, and some of the parts—and those that are treated at great length—have not at all aided the composer in his avowed intention of composing an oratorio "which should embody the Calling of the Apostles, their Teaching (schooling), and their Mission, culminating in the establishment of a Church among the Gentiles." If this rather pompous announcement had not been made in the form of a note to the published score, I am certain that no one would have left the Town Hall at Birmingham with any clear idea of the composer's intentions. The effect of "The Apostles" is fragmentary; and, except for "The Beatitudes" (the most successful number in the work), the main impression made on me was by the music assigned to Judas and by the scene in which Mary Magdalene repents of her life.

To say this of a work of the scope and ambition of "The Apostles" is to chronicle the composer's failure to impress himself on at least one member of the audience who did not listen to the music in any spirit of prejudice. Perhaps it may be that a musical composition should not be judged by what it should convey but by what it does convey. A subject should be held of no more account than it is held by painters. In the pictorial art only the veriest Philistines look on the subject depicted as the main question at issue. To painters themselves, the colour and design are everything. But I do not think that that [*sic*] I am a Philistine: for my position is that, if a musical composition pretends to make a certain effect by expressing certain ideas with the aid of words sung, it must to a great extent be judged by the measure of success with which it does realise those ideas. To me a work which is merely clever, ingenious and imaginative is a failure if it pretends to be, and should be, more. And as a rule the absence of great ideas in music means an absence of great workmanship. Cleverness piled on cleverness, complexity making complexity more obscure is not great workmanship. You might as well admire the over-ornate designs of certain decadent periods of furniture designing, merely because all kinds of unexpected things are done in the thick plastering of decorations. A real Sheraton sideboard, with its elegant and austere decorations designed with an idea of being appropriate to the uses of the piece of furniture is greater workmanship than the over elaborated and meaningless specimens of the *éboniste*'s art which the collector prizes so highly. In this particular sense Dr. Elgar's "The Apostles" is not great in workmanship. Many of the ingenious devices and well thought out complexities serve no end: they are mere scrolls and figures and gilding. You may admire each for itself, but you cannot pretend that each play its part in the whole design. And Dr. Elgar's complexities are sometimes the result of his working in the wrong materials. He attempts to use his chorus as if the singers were instruments, and the result is often mere confused noise. Again, his complex use of the *leit motif* system is too often only clever on paper. In performance the themes pass in the general hurly-burly without any particular significance; partly because many of them are not very distinctive in themselves and partly because the composer's use of them is so fragmentary. He seems disinclined to develop his themes to any great extent; and their recurrence, in slightly changed form, does appear mechanical,—a charge often brought against Wagner, who could develop his themes.

As a writer for the voice, Dr. Elgar has developed wonderfully since the days of "Caractacus." The music which Judas sings is declamation of varied and appropriate character. It has sprung from the words, and at once illustrates them and is illustrated by them. To a much less extent has Dr. Elgar been happy in his inspiration for Mary Magdalene. Everything in the picture is well conceived,—the glimpse of the storm on the Sea of Galilee (what a cheap musical storm it is, though!), the pathetic figure of Mary and the fascinating choral fantasia which comments on her penitence; but almost one might say that the section is typical of Elgar's comparative failure in treating his subject, for the most memorable is precisely the unessential,—the choral phantasy.

AFTER all, no man can give more than is in him. The most brilliant technical mastery will not enable a musician to say more than he has to say, however interesting may be the manner of speech. Elgar has never appealed to me as a strong man in music. Viewing his output as a whole, we see that in "The Light of Life" there is an almost sentimental vein; in "Caractacus" there is picturesqueness, and again a rather sentimental curve of melody; in "The Dream of Gerontius" this sentiment has become tinged with passion, but the music is fine just because it is so very personal and sincere.

Then there is the Elgar of fancy, imagination and Puck-like lightness, as in many of the "Enigma" variations. In "The Apostles" all these qualities are amalgamated. You have in that score an epitome of Elgar, except that the note of personal and lyrical sentiment is not prominent. In its place we have something new, something which has not the Elgarian stamp. It is stronger, more impersonal, more aloof, but it has not the same convincing force: it is not so real. Anyone might have written it who knows his Wagner and who loves his Richard Strauss. Roughly, my impression of the work is that its composer has handicapped himself in attempting to combine realism and mysticism, and that the subject is beyond his powers. By technical ability he has endeavoured to build up a great work, but the ringing tones of a great genius are not to be heard in the music.

APART from its specific merits and demerits, "The Apostles" has, at any rate, the distinction of being a new departure in oratorio, inasmuch as the orchestral portion of the work is really a big symphonic poem and the chorus does not take more than an appropriate part in the composition. For that experiment the future of oratorio in this country will probably owe Dr. Elgar a heavy debt.

Part II: Manchester and Covent Garden
(February 25 and March 15, 1904)

The Manchester performance, which took place under Hans Richter at the Free Trade Hall on February 25, 1904, formed the seventeeth concert in the Hallé Orchestra's winter season. Four of the soloists at the premiere sang here, and in the same roles: Foster (Mary Magdalene), Coates (St. John), Black (Judas), and Ffrangçon Davies (Jesus). Albani was replaced as the Blessed Virgin and the Angel Gabriel by Agnes Nicholls,[36] and Rumford was replaced as St. Peter by Frederic Austin.[37]

On March 15, 1904, Richter, the Hallé Orchestra, and Manchester Chorus performed the work again, this time at Covent Garden as part of a special three-concert Elgar Festival that also included a performance of The Dream of Gerontius on March 14, and on March 16 a concert of mostly orchestral works (among them In the South, which received its premiere). The festival was organized by the Grand Opera Syndicate, in conjunction with Richter's agent, Alfred Schultz-Curtius, who ensured the involvement of the German conductor and his orchestra. (It should be noted that these arrangements were made after the Hallé season had been finalized; thus the Manchester performance was not originally designed to be a dry run for the Elgar Festival.) Four of the soloists in Manchester also sang at Covent Garden, and in the same roles (Nicholls, Coates, Black, Ffrangçon Davies); Foster was replaced as Mary Magdalene by Louisa Kirkby Lunn, and Rumford replaced Austin as St. Peter.[38]

The festival concerts attracted large audiences (including, for the first two concerts, the king and queen), and were regarded as a triumph for Elgar and British music in general. Artistically, the only problem appears to have been that in both Gerontius and The Apostles the chorus was placed too far behind the orchestra and consequently sounded muffled.

"The Apostles."
(The Manchester Performance.)

Musical News 26, no. 679 (5 March 1904): 228

The author of this article, T. L. S., is Thomas Lea Southgate (1836–1917), one of the founders of both The Musical Standard and Musical News. A noted musical antiquary and organologist, he co-wrote The Music and Musical Instruments of Japan (London: B. T. Batsford, 1893) with Sir Francis Taylor Piggott.[39]

That considerable interest was felt in connection with the performance of Dr. Elgar's new oratorio at Manchester was apparent in the crowded attendance at the Free Trade Hall on the 25th ultimo, when this remarkable work was given under the direction of Dr. H. Richter, with the Hallé band and chorus. Every seat was sold out in advance of the concert, and the course of the work was followed with close attention, a considerable proportion of the audience having come provided with the vocal score.

Much has been written on this oratorio since its production at Birmingham; its method and text have been so carefully described that it would seem there need be nothing more said than to record what sort of a performance Dr. Elgar's music received, now that it is better known, and its text more clearly understood. But perhaps this is just the reason why some more matured impressions may be offered on the work from a constructive and effective point of view. "The Apostles" differs vastly from the customary oratorio type, indeed, so much so, that some may say it is only an oratorio in point of name. To those who look for an oratorio proper, set solos, duets, choruses, and a chain of vocal fugues, the work will be disappointing. Its form rather takes the narrative method of Bach, with something of the reflective comment of the ancient Greek dramas, conjoined to such passing impressions as much of the modern music since the time of Wagner presents to us. The work is one of close human interest, interest sustained throughout its entire course; conventionalism, and little of set form is to be found in its pages. Whether this independent mode of treating the subject chosen as a whole tends to make the oratorio an effective work for presentation to the general public is a question which each person must decide for himself. Those who reverence Handel and Mendelssohn will probably say No! Those who remember Bach and are attracted by the modern impressionist music will perhaps answer the contrary—though to be sincere they should require more than one hearing to form a judgment which is defensible.

Elgar is above all things independent, and "The Apostles" shews this in every page; the parts for the soloists, the choir, and the band do not depend on one another, though they unite to build up a harmonious whole. The band is rarely accompanimental, it has something to say by itself, some striking phrase of comment on what the voices are uttering, some particular note of colour to display, all helping to make a composite whole. A similar independence characterises all the sections of his score, and, in truth, adds not a little complexity to the proper understanding of the music. It is not uncommon to hear the voice singing quite a different [*sic*]—a clashing note to what is going on in the orchestra; or to find that voices sing for a moment in not the same key notation in which the instruments are playing. And this effect is apparent to the ear as well as to the eye. It may be said that no bad effect results, and the momentary discord over it comes all right. Since Strauss has rioted in sound we have become more accustomed to these concurrent lines of independence; they would have inexpressibly shocked the good men of old, and made a Handel throw his wig with much uncanonical language at the perpetrator. But we have got to reckon with modern music, with progress, invention, fresh modes of thought, and it is dangerous to say that music so entirely independent in its parallel construction as is much of that made to-day cannot be entertained. Whether it will live is more than doubtful, but there are many who feel that such emotional music as Elgar writes appeals to them, and are ready to accept it, if not to become enthusiastic over it.

One must remember that in the Church to which Dr. Elgar belongs there is more realism, more intensity than is felt over the scriptural narratives reflected in the music of Protestant composers. Perhaps this may account for his treatment of portions of this oratorio. For instance, the scene in the Tower of Magdala in which Mary Magdalene bewails her past is spun out and very unduly lengthened. At the same time it should be said that in the picturesque "Is Thy wrath against the sea," and in the passionate "Hide not Thy face far from me," with its complicated wind and string accompaniment, some quite remarkable effects are produced.[40] Then the scene "In Gethsemane," in which Judas plays so prominent a part, is far too much protracted; the remorse of the betrayer seems unending—as perhaps it was, but still too much is made of it considering the scope of the oratorio. Some may urge that not enough is made of the doings of the Apostles, as the title of the work would seem to imply; the author, who is responsible for the selection of the words, has explained that he has stopped at the Calling of the Apostles and their Teaching, leaving their mission for a second oratorio. Amidst much that is imposing and remarkable, the charge to Peter, "Upon this rock I will build my Church, and the gates of Hell shall not prevail against it," stands out with immense force; here, of course, Dr. Elgar expresses his own quite natural feelings. The conception of the scene "At the sepulchre," in which the Watchers, and the Angels with their ancient Alleluia take part, is a fine piece of contrapuntal work; in the long complicated finale, in which Earth and Heaven, with the soloists, are all intermingled, the vocal parts frequently number twelve, the accompaniments being *obbligato*. The effect here is truly magnificent. A flood of music pours forth from the three separate choirs employed, and with the independence of the four soloists, and the fine orchestration, it all brings the work to a thrilling conclusion.

The difficulties in securing an adequate performance of "The Apostles" are great, skill and close attention to the stick of the conductor are needed for every note, or unity in the presentation of its elaboration cannot be obtained. It is understood that not only did Dr. Richter have more than the customary chorus and departmental rehearsals, but for three nights previous to the performance extra rehearsals were held. No wonder then that the rendering was more than ordinarily satisfactory; the choral singing was fine all the way through, difficult points being taken up without hesitation, the accent and shading were all that the composer could have desired. The band parts had been so well studied that as far as could be judged from following the vocal score there was no hitch; all was pieced accurately together. It only remains to mention that the soloists were Miss Agnes Nicholls, Miss Muriel Foster, Mr. John Coates, Mr. F. Davies,[41] Mr. F. Austin, and Mr. Andrew Black; most of these artists took part in the work when it was produced at Birmingham in October last. Suffice to say that in each case full justice was done to Dr. Elgar's expressive, difficult text, and their efforts appeared to be appreciated by an audience by no means enthusiastic over the novel music so well presented to them.

—T. L.S.

The Elgar Festival.

Musical News 26/681 (19 March 1904): 268

No signature is appended to this article.

This notable fixture, organised by the Covent Garden Syndicate, and held in the Covent Garden Opera House, will certainly form a land-mark in the history of England's musical life. In several respects its occurrence must be regarded as deeply significant. Above all, it affords unmistakeable indication that interest in our national music is gradually becoming greater, and that the British public are beginning to realise fully the value of their own countrymen's genius. As, however, this side of the Festival, and some others kindred, are discussed in another column, we need not dwell on them here.[42] The fact that the King and Queen and members of the Royal Family personally attended the fixture was a happy omen for its success; and Their Majesties' patronage gives one more proof of the genuine interest they take in all things that appertain to native progress, whether in matters artistic or otherwise. The fact also that Richter, with the Hallé band and chorus was engaged for the Festival, promised well for the excellence of the performances, as far as these forces were concerned. And as to the two first concerts, this promise was to a great extent fulfilled.[43] These concerts consisted of "The Dream of Gerontius" and "The Atonement," the former being given on Monday, the 11th instant, which was the opening night.[44] It was evident that the many subtleties of Dr. Elgar's scores had been carefully rehearsed, and Richter showed all his well-known skill and care in interpreting these works. But many of the choral performances scarcely seemed to realise the composer's intentions, and especially was this so in "Gerontius." In the grim and sardonic chorus of "Demons" there was especially a lack of forcefulness and energy. The singers seemed mildly cynical rather than inspired with demoniac frenzy. Again, the strings in *forte* passages lacked somewhat in brilliance and power; this, however, was perhaps fully compensated for by the singularly clear phrasing and purity of tone displayed in this department. In respect to the choral defects, full allowance must be made for the disadvantages the singers suffered from in being placed far back on the stage amidst decorative arrangements which were obviously not conducive to good choral effects. It is, however, no doubt difficult to adapt a theatre to concert requirements, and at any rate the Covent Garden authorities managed to produce a pleasing picture to the eye. The performance of the "Apostles" was the better of the two as regards the band and chorus, and this fact was probably due to the thorough knowledge of the work which these forces gained in the Birmingham Festival. Under Richter, the finish, care, and intelligence shown by all concerned in this were beyond praise, and if only more verve had been shown by the chorus, the interpretation would have been almost ideal. As regards the solo portions of both oratorios, they were all excellently given, and in most instances by vocalists who have made them, in a sense, their own. In "Gerontius" Madame Kirkby Lunn, Mr. John Coates, and Mr. Ffrangçon Davies appeared, and in the "Apostles" these artists were joined by Miss Agnes Nicholls, Mr. Kennerley Rumford, and Mr. Andrew Black. Particularly impressive were Mr. Coates as *Gerontius,* and Mr. Davies both as the "Angel of the Agony" and as *Jesus* in the "Apostles."

It was of course the latter work which aroused most curiosity during the Festival, since this performance was the first in London. The juxtaposition of this oratorio and "Gerontius" also afforded a good opportunity of estimating their relative merits. We have heard the question debated whether the later creation is an advance on the earlier. Here was a favourable opportunity of throwing more light on this point, although perhaps it is hardly fair to the composer to make comparisons of this sort. It must be confessed that such a comparison is scarcely avoidable after hearing them consecutively. To us it does not seem that the "Apostles" is an advance. "Gerontius" is distinctly a stronger work, stronger both in subject and music. The composer has the inestimable advantage in the earlier work of having a great poem to work upon, a poem full of mystic and human interest, completely satisfying both intellectually and artistically, and exactly suiting Dr. Elgar's genius. The result is we do not feel that any of its effects are too laboured, as in the "Apostles." This work, in spite of its suggestive musical pictures, with their dramatic background and its extraordinary subtlety, lacks that symmetrical power and satisfying finality which characterises "Gerontius," and is an essential factor in the greatest creations.

Comments and Opinions

The Musical Standard 66, no. 2068 (full series) (19 March 1904): 179–80

The "Elgar Festival" article that appears here, published as part of the "Comments and Opinions" section of The Musical Standard *and signed E. E., is identifiable as the work of one of the two critics—a father (1844–1923) and son (1874–1945)— named Edwin Evans. The author of this article is more likely to be Evans Senior, a critic with a particular interest in Russian music, than his son, whose early writing was concerned mostly with contemporary French music. Moreover, the article lacks the progressiveness that was the hallmark of Evans Junior, a progressiveness which led to his playing an important part in the discussions that resulted in the creation of the International Society for Contemporary Music in 1922 (an organization of which he became president in 1938).*[45]

The Elgar Festival

For Londoners who did not attend Birmingham last year the event of the festival was undoubtedly the first performance in the metropolis of "The Apostles." I had long and eagerly looked forward to an opportunity of hearing his work, with which I had in the meantime made myself familiar. I will confess at the outset that I like it less than "The Dream of Gerontius," although there are many points in it where the composer has attained greater heights. The weakness lies in the construction, principally of the libretto, but in some respects of the music. As regards the former, the use of narrating voices, which is so effective in Vittoria and his contemporaries, is an element of disruption, dangerously affecting the coherence of the plan.

By the end of the first part I felt disappointed, in spite of a warm admiration of certain pages, such as the scene at dawn, the fantasy and some beautiful choruses. There was continual unevenness in the interest, which was increased by some notable lost opportunities. Neither was the treatment of the Beatitudes artistically convincing.

Matters improved considerably in the second part where the characterization and the handling of the dramatic forces is much more successful. The part of Judas, admirably sung by Mr. Andrew Black, is in itself a masterpiece of sufficient weight to place any work containing it upon a high level. A discordant note is struck, however, by the association of the glockenspiel with the thirty pieces of silver, which verges dangerously near the theatrical realism of a type utterly out of place in oratorio.

The close of the work is truly magnificent, and is approached by steps of cumulative power, the building of which reveals the master-hand.

On the whole, I repeat "The Apostles" contains pages which are greater than anything in "Gerontius," but it is inferior to that work, inasmuch as it is less complete and sustained in its effects. One misses the quality of inevitableness, both in the musical situations and in the setting of certain parts of the text, as, for instance, some of the most dignified utterances of the Saviour including the first of them. In "Gerontius" there is not a moment where the attention is not firmly held: in "The Apostles" there are many, though perhaps they are made more conspicuous by the intermittent grandeurs than they would have been in the earlier work. They cause one to speculate as to whether the music was not written too quickly or possibly put on paper before it had matured in the composer's mind.

Incidentally it may be noted that "The Apostles" is far from being so essentially a Roman Catholic work as "Gerontius."

As regards the performance, the solo voices were once more beyond reproach. Mme. Kirkby Lunn, Miss Agnes Nicholls, Mr. Ffrangçon Davies and Mr. Andrew Black (whom I have already mentioned) were in splendid form; but I must single out Mr. Kennerley Rumford, not for any superiority over the performances of the other singers, but over his former ones. Time was when I would scarcely have considered him equal to such a task. It is a pleasure to place on record that he rose fully to the occasion.

I was so unfortunately placed that I hesitate to speak of the orchestra and chorus, but I gained somehow the impression that there was rather less enthusiasm than on the previous evening. The strings particularly played over-rigidly with the result of making the prevailing four-beat rhythm more obvious than was entirely desirable. Once more there was a brilliant gathering, honoured by the presence of the King and Queen, to record.

—E. E.

The Elgar Festival

Monthly Musical Record 34 (April 1904): 62

This article is not attributed to any author, but its style and views—and its presence in the Monthly Musical Record—*indicate that it is the work of E. A. Baughan.*

THE "Elgar Festival"—to dignify by this somewhat grandiose appellation the three concerts of Dr. Elgar's music which were given in Covent Garden Theatre on March 14th, 15th, and 16th—from whatever point of view it was regarded, was an occasion of much significance. It was valuable as a proof of Dr. Elgar's popularity—a popularity acquired by sheer force of talent, unaided by any adventitious circumstances—it was perhaps more valuable still as an indication that Englishmen have at last realized that English music may be listened to without any loss of self-respect. Hitherto the English amateur who has wished to pose as an authority upon music has considered it his duty to praise nothing but the productions of foreign musicians. Dr. Elgar, aided by the ungrudging applause of German critics, has taught his countrymen that the music of an English composer is as well worthy of attention as that of any other man, and whatever his subsequent career may bring forth, this must be counted to him for righteousness. Fashion has much to answer for in matters of this kind. So long as it was fashionable to sneer at English music, it was useless for critics to complain of the neglect that our native composers had to endure. Dr. Elgar has been strong enough to turn the stream of fashion into a new channel; let us hope that his success in this respect will herald a new era of prosperity for English music. The "Elgar Festival" comprised performances of "The Dream of Gerontius," "The Apostles," and a miscellaneous selection, chiefly of orchestral music. Dr. Richter was at the head of affairs, supported by his Manchester orchestra, and the Manchester chorus took part in the two oratorios. Covent Garden is very far from being an ideal place for oratorio. The chorus has necessarily to be thrust to the back of the stage, and the result is that the main volume of sound goes straight up into the roof, and never reaches the auditorium at all. At the side of the stalls the softer choral passages were entirely inaudible, and a good deal of the orchestral work was lost into the bargain. Nevertheless, both oratorios were so well performed that, in spite of the disadvantages of the *locale,* they appeared to make a deep impression upon the audience; but there is no doubt that anywhere else the performances would have been twice as effective. Of the two, "Gerontius" is unquestionably the more popular, and, at the same time, the better work of art. It is more homogeneous in style than "The Apostles," and the composer's touch appears to be firmer in handling his material. Of its musical ability there can be no question; it is an extraordinarily vivid and sincere piece of work, marvellously truthful in interpreting the spirit of Cardinal Newman's poem. With regard to the poem itself, however, and its suitability for musical setting, there is room for considerable divergence of opinion. By reason of its subject, or rather the treatment of that subject—which, it need scarcely be said, represents the Roman Catholic view of death and the hereafter in its most orthodox form—the work must necessarily make but a limited appeal to those whose faith, like that of Tennyson, "has centre everywhere, nor cares to fix itself to form."[46] But, regarded as a work of art, "The Dream of Gerontius" is entitled to all the eulogies that have been showered upon it. Despite the adverse conditions that obtained at Covent Garden, the fervour and dignity of the music, its often beautiful melody and the composer's exceedingly fertile and judicious use of every modern orchestral device, combined to produce an effect of overpowering grandeur. Repeated hearings do but serve to convince us that "Gerontius" deserves to rank as one of the few masterpieces of modern oratorio.

The same cannot be said of "The Apostles," which is sadly lacking in the homogeneity of the earlier work. The libretto is poor in construction; it lacks a central idea and the feeling of unity that this should inspire. It is a succession of scenes, many of them vivid and interesting in themselves, but with little mutual coherence or connection. The music unquestionably suffers from this. Fine as much of it is, it does not show the mastery of material which is to be found in "Gerontius." There is a constant straining after effect, with no proportionate result—indeed, at times the mere piling up of one effect upon another seems to defeat its own object. The elaborate intricacy of the musical structure obscures the main outline of the composer's conception—one cannot see the wood for the trees. In certain scenes, too, Dr. Elgar's desire to heighten the dramatic value of the music has carried him dangerously near the confines of bad taste, as when Mary Magdalene, in the hour of her deep contrition, is haunted by recollections of the rioting and wantonness of her past life, or when Judas's reference to the thirty pieces of silver is illustrated by an accompaniment suggestive of the chinking of money—a device borrowed, by the way, from Verdi's "Falstaff," where it is appropriate enough, though it sounds oddly out of place in an oratorio. The performance of "The Apostles" was a constant struggle against unfavourable conditions. As in "Gerontius," the choral work did not create half the effect it should have done, and the appearance and general atmosphere of the theatre seemed strangely out of harmony with the solemnity of a work dealing with the subject of "The Apostles."

[…] The net result of the festival is to place Dr. Elgar in a position such as has probably never been occupied by an English musician before. His popularity is beyond question, and his influence upon the future of English music must necessarily be very important. It is to be hoped that he will recognize this to the full, and will take a serious view of the responsibility which his brilliant talent has laid upon him.

Musical Gossip
BY 'COMMON TIME'

Musical Opinion 27 (April 1904): 521–22

DR. EDWARD ELGAR has come out of the festival organised in his honour with flying colours. As a rule, a program [*sic*] devoted entirely to the work of one man is apt to prove wearisome, and there was every reason to think that three concerts of Elgar's music would be too much of a good thing. But the truth is that the composer, from the "Froissart" overture to "The Apostles," has had many styles which are only bound together by a thread of individuality. The temperament of the composer, of course, has not changed. What may be called the "Elgarian" cast of melody is as notice-able in the early works as in the later, although the workmanship is very different.

A SECOND hearing of "The Apostles" did not make me alter my first opinion of it in any essential degree. The score contains some glowingly imaginative pages which, in conception and technical mastery, are far above anything in "The Dream of Gerontius;" but, none the less, it does not seem to me so successful in an artistic sense. The subject, of course, is not so com-plete; not so pliable to the personal treatment which is the strength of the composer. It is laid out in a series of pictures which have no great connec-tion one with another; and Dr. Elgar has so seized on the picturesque side of the matter that the spiritual ideas are more or less swamped. The orchestra plays a large part in the work, and I must confess that I found it the most interesting part. But, after all, the vocal portion of an opera and an oratorio must predominate if the main idea of a work is to impress. Elgar's writing for the voice has greatly improved since he composed "The Dream of Gerontius;" but it still does not seem to me that he thinks in a vocal sense. His melodies do not come to him as song; they are not the natural outcome of the words that he sets. In "The Apostles," for instance, there is but very little vocal music that really would impress one apart from the harmony and the orchestral colour. Again, in his laying out of the cho-ruses, he is too inclined to make his voices part of the whole contrapuntal web, as if they were additional instruments. The effect in performance is not equal to the clever appearance of the music on paper. Much that one expects to come out well is comparatively ineffective.

APART from all these technical defects, however, the work fails to make the impression that it should, because the composer has not kept to a very central idea. He continually wavers between description and the expression of personal feelings; between the dramatic and the lyrical view of his subject. One finds this, to be sure, in the works of many a great composer. Handel, for instance, is descriptive in one chorus and in the next he is abstract and emotional; but Dr. Elgar has a fancy for mixing his point of view whenever musical exigences [*sic*] prompt him. As an instance, I may mention the realistic description of the pieces of silver (by a gong and shivering of cymbals) in the midst of the impressive Judas music.

"The Apostles," however, is not a work that can be finally judged by two hearings. It is to [be] performed again by the Royal Choral Society this month, and I shall go to its performance with an open mind. At present it impresses me in detail, but the cumulative effect is not impressive. The new overture, "In the South," in spite of a rather weak opening, and perhaps some diffuseness, is a work which should raise the composer's reputation. Once again I thought that Dr. Elgar finds his proper expression in orchestral composition rather than in oratorio.

Part III: The Gloucester Festival Performance
(September 8, 1904)

The Three Choirs Festival was perhaps the most important choral festival in Britain in the early twentieth century (indeed, it remains one of the most important to this day). It is an annual event whose venue rotates among the cathedrals of Worcester, Hereford, and Gloucester, and is so called because its festival chorus was traditionally drawn from the choirs of those three cathedrals. Typically, the festival began on a Sunday with a service that included an anthem and canticles specially written for the occasion; this was followed during the week by a series of morning and evening concerts that included several large-scale choral works (including Messiah *and* Elijah*) and a rather smaller number of orchestral works. The festival usually included several premieres of works by British composers.*

In 1904, the Three Choirs Festival took place in Gloucester and ran from September 4 to 9. The Apostles *was performed in Gloucester Cathedral on the morning of September 8 as part of a concert that also included Beethoven's Eighth Symphony.*

The soloists included four of those who had sung at the premiere (Albani, Foster, Coates, and Ffrangçon Davies); Dalton Baker sang St. Peter,[47] and Harry Plunket Greene, who had sung the Angel of the Agony in the premiere of Gerontius, *sang Judas.[48] As was customary for the festival, the cathedral organist (in this case A. H. Brewer) appeared on the program as well, conducting the Beethoven symphony.[49]*

The Gloucester Festival

Musical News 27, no. 708 (24 September 1904): 259

The author of this article, G. H., has not been identified.

[. . .]

The chief interest centred in "The Apostles," which was given, under the composer's direction, on the Thursday morning and afternoon. Since this work was first heard at the Birmingham Festival, last year, much has been written about it in these columns and elsewhere. The scheme and treatment of this oratorio, if such it can be called, has aroused much discussion, and created a variety of opinion. Those who are accustomed to and prefer the old orthodox style for oratorio would, doubtless, be disappointed at a first hearing of such a work as "The Apostles." Those, on the other hand, who are fascinated by a novel and vivid treatment of an old story will hail it with pleasure, as they will see in it a new method of oratorio.

But whatever may be the opinion, both sides must be struck by the magnitude of the work, its intricacy of treatment, and its novel effects, and both cannot fail to admire the genius of the man who created it. A detailed account of the work is superfluous, as it has now been performed in London and important musical centres, and has frequently been described and analysed. Briefly, it is the story of the "Calling of the Apostles," ending with the Ascension. This is presented in a series of musical pictures which are vivid in colour, varied in treatment, and dramatic in character. A broken chain of events rather than a connected whole. A story told by brilliant and picturesque episodes rather than by a continuous sequence of events. Hence it has not the structural finish or continuity of the composer's "Dream of Gerontius," but, technically, it is in advance of it, as, though the design is not so satisfactory, the details are more intricate. The composer's use of leit motif is peculiar and excessive. Some of his themes—notably the harsh progression of the "Christ-motif"—are startling. The orchestration is very complex. It needs only an examination of page 15 to see how closely the texture of the score is woven.[50] The main characteristic of the work is the curious blend of mysticism and realism. This, though very ingenious, has, occasionally, a disquieting effect. The "Fantasy" where the Magdalene bewails her sins, while the chorus suggests her past life in music of a different character, is daring and original, but it is doubtful if it produces the effect intended. Among many beautiful scenes, those that are memorable are the peculiar pathos of the "Betrayal" scene, the dramatic force of the "Judas" section, the peaceful beauty of the "Sepulchre" section. All these arrest the attention, either on account of their emotional depth, or by the power of their forcible dramatic presentation. As regards the performance, it was, on the whole, a satisfactory one. It was only natural that in a work making such exacting demands on chorus and orchestra, there should be some awkward moments. But they were few. The tone and precision of the chorus were splendid, and the fine playing of the orchestra was equally noticeable. The soloists performed their parts effectively. Mdme. Albani, as *The Blessed Virgin* and *The Angel*, sang with that devotional expression with which this great artist always interprets sacred music. Miss Muriel Foster sang the part of *The Magdalene* with rare emotional and dramatic power. Mr. Ffrangçon Davies, as *Jesus*, delivered the impressive music with due solemnity. As *Judas*, Mr. Plunket Greene was forcible and dramatic, but his intonation was not good, and occasionally the sentiment and passion of the words were too accentuated. Mr. Coates as *St. John*, and Mr. Dalton Baker as *St. Peter*, were both excellent in their respective parts. Beethoven's Eighth Symphony, which brought the afternoon programme to an end, provided a pleasing contrast to the emotionalism of the previous work, and was very well played, under Mr. A. H. Brewer's careful direction.

—G. H.

The Gloucester Festival
THE NEW WORKS.

Monthly Musical Record 34 (October 1904): 185–86

Another article by E. A. Baughan.

IN looking back on the festival the chief memory is of two British religious works which presented features so diverse that comparison of them is not without interest; need I say that I refer to Sir Hubert Parry's "The Love that casteth out Fear" and Sir Edward Elgar's "The Apostles."[51] The two oratorios seem at first blush to differ so radically in workmanship and musical aim that a comparison may appear to be out of place. In some ways that is so; but as being the religious musical expression of two of the most prominent English composers, there is room for thought in comparing the complexion of the two works.

I have now heard "The Apostles" thrice—at Birmingham, at Covent Garden and at Gloucester. From the first the oratorio struck me as disconnected, as wanting in a central idea carried out consistently. The composer has apparently desired to mix realism or description with abstract religious thought, perhaps taking some of Bach's cantatas and Wolfrum's "Christmas Mystery" as his models. Only on this ground of realistic naïveté can you explain the rather cheap realism of an instrumental description of the thirty pieces of silver on the cymbals, and of the opening choruses with the use of the shofar. Then, again, the repentance of Mary Magdalene, with its punctuation of a chorus describing the fascination of the old life, falls within the same type of treatment. There is no reason why a modern composer should not make use of this realistic background, but it must be laid on with tactful brush, otherwise it becomes of more importance than the principal figures. It is here that Elgar seems to me to have failed. His series of pictures are individually of interest, especially in their orchestral colour and general treatment. But the plan of the whole is by no means organic. The Apostles, whom the composer wished to draw as men, according to what he has told several interviewers, do not loom with importance. On the other hand, the figure of Christ is purposely made shadowy, and the unessential matter of the repentance of Mary Magdalene is given too much prominence. Apart from this weakness of the work I personally cannot put myself in sympathy with the composer's type of religious feeling. It is, if I may so put it, too servile. In "The Dream of Gerontius" the sentimental mysticism of the music is thoroughly in keeping with the character of Cardinal Newman's poem, and it has also the merit of seeming to be an expression of the composer's own religious outlook. At any rate, the music of the earlier work rises to a natural climax and has the air of personal sincerity, which I do not notice in "The Apostles." The story of their "call" does not bear that sentimental treatment. Yet though the composer has orchestrally given vigour to his musical picture, beneath the outside of the work there runs the same vein of sentiment. No doubt this is due to the faith which Sir Edward Elgar holds. To me, and, I have no doubt, to many others, this results in a monotony of style which becomes cloying in its sweetness. The same characteristic is to be noticed in all the composer's religious works, from "The Light of the World" to "The Apostles." It is not, in short, an English treatment of religious feeling; indeed, it is far removed from national character.

It is here that the work of Sir Hubert Parry is so different. His treatment of the big subject of the smallness of man and the largeness of Divine Love is full of a manly reverence and force. In his music man acknowledges the greatness of God without abasing himself. There is no sentimental "whine" in the music. In wholeness of conception, too, the short oratorio is organic. There is none of the wavering between realism and abstract thought that makes the treatment of "The Apostles" so unequal—an inequality that is the cause of the unsatisfactoriness of many of Richard Strauss's symphonic poems. One is almost tempted to think that the modern composer jumps from an abstract treatment of his subject to a realistic for the simple reason that realism gives so many openings for effective orchestral writing. Sir Hubert Parry has apparently no sympathies with that view of art. The form of oratorio rightly remains in his mind as a form of art in which abstract thought can be best expressed—indeed, it is the very essential of oratorio. In his "The Love that casteth out Fear," the composer has made a very effective use of a semichorus as the Divine voice. In the cathedral this had a fine effect of aloofness. In other ways the work is a good example of the composition of the "Job" period of the composer's creative career.[52] The sincerity of the music and its breadth of feeling, peculiarly characteristic of the composer, made their own impression, but the specific musical invention and inspiration of the work are not on the same level as the conception. Were they so the new Gloucester oratorio would be on an infinitely higher plane than "The Apostles."

That work of Elgar's has certainly more inspiration and shows a clearer call for musical composition. Indeed, many of its pages contain some of the most impressive music of modern days. As at first, the Judas music seems to me the most successful of the whole oratorio. It is a veritable inspiration and shows a great advance in the composer's grasp of declamatory style. The new point which the Gloucester performance brought out was the real power and beauty of the final "Ascension" section. Here the composer rises to a big musical climax—not a climax of mere orchestral noise and the piling up of choral complexities, but a climax of feeling and conception. There is nothing in "The Dream of Gerontius" to equal the glow of feeling of this section of the later work. The performance of the Gloucester choir, although by no means perfect in detail, was singularly expressive and intelligent. Evidently the work had been splendidly rehearsed by the organists of the Three Choirs, and the chorus sang as if it entered fully into the meaning of the oratorio. Sir Hubert Parry's work, on the other hand, was not well presented. The composer himself conducted, and his talents do not run towards the direction of large choral and orchestral forces.

—E. A. BAUGHAN

Part IV: The London Choral Society Performance
(February 13, 1905)

Founded in 1903 by the conductor of the Dulwich Philharmonic Society, Arthur Fagge, the London Choral Society specialized in performing British choral works, particularly those that were new or were perceived to be unjustly neglected.[53] Elgar was central to the Society's activities during its first two seasons; at least one work by Elgar was featured in all five of the Society's concerts in 1904–1905 (these included two performances of Gerontius*). This was presumably not because Elgar's music was felt to be underperformed but because it was well-known to the singers and attracted large audiences: two imperatives for a conductor attempting to establish the reputation of a new choir.*

    The Apostles was the third concert of the 1904–1905 season and took place, as did all the London Choral Society's concerts, at Queen's Hall. Among the soloists only Ffrangçon Davies had sung at the premiere. The American soprano Clementina De Vere-Sapio sang the Blessed Virgin and the Angel Gabriel;[54] Marie Brema, one of the soloists in the premiere of Gerontius, *sang Mary Magdalene;[55] Gregory Hast sang St. John;[56] Francis Braun sang St. Peter;[57] and Plunket Greene sang Judas, as he had done in Gloucester.*

From the Concert Room

The Musical Standard 68, no. 2116 (full series) (18 February 1905): 100

The author of this article, L. L., has not been identified.

"The Apostles" at Queen's Hall.

SIR EDWARD ELGAR'S "The Apostles" was performed on Monday evening, February 13, by the London Choral Society under the direction of Mr. Arthur Fagge. The idea of the work came to the composer in his school days at Worcester. The head-master had been discoursing on the Twelve to his pupils: "The Apostles" he said, "were poor men, young men at the time of their calling; perhaps before the descent of the Holy Ghost not cleverer than some of you here." This impressed the young musician and as he afterwards told his biographer, Mr. R. J. Buckley, the oratorio of 1903 was the result.[58] The impression one carries away from a first hearing of this fine work is one of admiration for the marvellous constructive unity of purpose in both libretto and music and for the vivid dramatic power in the second part. The cohesiveness and directness of aim seems greater than in "The Dream of Gerontius." It is more direct, the action more rapid, and therefore it seems stronger, more dignified. "I have been thinking it out from boyhood," Sir Edward Elgar said speaking of his libretto, "and have been selecting words for years, many years. I am my own librettist. Some day I will give you my ideas on the relationship between libretti and composer."[59] It will not fail to be of interest to many when Sir Edward makes public his theories on the subject. In "The Apostles" the music and words are of intimate unison and in closest sympathy. The work is divided into two parts, which are again subdivided into seven numbers. The two parts are strongly contrasted. The music of the first is reposeful, placid, suited to the early environments and circumstances of the chief characters. The opening bars of "By the Wayside," in which section Jesus first appears, are tender and melodious. They are heard again when He "came into the parts of Cæsarea Philippi," "By the sea of Galilee" and in the "Betrayal," when "He went throughout every town and village preaching and shewing the glad tidings of the Kingdom of God." In the first section two very beautiful little orchestral tone-pictures are given: "In the Mountain—Night," where "Jesus continued all night in prayer to God"; and "The Dawn," in which the Shofar is heard and the watchers are on the Temple roof. The poetical feeling of the early morn is restrained but none the less extremely effective and delicate; as the sun rises the chorus sings: "The face of all the East is now ablaze with light, the dawn reacheth even unto Hebron." The same musical subject is used again slightly altered "At the Sepulchre" on Easter morn when "early in the morning they came unto the Sepulchre at the rising of the Sun." In the second part from the "Betrayal" to "Golgotha" the great drama is unfolded with swift, nervous strokes. The figure of Judas stands out in strong relief. Elgar takes the modern view which lends infinite pathos to the character and which gives an added interest to the conception. There is not the slightest touch of theatricality in the "March to Calvary," and the blaspheming rabble are convincingly portrayed with their wild shout of "Crucify Him, crucify Him." Finally, of the fresh central Figure on the Hill of Crucifixion only a suggestion is given by seven bars of orchestration, over which, on the score are outlined the words, "Eli, Eli, lama sabachthani." The work concludes with the mystic semi-chorus and chorus in "Heaven" and soli and chorus on "Earth." Sir Edward Elgar's music is distinctive and individual. With an early love for, and knowledge of the old contrapuntists and classicists, he has constructed his work on their deep fine foundations. It is invidious to compare him, either to his detriment or to his advantage with Wagner, Brahms, Richard Strauss and others. His personality is not in any way akin to theirs. His works carry the impress of a calm, keen intellect; his genius is the product of a serious yet eminently genial English mind. Though apologies were made for Miss Marie Brema (Mary Magdalene) and Mr. Gregory Hast (St. John) on the score of colds, yet they sang the music allotted to them with great expression and sympathy. Mme. de Vere, Mr. Ffrangçon-Davies [*sic*] and Mr. F. Braun, as the Virgin Mary, Jesus and St. Peter sang their respective parts with fine artistic insight. Judas was most effectively rendered by Mr. Plunket Greene. The orchestra and choruses had been very carefully rehearsed and the result, allowing for certain discrepancies, was a good, all-round performance.

—L. L.

From the Concert Room

The Musical Standard 68, no. 2116 (full series) (18 February 1905): 100–101

The following article continues on from L. L.'s article above. The identity of its author, "J. H. G. B.," has caused some confusion. Jerrold Northrop Moore suggests that he was Percy Betts of The Daily News, *but this is incorrect: Betts's full name was Thomas Percival Milbourne, and he had died on August 27, 1904. J. H. G. B. was in fact J. H. G. Baughan, the brother of E. A. Baughan, whom he succeeded as editor of* The Musical Standard *in 1902 (a position that J. H. G. Baughan held until the end of June 1913.)*[60]

The Oratorio Musically Considered.

More than once has it been declared that the music of Elgar's "The Apostles" suffers from over-elaboration. On Monday evening, at the Queen's Hall, the writer felt that that criticism does not hit home at all, though it may possibly in the opinion of those who refuse to the oratorio any of the musical development that has taken place in other branches of the art. It is true, on the other hand, that "The Dream of Gerontius" and "The Apostles" mark a great advance in form and in detail over any previous choral works by the same or any other British composer. Yet it is impossible to believe Elgar has gone too far; it is, indeed, far easier to believe, from an artistic standpoint that he has not gone far enough. The writer, however, is not altogether certain whether the *leit-motif* method in composing music does or does not contribute in the first part of this latest manifestation of Elgar to the prevailing effect of boredom. Wagner did certainly not work his *motiven*, in such a bald, spasmodic and unvaried way. This defect is far less noticeable in

"The Dream of Gerontius." But it is probable, nevertheless, that Elgar would do better if he abandoned this Wagnerian device, as unsuited to his talent; that so his music would become more spontaneous in effect. Again, there is also much room for improvement in his writing for the vocal principals, both as regards melody and recitative. He writes beautifully and tellingly for the chorus, but for the solos he frequently assigns vague, meaningless and totally ineffective phrases. Wagner thoroughly understood, and was master of the human voice; he wrote phrases for his singers of which, with a few pardonable exceptions, they could make something; phrases that were well grown and nourished. Thus his vocalists were interested. If they are not interested, how can you expect them to sing well? Even, Miss Marie Brema made nothing of the melodic and recitative music assigned to Mary Magdalene. It is true that indulgence was claimed on the score of a cold, but really it must have been an extraordinarily slight cold, as her singing showed absolutely no signs of indisposition. And the same may be said of Mr. Gregory Hast, for whom indulgence was similarly claimed. The male singers are better served, though scarcely the tenor (Apostle St. John)—on this occasion, Mr. Hast. There is, undoubtedly, some really good and impressive writing for the baritones, more especially is this noticeable in the music that falls to Judas Iscariot. And Mr. Plunket Greene—though one cannot always admire what he does—made quite the most of it. I do not say that the music for the three low male voices is anything very remarkable in gratefulness or effectiveness, but, in my opinion, it is a world better than that the soprano and contralto have to sing, especially the contralto. The music becomes more interesting—Elgar was ever good at descriptive music—in the second part, and the vocal principals have considerably less to do, and what they do fully passes muster; or to put it another way, you are not worried by any great shortcoming on the part of the composer. The orchestral introduction, however, is, to speak plainly, a very poor thing. It is bald, means absolutely nothing; and must surely have been written in a hurry. That complaint made, I have to say that the remainder of the work really flows properly. It is not great music; it is not the music of genius; it has, as all Elgar, but little of the harmonic refinement and science of the great German School of Music—Bach, Beethoven, Wagner and Richard Strauss. But it is music of great talent, and that, of course, is a good deal. That Part I., however, can never appeal to me, with its faded Elgarisms and general oppressiveness. No music can be good that is laboured. And the fact should not be explained away—such as the book demanded that sort of treatment, etc., etc. Strange to say, there are a few who positively do not feel that it is laboured. Some musicians—plain men who are not always thought much of and who often know something about composition—are entirely of my opinion. The performance, conducted by Mr. Arthur Fagge, was extremely meritorious.

—J. H. G. B.

NOTES

The author wishes to thank Byron Adams, James Clement, Stewart Gilles, Geoffrey Hodgkins, and Charles Edward McGuire for their help in the preparation of this chapter; thanks also to the library and staff of the Bodleian Library, Oxford; the Faculty of Music Library, Oxford; the British Library; and the British Library Newspapers at Colindale.

1. Jerrold Northrop Moore, ed., *Elgar and his Publishers: Letters of a Creative Life* (Oxford: Oxford University Press, 1987), 1:414–16; "Dr. Elgar's New Oratorio: 'The Apostles,'" *The Musical Times* 44 (April 1903): 228–29; "The Apostles," *The Musical Times* 44 (July 1903): 449–50. The libretto referred to in the April article was not that of the oratorio in its final form, but that of the larger, three-part *Apostles* whose third part eventually became the basis of *The Kingdom*. Edwards had arranged with Elgar to submit the article on the music in time for publication in the June issue, but illness prevented the composer from doing so. See Moore, *Elgar and his Publishers*, 1:435–36.

2. Canon Gorton, "Dr. Elgar's Oratorio 'The Apostles,'" *The Musical Times* 44 (October 1903): 656–57; Jerrold Northrop Moore, *Edward Elgar: A Creative Life* (Oxford: Oxford University Press, 1984), 414; Meirion Hughes, *The English Musical Renaissance and the Press 1880–1914: Watchmen of Music* (Aldershot: Ashgate, 2002), 174.

3. C. V. Gorton, *The Apostles: sacred oratorio by Edward Elgar. An Interpretation of the libretto* (London: Novello, 1903); A. J. Jaeger, *The Apostles, Parts I and II, by Edward Elgar: Book of Words with Notes* (London: Novello, 1903).

4. See Hughes, *Watchmen of Music*, 85–88.

5. *The Musical Standard* 1, no. 1 (1862): 2; quoted in "Répertoire International de la Presse Musicale: *The Musical Standard* 1862–1871 [First Series]," prepared by Diana Snigurowicz; data processed and edited at the Center for Studies in Nineteenth-Century Music, University of Maryland, College Park (Ann Arbor, Mich.: University Microfilms, 1991), ix–xii.

6. "Musicians of the Day: Edward Elgar," *The Musical Standard* 51 (21 November 1896): 317; see Hughes, *Watchmen of Music*, 165. For the reasons behind the change of Elgar's original title of *Lux Christi* to *The Light of Life*, see Robert Anderson, *Elgar* (New York: Schirmer Books, 1993), 32.

7. "To Our Readers," *Monthly Musical Record* 1, no. 1 (January 1871): 1; "Notes of the Day," *Monthly Musical Record* 90, no. 1002 (November–December 1960): 202.

8. "To the Reader," *Musical News* 1, no. 1 (6 March 1891): 1.

9. Charles Maclean, "Music in England," *Zeitschrift der internationalen Musikgesellschaft* 1, no. 1–2 (September–October 1899): 23.

10. Ibid., 23.

11. "To the Reader," 1.

12. Hans Richter (1843–1916), Hungarian-born German conductor. A Wagnerian, best known for conducting the first complete *Ring* cycle at Bayreuth in 1876, he was conductor of the Birmingham Musical Festival between 1885 and 1911, and of the Hallé Orchestra between 1897 and 1911. Richter befriended Elgar when he directed the pre-

miere of the *Enigma* Variations in 1899. He also conducted the premieres of *Gerontius* in 1900 and the First Symphony (of which he was the dedicatee) in 1908. "Obituary: Hans Richter," *The Musical Times* 58 (January 1917): 22; Moore, *Elgar: A Creative Life,* 269–72.

13. Emma (after 1925, Dame Emma) Albani (1847–1930), Canadian soprano. Born Emma Lajeunesse in Chambly, near Montreal, she studied at the Catholic Cathedral of Albany, New York, then Paris (under Duprez), then Milan (under Lamperti). She made her debut at Messina in 1870, and her British debut at Covent Garden in 1872, in both cases as Amina in Bellini's *La Sonnambula*. In addition to her many operatic roles (including Eva, Desdemona, and Isolde) she sang in English provincial choral festivals for more than twenty years; Gounod's *Mors et Vita* was written for her. "Obituary: Dame Emma Albani," *The Musical Times* 71 (May 1930): 463; Alexis Chitty and Gilles Potvin, "Albani [Lajeunesse], Dame Emma (Marie Louise Cécile)," *The New Grove Dictionary of Music and Musicians,* 2nd ed. (London: Macmillan, 2001), 1:282.

14. Muriel Foster (1877–1937), English mezzo-soprano. Born in Sunderland, she studied under Anna Williams at the Royal College of Music, where, in 1900, she won the Musicians' Company Medal for the best student in the college. She became closely identified with Elgar's music after singing (in German) the part of the Guardian Angel at the Düsseldorf performance of *Gerontius* in May 1902; she also sang in the premieres of both *The Apostles* and *The Kingdom.* "Miss Muriel Foster," *The Musical Times* 45 (March 1904): 153–55; and "Obituary: Muriel Foster," *The Musical Times* 79 (January 1938): 67.

15. John Coates (1865–1941), English tenor. Born in Bradford, he began his career singing baritone in comic opera before changing to tenor. In the early years of the twentieth century he established a reputation as an opera singer in Germany and as a concert singer in Britain; after the First World War he became best known for his solo recitals, which often included unusual repertoire, including contemporary British works. Like Foster he became particularly identified with Elgar's music; indeed, Gerald Moore has claimed that the turning point in Coates's career was his performance as *Gerontius* at the 1902 Three Choirs Festival at Worcester. "Obituary: John Coates," *The Musical Times* 82 (September 1941): 351; Gerald Moore, "Coates, John," *The New Grove Dictionary of Music and Musicians,* 2nd ed., 6:69.

16. Robert Henry Kennerley Rumford (1870–1957), English baritone. He studied with Sbriglia and Bouhy in Paris, and then under George Henschel and Alfred Blume in London, making his debut under Henschel in 1893. In 1900 he married Dame Clara Butt. "Obituary: Robert Henry Kennerley Rumford," *The Musical Times* 98 (April 1957): 219. A. Eaglefield-Hull, "Rumford, R. Kennerley, A Dictionary of Modern Music and Musicians," ed. A. Eaglefield-Hull (London: Dent, 1924), 427.

17. David Thomas Ffrangçon Davies (1856–1918), Welsh baritone. Born in Bethesda, Carnarvonshire, he began his adult life as a Church of England clergyman but switched to singing, studying under Richard Latter, William Shakespeare, and Alberto Randegger. Initially, he worked mostly in America and Germany, but at the turn of the century he returned to Britain, where he established himself as an oratorio singer, notably in the London premiere of *Gerontius.* He suffered a nervous breakdown in 1907. "Obituary: David Thomas Ffrangçon Davies," *The Musical Times* 59 (May 1918): 214.

18. Andrew Black (1859–1920), Scottish baritone. Born in Glasgow, he studied under Randegger in London and under Scafati in Milan, making his London debut in 1887 and his festival debut at Leeds in 1892 as the Spectre in Dvořák's *The Spectre's Bride.* He later emigrated to Australia and died there. "Obituary: Andrew Black," *The Musical Times* 61 (December 1920): 837; Jean Mary Allan and Ruzena Wood, "Black, Andrew," *The New Grove Dictionary of Music and Musicians,* 2nd ed., 3:663.

19. The motif titled "Christ's Loneliness" first appears two measures before rehearsal number 20.

20. This figure, which bears the label "Christ the Man of Sorrows," first appears 6–7 measures after rehearsal number 2.

21. Gorton, *The Apostles*, 10.

22. Richard Whately (1787–1863), Archbishop of Dublin (1831–63). A liberal in both theology and politics—he favored Catholic emancipation and promoted nonsectarian education in Ireland—Whately was one of several nineteenth-century thinkers who argued that Judas's actions were motivated by a belief in a physical (rather than a spiritual) enactment of Christ's kingdom on earth. See Charles Edward McGuire, "Elgar, Judas, and the Theology of Betrayal," in *19th-Century Music* 23, no. 3 (Spring 2000): 236–72, esp. 247–49.

23. Both quotations are taken from Gorton, *The Apostles*, 21; the first is quoted in turn from Richard Whately, *Lectures on the Character of Our Lord's Apostles and Especially Their Conduct at the Time of His Apprehension and Trial*, 3rd ed. (London: J. W. Parker, 1859), 29–30, part of a lecture titled "Trials of the Apostles." (I am grateful to Geoffrey Hodgkins for providing me with this information.) Elgar would quote these words of Whately in his interview with *The Strand Magazine* in 1904. See Moore, *Elgar: A Creative Life*, 294.

24. According to Jerrold Northrop Moore, this review (15 October 1903) was by J. A. Fuller-Maitland (1856–1936), the chief music critic of the *Times* (London), and one of those members of the British musical establishment who was most hostile to Elgar (*Elgar: A Creative Life*, 417). The passage quoted in *Musical News* forms the central section of the review.

25. See Jaeger, *The Apostles*.

26. "Christ the Man of Sorrows" is one motif, not two; "Gospel" first appears one measure before rehearsal number 3.

27. The theme appears three measures after rehearsal number 120.

28. For some reason, the contribution of Andrew Black (Judas) was omitted in this sentence.

29. Charles William Perkins (1855–1927) was the city organist of Birmingham between 1888 and 1923. Prior to his appointment in Birmingham he studied under Arthur Deakin, Charles Swinnerton Heap, and, at Westminster Abbey, Sir Frederick Bridge. Barbara Padjasek, "Organist to the City of Birmingham," *The Musical Times* 130 (February 1989): 111.

30. "Obituaries: Mr. Alfred Kalisch," *Times* (London), 18 May 1933, 16.

31. Moore, *Elgar: A Creative Life*, 481, 244–45, 330, 333; Hughes, *Watchmen of Music*, 165; Byron Adams, "Elgar's Later Oratorios: Roman Catholicism, Decadence, and the Wagnerian Dialectic of Shame and Grace," in *The Cambridge Companion to Elgar*, ed. Daniel M. Grimley and Julian Rushton (Cambridge: Cambridge University Press, 2004), 86.

32. In stating that Judas was not an "Apostle," the author makes a semantic distinction between *disciple* (literally "one who learns") and *apostle* (literally "one who is sent out").

33. The oratorio *Ein Weihnachtsmysterium* (1899) by the German composer, conductor, and musicologist Philipp Wolfrum (1854–1919) made extensive use of both Gregorian chant (notably "Resonet in Laudibus") and Christmas carols (notably "Joseph Lieber, Joseph Mein"). It received its British premiere at Worcester on December 12, 1901; according to *The Musical Times*, "the credit of introducing it to England belongs to Dr. Elgar and the Worcestershire Philharmonic Society," so Baughan's reference was presumably not accidental. See "Philipp Wolfrum's Weihnachtsmysterium," *The Musical Times* 43 (January 1902): 39.

34. Arthur Nikisch (1855–1922), German conductor. Best remembered as the conductor of the Gewandhaus Orchestra of Leipzig (1879–89), he performed regularly in Britain between 1895 and 1914, both in London—where his Wagner received particular critical acclaim—and in the provinces. Alfred Kalisch, "Arthur Nikisch," *The Musical Times* 63 (March 1922): 172–74.

35. Felix Weingartner (1863–1942), German conductor and composer. The conductor of the Vienna Philharmonic between 1908 and 1927, he first visited England in 1898, conducted at the 1902 Beethoven Festival in London, and following his 1904 performance of *Gerontius* with the Sheffield Musical Union at Queen's Hall became conductor of the Sheffield Festival in 1906. "Obituary: Felix Weingartner," *The Musical Times* 83 (June 1942): 192.

36. Agnes Nicholls (1877–1959), English soprano. She studied at the Royal College of Music under Visetti and John Acton, making her London debut in 1895 as Dido in Purcell's *Dido and Aeneas* and her Covent Garden debut in 1901 as the Dew Fairy in *Hänsel und Gretel*. She later sang under Richter in the first English *Ring* cycle in 1908 and became established as a leading Wagnerian and Mozartian. She was married to the (Northern) Irish conductor and composer, Sir Hamilton Harty (1879–1941). See C. W., "Obituary," *The Musical Times* 100 (November 1959): 618–19; A. Eaglefield-Hull, "Harty, Agnes," *A Dictionary of Modern Music and Musicians*, 224.

37. Frederic Austin (1872–1952), English baritone and composer. Born in London, he studied under Charles Lunn and made his London debut in 1902. His career as a singer included opera (Gunther in the 1908 Covent Garden *Ring*); concert work, notably Delius's *Sea Drift* (of which he sang in the English premiere); and oratorio. In 1924 he was appointed artistic director of the British National Opera Company. H. C. Colles, "Austin, Frederic," *The New Grove Dictionary of Music and Musicians* (London: Macmillan, 1980), 1:706.

38. Louisa Kirkby Lunn (1873–1930), English mezzo-soprano. Born in Manchester, she studied at the Royal College of Music under Visetti. Her career began with the Carl Rosa Company; later she performed at Covent Garden in such roles as Brangäne, Amneris, and Kundry (a role which she was the first to sing in English in the United States). She was also a noted concert and Lieder singer. "Obituary: Louisa Kirkby Lunn," *The Musical Times* 71 (March 1930): 271; A. Eaglefield-Hull, "Lunn, Louise Kirkby," *A Dictionary of Modern Music and Musicians*, 306.

39. "Obituary: Thomas Lea Southgate," *The Musical Times* 58 (March 1917): 116.

40. See rehearsal number 94f. and five measures after rehearsal number 125, respectively.

41. As in Ffrangçon Davies.

42. O. I., "Homage to British Composers," *Musical News* 26, no. 681 (19 March 1904): 273–74.

43. The three concerts of the festival consisted of *The Dream of Gerontius* (March 14); *The Apostles* (March 15); *Froissart*, selections from *Caractacus*, the *Enigma* Variations, *In the South*, *Sea Pictures*, *Cockaigne*, and *Pomp and Circumstance* Marches nos. 2 and 1 (March 16).

44. Both the date and the piece are wrong here; *The Atonement* (1903) was a sacred cantata by Samuel Coleridge-Taylor (1875–1912), but it is to *The Apostles* that this article refers.

45. A. Eaglefield-Hull, "Evans, Edwin, jun.," *A Dictionary of Modern Music and Musicians*, 144; H. C. C[olles]. "Evans, Edwin (ii)," *Grove's Dictionary of Music and Musicians*, 5th ed. (London: Macmillan, 1954), 2:980–81.

46. Alfred, Lord Tennyson, *In Memoriam*, 33.3–4.

47. Dalton Baker (b. 1879), English baritone. He studied at the Royal Academy of Music, where he won the Mence Smith scholarship for singing and made his debut at St. James's Hall in 1902. After a career in the provincial festival circuit, which included the premiere of Bantock's *Omar Khayyám*, he emigrated in 1915 to Canada, where he became a member of staff at the Toronto Conservatory of Music. "Miscellaneous," *The Musical Times* 56 (January 1915): 50; L[eo] S[mith], "Baker, Dalton," in *A Dictionary of Modern Music and Musicians*, 25.

48. Harry Plunket Greene (1865–1936), Irish-born baritone. After periods of study in Dublin, Stuttgart, Florence, and London, he became renowned as one of the leading

interpreters of his generation of English and Irish song; according to his obituarist in *The Musical Times*, "By the beauty of sense and feeling in his utterance, by the frequency and popularity of his recitals, and by the extent of his repertory he did more than any other artist to encourage the new school of song-writing that sprang up in this country during the present century." Married to Parry's daughter Maud, he became very much part of the British musical establishment, notably as president of the Incorporated Society of Musicians (1933) and chairman of the Musicians' Benevolent Fund (1934). His musico-logical work included *Charles Villiers Stanford* (London: Arnold, 1935). See "Harry Plunket Greene," *The Musical Times* 77 (September 1936): 799–800.

49. (Sir) A(lfred) H(erbert) Brewer (1865–1928), composer and organist. Born in Gloucester, he was a chorister at the cathedral before studying organ in Gloucester (under C. H. Lloyd), Oxford, and the Royal College of Music (under Walter Parratt). After spells at Bristol Cathedral, St. Michael's, Coventry, and Tonbridge School, he returned to Gloucester as cathedral organist in 1896. His best-known works are his cantatas *Emmaus* (1901), with which Elgar assisted in the orchestration, and *The Holy Innocents* (1904). He was knighted in 1926. "Obituary: Alfred Herbert Brewer," *The Musical Times* 69 (April 1928): 367–68; "Some of Elgar's Friends," *The Musical Times* 75 (April 1934): 320.

50. See also rehearsal nos. 19 to 20.

51. Parry's oratorio received its premiere at the festival.

52. Parry's oratorio *Job* was premiered in 1892, also at the Three Choirs Festival in Gloucester.

53. Arthur Fagge (1864–1943), organist and conductor. Born in Kent, but based for most of his life in London, he founded the London Choral Society in 1903 as a vessel through which to perform British works, notably Elgar's three mature oratorios, and also Walford Davies's *Everyman* and Bantock's *Omar Khayyám*, both of whose London premieres the Society gave. "Obituary: Arthur Fagge," *The Musical Times* 84 (June 1943): 192.

54. Clementina De Vere-Sapio, American soprano, was a regular performer in the provincial festival circuit. She appears not to have performed in Britain any earlier than 1894 or any later than 1911.

55. Marie Brema (1856–1925), English mezzo-soprano, of German-American parentage. Born in Liverpool, she studied under Henschel and Alfred Blume, making her debut at St. James's Hall in 1891. Although remembered primarily as an operatic performer (particular in Wagner; she was the first English singer to sing at Bayreuth), she was also an accomplished oratorio singer; the Guardian Angel in *Gerontius* (which she sang at the work's premiere) was considered one of her finest roles. "Obituary: Marie Brema," *The Musical Times* 66 (May 1925): 461; A. Eaglefield-Hull, "Brema, Marie," *A Dictionary of Modern Music and Musicians*, 59.

56. (Harry) Gregory Hast (1862–1944), English tenor. A founder of the Meister Glee-Singers in 1890 and a member of the choirs of both Westminster Abbey and the Temple Church (under Walford Davies), he became a noted recitalist following his St. James's Hall debut in 1898, touring in both America and Europe. He published *The Singer's Art: Letters from a Singing Master* (London: Methuen) in 1925. "Obituary: Gregory Hast," *The Musical Times* 85 (October 1944): 319.

57. Arthur Francis Braun (1876–1940), English baritone (and Marie Brema's son), was a regular performer in provincial festivals in the first decade of the twentieth century. The high point of his career appears to have been singing the solo baritone part in a performance of Beethoven's Ninth Symphony with the London Symphony Orchestra in Paris under Stanford in January 1906. "The English Concerts in Paris," *The Musical Times* 47 (February 1906): 105.

58. Robert J. Buckley, *Sir Edward Elgar* (London: Jone Lane, 1905), 8.

59. Ibid., 74.

60. Moore's suggestion appears in *Elgar and His Publishers*, 1:111. The obituary for Percy Betts can be found in *The Musical Times* 45 (October 1904): 652; that for J. H. G. Baughan can be found in *The Musical Times* 69 (February 1928): 173.

Charles Sanford Terry and
Elgar's Violin Concerto

TRANSCRIBED AND INTRODUCED BY ALISON I. SHIEL

Since its first performance on November 10, 1910, much scholarly energy has been expended on certain mysterious aspects of Elgar's Violin Concerto in B Minor, op. 61. The significance of the dedication and the five dots that follow—*Aquí está encerrada el alma de*..... (Herein is enshrined the soul of.....)—and of Elgar's particular attention to the grammatical correctness of this Spanish quotation, drawn from Lesage's picaresque novel *L'Histoire de Gil Blas de Santillane,* has called forth pages of speculation by Elgar biographers. Scholars have subjected the concerto itself to detailed analysis, much of it in terms of the gender of its various themes, the implication being that the melodies are meant to represent some romantic entanglement of Elgar's, past or present. Names of several women have been invoked in these studies, including those of young Elgar's Worcester girlfriend, Helen Weaver, the mature composer's American friend Julia "Pippa" Worthington, and, most persistently, Alice Stuart-Wortley, whom the composer once described as the "stepmother" of the score.[1]

A volume now lodged in the British Library (Add. MS 62000) illuminates the history of the Violin Concerto. The first-proof copy of the full score, given by Elgar to his friend Professor Charles Sanford Terry, is bound with letters from Sir Edward and Lady Elgar to Terry, as well as Terry's own various notes and observations. Together, these documents provide a fresh approach to our understanding of the work.

Charles Sanford Terry (1864–1936), first lecturer and later professor of history at the University of Aberdeen (1898–1930) was the leading Bach scholar of his day in Britain. A pioneering historian, especially in the field of Scottish history, he had the reputation of being a brilliant lecturer, capable of "marshalling intricate masses of detail into lucid and balanced narrative."[2] Terry applied these formidable skills to his research into the life and music of J. S. Bach. His large number of publications on Bach and the Bach family attest to his industry and scholarly rigor, and several of these studies remain unsurpassed to this day. An able amateur musician—singer, violinist, and conductor, with musical abilities cultivated at both St. Paul's Cathedral and Cambridge—Terry conducted the Aberdeen University Choral and Orchestral Society (1898–1913), and in 1909 founded the first competitive music festival in Scotland.[3] Terry's activities consistently met with marked success.

Terry's regular attendance at festivals and other musical events in England encouraged his varied musical undertakings, and the resulting acquaintances with the musicians he met at such venues were of signal importance, including a close friendship with Elgar. In 1906, at Terry's instigation, Elgar traveled to Aberdeen to receive an honorary doctorate from the university, the first musician to be so honored; Terry's gesture appears to have further deepened the relationship between the two men.[4] In 1908 Terry was invited for the first time to be a member of the Elgars' Three Choirs Festival house party. Terry's charm and congeniality (and perhaps his academic status) quickly endeared him to Lady Elgar, and he soon became an "approved" friend. When Terry attended the premiere of *The Music Makers* in Birmingham, Alice Elgar was glad that the professor from Aberdeen was there to take care of her husband; she wrote in her diary on September 16, 1912, "Prof. Terry with him which made A. happy about him." The diaries also record the many occasions when Terry acted as a companion for both Lady Elgar and her daughter Carice, tactfully taking them off Elgar's hands when the composer was involved with rehearsals and other musical matters. Terry enjoyed an especially warm and friendly relationship with the young, often lonely Carice Elgar, and indeed, was affectionately referred to by Carice as "uncle." The Elgar diaries reveal the extent to which Terry was to become supporter, defender, mentor, and ally to all three members of the Elgar family.[5]

By 1910, Terry had become a regular visitor to the Elgar household. He arrived for a visit on Friday, October 7, 1910, the same day that Lady Elgar recorded the arrival of an important parcel in her diary: "Large parcel of proofs. E. very busy." Over the weekend, Terry helped considerably with the intensive and detailed labor of checking the proofs. Saturday, October 8, was a "Stuffy day. Prof. helping E. with proofs etc . . . Heavy air and damp," and the following day, "E. & Prof. comparing parts in score. Much good work."[6] As a token of thanks, Elgar presented Terry with the proof score, sending it to Aberdeen later that month. Writing to Alice Stuart-Wortley on October 11, Terry was enthusiastic:

<u>The</u> Concerto grows more and more <u>Dunter</u>esque![7] It is bound to create an enormous sensation on Nov. 10, and thereafter be acclaimed the compeer of those of Beethoven and Bach. It is a <u>glorious</u> work, and <u>what</u> a glorious man he is! When I leave Plas Gwyn I always feel like a schoolboy facing the awful blackness of a return to school.[8]

This letter indicates the extent of Terry's devotion to Elgar and explains the great care he subsequently took in preserving the full score that Elgar had given him out of "his goodness and to my vast pride and pleasure."[9] (Terry was not the only person to receive a gift in connection with the proofs of the concerto: Charles Stuart-Wortley, Alice's husband, and Ivor Atkins also received similar gifts.) With typical foresight, and in a fashion reminiscent of the large scrapbooks he assembled for each of Aberdeen's competitive music festivals, Terry assembled all the materials he had collected in connection with the Violin Concerto: the first-proof full score, his own typewritten comments, concert tickets (including his own and Carice's tickets for the premiere, suggesting that he escorted Carice to the event), photographs, newspaper cuttings, and letters from Sir Edward and Lady Elgar.[10] These assembled documents were among his treasures.[11]

Terry felt moved to record his unique association with the Violin Concerto in a series of informative typewritten sheets that are bound in the British Library volume with the rest of the material. As a friend—but clearly also as a music historian—Terry obviously felt a responsibility "for the benefit of posterity" to "place on record the facts and details" known to him in relation to the concerto. Having been an eyewitness to Elgar's uncertainty when inscribing the dedication on the score, Terry recorded his version of this event in the clearest of terms; but being a discreet person of unswerving loyalty to Elgar, he makes no reference whatever to any private history the dedication may have had, writing only that "there are matters too sacred and too intimate for even the biggest friendship to pry into." Terry's firm opinion is that it is Elgar's own soul that is enshrined in the work, and he perceives "a particular intimate relation between the Concerto and its creator."[12] In wholly characteristic fashion, Elgar seems to have relished the mystery surrounding the dedication. Writing to his friend Nicholas Kilburn on 5 November 1910, Elgar adds a tantalizing footnote that is unrelated to the rest of the letter:

Aqui está encerrada el alma de. . . . .
Here, or more emphatically *in here* is enshrined or simply enclosed—
buried is perhaps too definite—*the soul of* . . . ?

The final "de" leaves it indefinite as to sex or rather gender.
Now guess.

In a set of notes dated 11 November 1910, Terry, ever the historian, records in detail his role in the publication of the concerto and reveals the pride he took in his involvement:

> The subject of the Concerto had long been in the composer's mind, and I remember his playing the opening theme to me at Mr Schuster's house in Old Queen Street on January 7th, 1909, after conducting a performance of his first Symphony at Queen's Hall, London, that evening. He brought the whole work completed for Violin and Pianoforte to the York Festival in July 1910, and it was played to him, I think for the first time, by Mr W. H. Reed of the London Symphony Orchestra at Plas Gwyn, Hereford, on Tuesday July 26th, 1910. As appears from a letter dated August 5th, 1910, bound herewith, the scoring of the Concerto was completed at Plas Gwyn on that date. Herr Fritz Kreisler accepted in [blank] the composer's invitation to produce the work, and on Friday, September 2nd, 1910, he played the Concerto for the first time to the composer in the Board Room of Messrs Novello at 160 Wardour Street, London. The only other person present was myself, whom the composer had asked to turn over for him the pages of the piano score. During the Gloucester Festival, Kreisler again went through the work at a house in the Close taken for the Festival by Sir Edward and Lady Elgar. After a long rehearsal which lasted through the afternoon and part of the evening of Thursday September 8th, 1910, Elgar inscribed Kreisler's name on the work.

The letters to Terry from Elgar and Lady Elgar in the volume provide fascinating insights into the progress of the Violin Concerto and the circumstances surrounding its creation. Shining through all the letters is the pleasure that Alice and Edward Elgar took in Terry's company; as well as their disappointment when he was unable to be with them on occasions of celebration.

In view of his proud association with the concerto, it is rather surprising that in June 1919 Terry gave away the proof score bound with this precious memorabilia. The recipient of Terry's handsome gift was Sir John Marnoch, a keen amateur musician, professor of surgery at Aberdeen University, and, as such, one of Terry's colleagues. One can only speculate that Terry felt indebted to Marnoch in some way, possibly in relation to his own health. The volume is bound in cream-colored leather with "JM from CST June 4 1919" embossed in gold on the cover. In his prefatory letter to Marnoch, Terry expresses the accurate opinion that the volume is "a real historical document" and that "some day it will have to be recorded."

After Marnoch died in 1932, Terry regained possession of the volume. In 1934 when Fritz Kreisler visited Aberdeen as part of a concert tour of Scotland, he visited the now elderly Terry, and was invited to inscribe the volume—"In kind remembrance of Fritz Kreisler, March 22, 1934"— under a photo of the violinist that Terry had pasted into the book after the first performance of the Violin Concerto in 1910. One can only imagine the shared memories that this reunion brought back for both virtuoso and musicologist, especially since Elgar had died less than a month before Kreisler inscribed Terry's precious volume.

Terry died two years later, in November 1936. His distinguished contributions to historical research in the fields of Scottish history and musicology, especially dealing with Bach and his world, are set out in an extensive publications list. Less evident, but nonetheless extraordinarily valuable, is the information that Terry scrupulously preserved, in this bound volume and elsewhere, concerning his friendship with Edward Elgar.

NOTES ON THE INTRODUCTION

1. See Michael Kennedy, *The Life of Elgar* (Cambridge: Cambridge University Press, 2004), pp. 120–21. Oddly, Kennedy does not mention Lady Elgar's speculation to Dora Penny (enshrined as "Dorabella" in the *Enigma* Variations) that an inspiration for the Violin Concerto was Julia Worthington. See Michael De-la-Noy, *Elgar the Man* (London: Allan Lane, 1983), 149.

2. L. G. Wickham Legg, ed., *Dictionary of National Biography: 5th Supplement: 1931–1940* (London: Oxford University Press, 1949), 851–52.

3. See Alison I. Shiel, "Charles Sanford Terry and Aberdeen University Choral Society," *Aberdeen University Review* 49, no. 206 (Autumn 2001): 122–33; and "Aberdeen's Competitive Music Festivals 1909–13," *Northern Scotland*, 22 (August 2002).

4. See Alison I. Shiel, "Elgar's Visits to Aberdeen," *Elgar Society Journal* 13, no. 1 (March 2003): 36–40.

5. Alison I. Shiel, "Charles Sanford Terry in the Elgar Diaries; the Chronicle of a Friendship," *Elgar Society Journal* 12, no. 5 (July 2002): 193–96.

6. Alison I. Shiel, "Charles Sanford Terry and the Elgar Violin Concerto," *Elgar Society Journal* 12, no. 6 (November 2002): 254.

7. Elgar, writing to Terry on 5 August 1910, described the Violin Concerto as "a Dunter," referring to the powerful nature of the work. The *Oxford English Dictionary* gives two definitions for "dunt": the first is "to knock with

a dull sound, as with the fist in the back or ribs"; the second is "of the heart: to beat violently." Either is apposite to the concerto, as Elgar may have used "dunter" to suggest that the score would be a "knock-out."

8. Hereford and Worcester Record Office 705:445, parcel 22 (i) 7916.

9. Charles Sanford Terry, "Notes on Elgar's Violin Concerto," in British Library Add. MS 62000.

10. Aberdeen University Library, MS 3237/1–5.

11. 1919 letter from Charles Sanford Terry to Sir John Marnoch, in British Library Add. MS 62000.

12. Terry, "Notes on Elgar's Violin Concerto."

Notes on Elgar's Violin Concerto, by Charles Sanford Terry

It seems well, for the benefit of posterity, that I should place on record the facts and details known to me in relation to the Concerto. There are matters too sacred and intimate for even the biggest friendship to pry into, and though I was with Elgar when he was correcting the proof of the dedicatory page bound in this volume I did not attempt to obtain any solution of the mystery of the Spanish motto. At the same time I have not the slightest doubt that it is his own soul which the Concerto enshrines. In the first place it will be noticed that he originally wrote "del" before the blank, an indication that the name to follow was a masculine one. True, while I was looking over his shoulder, he wrote "de la" in red ink under "del," but thereafter he took the trouble to consult a Spanish friend, M. de Novaro [*sic*][1], as to whether the word "del" would leave the sex of the soul's possessor undetermined. Receiving an assurance that it did he retained it and deleted the "de la." In the second place there is evidence of a particular intimate relation between the Concerto and its creator. One of the most extraordinary and fascinating traits in Elgar's great and beautiful character is a curious attitude of detachment from his work, an utter absence of even the faintest trace of "side" or affectation in regard to it. To the genius, I suppose, even works of the most stupendous grandeur seem the inevitable result of forces within him. On the rare occasions when he spoke spontaneously of his work it was their construction on which he allowed himself to dwell. Thus of "The Apostles" he once remarked in answer to some attempt on my part to express its message to me, "Yes, it is a large canvas, isn't it." At York in July 1910 when he conducted "King Olaf" and heard it, so he told me, for the first time performed on the scale and with the accessories he required, he amused the orchestra vastly by saying out loud to himself, "By Jove, there's good stuff in this." Afterwards he told us that the constructional skill of one of the numbers had struck him and he pointed it out to us, adding curiously, "I <u>could</u> write in those days!" But I have never heard Elgar <u>speak</u> of the <u>personal</u> note in his music except in regard to the Concerto, and of it I heard him say more than once when he was playing it over before it was produced, "I <u>love</u> it." Again there is a fact for which Ivor Atkins of Worcester is my authority. Speaking of the Concerto Elgar said to him one day that he would like the Nobilmente theme in the Andante inscribed on his tomb. I remember how moved he was by that passage and the violin passage which heralds it 2 bars before figure 53 when Kreisler first played it to him, and how with his own left hand held as though it were supporting his own fiddle he reproduced the emotion and vibrato which Kreisler brought to the interpretation of that passage. Nor did I ever hear the Concerto played through by Elgar without his doing the same thing.

The first Rehearsal of the Concerto was called for the morning of Wednesday November 9th. A few privileged people were present, among whom I saw Ysaye, old Hollmann the Cellist, Landon Ronald and others. Before rehearsing the Overture (The Naiades)[2] Elgar turned at once to the Cadenza Accompagnata, evidently anxious to have the first opportunity of testing the effect of the novel tremolando which he has introduced there for the strings. He had originally used the word "drummed" at figure 101 in his direction as to how the tremolando was to be secured. I ventured however to point out to him that the word "Thrummed" had a more obvious meaning and expressed exactly the idea he wished to convey. He therefore made the change. At first the orchestra, unaccustomed to such a form of accompaniment, quite failed to obtain the soft shimmer of sound which Elgar required. The tone was hard and "naily" and observing one or two of the Double Basses actually "drumming" the strings I wondered after all whether Elgar had not been right in his choice of word. But after telling the men to put down their bows the tone became lighter and eventually at the performance the effect of the accompaniment of the Cadenza was quite extraordinary. When later Elgar rehearsed the Concerto with the orchestra alone I noticed that he was taking the first movement much slower than when he first played it to me and much slower than the metronome mark (crotchet 100) in the score. The tempo which he actually adopted was (I trust to memory here, for I was not able to test my memory by the metronome until the morning after the performance) crotchet 88. Elgar's first conception of the opening theme was certainly analogous to that of the vigorous and pressing second theme of the first movement of the Symphony, whose metronome mark is crotchet 104. Not only so, but in the last eight bars of the first movement, where the first subject is again brought in, as will be seen from the proof of the Full Score, Elgar marked it Piu Allegro increasing to Presto. But in the course of the rehearsals at Gloucester[,] to which reference has already been made, Kreisler pleaded the importance of a "broad presentment" of the first movement of a new work and Elgar agreed. I remember Kreisler laughingly telling Elgar[,] "You composers never know how to play your own works." Kreisler also made a few alterations in the solo part with the object of securing greater effectiveness or convenience for the solo instrument. These Elgar sanctioned. One very effective one is at the second bar before figure 47, where the whole of the nine notes before 47 are carried an octave higher. Another effective alteration which Elgar made on Kreisler's representation will be noticed just after figure 96. My proof Score shows the Violin part as it was originally written and without the alterations which Elgar made in the course of his rehearsals with Kreisler. Regarding those rehearsals there is a little incident which is perhaps worth record. Kreisler is an extraordinarily good linguist. But he occasionally uses the word he wants from a foreign language with the pronunciation of the language in which he is speaking for the moment. Thus it was amusing after a long rehearsal and in the midst of a violent passage when he suddenly stopped and said excitedly to Elgar[,] "Sir Edward, I must have a quart here," pronouncing the word as though it were the English liquid measure.

The first rehearsal of the Concerto roused extraordinary enthusiasm among the orchestra, who rose and cheered Elgar and Kreisler at the end of it. On the following morning Elgar did Landon Ronald the honour to ask him to conduct the first movement so that he might hear the effect from the auditorium. I lunched with Elgar at Schuster's after the rehearsal and we strolled after that through the old streets round Westminster. In so far as he touched on the Concerto at all, Elgar's talk was about the fine theme at figure 87. He described it as "ritterlich," and was pleased to have secured from the orchestra the atmosphere he wanted there. At the performance in the evening the Queen's Hall was packed. It was said that most of the musical celebrities of the country were present. For that I cannot vouch. But I can vouch for the fact, and it is I think remarkable, that in the audience were five of our Cathedral organists, namely Ivor Atkins of Worcester, G. R. Sinclair of Hereford, Herbert Brewer of Gloucester, Dr Bennett of Lincoln, and Tertius Noble of York. Kreisler was certainly nervous during the first movement, but the persistent applause at the end of the movement proved that already the audience had recognised a master-piece. The Andante was superbly played both by Kreisler and the orchestra. Indeed I cannot remember ever to have heard such wonderfully sympathetic accompaniments. During the wonderful Cadenza in the last movement the interest was tense and at the end of the Concerto there was such enthusiasm as I have never before witnessed. There was a long and persistent roar of applause which was continuous for about five minutes and never lessened in volume even when Elgar and Kreisler had escaped from their journeys to the centre of the platform. As usual Elgar tried to put himself in the background and refused to take himself the first applause which followed the end of the work. At length Kreisler himself refused to take the applause for himself and turning to Elgar bowed with a fine air to him. In the Artists room Elgar was again besieged by enthusiastic friends. "You have saved me from this before, can't you do it again?" he said to me. Kreisler was naturally exhausted. His magnificent interpretation of the work was the theme of all. Save at one point his memory did not fail him throughout. His wife, to whom he introduced me, was also clearly very proud and happy.

C. Sanford Terry

November 12, 1910.

1. The Spanish friend was M. Antonio de Navarro, whose wife was the well-known American actress Mary Anderson. The Elgars enjoyed the Navarros' lavish hospitality at Court Farm, Broadway, Worcestershire, on a number of occasions.

2. *The Naiades* concert overture is by the noted British composer William Sterndale Bennett (1816–75).

Letter from Charles Sanford Terry to Sir John Marnoch, 1919

Westerton of Pitfodels
By Aberdeen

Sunday [n.d.]

My dear Marnoch,

This is to introduce a volume which has been among my treasures and for that very reason I want to count among yours henceforth. It is the final proof of the Full Score of Elgar's Violin Concerto. Some of the corrections obviously are the proof reader's. The rest are Elgar's holograph. He gave the score to me because, as you will see when you read the typed memorandum bound up with the score, I had been so closely connected with the completion and production of the work. Certain letters of his relating to the Concerto are included, in particular one which definitively dates its completion.

As it stands the volume is a real historical document: the information it contains has never been published and is unknown outside a narrow circle, many of whom already have forgotten much of it, no doubt! Some day it will have to be recorded.

There accompanyies [*sic*] the Score three little water colours of local scenes by a local artist. They bring with them the deep and heartfelt gratitude of us both which strives to express itself in this imperfect form. I can hardly believe that it is only one week tomorrow since we were in your house. But what a deep gulf of relief divides the dates!

Yours ever gratefully,
C. Sanford Terry

I enclose a Hymn written for Maisie Smith's[1] wedding.

---

1. Eldest daughter of the Reverend Professor Sir George Adam Smith, principal of Aberdeen University, a close friend of Terry's. She married American army officer Charles Drew in June 1919. Terry dabbled in composition from time to time, and besides this hymn, his works include published songs and anthems, and a comic opera.

Letter from Elgar to Charles Sanford Terry, 5 August 1910

Aug 5 1910

Plas Gwyn
Hereford

My dear Terry,

It was good of you to send that cheery wire; we, deleerious devils, were hard at it & we wanted you. This moment I have put the last note to the last movement in the full score & have lit a pipe! Would you were here to join in. We shall play through the concerto at Gloucester & we hope to have an uproarious time: the concerto is (aiblins!) a Dunter. I think you will like it & I only hope something will bring you to London for the 10th Novr. Couldn't you be turned on to represent the University at the Lord Mayor's Show the day before—or something of that sort? Shall I write to the Senate to suggest this [?]

The weather has been awful with one or two glorious days & we hope for a fine autumn: turn up in good time at Gloucester. [Added in pencil] Saturday 3 Sept. The Hostel, College Green, quite by noon.[1]

Mrs Worthington is here till tomorrow, & the family & she & I send all messages to Mrs Terry & to you. I send this to Cults[2] but I expect you are leaving or already left. Good luck & love to you.

Yours ever,
E. E.

1. Terry was to be a member of the Elgars' Three Choirs Festival house party at the Cookery School, Gloucester.

2. The Aberdeen suburb where Terry lived.

Postcard from Elgar to Charles Sanford Terry, 16 October 1910

Athenaeum

October 16, 1910

So many thanks for your note from Leeds.[1] Kreisler was here and plays the thing superbly now & last night I had a very pleasant 2 hours with Saffery[2] & Legge[3] at the Savile[4]—we wanted you.

All good wishes,
Yrs ever
Ed: Elgar

1. Terry had been at the Leeds Festival, which the Elgars did not attend that year.
2. Terry's brother-in-law.
3. Robin Legge, music critic of the *Daily Telegraph*.
4. Terry was a member of the Savile Club.

Note from Elgar to Charles Sanford Terry, 19 October 1910

Q.A.M.
[Queen Anne's Mansions]

Oct 19 [1910]

My dear CST,

No time to write.

Here's a sweet-looking page for you & come the besmirched pages of the whilk[1] were despatched yesterday to N[orth]. B[ritain].[2]

Love
Edward E

Just off home.

1. "Whilk" is Old English for "which."
2. This note accompanied the first-proof score of the Violin Concerto, posted to Terry in Aberdeen.

Letter from Elgar to Charles Sanford Terry, 6 November 1910

Nov 6, 1910

Plas Gwyn
Hereford

My dear Terry,

This is to say that all goes well in the parish. Jake[1] has been missing for some three weeks but Carice & I found him on Friday on the road to our great joy—in which my wife does not join.

 The concerto goes well also but much tribulation over mistakes alas!

 We had a good time at Sunderland[2] & were geared up by your telegram & the whole evening was merry.

 Now we start to Gotham[3] tomorrow[4] & will make it truly Cockaigne before the week is out—you will come round to the artists room, won't you. All the folk will be there for a moment.

Love to you
from
Edward E.

I have made a new friend in the parish—a man who traps weasels: he knows little of concertos I find but the parish <u>is</u> backward.

1. "Jake" remains unidentified but seems to have been a local "character" whom Elgar befriended. On 24 December 1910 he wrote to Mrs. Sidney Colvin (soon to be Lady Colvin) that he had had "seasonable dealings (tobacco &c have passed)" with "Jake the Lawyer."

2. At the request of his friend Nicholas Kilburn, Elgar conducted part of a concert given by the Sunderland Philharmonic Society and the Hallé Orchestra in Sunderland on November 1.

3. Elgar refers to London with "Gotham" which was first used as a name for New York by the American author Washington Irving (1783–1859). The *Oxford English Dictionary*'s definition of *Gotham*—"the name of a village, proverbial for the folly of its inhabitants"—combined with the definition of *Cockaigne*—"an imaginary country, the abode of luxury and idleness"—provides the gist of Elgar's opinion of London.

4. Terry has written in the margin "to stay with Schuster for production of the Concerto." Both Terry and Elgar were friends of Frank Leo Schuster (1852–1927), a wealthy patron of music.

Letter from Lady Elgar to Charles Sanford Terry, 2 December 1910

2 December 1910

Ladies Imperial Club
Dover Street
Piccadilly

Dear Prof. Terry,

I feel we have been remiss in letting you hear, what curious English, I mean in <u>not</u> letting you hear, oh! it is all tied up in a knot. I have only time to tell you the 2nd performance was <u>more</u> wonderful even than the 1st.[1] More authority and more easy mastery, it seemed over too soon like a beautiful dream—many <u>lovely</u> sounds in the Orch.—came out, we heard before— Tremendous enthusiasm.

The 1st movement was so splendid. Much finer performance. Excuse such a blot. E. is looking rested & well again but this weather is <u>so</u> depressing, rain ceases not, & so dark. Impossible to go househunting.[2] So many <u>many</u> thanks for all the Archives. We have given over Plas Gwyn to the Arkwrights.[3] Trust he will have a splendid majority on the 5th at Hereford.

Best remembrances to you both. So glad apples are good.

Yrs. Very sincerely,
C. A. Elgar.

1. The second performance of the Violin Concerto took place on November 30, 1910. Terry was not able to attend.

2. The Elgars were looking for a larger property in London, eventually moving into Severn House in London in January 1912.

3. The Elgars were supporters of John Stanhope Arkwright, the young Conservative M.P. for Hereford. In the forthcoming general election, for which Arkwright was campaigning, he held his seat, although the Liberals remained in power.

Letter from Elgar to Charles Sanford Terry, 4 December 1910

[London]
Dec 4 1910

My dear Terry,

We wanted you badly last Wednesday to complete our joy. "It"[1] went well & we had the de Navarros & the Legges & Schuster to supper at Queen Anne's [Mansions] after—I borrowed a welkin & we made it ring till after 12. Since then—nothing—the weather has been awful. Saffery introduced a beaming smile, most welcome, into the artists' room & then we had a gathering of all sorts—& you not there to defend me: perhaps it was as well for you might have prevented an impulsive lady from kissing me (!) SHE DID &—well—I didn't mind so perhaps it's as well Scotland had ye in grip.

I have been better since that foggy evening[2] & shall never forget the delight I had in having you there. I hope all goes well in Aberdeen & that your journey home was not too trying.

They cut all the [illegible word, but possibly 'sermon' or 'scree'[3]] out of my speech[4] which was not bad but the room was too big for me to coruscate in—a week ago though & you will have forgotten.

We lunched with the Legg[e]s today & had a nice time. Now rain in torrents.

I fear these elections will do no good—yesterday was not much promising.

Send me a line soon. Carice is still in the Lalley County—I forget quite where it is—oh! with Granny Gandy[5]—she goes on to the Kilburns[6] I think.

Alice joins me in love. She has had a most delightful time at tea today at the Safferys: whither I could not wend.

My love to you and duty to Mrs Terry.

Yrs ever
Edward Elgar

[Addendum written sideways on the front page of the above]: I have no news of the parish. Jake is a bad correspondent though I believe I am discussed at length in the Bunch of Carrots & in less measure at the Whalebone[7], but no letters.

1. "It" refers to the second performance of the Violin Concerto.

2. A reference to the evening of the first performance of the Violin Concerto.

3. Definition of *scree* in the *Oxford English Dictionary*: "a mass of loose detritus." This may well describe what Elgar meant!

4. Elgar addressed the Institute of Journalists in London on November 26.

5. Mrs. Annie Gandy was a leading light at the Morecambe Music Festival; the Elgars met her through Canon Gorton. She was part of the Elgars' Three Choirs house party at Worcester in 1905 and on subsequent occasions. Elgar is said to have particularly enjoyed her wit and vivacity. Carice went to stay at the Gandys' country house, Heaves, near Sedgwick in the Lake District (then Cumberland).

6. Dr. Nicholas Kilburn (1843–1923) conducted choirs in Sunderland and Bishop Auckland in northeastern England and was an ardent champion of Elgar's works. Carice was to join the Kilburns while they were on holiday in Westmorland.

7. Two local pubs on the River Wye near Plas Gwyn. Both are still in existence, although the second is now named The Salmon. Elgar found inspiration in cycling along the country lanes around Hereford and would have been familiar with such local landmarks.

PART III
LONDON

Elgar's Critical Critics

AIDAN J. THOMSON

On December 6, 1905, Edward Elgar delivered the fifth lecture in his first series as Peyton Professor of Music at the University of Birmingham. Titled "Critics," it was concerned less with individual critics (although several were mentioned by name) than with their function. In Elgar's opinion, music criticism should be educational as much as judgmental, both for the composer, to whose work a critic should give "the final polish" and "help us [the composers], guide us and lead us to higher things," and for the listener, for whom the critic could provide musical analyses.[1] Too often, however, critics seemed unaware of these responsibilities. In Elgar's view, the journalist-critic was prone to write concert reviews too quickly, for an inappropriate medium (such as a general magazine with a nonmusical editor), and, above all, without sufficient time for reflection. For Elgar, the "real, lasting, educational good" was "gained from the mature slowly-wrought opinion."[2]

Such hasty assessments thus had considerable potential to affect adversely the performance history of a work. Yet despite these concerns, Elgar was imaginative enough to envisage a role for criticism more familiar to musicologists a hundred years later than it would likely have been to his audience in Birmingham. Enlarging upon his topic, Elgar opined:

> It is invariably interesting to read the opinions of various writers on the same work: I venture to suggest that such a collection might form a volume. If extracts from various criticisms on the same work, or on the same performance of a work, could be gathered together, it would form a valuable contribution to musical literature; not formed with any idea of playing off one critic against another, but to arrive at the result, which from a multitude of such counsellors should be wisdom.[3]

With these remarks, Elgar promotes "reception history" as a methodological approach decades before the term was coined, although it must be stressed that his conception of reception history—to find the essential "truth" that lay at the heart of a piece of music—is very different from that of musicologists today. The centrality to Elgar's vision of what Lydia Goehr has called the "work-concept" reflects both the idealist philosophy that underpinned nineteenth-century German music (particularly instrumental music) and the doctrine of "Art for Art's sake," whose prevalence in Britain had grown considerably since its original espousal in the 1860s by Matthew Arnold and Walter Pater.[4] To an aesthetic that denied anything beyond the artistic *Ding an sich,* the idea that the "final arbiter" in reception histories should be not the work but, as Carl Dahlhaus has described it, the "'moment in history,' i.e. the forces that condition reception," would have seemed utterly alien; to a composer as concerned as Elgar with his place in ahistorical, ideology-free posterity, it doubtless would have seemed a threat.[5] Indeed, the only historical *process* that Elgar is willing to countenance in reception history is the "conversion" of a critic from a negative to a positive point of view about a particular composer, which he felt would be "seriously instructive."[6] But this process, revealingly, is concerned primarily with the uncovering of an objective artistic "truth" which, once reached, is set in stone for all time. There is no suggestion that a critic's change of view might have any historically contingent or ideological stimulus behind it; rather, the "conversion" would appear to be a Damascene one.

Although Elgar's views on art are theoretically underpinned by an objective value system, it is far from clear what aesthetic criteria he used in making critical judgments. Elgar was no philosopher, and if, as Brian Trowell has observed, he shared Ruskin's "resolutely Platonic view of music as an art of great ethical power," this was no more than most of his contemporaries did.[7] If any ideological position is discernible in the Birmingham lectures, it is a bias for "absolute" music: Elgar praised Hanslick in his "Critics" lecture and would later describe the symphony without a program as the "highest development of art."[8] But, as Ernest Newman noted, this position was contradicted by virtually all of Elgar's oeuvre to date, and though the First Symphony would come close to realizing the ideal of absolute music, the quotations at the beginning of both the Second Symphony and the Violin Concerto seem to indicate that Elgar's view of art was not instinctively formalist.[9] Rather, Elgar's conception of music was that it "must be . . . a reflex, a picture, or elucidation of [an artist's] own life," a position that owed more to the early Romanticism of Elgar's "ideal," Schumann, than to either camp in the Brahms-Wagner debate.[10] This reflex was a multifaceted one, where different genres called for different approaches, thereby obscuring any specific agenda. Thus Elgar's large-scale instrumental works conform, more or less, to the criteria of absolute music (even if the "absolutism" is more honored in the breach); the mature oratorios adopt Wagnerian music-dramatic principles, at least externally; and the smaller vocal genres, marches, and occasional music reflect a functional approach that embodies Elgar's comparison of the composer's vocation to that of the "old troubadours and bards . . . [who] inspire the people with a song."[11] More to the point, however, a composer whose conception of music was as personal, even instinctive, as Elgar's was hardly likely to apply rigorously objective standards when evaluating the works of others. Instead, these works would be measured by their artistic sincerity, a criterion that was intuitive and justifiable in terms of common sense.

But such a commonsensical approach merely conceals biases that are far from objective, and which certainly do not transcend history; instead, they are inextricably connected to the historical and critical concerns of early-twentieth-century British music. These biases are all too apparent in Elgar's lectures, even, for example, in the critics of whom he approved and disapproved. It is clear that the composers most likely to suffer from the overhasty journalistic judgments that Elgar condemned would be young, unknown, and probably English—a particular concern for the composer given that, in his inaugural lecture, he had spoken of an "English School of Music" driven by a "younger generation [who] are true to themselves . . . and draw their inspiration from their own land."[12] So it is surely no coincidence that several of the contemporary critics he singled out for praise had all actively promoted English composers: Joseph Bennett (the chief music critic of the *Daily Telegraph*), Arthur Johnstone (of the *Manchester Guardian,* until his death in 1904), Ernest Newman (Johnstone's successor at the *Manchester Guardian*), and George Bernard Shaw. Conversely, Elgar's one example of the "shady side of music criticism" involved the disparagement of a British composer, namely the obituary of Arthur Sullivan in the *Cornhill Magazine* in 1900, written by J. A. Fuller-Maitland (although Elgar did not name him in the lecture). For Elgar, this was a "foul unforgettable episode"; Fuller-Maitland was simply wrong. But at no point did Elgar explain *why* Fuller-Maitland was wrong, let alone admit that his argument—that Sullivan was a composer capable of genius (notably in *The Golden Legend* and in his incidental music for *The Tempest*) who rarely fulfilled it because of his readiness to compromise his style to popular taste—might have some truth to it.[13] Not surprisingly, Elgar's comments attracted negative press coverage: *Musical News,* conscious of similar faux pas that Elgar had directed at Stanford in earlier lectures, observed that Elgar seemed unable to "open his mouth apparently without finding himself embroiled in some more or less lively controversy."[14]

That Elgar should have condemned Fuller-Maitland perhaps reflects another instinctive bias on his part. Fuller-Maitland (1856–1936) was no ordinary journalist, but the chief music critic of the *Times* and a distinguished scholar—he was the author of an important recent monograph on English music and, at the time of the lecture, was editing the revised edition of *Grove's Dictionary of Music*.[15] He was also a central figure in the English musical "renaissance" set of composers and critics, based around the Royal College of Music, where the group's two most important composers, Parry and Stanford, were professors. As Meirion Hughes has pointed out, the members of this set were mostly from the university-educated, upper-middle classes and Fuller-Maitland was particularly keen to emphasize their social and intellectual elitism.[16] He was less keen, however, to acknowledge the achievements of a lower-middle-class, self-taught, provincial Roman Catholic like Elgar. His reviews of Elgar premieres in the *Times* were frequently ambivalent and often hostile, as both Hughes and Jerrold Northrop Moore have noted. With the works that appeared before the *Enigma* Variations, Fuller-Maitland was often as concerned with Elgar's provincial background as with the music; the Variations themselves were damned for their "obscure" program; *The Dream of Gerontius* was compared unfavorably with Stanford's *Eden* and Parry's *Job*; and the Concert Allegro for piano suffered because of an alleged lack of "organic connection between one part and another."[17] Fuller-Maitland's attitude toward Elgar hardened with each of the composer's successes. The critic was absent from the premiere of the First Symphony in 1908 and, after criticizing the composer for his overcolorful orchestration at the work's London premiere, conducted an unsuccessful campaign against the piece in the *Times*.[18] It is uncertain exactly how aware Elgar was of Fuller-Maitland's later writing about him, given the composer's claim that after 1900 he never read any (negative) criticism of his own work. But even if that claim were true, the mixed reception of *Gerontius,* to which Fuller-Maitland contributed, had hurt Elgar and one could understand it if his rebuke of the critic were a way, subconsciously, of settling scores.

The significance of Fuller-Maitland's criticism of Elgar, however, is not the extent to which it was fueled by personal enmity, but that it provides any evidence of a negative view of the composer. Until recently, Elgar scholarship, perhaps understandably, has emphasized the many positive reviews of the composer's work and concentrated less on the dissenters; the one significant exception among the latter is Edward J. Dent, to whose infamous assessment of Elgar in the 1920s we shall return below.[19] But Fuller-Maitland and Dent are only the best known of a significant minority of critics who were skeptical of the popular and critical acclaim afforded to Elgar, particularly following the successful German performances of *Gerontius* in December 1901 and May 1902. For the most part, these

critics differed from their pro-Elgarian counterparts in their social provenance and in their philosophical and aesthetic views, particularly in their
attitude to Wagner. With the exception of the ultraconservative Bennett,
whose enthusiasm for Elgar stemmed more from their shared autodidac-
tic background than from purely musical reasons, the pro-Elgar critics
were generally pro-Wagner and/or pro-Strauss.[20] This group included
not only Newman and Shaw, but two other pro-Wagnerians: Alfred Kalisch
(1863–1933), from 1912 the critic of the *Daily News,* and Herbert Thompson
(1856–1945), between 1886 and 1936 the critic of the *Yorkshire Post.*[21]
Moreover, all of these critics shared with Elgar the fact that they were outside the London establishment of the "renaissance" clique: Bennett and
Newman were self-taught provincials; Shaw was Irish (and a socialist to
boot); Thompson, Cambridge-educated but Leeds-born and based, was
steeped in the conservative traditions of the English choral tradition (his
father-in-law, Frederick Spark, was the secretary of the Leeds Music Festival in 1898 when *Caractacus* received its premiere); and Kalisch, though
London-born, was of German-Jewish extraction. By contrast, the "critical
critics" were mostly part of (or close to) renaissance circles, and shared
the predominantly anti-Wagner views of Stanford and, especially, Parry,
who disliked Wagner's ideology and his late works—a consequence partly
of the failure of his opera *Guenever* (1886) and partly of his puritanical
sensibility.[22] The significance of this particular bias is considerable. A key
aim of the renaissance critics was, through their writing, to influence, rather
than simply reflect, musical "good taste": a concept that, in theory, was
ideologically neutral but, in practice, often betrayed the critics' anti-
Wagnerian aesthetic agenda. The value of their discourse on Elgar is
therefore not that they reveal the hidden "essence" of his music (insofar
as that objective was ever possible), but that they reveal much about the
forces that conditioned the reception of his works and those of his contemporaries. In doing so, they offer proof, if any were needed, that Elgar's
works, far from transcending the period in which they were written, are
grounded in the historical, critical concerns of the early twentieth century.

The aim of this essay, then, is not to revisit the positive criticism of
Bennett, Johnstone, Newman et al., which has been covered adequately
elsewhere in Elgar scholarship. Instead, it is to show how Elgar's detractors viewed him as an uncomfortably progressive addition to British musical
life: first, by consciously (and negatively) distancing him from the "safe"
figure of Parry; and second, by associating him with the ethically suspect
school of Wagner and his followers. Elgar emerges from this criticism as a
deeply politicized figure, the vessel through which particular critical critics
directed their arguments about the future of British music.

One such critic is Dr. Charles Maclean (1843–1916). Maclean's background was typical of the renaissance set: public school (Shrewsbury) and Oxford (where he was a classical scholar), further musical training under Ferdinand Hiller in Cologne, and then the musical directorship of Eton College between 1871 and 1875. His musical activities in Britain were curtailed somewhat during the twenty-two years in which he worked in the Indian civil service (as an inspector of schools, a magistrate, and a government translator), but they resumed on his retirement in 1893, whereupon he became active both as a critic and within the Musical Association (later the Royal Musical Association).[23] In 1899 he was invited to join a committee, chaired by Parry and including Stanford, John Stainer, Fuller-Maitland, and Ebenezer Prout among others, whose aim was to "further the objectives . . . in England" of the Internationale Musikgesellschaft (hereafter IMG), which had recently been founded in Leipzig by the German musicologist Oskar Fleischer.[24] In practice, this meant setting up a British national section, and Maclean, with his linguistic skills, was the obvious candidate to become group secretary and national group editor of the society's monthly periodical, *Zeitschrift der internationalen Musikgesellschaft*. The *Zeitschrift* was one of two IMG publications, but whereas the content of the quarterly *Sammelbände der internationalen Musikgesellschaft* was essentially scholarly, that of the *Zeitschrift* aimed at a wider readership. It included concert and book reviews, lists of forthcoming lectures and performances of old music, a comprehensive list of recent literature in music periodicals of all countries, reports of papers given at local group meetings, and short articles on musical subjects, most of which were written in either German or English. Its function was thus similar to that of *The Musical Times*, but with one vital difference: its readership extended beyond Britain to a larger, international audience. Consequently, the role of the national group editors of the *Zeitschrift* went well beyond being their countries' musical diarists. What they wrote about individual composers had the potential to shape the opinions of foreign readers who had little or no direct experience of those composers, as well as mold the scholarly discourse on their music. The columnists thus represented the music-critical voices of their respective nations. For Maclean this entailed the additional responsibility of making a case for British music to a readership that, by and large, still considered Britain to be *das Land ohne Musik*.[25]

At best, Maclean's attitude to Elgar was ambivalent; at worst, it was downright hostile. Writing about the performance of *Gerontius* at the 1902 Three Choirs Festival, he described the composer as a "polemic modernist," a comment that, given the generally negative tone of the article, was certainly not intended as a compliment.[26] Maclean's objections to Elgar can be classified as at least one of three forms: aesthetic (where Elgar's compositional style is weighed in the balance, on its own merits, against Maclean's preferred musical criteria, and generally found wanting); ad hominem (attacks on Elgar, as well as objections to composers who had clearly influenced him); and cultural (those where Elgar's music is deemed unmanly, un-English, or both). In practice, these factors were interlaced, for Maclean's aesthetic standpoint inevitably found its ideal in some composers more than in others, and given that his *Zeitschrift* column was frequently concerned with the future direction of English music, it is unsurprising that the composers whose works came closest to realizing his personal vision were lauded as models for emulation. Maclean's vision was a conservative one, but it is by no means untypical (as will become clear when we consider other writing about Elgar in this period). Indeed, paradoxically, a critical view of Elgar such as Maclean's actually serves to highlight the progressiveness of many of the composer's scores composed at this time.[27]

Maclean's influential position within the IMG and his consistent disparagement of Elgar make him a figure of more than marginal interest. Unaccountably relegated to a minor position in Elgar scholarship, Maclean assumes the role of a focal figure—perhaps *the* focal figure—in this essay due to his influential status and aspirations as an arbiter of musical taste. To use Maclean's opinions as a lens through which to view the reception of Elgar's music during this period brings into sharper focus the significance of several other critical critics, most notably Fuller-Maitland and W. H. (later Sir Henry) Hadow (1859–1937). Originally a classics don at Worcester College, Oxford, and later vice-chancellor of the University of Sheffield (where he was instrumental in establishing a professorial chair in music), Hadow was also the author of many significant books on music in the 1890s and 1900s, including two oft-reprinted volumes, *Studies in Modern Music* (which considered the careers of six leading nineteenth-century composers); a number of contributions to Fuller-Maitland's revised edition of *Grove's Dictionary;* and, perhaps most notably, the fifth volume of the *Oxford History of Music* series of which he became editor in 1896.[28] His interests also included British music. In 1921, he wrote a report on the history and prospects of British music for the Carnegie United Kingdom Trust and, in 1931, a monograph titled *English Music*, part of a series of books on English Heritage edited by Viscount Lee of Fareham and J. C. Squire.[29] A protégé of Fuller-Maitland, Hadow initially held views on Elgar mirroring those of his mentor, but, as will become apparent, Hadow's espoused views in *English Music* are quite different from those he had embraced twenty-five years earlier.[30]

Before returning to *English Music*, two key musical relationships that the critical critics identified in their writings about Elgar must be considered:

the musical debt he owed to Wagner and Wagnerites and, crucially, how he was compared to the composer at the heart of the renaissance establishment, Sir Hubert Hastings Parry.

Elgar and Parry

However else the critical critics might have disagreed with Elgar, they surely agreed with his high opinion of Parry. In his inaugural lecture at the University of Birmingham, Elgar drew attention to the fact that at the previous year's "Musical Festivals . . . the honours have fallen, save with one exception to the *younger men*." Identifying that exception, Elgar cited

> a name which shall always be spoken in this University with the deepest respect, and I will add, the deepest affection—I mean Sir Hubert Parry, the head of our art in this country . . . : with him no cloud of formality can dim the healthy sympathy and broad influence he exerts and we hope may long continue to exert upon us.[31]

Elgar's reservations about others associated with the Royal College of Music, notably Stanford, did not extend to Parry, for whom his admiration was genuine—and with good reason. Parry had been supportive in helping to secure Hans Richter's services for the premiere of the *Enigma* Variations in 1899 and had proposed Elgar for membership in the Athenaeum Club in 1904. In the latter year, Elgar publicly acknowledged his indebtedness to Parry's scholarship when he was interviewed by *The Strand Magazine*: "The articles [in *Grove's Dictionary*] which have since helped me the most . . . are those of Hubert Parry." Appropriately, Parry made the Latin oration when Elgar received his honorary doctorate from Oxford in 1905. Parry's music impressed Elgar sufficiently for him to comment in a letter to August Jaeger of Novello, sent 8 October 1907 that *A Vision of Life* was "*fine stuff* & the poem [which Parry had written himself] was literature"— a far more positive endorsement than his barbed allusion to Stanford in the inaugural lecture that "to rhapsodise is one thing an Englishman *cannot do*."[32] With the exception of a (relatively early) complaint to Jaeger that Parry's orchestration was "never more than an *organ part arranged*," there is no hint that Elgar disagreed with prevailing critical opinion about Parry's preeminence.[33]

Yet it was precisely this preeminence that led Elgar's detractors to compare him unfavorably with Parry, as Fuller-Maitland's assessments of both composers in *English Music in the Nineteenth Century* (1902) and the revised edition of *Grove's Dictionary* (1904–7) exemplify clearly. It might seem unfair to include *English Music* here, given that it would have gone to press before the Düsseldorf performance of *Gerontius* in December 1901 and the burgeoning critical interest in Elgar that followed it; but, as perhaps the first monograph to advance the thesis that 1880 (the year when Parry's *Scenes from Shelley's "Prometheus Unbound"* was premiered) represented a peripeteia for British music, it is an important illustration of how in certain quarters Parry's status was beyond dispute. Fuller-Maitland argued that the post-1880 renaissance was attributable to five "leaders" (Parry, Stanford, Mackenzie, Frederic Cowen, and Arthur Goring Thomas), who, in turn, had bred a generation of "followers" (essentially all other British composers born after 1850 and active in 1900). Not surprisingly, the five leaders are examined in considerable depth; conversely, the followers receive short shrift. Elgar, though the "most prominent among the older generation of the followers," is summarized in just a single page, in which *Froissart, The Light of Life, Caractacus, Dream of Gerontius [sic]*, and *Cockaigne* are mentioned only in passing, the *Enigma* Variations are described simply as "delightful," and *Sea Pictures* is characterized tersely as "popular." In all these works, Fuller-Maitland concludes, there were "evidences of a truly poetic gift, of imagination rightly held in control, and of great technical skill in the management of voices and instruments."[34] But that was all. Compared to these blandishments, Fuller-Maitland's ten pages on Parry are positively effusive, for instance his comment that it was "Parry's especial gift to 'bring all heaven before our eyes' by means of the mastery of his cumulative effect."[35]

This disparity did not go unnoticed in early reviews of the book. *Musical News* felt that Fuller-Maitland had drawn "totally inadequate notice" to Elgar's work; in *Musical Opinion* the pseudonymous columnist Common Time meanwhile declared that Fuller-Maitland's "prejudices [were] strong and often unaccountable," and proposed 1896 (the year of Stanford's opera *Shamus O'Brien*) as an alternate starting date for an English musical renaissance.[36] But Fuller-Maitland soon became more transparent in his prejudices, for his *Grove* entry for Elgar (1904) is laced with invective, particularly with regard to the composer's large-scale choral works: "Praise to the Holiest" in *Gerontius,* for instance, suffered from a "want of the cumulative power which some other masters have attained, and which would have brought into the whole work a unity and a sublimity which it was not felt to possess."[37] No sense here, then, of Elgar managing to "bring all heaven before our eyes" like Parry; if anything, quite the opposite, for the success of *Pomp and Circumstance* March no. 1 was achieved "in spite of the objections of some musicians"—including Fuller-Maitland himself, presumably—"to it on the score of its immediate appeal to hearers of every class." Meanwhile, *The Apostles* is portrayed as Elgar's artifice-laden overreaction to these objections:

> It is perhaps not to be wondered at that, after the compliments paid the composer by the most advanced of modern German composers, and the adverse opinion passed by some superior persons upon the "Pomp and Circumstance" tune, the composer should have adopted an ultra-modern style in this oratorio, and that it should be found so strange by some hearers as to call for censure.[38]

If Fuller-Maitland's entry for Elgar was marked by trenchant criticism, his entry for Parry, published in 1907, was full of praise—and praise that seems almost deliberately to promote Parry at Elgar's expense. Unlike Elgar's highly colored orchestration, Parry's symphonic works "laid more stress on the substance of the ideas and development, rather than on the manner of their presentment," and as such "must always appeal strongly to the cultivated musician." Compared with the "want of cumulative power" in "Praise to the Holiest," Parry's choral music was characterized by his "wonderful power" in "handling large masses with the utmost breadth and simplicity of effect, and of using the voices of the choir in obtaining climax after climax, until an overwhelming impression is created": this was "felt not only by the educated hearer, but even by the untrained listener." The implication is clear: without ever compromising his style, Parry wrote music whose authority was discernible to all; Elgar, by contrast, veered inconsistently between oversophistication (*The Apostles*) and vulgarity (the *Pomp and Circumstance* marches). Lest his readers be left in any doubt of Parry's stature, Fuller-Maitland concludes the dictionary entry by stating that Parry's "strong common sense" and the "purity of his artistic ideals" marked him "as the most important figure in English art since the days of Purcell."[39]

Fuller-Maitland was not Parry's sole apologist, however. In a *Zeitschrift* article from 1903, Maclean conflated Parry's social and musical elitism in terms very similar to those that Fuller-Maitland would use in *Grove*. Maclean wrote that Parry's art "stands above that of his fellows, as the Drachenfels above the Rhine; lofty, alone, perhaps even melancholy." His music is "a direct counterblast to preciosity":

> In contour it is wholly broad. While in harmony it is free from decadent subtleties; indeed almost absolutely diatonic, a trait in common more or less with all British composers who are true to themselves,

but carried in this beyond the practice of most of them. The amount of expression which Parry obtains with diatonic means is quite astonishing. . . . Nor does his art yield to emotional excesses; he is greatly subjective, but his introspection is steadied by reflection.[40]

Thus, not only did Parry's solidity of form and emotional moderation offer proof of his naturally good musical taste, but his avoidance of chromaticism provided evidence of his echt-Englishness—certainly much more than was the case with Elgar, against whom Maclean ends his article with a damning broadside. Recalling Strauss's toast to Elgar as the "first English progressivist" at the 1902 Lower Rhine Music Festival, Maclean pompously observed that with works of art, unlike with "physical and mathematical truths," there is "at least as much chance of what is older being superior to what is younger, as vice-versa." To prove his point, Maclean compared Elgar's *Coronation Ode* with Parry's symphonic ode of 1903, *War and Peace*. The latter work, in Maclean's opinion, was "Parry purified from mannerism or blemish, pushing new discoveries in poly-tonism without relinquishing his own diatonic habit . . . showing depths of harmonious sensibility in the solo numbers with long resistless forces in the choral numbers." The *Coronation Ode*, however,

consists musically of little else than this; first a decided mannerism of the composer in descending bass scale-passages and certain treble suspensions, secondly music based on quite the weakest form of the English part-song style, thirdly a march-tune imported from another composition which has no affinity whatever with this one and is in this place at least extra-ordinarily common.

"It seems next to impossible," Maclean concluded, "that any musician could hear or read these two works side by side, and not realise that the work of the older man is on an immeasurably higher plane than that of the younger."[41]

At least one periodical was moved to comment that Maclean's choice of works was disingenuous. In a review of the article, *Musical News* dismissed Maclean's claim that "composers must be judged by their latest productions," observing that as the *Coronation Ode* was "not up to its composer's highest standard" it was hardly the most appropriate piece to use for such a comparison.[42] Quite what the periodical would have made of Maclean's comments on the 1904 Gloucester Festival is debatable; for once again his praise for Parry is tempered by an implicit rebuke to Elgar. The main review of the festival for the *Zeitschrift* was written by the

pro-Elgar critic Herbert Thompson, who dwelt chiefly on the performances of *The Apostles* (which was receiving its Three Choirs premiere) and
Parry's oratorio *The Love that Casteth out Fear*.[43] Maclean added a postscript to Thompson's report, in which he extols Parry in terms similar to
his article of the previous year: *The Love* was the "master-work of the festival"; Parry's diatonic language showed "capacities for still further budding
and blossoming"; and "the effect . . . of this newest work of Parry's on all
right-minded musicians was prodigious." In his closing comments comes
the pointed gibe: "Such results achieved by a composer who never makes
a bid for popularity might give cause to those who are on the crest of a
wave to institute heart-searchings as to how much of the mountebank there
may not be mixed up in their own art."[44] This reference is so transparent
that Maclean hardly needed to invoke the composer's name; the Elgar
Festival at Covent Garden had taken place barely six months earlier and,
as Thompson had noted, *The Apostles* attracted a larger audience at Gloucester
than *Elijah*.

As it is Elgar's popular appeal, once again, that damns him, it is worth
putting Fuller-Maitland's and Maclean's objections into context, for their
remarks are the ancestors of Edward J. Dent's notorious critique of the
composer in Guido Adler's *Handbuch der Musikgeschichte* (1924, rev. 1930),
in which Elgar's music is described as "too emotional and not quite free
from vulgarity."[45] That vulgarity was a concern for early-twentieth-century
British music critics should not be surprising. The development of mass
consumer culture in cities, epitomized by the growth of urban popular
song and the growing respectability of music hall, provided attractions
for potential audiences that were far removed from the internationally
respected *Tonkunst* the critics were seeking to establish. Admittedly, these
new stimulations might ignite a creative spark; Elgar himself argued that
vulgarity "often goes with inventiveness" and that "in the course of time
[it] may be refined."[46] But his was a minority view. More typical was that
of C. Fred Kenyon, who saw musical vulgarity not as a raw material from
which works of art might be fashioned, but as an unwelcome by-product
of success: vulgarity was "the most insidious, and most deadly, and yet most
popular of all vices." In Kenyon's eyes, a composer who possessed genius
("the highest gifts that the gods can bestow") had no business seeking
worldly pleasures, which was simply greediness on his part.[47]

Elgar's detractors do not accuse him of greed; indeed, if anything, the
remarks above suggest that the resentment toward the composer from
some within renaissance circles owed less to vulgarity per se, and more to
Elgar's post-Düsseldorf fame—hardly surprising, perhaps, given that
Strauss's toast had been dismissive of those who had spent the previous

twenty years trying to advance the prospects of British music. Maclean's defensive comment that "we have more than one composer" reveals just how sensitively the higher echelons of British musical opinion reacted to Strauss's possibly tipsy reflections, but their attempts to promote other composers met with mixed success.[48] Proposals to hold a National Festival of British Music in November 1903 at which "too much attention will not be given to the music and musicians who have been unduly prominent of late" came to nothing. Indeed, the prospect that this festival might be run on "Royal College lines" caused *Musical Opinion*'s columnist Common Time to remark that the Royal College had a reputation for self-advancement, and that "their idea of the best interests of the art [was] too limited by personal considerations."[49] By contrast, the Elgar Festival at Covent Garden in March 1904 was both artistically and financially successful—more so, indeed, than the Beethoven and Strauss festivals that had taken place in London the previous year.[50]

Ironically, this London success occurred within a year of another source of resentment toward Elgar among London critics: the composer's pronouncement, in a public letter to Rev. Canon Charles Gorton prior to the 1903 Morecambe Festival, that "unknown to the sleepy London press . . . the living centre of music in Great Britain is not London, but somewhere farther North."[51] The letter was reprinted in the festival brochure, from where it was copied by the *Musical Times*. The heated response it generated from critics was considerable: as one *Musical Standard* editorial put it, London's critics were "annually driven near crazy during the months of May, June and part of July in the process of deciding which of the forty (or more) concerts per week need their personal attention . . . [Elgar] should remember, at all events, that there is other music besides part-songs and oratorios."[52] Whether Fuller-Maitland, Maclean et al. took personally Elgar's description of a "sleepy" London press, uninterested in provincial music making, is a moot point. But it is hard to imagine that it did not color their views of the composer. It is surely no accident that this period coincided with a hardening of Fuller-Maitland's stance toward Elgar. It is likely, too, to have contributed to the often negative reaction to Elgar's professorial lectures two years later, when the composer appeared at times to take a consciously anti-metropolitan stance, notably when he hinted that Leipzig (rather than London) might prove the most appropriate model for music making in Birmingham.[53]

A more profound reason for this resentment of Elgar's popularity was his unsuitability as an exemplar. The future of British music was a major concern for many critics, who saw one of their functions as promoting the best British composers and their works to as wide an audience as possible in the hope that a younger generation, an elusive "School of British

Composition," might be inspired to follow in their wake. (Maclean's articles in the *Zeitschrift* are one manifestation of this; Fuller-Maitland's favorable comparison of his five renaissance "leaders" with the Russian *Kuchka* is another.)[54] But the "School of British Composition" had to consist of the right kind of composer; not everyone was welcome to join this exclusive club. In the critical critics' eyes, the aristocratic Parry qualified for membership, but Elgar, the tradesman's son, did not. A comparison of the language used to describe the two composers is most revealing. Parry's "loftiness" and "aloofness" hint at a social and artistic elitism from which Elgar's "extra-ordinarily common" writing (and ordinary background) automatically excluded him. Parry's music was described by Maclean as a "direct product of academic olive-groves." Elgar, however, was not only uneducated but implicitly undisciplined, trusting "little if at all to intellect" and "rush[ing] wholly on impulse."[55] Parry's diatonicism and his emphasis on musical ideas rather than color provided evidence for the "purity of his artistic ideals"; Elgar was overreliant on virtuosic orchestration and "ultra-modern" chromaticism that might mask a deficiency in technique elsewhere.[56] Above all, Parry possessed a "power" and emotional control that had its roots in the manly self-restraint of "muscular Christianity," the very embodiment of Victorian public school values. It is not without significance that Fuller-Maitland refers to the "purity" of Parry's artistic ideals. That same self-restraint and, implicitly, purity was lacking in the more volatile, stylistically protean Elgar.

In short, the critical language used to describe the two composers forms part of a system of binary oppositions: Parry consistently embodies the positive, hegemonic values of the normative Self, Elgar the negative values of the Other. Given this construction of the two, there was no way that Elgar might have been held up as a model for younger composers to emulate because he was defined expressly in opposition to the one composer, Parry, who was regarded as a salutary—and characteristically British—influence for the young. Ironically, the discourse used by Fuller-Maitland and Maclean to describe Parry's music is used by pro-Elgar critics to describe *his* work, as is illustrated by three comments about *The Apostles:* Alfred Kalisch wrote of the score's "power and beauty and spiritual elevation"; Herbert Thompson referred to Elgar's "masterful" weaving together of the score; and Robert Buckley, comparing the work to *Gerontius*, commented that it is "of more masculine fibre, and with all its passion, has greater reserve. And greater reserve means greater dignity."[57] The ideological values shared by these three writers were the same as those of the critical critics; even the vocabulary is virtually identical. The only difference is in the object of approbation.

The binary oppositions outlined above can perhaps be summed up by reference to an article by Henry Hadow, titled "Some Tendencies in Modern Music," which appeared in the *Edinburgh Review* in October 1906. Once again, Parry is praised for his depth of purpose ("his prevalent mood is one of serious earnest[ness]"), his emotional restraint (Parry "minimis[ed] the appeal to the senses, concentrating his whole force on the intimate expression of religious or philosophic truth"), and his ability to depict "the awe and mystery which surround the confines of human life" in musically simple ways. Above all, Parry embodied the national character, and in a way that drew sustenance from his artistic forebears:

> Throughout his work he employs an idiom of pure English as distinctly national as that of Purcell himself. He is the spokesman of all that is best in our age and country, its dignity, its manhood, its reverence; in his music the spirit of Milton and Wordsworth may find its counterpart.[58]

Conversely, Hadow's criticisms of Elgar echo those of Fuller-Maitland and Maclean. *Gerontius* offered proof that Elgar's music "invariably falters" before the "highest and noblest conceptions" and that his "extraordinary skill of orchestration covers . . . an occasional weakness of idea," while in *The Apostles*, there is a "want of largeness and serenity" in Elgar's handling of the music. This, Hadow claimed, was caused by Elgar's leitmotif technique: the motifs were "all broken up into little anxious 'motives,' which are not blended together but laid like tesseræ in a mosaic, each with its own colour and its own shape. No work of equal ability has ever displayed so little mellowness of tone." In general, Elgar's style is "somewhat tentative and transitional; it often moves with uncertain step, it often seems to be striving with a thought which it cannot attain." For these reasons Hadow likened Elgar to Berlioz, as the Frenchman possessed something of the same "wayward brilliance."[59]

"Wayward brilliance," however, was scarcely a sure foundation for an English school of composition. Elgar's tentativeness, uncertainty, and mosaic-like orchestration seemed to offer a fragmented, even emasculated, future for English music, compared with the philosophical certainties and wholeness of Victorian manliness embodied in Parry's music. Not surprisingly, it is Parry, the spiritual heir of English poets, rather than Elgar, the artistic heir of Berlioz, who emerges as the true musical voice of the nation: the Balakirev at the head of Britain's *Kuchka* to Elgar's Tchaikovsky.[60]

Elgar, Wagner, and Lyricism

Hadow's concerns about Elgar's use of leitmotifs were as much a matter of personal aesthetics as of technique. As noted above, opinion on Wagner in Britain was divided, with many leading figures within the renaissance set skeptical of the composer, at least as a compositional model and certainly as an ideologue. Hadow was less explicitly anti-Wagner than some, but his pronouncement in 1893 that it was "neither likely nor advisable that [Wagner] should exercise any permanent influence" on composers working in musical genres other than opera or music drama was somewhat ingenuous, to put it mildly.[61] Yet this rejection of Wagner outside the theater was consistent with the idealism, derived largely from the critical writings of Hanslick, that pervaded contemporary British musical thinking. Such idealism found its perfect exemplar in the music of Hanslick's hero, Johannes Brahms, who provided British composers with a "safe" compositional model that eschewed the extremes associated with Bayreuth.[62] The Brahmsian model was realized most fully in Britain by Parry, whose emotional control and moderation in orchestration seems almost the antithesis to Wagner. For Elgar to make use of a Wagnerian orchestra, Wagnerian chromatic harmony, and an extensive network of leitmotifs in *Gerontius* and *The Apostles* was, to some extent, to state his allegiance to a composer against whom the leading faction in modern English music had defined itself. Moreover, despite Elgar's plausible claim that his earliest acquaintanceship with reminiscence motifs had not been in Wagner but in Mendelssohn's *Elijah*, the "thematic analyses" to *Gerontius*, *The Apostles*, and *The Kingdom*, which were written by Jaeger under the composer's supervision, and which listed the works' different motifs, were clearly based on Hans von Wolzogen's *Handbücher* for audiences at Bayreuth.[63] Comparisons with Wagner were thus inevitable.

These comparisons were often negative, notably with regard to *The Apostles*, where the composer's leitmotif technique attracted unfavorable comments. For instance, J. H. G. Baughan of the *Musical News* felt that the piece lacked spontaneity and that Elgar's use of leitmotifs elicited only boredom; the opening of Part II, indeed, was castigated as "bald, means absolutely nothing; and must surely have been written in a hurry."[64] This much we might expect from a critic who had previously claimed of *Gerontius* that it "lacked novelty and real inspiration," that "the feminine whine and excessive love of minor harmonies" made "many of the score's pages more painful than artistically impressive," and that its "frequent faded feeling and morbidity" compared unfavorably with the "virility" and "robustness" of Elgar's earlier (and more conservative) *King Olaf*.[65] But criticism of this same passage in *The Apostles* also came from one of the most ardent advocates of *Gerontius*, Ernest Newman, for whom it had "no musical *raison d'être*. You could play the themes in any order you liked without any sense of discontinuity." The problem with the oratorio, Newman argued, was that Elgar's primary concern was to depict a literary narrative, which he achieved through juxtaposing motifs irrespective of musical sense. According to Newman, the music was incapable of developing "an organic life of its own. . . . In no modern work have leading motives been employed so woodenly and with such lack of variety."[66] This charge was echoed by a critic whose views of the composer generally fell between J. H. G. Baughan and Newman, namely Common Time:

> His complex use of the *leit motif* system [in *The Apostles*] is too often only clever on paper. In performance the themes pass in the general hurly-burly without any particular significance; partly because many of them are not very distinctive in themselves and partly because the composer's use of them is so fragmentary. He seems disinclined to develop his themes to any great extent; and their recurrence, in slightly changed form, does appear mechanical,—a charge often brought against Wagner, who could develop his themes.[67]

The observation that Elgar's leitmotifs tended to fragment rather than coalesce—a point that echoes Hadow's comments about unblended tesserae—is highly significant, for the notion of fragmentation lies at the root of much of the anti-Wagnerist criticism of Elgar. Musically, the concerns with fragmentation were twofold: first, the suspicion that Elgar's use of leitmotifs compensated for a lack of skill in writing periodic, lyrical melodies; and second, that Elgar's highly colored scoring masked an underlying formlessness. Both these suspicions were articulated, indeed fostered, by Maclean, for whom Elgar's career seemed to be a long, mostly downward slide from the somewhat unlikely high point of *Caractacus*. According to Maclean, *Caractacus* was "a pleasure to listen to from start to finish" on account of its "good rhythm, . . . fair hold of tonality, judicious prevalence of the major key, broad long phrases, and . . . melody-line often beautiful."[68] With the *Enigma* Variations, however, the long phrases and beautiful melodies disappeared. Maclean opined that the melodies in that score were "downright ugly at their core," largely because the melody was "scarcely lyric" and the minor-major alternation in the theme of "doubtful beauty."[69] Matters worsened for Maclean in the large-scale choral works, in which Elgar abandoned traditional melodic writing for a word painting, driven by leitmotifs, whose sensational immediacy was antithetical both to lyricism and to form. In a review of *The Apostles,* Maclean was moved to write: "To those who believe in the doctrine 'follow the words,' [there is] no example finer. To those who ask for backbone, [there is] little or none, though perhaps more than in *Gerontius.*" Similarly, in *The Music Makers,* the "extensive word-painting" acted "to the detriment of the general jubilancy which is the tenor and purport of the poem." Indeed, of Elgar's mature works, only the First Symphony and the *Crown of India* Suite escaped Maclean's vituperations.[70]

Maclean's complaints about Elgar's alleged lack of lyricism reflect a dislike less of Wagner than of his English disciples. Maclean certainly had grave reservations about the morality of Wagner's mature stage works, but in his eyes moral lapses in plot did not necessarily taint the German composer's music.[71] On the other hand, he expressed contempt for Ethel Smyth, whose *Der Wald* he damned as "one of the dreariest specimens of pseudo-Wagner ever presented to an audience on a first-class occasion."[72] His objection to the work stemmed partly from the extent to which Smyth's scenario mirrored passages in *Siegfried* and *Tristan,* but more from her use of what he considered an alien style of vocal writing. In his view, English opera (and, implicitly, English choral writing in general), "has remained to this day instinctively lyrical. . . . Italian examples, Weberian influences, Wagnerian temptations, have all left that main tendency much as it was."[73] The implication is that any English composer who wrote in an anti-lyrical manner was at the very least unpatriotic and, given the reference to "Wagnerian temptations," quite possibly immoral.[74] As one who had consistently yielded to such temptations, Elgar was thus guilty as charged in the court where Maclean served as both judge and jury.

Elgar, Orchestration, and Strauss

If the decline of English lyricism was primarily a concern of Maclean, the charge that Elgar's highly colored scoring led to formlessness was made by several writers. Ernest Walker, in *A History of Music in England* (1907), felt that there was a "lack of sustained thematic inventiveness" to Elgar's music: "Even when, in a way, quite original, the material sometimes consists of scraps of music, neither individually nor collectively of any particular interest beyond mere colour, joined together by methods not altogether convincing."[75] Walker was not alone. Common Time, for instance, wrote that for all its brilliance in orchestration, there was a "scrappiness of effect" in the *Cockaigne* Overture, and that Elgar had "worked from detail to detail": "There does not seem any reason why the composition should come to an end when it does; simply because there is formality there is no real musical form or architecture."[76] Walter Bernhard, writing in *Musical Opinion*, noted the claim of the music critic of the *Observer* that the "'magnificently modern' orchestration" of the First Symphony had acted "as a dress efficiently disguising the skeleton."[77] One suspects, however, that those critics who valued Parry's soberly delineated forms more highly than Elgar's variegated orchestral kaleidoscope in such works as *Cockaigne* would have considered this orchestral dress to be less Savile Row and more the emperor's new clothes.

The concern that English critics of this period had for formal coherence is well illustrated by a paper that Maclean presented to the Musical Association in 1896, in which the author argued that established forms, such as sonata or rondo, were essentially elaborate versions of simpler (and implicitly universal) formal procedures: the strophic, the episodic, and the balanced. Maclean concluded this paper by remarking that it would be more difficult to find a work that did not reflect these procedures than one that did.[78] The only contemporary genre that might have been charged with formlessness was the symphonic poem, so it should come as no surprise that over the next two decades Maclean would frequently decry its shortcomings: overly chromatic harmony, excessively elaborate orchestration, and structures derived from nonmusical scenarios. While a handful of leading composers could compose in the genre, Maclean felt that "for the rank and file, and for our own times, the 'symphonic poem,' which is understood to be programme-music liberated from all troublesome forms, has proved the haven of the tuneless."[79] The immediate stimulus for the composition of symphonic poems in Britain was the growing popularity of Richard Strauss, whose status as the "world's leading composer" was accepted by conservative and liberal critics alike by the early 1900s.[80] In the eyes of some, however, Strauss's popularity had developed into a virtual cult. "Ours is not the only country where concern is felt at the neglect of native composers," ran a *Musical News* editorial. "This perhaps has arrived at a more advanced stage with us than the French. They only seem as yet to be involved in the Wagner cult. We have to reckon with the Straussians."[81]

But with Straussians came an anti-Straussian backlash—and one which indirectly affected Elgar. As we have seen, Strauss's toasting Elgar as the "first English progressivist" meant that a number of touchy British musicians had a personal reason to dislike the German composer, and it is interesting how certain critics managed to promote anti-Strauss sentiment without in any way questioning his preeminence. In Maclean's case, this took a patriotic form that, given his criticism of Strauss's Düsseldorf speech noted above, as well as his promotion of a leading renaissance composer, is a clear dig at Elgar:

It is to be hoped that the Nile will not inundate here with imitation-Strauss. Our younger composers will get little good from that, and had much better follow their own leaders (admirably typified by a new Stanford Irish Rhapsody at an extra Platt–Strauss concert) and develop the genius of their own country.[82]

More common, however, was the criticism that Strauss's musical language emphasized realism rather than beauty. In a review of the English premiere of the *Sinfonia Domestica,* for instance, Fuller-Maitland, though admiring Strauss's orchestration, questioned whether it could depict anything more than everyday banality: "We cannot enter into the question whether all this array of instruments . . . was worthwhile in order to enforce upon the hearers no idea of greater value than the facts that in Germany some couples fall out and agree again, while some babies are washed both morning and evening."[83] (Such a critical mind-set perhaps explains why E. A. Baughan had a few months earlier dismissed Elgar's most conspicuous piece of Straussian realism, namely Judas's glittering repudiation of the thirty pieces of silver in *The Apostles,* as "cheap.")[84] Fuller-Maitland's flippant point is developed by Hadow, who, in his "Some Tendencies" essay, points out that "in the first place the function of music is to beautify and idealize; and not everything can be expressed in terms of beauty, but only those aspects of life and nature which are capable of idealization." Strauss's music could "excite," "intoxicate," and "dazzle us with coruscations of brilliance and set us tingling with a pleasure that is sometimes very near to pain, but it leaves out of account all the nobler side of human nature; the tenderness that is too deep for tears, the chivalry that is too high to threaten, the indwelling spiritual power with which all great music has held communion." For Hadow, Strauss's tone poems lacked the idealistic qualities and, above all, the moderation that was required to underpin a healthy aesthetic. "All this," he concluded, "bears the clear impress of a decadent and sophisticated art."[85]

Elgar, Decadence, and Debussy

Hadow's comments about Strauss make for an interesting comparison with those of Herbert Thompson about the orchestration of *The Apostles.* Thompson, a critic disposed to favor Elgar, inadvertently revealed the difficulty many critics had with Elgar's scoring when he remarked that "the magnificence and variety of the colouring are almost bewildering, and one only fears lest they should dazzle one's critical faculties and make it difficult to judge dispassionately so striking a work."[86] The danger that aesthetic judgments might be made as a result of sensual rather than intellectual processes was one that unnerved many British critics, as their comments about Elgar's music bear witness. A particularly striking example is C. L. Graves, the music critic of the *Spectator,* who described the effect of the "musical pandemonium" of Elgar's concert overture *In the South* in almost pathological terms as "painfully stimulating." He harbored similar doubts about the First Symphony, where the working out of themes "borders at times on feverishness." Graves continued by asserting that the "human ear is only capable of absorbing a certain volume of sound at a single hearing, and the continuous sonority of this symphony, which eschews those pauses and silences which furnish some of the most eloquent and affecting moments in the works of Beethoven and Schubert, begets a sense of physical fatigue."[87] Such "unhealthiness" was also noted by Ernest Walker. A fellow of Balliol College, Oxford, Walker's views typify some of the academic skepticism toward Elgar that we have already encountered with Fuller-Maitland and Hadow. Walker believed that Elgar's music lacked the "bracing sternness that lies at the root of the supreme music of the world," and instead relied upon "a rather hot-house type of emotionalism." That Walker considered this emotionalism to be inherently unnatural is made clear by his remark that the eponymous protagonist's confession of faith in *The Dream of Gerontius,* "though sincere, nevertheless suggest[s] an atmosphere of artificial flowers," a choice of metaphor that hints at the work's evident affinities with *Parsifal.*[88]

Walker's juxtaposition of Elgar's emotionalism with *Parsifal* is surely more than coincidence. As Byron Adams has noted, the so-called decadent aesthetic movement of 1890s Britain and France placed Wagner on a pedestal above all other composers, and *Parsifal* above his other works.[89] Quoting Ellis Hansen, Adams observes that decadent aesthetics were pervaded by a connoisseurship of "failure and decay," in art, language, or society, for decay itself was considered by the decadents as "seductive, mystical, or beautiful." *Parsifal,* a work that celebrated the degeneration of a sick society at least as much as the regeneration which was the work's notional raison d'être, was thus particularly attractive to the decadent movement.[90] Consequently, when critics write about Elgar's music in terms that suggest some sort of mental illness—or if they draw attention to excessive color, emotionalism, or sensuous beauty—they allude to decadent traits within his work. Perhaps no decadent signifier was more significant than fragmentation itself (whether motivic, thematic, or formal), as the following example from the review of *The Apostles* by Common Time illustrates:

Cleverness piled on cleverness, complexity making complexity more obscure is not great workmanship. You might as well admire the over-ornate designs of certain decadent periods of furniture designing, merely because all kinds of unexpected things are done in the thick plastering of decorations. . . . Many of the ingenious devices and well thought out complexities serve no end: they are mere scrolls and figures and gilding. You may admire each for itself, but you cannot pretend that each plays its part in the whole design.[91]

Alongside fragmentation, the most striking decadent signifier for Elgar (and certainly the most Wagnerian) was the composer's harmony, then considered far more radical and colorful than perhaps it is today. Indeed, Maclean linked the names of Elgar and Debussy, labeling both as harmonic "extremists" in whose music it was difficult to recognize the "ordinary chords" of traditional harmony. (Maclean raised no such objections to Richard Strauss, whose harmonies "are not particularly strange and are in any case quite clear through all his orchestration and passing-notes.")[92] This view was echoed, though less pejoratively, by F. J. Sawyer, in a paper he delivered to the Incorporated Society of Musicians at their Lowestoft conference in January 1906, which subsequently appeared as an eight-part article in *Musical Opinion* titled "Modern Harmony: Exemplified in the Works of Elgar, Strauss and Debussy." Almost three-quarters of Sawyer's article was concerned with the "richness of harmonic invention" of Elgar's most recent works, particularly *Gerontius*, *The Apostles*, and *In the South*. Compared with Elgar's daring, Strauss's harmony was "generally more normal and ordinary. . . . He does not seem so decidedly to have gone out of his way to invent fresh passages as Elgar has done; but, when we turn from these composers to the Frenchman Debussy, we seem to have left behind all former ideas and to be lost in a new world of sound."[93] For Sawyer, Elgar provided a link between Strauss and Debussy.

In his monograph on Elgar, Ernest Newman compares Debussy unfavorably to the English composer, describing the Frenchman's music as "neurotic, wherein the intellect plays so little part, while the nerves are just whipped or soddened by floods of tone of which the main element is the merely sensuous."[94] This depiction of Debussy as anti-intellectual, sensational, possibly febrile, and certainly feminine, provided Newman with a Mediterranean Other against whom he could posit Elgar as a strong, intellectual, masculine, pan-Germanic Self. But if one turns to Hadow's article a markedly different picture emerges. Hadow explicitly described Strauss as "decadent" while Debussy is "almost too fragile for daily life . . . never robust or vigorous"—and unable to "express the larger and broader aspects of humanity."[95] The similarity of Hadow's comments about Elgar's music—"Before the highest and noblest conceptions it invariably falters" and "want of largeness and serenity often appears in the handling of the music"—to his description of Debussy's art is striking: both compose miniaturist musical material that compares unfavorably to Parry's broad melodies and relies excessively on timbre. As post-Wagnerians, albeit of differing hues, Elgar, Debussy, and Strauss are all, to some extent, tarred with the same decadent brush.

Autres temps, autres moeurs

Elgar's biographers have generally considered the reaction against the composer in the 1920s as evidence of a post–World War I generational and ideological shift. To some extent they are correct, but it is clear that even between 1899 and 1919 (and especially between 1902 and 1908), when Elgar was at his creative and popular peak, there was already a significant body of opinion that was consistently hostile to the composer, and for reasons that reflected a very particular aesthetic standpoint. Dent's notorious condemnation of Elgar's vulgarity is thus as much a continuation of this critical tradition as it is a curt dismissal by the president of the International Society for Contemporary Music of a composer who, by 1930, could be portrayed as a creatively inactive, late-Romantic musical dinosaur; the concerns of his article (vulgarity, emotionalism, brilliant orchestral timbre) are identical to those of Maclean and Fuller-Maitland.

But not to those of the Hadow who in 1931 published *English Music*. The structure of this volume is clearly modeled on Walker's *A History of Music in England:* the Middle Ages provide a preparation to the musical heights of the sixteenth and seventeenth centuries, before descending into the "Dark Age" of the eighteenth century, from which emerges the "Dawn and Progress of the English Renascence" and the music of the present day (whose leading exponent, Vaughan Williams, provides the book's introduction). The "Renascence" chapter closes with an assessment of Elgar's career that is far more appreciative than Hadow's *Edinburgh Review* article a quarter of a century earlier. *Gerontius,* a work about which Hadow had previously commented that the orchestration sometimes concealed "an occasional weakness of idea," receives particular praise; moreover, in writing that "there should have been no question, as there is none now, about the hymn 'Praise to the Holiest,' or the pathos of the death-scene, or the mystic beauty of the ascent toward the Throne," Hadow distances himself from Fuller-Maitland, who had raised those very questions. Whereas in 1906 Hadow had written that Elgar and Berlioz possessed "something of . . . the same wayward brilliance," in 1931 there was no parity between the two composers. Elgar, though having something of the Frenchman's revolutionary spirit, was "a greater man than Berlioz, greater in sustained power of thought, in elevation of sentiment, in dignity and control of expression." The "*gaucherie*" of his earlier works had given way to a "serenity of manner" and a "variety of utterance which will be a heritage for all our generations to come." In short, Hadow concluded, Elgar had "remodelled the musical language of England: he [had] enlarged its style and enriched its vocabulary, and the monument of his work is not only a landmark in our present advance but a beacon of guidance for its future."[96]

Thus did one septuagenarian member of the British establishment pay homage to another, in a period when British society was in crisis, threatened both economically (the aftermath of the Wall Street crash) and politically (the rise of socialism at home). How better to ameliorate such a situation than address an imagined national community—"a heritage for all *our* generations to come," "a landmark in *our* present advance"—in praise of a figure now identified in the public mind with Englishness itself?[97] If any proof were needed of the fundamentally historical and contextual nature of reception history, this would be it. But I suspect that Elgar, ever the idealist, might have regarded Hadow's tribute to him as evidence of a "real, lasting educational good"—truth—"gained from the mature slowly-wrought opinion." Indeed, he might even have considered it a belated "conversion."

NOTES

1. Edward Elgar, *A Future for English Music and Other Lectures,* ed. Percy M. Young (London: Dobson, 1968), 163, 177, 167.

2. Ibid., 163.

3. Ibid., 183.

4. Lydia Goehr, *The Imaginary Museum of Musical Works: An Essay in the Philosophy of Music* (Oxford: Clarendon Press, 1992).

5. Carl Dahlhaus, *Foundations in Music History,* trans. J. B. Robinson (Cambridge: Cambridge University Press, 1983), 151.

6. Elgar, *A Future for English Music,* 167.

7, Brian Trowell, "Elgar's Use of Literature," in *Edward Elgar: Music and Literature,* ed. Raymond Monk (Aldershot: Scolar Press, 1993), 230, 280. Compare Rev. H. R. Haweis's similarly Platonist *Music and Morals* (London: W. H. Allen, 1871), which was sufficiently celebrated to go through twenty editions; see Meirion Hughes, *The English Musical Renaissance and the Press 1850–1914: Watchmen of Music* (Aldershot: Ashgate, 2002), 6–8.

8. Elgar, *A Future for English Music,* 167–73, 207.

9. Ibid., 105; Trowell, "Elgar's Use of Literature," 254–56. The extent of the "absolute" character of the First Symphony is also debateable; see Aidan J. Thomson, "Elgar and Chivalry," *19th-Century Music* 28, no. 3 (2005): 259–67.

10. Letter to Ernest Newman, 4 November 1908, quoted in Jerrold Northrop Moore, *Edward Elgar: A Creative Life* (Oxford: Oxford University Press, 1984), 537.

11. *The Strand Magazine* (May 1904): 543–44, quoted in Moore, *Elgar: A Creative Life,* 339.

12. Elgar, *A Future for English Music,* 51, 53.

13. Ibid., 187. Fuller-Maitland intended his obituary to act as a rejoinder to the over-the-top (and sometimes inaccurate) articles that followed Sullivan's death in 1900, but his description of these accounts as an example of "Jumboism" was somewhat crass. See J. A. Fuller Maitland [*sic*], "Sir Arthur Sullivan," *Cornhill Magazine* 495 (1901): 300–309.

14. *Musical News* (9 December 1905), quoted in Moore, *Elgar: A Creative Life,* 480. In his inaugural lecture, for instance, Elgar criticized British composers who had written rhapsodies ("Could anything be more inconceivably inept. To rhapsodise is one thing Englishmen *cannot* do"). Stanford, the composer of several Irish rhapsodies, was almost certainly his target. Elgar, *A Future for English Music,* 51, 53.

15. J. A. Fuller-Maitland, *English Music in the Nineteenth Century* (London: Grant Richards, 1902).

16. Meirion Hughes and Robert Stradling, *The English Musical Renaissance 1840–1940: Constructing a National Music* (Manchester: Manchester University Press, 2001), 41; Hughes, *Watchmen of Music,* 29–38.

17. Hughes, *Watchmen of Music,* 164, 167–68, 172; Moore, *Elgar: A Creative Life,* 359.

18. Hughes, *Watchmen of Music,* 181–82; Moore, *Elgar: A Creative Life,* 549.

19. Moore, for instance, dismisses Fuller-Maitland as "a notorious reactionary," ironically only a few lines after he refers, in far less loaded terms, to the even more conservative, but pro-Elgar, Joseph Bennett as an "old stager." See Moore, *Elgar: A Creative Life,* 333.

20. Hughes, *Watchmen of Music,* 55–56.

21. Kalisch was a progressive critic who not only translated the libretti of both *Elektra* and *Der Rosenkavalier,* but "as secretary of the old Concert-goers' Club and chairman of the later Music Club . . . was able by lectures and demonstrations to introduce a wide public to the new works as they were produced." See Kalisch's obituary in the *Times* (London), 18 May 1933, 16. Thompson was an enthusiastic Wagnerian, whose one music mono-

graph was titled *Wagner and Wagenseil: A Source of Wagner's Opera "Die Meistersinger"* (London: Oxford University Press, 1927). Both critics befriended Elgar.

22. Vaughan Williams recalled that Parry described the Prelude to *Parsifal* as "mere scene painting," and that he was "always very insistent on the importance of form as opposed to colour," and further, that he possessed an "almost moral abhorrence of mere luscious sound." See Hughes and Stradling, *The English Musical Renaissance*, 31, 26; Jeremy Dibble, *C. Hubert H. Parry: His Life and Music* (Oxford: Clarendon Press, 1992), 243; and Ralph Vaughan Williams, *National Music and Other Essays*, 2nd ed. (Oxford: Oxford University Press, 1987), 182. For a fuller examination of British attitudes to Wagner in this period, see Anne Dzamba Sessa, *Richard Wagner and the English* (London: Associated University Presses, 1979); and Emma Sutton, *Aubrey Beardsley and British Wagnerism in the 1890s* (Oxford: Oxford University Press, 2002).

23. H. C. Colles, "Maclean, Charles (Donald)," in *Grove's Dictionary of Music and Musicians*, 5th ed., ed. Eric Blom (London: Macmillan, 1954), 5:480; *Who's Who on CD-ROM, 1897–1998*. Oxford University Press.

24. *Zeitschrift* 1, no. 5 (February 1900): 120. According to Fleischer, the society aimed to be "a federation of the musicians and musical connoisseurs of all countries, for purposes of mutual information on matters of research or on more current matters." Charles Maclean, "International Musical Society," *Grove* 5th ed., 4:518.

25. My use of Oscar Schmitz's famous denunciation of English music is intentional: as one might expect, given its Leipzig origins, the IMG had more members from Germany than from any other country between 1899 and 1914. German scholarly attitudes to English music at the time are perhaps best summed up by Wilibald Nagel's *Geschichte der Musik in England* (Strasbourg: Trübner, 1894), which ended with the death of Purcell; see also "Two Histories of English Music," *Zeitschrift* 12, no. 3 (December 1910): 72–75.

26. Charles Maclean, "Worcester," "Notizien," *Zeitschrift* 4, no. 1 (October 1902): 31.

27. My thanks to Julian Rushton for suggesting this argument.

28. W. H. Hadow, *Studies in Modern Music: Hector Berlioz, Robert Schumann, Richard Wagner* (London: Seeley, 1893; hereafter *Studies 1*); *Studies in Modern Music: Frederick Chopin, Antonin Dvořák, Johannes Brahms* (London: Seeley, 1895; hereafter *Studies 2*); *The Oxford History of Music*, Vol. 5, *The Viennese Period* (Oxford: Clarendon Press, 1904).

29. W. H. Hadow, "British Music: A Report upon the History and Present Prospects of Music in the United Kingdom" (Dunfermline: Carnegie Trustees, 1921); *English Music* (London: Longmans, Green, 1931). The English Heritage series also included "Cricket" by Neville Cardus and "English Humour" by J. B. Priestley.

30. Hughes, *Watchmen of Music*, 37.

31. Elgar, *A Future for English Music*, 49.

32. Moore, *Elgar: A Creative Life*, 85, 259, 438; Jerrold Northrop Moore, ed., *Elgar and His Publishers: Letters of a Creative Life* (Oxford: Clarendon Press, 1987), 2:613, 677; Elgar, *A Future for English Music*, 51, 53; Jeremy Dibble, "Elgar and his British Contemporaries" in *The Cambridge Companion to Elgar*, ed. Daniel M. Grimley and Julian Rushton (Cambridge: Cambridge University Press, 2004), 20 (Elgar's italics). Jaeger himself was not always uncritical of Parry's work, describing the latter's *Magnificat* privately to Elgar as "poor stuff" (28 February 1898; Moore, *Elgar and His Publishers*, 1:66), and commenting disparagingly of the *Thanksgiving Te Deum*, "[O]h. Parry!! very MUCH Parry!!! Toujours Parry!!!! Fiddles sawing all the time!!!!! DEAR old Parry!!!!!!" 12 July 1900; Moore, *Elgar and His Publishers*, 1:213.

33. Letter to Jaeger, 9 March 1898, quoted in Moore, *Elgar and His Publishers*, 1:69 (Elgar's italics). Elgar's views on Parry's orchestration would change over time: many years later Elgar took Vaughan Williams to task for his criticism of Parry's scoring in the *Symphonic Variations*; see Dibble, "Elgar and his British Contemporaries," in *Cambridge Companion to Elgar*, 23.

34. J. A. Fuller-Maitland, *English Music in the Nineteenth Century* (London: Grant Richards, 1902), 252.

35. Ibid., 201. In addition to the ten pages on Parry, Fuller-Maitland devoted eight to Stanford and five to Mackenzie.

36. J.E.B., "Reviews: English Nineteenth Century Music," *Musical News* 22 (19 April 1902): 378; Common Time, "Musical Gossip of the Month," *Musical Opinion* 25 (April 1902): 510.

37. "Elgar, Sir Edward," in J. A. Fuller-Maitland, ed., *Grove's Dictionary of Music and Musicians,* 2nd ed. (London: Macmillan, 1904), 1:773–74.

38. Ibid., 774.

39. "Parry, Sir Charles Hubert Hastings Bart," *Grove* 2nd ed. (London: Macmillan, 1907), 3:625.

40. Charles Maclean, "Hubert Parry's Latest Work," *Zeitschrift* 4, no. 12 (September 1903): 676, 678.

41. Ibid.: 678–79.

42. "Parry and Elgar," "Comments on Events," *Musical News* 25 (26 September 1903): 255.

43. Herbert Thompson, "Gloucester," "Notizien," *Zeitschrift* 6, no. 1 (October 1904): 41–42. For a similar perspective see also E. A. Baughan, "The Gloucester Festival: The New Works," *Monthly Musical Record* 34 (1904): 185–86.

44. C[harles] M[aclean], "Gloucester," "Notizien," *Zeitschrift* 6, no. 1 (October 1904): 43.

45. Quoted in Basil Maine, *Elgar: His Life and Works* (London: G. Bell, 1933), 2:278. While Dent's comments seemingly passed unnoticed in the first edition of the *Handbuch,* they caused an outcry when the revised edition was published, even though, as Brian Trowell has pointed out, the two versions of the article were identical; see Trowell, "Elgar's Use of Literature," 183. An earlier accusation of vulgarity with a particularly Elgarian twist came from Francis Toye in an article entitled "Velgarity" [*sic*] that appeared in *Vanity Fair* shortly after the premiere of the Violin Concerto. Toye drew attention to the "torrents of snobbery, advertisement and flattery that now accompany the production of [Elgar's] every new work," and warned that "this untroubled enthusiasm is bound to produce a reaction sooner or later, and that the cause of Elgar is best served by a total abstention from 'velgarity.'" Quoted in Moore, *Elgar: A Creative Life,* 594.

46. Elgar, *A Future for English Music,* 47.

47. C. Fred Kenyon, "The Destroyer of Genius," *Musical Opinion* 24 (July 1901): 696. Kenyon wrote under the psuedonym "Gerald Cumberland."

48. Maclean, "Hubert Parry's Latest Work," 680.

49. Common Time, "Musical Gossip of the Month," *Musical Opinion* 26 (April 1903): 522–23. The author noted that the presence on the committee of Henry Hadow, and his closeness to the Royal College clique, raised questions about the committee's professed impartiality.

50. "The Musical Season" in "Comments and Opinions," *The Musical Standard* 65 (18 July 1903): 36.

51. Moore, *Elgar: A Creative Life,* 401; "'Somewhere Farther North': Echoes of the Morecambe Festival," *The Musical Times* 44 (July 1903): 460.

52. "'The Sleepy London Press'" in "Comments and Opinions," *The Musical Standard* 65 (4 July 1903): 3.

53. See Hughes and Stradling, *English Musical Renaissance,* 66–74, and Elgar, *A Future for English Music,* 53, 284.

54. Fuller-Maitland, *English Music in the Nineteenth Century,* 185.

55. Maclean, "Gloucester," 43; and "Hubert Parry's Latest Work," 679.

56. "There is an oddity at the core of Elgar's music which does not lie in the line of beauty, but consummate skill in figuration and orchestration conceals this." Charles Maclean, "Music in London," *Zeitschrift* 2, no. 11 (August 1901): 401.

57. Alfred Kalisch, "Musikberichte: Birmingham," *Zeitschrift* 5, no. 3 (December 1903): 132; Herbert Thompson, "The English Autumn Provincial Festivals," *Zeitschrift* 5, no. 4 (January 1904): 176; R. J. Buckley, *Sir Edward Elgar* (London: John Lane, 1904), 80.

58. W. H. Hadow, "Some Tendencies in Modern Music," *The Edinburgh Review* 204, no. 418 (1906): 397. Hadow is not identified as the author of the article in the *Review* itself but is in a review of the article by Charles Maclean in the *Zeitschrift;* see C[harles] M[aclean], "London," "Notizien," *Zeitschrift* 8, no. 3 (December 1906): 99.

59. Hadow, "Some Tendencies," 398–99.

60. This allusion has some basis in fact. It was no accident that five "leaders" of the English musical renaissance were highlighted in *English Music:* Fuller-Maitland explicitly compared Parry and his colleagues favorably with the Moguchaya Kuchka (the Mighty Fire), claiming that there was "more stability in their aims" (186); similarly, Hadow saw the development of nationalism in Russian music as "the best of auguries for the further progress and development of our own"; see "Some Tendencies," 396. The columnist Common Time of *Musical Opinion* argued that Elgar and Bantock were influenced by both Tchaikovsky and Wagner; see "Musical Gossip of the Month," *Musical Opinion* 25 (December 1901): 190. Similarly, Charles L. Graves identified Tchaikovsky, Berlioz, and Wagner as influences on Elgar's First Symphony; see *Post-Victorian Music with Other Studies and Sketches* (London: Macmillan, 1911), 39.

61. Hadow, *Studies 1*, 325.

62. This idealism prevailed outside the renaissance set, too. Ernest Newman, in his monograph of Elgar's early works, *Elgar* (London: John Lane, 1906), ostentatiously avoids any discussion of nonmusical issues until the final chapter. Elgar's admiration for Hanslick has been noted earlier.

63. Michael Kennedy, *Portrait of Elgar,* 3rd ed. (Oxford: Clarendon Press, 1984), 76.

64. J. H. G. B[aughan], "The Oratorio Musically Considered," From the Concert Room, *The Musical Standard* 68 (18 February 1905): 100–101. The identity of this critic has caused some confusion. Jerrold Northrop Moore claims that J. H. G. B. was Percy Betts of the *Daily News* (a critic whom, like Baughan, Elgar described as a "pig"; see Moore, *Elgar and His Publishers*, 1:111), but this is incorrect: Percy Betts's full name was Thomas Percival Milbourne, and he had died on August 27, 1904. See "Obituary: Mr. Percy Betts," *The Musical Times* 45 (October 1904): 652. Rather, J. H. G. B. was J. H. G. Baughan (d. 1927), who succeeded his brother, the better-known E. A. Baughan, as editor of the *Musical Standard* in 1902, a post he held until June 1913. Baughan wrote regularly for other periodicals, and for the *Daily Mail.* See "Obituary: J. H. G. Baughan," *The Musical Times* 69 (February 1928): 173.

65. J. H. G. B[aughan], "The Elgar Festival," Some Events of the Week, *The Musical Standard* 66 (19 March 1904): 185; "Dr. Elgar's 'King Olaf,'" Some Events of the Week, *The Musical Standard* 66 (30 April 1904): 277.

66. "Ernest Newman on Elgar's 'The Apostles,'" Comments and Opinions, *The Musical Standard* 69 (23 September 1905): 192.

67. Common Time, "Musical Gossip of the Month," *Musical Opinion* 27 (November 1903): 112.

68. Charles Maclean, London Notes, *Zeitschrift* 14, no. 3 (December 1912): 79.

69. Charles Maclean, "International Musical Supplement: Local," *Zeitschrift* 10, no. 3 (December 1908): 64b. This was an editorial that though lacking any authorial attribution would have been written by Maclean. Charles Maclean, "Music in England," *Zeitschrift* 1, no. 1–2 (October–November 1899): 16.

70. Charles Maclean, "Three Recent English Productions," *Zeitschrift* 5, no. 9 (June 1904): 362; London Notes, *Zeitschrift* 14, no. 3 (December 1912): 79. The *Crown of India* Suite was "Elgar up to date, discarding early puerilities and uglinesses, and leaning on his own matured individuality." "London Notes," *Zeitschrift* 13, no. 7 (April 1912): 238. The praise for the First Symphony perhaps reflects that work's apparently more conservative idiom (in comparison with, say, *The Apostles*): "At last. As on a surf-board coast a boat drifts backwards and forwards, then recoils, then suddenly on the crest of a high wave touches land, so with England in this case. In respect of the latest developments of highly charged emotional music her attitude has been indeterminate, baffling. Now at the hands of one of her own veritable sons, not those of an alien or a naturalized person, a work has been produced so absolutely up to date in every sense, of such commanding merit, and of such extraordinary and immediate success, that no one can doubt land has been touched, nay a definite territorial point in music-evolution has been annexed. All honour to Elgar, who has secured this for England." "International Musical Supplement," Local section, *Zeitschrift* 10, no. 3 (December 1908): 64a–64b. See also Thomson, "Elgar and Chivalry," 266–67.

71. Maclean considered *Parsifal* to be blasphemous ("It is revolting to Christians, who know of but one Redeemer, to have a second mediæval one staged") and claimed that *Tristan* was "a glorification of that which all the rest of the world condemns; an offence against everyone who takes satisfaction in the fact that Aphrodite has no power over Athene goddess of the mind or Hestia goddess and guardian of the hearth." But on another occasion he praised the music of *Parsifal* for "go[ing] on its majestic course in its own way, following the mood merely of the text, the words being fitted subsequently with consummate art into the stream of sound". See C[harles] M[aclean], review of Ernest Newman, *Wagner,* "Music of the Masters" Series (London: Wellby, 1904); "Kritische Bücherschau," *Zeitschrift* 6, no. 10 (July 1905): 443; Charles Maclean, "Music and Morals," *Zeitschrift* 8, no. 12 (September 1907): 462; "London Notes," *Zeitschrift* 13, no. 7: 238.

72. Charles Maclean, "'La Princesse Osra' and 'Der Wald,'" *Zeitschrift* 3, no. 12 (September 1902): 487.

73. Charles Maclean, "London Notes," *Zeitschrift* 15, no. 10–11 (July–August 1914): 295. Maclean advocated using ballad opera—a genre that was lyrical by its very nature— as the basis for developing a contemporary, consciously English operatic tradition. A composer whose work might be a model for this tradition, he suggested, was Mackenzie, as his style was "one of the most national . . . we have ever possessed" on account of its "fresh melody, complete individuality, and freedom from foreign models." By "foreign" Maclean almost certainly meant German, since Mackenzie's *Colomba* (1883), about which these remarks were made, owes much to *Carmen* in both its plot (which is based on a scenario by Mérimée) and musical language. See Charles Maclean, "Mackenzie's 'Colomba,'" *Zeitschrift* 11, no. 5 (February 1910): 142–45.

74. For a further example of a critic who regarded Elgar's approach to melody as unpatriotic, see George Lowe and Diogenes, "English Music: Two Views," *Musical Opinion* 31 (December 1907): 179–81. According to the pseudonymous Diogenes, "In the place of clear straightforward understandable writing, we find vague heavy most un-English and uninspired phrases loosely and often incoherently strung together. 'Musical mosaics' never have been and never will be great music; and great music is what we want and what we must have if we are to be a musical nation" (180).

75. Ernest Walker, *A History of Music in England* (Oxford: Clarendon Press, 1907), 306.

76. Common Time, "Musical Gossip of the Month," *Musical Opinion* 24 (July 1901): 683.

77. W[alter] B[ernhard], "My Note Book," *Musical Opinion* 32 (February 1909): 245.

78. Charles Maclean, "On Some Tendencies of Form as Shown in the Most Modern Compositions," *Proceedings of the Musical Association* 22 (1895–96): 153–81, 179.

79. C[harles] M[aclean], "London," "Notizien," *Zeitschrift* 7, no. 5 (February 1906): 204.

80. Maclean described him as the "greatest of living musicians" in "Music and Morals," *Zeitschrift* 8, no. 12: 462. The more liberal Alfred Kalisch described him as "the greatest, if not the only great force in the music of to-day, and destined to have a permanent and prominent place in the history of music." "Musikberichte," London section, *Zeitschrift* 4, no. 10 (July 1903): 627.

81. "Teutonised France," in "Comments on Events," *Musical News* 24 (10 January 1903): 30.

82. "Musikberichte," London section, *Zeitschrift* 4, no. 10 (July 1903): 631. Indeed, Maclean follows this quotation with a negative review of the London premiere of *Gerontius* at Westminster Cathedral on June 6, 1903.

83. Quoted in C[harles] M[aclean], "Musikberichte," London section, *Zeitschrift* 6, no. 7 (April 1905): 294. See also "Richard Strauss's Music," in "Comments on Events," *Musical News* 24 (18 April 1903): 363, for a report of a debate between the decadent poet Arthur Symons (in the *Monthly Review*) and Ernest Newman (in the *Speaker*) regarding the merits of Strauss's orchestral music. Symons had argued that "Strauss has no fundamental musical ideas (ideas, that is, which are great as music apart from their significance to the understanding, their non-musical significance)." Newman defended the German composer.

84. E. A. Baughan, "The Gloucester Festival: The New Works," 185. A similar point was made by E[dwin] E[vans, Sr.], "Comments and Opinions," "The Elgar Festival: Second Evening," *The Musical Standard* 66 (19 March 1904): 180.

85. Hadow, "Some Tendencies," 393–94.

86. Thompson, "The English Autumn Provincial Festivals," 176.

87. Quoted in "Notes on News," *Musical Opinion* 28 (October 1904): 18; Charles L. Graves, "Elgar's First Symphony" (2 January 1909), chap. 5 in *Post-Victorian Music with Other Studies and Sketches*, 38.

88. Walker, *A History of Music in England*, 306–7.

89. Byron Adams, "Elgar's Later Oratorios," in *Cambridge Companion to Elgar*, 81–105.

90. Ellis Hanson, *Decadence and Catholicism* (Cambridge, Mass.: Harvard University Press, 1997), 2–5, quoted in Adams, "Elgar's Later Oratorios," 85.

91. Common Time, "Musical Gossip of the Month," *Musical Opinion* 27 (November 1903): 112.

92. Charles Maclean, review of Hugo Riemann, *Introduction to Playing from Score* (London: Augener, 1905), "Kritische Bücherschau," *Zeitschrift* 7, no. 7 (April 1906): 296.

93. F. J. Sawyer, "Modern Harmony: Exemplified in the Works of Elgar, Strauss and Debussy," *Musical Opinion* 29 (August 1906): 816–17; *Musical Opinion* 30 (October 1906): 26.

94. Newman, *Elgar*, 80–81.

95. Hadow, "Some Tendencies," 391–92.

96. Hadow, *English Music*, 158–59.

97. Italics added. The importance of "imagined communities" in modern nationalism has been identified by Benedict Anderson; see his *Imagined Communities: Reflections on the Origin and Spread of Nationalism*, 2nd ed. (London: Verso 1991).

Elgar and the Salons:

The Significance of a Private Musical World

SOPHIE FULLER

The Bank of England has a tradition of embellishing its banknotes with famous British public figures. Those celebrated have included an engineer (George Stephenson), an architect (Christopher Wren), a statesman (the first Duke of Wellington), scientists (Charles Darwin, Isaac Newton, and Michael Faraday), writers (Charles Dickens and William Shakespeare), and social reformers (Elizabeth Fry and Florence Nightingale). In June 1999, the Bank issued a new 20-pound note, replacing Michael Faraday (who had himself replaced William Shakespeare) with its first musician, Edward Elgar.[1] Elgar is represented from the shoulders up, staring into the distance, in a drawing probably made from a photograph taken sometime in the first decade of the twentieth century. His hair is starting to thin and turn gray but the famous, resplendent moustache is still dark.[2] The rest of the banknote shows a reclining female figure, labeled "St. Cecilia," resting a portative organ on her lap; a trumpet-playing angel (presumably a reference to *The Dream of Gerontius*); and the west face of Worcester Cathedral, the Three Choirs Festival venue associated with many of Elgar's public triumphs, and also, of course, the cathedral of the town in which he grew up, and close to which he lived for much of his life.

The banknote is a pertinent acknowledgment of Elgar as one of England's leading cultural figures—a clear demonstration of the place he holds in the British public consciousness at the start of the twenty-first century. It is above all as a public figure that Elgar is celebrated today. Knighted in 1904, made Master of the King's Musick in 1924 and a baronet in 1931, he is most widely celebrated as the composer of the *Pomp and Circumstance* March no. 1 ("Land of Hope and Glory"), played every year without fail during the Last Night of the Proms—the culmination of a concert series modestly billed by the BBC on their website as "The World's Greatest Classical Music Festival."[3] Despite the best efforts of a new generation of Elgar scholars to show other sides to the composer, Elgar the man is popularly regarded as an example of the stereotypical English Edwardian, whose gruff, pompous exterior masked considerable inner turmoil and emotion. The musical compositions that Elgar is most respected for, by both scholars and music lovers, are large-scale orchestral and choral works: the two symphonies, the two concertos, the three mature oratorios, and the Variations on an Original Theme, op. 36 (the *Enigma* Variations).[4] During his lifetime, however, probably the most commercially successful and best known of Elgar's works was the short *Salut d'amour* for violin and piano (1888), an elegant salon piece, endlessly arranged for other instrumental combinations and still widely available on a range of compilation albums, including *Radiance 2: Music for Wine and Candlelight* and *Perfect Summer Wedding*.[5]

Music and the composers who created it have long held a conflicted place in British cultural life. As far back as the eighteenth century, music was generally regarded as the domain of those standing outside the mainstream of intellectual and artistic thought. The professional musician was usually expected to be a lower-class foreigner, and amateur music was stigmatized and dismissed as an upper-class female accomplishment.

The position of the musician and assumptions about his, and increasingly her, class or nationality were rapidly changing during the nineteenth century. Nevertheless, throughout that century and well into the next, male musicians faced the stigma of being perceived as effeminate or womanly. During the period usually characterized as the "British Musical Renaissance," and in the retelling of the musical history of that period throughout the twentieth century, there was a continual self-conscious attempt to move music away from its associations with the feminine and the foreign—to create a full-blooded "masculine" and British music. In 1889, for example, an anonymous writer in *The Musical Times* tried to dissociate male musicians from the female, feminine, and effeminate, arguing that "effeminacy and capriciousness, so far from being essential characteristics of all musicians, are only the accidental qualities of some," and that "the manlier an artist has proved himself to be, the better musician, *ex ipso facto*, has he generally been." Drawing clear parallels between the effeminate and the drawing room, he wrote:

> About these pests of the drawing-room congregates a swarm of pallid *dilettanti*, cosmopolitan in sentiment, destitute of any manly vigour or grit, who have never played cricket or been outside a house in their lives. It is from contact with these nerveless and effeminate natures that the healthy average well-born Briton recoils in disgust and contempt.[6]

From Hubert Parry to Ralph Vaughan Williams and beyond, male composers created images—or had images created for them—that stressed suitable vigor and grit. In his 1926 biography of Parry, Charles L. Graves passes swiftly over Parry's socialism and feminism to concentrate on portraying him as above all a sportsman and gentleman, "robust, manly, and intrepid."[7] Images of Elgar, images encouraged by the composer himself and constructed for him by contemporary and later commentators, are similarly full of contradictions. As early as 1903, a journalist wrote, "Dr. Elgar gives no hint of the popular notion of a musician, and might pass for an Army officer in mufti [more] than anything else."[8] One of his close friends was to remark: "Elgar possessed extreme sensitivity, great tenderness of feeling and pronounced emotional qualities. . . . Outbursts of almost boisterous humour often alternated curiously with his reticence."[9] The upright, military figure who seemed reluctant to admit to being a musician, who loved golf, bicycling, and dogs, and sold his violin to buy a billiard table seems far removed from the man who cried when he conducted his own music and could write of that music (in this case the Violin Concerto): "It's *good!* Awfully emotional! Too emotional but I love it."[10] It would be too simplistic to see this dichotomy merely as a tension between a public facade and a private personality. But it does seem bound up with the tensions between late-Victorian and Edwardian expectations of manliness and an expressive sensitiveness associated with femininity.

It is certainly clear that Elgar desired to be a public figure, aching for recognition in the form of civic honors, longing for enthusiastic capacity audiences for performances of large-scale works at prestigious venues.[11] He was always acutely aware that his Catholic, provincial, lower-class, self-educated background set him apart from the apparently effortless ease and confidence of those from the Protestant, upper-middle-class, Oxbridge, conservatory musical establishment—men such as Hubert Parry or Charles Villiers Stanford. But it is worth remembering that he shared his outsider status with several other contemporary composers such as Samuel Coleridge-Taylor (whose father was African), Rutland Boughton (a political radical), and Ethel Smyth. Smyth, like Elgar, felt perpetually slighted by what she called "the Machine," blaming her gender and her German musical education for the establishment's neglect.

The public musical world of the late nineteenth century that Elgar and Smyth aspired to was one of large choral festivals, such as the long-established annual Three Choirs Festival held alternately in the three cathedral towns of Gloucester, Worcester, and Hereford; of orchestral concert series at venues such as London's St. James's Hall and the Crystal Palace in Sydenham; of ballad concerts where the best-selling songs of the day were sung by the most popular vocalists of the day; and of chamber music series such as the high-brow Monday and Saturday Popular concerts at which leading performers such as pianist Clara Schumann or violinist Joseph Joachim were heard. This was a world closely connected to the music conservatories such as London's Royal College of Music and endlessly chronicled in the music reviews of the daily newspapers. But it was by no means the only musical world of fin de siècle Britain. This was a time when private music making provided vibrant, stimulating, yet now virtually unacknowledged opportunities for performers, composers, and audiences.[12] Private music making took place in the lavish music rooms of the artistically inclined upper classes, the drawing rooms of the well-to-do middle classes, and around the family piano in rather less well-off homes. In these private worlds the audience—if there was one—was invited rather than paying. The amateur musician played an important part in such private milieus, often—in upper-class venues—on the same platform or in the same room as the professional, insofar as the two categories could easily be distinguished in these settings. Private music making provided a space for more than the genres categorized as "salon music," now denigrated works such as character piano pieces, songs, and ballads.[13] Such works were certainly heard in drawing rooms, but so were both established classics and adventurous new music.

Besides groups of friends and family gathering to play together (often but not exclusively from the educated middle classes), private music making included the society gatherings organized by the celebrated music patrons of the day, such as Mabel Veronica Batten, Lady Gladys de Grey (later Marchioness of Ripon), Lady Radnor, Frank Schuster, and Edgar Speyer, women and men who also gave considerable support to struggling performers, composers, and institutions. At a time when women were only gradually moving into a more public musical sphere—whether as instrumentalists, composers, critics, or conductors—these gatherings provided a supportive space where they were able to work and perform alongside their male contemporaries. It helped, of course, that many of the women patrons and amateur musicians came from the assured, confident upper or upper-middle classes. Their education had stressed the acquisition of accomplishments—including singing and piano playing, alongside painting with watercolors or learning European languages—and many of them acquired considerable musical skills. The private musical world of the late nineteenth and early twentieth centuries was a decidedly feminized space.[14]

The world of society musicians is one that Mary Gladstone (1847–1927), the music-obsessed daughter of prime minister William Gladstone, recorded extensively in the thirteen volumes of her diaries.[15] Mary Gladstone was an accomplished pianist who endlessly accompanied her friends (usually

when they played arrangements of "great works" for concertina and piano)
as well as performing at more formal private events and public charity concerts. Her diaries are invaluable in providing one of the few detailed accounts
of society musical gatherings in the late nineteenth century. Gladstone
attended enormous numbers of musical events—from opera at Covent
Garden and orchestral concerts at St. James's Hall or Crystal Palace to
private, society concerts—often given after dinner and involving the same
high-profile performers as the public concerts. One of her early entries
records an after-dinner party in 1870:

> Oh, my winkie, Joachim played. It was marvellous. I was introduced
> to him and my feelings were nearly too many for me. An Andante
> of Mozart's, but the great thing was a Concerto of Mendelssohn's,
> Sullivan accompanying on the P[iano].F[orte]. I am so excited with
> the remembrance, I can hardly write.[16]

Other entries record events such as an 1876 house party at Lord
Brownlow's estate at Ashridge Park, with guests including the violinist
Wilma Neruda (later Lady Hallé), whom Gladstone herself accompanied
in the slow movement of a Beethoven violin sonata.[17] British composers
of the musical establishment, as well as performers, writers, and critics were
also to be found at these private musical parties. In 1877, Gladstone went
to Frank Balfour's "very higher ground Concert. Not a thing I had heard
before. The new Brahms Liebeslieder were really beautiful, Henschell
[*sic*] sang most satisfactorily, and Richter, and Hubert Parry's delightful
Violin Suite took extremely well."[18] In 1880 she recorded J. A. Fuller-
Maitland playing Chopin "beautifully" at a party given by the Tennysons.[19]
In May 1883 she dined with the Stanfords in Cambridge: "After dinner
Gompertz came and played Joe's [Joseph Joachim's] Hungarian concerto. Mr. S[tanford] played some of Hubert's [Hubert Parry's] new
symphony, the Scherzo and Trio delicious."[20]

While Gladstone was accompanying Neruda at Ashridge or listening
to new music at Frank Balfour's soirees, Elgar was still firmly ensconced
in the musical world of Worcester, coming up to London for the occasional violin lesson or orchestral concert. One wonders if Elgar also attended
the Rubinstein concert on April 21, 1877, which Gladstone vividly described
as "a real rotten Concert, bad, flashy, vulgar music played to perfection,
such a sarcasm, it was fun watching him and his marvellous performance
on the [Piano Forte], but *really* as a composer!?"[21] Elgar, like Gladstone, was
involved in musical events in which both amateurs and professionals, women
and men, took part. In the late 1870s he was the leader of the Worcester

Amateur Instrumental Society and the Worcester Philharmonic as well as a violinist in the orchestra for the Three Choirs Festival when it came to Worcester. This was public music making, but Elgar also spent much time playing music with friends in private. This was not yet the society world he was to start moving in after his marriage and the success of the *Enigma* Variations, but it was still one in which talented women played a significant part. In the 1880s, he frequently took part in musical evenings at Severn Grange, home of the proprietor of an organ-building firm. Among the other regular musical guests here was Harriet Fitton, an amateur pianist who had studied in Germany and London and who played for the Herefordshire Philharmonic Society.[22] Elgar frequently played chamber music with Fitton and anyone else staying at her Malvern house, including her two daughters, Hilda and Isabel. Isabel, to whom he gave viola lessons, was immortalized in the sixth *Enigma* variation as "Ysobel."

Several of the musicians with whom Elgar played chamber music at this early stage in his career were men: Charles Buck, Basil Nevinson ("B.G.N." of the twelfth *Enigma* variation), Hew David Steuart-Powell ("H.D.S-P." of the second *Enigma* variation), Frank Webb, and others. But just as many were women: the Fittons, Buck's mother, Webb's sisters, and others. Women also played important roles in organizing local musical institutions. Pianist Winifrid Norbury ("W.N." of the eighth *Enigma* variation) was one of the cofounders and first secretaries of the Worcestershire Philharmonic Society, formed in 1897 with Elgar as its conductor. Serving on the society's committee was the one member of the aristocracy with whom Elgar developed a friendship at this early stage in his career: Lady Mary Lygon (1869–1927), daughter of the sixth Earl Beauchamp. Lygon was a dynamic character and enthusiastic musician who founded and often conducted at a local competition festival at the family estate, Madresfield Court. She, too, was almost certainly immortalized in an *Enigma* variation— the contested thirteenth variation, headed "***."

Much of Elgar's working life from the 1870s on was spent teaching the violin, usually to women. It is hardly surprising that he hated teaching the violin, as the need to earn his living by teaching was a constant reminder that he had not succeeded either as a soloist or a composer. By the 1890s he was giving numerous private lessons in Worcester and Malvern and at two girls' schools (The Mount and Worcestershire Girls' High School). One of the musical manifestations of women's expanding opportunities at the end of the nineteenth century was the "violin craze" of the 1880s and '90s, when increasing numbers of women took up the violin, despite the fact that in the earlier part of the century the violin had not been considered a suitable instrument for a "lady." Contemporary critics were quick to comment on this phenomenon. In 1885 a journalist noted that "female violin *virtuosi* (beg your pardon, *virtuose*) are now springing up like mushrooms."[23] Four years later a reviewer of the all-female Shinner Quartet waxed lyrical: "In no instance is the present expansion of female emancipation more *apropos* than in the cultivation of the 'queen of instruments' by the *doights effilés* of the *beau sexe*."[24] Many of these female violin pupils wanted to take their playing outside the home and play with others, though still retaining their genteel status as amateurs. One of the earliest references to a British women's amateur ensemble dates from 1880 when an "Orchestra of Ladies" (although five of the twenty-five players were men) played at a Musical Festival in Newbury. The orchestra was led by a Mr. J. S. Liddle, violin teacher of many of the performers.[25]

A year later, in 1881, the Dundee Ladies' Orchestra gave its first performance. This group was a string orchestra of thirty-one women who were all pupils of the conductor, Arthur Haden.[26] Their accompanist was Florence Marshall, who was later to start her own predominantly female amateur orchestra.[27] Hildegard Werner, a Swedish teacher and journalist who had settled in Newcastle, banded her pupils into her Ladies' Mignon String Orchestra in 1885.[28] One of her pupils was Marie Hall (1884–1947), Britain's first native-born violin virtuoso.[29]

Elgar was quick to realize the financial possibilities of organizing a similar amateur ensemble of his own female violin pupils. In December 1887 he wrote to his friend Buck: "Jape! I have started a Ladies Orchestral Class & have sixteen fair fiddlers all in two rows & I direct their graceful movements; it is doing well & I think will pay very well & flourish another season."[30] He also used the group for playing through new works—in 1892, for example, rehearsing his Serenade for Strings with them. One member remarked wryly of this practice: "He's always writing these things and trying them out on us."[31]

Like Werner, Elgar gave Marie Hall some violin lessons; these lessons paid off many years later when in 1916 she made the first recording of his Violin Concerto.[32] The headmistress of The Mount school in Malvern, Rosa Burley, who was to become one of Elgar's friends, also took violin lessons from him. Yet another significant pupil, this time studying piano accompaniment, was a local major-general's daughter, Caroline Alice Roberts. In 1889, Alice Roberts became Elgar's devoted and endlessly supportive wife in defiance of family and friends horrified at the very thought of knowing someone whose father was "in trade."

An enormous amount has been written over the years on Alice Elgar and the various women in Elgar's life, from Helen Weaver and Rosa Burley to Alice Stuart-Wortley and Vera Hockmann. These writings have explored the often intense and passionate nature of Elgar's relationships with these and other women—all of whom, in various ways, invested vast amounts of energy in nurturing and supporting the moody and self-doubting composer. But little has been written about the keen musicality of many of these women or that it was their musical talents rather than (or at least as well as) their feminine charms that inspired Elgar to write pieces for them and dedicate works to them. In many ways the musical worlds in which Elgar felt most comfortable and at ease were the feminized spaces of the private drawing room or the society salon.

In the years after his marriage and the success of the *Enigma* Variations, Elgar started to move in somewhat different, more exalted musical circles. He became an honored denizen of the world of upper-class music making, a milieu similar to that which Mary Gladstone had written about in the 1870s and '80s. Some of these society contacts were made through his increasingly high public profile as a composer and some through his wife, Alice, as she was born into a higher social class and so was at ease with and had an entrée into this world. She was also a creative, artistic woman in her own right, described by one of her friends as "a woman of great culture."[33] She had published a novel (*Marchcroft Manor,* 1882) as well as stories, essays, and poems before her marriage, and had also studied the piano in Brussels.[34]

One of Elgar's most useful and supportive contacts was made directly through Alice in 1901 when, at the Leeds Festival, she renewed her acquaintance with Antonia Kufferath (1857–1939), the daughter of her Brussels piano teacher.[35] Antonia was a talented singer who was now married to Edward Speyer (1839–1934), a wealthy German-Jewish banker and enthusiastic music lover whose father had been a friend of Weber, Spohr, Mendelssohn, Liszt, Meyerbeer, and Rossini.[36] Edward Speyer had settled in England in 1859 at the age of twenty, becoming an English subject in 1869. Antonia was his second wife. He first saw her singing at a concert in Frankfurt in 1885 and was later to describe the impact of her artistry in his memoirs:

> Her soprano voice, though not of a particularly robust or bravura character, was of considerable compass, of the finest quality, & trained to a state of perfection. Her diction was exceptionally clear . . . but it was the truly musical & aesthetic side of her art, with its exquisite poetry & warmth of passion, which completely overwhelmed me.[37]

Antonia's public career ended with her marriage, but she continued to sing in private. In 1902 Elgar dedicated the song "Speak, Music" (text by

A. C. Benson) to Antonia. The Elgars soon became frequent guests at the Speyers' estate, Ridgehurst in Hertfordshire, where their hosts' musical parties provided numerous opportunities for the composer's new works or works-in-progress to be heard, as, for example *The Apostles* in January 1903 and the Cello Concerto in 1919.[38] Elgar wrote the recently discovered 42-second "Smoking Cantata" for baritone and very large orchestra on a visit to the Speyers' home. This whimsical work was a dig at Edward Speyer's request that his guests not smoke in the house. According to Elgar's words on the score, this exercise in drollery is a "specimen of an edifying, allegorical, improving, expostulatory, educational, persuasive, hortatory, instructive, dictatorial, magisterial, inadautory work."[39]

The mixture of sport and music at Ridgehurst, unusual for stately homes of the period, would have appealed to Elgar. Among the many musicians who were frequent visitors there in the early twentieth century was Pablo Casals, who recalled arriving to stay with Speyer and announcing: "First we'll play six sets of tennis and then the two Brahms sextets."[40] Edward Speyer's cousin Sir Edgar Speyer (1862–1932) was another influential musical patron and friend of Elgar. Edgar Speyer, born in New York and educated in Frankfurt, settled in England in 1886 as senior partner of the Speyer Brothers Bank.[41] He was chairman of the Underground Electric Railways Company of London from 1906 to 1915, contributed to the founding of the Whitechapel Art Gallery, and from 1909 was Honorary Treasurer of the British Antarctic Expedition's fund.[42] He was also head of the Queen's Hall syndicate and, according to John Bird, was in 1906, "the sole monetary force which kept the Queen's Hall Orchestra afloat."[43] He was host to many musicians when they visited London, including Debussy, Grieg, and Strauss. Elgar encountered Strauss at Edgar Speyer's house in 1902.[44] In 1921 Speyer was expelled from the Privy Council for so-called pro-German activities during the First World War.[45] He had earlier resigned from the Queen's Hall syndicate and eventually left a hostile and ungrateful Britain.[46]

Edgar Speyer married the American violinist Leonora von Stosch (1872–1956), whom he met when she performed at a concert organized by composer Maude Valérie White in the Cotswold village of Broadway.[47] Lady Speyer, as she became, had studied with Ysaÿe and made a successful career in the States, following her debut with the Boston Symphony Orchestra.[48] She does not appear to have played professionally after her marriage but was still firmly associated with the violin, as can be seen in John Singer Sargent's 1907 portrait of her in action. It was Lady Speyer to whom Elgar turned for the earliest private performances of the slow movement of his Violin Concerto in early 1910.[49]

The Violin Concerto is, however, more closely associated with one of Elgar's closest musical women friends, Alice Stuart-Wortley (1862–1936), or "Windflower" as Elgar called her in order to distinguish between the two women named Alice in his life. Stuart-Wortley was not a violinist but rather an accomplished amateur pianist. She was the daughter of the painter John Everett Millais and Effie Gray, and used to play the piano to her father as he worked in his studio.[50] Her musicality was clearly helpful to Elgar: apart from reviewing and playing works-in-progress she also helped him prepare for conducting César Franck's symphony with the London Symphony Orchestra in 1912 by playing it through with him as a piano duet.[51] In 1913 Elgar also asked her to learn part of a piano concerto which he had begun to sketch, but even his beloved "Windflower" could not inspire him to finish this score.[52]

Many other women active in society musical circles knew and worked with Elgar. Lady Maud Warrender (1870–1945), daughter of the eighth Earl of Shaftesbury, was born Ethel Maud Ashley-Cooper and married naval officer Sir George John Scott Warrender. After his death in 1917 (if not before) she became the lover of American soprano Marcia van Dresser, with whom she lived at her house, called "Leasam," near Rye.[53] Music was central to Maud Warrender's life. At the age of twenty-one, a family friend persuaded her mother to allow Warrender to take singing lessons from a Signor Caravoglia.[54] She soon became a celebrated amateur contralto who organized and participated in innumerable charity concerts, both private and public. Always a supporter of the suffrage movement and women's rights, Warrender knew and worked with many women musicians and composers including Rebecca Clarke, Ethel Smyth, and Maude Valérie White.[55] Alice Dew-Smith once summed up Warrender's musical reputation in the following limerick:

There is an enchantress called Maud,
Her voice!—let me hereby record
   That the angels who hear it
   Turn pale, for they fear it
May rival *their* singing to Gawd.[56]

In 1908 Elgar wrote one of his best-known songs for her, "Pleading" (text by Arthur Salmon).[57] She had earlier, in 1903, organized a concert with the Leeds Choral Union in aid of the Union Jack Club at the Albert Hall, which included the first performance of Elgar's *Coronation Ode*. Elgar was one of many musical visitors to Leasam.[58]

Warrender clearly became a close friend. Lady Radnor and Mabel Veronica Batten, both notable amateur musicians and patrons, were less close to Elgar but his acquaintance with them served to reinforce the significance of talented, assured, amateur women musicians in his life. Helen Bouverie, Viscountess Folkestone, and later Lady Radnor (?–1929) had studied singing with, among others, Ciro Pinsuti, Pauline Viardot, and Paolo Tosti. Like Warrender, Radnor put her musical talents to use in charitable ventures. She was involved in the People's Entertainment Society, regularly performed at concerts for "the working men of Battersea," and started singing classes in Bermondsey.[59] But she was best known for her String Band, an ensemble of women string players that she first assembled and conducted in 1881 for a concert that raised £1,000 for the Royal College of Music. The reviewer for the *World* was impressed: "Imagine a string band of twenty-four young girls of the highest station from about 12 to 17 years old, beautiful for the most part, playing magnificently, producing a pianissimo which would do honour to a professional band. . . . Lady Folkestone handled the baton like a Costa."[60] Parry composed his *Lady Radnor's Suite* for the ensemble; the premiere, with Radnor conducting from memory, was given in June 1894.[61] The String Band gave its last performance in 1896, before Elgar became part of the circles in which Lady Radnor moved. But he had taught her eldest son Jack the violin in Malvern and when Elgar first tried to make a name for himself in London, Lady Radnor gave him a letter of introduction "to some of the leading musicians in town."[62] She later became a staunch supporter of his music; Elgar valued her encouragement, treasuring the letters that she wrote to him.[63]

Elgar appears to have first met Mabel Veronica Batten (1856–1916) and her lover, novelist Radclyffe Hall (1880–1943), in 1911.[64] Batten and Hall were Catholic converts who had a house in the Malverns—both useful qualities for cultivating a friendship with Elgar. Elgar may have met Hall several years earlier as a guest at the house of her stepfather, singing teacher Alberto Visetti.[65] Batten had been a renowned society singer who had studied harmony and composition in Dresden and Bruges. In 1902 she was described in an unidentified newspaper as "a pretty, vivacious lady, with a lovely voice and a distinct talent for music."[66] Both Edward and Alice Elgar enjoyed Batten's company. In 1913, for example, Batten's diary recorded lunching with Alice Elgar and the composer Liza Lehmann at the Berkeley Hotel.[67]

Elgar knew several of the successful women composers who were his contemporaries, many of whom had careers that centered around the private musical world.[68] Liza Lehmann (1862–1918), having achieved considerable fame as a professional concert-hall singer, turned to composition after her marriage in 1894. Her first major work was the song cycle for four voices and piano, *In a Persian Garden* (1896), a setting of extracts from *The Rubáiyát of Omar Khayyám* in Edward Fitzgerald's popular translation. This work, however, might never have come to public attention were it not for the private musical world. Lehmann had been unable to get the work heard or published, but her friend, the society hostess Angelina Goetz, arranged a performance of it at one of her musical soirees and persuaded the firm of Metzler to publish it. One of the guests at Goetz's soiree was Hermann Klein, music critic for the *Sunday Times,* who was so impressed that he took the unusual step of reviewing a work that had been presented at a private concert. With such support, musicians soon took an interest in the cycle, which was to become extraordinarily popular throughout Britain and the United States.[69] Elgar, however, was obviously not overly impressed with Lehmann's work, writing to Alice Stuart-Wortley in 1923, apropos of a stage version of Omar Khayyám at the Court Theatre: "I am *not* drawn to Liza Lehmann's music."[70]

Elgar also knew Maude Valérie White (1855–1937). They had several friends and acquaintances in common, such as Frank Schuster, Lady Maud Warrender, and, especially, White's Broadway neighbor and close friend, the American actor Mary Anderson, later de Navarro. In a letter to Alice Stuart-Wortley of 1927, Elgar records Anderson coming to tea "with messages from Maude White."[71] Both White and de Navarro were Catholics. Elgar's opinion of White's songs does not appear to have been recorded but they were so ubiquitous he must have known them, and the question of her influence over his own songwriting, an intriguing topic, is unfortunately beyond the scope of this essay.

It also seems probable that Elgar met Adela Maddison (1863–1929)— they too had several friends and acquaintances in common, including Schuster and Fauré. But no record of a meeting has survived.[72] Another composer whose contact with Elgar appears to remain unrecorded is Ethel Smyth (1858–1944). He certainly heard her conduct her own music on at least one occasion, at the first meeting of the Musical League, of which he was president, in Liverpool in 1909.[73] Smyth has left her opinion of Elgar's music, recording in her memoirs John Singer Sargent's request to her sister: "Do persuade your sister to *pretend* she likes Elgar's music."[74]

Whereas Lehmann, Maddison, and White all found a supportive space in the private musical world of turn-of-the-century England, Smyth was rather more ambivalent, perhaps resisting the expectation that, as a woman, this was the sphere in which she was expected to succeed and flourish. With typical stubbornness Smyth refused to make use of or enjoy this kind of musical support. Smyth's view of amateur musicians was harsh, coming from someone who herself did not need to make a living through her music. Her disparaging remarks about Lady Radnor's String Band, written in retrospect, contrast sharply with the critical acclaim they attracted from contemporary commentators.[75] Maybe, as a woman and a composer, Smyth feared her art might be compromised by too great an association with this private society world, one that was so clearly regarded as a feminized space, chiefly inhabited by women and by foreigners, often German-Jewish musicians or patrons.[76]

Perhaps the most important and most unacknowledged figure in this private world of music was not only German and Jewish but further set apart by his homosexuality. Leo Francis Schuster (1852–1927), known as Frank (or Frankie), was undoubtedly prominent in British musical society and in Elgar's life and career. Yet, with the exception of Byron Adams, writers on Elgar have curiously downplayed the importance of Schuster's role both in Elgar's life and in the musical world of which the composer became a part. The most often quoted pen portrait of Schuster, used by both Jerrold Northrop Moore and Michael Kennedy, is the unpleasant one found in the diary of the poet Siegfried Sassoon:

> Unable to create anything himself, he loved and longed to assist in the creation of music. . . . He was something more than a *patron* of music, because he loved music as much as it is humanly possible to do. In the presence of great musicians he was humble, bowing before them in his Semitic way, and flattering them over effusively. . . . He lacked essential good-breeding and was always the Frankfurt Jew among aristocrats.[77]

Sassoon, himself a Roman Catholic convert of Jewish origin (on his father's side) and a man deeply troubled by his own homosexuality, had a somewhat uncomfortable friendship with Schuster, with whom he traveled in Europe and at whose various houses he was a frequent guest. When Schuster died he left Sassoon his collection of poetry books. Sassoon commented in his diary: "A meagre little collection: I wish he had left me a better feeling about his character. What I learnt from him was mostly negative. How not to live on £8,000 a year."[78] One of the aspects of Schuster's character that Sassoon may have found difficult to bear was Schuster's gentle teasing about the poet's sexual relationships with men.[79]

But Sassoon's uncharitable description of Schuster has persisted among Elgar scholars. Percy Young, for example, dismissed Schuster as "one of Edward's wealthy friends, a homosexual dilettante whom Alice did not like," and few commentators go beyond pointing out that Schuster was homosexual, of Jewish and German background, and a musical patron who gave Elgar financial help. Re-creating Schuster's life or character is difficult.[80] Few letters either to or from him (other than those written by and to Elgar) have survived and few other documents or records trace his activities.[81] But it is known that Schuster's family settled in England in the mid-nineteenth century, presumably before or not long after he was born, and that he was educated at Eton. He inherited considerable wealth and decided not to work in the family business but to live off that wealth and use it to promote the arts, with music being his particular passion. Young writes that he had a "deformed foot" as the result of a childhood accident.[82]

The remembrances of other friends provide a more generous picture than that given by Sassoon. Maude Valérie White, in her 1914 memoirs, wrote:

> Mr. Frank Schuster is so very well known as one of the most ardent music lovers in London, that it is hardly necessary to explain who he is. But he is the kindest and most constant of friends, and a most congenial comrade into the bargain, for his happy sense of humour is absolutely unique, and surrounds him as the sea surrounds Sicily! . . . His lovely little house in Great Queen Street, Westminster, has been for years and years one of the chief centres of musical London, and few indeed are the artists of distinction, both English and foreign, who have not at some time or other enjoyed the hospitality of this kindest of hosts.[83]

In 1883 Schuster had found White somewhere to stay when she went to study in Vienna, and in 1889 invited her to stay at Casa Wolkoff in Venice.[84] Due to the last minute cancellation of Lady Gladys de Grey, White was the only woman in the house party, somewhat to Schuster's, although not White's, consternation.[85] He also, of course, provided a venue for performance of her songs. A letter survives from baritone Charles Santley to Schuster, written in 1887, in which Santley agrees, presumably at one of Schuster's parties, to sing White's "The Devout Lover."[86] Other letters, as well as Elgar's travel diary, attest that Schuster was himself a proficient pianist. In 1886 Jacques Blumenthal reminded Schuster that he had accompanied the "Preislied" from Wagner's *Meistersinger* publicly in St. James's Hall "better than any professional."[87] Elgar's travel diary records an evening in Teraphia while on a cruise in the Mediterranean in the autumn of 1905 when "Lady M. [Maud Warrender] sang many songs & Frank accompanied beautifully."[88] He was certainly enough of a musician to be a valued recipient (as both reader and listener) of Elgar's latest scores and music.

Schuster's obituary in the *Times* was provided by two correspondents. The first described Schuster's "wonderful music parties" and added that he "was an admirable pianist himself. . . . He was an artist, too, and had a remarkable *flair* for distinguishing and encouraging the best in all that work." The second talked of

> that enthusiasm which was most astonishing as it was one of the most delightful of his characteristics. It was communicative; his joys he gave to others, his sorrows he kept to himself. . . . In the depths of that singular heart, at once so simple, so odd, and so willing to pass for what it was not, there were hidden three jewels—humility, patience, and love.[89]

Besides his renowned musical parties, which frequently showcased Elgar's music, Schuster was involved in more public music-related activities and institutions. He was closely involved with the Royal Academy of Music for many years and appears to have been a member of the committee of management.[90] In 1882 he was present at a meeting convened by the Lord Mayor of London to discuss establishing a Royal College of Music and in 1891 he was involved in the Dramatic and Musical Benevolent Fund.[91] In 1899 he served on the council of the Sunday Concert Society, together with Hubert Parry, and later that same year, with the Hon. Alexander Yorke and Paolo Tosti, organized a concert under the patronage of the Queen and the Duke of Wales at Grosvenor House in aid of the Royal Sea Bathing Hospital in Margate.[92]

In 1911 Schuster was named, together with Leonard Borwick, Fanny Davies, Percy Grainger, Irene Scharrer, Emil Sauer, Alice Stuart-Wortley, three members of the Verne family and others, as a supporter of a scheme to endow a "Chopin Bed" for professional pianists in a sanatorium or convalescent home.[93] Shortly before his death he demonstrated his awareness of the possibilities of new technology by serving on the advisory body for a scheme to popularize Beethoven's music "by means of the gramophone."[94]

But it was through private music making that Schuster made the most significant impact on the British musical world of his day. He was only too aware of the limitations of British public musical events, writing to Adrian Boult in 1906:

> I received yesterday another precious installment from E^d Elgar of first proofs of his "Kingdom" this is a work of extraordinary subtlety and delicacy & of more than usual 'intimacy' of atmosphere.

Heaven help it when produced in the respectable *stodgy* manner of a Birmingham Festival!—but of course I can't resist going for all that.[95]

Schuster clearly adored Elgar's music and devoted much of his considerable energy to promoting it and to supporting the composer through his bouts of depression. His first party for Elgar and his music appears to have been a reception after the performance of the "Meditation" from *The Light of Life* conducted by Henry Wood at Queen's Hall on May 9, 1899.[96] This was before the success of the *Enigma* Variations at its first performance on June 19 that year. By autumn, Elgar was sitting for a life-sized bronze bust by Percival Hedley for Schuster's music room.[97]

Elgar's letters to Schuster show his deep gratitude to the man who promoted his work to influential musical figures, provided financial backing, and opened both his London home and his country retreat, The Hut, near Maidenhead, as venues for exciting musical evenings. Schuster introduced Elgar to a wide variety of interesting cultural and society figures, from art critic Claude Phillips and painter John Singer Sargent to the other composer whose music he was so instrumental in promoting in England—Gabriel Fauré.[98] Music patron Winaretta Singer, the Princesse de Polignac, recalled an early Fauré appearance in London:

He first came to London with me in 1896 to give a concert in Frank Schuster's new music room in Old Queen Street, which was to be inaugurated by an orchestral and vocal concert entirely devoted to Fauré's music. It was an unforgettable evening, for the music had been well rehearsed and the greatest artists had gathered together to sing or play.[99]

At The Hut, Schuster also provided an important composing refuge for Elgar, and significant parts of the First Symphony, Violin Concerto, and *Falstaff* were composed there. As early in their relationship as 1901, Schuster had written to Elgar from Dresden:

Anything you do—or think of doing—will *always* interest me—and I shall do what I can to further your interests, the moment I get back and go *amongst people again*. It can only be done by talking—and when I run against the right person—as I hope to do—I shall *talk* no end![100]

Elgar's letters show that Schuster soon became a valued friend. During 1903 the form of address changes from "My dear Schuster" (signing off "Ever yours, Edward Elgar") to "My dear Frank" (signing off "Yours always,

Edward").[101] In 1904 Elgar dedicated the overture *In the South* to Schuster, writing to him: "You will find sunshine & romance &, . . . light-hearted gaiety mixed up in an orchestral dish which with my ordinary orchestral flavouring, cunningly blent, I have put in a warm cordial spice of love for you."[102] In 1904 Schuster came to stay with the Elgars at Plas Gwyn and gave them a sundial. Elgar wrote to thank him: "I love having it & am really happy; coming from you makes it perfect. . . . Also it is feminine, & only beams & smiles in sunshine."[103]

Schuster traveled all over England to hear performances of Elgar's music as well as organizing them himself. He also specialized in lavish parties to celebrate premieres. The day before the opening of the Covent Garden Elgar Festival in 1904, for which Schuster acted not only as instigator but also as guarantor, he threw a dinner party and decorated the walls of his dining room with Elgar's initials and the names of his works spelled out in flowers.[104] After the premiere of the Violin Concerto in 1910, Schuster gave a dinner party complete with menus headed with a theme from each of the three movements of the concerto at each of the three tables.[105]

With just as much thought, Schuster also arranged for important private hearings of Elgar's music. It was at his suggestion that W. H. Reed gave a private performance of the Violin Concerto (before Kreisler's London premiere) at the Gloucester festival of 1910. Of this event, Reed recalled, "Nearly all the prominent musicians engaged at the Festival were there. . . . The room was full; and all the lights were turned out except for some device arranged by Frank Schuster for lighting the piano and the violin stand."[106] Other notable performances included a concert at Schuster's London home in 1919 in which Albert Sammons, W. H. Reed, Raymond Jeremy, Felix Salmond, and William Murdoch played Elgar's string quartet, the quintet, and the slow movement from the violin sonata, with Adrian Boult turning the pages. This concert was repeated in public at the Wigmore Hall a month later.[107] At Alice Elgar's funeral it was Schuster who suggested and organized W. H. Reed's quartet to play the slow movement from the string quartet—a touching gesture of friendship for which Elgar was deeply grateful.[108] To celebrate Elgar's seventieth birthday in 1927, Schuster presented an "Homage to Elgar" in the form of a chamber music concert at The Hut. This was the occasion famously described by Osbert Sitwell, one of several members of the younger generation who were present, as a ghostly gathering of relics of the Edwardian age, with Elgar himself as "a personification of Colonel Bogey."[109]

Schuster was clearly extremely important to Elgar, and not just for his money and contacts. After Schuster's death in 1927, Elgar wrote to Frank's sister Adela:

I have said in music, as well as I was permitted, what I felt long ago,—in F[rank]'s own overture "In the South" & again in the final section of the second symphony— both in the key he loved most I believe (E flat)—warm & joyous with a grave & radiating serenity: this was my feeling when the overture was dedicated to him 24 years ago & is only intensified now.[110]

Elgar's occasional discomfort in Schuster's world of high society and his embarrassment at the loud behavior of some of Schuster's more outrageous young friends has also been documented. Henry Wood described Elgar being "very silent and stand-offish" at the party Schuster gave before the 1904 Elgar Festival.[111] However, most of Elgar's discomfort and rudeness seems to have started in the early 1920s.[112] This was a time when Schuster, like many hitherto wealthy people, found himself in reduced financial circumstances, possibly due to the economic aftermath of the world war. An emotional letter to Boult, written on September 3, 1921, describes Schuster's last moments at his London home: "It is 9.25, and in five minutes the Juggernaut vans will be here to tear my household goods from my arms." The letter ends: "22 Old Queen St. bids farewell to its dear schoolboy [illegible] friend."[113] A couple of years later Elgar wrote to Alice Stuart-Wortley:

> Frank called one day—he is at the Hut—Bankrupt he says & very vague: this afternoon he was sitting in the back of a smart car—the young man was driving with an *odd looking*—I hate to say it—"*bit of fluff*"!! in flamboyant PINK on the front seat, all laughing loudly; they did not see me & I was glad for I shd. have been thoroughly ashamed.[114]

Would a less wealthy Schuster perhaps have become a less attractive friend to Elgar? Schuster remained a loyal supporter to the end and his financial situation seems to have improved gradually. He was certainly able to leave Elgar a considerable sum of money. In 1928 Schuster's sister Adela wrote to Elgar to tell him about one of the clauses of Schuster's will: "To my friend, Sir Edward Elgar O.M. who has saved my country from the reproach of having produced no composer worthy to rank with the Great Masters, the sum of £7,000."[115]

Immersed in a private musical world that occasionally overlapped with the public world of the big choral festivals, clearly homosexual and continually perceived as "not English" (despite the Eton education), Schuster is a central figure of the feminized and overlooked space that was so supportive and vital to Elgar's musical career. Adams suggests that it was Schuster's homosexuality that made Elgar so ambivalent toward him.[116] Given the late-nineteenth-century preoccupation with establishing the general manliness of British musicians, Schuster's remarkable yet discomfiting influence thus begins to raise many important questions about Elgar's relationship to the private musical world over time.

Perhaps Elgar's discomfort was a reaction not only to Schuster's camp behavior and what it signified but also to the general frivolity sometimes apparent in Schuster's upper-class friends. Did Elgar feel that this private musical world was one in which he—the self-made, hardworking son of a shopkeeper—never really belonged, despite all attempts to welcome him? It is also possible that Elgar's behavior toward Schuster reflects establishment unease at a musical world so different from the official world of British music. As Elgar himself became a fixture of the British musical establishment—as his works were widely performed at important public venues and he received official honors and recognition—so he may have taken on more of those conventional beliefs and attitudes.

There is a distinct discomfort, not just from Elgar but from later commentators and scholars as well, in acknowledging the importance of a world that was not obsessed with finding manly qualities in its musicians or their music. This was a world that opened its doors to women, to lesbians and gay men, to foreigners, to Catholics and Jews—to all those who were different and faced exclusion from the Anglican, patriarchal mainstream.

In 1907 Ernest Walker published his *History of Music in England*. He described Elgar as a composer who has "preferred to live outside the whirl of the recognized musical circles, and has held no official position of any importance."[117] Walker continued by dismissing the private musical world in ways that were echoed throughout the twentieth century by other commentators:

> Elgar, till he was considerably over thirty years of age, was known chiefly by, so to speak, "smart society" music—the *Salut d'amour* kind of production that seeks and finds its reward in the West End drawing room, clever and shallow and artistically quite unpromising; and even in the days of his high fame, he has had . . . the heavy millstone of aristocratic fashionableness hanging round his neck, and may over and over again well have prayed to be delivered from his friends.[118]

With this paragraph, the misunderstanding of the West End drawing room, as well as the attempts to distance Elgar from the musical salons—surely the most nurturing of the musical worlds that he inhabited—had begun in earnest.

On the current British 20-pound note Elgar is depicted not only by an angel representing one of his works and a venue representing his public triumphs but also by the reclining figure of St. Cecilia, female patron saint of music. Probably unwittingly, the Bank of England designers have acknowledged that beyond the military moustache, music itself is perhaps best and most immediately symbolized by a feminine image. And despite himself, did Elgar ever acknowledge that he might have been lost without a world that gave him a space in which he could drop the mask of manly grit and vigor, and which gave his music such an appreciative, knowledgeable, and supportive audience?

NOTES

1. See www.bankofengland.co.uk/banknotes/about/withdrawn_notes.htm.

2. The Bank of England has claimed that Elgar's bushy moustache acts as a useful deterrent to forgers. Wulstan Atkins remarked: "He would be the first to appreciate that the complexity of that would be very difficult to copy, and it would have given him real pleasure to know that." See BBC News, 22 June 1999. http://news.bbc.co.uk/1/hi/business/the_economy/375091.stm.

3. Proms 2006 (http://www.bbc.co.uk/proms/) offered the world premiere of *Pomp and Circumstance* March no. 6, realized from sketches by Anthony Payne. Charlotte Higgins, "'New' Version of Pomp and Circumstance for the Proms," *Guardian*, 28 April 2006; http://arts.guardian.co.uk/news/story/0,,1763456,00.html.

4. In March 2006, "Nimrod" from the *Enigma* Variations came sixth in the top ten classical downloads from iTunes. *Pomp and Circumstance* March no. 1 was seventh. Charlotte Higgins, "Big Demand for Classical Downloads Is Music to Ears of Record Industry," *Guardian*, 28 March 2006. http://arts.guardian.co.uk/netmusic/story/0,,1741087,00.html.

5. *Radiance 2: Music for Wine and Candlelight* (Denon DEN 17488, 2005); *Perfect Summer Wedding* (Naxos Regular CD 8.557979, 2006).

6. "Manliness in Music," *The Musical Times* 30 (August 1889): 460–61.

7. Charles L. Graves, *Hubert Parry: His Life and Works* (London: Macmillan, 1926), 365.

8. "'The Sketch': Photographic Interviews LXII—Dr. Edward Elgar," *The Sketch* (7 October 1903): 419.

9. Edward Speyer, *My Life and Friends* (London: Cobden-Sanderson, 1937), 174.

10. Edward Elgar to Frank Schuster, 8 May 1910, quoted in *Letters of Edward Elgar and Other Writings*, ed. Percy M. Young (London: Geoffrey Bles, 1956), 195.

11. Elgar immediately offered himself as Master of the King's Musick when the post fell vacant in 1924; at the same time he was hoping for a peerage. See Jerrold Northrop Moore, *Edward Elgar: A Creative Life* (Oxford: Oxford University Press, 1984), 769–70.

12. It is surprising how little attention has been paid to the private musical milieus by scholars working in the field of British music studies. Work such as Jeremy Dibble's essay "Edward Dannreuther and the Orme Square Phenomenon," in *Music and British Culture,*

1785–1914: Essays in Honour of Cyril Ehrlich, ed. Christina Bashford and Leanne Langley (Oxford: Oxford University Press, 2001), are all too rare.

13. For a discussion of Elgar's attitude toward his own "salon music," see Daniel M. Grimley's essay in this volume.

14. That the private musical world was such a feminized space is doubtless largely responsible for its neglect by musicologists and music historians. In the world view of these scholars, it was only the public, masculine musical spaces that were worth investigating. Feminized spaces were simply assumed to be trivial, frivolous, and insignificant.

15. The diaries are in the British Library: Additional Manuscripts 46254–46266. A useful selection has been published: *Mary Gladstone (Mrs. Drew) Her Diaries and Letters,* ed. Lucy Masterman (London: Methuen, 1930).

16. Masterman, *Mary Gladstone,* 52.

17. Ibid., 100–101. Wilma Neruda (1839–1911), born in Moravia, was a frequent visitor to England where she was a much celebrated and loved performer, appearing at high-profile concerts throughout the country and doing much to popularize the violin as an instrument suitable for women to play. In 1888 she married the naturalized English pianist and conductor Charles Hallé.

18. Ibid., 123.

19. Ibid., 191.

20. Ibid., 291.

21. Ibid., 121.

22. Moore, *Edward Elgar: A Creative Life,* 89–91.

23. "Musical Notes," *The Monthly Musical Record* (September 1885): 208.

24. *The Monthly Musical Record* (June 1889): 137.

25. *The Musical Times* 21 (1880): 600.

26. *The Musical Times* 23 (1882): 82.

27. *The Musical World* 64 (5 June 1886): 366.

28. Margaret Myers, *Blowing Her Own Trumpet: European Ladies Orchestras and Other Women Musicians 1870–1950 in Sweden* (Göteborg: Göteborg University, 1993), 144.

29. Writing in 1946, Edmund Horace Fellowes noted that "her name is not now very generally remembered. Yet she stands alone among British-born violinists in the same rank as the great foreign virtuosi, Sarasate, Kubelik, Mischa Elman, Heifetz, and even Kreisler." Edmund H. Fellowes, *Memoirs of an Amateur Musician* (London: Methuen, 1946), 79–80. At her London debut in 1903, Hall was encored six times for her performance of Tchaikovsky's Violin Concerto with Henry Wood and the Queen's Hall Symphony Orchestra. That year, a *Musical Times* critic wrote: "We may be proud of her nationality, and wish for her a long and brilliant career." *The Musical Times* 44 (March 1903): 186, 173.

30. Jerrold Northrop Moore, *Edward Elgar: Letters of a Lifetime* (Oxford: Clarendon, 1990), 22.

31. Moore, *Elgar: A Creative Life,* 160–61.

32. Michael Kennedy, *The Life of Elgar* (Cambridge: Cambridge University Press, 2004), 147.

33. Speyer, *My Life and Friends,* 174.

34. See Percy M. Young, *Alice Elgar: Enigma of a Victorian Lady* (London: Dennis Dobson, 1978).

35. The Kufferath family was of German origin and were distinguished as performers and pedagogues, especially in Belgium.

36. Speyer, *My Life and Friends,* 3–11.

37. Ibid., 71.

38. Moore, *Edward Elgar: A Creative Life,* 390.

39. David Ward, "Unknown Elgar Is Just a Puff of Smoke," *Guardian*, 11 December 2003; http://arts.guardian.co.uk/news/story/0,,11711,1104249,00.html. As this witty little "cantata" was never intended for performance, Elgar described it as "inadautory."

40. *Joys and Sorrows: Reflections by Pablo Casals*, as told to Albert E. Kahn; available at http://www.cello.org/heaven/joys/chap10.htm.

41. Cyrus Adler and Frederick T. Haneman, "Speyer" in JewishEncyclopedia.com; http://www.jewishencyclopedia.com/view.jsp?artid=1004&letter=S.

42. "Grosvenor Street: South Side," Survey of London, vol. 40, Grosvenor Estate in Mayfair, Pt. 2 (The Buildings) (1980), 44–57. www.british-history.ac.uk/report.asp?compid=42104; "Archives in London and the M25 Area: Whitechapel Art Gallery"; www.aim25.ac.uk/cgi-bin/frames/fulldesc?inst_id=80&coll_id=7210; "Robert Falcon Scott 1868–1912: The *TERRA NOVA* Expedition 1910–13"; www.south-pole.com/p0000090.htm.

43. John Bird, *Percy Grainger* (London: Paul Elek, 1976), 116.

44. Moore, *Elgar: A Creative Life*, 383.

45. Richard Norton-Taylor, "Privy Council Agrees Aitken Resignation," *Guardian Unlimited* (June 27, 1997); http://www.guardian.co.uk/aitken/Story/0,,208491,00.html.

46. Kennedy, *Life of Elgar*, 141. According to Kennedy, the "pro-German" activities consisted of sending food parcels to relatives.

47. Maude Valérie White, *Friends and Memories* (London: Edward Arnold, 1914), 369.

48. John Farrar, ed., *The Bookman Anthology of Verse* (New York: George H. Doran Company, 1922); http://www.geocities.com/~bblair/bav22_5.htm.

49. Moore, *Elgar: A Creative Life*, 566–68. Leonora Speyer was later to turn to writing, winning the Pulitzer Prize for Poetry in 1927 for her collection *Fiddler's Farewell* (1926); http://www.poetrysociety.org/journal/articles/pulitzer.html.

50. Before she married Millais, Effie Gray had been married to John Ruskin. Since this first marriage was never consummated, she managed to get it annulled, but still faced the condemnation of much of Victorian society. On the Ruskin, Gray, Millais triangle see Phyllis Rose, *Parallel Lives: Five Victorian Marriages* (Harmondsworth: Penguin, 1985), 51–98; re playing piano in father's studio, Jerold Northrop Moore, *Edward Elgar: The Windflower Letters. Correspondence with Alice Caroline Stuart Wortley and her Family* (Oxford: Clarendon, 1989), 3.

51. Moore, *Elgar: A Creative Life*, 641.

52. Ibid., 658.

53. Sally Cline, *Radclyffe Hall* (London: John Murray, 1997), 288; http://www.thepeerage.com/p15927.htm.

54. Maud Warrender, *My First Sixty Years* (London: Cassell, 1933), 179, 185–86.

55. See Warrender, *My First Sixty Years*, 184, 205, 210–11, 238 passim.

56. Ibid., 199.

57. Moore, *Elgar: A Creative Life*, 543.

58. Warrender, *My First Sixty Years*, 187.

59. Helen, Countess-Dowager of Radnor, *From a Great-Grandmother's Armchair* (London: Marshall Press, 1927), 96–99; 102–5.

60. Radnor, *From a Great-Grandmother's Armchair*, 112.

61. Jeremy Dibble, *C. Hubert H. Parry: His Life and Music* (Oxford: Clarendon Press, 1992), 313.

62. Radnor, *From a Great-Grandmother's Armchair*, 100–101.

63. Ibid., 264.

64. Michael Baker, *Our Three Selves: A Life of Radclyffe Hall* (London: Hamish Hamilton, 1985), 41.

65. Diana Souhami, *The Trials of Radclyffe Hall* (London: Weidenfeld & Nicolson, 1998), 18.

66. Unidentified press cutting, dated 15 March 1902. Mabel Batten Papers, in the possession of Cara Lancaster.

67. Sally Cline, *Radclyffe Hall: A Woman Called John* (London: John Murray, 1997), 92.

68. See Sophie Fuller, "Women Composers During the British Musical Renaissance, 1880–1918," Ph.D. diss., King's College, London University, 1998.

69. Liza Lehmann, *The Life of Liza Lehmann*, (London: T. Fisher Unwin, 1919), 73–77.

70. Young, *Letters of Edward Elgar*, 284.

71. Moore, *Windflower Letters*, 313.

72. On Maddison, see Sophie Fuller, "'Devoted Attention': Looking for Lesbian Musicians in Fin-de-Siècle Britain," in *Queer Episodes in Music and Modern Identity*, ed. Sophie Fuller and Lloyd Whitesell (Urbana: Illinois University Press, 2002), 85–87.

73. Moore, *Elgar: A Creative Life*, 555.

74. Ethel Smyth, *As Time Went On . . .* (London: Longmans, Green, 1936), 252.

75. "I well remember that no one looked on Lady Folkestone's String Band of women-amateurs as an outlet for serious musical energy and passion, but merely as an aristocratic fad; a resource for such bored and elegant ones as to-day eke out the hours with feeble bridge." Ethel Smyth, *Female Pipings in Eden* (Edinburgh: Peter Davies, 1933), 7.

76. Another German-Jewish musical patron who became a fervent supporter of Elgar was Marie Joshua, renowned for her musical gatherings and support of various musicians and artists. In 1918 Elgar dedicated his Violin Sonata to her. Moore, *Elgar: A Creative Life*, 725

77. Rupert Hart-Davis, ed., *Siegfried Sassoon Diaries 1920–1922* (London: Faber & Faber, 1981), 293–94.

78. Unpublished diary quoted in John Stuart Roberts, *Siegfried Sassoon (1886–1967)* (London: Metro, 2005), 220.

79. As, for example, Schuster's teasing over the possibility of Sassoon's relationship with Philipp of Hesse being made public. See Roberts, *Siegfried Sassoon*, 172.

80. Young, *Alice Elgar*, 157. In fact, Alice was clearly very fond of and grateful to Schuster. The Elgars appointed him as one of their daughter's legal guardians, a clear demonstration of their respect and trust. See Richard Smith, *Elgar in America: Elgar's American Connections between 1895 and 1934* (Rickmansworth: Elgar Editions, 2005), 27.

81. I havé been unable to locate a copy of his will.

82. Young, *Letters of Edward Elgar*, 350.

83. White, *Friends and Memories*, 256. Correctly, it is "Old Queen Street."

84. Ibid., 255–56.

85. "Poor Mr. Schuster, who thought, with every reason, that the situation was rather embarrassing for a still youngish woman, rushed off to call on every nice woman he knew in Venice, and to one and all he said the same thing. 'You absolutely *must* come and call on Miss White as soon as she arrives, so that she may feel that everything is all right.' . . . I enjoyed every minute of my stay." Ibid., 336. Casa Wolkoff, a small palazzo at San Gregorio, belonged to the Russian painter and friend of Wagner, Aleksandr Volkov. It was used at various times by the Princesse de Polignac (who invited Gabriel Fauré to stay there) and Eleanora Duse, as well as Schuster. See Princesse Edmond de Polignac, "Memoirs of the Late Princesse Edmond de Polignac," *Horizon* 12, no. 68 (August 1945): 129; Jean-Michel Nectoux, ed., *Gabriel Fauré: His Life Through His Letters*, trans. J. A. Underwood (London: Marion Boyars, 1984), 156; and "Eleanora Duse: I Luoghi—Venezia"; http://spazioinwind.libero.it/eleonoraduse/_private/luoghiVenezia.htm.

86. Santley to Schuster, 19 July 1887. Extracts available at www.farahardupre.co.uk/index.htm (accessed June 28, 2005).

87. Blumenthal to Schuster, 7 June 1886. Extracts available at www.farahardupre.co.uk/index.htm (accessed June 28, 2005).

88. Quoted in Moore, *Elgar: A Creative Life*, 467.

89. *Times*, 2 January 1928, 19.

90. See *Times*, 26 June 1895, 6; 23 July 1897, 12; 23 July 1898, 14; 23 July 1904, 5; 22 July 1911, 6.

91. *Times*, 21 March 1882, 12; 24 February 1891, 10.

92. *Times*, 13 January 1899, 7; 16 May 1899, 12.

93. *Times*, 19 May 1911, 12.

94. *Times*, 2 March 1927, 14.

95. Frank Schuster to Adrian Boult, n.d., British Library, Add. Ms 72625 f.16.

96. Moore, *Elgar: A Creative Life*, 268.

97. Ibid., 292. The bust is currently on display at the National Portrait Gallery in London. See http://www.npg.org.uk/live/search/portrait.asp?mkey=mw02064. Note that the date given for the bust appears to be 1927 although this was presumably the year that the NPG acquired it, following Schuster's death.

98. In December 1908, for example, Schuster took Fauré to a rehearsal of Elgar's Second Symphony, followed by a dinner party for both composers. Moore, *Elgar: A Creative Life*, 547.

99. Polignac, "Memoirs of the Late Princesse," 119. This was not the first time that Fauré had been to London. According to Fauré's biographer, Robert Orledge, his first visit was in 1882, followed by a concert at St. James's Hall in November 1894. Robert Orledge, *Gabriel Fauré* (London: Eulenburg Books, 1979), 16.

100. Quoted in Moore, *Elgar: A Creative Life*, 348.

101. Ibid., 116 and 123–24.

102. Moore, *Letters of a Lifetime*, 144.

103. Ibid., 157.

104. Moore, *Elgar: A Creative Life*, 435.

105. Ibid., 592.

106. Quoted in Moore, *Elgar: A Creative Life*, 589.

107. Moore, *Elgar: A Creative Life*, 740.

108. See Young, *Letters of Edward Elgar*, 263–64.

109. See Moore, *Elgar: A Creative Life*, 775.

110. Young, *Letters of Edward Elgar*, 300. See also Byron Adams, "The 'Dark Saying' of the Enigma: Homoeroticism and the Elgarian Paradox" in *Queer Episodes in Music and Modern Identity*, 226–28; and Adams's essay in this volume. Schuster's sister Adela, also a friend of Elgar's, frequently acted as hostess at her brother's parties and is best known for her support of her friend Oscar Wilde, giving him £1,000 at the time of his trial in 1895 and sending a wreath to his funeral five years later. Wilde apparently regretted not making her the dedicatee of any of his work and so Robert Ross posthumously dedicated *The Duchess of Padua* to her. See Richard Ellmann, *Oscar Wilde* (New York: Alfred A. Knopf, 1988), 523, 584; and Vyvyan Holland, *Son of Oscar Wilde* (London: Rupert Hart-Davis, 1954), 187.

111. Quoted in Moore, *Elgar: A Creative Life*, 435.

112. See, for example, Elgar's snubbing of Schuster after a concert as recounted in Sassoon's diaries. Adams, "The 'Dark Saying' of the Enigma," 227.

113. Frank Schuster to Adrian Boult, 3 September 1921, British Library, Add Ms 60499 f.85.

114. Moore, *Windflower Letters,* 290. The "young man" driving was Anzy Wylde, a soldier from New Zealand who lost a leg at Gallipoli. The "bit of fluff" may have been Wylde's future wife, the artist and Sickert pupil Wendela Boreel. Schuster built an annex for the couple at The Hut.

115. Moore, *Elgar: A Creative Life,* 776. It is interesting that neither Elgar nor the Stuart-Wortleys and Siegfried Sassoon attended Schuster's funeral, apparently due to a snowstorm. See Moore, *Windflower Letters,* 318; and Max Egremont, *Siegfried Sassoon: A Biography* (London: Picador, 2005), 316.

116. See Adams, "The 'Dark Saying' of the Enigma," 227.

117. Ernest Walker, *A History of Music in England* (Oxford: Clarendon Press, 1907), 286. Elgar, of course, would have loved to hold an important official position (and successfully angled to be named Master of the King's Musick) and in many ways felt that his life outside recognized musical circles had been imposed on him against his wishes.

118. Walker, *A History of Music in England,* 304.

Elgar and the British Raj:
Can the Mughals March?

NALINI GHUMAN

Sir Edward Elgar touches us at home by his declared intention to write a "musick masque" on the theme of the "Crown of India," and make it celebrate the "pomp and circumstance" of the Imperial Coronation Durbar . . . India has lavished her arts of splendour on the Royal visit, and it is only fitting that a great master in the West should spend the wealth and range of his powers on interpreting for us "the kingdom, the power, and the glory" of the highest manifestation of empire that the world has seen.

—*Pall Mall Gazette*, 9 January 1912

In January 1912, at the height of its imperial fervor, the British public eagerly devoured colorful newspaper reports of King George V's visit to India the previous month.[1] This royal visit celebrated the king's assumption of the title "Emperor of India" that had been bestowed upon him during his coronation in Westminster Abbey on June 22, 1911. The focus of the new king's Indian sojourn was the Delhi "Durbar," the court ceremony held in his honor in December 1911, and presented in "Kinemacolour" film to packed London picture houses the following year. A magnificent imperial occasion lasting some ten days, the Durbar involved over 16,000 British and 32,000 Indian officials, and displayed the obeisance paid by all the Indian princes to their rulers.[2] An Australian visitor marveled at "the pomp and solemnity of it all; the gorgeous hues . . . the rhythmic march of regiments; the masses of white-robed, keen-eyed natives; the blended colours where East and West met . . . the thousand sights seen beneath the glamour of that old Indian sun."[3] The event was widely reported and attracted praise from all corners of the empire.

Contrary to appearances and popular belief, however, the Durbar was more than a "pageant of splendour," as one spectator termed it.[4] It afforded an opportunity for the king-emperor to announce several crucial measures to bolster England's weakening hold on India. The first, the shift of the imperial capital from Calcutta to Delhi, had been the subject of debate, and the suitability of other cities as capital had been considered. The king-emperor's second announcement was, in the words of an American spectator, "surely the best-kept secret in history . . . it literally took away the breath of India." He announced the reunification of Bengal, repealing Lord Curzon's partition of the region in 1905 as part of the English "divide and rule" policy.[5] The partition repeal was reportedly "fraught with such vast import" that the king's announcement left "astonishment and incredulity on every face."[6]

In 1905 Curzon, then the viceroy, had split Bengal down the middle, creating Eastern Bengal and Assam, which included the Muslim-majority eastern districts.[7] This arbitrary division caused seven years of communal violence and bloodshed among the Hindu and Muslim populations of Bengal, along with a sharp rise in anticolonial activity and general political anarchy.[8] *Hindi Punch* sought to convey the gravity of the 1905 partition in a cartoon entitled "Vandalism! Or, The Partition of Bengal!" that featured a woman (representing Bengal) who has been chopped by an ax into pieces that represent Assam and East Bengal (figure 1).[9] The tumult surrounding the partition had marred George's reception in India as Prince of Wales in 1905 and led him to conclude that the decision had been a serious political error. The repeal, advocated by George V, was agreed upon after a year of secretive debate concerning "the partition crisis," as the home secretary put it, in which British officials "surveyed the widening cracks in the wall of British authority as a consequence of five years of chaos."[10] The Delhi Durbar thus provided "a unique occasion for rectifying what is regarded by Bengalis as a grievous wrong."[11] But the repeal also signaled the beginning of imperial disintegration, for the partition decision had provided the needed catalyst for effective Indian resistance.[12]

Masking the Durbar

The Durbar, whose Indian memorial will be the buildings of the new capital, is to be commemorated in England by a masque composed by Sir Edward Elgar.

—*The Globe,* 9 January 1912

To mark the occasion of the Delhi Durbar, Elgar collaborated with Henry Hamilton on *The Crown of India,* an "Imperial Masque" produced by Oswald Stoll at the London Coliseum and performed in a mixed music hall program that opened on March 11, 1912.[13] *The Crown of India* was advertised

Figure 1. "Vandalism! Or, the Partition of Bengal!" from *Hindi Punch,* July 1905. Courtesy the British Library.

by the London *Times* as "a project which will evoke extraordinary interest and will, no doubt, prove, under Sir Edward Elgar's treatment, worthy of the historic event that it is designed to commemorate in so graceful a fashion."[14] Not only graceful, but also elaborate: production costs exceeded £3,000, a huge sum at the time, with ornate costumes and lavish settings by Percy Anderson; after all, the *Daily Telegraph* remarked, "so vast and dazzling a subject cannot, obviously, be treated in the spirit of parsimony."[15] And the *Eastern Daily Press* assured readers that "no effort is being spared to imbue the spectacular symbols of the durbar with all the glowing, gorgeous colour of the Orient, and . . . the score . . . casts a powerful spell over the whole production."[16] Photographs of scenes from *The Crown of India*, viewed alongside the colorful illustrated reports that described the spectacle of the Delhi Durbar to the British public, show how closely the masque's sets resembled those of the actual occasion (figure 2).[17]

Press reviews claimed that the masque "put the events of the Durbar in front of the British public in an attractive and concrete form" and that it was "a reconstitution of the scene of the Durbar."[18] Yet the masque staged only part of the events. The first tableau was dominated by the dispute between the cities of India as to whether Delhi or Calcutta should become the new imperial capital and the second tableau featured India and all

Figure 2. India, from the steps of the throne, hails the advent of the King-Emperor and Queen-Empress: A scene from the *Crown of India* masque, *Daily Graphic*, 12 March 1912. Courtesy the British Library Newspapers at Colindale.

her cities assembling with the character of St. George and the East India Company to do honor to England and the British Raj.[19] That the masque represented (in great detail) transfer of the capital to Delhi is unsurprising, since the move was a calculated step to guarantee the continuance of British rule in the face of ever-increasing Indian demands for political power: Delhi had a long history as the site of India's imperial throne.[20] Yet the most significant moment of the Durbar, the reunification of Bengal, found no mention in *The Crown of India,* despite the king's dramatic announcement (reportedly "making history and geography at once"), which might have seemed ideal material for the Coliseum masque.[21] Bengal could not be represented because it alluded to a spectacular policy failure and also suggested the narrowing limits of imperial authority. Thus a selective view of the Delhi Durbar, achieved by ignoring successful native resistance to the Raj that led to the partition repeal, served the interests of both the Raj and British sovereignty.

The Crown of India was, accordingly, a tool for manipulating popular consciousness.[22] India's personification in the masque, a vivid depiction of how the English spoke for India and represented Indians, determined both what could be said about India and what could count as truth. The words put into the mouth of the figure of India parrot the sentiments and ideology that the British used both to justify their reign in India and to make it palatable for themselves:

Each man reclines in peace beneath his palm,
Brahman and Buddhist, Hindu with Islam,
Into one nation welded by the West,
That in the Pax Brittanica is blest . . .

Oh, happy India, now at one, at last;
Not sundered each for self as in the past!
Happy the people blest with Monarch just!
Happy the Monarch whom His People trust!
And happy Britain—that above all lands
Still where she conquers counsels not commands!
See wide and wider yet her rule extend
Who of a foe defeated makes a friend,
Who spreads her Empire not to get but give
And free herself bids others free to live.[23]

Having the figure of India express such uncontested judgments about India and its rulers allowed Hamilton and Elgar to demonstrate to their audience that Indians accept British rule because it is "a mild and beneficent, a just and equitable, but a firm and fearless rule."[24] This has historically always been the way that European imperialism represented its enterprise, for, as Edward Said has argued, nothing could be better for imperialism's self-image "than native subjects who express assent to the outsider's knowledge and power, implicitly accepting European judgment on the undeveloped, backward, or degenerate nature of native society."[25] Moreover, by studiously omitting any reference to the partition repeal and excluding the all-too-present challenges to British rule, Hamilton and Elgar eliminated any chance of showing two worlds in conflict. *The Crown of India*, masquerading as a colorful depiction of the Delhi Durbar, was carefully inscribed with its creators' considered beliefs and suppressions.

The Composer's Burden

Edward Elgar had a personal connection with the ventures of the British in India. His father-in-law, Major-General Sir Henry Gee Roberts (1800–61), joined the East India Company in 1818, launching a distinguished military career. During the 1857–58 Indian Rebellion, he commanded the Rajputana Field Force that succeeded in capturing the town of Kota in March 1858.[26] Later he was honored in a parliamentary motion of thanks for the skill "by which the late Insurrection has been effectively suppressed."[27] Caroline Alice, Sir Henry Roberts's daughter, who was born in October 1848 in the residency at Bhooj in Gujarat, married Elgar in 1889, and they lived in a house scattered with Indian artifacts collected by her father.[28] Following in the footsteps of his father-in-law, Elgar himself was knighted in 1904, later receiving the Order of Merit in July 1911.[29]

The family's links with the Raj can be seen in the larger context of the extraordinary presence of "India" within English life during the years surrounding the turn of the century.[30] Following the 1857 Rebellion, the English sought to strengthen their increasingly precarious hold on the subcontinent by perpetuating the powerful fictions (of civilizing savages, of liberal philosophy, of democratic nationalism) that justified the Raj.[31] After Queen Victoria was proclaimed Empress of India in 1876, displays of the glories of British rule in India became immensely popular. The 1886 India and Colonial Exhibition, for example, attracted nearly four million visitors.[32] International exhibitions that drew attention to India were hosted by Glasgow in 1888, 1901, and 1911, and by London's Shepherd's Bush in 1909, 1910, 1911, 1912, and 1914.[33] The 1895 Indian Empire Exhibition and the 1896 India and Ceylon Exhibition, both at Earl's Court, together with the 1908 Franco-British Exhibition at Wembley were renowned for their displays of the arts, music, architecture, crafts, and "tribes" of India.[34] These cultural practices were exhibited before the British as microcosms of the larger imperial domain.

Outside these exhibitions, representations of "India" and of the historic events of the Raj became a central subject for musical spectacles during the decades around 1900, including *The Grand Moghul* (1884), *The Nautch Girl* (The Savoy, 1891), *The Cingalee* (Daly's, 1904), and H. A. Jones's *Carnac Sahib* (1899). The last of these was much admired both for its jeweled palace at (the fictional) Fyzapore and for its evocative music, including excerpts from Delibes's *Lakmé* and "a Hindu march."[35] Perhaps the most striking of all was the grand pageant *India*, produced by Imre Kiralfy, director-general of several Indian and colonial exhibitions.[36] Staged at the 1895 Earl's Court Indian Exhibition, Kiralfy's "historical play," with music by Angelo Venanzi, was an affirmation of English rule in India. It presented a selective account of Indian history that led naturally from the "Fall of Somnath—The Muhammadan Conquest" in 1024 to Victoria's imperial coronation at the 1877 Delhi Durbar, culminating in a "Grand Apotheosis" in 1895 (during which "Britannia Crowns Her Majesty the Goddess of India").[37]

The 1897 Diamond Jubilee celebrations had established Elgar as England's imperial bard, a composer whose music glorified colonial policy. Elgar certainly took up "The Composer's Burden."[38] His contribution to the Jubilee celebrations included the following works: the *Imperial March* (attributed to *Richard* Elgar!) played by vast military bands at the Crystal Palace early in 1897 and later by special command of the queen at the State Jubilee Concert (the only English work on the program); the two cantatas, *The Banner of St. George,* with its grand finale glorifying the Union Jack, and *Caractacus,* its ancient context encompassing the fall of the Roman Empire and prophesying the rise of the British nation.[39] Performances of the *Imperial March* during that year—at the Albert and the Queen's Halls, at a royal garden party and a state concert, and at the Three Choirs Festival—placed Elgar in the position of laureate for imperial Britain. The Crystal Palace hosted another grand occasion that year at which a new Elgar work was premiered. For this event, held in October 1897, "Ethnological Groups," including "Indians, Bushmen, Zulu Kaffirs, Mexican Indians, Hindoos [*sic*], Tibetans," were put on display in the south transept. Elgar contributed *Characteristic Dances* to the program.[40] Five years later, Henry Wood gave the London premiere of Elgar's *Pomp and Circumstance* Marches in D Major and A Minor, conducting two encores of the former.[41] Charles Villiers Stanford remarked that "they both came off like blazes and are uncommon fine stuff" that "translated Master Kipling into Music."[42] In October 1902, Elgar composed the *Coronation Ode* to commemorate the accession of Edward VII and his crowning as Emperor of India. At the king's suggestion, the *Ode* included the choral setting of the expansive trio melody of *Pomp and Circumstance* March no. 1, a tune that would in Elgar's words "knock 'em flat" and which became known across the world (with words by A. C. Benson) as "Land of Hope and Glory," the anthem of British imperialism.[43]

Yet, as inferred from the policies announced at the Delhi Durbar, these imperial festivals, resounding with marches and hymns, marked a high point for the public face, but not the imperial power, of British rule in India. An apologist for the Raj, Tarak Nath Biswas, prefaced his 1912 study of the Durbar by emphasizing how far relations had deteriorated within the Anglo-Indian colonial encounter:

> The present peculiar situation of India demands a popular exposi-
> tion of the bright side of the British rule, for the shade of discontent
> that one unfortunately notices in the country, can only be removed
> by a better understanding of our rulers and their beneficent and well-
> meaning administration.[44]

The "shade of discontent" is an oblique reference to the seven years of horrors unleashed by the Bengal partition, and the "bright side of British rule" masks the fact that radical Bengali nationalists and other "enemies of empire" were sent to a prison of death on the Andaman Islands in the Bay of Bengal.[45] While *The Crown of India* boasted of Britain's "beneficent and well-meaning administration" to a packed Coliseum during March 1912, English officials were hanging Indian dissidents in a desperate attempt to avoid a full-scale mutiny. As with so many of Elgar's imperialist works, *The Crown of India*, in its subject matter, march topoi, brassy scoring, and massive performing forces, was secretly addressing a crisis of imperial—and thus national—self-assurance.

"East Is East and West Is West."

Remarks by Elgar during the masque's composition indicate the composer's enthusiasm for the project. His earliest thoughts about the masque, out-lined to Alfred Littleton of Novello, his publisher, on January 8, 1912, describe it as "very gorgeous and patriotic."[46] By February 3, the *Daily Telegraph* reported that Elgar had "expressed the keenest satisfaction with Mr. Hamilton's work."[47] Later that month the composer declined an invi-tation from friends, explaining, "I must finish the Masque—which interests and amuses me very much."[48] Elgar divided Hamilton's elaborate reconstruction of the Delhi Durbar into two tableaux comprising some twenty musical numbers together with passages of *mélodrame*.[49] The cast was headed by "India" (played by Nancy Price), with twelve of her most important cities, Delhi, Agra, Calcutta (now Kolkata), and Benares (now Varanasi), as female singing roles; in addition, the masque featured St. George, Mughal emperors, the King-Emperor and Queen-Empress, and a herald called Lotus.

At rehearsals Elgar told the press he found the work hard but "absorbing, interesting."[50] The composer himself conducted the masque twice a day for the first two weeks of its successful run, often running rehearsals between performances.[51] His dedication paid off, not least financially: "God Bless the Music Halls!" he exclaimed to a friend, Frances Colvin, at the thought of his emolument.[52] The masque—and particularly its "gorgeous and patriotic" music—proved enormously popular with audiences and critics alike. In the production's fourth week it was still, the *Daily Telegraph* reported, "a case of 'standing room only' at the Coliseum soon after the doors were opened for both the afternoon and evening performances."[53] England's popular tabloid, the *Daily Express*, trumpeted Elgar's "great triumph at the Coliseum," declaring that "the call was for Elgar at the fall of the curtain. . . . Truly, *The Masque of India* is the production of the year."[54]

The success of Elgar's music was due at least in part to the manner in which the score drew on representations of India and its music that were then all the rage in popular culture. The London *Times* told readers that "the score contains ideas drawn from Oriental sources," pointing to inclusion of the most un-Indian of instruments, "a new gong" contrived by Elgar "for his special purpose."[55] A "native musician with tom-tom" and a pair of "snake-charmers with pipes" also figured in the opening scene, the former by way of the tenor drum, and the latter by oboes. These touches suggest that Elgar must have absorbed the manner in which Indian music was routinely represented at exhibitions, to wit by "snake-charmers . . . dancers, musicians, jugglers, and beautiful Nautch girls."[56] Nothing in *The Crown of India* would have been recognizable as Indian music to an Indian musician, but for audiences caught up in the celebrations of the Delhi Durbar, and with exhibition entertainments ringing in their ears, these allusions were more than sufficient to establish the proper atmosphere. *The Crown of India*'s libretto, together with the elaborate costumes and stage design of its Coliseum run, brought it close to the late-nineteenth-century "Indian" stage spectacle in which *bayadères* and Mughal emperors appeared in London's music halls and theaters. Moreover, similar in theme, representational style, and imperial purpose to Kiralfy's *India*, *The Crown of India* was intended as an edifying, historically accurate entertainment.

After completing the score, Elgar explained that "the subject of the Masque is appropriate to this special period in English history, and I have endeavored to make the music illustrate and illuminate the subject."[57] A perceptive review in *The Referee* addressed the difficulties of representing the Durbar musically:

> When Sir Edward Elgar undertook to write music for a masque dealing with historical events in India for the Coliseum he was faced by several problems not easy to solve harmoniously. It was essential that the patriotic note should be made prominent. It was also distinctly necessary to suggest the mystery of the East. . . . Sir Edward might have made use of the Indian scales . . . and, by contrasting the two systems of music, reflected in his score the difference of Indian and British outlook. Mr. Hamilton's libretto, however, mainly regards India from a British standpoint. . . . The result is that while his music illustrating the Indian portion of the libretto appeals to musicians who will distinguish with pleasure the hand of a master in subtleties of tone-colour and cross rhythms, the chief effect on the ordinary listener is almost entirely confined to the song, "The Rule of England." This, with its diatonic refrain, sounds the imperial note of popular patriotism.[58]

Audiences did indeed delight in St. George's song: critics described it as "a patriotic song of honest ring," "very stirring," and "destined to be heard for many a day outside the Coliseum walls."[59]

The appeal of St. George's rousing solo "Rule of England" can be understood in the context of its popular musical language, for which Elgar drew on several well-known idioms of the day. The chorus's energetic four-square melody and marching bass, along with the text's call to arms and imperialist sentiments, is akin to the "crusader" hymn tradition in general and to the popular exemplar "Lift High the Cross" in particular. The militaristic idiom and lofty imperialism expressed in such hymns and patriotic songs had been caricatured in Gilbert and Sullivan's operettas to great acclaim at the Savoy Theatre since the 1870s.[60] Elgar owned several of these libretti and had seen, played in, and conducted many of Sullivan's works in the 1880s and '90s, including *Iolanthe* which, along with *HMS Pinafore*, seems to have inspired "Rule of England."[61] Ironically, or perhaps with original irony intact and intended, echoes of Sullivan's imperialist spoof, "He is an Englishman" (*HMS Pinafore*) can be heard in the male chorus section of St. George's song with its marching bass and nationalistic text. And "Rule of England's" risoluto section, with its ostinato, marked *marcato*, and lofty sentiments, appears to have strayed out of Lord Mountararat's song with chorus: "When Britain really ruled the waves . . . in good King George's glorious days." Elgar even invoked his own "Land of Hope and Glory" in the song's accompaniment to tug at nationalistic heartstrings.[62]

In contrast to this popular patriotism, the "Dance of the Nautch Girls" is one of the pieces "illustrating the Indian portion of the libretto" that "appeals to musicians who will distinguish with pleasure the hand of a master in subtleties of tone-colour and cross rhythms." In writing a nautch girl's dance, Elgar was tapping in to one of the most pervasive cultural signifiers of India in late-nineteenth and early-twentieth century England. From the early days of the Raj, Indian dance had been a popular form of entertainment for the English. Yet, familiar with such dances as the waltz, the colonizers tended to misunderstand the dance they came across most often: kathak, the north Indian performance genre that includes mime, singing, accompanying music (usually *tabla* and *sarangi*) and intricate rhythmic improvisations with the feet in response to virtuosic tabla sequences.[63] Kathak has a strong erotic character, as it often depicts the amorous exploits of Krishna with his consort Radha. Although traditional kathak dates back to the progressive Bhakti movement of medieval times and was later danced by skilled courtesans, or *tawaifs*, at the royal courts, it had, by the turn of the twentieth century, become synonymous with what foreigners termed "nautch" dancing (from the Hindi *nach*, meaning dance), a derogatory term associated with prostitution.[64]

Nautch songs and dances in all kinds of instrumental and vocal guises had become all the rage in England; these included Venanzi's "Dance of the Bayadères" in Kiralfy's *India,* Walter Henry Lonsdale's "Nautch Dance" for piano (1896), Frederic H. Cowen's "The Nautch Girl's Song" (1898), a setting of words by the well-known authority on Indian literature, Sir Edwin Arnold.[65] In June 1891, the London populace first became privy to the secrets of the nautch girl when Edward Solomon's opera *The Nautch Girl* began a successful run at the Savoy in a production designed, like *The Crown of India,* by Percy Anderson. As Hollee Beebee, a character in the opera, explained in tantalizing detail:

First you take a shapely maiden . . .
Eyes with hidden mischief laden, Limbs that move with lissom grace,
Then you robe this charming creature, so her beauty to enhance:
Thus attired you may teach her all the movements of dance . . .
Shape the toe, point it so, hang the head, arms out spread
Give the wrist graceful twist, eyes half closed now you're posed . . .

Slowly twirling, creeping, curling . . . gently stooping, sweeping,
  drooping
Slyly counting one, two, three . . .

Bye and bye this shapely creature will have learned the nautch
  girl's art,
And her eyes . . . throwing artful, furtive glances . . .
Wringing heartstrings as she dances, making conquests all along.[66]

In his "Dance of the Nautch Girls," Elgar evoked the (imagined) intricacies of kathak dance in an almost pointillistic sequence of musical gestures
suggestive—to his Coliseum audience, at least—of the perceived eroticism of the dancing girl's hand, head, and eye movements ("Limbs that
move with lissom grace"/"Slowly twirling, creeping, curling"/"Eyes with
hidden mischief laden"): pianissimo muted violin and flute running thirds
in triplets and sextuplets with scrupulous attention to articulation; trills;
tempo changes; muted string chords; and touches of muted horn, harp,
and bass drum. Later, the Allegro molto features a repetitive rhythmic
pattern on Elgar's Indian drum ("Tomtoms"), along with fortissimo parallel fifths, flat leading tones, and a swirling sixteenth-note figure in flutes
and piccolo to evoke the perceived wild or barbarous nature of the nautch
as described by one onlooker in the late 1870s: "She wriggled her sides
with all the grace of a Punjaub [sic] bear, and uttering shrill cries which
resemble nothing but the death-shriek of a wild cat." (See Example 1).[67]

Following the London premiere of the *Crown of India* Suite, one critic
described the effect of hearing the "Menuetto" after the "Dance of the
Nautch Girls":

This movement follows as if to illustrate the statement that "East is
East and West is West" in the dance as in other matters. Nothing
could be in more effective contrast to the tempestuous conclusion
of the Nautch Dance than this quiet and majestic old-world Minuet.[68]

Beyond the irony that the minuet could be considered "old world" in
comparison with the centuries-old tradition of kathak, the critic's reference to Kipling's "Ballad of East and West" ("Oh, East is East, and West is
West, and never the twain shall meet") lends perspective to our understanding of *The Crown of India*'s music.[69] In the masque, the stately E-flat
minuet, titled "Entrance of John Company," heralded the highest officials of "the Honourable East India Company" including Clive of India,
Lord Wellesley and Warren Hastings, as well as several "heroes" of the

Example 1. Allegro molto, "Dance of the Nautch Girls," *Crown of India*.

Example 1 continued

Indian Rebellion of 1857 such as Sirs Henry Lawrence, Colin Campbell, and Henry Havelock. Marked *dolce e maestoso, stilo antico,* its trills and rhythmic gestures conjure up the social hierarchy of courtly eighteenth-century European aristocracy in which the minuet promoted a particular kind of grace, agility, and control (Example 2). The minuet exemplified the European idea of dancing as a social activity in which both sexes participated. It would be difficult, then, to find two more contrasting dance forms and musical accompaniments than the European and Indian styles that Elgar depicted in his masque.

Perhaps Elgar's most exotic composition in the masque, and indeed in his entire output, is Agra's "Hail, Immemorial Ind!" Yet, far from displaying the kind of studied musical orientalism of the "Dance of the Nautch Girls," Agra's song has a refined musical setting in which Elgar drew on elements of his personal idiom and, inspired by the Indian subject, expanded their expressive capacities.[70] The name Agra was evocative both for Elgar and his audience: it was the former capital of the Mughal Empire and the location of several wonders of the Muslim world, including Emperor Akbar's city Fatehpur Sikri and Shah Jehan's Taj Mahal, which served as Agra's backdrop at the Coliseum.[71] The song unfolds in the form of a historical "mythography" of India's glories from ancient times to British conquest and rule and is, as Benares explains, essentially an homage to India:

O Mother! Maharanee! Mighty One! . . .
Thy daughters bless thee and their voices blend
With that unceasing song.[72]

Written for alto solo and an orchestra scored to depict the mysterious delights of the distant land of its text, Agra's song recalls Elgar's earlier

Example 2. Moderato, "Menuetto," *Crown of India*.

song cycle for alto and orchestra, the well-known *Sea Pictures* (1897–99). The sea—Shakespeare's realm of "strange sounds and sweet aires"— inspired a highly evocative, often exotic musical language for Elgar (as it did for other composers, including Debussy, Ravel, and later, Britten). While Elgar seems to have used these earlier songs as a touchstone for Agra's aria, the Indian imagery of Hamilton's verse evidently suggested to Elgar an extended and more nuanced vocabulary of musical expression with which he evokes every detail of this historical paean to India.[73] Agra's rich contralto, timbrally redolent (for an audience brought up on nineteenth-century exotica) of the feminized East, begins with a refrain colored by an insistent and exotic augmented triad (A–C♯–F), and closes with a suspended ninth resolving downward in the lowest regions of the orchestra (bass tuba, basses, bass drum). This gesture is derived from Agra's singing of "Ind" and it musically suggests the ancient, mystical, and, in Agra's own description, "dark" depths of "immemorial" India (see the first return of this refrain as it is taken up by the chorus of Indian cities in Example 3). Agra's "quasi recitative" is peppered with tritones that call to mind "the Orient," as Elgar's setting of those words to a rising G♯–D attests.

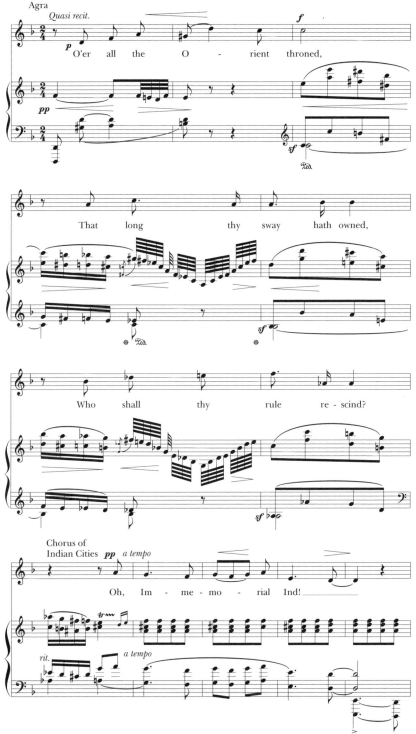

Example 3. Agra's aria, "Hail, Immemorial Ind!" *Crown of India*.

Her vivid descriptions are brought to life by an attendant orchestra of shimmering ponticello tremolo strings, harp, flute, oboe, bassoon, clarinet, piccolo, cymbals, triangle, and glockenspiel that lead Agra's narrative through a harmonic sequence of chromatic lines punctuated by diminished-seventh harp glissandi and ornaments (see fourth bar of Example 3).

Agra's aria, along with the rest of the masque, has largely been condemned to the obscurity its colonialist premise might seem to deserve.[74] The complete music from the masque was published in vocal score by Enoch & Sons in 1912, but only the well-known orchestral suite, originally published separately by Hawkes & Son (owing to the demise of the Enoch firm in the 1920s), is extant in full score and parts.[75] When, in 1975, Leslie Head wished to conduct the complete masque, only two movements could be found (Agra's song and the "Crown of India March"), and any performance of the work today would involve orchestrating the vocal score. How far, though, do memories of the masque inform our hearing of the *Crown of India* we know today, the orchestral suite, op. 66?

Can the Mughals March?

Martial music, in a decidedly Indian vein.
—*The Daily Sketch,* 12 March 1912

In September 1912, six months after the successful run of his imperial masque, Elgar conducted the premiere of his *Crown of India* Suite, comprising five movements: Introduction, Dance of the Nautch Girls, Menuetto, Warriors' Dance, Intermezzo, and March of the Mogul Emperors.[76] Praised as one of Elgar's exemplary marches, this last was favored by its composer, who chose to record it several times, the last being with the Gramophone Company in 1930.[77] These recordings were made, along with "Dance of the Nautch Girls," to the delight and approval of Elgar who declared "Mogul Emperors" to be "a terrific! record."[78] The following year, Alan Webb recalled his first meeting with Elgar: "It at once became evident that most of the evening would be taken up with listening to records. . . . I was fascinated by his choice . . . of his own music, we had 'March of the Mogul Emperors' from *The Crown of India*, the new *Pomp and Circumstance* March no. 5, and the opening and close of the *First Symphony*."[79]

Soon after the *Crown of India*'s run at the Coliseum, the "March of the Mogul Emperors" was singled out as a popular choice for patriotic and imperial occasions. A fine example of the former is the "great patriotic concert" held at the Royal Albert Hall in April 1915 which involved more than four hundred performers drawn from army recruiting bands, and from which all proceeds went to the Professional Classes War Relief Council and the Lord Mayor's Recruiting Bands.[80] At the concert, "Mogul Emperors" was featured alongside "Land of Hope and Glory" and such favorites as "Tipperary" and "Your King and Country Need You." Nearly a decade later, Elgar contributed music for the British Empire Exhibition held at Wembley in the summer of 1924.[81] His name appeared some twenty times on the program of the grand Pageant of Empire, most prominently in "The Early Days of India" that featured his *Indian Dawn* (setting of Alfred Noyes) written for the occasion, along with three numbers from *The Crown of India*: the Introduction, the "Crown of India March," and the "March of the Mogul Emperors."[82] These, interspersed with the other exemplary "Indian" works such as *Old Indian Dances* by an unidentified Shankar (undoubtedly Uday), represent what best depicted India for the British public and how India was perceived.[83] For an England intoxicated by imperial power, India could be no more vividly evoked than by Elgar's "Indian" March.

In a preview of the masque, a critic for the *Daily Telegraph* had noted that "the score fairly bristles with marches, in the composition of which we all know Elgar to be an expert."[84] Some seventy years later Michael Kennedy exclaimed that the "clue" to Elgar's marches is "how *nostalgic* they are," and that "they also represent aspiration and hope"; he described the "March of the Mogul Emperors" in particular as "a fine piece of Elgarian imperialism which requires no apology."[85] More recently, in her article on the composer for the *New Grove Dictionary of Music and Musicians,* Diana McVeagh suggests:

> [Elgar's] unaffected love of English ceremonial, and of the grand moments in Meyerbeer and Verdi, prompted him to compose marches all his life: independent pieces like [the *Pomp and Circumstance* marches], or for particular occasions (*Imperial March,* 1897; *Coronation March,* 1911; *Empire March,* 1924) or as parts of larger works (*Caractacus, The Crown of India*). Mostly they are magnificent display pieces, apt for their time, and still of worth, if they can be listened to without nostalgia or guilt for an imperial past . . . Elgar's march style causes embarrassment only where it sits uneasily, as in the finales of some early choral works, or as an occasional bluster in symphonic contexts.[86]

We might, however, also understand Elgar's celebrated marches, especially "Mogul Emperors," as belonging, musically and ideologically, to the late-nineteenth-century tradition of the march as the favorite signifier of the Raj. By midcentury, the prevailing militarism was generating marches with titles such as "Empire," "Oriental," "Battle," "Hindu," "Cavalry," "Delhi," and even an "Indian Wedding March."[87] In Adolphe Schubart's fantasia *The Battle of Sobraon,* published in London in 1846, Sikhs can be heard marching to their entrenchments to the strains of "There Is a Happy Land."[88] Queen Victoria's crowning as Empress of India in 1876 inspired a further plethora of the genre, including John Pridham's *The Prince of Wales' Indian March* (1876) and *General Roberts' Indian March* (1879), whose title refers to Elgar's father-in-law.[89] Kiralfy's *India* featured two "grand" marches, those of "the Rajahs at Delhi" and of "the Mogul Court." By the 1897 Diamond Jubilee, the march had come to signify both imperial expansion and national celebration; in the process, it had become linked specifically with British India, as exemplified by Thomas Boatwright's 1898 *Indian March: The Diamond Jubilee.*[90]

The "Mogul Emperors" was not Elgar's first exotic march. It followed by eleven years *Pomp and Circumstance* March no. 2, dedicated to the master of Indo-Persian exotica, Granville Bantock. In that earlier (non-programmatic) A minor march, Elgar created an exotic sound chiefly by omitting the leading tone in the main theme. For these marching Mughals, Elgar expanded his orientalist musical armor considerably. At first glance the stately moderato maestoso with its marziale and pomposo sections played by a vast orchestra of full brass and percussion (cymbals, timpani, bass drum, side drum, tambourine, tom-tom, and large "Indian" gong) does seem to be an unequivocal instance of Elgarian imperialism. Listening to the music with insight, however, suggests a rather different interpretation. The first sounds we hear hint at the march's unconventional character; the piece begins not, as we have come to expect from such a genre, with consonant affirming triads but with an accented diminished seventh (E♯–D) followed by a dissonant tritone (D–G♯ / G♯–D) as if to conjure up the oriental despotism of the Mughal emperors depicted within (Example 4).[91]

In *The Crown of India* masque, this was the music that accompanied the emperors Akbar, Jehangir, Shah Jahan, and Aurangzeb onto the Coliseum stage: "Four names," Delhi announces, "whose splendours nothing shall annul . . . Come, oh ye mighty ones from out the Past."[92] Unusually for Elgar's marches, the music is cast in 3/2 with a distinctly triple-meter feel, lest we forget Kipling's rejoinder that it was, after all, "well for the world" only if the "White Men tread their highway side by side," marching in 2/4 or 4/4 naturally![93] Indeed, Elgar's Mughals do not march at all, but rather "process" to a (thinly disguised) polonaise, with all its ceremonial associations, just as Rimsky-Korsakov's Nobles did in *Mlada* (1892).[94] Elgar's three swaggering beats divided by two; second-beat accents (see Example 4); striking eighth-note fanfare figures; and the appearance

Example 4. Opening, "March of the Mogul Emperors," *Crown of India*.

of the rhythm popularized in examples of this genre by Chopin, Glinka, Tchaikovsky, and others, reveal this "march" to be a polonaise. (Example 5, a rare passage of thematic development, shows the polonaise rhythm that permeates the final section.) For these courtly Mughals of bygone times, Elgar drew on the polonaise's history in nineteenth-century Russian art music as a stately, processional dance associated with the court; in this guise the polonaise often replaced the march where official "pomp

Example 5. Polonaise, "March of the Mogul Emperors," *Crown of India.*

and circumstance" was desired.[95] While the "Mogul March" emulates the particular style of Rimsky-Korsakov's grand maestoso polonaise with its brassy fanfares and prominent timpani, Elgar may also have known the "parade-ceremonial" polonaises with patriotic overtones in Tchaikovsky's *Vakula the Smith* and *Yevgeny Onegin,* and in the opening choral pageant of Borodin's *Prince Igor.*[96]

The generic resonance of the polonaise with which Elgar tacitly casts his Mughal music effectively invokes not only noble or martial associations but also, more significantly, the borderline between dance and processional. Elgar thereby suggests, with the help of several orchestral effects designed specifically for his Mughal depiction, the image of a colorful, festive oriental parade. As the motif introduced in bars 5–8 (see Example 4) is extended upward in a series of trills and pseudo-glissandi, it seems to mimic the trumpeting of elephants as they carry their Mughal masters. This is particularly striking when trumpets, muted (for effect rather than volume), repeat the phrase portamento (with slides) and fortissimo; they are punctuated by bass tuba, trombones, bass clarinet, contra-bassoon, double-bass, timpani, bass drum, and "Indian" gong (tam-tam) in second-beat accents (*à la polonaise*) suggestive of ponderous elephant steps (Example 6). These trumpet trills, used earlier in the masque's minuet to portray European gentry in the entrance of the East India Company, now gaudily cloaked by tambourine, cymbals, and gong, become audible manifestations of Indian ornamentalism (opulent Mughal costumes and jewelry, lavishly decorated elephants, bejeweled Mughal swords, and so on). A series of illustrations of "Greater Britain" published in *The Sketch*, a popular London weekly, demonstrates how the Mughal emperors and elephants Elgar depicted in the march served, at the time, as symbols of India itself (figure 3).[97] India, for the British, in Elgar's march as in *The Sketch's* illustration, is represented as a bejeweled, hedonistic, and trumpeting elephant-Emperor, an allegory of wealth and self-indulgence.[98]

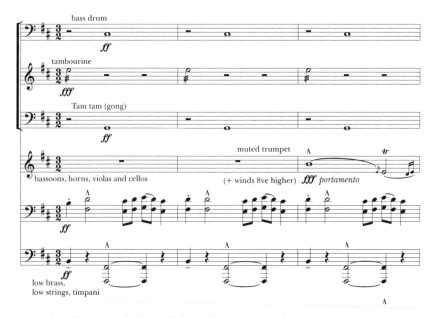

Example 6. "Trumpeting" motif, "March of the Mogul Emperors," *Crown of India*.

Example 6 continued

Figure 3. "India." Part of "Greater Britain." *The Sketch*, 21 April 1897.
Courtesy the Bancroft Library collections, University of California at Berkeley.

Elgar's marches, like most examples of the genre (and famously on account of *Pomp and Circumstance* March no. 1), contain a central trio section of a less martial, more lyrical or *nobilmente* character. Yet the Mughal emperors' polonaise has no such trio to interrupt the fanciful orientalist procession. Instead, the "trumpeting" motif dominates, taken up by all the instruments in turn and juxtaposed with the dissonant opening theme. This trumpeting, together with the militaristic polonaise rhythm reiterated by timpani and side drum, and the heavy second-beat polonaise-style elephant steps punctuated by cymbals and bass drum conjure what the *Musical Times* referred to as "the magnificent barbaric turmoil" of this inspired, and somewhat eccentric, polonaise.[99]

Elgar the Barbarian

The cymbal-crashing, gong-ringing fortississimo that brought to a close the "Mogul March," and hence *The Crown of India* Suite, came to embody the acme of Elgarian imperialism for the musical intelligentsia after the First World War. In *A Survey of Contemporary Music* in 1924, Cecil Gray, Scottish critic and composer, established what was to become a trope (with minor alterations) in Elgar criticism: the distinction between "the composer of the symphonies and the self-appointed Musician Laureate of the British Empire."[100] Concluding that "the one is a musician of merit; the other is only a barbarian," Gray denounced all of Elgar's marches, odes, and other occasional pieces, particularly *The Crown of India*—which he found "undoubtedly the worst of the lot"—as "perfect specimens" of jingoisim. By 1931, *The Crown of India* was, for F. H. Shera, professor of music at the University of Sheffield, an almost unmentionable piece of Elgar's imperialism that had been "allowed to fade into deserved oblivion."[101]

While Gray's and Shera's criticisms reveal the contemporary attitudes of many critics and modernists of their generation, they tell us little about the continuing popularity of Elgar's music with the British public. In his study, "Elgar and the BBC," Ronald Taylor states that by 1922, Elgar's music could be heard on at least one of the BBC stations most days of the year.[102] Significantly, not only were his imperial works among the most regularly broadcast but, of them (apart from the literally countless broadcasts of "Land of Hope and Glory" and *Pomp and Circumstance* March no. 1), *The Crown of India* suite (the "worst" product of Elgar's "barbarian" mind) was heard most frequently—102 times between 1922 and 1934.[103]

Radio Times, a magazine reflective of popular tastes, featured an article in December 1932 that appears to have been crafted in response to the criticisms of Gray, Shera, and others. The author, Alex Cohen, in a spirit of fervent support for the Raj, suggested that "superior folk" had "sniffed" at Elgar's imperialism and that these detractors thought the composer "should have adequately equipped himself . . . first by a study of oriental mysticism . . . followed by a few years apprenticeship as a Hindu ascetic."[104] Cohen's contempt for such criticism of Elgar's lack of engagement with India in his music is evident in his retort, in which he derided not only the Indian practice of meditation but also Mohandas K. Gandhi's satyagraha in particular as years of Hindu asceticism Elgar "might have spent standing on one leg and contemplating the very essence of things until he grew talons a yard long and could subsist on air alone." (Gandhi's staunch adherence to satyagraha was widely considered by many British at best eccentric and at worst an extremely effective form of resistance.) Cohen concluded that "west is not east and the miracle has never been achieved . . . he was the child of his environment" who, accordingly, had mixed in his music "the faith of St Francis the Visionary and an admiration for Cecil Rhodes, the Empire-builder."[105]

Along with the position accorded *The Crown of India* by Gray, Shera, and others in their censure of Elgar's imperialist music, Cohen's perceived connection between Elgar's orientalism and the maintenance of colonial rule in India suggests a way of understanding the critics' changing interpretations. Their rejection of *The Crown of India* and other imperialist works in the late 1920s and early 1930s coincides with significant changes in Anglo-Indian colonial relations and policies during that time. In 1930, Gandhi broke the salt law, thereby setting in motion a flurry of civil actions against British authorities; that year also saw the first roundtable conference summoned by the British concerning a new Indian constitution. Anticolonial sentiments from English liberals intensified in the face of negligible native participation in the constitution's makings and even more in 1932 when the Indian Congress was declared illegal and Gandhi was arrested. It was perhaps neither Elgar's death in 1934 nor a received view that his music had become outmoded but rather the passing of the Government of India Act in 1935 that proved the most potent catalyst for his music's reinterpretation as pastoral. The India Act provided for the establishment of an All-Indian Federation and a new system of government on the basis of provincial autonomy—signaling the beginning of the end of colonialism. As Jeremy Crump argues:

> Only in the 1930s, at the time of the Peace Pledge Union and concern for the League of Nations, when the Indian Act [of] 1935 marked a commitment to a less expansionist phase of colonial imperialism, [did] the pastoral became dominant in some interpretations of Elgar. The retreat to rural values was consonant with the view of "sunset splendour" in the Edwardian Elgar, and coincided with a cultural conservatism, marked in music by the decline in the fashion for experimental works like Walton's *Façade* (1921).[106]

Thus, the earlier association of empire and the war was dismissed from Elgar's music so that it could provide a locus of nostalgia for the Edwardian era. Along with the ever-growing resistance to English imperial might in India, the breakup of landed estates and economic crisis all contributed to what Crump describes as "a yearning for past glories and a mythical, stable social order"—at home and in the colonies.[107] In response to this yearning, Elgar's music was reinterpreted as redolent of the imagined virtues of a preindustrial rural Britain that many sought. His music was not only increasingly related to the English countryside but was also seen as belonging to the folk music revival, particularly by Ralph Vaughan Williams, who suggested that Elgar's exploitation of the musical idiom of "the people" was comparable with Burns's and Shakespeare's use of the vernacular.[108] Writers at this time often emphasized the English spirit of Elgar's music, asserting its power to "express the very soul of our race," as Ernest Newman put it in 1934, much as during previous decades.[109]

One of the strategies used to distance this intangibly English Elgar from the English imperial enterprise is to largely ignore his nationalistic works (except at graduation time or the Last Night of the Proms). Lovers of Elgar's music have, since the 1930s, regularly tried to save the composer from himself. As a result, the established Elgar canon is based on the *Enigma* Variations, the symphonies and concertos, the overtures, *Dream of Gerontius,* and some smaller instrumental works, including the Serenade, and Introduction and Allegro for strings. The subsequent dismissal of a large body of Elgar's music has been justified by denying the integrity of his output and appealing to the "two Elgars" theory, seen in embryo in Gray's criticism.[110] In 1932, A. J. Sheldon claimed that "political ideas can never inspire the artist in the same way, or to a like extent, as poetical ideas can." Thus he declared that Elgar's music connected with imperialism "should be buried soon; at present it is a clog on the endearing place Elgar holds in our estimation."[111] Three years later, Frank Howes clarified this view of the two Elgars, with only one worthy of retaining, stating that "the two Elgars may be roughly described as the Elgar who writes for strings and the Elgar who writes for brass."[112]

The result has been that long-established nationalistic myths (pastoral, spiritual, and nostalgic) have dominated interpretations, forming the basis of the composer's revival in the 1960s.[113] Historian Jeffrey Richards has noted that the pillars of this revival, Ken Russell's BBC documentary *Elgar* (1962) and Michael Kennedy's *Portrait of Elgar* (1968), "seriously distort the picture" because of a desire to "exculpate Elgar from imperialism."[114] Works like *The Crown of India* have thus either been put off limits or uncritically celebrated. Yet, listening insightfully to Elgar's music with attention to its political subtext can tell us far more about the music and its times than abstract notions of imperialism.

The emergence of a postcolonial consciousness has sparked discussion about the British Empire that promotes a new understanding of what Britain was—and is. Landmark scholarship has done much to remedy the historiographical distortions surrounding the composer and his music.[115] Alain Frogley recently argued that consideration of imperialism by scholars

of English music is a necessary part of challenging "the prevailing ortho-
doxies of British music historiography."[116] Thus, while a reevaluation of Elgar
is well under way, one of the challenges for historians of early-twentieth-
century England today is to connect the musical works of Elgar and his
contemporaries not only with the pleasure of listening but also with the
British imperial enterprise—particularly the Raj, "a reign of such immense
range and wealth as to have become a fact of nature for members of the
imperial culture."[117]

In this context, Elgar's *Crown of India*, like Rudyard Kipling's *Kim* (1901),
can be understood to be central to the high point of the Raj and in some
ways to represent it. The masque is a fascinating work of imperialism:
historically illuminating and often musically rich, it is nevertheless a profoundly embarrassing piece—a significant contribution to the orientalized
India of the English imagination.[118] We might hear it, in some ways, as
the realization of British imperialism's cumulative process: the control and
subjugation of India combined with a sustained fascination for all of its
intricacies. As *The Crown of India*'s emphases and omissions suggest, Elgar
not only recognized the nature of imperialism, but also recognized the
situation of the Empire in the early years of twentieth century, when it
began to dawn on the British that India was once independent, that England
now dominated it, and that, in time, growing native resistance to British
rule would inevitably win back India's freedom.[119]

But there is, I think, a larger conclusion. The works of the "real" Elgar
have, for the most part, been received as powerful artistic statements
from the pioneer of English musical nationalism. Yet the critical obsession
with identifying in them an essential Englishness, while ostensibly intended
as an affirmation of their worth, has served only to separate the music from
the mainstream and confine it within the nation's boundaries. That Elgar
has often been drawn on to define England musically has set the limits on
what should—and can—be heard in his music. Reluctance to acknowledge that Elgar's music is imbued with traces of the empire it played a
part in promoting is reflective of a larger and equally counterproductive
unwillingness to understand modern England as having been, in many
ways, shaped by its colonial rule and its colonial Others.

NOTES

I am indebted to Richard Taruskin who helped me at every stage in my examination of Elgar's musical relation to the British Empire. Thanks also to Roger Parker and Bonnie C. Wade for their enormously helpful critical input on an earlier version of this chapter. I am also grateful to Mariane C. Ferme, Paul Singh Ghuman, and the late Edward W. Said for their role in shaping my work on imperialism and music. Thanks also to Byron Adams, Alain Frogley, Mary Ann Smart, and Paul Flight for their suggestions, advice, and encouragement at various stages of my work. Finally, I appreciate the assistance offered to me by staff at the Elgar Birthplace Museum during my research visits there.

1. The *Pall Mall Gazette* from which this essay's epigraph was drawn was found in the cuttings files, Elgar Birthplace Museum, Lower Broadheath, Worcester, vol. 7 (June 1911–June 1914), ref. 1332, 9; hereafter, *EBM Cuttings*.

2. A "Kinemacolour" film of the Delhi Durbar, titled *With Our King and Queen Through India*, was shown in London from February 1912. E. A. Philp, *With the King to India, 1911–12* (Plymouth: Western Morning News Co., 1912); *The Historical Record of the Imperial Visit to India, 1911*, compiled from the official records, with illustrations (London: John Murray, 1914). The "Programme of Ceremonies" is included in *The Delhi Durbar Medal 1911 to the British Army*, ed. Peter Duckers (Shrewsbury: Squirrel Publishing, 1998); John Fortescue, *Narrative of the Visit to India of Their Majesties King George V and Queen Mary and of the Coronation Durbar Held at Delhi 12 December 1911* (London: Macmillan, 1912).

3. N. D. Barton, "The Durbar Ceremonials," in *At the Delhi Durbar 1911: Being the Impressions of the Head Master and a Party of Fourteen Boys of the King's School, Parramatta, New South Wales, Who Had the Good Fortune to be Present (March 1912)*, ed. Stacy Waddy, British Library, India Office: ORW 1989, A.2237, 22–28.

4. Ibid., 71.

5. Gargi Bhattacharyya has observed that the dutiful use of the term *British* rather than *English* glosses over the fact that in power relations there is no difference between them: *British* was imposed by the English on the non-English. For this reason, I generally use these terms interchangeably. "Cultural Education in Britain," from the Newbolt Report to the National Curriculum, in Robert Young, ed., "Neocolonialism," *Oxford Literary Review* 13 (1991): 4–19, 19n.

6. Quoted in Shelland Bradley, *An American Girl at the Durbar* (London: John Lane, 1912), 162–63.

7. The boundaries of the old province of Bengal, those of the provinces in 1905, and the provinces as rearranged in 1911 are shown in *Muir's Historical Atlas—Mediaeval and Modern*, 9th ed., ed. R. F. Treharne and Harold Fullard (London: George Philip and Son Ltd., 1962), 73.

8. For a detailed account of these years, see Nirad Chaudhuri, "Enter Nationalism," *The Autobiography of an Unknown Indian* (1952); repr. in *Modern India: An Interpretive Anthology*, ed. Thomas Metcalf (New Delhi: Sterling Publishers Private Ltd., 1994), 303–22.

9. Barjorjee Nowrosjee, ed., *Cartoons from the "Hindi Punch" 1905* (Bombay: Bombay Samachar Press, 1905), 57.

10. Richard Paul Cronin, *British Policy and Administration in Bengal, 1905–1912: Partition and the New Province of Eastern Bengal and Assam* (Calcutta: Firma KLM Private Ltd., 1977), 207–13.

11. Ibid., 441.

12. Ibid., introduction, in which Cronin analyzes the implications of the partition and its repeal.

13. The London Coliseum program for the opening week of the masque (commencing March 11, 1912) is in the British Library (BL): London Playbills (1908–13), ref. 74/436. Two copies are also held at the Elgar Birthplace Museum: Concert Programmes (Jan–July 1912), ref. no. 1126.

14. *Times*, 9 January 1912, 6.

15. *Daily Telegraph*, 4 March 1912, EBM Cuttings, 16.

16. *Eastern Daily Press*, 24 February 1912, EBM Cuttings, 16.

17. Three photographs from the masque appeared in *The Daily Sketch*, 12 March 1912, 8–9. Illustrations and photographs of the Delhi Durbar abound: see, for instance, John Peeps Finnemore, *Delhi and the Durbar with Twelve Full-page Illustrations in Colour by Mortimer Menpes* (London: Adam and Charles Black, 1912); Sir Stanley Reed, KBE, *The King and Queen in India. A Record of the Visit of Their Imperial Majesties to India, from December 2nd 1911 to January 10th 1912* (Bombay: Bennet, Coleman & Co., 1912); *The Great Delhi Durbar of 1911*, written to accompany a series of lantern slides (1912), BL: 010056.g.26.

18. *The Standard*, 1 March 1912, EBM Cuttings, 16.

19. *The Crown of India: An Imperial Masque*, written by Henry Hamilton, composed by Edward Elgar, op. 66 (London: Enoch & Sons, 1912); BL 11775.h5/2; hereafter, Hamilton, *The Crown of India:* libretto.

20. For a discussion of the motivation behind the transfer of the capital, see Cronin, *British Policy*, 217.

21. Barton, *At the Delhi Durbar 1911*, 75.

22. Such interpretation of pageants, masques, and other imperial entertainments as pieces of popular propaganda dates back to J. A. Hobson, *The Psychology of Jingoism* (London: G. Richards, 1901). For more recent examples of this general view see two important books, John M. MacKenzie, *Propaganda and Empire: The Manipulation of British Public Opinion 1880–1960* (Manchester: Manchester University Press, 1984); and *Imperialism and Popular Culture*, ed. John M. MacKenzie (Manchester: Manchester University Press, 1986).

23. Hamilton, *Crown of India:* libretto, 7 and 18. For detailed analyses of the belief systems that justified the Raj, see Thomas Metcalf, *Ideologies of the Raj* (Cambridge and New York: Cambridge University Press, 1995); and Bernard S. Cohn, *Colonialism and Its Forms of Knowledge: The British in India* (Princeton, N.J.: Princeton University Press, 1996).

24. This was how the *Illustrated London News* described Victoria, Empress of India's rule of India during the 1886 India and Colonial Exhibition, 8 May 1886; quoted in Kusoom Vadgama, *India in Britain: The Indian Contribution to the British Way of Life* (London: R. Royce, 1984), 61. In the masque, these sentiments are echoed by "India" as she pays homage to the King-Emperor and Queen-Empress at their feet; Hamilton, *Crown of India:* libretto, 22.

25. Edward Said, *Culture and Imperialism* (London: Vintage, 1994), 180.

26. Robert Anderson, "Elgar's Passage to India," *Elgar Society Journal* 9, no.1 (March 1995): 15–16.

27. Anderson, *Elgar* (New York: Schirmer Books, 1993), 16–17.

28. Anderson, "Elgar's Passage to India," 16, 19. See also Anderson, "Immemorial Ind," in his *Elgar and Chivalry* (Rickmansworth: Elgar Editions, 2002), 312–13. In addition, Elgar would have come to know of the opulence of Indian arts and crafts from his mother, Ann; Anderson notes that she kept a scrapbook of cuttings that included some on Indian art.

29. Elgar clipped and kept the following announcement in *The Bystander:* "Sir Edward Elgar, strongest and most individual of all English composers, has, by assuming the Order [of Merit], redeemed knighthood from being the charter of mediocrity in music"; 15 November 1911. EBM Cuttings, 1.

30. The presence of Indians living in Britain around the turn of the century, as distinct from the idea of "India" constructed at the exhibitions, was not large. Although no official statistics are available before 1947, the Indian National Congress conducted a survey of "all Indians outside India" in 1932, which estimated 7,128 Indians in the United Kingdom. Some idea of the numbers of Indians in England's cities can be gleaned from these figures: in 1939 the Indian population in Birmingham was about 100, which included some twenty doctors and students; by 1945 it was 1,000. Of professional-class Indians, the largest group was in the medical profession: it is estimated that before 1947 about 1,000 Indian doctors practiced throughout Britain, 200 of them in London. Three Indians/ Pakistanis were elected to the House of Commons between 1893 and 1929. Rozina Visram, *Ayahs, Lascars, and Princes: Indians in Britain, 1700–1947* (London and Dover, N.H.: Pluto Press, 1986), 190–94.

31. The Indian Rebellion (also known as the Indian Mutiny) of 1857, began in Meerut on May 10 and spread quickly to the capture of Delhi by the mutineers. The British slaughtered the mutineers, and this act was celebrated as a victory over native resistance. For many in India, the Mutiny was a nationalist uprising against foreign rule and came to be considered the First War of Independence. An enormous amount of writing, British and Indian, covers this important event; it has been acknowledged as having provided a clear demarcation for both Indian and British history; see, for example, Christopher Hibbert, *The Great Mutiny* (London: Viking 1978).

32. H. Trueman Wood, ed., *Colonial and Indian Exhibition Reports* (London: William Clowes & Sons Ltd., 1887).

33. The 1901 Exhibition, for example, opened May 2 and closed November 9; it covered some 73 acres in Glasgow's Kelvingrove Park. Admission was one shilling, season tickets were one guinea. The attendance figures were 11,497,220; profits were £39,000 (pub. figure of 1905). Free music was a big selling point for the exhibition; Perilla and Juliet Kinchin, *Glasgow's Great Exhibitions* (Bicester: White Cockade, 1988), 15, 87–88.

34. For instance, a complete "Indian City" was erected for the Empire of India Exhibition in 1895. Raymond Head notes that "the apotheosis of the use of an Indian style at an exhibition was at the Franco-British Exhibition in 1908," which featured Mughal or Indo-Saracenic rather than Hindu forms, in *The Indian Style* (London: George Allen & Unwin, 1986), 128–29, 141–42. See also *Franco-British Exhibition Official Guide* (London: Bemrose & Sons Ltd.,1908); F. G. Dumas, *Franco-British Exhibition Illustrated Review* (London: Chatto & Windus, 1908), esp. 295; *Illustrated London News,* 15 June 1901; Imre Kiralfy's notes for his India and Ceylon Exhibition (1896), BL India Office, V 26652, 37–40.

35. John M. MacKenzie discusses these productions in his *Orientalism: History, Theory and the Arts* (Manchester and New York: Manchester University Press, 1995), 194–96; quotation, 196.

36. Imre Kiralfy, *India* (1895), BL1 1779, Kb, folio 5.

37. Ibid., 41. For a more detailed discussion of Kiralfy's *India*, see "The English Musical Renaissance, An(other) Imperial Myth," in A. Nalini Ghuman Gwynne, "India and the English Musical Imagination," Ph.D. diss., University of California at Berkeley, 2003, 25–28; see also MacKenzie, *Orientalism,* 196–97.

38. The reference is to Rudyard Kipling's poem "The White Man's Burden: The United States & The Philippine Islands, 1899" which begins "Take up the White Man's burden / send forth the best ye breed . . . " in *Rudyard Kipling's Verse: Definitive Edition* (Garden City, N.Y.: Doubleday, 1929).

39. Anderson, *Elgar*, 35.

40. *Crystal Palace Programme* and *Guide to the Entertainments*, 1901, BL Miscellaneous Programmes 1898–1923, Shelfmark 341, no. 4. See also Anderson, *Elgar*, 36.

41. Sir Henry Wood recalled the historic Promenade Concert held at the Queen's Hall at which the D major march was premiered and "accorded a double encore": "The people simply rose and yelled. I had to play it again—with the same result; in fact, they refused to let me go on with the programme. . . . Merely to restore order, I played the march a third time." Wood, *My Life of Music* (London: Gollancz, 1946), 154.

42. Quoted in Anderson, *Elgar*, 49–50.

43. Robert Anderson surmises that it was probably Clara Butt (rather than King Edward VII) who suggested the use of the trio tune from *Pomp and Circumstance* March no. 1, in *Elgar*, 53. For further details on such national and imperial occasions as the 1902 coronation, including the Second British Empire Festival of 1911, see Michael Musgrave, *The Musical Life of the Crystal Palace* (Cambridge: Cambridge University Press, 1995), esp. "National and Imperial Festivals," 211–12. See also David Cannadine, "The Context, Performance and Meaning of Ritual: The British Monarchy and the 'Invention of Tradition,' c. 1820–1977," in *The Invention of Tradition*, ed. Eric Hobsbawm and Terrence Ranger (Cambridge: Cambridge University Press, 1983; repr. 1989), 101–64.

44. Tarak Nath Biswas, *Emperor George and Empress Mary: The Early Lives of Their Gracious Majesties the King-Emperor and Queen-Empress of India*, rev. Panchanon Neogi, 4th ed. (London: New Britannia Press, 1921).

45. See Cathy Scott-Clark and Adrian Levy, "Survivors of Our Hell," *The Guardian Weekend*, 23 June 2001, 30–36.

46. Quoted in Anderson, "Elgar's Passage to India," 16.

47. *Daily Telegraph*, 3 February 1912, EBM Cuttings, 11.

48. Letter (January 1912), reproduced in Jerrold Northrop Moore, *Letters of a Lifetime* (Oxford: Clarendon Press, 1990), 242.

49. *The Crown of India: An Imperial Masque*, arranged for the piano by Hugh Blair (London: Enoch & Sons, 1912), 52–64, BL g.1161.e; hereafter, Elgar, *Crown of India:* vocal score.

50. From a report in *The Standard*, 1 March 1912; quoted in Moore, *Edward Elgar: A Creative Life* (Oxford and New York: Oxford University Press, 1984), 629. See also EBM Cuttings, 7.

51. Moore, *Edward Elgar: A Creative Life*, 630.

52. Cited in ibid.

53. *Daily Telegraph*, 9 April 1912, EBM Cuttings, 23.

54. *Daily Express*, 12 March 1912, EBM Cuttings, 18.

55. *Times* (London), 7 March 1912, EBM Cuttings, 15.

56. Franco-British Exhibition held at Shepherd's Bush, London, 1908, *Official Guide*, 47–48.

57. *The Standard*, 1 March 1912; quoted in Moore, *Edward Elgar: A Creative Life*, 629.

58. *The Referee*, 17 March 1912.

59. Excerpts from 1912 reviews in the *Morning Post* (12 March) and the *Daily Telegraph*, 24 February and 12 March, respectively; EBM Cuttings, 17.

60. "Stand Up, Stand Up for Jesus" is another such hymn popular at the time. *Hymns Ancient and Modern Revised* (London: William Clowes and Sons Ltd., 1950), 872–73.

61. Raymond Monk, ed., *Elgar Studies* (Aldershot: Scolar Press, 1990), app. 1 and 4, 16–33.

62. The quotation from "Land of Hope and Glory" appears in St. George's final verse to accompany the words "Dear Land that hath no like!" Elgar, *Crown of India:* vocal score, 61.

63. Gerry Farrell discusses European reactions to kathak in his *Indian Music and the West* (Oxford and New York: Oxford University Press, 1997), 29–30, 54.

64. The O. E. D. definition of *nautch:* "An east Indian exhibition of dancing, performed by courtesans or professional dancing girls." Due to the impact of the anti-nautch movement in 1892, the courtesans who danced traditional kathak were stigmatized as the infamous nautch.

65. Walter Henry Lonsdale, *Nautch Dance* (London: Alphonse Cary, 1896); Frederic H. Cowen, "The Nautch Girl's Song." (London: Joseph Williams & Co., 1901).

66. Edward Solomon, *The Nautch Girl,* comic opera in two acts (London: Chappell & Co., 1891).

67. Richard Burton, *Sindh Revisted: In Two Volumes* (Karachi: Department of Culture and Tourism, Gov. of Sindh, 1993), 2:53.

68. Unidentified review of *The Crown of India* Suite performed at the Proms on September 7, 1912, EBM Cuttings, 41.

69. Rudyard Kipling's "The Ballad of East and West" begins: "Oh, East is East, and West is West, and never the twain shall meet." *Gunga Din and Other Favorite Poems* (New York: Dover Publications Thrift Editions, 1990), 6–9.

70. "Hail, Immemorial Ind!" Elgar, *Crown of India:* vocal score, 21–31.

71. Scene description for *Tableau I,* Hamilton, *Crown of India:* libretto, 3.

72. Hamilton, *Crown of India:* libretto, 5.

73. For a detailed analysis of Agra's song, see "Elephants and Moghuls, Contraltos and G-Strings: How Elgar Got His Englishness," in A. Nalini Ghuman Gwynne, "India and the English Musical Imagination," 134–63.

74. Agra's song and the "Crown of India March" can be heard on *Classico CD 334* (Olufsen Records, 2000); a 1912 recording of the "Crown of India March" by the Black Diamonds Band was released by the Elgar Society, CDAX 8019, 1997. A new edition of the masque has recently been published that includes Henry Hamilton's libretto, the orchestral suite of five numbers from the masque arranged by the composer, the vocal score of the masque, and two numbers reconstructed from the extant orchestral parts: Agra's song, "Hail, Immemorial Ind!," and "Crown of India March." *The Crown of India,* 3rd ed., ed. Robert Anderson (London: Elgar Society, 2005), 18.

75. *The Crown of India* Suite, op. 66, score (Hawkes and Son, H. & S. 4936), BL h.3930.w.(1.); and orchestral parts, BL h.3930 (42). The suite is published in full score by Edwin F. Kalmus & Co.

76. Elgar conducted the London Symphony Orchestra in the suite's premiere at the Three Choirs Festival, Hereford, on September 11, 1912; program held at the Elgar Birthplace Museum, ref. 1037. Elgar used the Anglicized spelling *Mogul,* rather than the correct *Mughal.*

77. See Elgar's letter, 13 August 1930, quoted in Moore, *Elgar on Record: The Composer and the Gramophone* (Oxford: Oxford University Press, 1974), 113. The recordings were made between September 15 and 18 with the London Symphony Orchestra in the Kingsway Hall. The "March of the Mogul Emperors" was recorded, as was the "Menuetto," and the "Warriors' Dance." These were transferred from shellac by A. C. Griffith to LP (RLS 713). The "Introduction" and "Dance of the Nautch Girls" was also recorded. For further details, see Moore, *Elgar on Record,* 114–15. See also the letter from Gaisberg to Elgar, 16 October 1930, in Moore, *Elgar on Record,* 117.

78. Letter from Elgar to Fred Gaisberg, 15 October 1930, in Moore, *Elgar on Record,* 116.

79. Quoted in ibid., 128.

80. *Times* (London), 26 April 1915. This concert is described by Jeremy Crump in "The Identity of English Music: The Reception of Elgar 1898–1935," in *Englishness: Politics and Culture 1880–1920,* ed. Robert Colls and Philip Dodd (London and Dover, N.H.:

Croom Helm, 1986), 164–90, 173. The event was, perhaps, an attempt to bolster public morale during the war years, at a time of increasing pressure for conscription; Crump suggests that the concert was "an apotheosis of self-confident militarism."

81. British Empire Exhibition pamphlet no. 7: *Pageant of Empire* Programme—Part II July 21–Aug 30 1924 (Fleetway Press Ltd., London), Elgar Birthplace Museum Concert Programmes 1912, Ref. 1126: 5. The oft-quoted letter that Elgar wrote to Alice Stuart-Wortley deploring the vulgarity of the event might suggest the composer's renunciation of overt celebrations of the British Empire. See Jerrold Northrop Moore, ed., *Edward Elgar: The Windflower Letters. Correspondence with Alice Caroline Stuart Wortley and Her Family* (Oxford: Clarendon Press, 1989), 289–90.

82. I have not been able to locate a score of *Indian Dawn*, nor find any further references to it.

83. Similarly, Samuel Coleridge-Taylor's *Bamboula* represented South Africa in the pageant, along with Hamish McCunn's *Livingstone Episode*, Elgar's "The Cape of Good Hope," "Dutch Boat Song," and "Old 'Hottentot' Melodies," et al. Uday Shankar came to London in 1920 to study art; his father, Shyam Shankar produced an Indian ballet in London in 1924 in which Uday danced. Ravi Shankar, *My Music, My Life* (New York: Simon & Schuster, 1968), 63.

84. "Elgar's New Masque," *Daily Telegraph,* 24 February 1912, EBM Cuttings, 15.

85. Michael Kennedy, "Elgar the Edwardian," in Monk, *Elgar Studies,* 116–17; and Kennedy, notes to CD Hamburg Deutsche Grammophon 413 490–2 (1982) that includes the *Enigma* Variations, *Pomp and Circumstance* March, op. 39, along with the *Crown of India* Suite, Leonard Bernstein.

86. Stanley Sadie, ed., *The New Grove Dictionary of Music and Musicians,* 2nd ed. (London: Macmillan, 2001), 8:125.

87. *Hindu Marches* by Raymond Roze and Sellenick, 1899. Many other pieces are "Indian" marches in all but name, such as Edward Clarke's "Song of the Indian Army" to words by B. Britten (London: F. Moutri, 1859). Carl Bohm's *Miniature Suite* for piano includes an "Indian March" (Leipzig: Arthur P. Schmidt, 1907). See also Austin C. Ferguson's *Indian Wedding March* for piano (London: West & Co., 1914); and John Faulds, *The Indian: Grand March* for piano (London: E. Marks & Sons, 1913). The spelling of the composer's name here is not one John Foulds (1880–1939) seems ever to have used, unless it is an error. Foulds scholar Malcolm MacDonald states that, as far as he is aware, there is no mention of such a piece in Foulds's work lists, and that no work of Foulds is known to have been published by Marks & Son (personal correspondence, 25 May 2006). Foulds did, however, write a "Grand Durbar March" in 1937 when he was in India, which is a suggestive parallel.

88. Along with other Indian exotica, this piece is discussed in Derek B. Scott, *The Singing Bourgeois: Songs of the Victorian Drawing Room and Parlour* (Milton Keynes: Open University Press, 1989), 177–78.

89. John Pridham, *The Prince of Wales Indian March* (London, 1876) and *General Roberts' Indian March* (London, 1879). Other examples include Stephen Glover's *The Fall of Delhi* "characteristic march for the pianoforte" (London, 1857) BL h.745 (5), and *The Oriental March of Victory* (London, 1858), BL h.745 (9).

90. Thomas Boatwright, *Indian March: The Diamond Jubilee* (London: Klene & Co., 1898): BL g.605.k (1). See also Richard F. Harvey, *The Royal Indian March* for piano (London: Francis Day & Hunter, 1901).

91. "March of the Mogul Emperors" no. 5, *The Crown of India* Suite, op. 66, full score (Miami: Edwin Kalmus & Co.), 35–53. For an artistic and political study of Mughal court culture, see Bonnie C. Wade, *Imaging Sound: An Ethnomusicological Study of Music, Art and*

Culture in Mughal India (Chicago: University of Chicago Press, 1998), which includes an extensive bibliography for further reference.

92. Quotation from Delhi's speech, First Tableau; Hamilton, *Crown of India:* libretto, 12–13. These are four of the great Emperors of the Mughal Dynasty: Akbar (reign: 1556–1605), Jehanghir (r.: 1605–27), Shah Jahan (r.: 1627–58), and Aurangzeb (r.: 1658–1707). After the last Mughal emperor, Bhadur Shah Zaffar, was exiled to Rangoon, Burma (now Yangon, Myanmar) in 1858 following his post-Rebellion capture by the British, a formal end was declared to the Mughal Dynasty (that began with Babur in 1526). The title of Emperor of India was eventually taken over by the British monarch (in 1877), in the person of Queen Victoria, and held until India won independence from Britain in 1947.

93. The Kipling quotation, from his poem "A Song of the White Men," reads: "Oh, well for the world when the White Men tread / Their highway side by side!" *Verse* (Garden City, N.Y.: Doubleday, 1954), 280.

94. A five-movement orchestral suite was extracted from *Mlada* in 1903 and published the next year. Including a suggestively titled "Indian Dance," Rimsky-Korsakov's suite concludes with the grand "Procession of the Nobles."

95. For a detailed tracing of the history of the polonaise in Russia, see Richard Taruskin, *Defining Russia Musically* (Princeton, N.J.: Princeton University Press, 1997), 281–91.

96. Elgar certainly knew Rimsky-Korsakov's music: he had conducted the *Fantasia on Serbian Themes* and the suite from *The Snow Maiden* in 1899. Monk, *Elgar Studies,* App. 2, 25.

97. "India," part of "Greater Britain," *The Sketch* 17, no. 221 (21 April 1897): 556–57. Images of Ganesh, the elephant-headed god of the Hindu pantheon, also contributed to *The Sketch*'s representation of India.

98. Such imagery endures: the cover of Sony's 1992 recording of *The Crown of India* Suite (SBK 48265) features a painting of finely decorated elephants carrying Akbar and his cohorts who are engaged in military activities using ornate swords and shields. The painting *Akbar, Grossmogul von Indien (1542–1605),* is in the Archiv für Kunst und Geschichte, Berlin.

99. *Musical Times* 53, no. 836 (1 October 1912): 665–66; *The Referee* similarly spoke of "a touch of the barbaric appropriate to the situation" in the "March of the Moghul Emperors" (17 March 1912), EBM Cuttings, 19.

100. Cecil Gray, *A Survey of Contemporary Music* (London: Oxford University Press, 1924), 78–79.

101. F. H. Shera, *Elgar: Instrumental Works* (London: Oxford University Press, 1931), 6.

102. Ronald Taylor, "Music in the Air: Elgar and the BBC," in *Edward Elgar: Music and Literature,* ed. Raymond Monk (Aldershot: Scolar Press, 1993), 337.

103. Ibid., 336.

104. Alex Cohen, "Elgar: Poetic Visions and Patriotic Vigour," *Radio Times,* 2 December 1932, 669.

105. Ibid., 669.

106. Crump, "Identity of English Music," 184.

107. Ibid., 184.

108. Ibid., 181.

109. Ernest Newman in the *Sunday Times* (25 February 1934); quoted in Crump, "Identity of English Music," 180.

110. Frank Howes, "The Two Elgars," *Music and Letters* 16, no. 1 (January 1935): 26–29.

111. A. J. Sheldon, *Edward Elgar* with an introduction by Havergal Brian (London: Office of "Musical Opinion," 1932), 16.

112. Howes, "Two Elgars," 26–29.

113. A recent manifestation of this is Roger Scruton's *England: An Elegy* (London: Chatto and Windus, 2000), which, as its title suggests, mourns the loss of "traditional val-

ues" associated with Victorianism while celebrating "the virtues of England" (preface). Elgar's music, along with that of other supposed purveyors of English pastoralism, is called on as a witness of the now-lost Golden Age: "Hardy, Housman and Edward Thomas; Elgar, Vaughan Williams and Holst, offer the last united invocations of a regional England, in which people were united by the history that divided them. . . . Theirs was a country of varied agriculture and localised building types, of regional accent and folk song, of local fairs and markets and shows." (183).

114. Jeffrey Richards, "Elgar's Empire," in *Imperialism and Music: Britain 1876–1953* (Manchester and New York: Manchester University Press, 2001), 44–87; 45. Richards goes on to reveal his desire to exculpate imperialism from its driving force: profit. Thus, like those Elgar scholars he so readily criticizes, he tries to save Elgar from himself, in this instance by claiming that (British) imperialism was "altruistic," (53) and that it was "the noble vision at the heart of British imperialism" (84) that inspired Elgar: "The problem is that people have misunderstood the meaning of imperialism, equating it with jingoism and exploitation. To apply the term 'jingoistic' to Elgar's work is to misunderstand his view entirely. His critics should have had more confidence in Sir Edward. Elgar's vision of Empire was clearly set out at the end of *Caractacus:* it is a vision of justice, peace, freedom and equality, of the pax Britannica—and of the fulfillment by Britain of its trusteeship mission, to see the countries in its charge brought safely and in due course to independence—a far from ignoble dream." (51). Actually, the facts are quite to the contrary—far from other people having misunderstood imperialism, it is Richards himself who has failed to grasp the driving force of imperialism, concentrating merely on the pillars of arguments that were constructed to support the colonial enterprise, and which have been laid bare by a generation of postcolonial scholars. Moreover, far from Britain "bringing [them] safely and in due course to independence," all colonized peoples have fought for their independence, many for over half a century and with considerable loss of life, before forcing the British to leave (especially India, which fought for over fifty years for its freedom).

115. The most recent volume that contributes to the revisionist Elgar-bild is *The Cambridge Companion to Elgar,* ed. Daniel M. Grimley and Julian Rushton (Cambridge: Cambridge University Press, 2004), see esp. the editors' introduction, 1–14. See also the two books edited by Raymond Monk, *Elgar Studies* and *Edward Elgar: Music and Literature;* Charles Edward McGuire, "Functional Music: Imperialism, the Great War, and Elgar as Popular Composer," in *Cambridge Companion to Elgar,* 214–24; Byron Adams, "The 'Dark Saying of the Enigma': Homoeroticism and the Elgarian Paradox," in *Queer Episodes in Music and Modern Identity,* ed. Sophie Fuller and Lloyd Whitesell (Urbana: University of Illinois Press, 2002), 216–44; Stephen Banfield, "Three of a Kind: Elgar's Counterpoint," *Musical Times* 140 (Summer 1999): 29–37; Michael Allis, "Elgar and the Art of Retrospective Narrative," *Journal of Musicological Research* 19 no. 4 (2000): 289–328; Crump, "Identity of English Music," and John Gardiner, "The Reception of Sir Edward Elgar, 1918–1934: A Reassessment," *Twentieth Century British History* 9 (1998): 370–95.

116. Alain Frogley, "Rewriting the Renaissance: History, Imperialism, and British Music Since 1840," *Music and Letters* 84, no. 2 (May 2003): 241–57, 252.

117. Said, *Culture and Imperialism,* 39. An entirely contrary tendency, involving the celebration of imperialism and its orientalist works, is visible in the recent work of a number of writers including Richards, "Elgar's Empire" (see n. 117); MacKenzie, who tries to resurrect a respectable face for orientalists of all kinds in his book *Orientalism: History, Theory and the Arts;* James Day, who celebrates the "noble" empire he hears in Elgar's music, in his book *"Englishness" in Music: From Elizabethan Times to Elgar, Tippet and Britten* (London: Thames Publishing, 1999); David Cannadine, who attempts to erase race from the imperial equation in his book *Ornamentalism: How the British Saw Their Empire* (London: Allen Lane, 2001); Bernard Porter, who concludes that "imperialism was a veneer," not only for

Elgar but, he suggests, also for Britain in general, in his "Elgar and Empire: Music, Nationalism and the War," in *"Oh My Horses!": Elgar and the Great War,* ed. Lewis Forman (Rickmansworth: Elgar Editions, 2001), 133–73, 162; and Scruton, who, in his recent article "Islam and Orientalism," claims that "we" should acknowledge that "Eastern cultures owe a debt to . . . those noble orientalists [who undertook] the task of rescuing a culture other than their own." *The American Spectator,* May 2006, 10–12. This tendency began in the 1980s: Salman Rushdie has argued that the vogue of "Raj revivalism" in that decade—the period of such films as *A Passage to India* and *Gandhi,* and of the televised serialization of M. M. Kaye's *The Far Pavilions* and Paul Scott's *Raj Quartet*—was an attempt to restore the prestige, if not the reality, of the British Empire; see his "Outside the Whale," in *Granta* 11 (1984): 125–38; repr. in *Imaginary Homelands: Essays and Criticism 1981–1991* (New York and London: Granta Books, 1991), 87–101.

118. Francis G. Hutchins analyzed the orientalizing of India in his *The Illusion of Permanence: British Imperialism in India* (Princeton, N.J.: Princeton University Press, 1967).

119. Even though Elgar, along with many of his generation, may have resisted this reality, India had been engaged in a dynamic of opposition to colonial rule from the First War of Independence in 1857, with the first Indian National Congress established in 1885 and the Swadeshi, or home rule movement, in 1905.

Working the Crowd:

Elgar, Class, and Reformulations of Popular Culture

at the Turn of the Twentieth Century

DEBORAH HECKERT

Opened in 1904 by the visionary impresario Oswald Stoll, the London Coliseum was arguably the most opulent of the Edwardian music halls. It had a particularly unusual feature: an enormously expensive conveyance christened the "King's Car." This clumsy, elephantine contraption was a lavishly decorated anteroom on wheels that ran for twenty-six yards on a series of tracks; it was designed to whisk the king and his guests from their carriages directly through a special Royal Entrance to the door of his box. Thus His Majesty would not have to mingle with—or indeed, so much as glance at—any of his subjects. Instead, unsullied by propinquity to the lower classes, the monarch could partake of an entertainment only recently beginning to distance itself from working-class associations. In his lively history of the London Coliseum, *The House That Stoll Built,* Felix Barker relates the tragicomic fate of the King's Car:

> The only recorded occasion on which this unique piece of transport had a chance to prove itself came on a visit by Edward VII. This was shortly after the opening of the theatre, and was the first visit ever paid by a member of the Royal Family to a variety theatre. The royal party climbed in, the manager gave the signal. But instead of moving softly along its tracks, the car stayed quite still. The King passed it off as a joke, but the car never recovered from the disgrace.

Covered in ignominy, the King's Car was banished to the Stoll Theater where it gathered dust until it was eventually converted into a supplemental box office during the 1920s.[1]

Figure 1. An early photograph of the King's Car at the London Coliseum.

Elgar, too, might have wished for a hermetically sealed (or hermeneutically sealed) "Composer's Car" to whisk him through the portals of his fraught interactions with the popular culture of his day. For the composer's engagements with mass culture—and the attendant accusations of "vulgarity" leveled at him by elitist critics—have raised some of the most problematic questions in the study of Elgar reception by both his contemporaries and later commentators.[2] Since the topic of Elgar's relationship to popular culture is extraordinarily complex, this essay seeks to explore ways in which envisioning Elgar crossing the Coliseum's threshold might open the doors for an investigation of the popular, vulgar spaces available to artists during the fin de siècle. Barry J. Faulk and others have argued that new forms of entertainment arising in the late nineteenth century allowed for the transcending of class barriers. In marked contrast to the dubious working-class entertainments of the mid-Victorian period, widely considered by the authorities to be socially disruptive and unsuitable, a new version of popular culture developed as part of a bourgeois field of activity.[3] By turning a critical eye on Elgar's participation in the popular culture of his era, we may well arrive at a clearer understanding of his engagement with modernity.

For Elgar, who reached the height of his fame in the early years of the twentieth century, an aspect of being a "modern" composer was to step boldly into the arena of mass popular culture, especially as the "popular" had gained new respectability due to its associations with the genteel middle classes. Given Elgar's family background, his alliance with the middle class was a comfortable and natural step up in social status. Elgar's father was a provincial piano tuner and freelance musician who raised himself from working class to the lower-middle class by going into trade as part owner of a music shop in Worcester. Despite Elgar's marriage to a woman who enjoyed a markedly higher social status and his subsequent conflicted attempts to play the county gentleman, the composer was forever branded by some denizens of upper-class society as a social climber from the lower-middle class.[4] The extent to which Elgar's biographers dwell on the class conflicts inherent in his career and character attests to the centrality of this issue. Positioning Elgar against the backdrop of a newly respectable and increasingly uniform middle-class version of mass culture now helps us gain insight into a whole range of Elgar's compositions that were regarded, in his lifetime and after, as problematic because of their supposed vulgarity. A partial list of such "vulgar" scores might include the *Pomp and Circumstance* marches and the many works designed to celebrate coronations and other civic occasions; "salon" music, such as *Salut d'amour;* and much of the incidental music written for theatrical productions. All of this music may be viewed, as it is by Charles Edward McGuire, as "functional music."[5] By composing functional music that appealed to an expanding bourgeois audience, Elgar demonstrated that he was a savvy professional who accurately assessed the possibilities, fiscal and otherwise, that popular culture offered to a British composer during the first decade of the twentieth century.[6]

A prerequisite to gaining greater insight into this phenomenon is an exploration of the times and places in which Elgar purveyed music to the masses. Such an investigation must take place on multiple planes, encompassing both the metaphorical and the concrete. An apt place to begin is in the music halls (also known as "variety palaces" or "variety theaters"), which functioned, as noted above, as prominent *loci* of popular entertainment in the years preceding the First World War. The culture of the music halls has recently attracted a lively amount of attention from historians who study the rise of popular culture, but Elgar's place in this milieu has rarely been examined in depth.[7]

In 1912, Elgar composed a spectacular masque, *The Crown of India,* op. 66. By creating this piece of functional music, the composer passed the threshold of more than the Coliseum, for he also entered into a metaphorical space understood at the time as "modern." Furthermore, in that same step, he traversed a series of class boundaries: the slumming royals, the boisterous working classes, and the respectable bourgeoisie. Recent scholarly work on *Crown of India* rightly investigates its overt imperialistic and orientalist aspects: the score can be viewed as a nexus for issues of national identity and colonial "otherness" that permeated British cultural productions during the late-Victorian, Edwardian, and, indeed, Georgian, eras. Nalini Ghuman, for example, offers an insightful exploration of the imperialist underpinnings of *Crown of India* in her essay "Elgar and the British Raj: Can the Mughals March?" in this volume. These accounts present a fascinating picture of how the details of the music and production commingled to uphold a set of musical and dramatic conventions that served to encourage (and maintain) the then popular ideologies of empire. Instead of viewing the score through the lens of colonial studies, however, this essay concentrates on the particularly modern artistic and public stance that Elgar adopted in exploiting imperialist tropes within the larger contexts of audience and mass culture.

The Crown of India as Popular Entertainment

The commission for the *Crown of India* masque came from impresario Oswald Stoll, who sought Elgar's prestige and popularity for the London Coliseum in order to celebrate the state visit of King George V to India in December 1911.[8] Stoll planned a sumptuous production for the Coliseum, with a budget of over £3,000 for fabulous costumes and elaborate sets. He hired popular actors and actresses, including the celebrated Nancy Price in the role of "India" (figures 2a and 2b).

The elaborate libretto was concocted by the playwright and littérateur Henry Hamilton. His text for *Crown of India* exalted British colonial power as if it were still at its historical peak rather than already in the process of an inexorable decline. (Nalini Ghuman has provided a synopsis of Hamilton's libretto in her discussion of *Crown of India*.) Not content to fill the stage with the several groups of dancers, personifications of cities, and the putative national characteristics of both Britain and India, Stoll crowded in courtiers, soldiers, attendants, pages, natives, and a multitude of "etceteras," providing an opulent visual display that played directly to his public's colonialist fantasies. In Stoll's vision, India was characterized as an exotic dreamland firmly controlled by a benign British military, abetted by commercial interests. India was therefore controlled within the space of the theater by the modern gaze of an audience of British consumers.

Figures 2a and 2b. Publicity stills of
Nancy Price as India from the Coliseum
production of *The Crown of India*.

For this spectacle, designed to cater to the longings of the newly emerging lower-middle and middle classes, Elgar created a richly varied score:
introductions, melodramas to support speeches, songs, interludes, and
marches that reflect the stereotyped characteristics of an orientalist mode.
These sections mined musical representations of non-Western locales that
were used throughout the nineteenth century and into the early twentieth.[9]

Such characteristics—including discreet chromaticism, "exotic" percussion, and piquant harmonies—had long been exploited by British composers who specialized in short, light orchestral works often featured prominently in concert halls such as the Crystal Palace. Such exotic tropes are also found in music for the theater, both serious and comic, and above all in the extensive corpus of parlor songs with orientalist lyrics, such as Amy Woodforde-Finden's famous "Kashmiri Song."[10] In *Crown of India*, these standard elements of exoticism emerge in music designed to characterize the "East," whereas British characters are portrayed through hearty diatonic tunes.

Once the score was complete, Elgar threw himself enthusiastically into preparations for the premiere.[11] He conducted cast rehearsals, both for the chorus and the soloists, often as accompanist at the piano. He rehearsed the pit orchestra as well. During the first two weeks of the run, Elgar conducted two performances of the masque daily, and often called additional rehearsals as needed. This tremendous effort exhausted the aging composer and, by its end, exacerbated an inner ear problem that ultimately required a stay in a nursing home.[12]

Crown of India was first performed on March 11, 1912; Elgar's participation in its run ended on March 23 (figures 3a and 3b). The production was unquestionably a commercial success. Nevertheless, some critics at the time—and several commentators since—considered it beneath a composer of Elgar's stature: the creation of such a frankly commercial score could not be received with universal approbation.[13] Concerns about the composer's involvement in a populist spectacle were voiced by a reporter who interviewed him for the *Standard* just before the premiere of *The Crown of India*. In response, Elgar mounted a public defense:

> Sir Edward Elgar would commit himself to no special opinion regarding his first definite contribution to the programme of a big music-hall. "It is hard work, but it is absorbing, interesting," he said, during pause in the proceedings. "The subject of the Masque is appropriate to this special period in English history, and I have endeavoured to make the music illustrate and illuminate the subject."[14]

Elgar's statement reads as a thinly veiled attempt to give the commission greater dignity through an appeal to patriotism. However, the composer's motives for accepting such commercial projects were more personal in nature.

In his account of the period from 1910 to 1912 when the masque was composed, Jerrold Northrop Moore reveals Elgar's anxiety over his persistent financial difficulties, especially the debts accrued through the

Figure 3a. A playbill publicity insert for the
Coliseum production of *The Crown of India*.

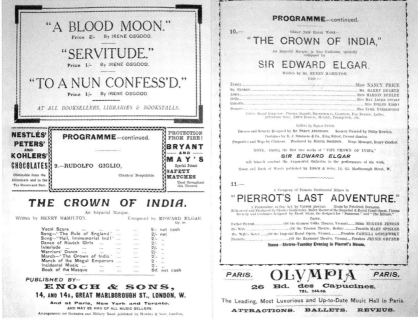

Figure 3b. A program for an evening at the Coliseum in March 1913, including
The Crown of India.

composer's ill-considered move into Severn House, a large and expensive edifice in Hampstead. Stoll's lavish budget for the masque included a sizable fee for the composer, with additional funds for Elgar if he agreed to conduct it during the first two weeks.[15] Elgar wrote a somewhat defensive letter to Frances Colvin outlining the fiscal benefits of the masque:

> When I write a big serious work e.g. Gerontius we have had to starve & go without fires for twelve months as a reward: this small effort allows me to buy scientific works I have yearned for & I spend my time between the Coliseum & the old bookshops . . . Also I can more easily help my poor people [his brother and sisters' families]—so I don't care what people say about me—the real man is only a very shy student & now I can buy books. . . . I go to the N. Portrait Gallery & can afford lunch—now I cannot eat it. . . .
>
> My labour will soon be over & then for the country lanes & the wind sighing in the reeds by Severn side again & God bless the Music Halls![16]

Whether the money was spent on such purchases, or whether Lady Elgar used it to pay the servants' salaries at Severn House, is unknown.

Although the pecuniary rewards of such popular commissions obviously held their appeal for Elgar, he also respected his colleagues at the Coliseum. The timing of the *Crown of India* commission was suspiciously apposite, as Stoll's extensive connections in society may have let him hear rumors of the composer's unstable finances. Stoll was well-known for his successful approaches to "serious" music and theatrical personalities, overtures that were timed to coincide with periods when these artists were short of ready money.[17] Stoll's shrewd premise was that once the great and good, baited by cash, encountered the Coliseum's high artistic standards and respectability, they would become advocates.[18] Clearly, Stoll's strategy worked with Elgar: in the letter to Colvin quoted above, Elgar also wrote, "It's all very curious & interesting & the *people* behind the scenes so good & so desperately respectable & so honest & straight-forward—quite a refreshing world after Society—only don't say I said so."

The obvious financial rewards of this commission were clearly not the only inducement for Elgar. As Corissa Gould has observed, he had no qualms about turning down commissions he did not feel suited his temperament, either musical or ideological.[19] Rather, Elgar and his wife enjoyed the Coliseum. During the production's run, Alice Elgar, whose standards of propriety were high indeed, repeatedly took friends and family to the Coliseum to view the entertainment.[20] She wrote proudly in letters and diaries of the glories of the production and her husband's music in a way that strongly conflicts with the notion that either Edward or Alice was embarrassed by the composer's involvement with the Coliseum.[21] Indeed, Elgar relished attending the Coliseum over the years: seeing a performance there of the ballet *Little Boy Blue* danced by Anton Dolin and Ninette de Valois inspired the composer to send Dolin his *Nursery Suite* to choreograph as a ballet.[22] In 1918 Elgar wrote another work for Stoll and the Coliseum, *Fringes of the Fleet,* a setting of verse by Rudyard Kipling. In producing works for the Coliseum and its mass audiences, then, Elgar sought to fulfill at least part of what he conceived to be his responsibility as a modern British composer.

The Nineteenth-Century Music Hall

If neither Elgar nor his wife were embarrassed by the composer's sally into Stoll's Coliseum, then we should not be surprised at the imperialist ideology embedded in his music hall pieces. Recent investigations by Dave Russell, Penny Summerfield, and Peter Bailey have shown that jingoistic sentiment— a chauvinistic celebration of the British Empire—was an essential feature of a successful music hall revue.[23] New data on the content of music hall acts reveal that the sorts of imperialist ideologies represented by *Crown of India* were present even in the performances by comic singers in working-class variety palaces. Imperialism was therefore joined inextricably with popular culture in late-Victorian, Edwardian, and Georgian music halls. The songs of the music hall stars were at times ambivalent about particular aspects of Britain's imperialist ambition and the impact of empire building on the lives of workingmen and women, especially during the Second Boer War. Overall, however, support for Britain and its empire, found in overt displays of patriotic sentiment, was a signal way in which the music halls managed to create a unified audience from a disparate group of spectators across a spectrum of class backgrounds.

But even as positive sentiments toward imperialism seemed to transgress the class boundaries of fin-de-siècle Britain and imply some sort of unity between these classes, the reality was that class distinctions were sharply drawn even within the walls of the music halls—as the very existence of the King's Car suggests. Any reading of the popular culture found in the middle-class Edwardian and Georgian music halls must take into account the populist (and at times rowdy) characteristics of the earlier incarnations: the variety palaces that flourished during the second half of the nineteenth century that were also known as the "late-Victorian" or "working-class" music halls.

During the transition between the Victorian and Edwardian eras, the "new" and "modern" music halls (as well as other emerging forms of mass entertainment) provoked both fascination and anxiety on the part of contemporary commentators. Such commentators lacked an adequate frame in which to position inherited attitudes against the onrush of modern influences. Since the general populace enjoyed a previously unknown amount of leisure time, access to early twentieth-century sites promoting popular entertainments increased. These venues were surrounded by anxieties emanating from late-Victorian attitudes toward social control. Music and music making were particularly implicated in Victorian strategies for controlling the actions and attitudes of society, especially those of the working class.

Music was securely bound to the Victorian ideal of "moral uplift." Victorians of the ruling class sought to use didactic imperatives to support the continuance of a class-based system; in this context they tried to control the putatively undisciplined and volatile working classes through the medium of an artistic culture imposed from above. The result was an attempt to denigrate—or at times erase—popular music making that originated from within the working classes themselves. But for all the Victorian rhetoric of disapproval, which was often a nostalgic attempt to deny contemporary reality, popular music that arose from the working classes forced its way into visibility within institutions that were valued as modern. To the Victorians, the music halls represented a dangerous but enticing brand of modernity.[24]

One British artist who celebrated the music halls was the painter Walter Sickert (1860–1942), who created several canvases dating from the 1890s that portray the variety palaces in ways that suggest their modernity.[25] Sickert's writings frequently valorized the music hall as an appropriate topic for the modern artist, and he practiced what he preached.[26] Sickert was particularly drawn to the lively music halls in Islington and Camden; his nocturnal jaunts were habitual and became legendary, since he walked miles to attend these variety palaces, returning late at night on foot to his residence in the much more exclusive suburb of Hampstead.

Sickert's keen, unsentimental eye is evident in such paintings as *The P.S. Wings in the O.P. Mirror*. (Sickert's title alludes to the "prompt side" and "off prompt" side of the stage.) In this canvas, a reflecting mirror separates the space of the painting into two contrasting perspective planes, heightened by differences in scale (figure 4). Sickert's other music hall paintings present even more of a visual puzzle evoking his multivalent and essentially modern attitude to his subject. Indeed, Sickert's paintings can be viewed as a mirror that reflected, through the use of new techniques such as skewed perspective, the tensions—class, gender, and aesthetic—that arose as the new lower-middle and middle classes began to define themselves within the 1890s variety palaces. An example of Sickert's ingenuity in this regard is his canvas of a lone audience member propped up

Figure 4. Walter Sickert, *The P.S. Wings in the O.P. Mirror.* Rouen, Musée des Beaux-Arts.

against a mirror, which creates a vertiginous array of backdrops, wings, mirrors, and raking perspectives (figure 5). The intricacies of Sickert's paintings constitute an eloquent portrayal of the music hall during the 1890s, as well as how perspectives, both literal and figurative, were changing during this period of transition.

The predecessors to the music halls that Sickert painted in the 1890s were various kinds of public meeting places that combined drinking and music, such as the supper club and music-licensed taverns. Music halls as such did not appear until the 1850s.[27] During the 1860s, they multiplied until there were over three hundred such establishments in greater London alone. By the early 1870s, music halls had assumed a regular design: a proscenium arch marking a definitive stage area, bars serving alcohol at the back of the hall, and frequently a promenade area where men and prostitutes might open negotiations.

The Oxford Music Hall was the most notorious of these establishments. When it came time to renew its license, this particular hall served as a target for attacks by several organizations dedicated to the preservation of public morality; these attacks represented just a few of the many overt attempts to close or constrain these variety theaters.[28] Perceived as contested sites of modernity as well as immorality, the music halls and the debates that swirled around them reflected larger ideological concerns that flared up during the 1880s and '90s. These centered on the dangers of popular culture and the frightening instability of the urban working classes.

By the 1890s, music halls had sprung up in London's suburbs such as Camden Town and Islington—the halls frequented by Sickert—as well as in the new theater and entertainment district around Leicester Square in London's West End.[29] Neighborhoods determined the style of hall; suburban halls catered to the new "clerk" class of the petit bourgeois, a direct result of a dramatic increase in white-collar workers on the lower end of the pay scale. The older, poorer neighborhoods of the East End were home to halls frequented by members of the working class. Larger, more opulent establishments were clustered around Leicester Square and Charing Cross, where proximity to rail stations allowed travelers of all sorts to stop in at the Oxford, the Empire, and the Alhambra—which meant that these halls had to maintain at least a veneer of respectability.

In the early 1890s, these larger venues began to diversify their programs in order to appeal to new middle-class audiences by including variety acts; the Alhambra even made ballets a particular feature of their nightly offerings. However, this high-toned fare was more the exception than the rule; most music halls still appealed predominantly to working-class and lower-middle-class audiences. The success of the halls relied heavily on stars,

Figure 5. Walter Sickert, *Vesta Victoria at the Bedford*. Private collection of
Richard Burrows.

especially comic singers such as Albert Chevalier, Harry Lauder, Marie Lloyd, and Katie Lawrence. Their songs were popularized not only by performances in the halls, but through sheet music which sold widely across Britain. A song's success was based solely on the reputation of the star with which it was associated rather than the composer or lyricist. The songs dealt mostly with quotidian topics, some sentimental, most comical, and many pervaded by sly sexual innuendo. These popular songs were designed to mirror the audiences they targeted, treating with humor the trials and tribulations of love, courting, marriage, work, and other subjects. Recent discussions of music hall songs stress their conservative nature: these songs were hardly a call to revolution. Despite this conservatism, the songs nevertheless expressed a particularly working-class perspective that would have been considered modern at the time.

Although it would be a mistake to downplay the wide variety of social, political, and ethnic backgrounds represented by the individuals who made up the music hall audiences—London audiences in particular were notable for their diversity—music hall songs articulated a shared experience, creating both solidarity and camaraderie. The sense of solidarity is attested to by the audience's participation in refrains of their favorite songs, and the give-and-take between audience members and the "Chairman" who acted as a master of ceremonies, as well as with the stars themselves.[30] There were a number of opportunities for an audience to interact with the stars, as these privileged performers appeared more than once during the course of an evening. Acts were paid by the "turn," or appearance onstage, and only established stars would perform more than one turn a night. The second turn, usually scheduled for around 10 P.M., was always the most desirable, since it was then that the hall had the largest audience, as opposed to the first turn at 8 P.M. and the third at midnight.

Another reason for the music hall's popularity among working-class clientele was the relatively cheap admission prices: a seat in the stalls by the Chairman's table cost two shillings, a seat in the gallery a mere sixpence. Furthermore, an audience member could get back in drink half the cost of admission. With prices like these, affordable even to a member of the urban working class, it is unsurprising that the music halls were hugely popular, sometimes with nearly a thousand people crowding into the theater.

But as the popularity of the music halls rose in the 1880s, so did governmental fears about the putatively deleterious effects of such raucous and risqué entertainments on public morals, and the variety palaces came under a closer scrutiny. Increased governmental intervention resulted in the growth of licensing laws and regulations controlling safety in the halls and the content of variety acts. The mid-to-late 1890s was a transitional period as these new regulations began to take effect. Music hall proprietors, fully cognizant of social pressures—and aware of the profitable potential of more genteel audiences—sought to gentrify their establishments.

Edwardian Reconfigurations

Hastening the changes that occurred during the second half of the nineteenth century, initiatives were made in the early twentieth by newly formed music hall amalgamates to avoid confrontations between theater owners and local governments over the issues of working-class rowdiness, temperance, and prostitution. The key to the success of these initiatives was modification of outdated formulas in order to appeal to a new middle-class clientele. Music hall proprietors shrewdly realized that the most important change needed to cultivate this particular audience was to attract middle-class women. If they could entice middle-class feminine spectators into their establishments, the families of these women would quickly follow. By this time, Stoll's Coliseum, like halls in London's West End, with its "round-the-clock variety" that ran from noon to midnight, was designed specifically to appeal to an audience that included large numbers of women with their families in tow. These respectable audience members were often suburban visitors to London who sought harmless but diverting entertainment on their excursions. Catering to this new kind of audience obviously had an enormous impact on the kinds of acts presented in Edwardian music halls: the Victorian working-class halls' emphasis on the comic solo was sharply reduced, if not eliminated totally, and replaced instead by an array of acrobats, dancers, animal acts, and extended spectacular features that appealed to patriotic sentiment—as in *The Crown of India*.

Given the highly varied composition of the audience on any given night, a convenient fiction was thus perpetrated by the impresarios and amalgamates who had a financial stake in the success of the variety palaces: an imaginary audience consisting entirely of middle-class families. This construct, at odds with reality, proved powerful and successful. It was attractive to consumers of all classes who were invested in maintaining a facade of social respectability—especially the lower-middle class aspiring upward. The fiction flattered both the bourgeoisie and those who aspired to be so, and was invoked to determine the acts' content and, by extension, generate ideologies of representation and consumerism.

The result of these reforms was that widely mixed audiences from all strata of the urban and suburban population flocked to the music halls. This diversity was reflected by the wide range of entrance prices, which theoretically made seats available for every income bracket. Along with aristocrats and the bourgeoisie, working-class spectators of both sexes still attended the variety palaces, of course, as well as the grandees who had patronized the *louche* late-Victorian halls.

The theater's cleverly calculated appeal to a decorous, feminized middle class is evident in a brochure published and distributed by Stoll in 1906.[31] Lavishly illustrated, on heavy paper and embellished with gold, the publication concretized in its materials the goals of the management; it was cannily designed to convince a wide audience of the opulence, distinction, "culture," and above all, propriety of the Coliseum (figure 6). But Stoll's genius in promoting this perception of respectability served a related function that further legitimized his claims. Stoll used his advertisements, along with promises of lavish remuneration, in order to woo performers, composers, and artists who normally inhabited the world of high culture, such as Elgar. Like a set of facing mirrors reflecting off each other, the prestigious cultural products of such creators further confirmed the essential respectability and high tone of the Coliseum.

The pamphlet stated that the Coliseum was built "to attract that huge class which believed the variety theatre to be in bad odour and would not in consequence visit it."[32] Much of the brochure is devoted to vivid descriptions of the beauty and tastefulness of the decorations, up-to-date stage machinery, and the Coliseum's restaurants and cafés. The pamphlet forcibly outlined the dramatic changes to the music halls, stating, "It would be very little if the atmosphere and environment had not undergone a similar process of purification. It was desired to make attendance at this playhouse as respectable as going to church."[33] The brochure further claimed that "the Coliseum is like going to a friend's house—everything is so homely and domestic and in good taste" (figure 7).[34] Statements expressing Edwardian and Georgian ideologies of class and gender run through the brochure's text. Moreover, sharp distinctions along class lines between the old music hall—which was "only the resort of a class"— and the modern Coliseum, a "space sufficient for each of the little worlds that go to make up society, each to enjoy equal facilities and, in a way, equal accommodation"[35] (figure 8). Finally, the feminization of this space was linked to the broadening of the audience's class base:

> It must be noticed by all visitors to the Coliseum that its audience is largely made up of women and children, conspicuously in all parts of the house. Society ladies, sitting in the boxes and stalls with their children, have not been quicker to seize the opportunity which are offered for bright, wholesome entertainment than the wives of the

Figure 6. Opening illustration in the publicity publication *To the Coliseum*.

artisan, who, with their numerous progeny, crowd the balconies, proving in the most conclusive manner that the pit is quite as eager and capable as the stalls of responding to a genuinely artistic appeal."[36]

Music was a serious and carefully considered part of the ideological program advanced by Stoll and the management of the Coliseum: "It will surprise the uninitiated to know what infinite pains are taken to promote in the public a love for good music." A considerable amount of space in the promotional brochure was expended on describing the classically trained vocalists in the house choir, the organ and organist, and the quality of the music (figure 9): "It is not a music hall in any acceptance of the term; but a 'music-theatre,' where high-class renderings of the greatest scores may be heard which, aided by the cultured interpretation given them, can be thoroughly enjoyed."[37] The pamphlet specifically mentioned opera scenes presented by the noted diva Alice Estey and a staged excerpt from Gounod's popular *Faust* that had recently been featured at the Coliseum.

Despite such claims, the frequency with which "serious" art music was programmed at the Coliseum was erratic. Stoll's commission of *Crown of India* represented an exception rather than the rule, and Elgar's music was, after all, commissioned to adorn the elaborate libretto rather than as a serious extended piece of music in its own right. At the Coliseum, like most variety palaces, art music was considered just one of the many building blocks used to construct the elaborate edifice of an evening's entertainment. Sometimes these classical selections were unexpected, as when Stoll staged scenes from *Parsifal* during the 1913 season, the first time extended excerpts from Wagner's music drama had been heard in London.[38] In 1912, the year before this excursion into Wagnerian territory, the "Milan Opera" performed Leoncavallo's *I Pagliacci* at the Coliseum. More often, however, scenes and selections from longer works were scheduled as part of the rotation of turns within the three-hour shows, and light orchestral pieces were used as filler. Elgar's *Salut d'amour,* for instance, turns up occasionally on the list of an evening's offerings.[39] It was mainly through the popular ballets that audiences heard music by serious composers, since spectacular ballets and pantomimes—of which *Crown of India* was just one example—were hallmarks of the Coliseum, the Alhambra, and the Empire. For instance, the new revue of January 1913, titled *Keep Smiling*, included an "Assyrian" ballet featuring music by Glazunov, Rimsky-Korsakov, Borodin, Goldmark, Ravel, Arends, and Montague Ring.[40]

The quantity of art music played in the various Edwardian and Georgian music halls is less important than the belief, shared by management and audiences alike, that such high-class works belonged there. At the same

Figure 7. "Domesticity" at the Coliseum—one of the several tearooms.

Figure 8. A view of the Coliseum's auditorium.

Figure 9. The "cultured interpreters" of the Coliseum as "music theater"—the Coliseum choir.

time, audience and management seemed to agree that just a smattering of highbrow music was enough, and such pieces were squeezed in between the acrobats, shadowgraphists, sharpshooters, and comic singers. This unspoken agreement, too, helped to constitute the modern identities of the new music hall audiences.

The presentation of scenes from *Parsifal* is a case in point. This production attracted great attention at the time: the distinguished conductor Henry Wood directed an augmented orchestra; the noted designer Byam Shaw created the sets and costumes; and an elaborate program was printed to provide spectators with the story, background materials, and brief discussion of the selections, all designed to whet their appetite and enhance their enjoyment.[41] But the *Parsifal* excerpts occurred within the context of a normal night out at the Coliseum. The bill began with an overture, followed by Australian dancers, a comic duo, ragtimers, and a female comic singer. The big novelty of the season, the *Parsifal* tableaux, appeared in the spot immediately after intermission. It was followed by a short play with music, Max Pemberton's *David Garrick*. The evening ended with Austrian woodcutters and a "Kinemacolour" presentation. The sequence of turns preceding and succeeding *Crown of India* was similar.[42]

Significantly, a new version of popular culture emerged from these evolving forms of mass entertainment for middle-class audiences. John MacKenzie has asserted that during the Edwardian period intellectual and popular tastes converged to an extent encountered at perhaps no other time.[43] Elgar certainly hoped to appeal to the broadest possible Edwardian audience. By crossing the threshold of the Coliseum, however, Elgar became a pawn in the Edwardian game played by Stoll and other impresarios that sought to efface class distinctions, especially with respect to artistic taste, for commercial gain.

Elgar as "Public Poet"

How might Elgar be positioned as a voice for (or against) this newly emerging popular culture linked to the middle class? J. H. Grainger has identified and characterized the role of the "public poet" during the first decade of the twentieth century, and it may well be useful to imagine Grainger's description as a metaphorical space into which a composer of functional music, such as Elgar, might enter profitably. The role of "public poet" is especially relevant if this composer chose to address the issue of imperialism within the context of mass culture, as Elgar did so conspicuously in *Crown of India*. Grainger has defined the "public poet" as one who

> reminded, reassured, mobilized, sang praises and identified enemies within an objective, easily recognized world. Far from illumining their own subjective wholenesses, they were content to tell men what they already knew. . . . The poet repeatedly affirmed sentiments and told

the tale again and again. As the public poet of a wide successful *imperium* he was not bardic. Bards are for lost or submerged patriae. Yet like the bard he looked for the heroic, the singular in the familiar story, emphasizing not freedom broadening down from precedent to precedent, not the long slow march of everyman, but deeds that made the realm and Empire. . . . The public poet invoked, exhorted, clearing not muddying the springs of action.[44]

Grainger's description of the poet who rehearsed over and over what the people already implicitly felt about England aptly fits much of Elgar's functional music. A persistent demotic attitude characterizes scores, such as *Pomp and Circumstance* March no. 1, as the veritable embodiment of English national identity. It is therefore illuminating to think of Elgar reflexively assuming the voice of a "public poet" in music, one who sings on behalf of his entire nation.[45] With *Crown of India*, Elgar's assumption of a public voice is augmented by the nationalist implications of its genre, that of the "masque."

To have written a masque during the Edwardian period meant that the composer firmly positioned such a work within a venerable and uniquely British tradition stretching back hundreds of years, through Purcell to the Elizabethans. The Edwardian and Georgian masque composers sought to signify "Englishness" musically in ways that gestured toward popular culture, especially in the mediation of traditional components like spectacle and allegory.[46] Many of these elements of the masque are clearly present in *Crown of India;* thus Elgar's entrance into the Coliseum was made through an aesthetic portal provided by a genre that has traditionally linked celebrations of "Englishness" with popular spectacle.

Younger contemporaries of Elgar who also participated in the revival of the masque, such as Ralph Vaughan Williams, were enticed in part by the genre's historical resonances, combining the musical and the literary with the artistic. Vaughan Williams pointedly used the designation "masque" to imply connections between his own music and that of the glorious Tudor past.[47] While this is far from the only reason that he was interested in the genre, part of Vaughan Williams's ambition was to validate certain constructs of British history, such as the glorification of the Elizabethan age. In this way, composers like Vaughan Williams were inoculated to a degree from the contagion of vulgar, popular modernity—the contemporary life that Elgar seemed to promote in accepting the commission for *Crown of India*. But unlike the putatively "historical" masques of his younger colleagues, Elgar's work confronts instead the hunger of the middle class for a reflection of their own concerns. By writing for the Coliseum, Elgar avoided historical nostalgia and instead cultivated the role of the "public poet."

Elgar was usually unwilling to claim explicitly the status of "public poet." He displayed the same ambivalence in this regard as he did for most of the *personae* that he adopted, preferring—especially as he grew older—to let others, such as George Bernard Shaw and Ernest Newman, make such claims on his behalf. Elgar, however, permitted occasional glimpses of his outlook on the relationship he had with the British public. The most famous (or notorious) of these instances occurred during lectures he delivered in 1905 as part of the Peyton Professorship at the University of Birmingham.[48] Among several controversial assertions found in these lectures, Elgar repeatedly criticized those British composers (clearly referring to his archenemy Stanford) who eschewed the challenge of the contemporary through recourse to historical materials. When alluding to the musical glories of the past, he stated unequivocally, "I think it unnecessary to go back farther than 1880." In Elgar's opinion, the trend in English music toward a dry academic historicism—"to sing 'Ca ira, ça ira' chanted to the metrical tune of the 'Old Hundredth'"—would cause irrevocable damage to the development of native art, since from the "big music" of the last twenty-five years "we had inherited an art which has no hold on the affections of our own people." His severest criticism of such music is that it is "commonplace":

> Critics frequently say of a man that it is to his credit that he is never vulgar. Good. But it is possible for him—in an artistic sense only, be it understood, to be much worse; he can be commonplace. Vulgarity in the course of time may be refined. Vulgarity often goes with inventiveness, and it can take the initiative—in a rude and misguided way no doubt—but after all it does something and can be and has been refined."[49]

Obviously, Elgar evinced no distaste of vulgarity per se—by which he meant strong emotion, not the bawdiness of the late Victorian comic song. Instead, he distrusted any music, high or low, that does not engage with its audience, no matter how that audience was constituted. Accusing his more academic colleagues of composing music for one another's delectation, Elgar states forthrightly, "Is it possible to conceive that Bach or Beethoven or Brahms so wrote for a narrow circle? No, they addressed a larger party, a responsive, human and artistic mass, and amongst these we find our greatest supporters." He warned the "youthful English composer" not to "misjudg[e] his own strength—the public his works are to meet: I mean, of course, not that he should compose with a view to please

a certain audience, but he should, on the rare occasions of a performance, choose a work suited to the occasion."[50]

In 1905, there were cogent distinctions to be made about audiences, the
absence of which reveals a certain lack of clarity in Elgar's bold assertions,
as well as his ambivalence about what sort of listeners constituted an audience for meaningful English music. On the one hand, he repeatedly warned
young composers not to pander to the "popular public," but in his lectures he seemed to be concerned with the cynical exploitation of the
wider public just for fame and easy profit.[51] As an alternative to easy
fame, Elgar urged young British composers to imagine an audience consisting of thoughtful people drawn from all walks of intellectual and artistic
life. Yet as some of the assertions quoted above demonstrate, Elgar demanded
that composers take a wider public into consideration as well, even going
so far as to recommend that, in giving "people's" or "cheap concerts,"
organizers should eschew condescension in the selection of repertory:

> *When good music* is offered to the people, there is too much of an atti-
> tude of Sterne about the givers. When Sterne saw the hungry ass—he,
> *after much thought,* gave him a macaroon. His heart, he says, smites
> him that there presided in the act more pleasantry in the conceit of
> seeing how an ass would eat a macaroon than of benevolence in giv-
> ing him one. *Now—the English working-men are intelligent: they do not
> want treating sentimentally,* we must give them the real *thing, we* must
> give them of the best because we want them to have it, not from
> mere curiosity to see HOW they will accept it.[52]

In this quotation, Elgar's remarks demonstrated an implicit tension, if
not contradiction, between Victorian assumptions about what sort of music
was appropriate to each social class and an instinctual realization by the
composer of "Land of Hope and Glory" that the new century had ush-
ered in a decided shift in cultural power. Elgar's assertions also shed light
on his relationship with the Coliseum, as the music halls of the early twentieth century helped to amalgamate the previous disjunctions between
lowbrow and highbrow into a somewhat disjointed but powerful middle-
class cultural aesthetic, that of the "middlebrow." Just like the music halls
that he so enthusiastically blessed in his letter to Colvin quoted earlier,
Elgar self-consciously desired to create a relationship with wider modern
audiences that provided new compositional stances but still maintained an
overarching musical aesthetic aimed squarely at the educated bourgeoisie.

The unresolved tensions and inconsistencies found in Elgar's opinions
have given rise ever since to problematic views concerning the relationship

between Elgar's music and popular culture. For Elgar to have written music
for Stoll's Coliseum was not, as some have suggested since the premiere
of *Crown of India*, merely egregious opportunism by a great composer in
need of ready cash. He did need the money at that point, surely, but as
we have seen, remuneration was not the whole story. Elgar took this compositional opportunity as a means of reaching eclectic new audiences,
and he achieved this goal by assuming the role of a "public poet."

When Elgar strode into the Coliseum, he entered a space peopled in
large part by an exuberant audience who demanded contemporary music
that reflected its concerns. The later reputation of Elgar's popular commercial works, considered in many twentieth-century histories of British
music as subsidiary to his art music, should not blind us to the composer's
personal interest and enthusiasm when he composed *Crown of India* in
1912. Elgar's willingness to adopt a compositional attitude calculated to
appeal to a diverse public—to adopt the emerging popular culture of that
public—was a daring gesture for a serious composer of his time. Taking
their cue from this model, musicologists might profitably explore the different environments, both physical and metaphorical, that Elgar inhabited
and explored throughout his career, positioning them against the rapidly
changing ways by which these spaces were being defined (and redefined)
during the socially transitional years of the Victorian, Edwardian, and
Georgian periods. Such efforts will surely result in a more nuanced view
of the composer and his music, for, beyond the Coliseum, where else can
we find Elgar?

NOTES

I wish to thank Jenny Doctor and Byron Adams for their help and advice
in the course of completing this essay, as well as express gratitude for the
pioneering work of Robert Anderson, Nalini Ghuman, and Corissa Gould
on *The Crown of India*. Also, thanks to the Victoria and Albert Museum for
all the images related to the London Coliseum.

1. Felix Barker, *The House That Stoll Built* (London: F. Muller, 1957), 18. The Coliseum
is now the home of the English National Opera.

2. One notorious example of a musicologist characterizing Elgar's music as "vulgar"
was E. J. Dent's tart opinion of the composer written in 1924 for Adler's *Handbuch der
Musikgeschichte*. Dent's assertions were only seriously challenged when the second edition
of the *Handbuch* appeared in 1930. An anguished cry of indignation was then sounded by
Elgar's defenders. Somewhat unexpectedly, it was the sardonic modernist composer
Peter Warlock who gathered signatures from leading musicians of the day, as well as emi-

nent supporters such as George Bernard Shaw and Augustus John, for an "open letter" of protest praising Elgar. See Robert Anderson, *Elgar* (New York: Schirmer Books, 1993), 167. Dent's opinions are frequently cited in discussions of Elgar's character, popular appeal, and literary pretensions. Brian Trowell neatly summarizes the reception of Dent's comments over the years in his "Elgar's Use of Literature," in *Edward Elgar: Music and Literature,* ed. Raymond Monk (Aldershot: Scolar Press, 1993), 182–287.

3. Barry J. Faulk, *Music Hall and Modernity: The Late-Victorian Discovery of Popular Culture* (Athens: Ohio University Press, 2004). The classic discussion of emerging forms of Victorian leisure activity and the attendant class ideologies remains Peter Bailey, *Leisure and Class in Victorian England: Rational Recreation and the Contest for Control, 1830–1995* (London: Routledge & Kegan Paul, 1978).

4. Most of the current biographies of Elgar discuss this aspect to a greater or lesser extent. An essay by Meirion Hughes offers perhaps the most focused discussion of Elgar's problematic relationship to his family background and subsequent efforts to project a more genteel identity. Meirion Hughes, "The Duc d'Elgar: Making a Composer Gentleman," in *Music and the Politics of Culture,* ed. Christopher Norris (New York: St. Martin's Press, 1989), 41–68.

5. Pertinent chapters on Elgar's functional music found in *The Cambridge Companion to Elgar,* ed. Daniel M. Grimley and Julian Rushton (Cambridge: Cambridge University Press, 2004) include J. P. E. Harper-Scott, "Elgar's Unwumbling: The Theatre Music," 171–84; Charles Edward McGuire, "Functional Music: Imperialism, the Great War, and Elgar as Popular Composer," 214–24; and Diana McVeagh, "Elgar's Musical Language: The Shorter Instrumental Works," 50–62. See also Daniel M. Grimley's essay in this volume.

6. Not that Elgar was alone in this ambition by any means; for instance, his archrival Charles Villiers Stanford also sought to compose popular, lucrative works and succeeded with oft-performed (and patriotic) choral works such as *The Revenge.* See Jeremy Dibble, *Charles Villiers Stanford: Man and Musician* (Oxford: Oxford University Press, 2002), 178–79. Stanford never ventured into the music halls, however.

7. There is a large, fascinating bibliography on the music hall, truly interdisciplinary in the range of fields from which it has emerged. Besides Barry J. Faulk's magisterial book, a list might include the collection of essays *Music Hall: The Business of Pleasure,* ed. Peter Bailey (Milton Keynes: Open University Press, 1986); Dagmar Kift, *The Victorian Music Hall: Culture, Class, and Conflict,* trans. Roy Kift (Cambridge: Cambridge University Press, 1996); and the wonderful section on the music hall in Dave Russell's *Popular Music in England, 1840–1914,* 2nd ed. (Manchester: Manchester University Press, 1997).

8. King George V's Delhi Durbar was a huge event, exciting intense interest in the British media. Part of the royal tour of India, the Durbar was a modern court occasion, when Indian princes assembled to pay homage to the ruler. As an "invented tradition," in Eric Hobsbawm's terms, this sort of ceremony was perfectly geared for the imposition of a new British ruler on Indian soil. For more on the fascinating impact of the event on the imaginations of the British people, and how this was fueled by emerging media technologies, see Corissa Gould, "Edward Elgar, *The Crown of India,* and the Image of Empire," *Elgar Society Journal* 13, no. 1 (March 2003): 25–35.

9. Robert Anderson has recently prepared an edition of the score for the masque for the *Elgar Complete Edition,* vol. 18, (London: Elgar Society with Novello, 2004). Despite the pervasiveness of the exotic idiom in music during the nineteenth century, particularly in Britain, musicological investigations of the ways in which the orientalist impulse mapped onto British musical composition and its reception are relatively limited. Recently there has been a rise of interest. See especially Nalini Ghuman Gwynne, "India in the English Musical Imagination, 1890–1940," Ph.D. diss., University of California, Berkeley, 2003. Jeffrey Richards offers an overview of the subject in *Imperialism and Music: Britain 1876–1953*

(Manchester: Manchester University Press, 2001). Finally, for a pan-European look at critical approaches to the subject of orientalism, see the collection of essays edited by Jonathan Bellman, *The Exotic in Western Music* (Boston: Northeastern University Press, 1998).

10. For a discussion of such songs, see Derek B. Scott, *The Singing Bourgeois: Songs of the Victorian Drawing Room and Parlour,* 2nd ed. (Aldershot: Ashgate Press, 2001), 177.

11. Barker, *House That Stoll Built,* 179.

12. Jerrold Northrop Moore, *Edward Elgar: A Creative Life* (Oxford: Oxford University Press, 1984), 629–30.

13. Diana McVeagh, for example, has characterized the music of *Crown of India* as "trumpery in a colourful and dashing manner." See Diana McVeagh, "Elgar" in *The New Grove Twentieth-Century English Masters,* ed. Stanley Sadie (New York and London: W. W. Norton, 1986), 44.

14. 1 March 1912, as quoted in Moore, *Elgar: A Creative Life,* 629.

15. Gould, "Edward Elgar, *The Crown of India* and the Image of Empire," 25.

16. Letter to Frances Colvin, 14 March 1912, as quoted in Moore, *Elgar: A Creative Life,* 630.

17. Barker, *House That Stoll Built,* 179. In the first three chapters, Barker paints a vivid picture of Stoll's peculiar but successful style of management.

18. Stoll was right: Elgar convinced the actress Mary Anderson to appear at the Coliseum in 1917, citing his own happy experience there; see Barker, *House That Stoll Built,* 135.

19. Gould, "Edward Elgar, *The Crown of India* and the Image of Empire," 29.

20. Both Edward and Alice Elgar may have been further reassured by Stoll's own high standards of respectability, for he neither drank nor smoked and swore only on the rarest of occasions; see Barker, *House That Stoll Built,* 53.

21. Ibid., 27.

22. Anton Dolin, a major star, had been *premier danseur* with the Ballets Russes; see Richard Buckle, *Diaghilev* (New York: Atheneum, 1984), 413ff. For Elgar's interest in having Dolin choreograph his *Nursery Suite,* see Barker, *House That Stoll Built,* 158–59.

23. See Russell, *Popular Music in England, 1840–1914;* and Bailey, *Leisure and Class in Victorian England;* as well as an essay by Penny Summerfield, "Patriotism and Empire: Music Hall Entertainment, 1879–1914," in *Imperialism and Popular Culture,* ed. John M. MacKenzie (Manchester: Manchester University Press, 1986), 17–48.

24. For more on the anxiety over musical halls and their role in working-class life, see Kift, *The Victorian Music Hall: Culture, Class and Conflict,* in particular chaps. 5 ("1860–1877: The Demon Drink") and 6 ("1875–1889: Programs and Purifiers").

25. Walter Sickert was one of the most important British artists in the decades surrounding the turn of the twentieth century. A student of the self-consciously modern Whistler, he came under the influence of Degas and thus was firmly rooted in French Impressionism and committed to the "painting of modern life." Sickert remained a successful artist throughout his life, his style changing with the times, and also was extremely important as a teacher and mentor to younger British artists. For more information about Sickert and his music hall paintings in particular, see David Peters Corbett, "Seeing into Modernity: Walter Sickert's Music-Hall Scenes, c. 1887–1907," in *English Art 1860–1914: Modern Artists and Identity,* ed. David Peters Corbett and Lara Perry (Manchester: Manchester University Press, 2000), 150–67, and *Walter Sickert* (London: Tate Gallery Publishing, 2000). Anne Greutzer-Robins discusses Sickert's knowledge of the music hall scene in "Sickert 'Painter in Ordinary' to the Music Hall," in *Sickert Paintings,* ed. Wendy Baron and Richard Stone (New Haven: Yale University Press, 1992).

26. Walter Sickert, *Writings on Art* (Oxford: Oxford University Press, 1933), 14.

27. Barker, *House That Stoll Built*, 29–30.

28. For the politics and social conditions involved in this contest over relicensing, see Tracy C. Davis, "The Moral Sense of the Majorities: Indecency and Vigilance in Late-Victorian Music Halls," *Popular Music* 10, no. 1 (1991): 39–52. For the Oxford Music Hall controversy, see Faulk, *Music Hall and Modernity*, 75–110. Oswald Stoll's own churchgoing in-laws considered such theaters as "sinful homes of the devil"; see Barker, *House That Stoll Built*, 50.

29. Such "variety palaces" were found in most of the larger towns and cities across England as well as in London.

30. The Chairman played an important role in the music halls until the 1890s, introducing the turns and keeping order; see Barker, *House That Stoll Built*, 30.

31. Anon., *To the Coliseum* (London: Raphael Tuck and Son, 1906).

32. Ibid., 8.

33. Ibid., 6.

34. Ibid., 6

35. Ibid., 3, 7.

36. Ibid., 6

37. Ibid., 18.

38. The timing of these excerpts from *Parsifal* was largely the result of a copyright issue. See Barker, *House That Stoll Built*, 177.

39. For instance, the program on February 9, 1913, was sponsored by the National Sunday League. "A Grand Orchestral Concert with the Meistersingers Orchestra, conducted by Mr. Norfolk Megone. Mix of songs, orchestral favorites, Viennese waltzes, the *William Tell* overture, Elgar's 'Salut d'Amour' and Three Dances from German's *Henry VIII*." The Coliseum program is in the collection of the Victoria & Albert Museum Theatre Archives.

40. I have not been able to trace the identity of the composer "Arends" mentioned in this program. But given the frequent misspellings of the foreign composers' names in ephemeral documents of the time such as this one, it is entirely possible that this composer was actually Anton Arensky, a Russian who had written ballet works in an orientalist vein.

41. The program even included musical examples explicating Wagner's musical dramas. The scenes from *Parsifal* presented:

    1. Killing of the Swan

    1b. Towards the Castle of the Grail

    2. Amfortas Administering the Grail

    3. Ejection of Parsifal from the Castle of the Grail

    4a. The Magic Garden

    4b. The Temptation of Parsifal by Kundry

    4c. Kundry Repulsed by Parsifal

    4d. Parsifal and the Spear

    5. The Overthrow of Klingsor's Splendour

    6. The Flowery Mead

    7. The Healing of Amfortas

    8. Redeeming Love

Coliseum program, March 1913, Victoria & Albert Museum Theatre Archives.

42. On the program: A family of gymnastic equilibrists / Tom Stuart in dramatic and burlesque impressions / Thora, a ventriloquial novelty / Billy Merson, the new London eccentric comedian / Dmitri Andreef, the famous Russian solo harpist / Miss Irene Vanbrugh in J. M. Barrie's "The Twelve-Pound Lock" / Rudolfo Giglio, chanteur napolitain / *Crown of India* / A company of famous Continental mimes in "Pierrot's Last Adventure," with music by Fridrich Bermann and produced by the Viennese ballet master Charles Godlewsky. Coliseum program, March 1913, Victoria & Albert Museum Theatre Archives.

43. John M. MacKenzie, "Introduction," *Imperialism and Popular Culture*, 1–16.

44. J. H. Grainger, *Patriotisms: Britain 1900–1939* (London: Routledge & Kegan Paul, 1986).

45. It is important to emphasize that the voice of the "public poet" was only one of many personae adopted by Elgar, both in his life and works. It is enough to say here that the negation of personal subjectivity, which is in some way demanded by the utterances of the "public poet," was a source of personal conflict for a composer whose work seems in many ways replete with autobiography and self-representation. Few Elgar scholars today, influenced by the seminal work of Jerrold Northrop Moore and Byron Adams, would argue that Elgar could ever project a unitary identity.

46. See Deborah Heckert, "Composing History: National Identity and the Uses of the Past in the English Masque, 1860–1918," Ph.D. diss., Stony Brook University, 2003.

47. Ibid., passim.

48. In 1905, Elgar was offered the new Peyton Chair in Music at the University of Birmingham. Richard Peyton had endowed this position with the stipulation that it would be offered to Elgar. Elgar was not enthusiastic about the offer, worried that his lack of academic credentials made him unqualified for the job, and justly fretted that his busy schedule would be further complicated by the addition of new responsibilities. However, with the creation of the professorship at stake, and with persuasive arguments from friends and colleagues in Birmingham, Elgar accepted the post. Part of his responsibilities included delivering a set of public lectures. Elgar gave seven lectures between 1905 and 1906, many of which proved quite controversial, before his resignation in 1907. See Percy Young's introduction and commentary to Edward Elgar, *A Future for English Music and Other Lectures*, ed. Percy M. Young (London: Dennis Dobson, 1968). See also Moore, *Elgar: A Creative Life*, 446–48, 456.

49. Elgar, *A Future for English Music*, 33, 41, 47–49.

50. Ibid., 37, 89.

51. Ibid., 41–43.

52. Ibid., 213.

Elgar's War Requiem

RACHEL COWGILL

> This is already the vastest war in history. It is war not of nations, but
> of mankind. It is a war to exorcise a world madness and end an age.
> —H. G. Wells, *The War That Will End War*

While Elgar's patriotism and sense of Empire have been treated with considerable insight in recent years, Elgar scholarship seems to have found it
relatively difficult to explore objectively the religious and denominational contexts in which he lived, and their significance or otherwise for
his music.[1] Indeed, in some cases emphasis on the former has obscured
the latter, as with Jeffrey Richards's suggestion that *The Dream of Gerontius*
can be considered an imperialist work on the grounds of Elgar's identification with "the idea of Christian heroism," exemplified by General Gordon
of Khartoum.[2] Where Elgar's Catholicism has been broached in the literature, as Charles Edward McGuire discusses elsewhere in this volume,
there has been a tendency to accept without much question two tropes
that emerged shortly after Elgar's death, which can be seen at least in part
to have originated from remarks made by Elgar himself: the first of these,
that a crisis of faith had rendered religion no longer of significance in his
life (an identity McGuire refers to as the "Weak Faith" avatar); and the
second, that as an English Catholic he had learned to appreciate and
operate within the codes of Protestantism (the "Pan-Christian" avatar). Just
as these avatars arguably offered Elgar himself a means of appeasing his
Protestant countrymen and for dulling his often sharply felt sense of otherness within British society, they have also offered convenient strategies
for his past biographers who perhaps either did not recognize the centrality of religious identity as a social dynamic in British society of the
Victorian and Edwardian eras, reflecting the increasing secularization of
subsequent generations, or whose view of their subject was filtered by a
particular denominational position or personal belief.[3]

Scholars who have tackled the topic of Elgar's Roman Catholicism directly have done so, understandably, in relation to his sacred and organ music.[4] But Elgar's Catholic identity can be seen to have a broader significance both for his art and for its place within English culture, as will be explored here in relation to one of his ostensibly secular vocal works, *The Spirit of England,* op. 80 (1915–17). This is a setting for tenor or soprano soloist, orchestra, and chorus of three poems from *The Winnowing-Fan,* a collection of verse published in the early months of the Great War by the poet, dramatist, and art scholar Laurence Binyon (1869–1943).

In his 1984 study of Elgar's life and works, Jerrold Northrop Moore points to an interrelationship between the themes the composer worked with in his music and his religious beliefs:

> The fortunes of Elgar's faith can be traced in the subjects he chose
> for his major religious choral works, his treatment of those subjects,
> and how they intertwined with the more purely literary heroes for
> compositions, also of his own choosing.[5]

Yet Moore places *The Spirit of England* among Elgar's imperialist works, reserving discussion of it for the chapter titled "Land of Hope and Glory" and denoting it "the other face of the *Coronation Ode* of 1902."[6] In this regard he echoes Donald Mitchell, who had remarked earlier on "Elgar's convinced committal to what we may generally term 'imperial' topics (the *Coronation Ode, Crown of India, Spirit of England* and the rest)."[7] Both writers are surely correct to highlight the overt nationalism of this score, which Moore emphasizes further by adopting its title for his book (*Spirit of England: Edward Elgar in His World*). At first glance Binyon's poetry does not seem far removed from A. C. Benson and indeed many British poets writing in the autumn and winter of 1914. The opening stanzas revel in a version of Kipling's "White Man's Burden"—England's mission to free those enslaved by ignorance and tyranny, to vanquish the forces of evil, and to spread the beacons of civilization—all couched in heady imperial imagery designed to stiffen the backbone in the face of mounting death tolls on the western front. Musically Elgar seems to respond in a like manner, with expansive, aspirational melodies built around upward leaps and rising sequences in full choir and orchestra, marked *grandioso, nobilmente,* and *sonoramente.*[8] However, to accept unquestioningly this bracketing of *The Spirit of England* with Elgar's imperialist works without further investigation would be to perpetuate the whiff of jingoism and propaganda that has lingered around the work, and which probably accounts for its neglect both in the concert hall and in the literature, despite the quality of the music and its significance within Elgar's creative output.[9] As will be seen, *The Spirit of England* can be interpreted as a specifically Catholic response to the outbreak of war in Europe, and understanding it as such can yield insights into Elgar's changing attitudes to his faith—the faith in which he was immersed as a young child—and its relationship to his sense of heroic nationalism in the turbulent second decade of the new century.[10]

When taken out of context, Elgar's words to Frank Schuster on hearing of the commencement of hostilities against Germany on August 4, 1914, can seem startlingly inhumane:

> Concerning the war I say nothing—the only thing that wrings my heart & soul is the thought of the horses—oh! my beloved animals—the men—and women can go to hell—but my horses;—I walk round & round this room cursing God for allowing dumb brutes to be tortured— let Him kill his human beings but—how CAN HE? Oh, my horses.[11]

Volunteers were flooding to join the British Expeditionary Force across the Channel, but the British army was still perceived as a body of professionals; conscription would not be instituted for two years and the full horrors of trench warfare had yet to become a reality. Like many of the aristocracy with whom he aligned himself, especially as an enthusiastic race-goer, Elgar's concerns were thus for the noble beasts that as cavalry mounts and draught animals had been crucial to Britain's pursuit of the Boer War, and which epitomized the ideal of unwavering service and loyalty until death, most poignantly when slaughtered in their hundreds to sustain the besieged citizens of Mafeking (1899–1900).[12] Frustrated that he was "too old to be a soldier," Elgar signed up as a Special Constable within two weeks of the outbreak of war, and a few months later switched to the Hampstead Volunteer Reserve, involving himself in regular drills and rifle practice.[13] He mobilized A. C. Benson into revising the words for "Land of Hope and Glory" and was soon devoting his creative energies to a range of small-scale compositions, including recitations with orchestral accompaniment of poetry by the Belgian patriot Émile Cammaerts (1878–1953): *Carillon* (op. 75, 1914), *Une voix dans le désert* (op. 77, 1915), and *Le drapeau belge* (op. 79, 1916).[14]

British poetic responses to the conflict began to flood the pages of newspapers and periodicals, and among the first were those published in the London *Times* by Elgar's friend Laurence Binyon. By Christmas Binyon had gathered twelve of his poems into a single volume, *The Winnowing-Fan: Poems on the Great War;* from this collection, probably working from a copy given to him by the poet himself, Elgar took the following as the basis for a new cantata: I. "The Fourth of August" (referring to the day war was declared); X. "To Women"; and XI. "For the Fallen"; all of which are presented below.[15] The elegy "For the Fallen" would become the most famous and lasting of Binyon's poems, containing the prescient fourth stanza:

> They shall grow not old, as we that are left grow old:
> Age shall not weary them, nor the years condemn.
> At the going down of the sun and in the morning
> We will remember them.

Over the decades to come this quatrain would be recited during countless Armistice and Remembrance Day services and carved on many of the cenotaphs and war memorials erected across the British Empire. After the war, at the behest of the League of Arts, Elgar would rearrange his setting of "For the Fallen" for "Military or Brass Band, or Organ or Pianoforte" (later replaced by full orchestra), omitting the solo part, cutting three stanzas, more than halving the movement in length, and reworking his treatment of the central quatrain into a more consoling, luminous, and sparsely accompanied passage in E major. Renamed *With Proud Thanksgiving*, this version was intended for performance at the dedication of Edwin Lutyens's Whitehall Cenotaph and the entombment of the unknown warrior in Westminster Abbey in 1920, though in the end hymn singing would be preferred by the organizers.[16] As the third movement of Elgar's *The Spirit of England*, "For the Fallen" would become a stock item in the BBC's Armistice Day broadcasts, sometimes conducted by the composer himself.[17] Elgar considered it equal in merit to *The Dream of Gerontius* and *The Kingdom*, and by 1933, Basil Maine could confirm that "for many [*The Spirit of England*] has become a national memorial to which they instinctively turn each year on Remembrance Day."[18]

The idea of setting poems from Binyon's *The Winnowing-Fan* appears to have been triggered by Elgar's friend Sir Sidney Colvin (1845–1927), who, until his retirement as Keeper of the Department of Prints and Drawings, had been a colleague of Binyon's at the British Museum. It was widely believed by the Allies that the war would be over by Christmas, and so by the first weeks of New Year 1915 the need was keenly felt for something that could help to make sense of the escalating carnage and offer consolation to the growing mass of the bereaved.[19] Colvin probably discussed this with Elgar, for after spending the day with him he jotted the following postscript to a letter dated 10 January 1915:

Why don't you do a wonderful Requiem for the slain—something in the spirit of Binyon's "For the Fallen," or of that splendid homage of Ruskin's which I quoted in the Times Supplement of Decr 31—or of both together? —SC.[20]

That Elgar found Colvin's citation of "For the Fallen" sufficiently appealing to set the text itself, along with others from the same collection, is perhaps not surprising. The verses are replete with musical references, which Binyon enhanced in an extra stanza he wrote for Elgar's "Marziale" section (quoted below). As the son of an Anglican clergyman, Binyon also drew on a long familiarity with the language and imagery of the Bible in his poetry: for the famous quatrain in "For the Fallen" he later described how he had "wanted to get a rhythm something like 'By the Waters of Babylon we sat down and wept' or 'Daughters of Jerusalem, weep not for me' . . . and having found the kind of rhythm I wanted, varied it in other stanzas according to the mood required."[21] His disillusionment with institutionalized religion, however, and fascination with Eastern art and cultures (the main focus of his scholarship in adult life) brought to his poetry both an emphasis on humanism and a broad frame of reference, giving it an appeal that crossed denominational boundaries. His studies of William Blake's apocalyptic visions might also have helped him to find a voice with which he could speak of the harrowing events of the war; and in "Louvain," the sixth poem from *The Winnowing-Fan,* he expressed both a deep love for Flanders and his personal pain at the sacking of this ancient university town. (He did not at this stage know of the murder of his close friend Olivier Georges Destrée, who had entered a Benedictine monastery there.)[22] The extent to which in early 1915 "For the Fallen" seemed to capture the mood particularly of the nation's noncombatants, and would do so increasingly over the course of the war, is underlined by Binyon's biographer, John Hatcher:

"For the Fallen" is one of the few great war poems to include in its tragedy those "that are left." It takes Henry's St. Crispin's Day speech from [Shakespeare's] *Henry V* IV. iii, the key text of English chivalric patriotism, and turns it inside out, seeing the war and its aftermath from the point of view of those at home, the older generation too old to fight, including those who found their jingoistic platitudes stilled in their throat by the surreal nightmare the war had become.[23]

Colvin, Binyon, and Elgar all belonged to this "older generation"—"Do you realize that nearly half my life belongs to Victoria's days?" Binyon quizzed T. S. Eliot in 1940—and of the three, only Binyon had direct experience of the fighting.[24]

The second text to which Colvin referred Elgar came from the final chapter in volume 3 of John Ruskin's *Modern Painters*—this was an important, indeed crucial, book for Colvin, who had idolized Ruskin all his life.[25] Writing during the Crimean War (1853–56), Ruskin takes as his theme "righteous" warfare, which he argues is essentially a better, more ennobling state for England than peace, referencing ancient codes of Christian chivalry:

> I ask *their* witness, to whom the war has changed the aspect of earth, and imagery of heaven, whose hopes it has cut off like a spider's web, whose treasure it has placed, in a moment, under the seals of clay. Those who can never more see sunrise, nor watch the climbing light gild the Eastern clouds without thinking what graves it has gilded, first, far down beneath the dark earth-line—who never more shall see the crocus bloom in spring without thinking what dust it is that feeds the wild flowers of Balaclava. Ask *their* witness, and see if they will not reply that it is well with them and with theirs; that they would have it no otherwise; would not, if they might, receive back their gifts of love and life, nor take again the purple of their blood out of the cross on the breastplate of England. . . . They know now the strength of sacrifice, and that its flames can illumine as well as consume; they are bound by new fidelities to all that they have saved—by new love to all for whom they have suffered; every affection which seemed to sink with those dim life-storms into the dust, has been delegated, by those who need it no more, to the cause for which they expired; and every mouldering arm, which will never more embrace the beloved ones, has bequeathed to them its strength and its faithfulness.[26]

Elgar's own affection for Ruskin is apparent in his quotation of a passage from *Sesame and Lilies* on the last page of his score of *The Dream of Gerontius*. That he considered working directly with the text Colvin highlighted for him seems unlikely—it is, after all, prose rather than poetry—but in its message and atmosphere of heroic idealism it comes close to the poem he would choose for the opening movement of *The Spirit of England*, Binyon's "The Fourth of August" (text quoted below). By 1915 most Englishmen believed their country was engaged in a just war, necessary to honor treaties and avenge the "rape of Belgium" by going to the aid of the smaller, weaker country overwhelmed by a foreign aggressor. In this manner, the war engaged highly developed notions of chivalric honor, manliness, patriotic duty, and, as David Cannadine has observed, an increased confidence that death, when it came, would come naturally and in old age, encouraged by the lengthening of life expectancy and decline in infant mortality in Britain since the 1880s. Combined with growing international tensions (including a concern that colonial youths were outstripping their home-grown counterparts in prowess and vigor) and the increasing appeal of social Darwinism in the 1900s, these factors had created the "strident athletic ethos of the late-Victorian and Edwardian public school . . . in which soldiering and games were equated, in which death was seen as unlikely, but where, if it happened, it could not fail to be glorious."[27] Such conditioning determined the conduct not only of the officers drawn from the public-school elite, but also those from the lower social ranks who emulated them, and can be seen to have been effected through music as much as through the literature and imagery of the 1900s (see, for example, figure 1).

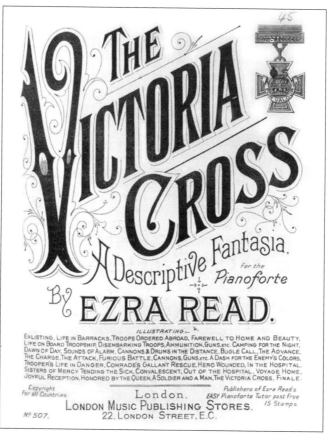

Figure 1. Ezra Read, *The Victoria Cross: A Descriptive Fantasia for the Pianoforte* (London: London Music Publishing Stores, c. 1899). Note the detailed program.

The most striking aspect of Colvin's proposal is that he should have prompted his Catholic friend Elgar to compose a "requiem for the slain," a phrase that may owe something to Binyon's habit of referring in private to "For the Fallen" as his "requiem-verses."[28] To someone with a Protestant background, like Colvin, the word *requiem* could be bandied quite lightly. Over the 1890s and 1900s English audiences had shown a greater willingness to accept choral works based on Roman Catholic liturgy; and in his discussion of Stanford's decision to compose a requiem for the 1897 Birmingham Festival, Paul Rodmell cites freedom from librettists and potential copyright entanglements among the attractions of setting such a text.[29] Yet to Elgar, raised as a Roman Catholic, *requiem* was inseparable from a particular view of the afterlife, especially the doctrine of purgatory—a process that allowed for the purification of the souls of repentant sinners in a slow agony and which could be hastened and even curtailed by the prayers of the living. By contrast, Protestant theology on the afterlife during the Victorian era was far more rigid: God's judgment determined whether a soul ascended to heaven or was cast into the fires of hell for eternity, and the doctrine of purgatory was excoriated in the Thirty-Nine Articles of the Anglican Church.[30]

Byron Adams has described Elgar's faith as never more than "a flickering light" and in a compelling narrative tracks the faltering of that faith through a downward spiral of physical and psychological corrosion as the composer struggled to complete his massive trilogy of oratorios, especially the final work *The Last Judgement*.[31] Such was the extent of this apparent spiritual decline that the doctor who diagnosed Elgar's terminal cancer remembered the composer telling him that "he had no faith whatever in an afterlife: 'I believe there is nothing but complete oblivion.'"[32] This must have seemed an astonishing remark to hear from the man who had composed *The Dream of Gerontius* over thirty years earlier. Similarly, in his last weeks Elgar's friends and daughter were unsettled by his request to have his body cremated and his ashes scattered at the confluence of the rivers Severn and Teme; and although he reportedly received the "last rites," it was only after he had slipped into morphine-induced unconsciousness. Elgar's daughter Carice finally persuaded him to be buried alongside his wife, Alice, at St. Wulstan's Roman Catholic Church, Little Malvern, and though a requiem mass was celebrated in his memory, it was a low mass without music.[33]

Whether one can fully accept Adams's narrative of a crushing loss of faith, or set Elgar's apparent ambivalence toward his Catholicism down to the obfuscation necessary for acceptance in Protestant British society, two considerations are fundamental to any discussion of Elgar's spirituality.

First, whatever his experience in late adulthood, and whatever the strength or otherwise of his faith, Elgar's outlook and personal history were steeped in Catholicism: culturally, he always remained a Catholic. Until his departure from Worcester to London in his early thirties, he lived life in a Catholic context dominated by his mother, a fervent convert to the faith; he had attended Catholic schools and a Catholic church, had socialized with Catholics, and was organist at St. George's Catholic Church in Worcester, which provided him with many of his earliest musical experiences including exposure to repertoire from the continental Catholic traditions. Catholicism would remain a strong influence on the women in his life— his wife would convert to Catholicism, and his sister became a senior nun at a Dominican convent near Stroud. Memories of boyhood would forever be inseparable from this "Catholic ethos," to borrow John Butt's phrase, as when Elgar reminisced about priests he had known as a child, for example, in conversation with the Leicester family on June 2, 1914.[34]

Second, in the sphere of religious music Elgar had to become adept at negotiating Protestant sensibilities. In his early career, before 1898, he composed a great deal of Latin sacred music, including a short hymn tune for the Marian devotion "Stabat Mater Dolorosa" and a number of individual mass movements, though he never attempted a complete setting of the Ordinary.[35] In the years before the Great War, Elgar turned his attention to the composition of Anglican liturgical music, to the extent that John Butt describes him as "an Anglican *manqué*," but his interest in Catholic music continued unabated.[36] While on a trip to Italy in 1907–8, Elgar planned to obtain a copy of Giovanni Sgambati's *Messa di Requiem*, which had been sung at Italian royal funerals and had been heard twice to great acclaim in Germany; perhaps he hoped this might reignite his inspiration as he struggled to complete his oratorio *The Last Judgement*.[37] He suggested to Ivor Atkins, organist of Worcester Cathedral, that Sgambati's Requiem might be suitable for a Worcester Festival Choral Society concert, or even the Worcester Festival of 1908, and laid plans to meet the composer personally while in Rome to discuss the loan of orchestral parts. In the end, however, the festival committee chose Stanford's *Stabat Mater* (1906), a setting of a Catholic text by a safely Anglican composer.[38]

The most eloquent evidence of Elgar's willingness to appease his Protestant countrymen remains his approach to the setting of Cardinal Newman's "The Dream of Gerontius." Newman's poem required considerable truncation and simplification in order to render it suitable as a libretto. Elgar also seems to have wanted to shift the focus of attention away from Newman's conception of the afterlife, toward Gerontius as a universalized suffering human figure, which, as McGuire observes, was characteristic of his approach in his later oratorios.[39] Among the cuts Elgar was prepared to make were several passages of Catholic doctrine. The Guardian Angel's words on leaving Gerontius in the care of the Angels of Purgatory were left out, for example, although the remaining text still clearly described a purging of the soul hastened by masses said by the living.[40] Passages from Newman such as these caused Dean Spence-Jones of Gloucester to ban the work from performance in the cathedral there in 1901 and the Anglican authorities to stipulate textual alterations before *Gerontius* could be heard in Worcester Cathedral the following year.[41] As Elgar outlined in a letter to Jaeger, on May 9, 1902, the problematic sections were the Litany of Saints recited at the dying man's bedside, Gerontius's beseeching of the Virgin Mary to intercede for him, and the references to the doctrine of purgatory in the final scene:

> What is proposed is to omit the litany of the saints—to substitute other words for Mary & Joseph—& to put "Souls" only over the chorus at the end instead of "Souls in Purgatory" & to put "prayers" instead of Masses in the Angel's Farewell. . . . So far I have only said I have no objection to the alterations or that I concur—permission *I* cannot give.[42]

For that permission the approval of Newman's executor, Father Neville, had to be sought. In the end Neville concurred with Elgar on a bowdlerized version of the work designed for performance in an Anglican church; Elgar was sufficiently content to conduct this version himself at Worcester in 1902 and finally at Gloucester in 1910.[43] Clearly, Elgar learned from these experiences: he took the precaution of having the text of *The Apostles* vetted by two Anglican clergymen before committing himself to the final version.[44]

In view of Elgar's cultural roots in Catholicism, the faltering of his inspiration for *The Last Judgement,* his preparedness to make compromises for his Protestant audiences and patrons, and the fervency of his nationalism, we can speculate that Colvin's invitation to write a requiem for the slain in the early months of the Great War would have been a powerful stimulus to the composer's creative imagination. Having suffered Anglican censure of *The Dream of Gerontius,* however, Elgar would surely have been reluctant to court controversy again by composing a setting of the Latin Mass for the Dead. A requiem from his pen, as opposed to those of his Protestant countrymen, would need to take a less overtly Roman Catholic (and therefore less provocative) form; Binyon's poetry would prove ideal for the composer's purpose.

The verses Elgar selected from Binyon's *The Winnowing-Fan* had been published in the *Times* at the outset of the conflict on August 11, August 20, and September 21, 1914. Elgar emphasized their local significance in an inscription on the completed score: "My portion of the work I humbly dedicate to the memory of our glorious men, with a special thought for the Worcesters," and at the end, *"For the Fallen* & especially my own *Worcestershires."* The text is as follows:

Movement I (*Moderato e maestoso*)
I. *The Fourth of August* [45]
Now in thy splendour go before us,
Spirit of England, ardent-eyed,
Enkindle this dear earth that bore us,
In the hour of peril purified. [46]

The cares we hugged drop out of vision.
Our hearts with deeper thoughts dilate.
We step from days of sour division
Into the grandeur of our fate.

For us the glorious dead have striven,
They battled that we might be free.
We to their living cause are given;
We arm for men that are to be.

Among the nations nobliest chartered,
England recalls her heritage.
In her is that which is not bartered,
Which force can neither quell nor cage.

For her immortal stars are burning
With her the hope that's never done,
The seed that's in the Spring's returning,
The very flower that seeks the sun.

She fights the fraud that feeds desire on
Lies, in a lust to enslave or kill,
The barren creed of blood and iron,
Vampire of Europe's wasted will . . .

Endure, O Earth! and thou, awaken,
Purged by this dreadful winnowing-fan,
O wronged, untameable, unshaken
Soul of divinely suffering man.

Movement II (*Moderato*)

X. *To Women*
Your hearts are lifted up, your hearts
That have foreknown the utter price.
Your hearts burn upward like a flame
Of splendour and of sacrifice.

For you, you too, to battle go,
Not with the marching drums and cheers
But in the watch of solitude
And through the boundless night of fears.

Swift, swifter than those hawks of war,
Those threatening wings that pulse the air,[47]
Far as the vanward ranks are set,
You are gone before them, you are there!

And not a shot comes blind with death
And not a stab of steel is pressed
Home, but invisibly it tore
And entered first a woman's breast.

Amid the thunder of the guns,
The lightnings of the lance and sword
Your hope, your dread, your throbbing pride,
Your infinite passion is outpoured

From hearts that are as one high heart
Withholding naught from doom and bale
Burningly offered up,—to bleed,
To bear, to break, but not to fail!

Movement III (*Solenne*)
XI. *For the Fallen*[48]
With proud thanksgiving, a mother for her children,
England mourns for her dead across the sea.
Flesh of her flesh they were, spirit of her spirit,
Fallen in the cause of the free.

Solemn the drums thrill: Death august and royal
Sings sorrow up into immortal spheres.
There is music in the midst of desolation
And a glory that shines upon our tears.

They went with songs to the battle, they were young,
Straight of limb, true of eye, steady and aglow.
They were staunch to the end against odds uncounted,
They fell with their faces to the foe.[49]

[Stanza written by Binyon especially for Elgar:]
They fought, they were terrible, nought could tame them,
Hunger, nor legions, nor shattering cannonade.
They laughed, they sang their melodies of England,
They fell open-eyed and unafraid.

They shall grow not old, as we that are left grow old:[50]
Age shall not weary them, nor the years condemn.
At the going down of the sun and in the morning
We will remember them.

They mingle not with their laughing comrades again;
They sit no more at familiar tables of home;
They have no lot in our labour of the day-time;
They sleep beyond England's foam.

But where our desires are and our hopes profound,
Felt as a well-spring that is hidden from sight,
To the innermost heart of their own land they are known
As the stars are known to the Night;

As the stars that shall be bright when we are dust
Moving in marches upon the heavenly plain,
As the stars that are starry in the time of our darkness,
To the end, to the end, they remain.

Elgar took his title for *The Spirit of England* from the opening stanza of "The Fourth of August," the first of the three poems he selected from Binyon's book. In this he was probably influenced by the publication of *The Spirit of Man,* a popular anthology of poetry and philosophy compiled by Robert Bridges (1844–1930), who had been made poet laureate in 1913 following Kipling's refusal of the post. In his preface, Bridges stated the intention of his volume—to uphold and nourish spirituality among the Allies in the face of "the miseries, the insensate and interminable slaughter, the hate and filth" brought on by the "evil" of Prussian materialism, militarism, and conscious criminality.[51] In "The Fourth of August" Binyon associates the "Spirit of England" with qualities such as mettle, courage, ardor, and steadfastness, which, he implies, define the English as individuals, as an army, and as a nation with a noble destiny. Other meanings are also brought into play, however, which remove the poem from its immediate time and place to the realms of the metaphysical and the eschatological: among those

Example 1a. "Novissima hora est" motif, *The Dream of Gerontius,* Part I, rehearsal no. 66.

Example 1b. "Endure, O Earth!" *The Spirit of England,* first movement, "The Fourth of August," rehearsal no. 13.

who make up the "Spirit of England" are the "glorious dead" who in the battle for freedom have already "gone before" (in both senses of the phrase). Here, as in the Ruskin extract Colvin cited for Elgar, war is presented not only as a fight for good against evil, but as a purgation of the spirit of the English, from whom self-sacrifice is required to secure the cleansing, revivification, and salvation of Europe. Binyon encapsulates this in his image of the winnowing-fan, a tool from which crops are thrown up into the air as the fertile grain is sorted from the lightweight chaff. That this was an attractive metaphor for Elgar is evident in his decision to reprise the opening stanza at the end of the first movement, thereby bringing *purged* (seventh stanza) and *purified* (first stanza) into a direct relationship with each other through juxtaposition and reinforcing the interpretation of *spirit* as *soul*, that is, along eschatological lines. At its first appearance the word *purified* falls on a weak beat but is accented, and in its final iteration is given musical expression with a movement sharpwards in the harmonies.

More significant are the motivic links Elgar establishes between this movement and *The Dream of Gerontius*, connections that confirm a bond between these two works in his imagination. For the phrase "Endure, O Earth!" (seventh stanza), Elgar quotes his setting of the phrase "Novissima hora est" ("This is the final hour") from *Gerontius* (compare Examples 1a and 1b), probably prompted by the phrase "hour of peril" in the fourth line of the first stanza, but again focusing attention on the afterlife: this poignant phrase is sung by Gerontius in the final agonies of corporeal death (Part I, rehearsal no. 66), on encountering God (Part II, at "Take me away," two measures after rehearsal no. 120), and by the Angel of the Agony pleading with Christ for deliverance of the Souls in Purgatory (Part II, at "that glorious home," five measures before rehearsal no. 113—"Hasten, Lord, their hour, and bid them come to Thee, / To that glorious Home, where

Example 2a. "Christ's Peace" motif, *The Dream of Gerontius*, Part I, five measures after rehearsal no. 22.

Example 2b. "Christ's Agony" motif, *The Dream of Gerontius*, five measures after rehearsal no. 62.

they shall ever gaze on Thee").[52] Elgar's reuse of this distinctive motif here also gives musical utterance to Binyon's implied parallel between the "Spirit of England" and the figure of Christ in the lines that follow ("O wronged, untameable, unshaken / Soul of divinely suffering man"), for in *Gerontius,* as Moore points out, the "novissima hora est" motif takes its shape from those associated both with Christ's peace ("Thou art calling me") and with the agony of the crucifixion ("in Thine own agony") (compare Example 1a with 2a and 2b).[53] For the closing lines of the seventh stanza, as he did in the opening of Part II of *The Dream of Gerontius,* Elgar seems to suspend time, delivering the direct address in a hushed, unaccompanied chorale, marked *più lento* and *espressivo*:

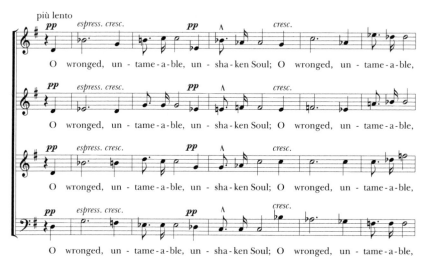

Example 3. *The Spirit of England,* first movement, "The Fourth of August," rehearsal no. 14.

The "Novissima hora est" motif also resurfaces in the second movement, "To Women," where it is heard (over the "Spirit of England" theme from the first movement) in the solo part and taken up by the chorus at "but not to fail!" (Example 4).[54] For added emphasis, the melody used for "this dreadful winnowing-fan" in the previous movement is alluded to in the violins in the measure before rehearsal no. 11, where the chorus reenters with "to bleed, to bear, to break." Once again the connections with Christ are significant, emphasizing both divine sacrifice and endurance, for the text of this movement can be interpreted as a latter-day Stabat Mater Dolorosa. As mothers, but also wives and lovers, women of England witness in spirit the corporeal suffering and death of their men on the battlefield, just as Mary stood weeping for her Son at the foot of the Cross on Golgotha. Binyon's choice of language seems to echo the opening verses of the thirteenth-century Latin hymn, particularly in his fifth and sixth stanzas that refer to the "infinite passion," seemingly anachronistically to "lance and sword," and to the scourging of Christ with the phrase "to bleed, to bear, to break." (Here Elgar links the motif of endurance with immortality by anticipating in the orchestra the climax of the third movement, the ghostly legion "moving in marches upon the heavenly plain," as well as "Flesh of her flesh they were, spirit of her spirit" and "There is music in the midst of desolation.")[55] The connection is lost for us, however, in his association of "passion" with "throbbing pride." Elgar's biographer Basil Maine heard further echoes of *The Dream of Gerontius* in this movement:

> At more than one point in this deeply moving music but especially in the brief orchestral passage at the end, the spirit that pervaded the "Angel of the Agony" episode in "Gerontius" is perceptibly at work.[56]

Example 4. *The Spirit of England,* second movement, "To Women," rehearsal no. 10.

Example 4 continued

The chromaticism and the repeated rhythm (short-long) forge this link, which again transports us to Calvary and an invocation to the crucified Christ; for as Gerontius is told just before the appearance of this heavenly being, the Angel of the Agony is "the same who strengthened Him, what time He knelt / Lone in the garden shade, bedewed with blood. / That Angel best can plead with Him for all / Tormented souls, the dying and the dead."

A further motivic link with *Gerontius* is established in the first movement for the sixth stanza (rehearsal nos. 9–13), which culminates in the line "Vampire of Europe's wasted will." At this point Elgar quotes the Demons' Chorus from the second part of the oratorio, thus connecting implicitly the architects of the Prussian war machine with the depraved beings who howl and snatch at the soul of Gerontius as it passes on its way to Judgment. On June 17, 1917, after completing *The Spirit of England*, Elgar sent an explanation of this decision to Ernest Newman, who was to write an account of this movement for the *Musical Times:*

Example 4 continued

Do not dwell upon the Demons part:—two years ago I held over that section hoping that some trace of manly spirit would shew itself in the direction of German affairs: that hope is gone forever & the Hun is branded as less than a beast for very many generations: so I wd. not invent anything low & bestial enough to illustrate the one stanza; the Cardinal invented (*invented* as far as I know) the particular hell in Gerontius where the great intellects gibber & snarl *knowing they have fallen*:

This is exactly the case with the Germans now;—the music was to hand & I have sparingly used it. A lunatic asylum is, after the first shock, not entirely sad; so few of the patients are aware of the strangeness of their situation; most of them are placid and foolishly calm; but the horror of the fallen intellect—*knowing* what it once was & *knowing* what it has become—is beyond words frightful.[57]

The words "held over" in this letter have often been interpreted to mean that Elgar had difficulty composing this passage—that with his style so firmly rooted in the Austro-German tradition, he struggled to position the Hun musically as the "Other," in a way he had not in his depiction of the "otherness" of the Mogul emperors for the *Crown of India* three years earlier—and that it had taken him well over a year to arrive at this solution.[58] If this was indeed a troublesome passage that held up the completion of the work for so long, however, it seems odd that among the sketches so few are devoted to this particular section.[59] A more plausible explanation is that Elgar arrived at his solution early on, and held this particular movement back—the first performances (from May 3, 1916, until the premiere of the completed trilogy on October 4, 1917) were of the second and third movements. His reasons for this decision were probably twofold. First, he would have wanted to avoid offending certain friends, most notably Edgar Speyer, the wealthy patron of London's transport system, hospitals, and concert life. Despite having English nationality, the Speyer family had rapidly become the target of anti-German harassment in the early months of the war: Edgar Speyer was ostracized by former associates, accused of collusion with the enemy, and pressured to relinquish his baronetcy and membership in the Privy Council. Ultimately, on May 26, 1915, Speyer and his family left England for the United States. Elgar had been supportive under these difficult circumstances and might well have remained reluctant to place "The Fourth of August" before the public until the Speyers had settled abroad.[60] Elgar's great German musical ally, the conductor Hans Richter, was dead by the end of December 1916.

From Alice Elgar's diaries we know that German forces were frequently described as demonic and brutal in the Elgar household during the early stages of the Binyon project. On December 31, 1914, she wrote, "Year ends in great anxieties but with invaluable consciousness that England has a great, holy Cause—May God keep her," and from Severn House the following month she recorded outright condemnation of the latest Zeppelin activity:

[19 January 1915:] Seemingly tranquil but at night a German air raid on Yarmouth & that part of East Coast. They damaged houses & caused some loss of life, engulfing themselves more deeply in crime than ever. Brutes—

[20 January 1915:] Long accounts of air raid. Hope it has shown the U.S.A. what lengths uncivilised fiends will go

[27 January 1915:] Splendid accounts of naval action. Must have immense moral *effect*—No truth in the elaborate German *lies*. Almost impossible to conceive that their airships dropped bombs on the sailors

while they were trying to save German drowning men—Demons
might have acted better.[61]

This intemperate language resurfaced twelve months into the war, when
Alice, who had ambitions as a versifier, tried her hand at a war sonnet
after Binyon for publication in *The Bookman*. The Handel scholar R. A.
Streatfeild, acting as go-between for the editor, advised her that he would
"(probably) suggest another adjective in the place of 'devilish,'" but the
original word was retained when the poem went into print.

England. August 4, 1914. A retrospect.

Holding her reign in kindly state and might,
Still deeming honour trod in knightly ways,
Half armed, lay England, through the summer days;
Her rule, outspeeding dawn, outchecking night,
Welded the sphere in wide, majestic flight.
When lo! a foe appears who neither stays
Nor warns, but sweeps the Belgian plains and sways
Grim hosts and arrogates a devilish right.
'England still sleeps,' he said 'and dreams of gain,
She will not stir, who once was battle's lord,
Or risk the clash of squadrons on the main;
Her treaties may be torn, while 'gainst the horde
These lesser folk may plea[d]e for help in vain . . .'

Then, throned amidst the seas, She bared her sword.[62]

Such rhetoric is a reflection of the propaganda that was disseminated
widely in the early months of 1915, particularly concerning alleged German
atrocities in Belgium, which were detailed in the Bryce report, published
in May 1915.[63] Characterization of the German army as a demonic horde
was encouraged in response to the use of poison gas and flame throwers
against Allied combatants, air raids that resulted in civilian casualties, and
incidents such as the torpedoing of the British passenger liner *Lusitania*
and the "martyrdom" of nurse Edith Cavell, all of which were dwelt on
at length by the British press in horror and outrage (see figure 2).[64]

For Elgar, however, setting the sixth stanza of "The Fourth of August" to
the music he had hitherto used for Newman's demons was not an exercise
in cheap propaganda, but part of his conception of the war as a metaphysical
struggle between hell and heaven, of darkness and light, for the soul of

Figure 2. "The Murder of Nurse Cavell," *The War Illustrated: A Picture-Record of Events by Land, Sea and Air* (30 October 1915). Reproduced by permission of the British Library.

humanity. Concern that he should not be seen to be peddling anti-German propaganda, fueling popular hatred, and endorsing simplistic views of the war as a conflict between English knights and German devils, might well have been a second factor in his decision to suppress the first movement for so long. And on this point Elgar's dialogue with the critics is revealing.

In April 1916, Ernest Newman wrote an article on *The Spirit of England* for *The Musical Times* in anticipation of the premiere of the second and third movements, which was scheduled for the following month (described in greater detail below). In his essay, Newman extemporized on material Elgar had supplied for that purpose in a personal letter, but the critic also indulged in explicit anti-German sentiments couched in "holy war" rhetoric:[65]

> We gladly leave the writing of Hymns of Hate to the race that has shown us in too many other respects also how near its instincts are to those of the barbarian. An older and better civilisation looks to its leading artists for something different from the German froth and foam, bellowing and swagger. We are not "too proud to fight," but we are too proud to abase our emotions about the war to the level of those of our bestial foe; to do that would be disloyalty to the memory of our holy dead.[66]

These references to "Hymns of Hate," which incensed Newman so deeply, allude to settings of a poem penned in 1914 by a German-Jewish writer, Ernst Lissauer, which had been used to whip up a fury of Anglophobia throughout Germany in the early months of the war. It was from this that the German army derived the slogan "Gott strafe England" (God punish England), for, as Stefan Zweig recalled, Lissauer's poem had "exploded like a bomb in a munitions factory":

> The Kaiser was enraptured and bestowed the Order of the Red Eagle upon Lissauer, the poem was reprinted in all the newspapers, teachers read it out loud to the children in school, officers at the front read it to their soldiers, until everyone knew the litany of hate by heart. As if that were not enough, the little poem was set to music and, arranged for chorus, was sung in the theatres.[67]

Copies reaching England were seized upon by the press, the text appearing in the *Times* on October 29, 1914 (in a translation prepared by Barbara Henderson for the *New York Times*), and a musical setting (attributed to Franz Mayerhoff) in the *Weekly Dispatch* of March 7, 1915. This stoked anti-German hatred in turn, triggering a series of musical retorts, particularly from the music halls: Whit Cunliffe, for example, popularized Robert P. Weston and Bert Lee's *Strafe'em!;* Thomas Case Sterndale Bennett produced *My Hymn of Hate;* and a lesser-known composer, Harold Whitehall, composed a *Tyneside Hymn of Hate*.[68] A satirical rendition of Lissauer's "Hymn" in its musical raiment was given on March 15, 1915, at the Royal College of Music by Hubert Parry, Walter Parratt, and an impromptu choir: "Sir Walter asked them to sing the hymn with plenty of snarl, to express honestly the intentions of the composer . . . but they laughed too much to snarl." Later burlesque performances included those by Major Mackenzie Rogan and the band of the Coldstream Guards in morale-building concerts behind the lines in France and Flanders, on ships, and in munitions factories, with "a second verse punctuated by snatches of British melodies, patriotic and profane, expressing Tommy's reply from the trenches to the comminatory bitterness of Prussianism."[69]

It was probably reluctance to be seen participating in this venomous exchange that prompted Elgar's exhortation to Newman not to "dwell upon the Demons part" when writing his introductory article about the first movement for the *Musical Times* a year later.[70] Although Newman took care to distinguish Elgar's *Spirit of England* from "the strut and swagger of the commoner 'patriotic' verse and music" in this essay, "the foul thing" that Germany had become was still to be roundly denounced: "For the first time in the lives of many of us we find ourselves indulging in a national hatred and not seeing any reason to be ashamed of it," he declared, for "even Fafner, Wagner's last word in brutishness, would not have decorated himself with a *Lusitania* medal."[71] Despite Elgar's instruction, Newman emphasized the "Demons part," predicting:

> We shall henceforth listen to the Demons' Chorus with a new imagery flashing across our minds. . . . We shall have a new appreciation of the "con derisione" that Elgar, with a prophetic intuition, has written in the score of "Gerontius" over the reiterated "gods" [musical example inserted here]—And at the end of it all the Demons' theme, as in the oratorio, goes panting and growling into the depths of hell.[72]

Other critics observed a heightened sense of violence in Elgar's own performances of the "Demon's Chorus" from *Gerontius* around this time. Herbert Thompson, reviewing for the *Yorkshire Post* a Leeds Choral Union performance of *The Dream of Gerontius* (programmed alongside *The Spirit of England*, complete) under Elgar's baton on October 31, 1917, noted, "The only thing that jarred was the nasal tone in the Demons' chorus, which was so exaggerated that it ceased to be impressive, and was merely grotesque"; moreover, the critic records that he had begun to notice an increasing cynicism in Elgar's delivery of this passage at least six months earlier.[73] In his response to *The Spirit of England,* however, Thompson made a point of trying to rescue "The Fourth of August" from the taint of anti-German propaganda, as his comments on the premiere of the complete work, conducted in Birmingham by Appleby Matthews, suggest:

> The general character of the poems by Lawrence Benyon [*sic*], which Sir Edward Elgar has chosen to set, is that of patriotism, which rings true, the more so since it is utterly devoid of vulgar bluster, and is dignified and restrained in sentiment. . . . There is a touch of indig-nation in an outburst concerning the barren creed of blood and iron, but there is no indication of any futile and childish "Hymn of Hate," either in the verse or in the music, which never loses control or degenerates into mere abuse.[74]

Elgar's own words on the subject in his June 1917 letter to Newman, give us a sense of how his thinking on the war had changed over the three years since his 1914 comment to Schuster (yet another of Elgar's friends with German origins), quoted above, and a year after the catastrophe of the Somme. It is the imagery of the madhouse that now seems most elo-quent to him, of which he had had firsthand experience as a young man, providing musical distractions to inmates of Powick Lunatic Asylum. The careful distinctions he draws between the innocent, the obliviously mad, and the knowingly corrupt and depraved is a telling one, as is the image of the remnants of noble souls overtaken by demons who, by implication, respect no national boundaries. In this the composer echoed sentiments expressed on the debasement of German culture in another of Binyon's poems from *The Winnowing-Fan,* the seventh, titled "To Goethe."[75] But Elgar also mirrors the thoughts of another writer with whom he is not so readily associated—H. G. Wells (1866–1946), who had delivered the fol-lowing statement in his pamphlet *The War That Will End War,* issued in August 1914:[76]

> We are fighting Germany. But we are fighting without any hatred of the German people. We do not intend to destroy either their free-dom or their unity. But we have to destroy an evil system of government and the mental and material corruption that has got hold of the German imagination and taken possession of German life. . . . This is already the vastest war in history. It is war not of nations, but of mankind. It is a war to exorcise a world madness and end an age.[77]

That Elgar shared Wells's vision of an impending Armageddon brought on by the materialism and corruption of those who would cast themselves as gods, and requiring the sacrifice of heroes, is further suggested by his song "Fight for Right" (London, Elkin, 1916)—a setting of Brynhild's words on sending Sigurd off to deeds of glory in William Morris's epic poem *The Story of Sigurd the Volsung and the Fall of the Niblungs* (1876), which was based on the same sources as Wagner's *Götterdämmerung*.[78]

Elgar had *The Dream of Gerontius* almost constantly in mind through the early years of the war. On September 8, 1914, Alice wrote in her diary, "It wd. have been 'Gerontius' tonight at Worcester Fest[ival]—but for Hun Kaiser"; and on November 19, Charles Mott sang the "Proficiscere" from *Gerontius* during an organ recital at Worcester in memory of Lord Roberts, colonel in chief of the empire troops in France, who had succumbed to pneumonia while visiting Indian soldiers at St. Omer. Elgar could not attend the recital, but approved organist Ivor Atkins's "excellent choice."[79] In February the following year, just after Elgar had begun work on the Binyon settings, Alice noted that he met with Clara Butt "to go through Gerontius" in preparation for her first performance of it at the Royal Albert Hall on the twenty-seventh of that month, in the role of the Guardian Angel.[80] In March 1916, he and Alice met again with Clara Butt, this time to plan what would become one of the most extraordinary musical events of the war.[81] At a time when "music-making on a large scale had almost completely ceased," as Basil Maine recalled, and nocturnal transportation around London was restricted and hazardous due to the blackout, Butt's plan was to present a week of six consecutive oratorio performances at the Queen's Hall (preceded by two performances in Leeds and Bradford respectively) of *The Dream of Gerontius* and the second and third movements of *The Spirit of England* (their initial performances) to raise funds for the Red Cross and Order of St. John of Jerusalem in England.[82] The London performances took place in the week of May 8–13, 1916, with John Booth and Agnes Nicholls taking the solo parts in "To Women" and "For the Fallen" respectively, and Clara Butt herself taking the Guardian Angel in *Gerontius*.

The success of these performances was remarkable. King George V, Queen Mary, and Queen Alexandra attended twice, and in total the week of performances netted the then considerable sum of £2,707.[83] In a letter to Lady Elgar, R. A. Streatfeild described the Thursday night performance as "wonderful & unforgettable . . . I still feel as if I were vibrating all over."[84] For Elgar, this must have been an overwhelming experience. His *Dream of Gerontius* was almost certainly given in its original form (that is, not the bowdlerized version produced for performance in a consecrated

Anglican space) at these concerts. With the first movement of *The Spirit of England,* "The Fourth of August," still unfinished, he must have been greatly encouraged by the reception accorded his interpretations of the Binyon poems, not least by the publicity put out by Clara Butt for these performances, the main points of which were summarized as follows by her authorized biographer:

> She had other motives in mind in this unusual enterprise besides the obvious ones of raising money for a patriotic cause. She had a religious motive as well. She felt it was time that the people who were passing through the sorrows and anxieties of war should hear music that was definitely spiritual, and that English art should try to express the attitude of the English mind to the life after death.
>
> She determined to challenge London with something really beautiful and mystic. "We are a nation in mourning," she said, discussing the project. "In this tremendous upheaval, when youth is dying for us, I want to give the people a week of beautiful thoughts, for I am convinced that no nation can be great that is not truly religious. I believe that the War has given us a new attitude towards death, that many who had no faith before are now hungering to believe that after death there is life."[85]

Though the first movement of *The Spirit of England*—the most explicit in its connections with *The Dream of Gerontius*—was not heard at these performances, the combination of *Gerontius,* "To Women," and "For the Fallen" was a powerful one, as a letter written to Elgar by Sidney Colvin's wife, Frances, after the Monday afternoon performance confirms:

> How can I ever tell you dear Edward what we felt today or how deeply moved we both were—it is all quite wonderful & just what one wants at this time—& at all times—it will live always—"For the Fallen" especially will always be the one great inspiration of the War. My heart is full of warm gratitude to you—but my eyes are sore with *tears* and I can't write—but we both send you our heartfelt love and congratulations—Bless you. . . . How lovely the choir was! Sidney has a bad cold but *nothing* would have kept him from going.[86]

These Red Cross concerts fused *The Spirit of England* with *Gerontius* in the public imagination, forming the two works into a diptych that provided a communal focus for grief and prayer and assumed a quasi-liturgical function. As Maine relates:

The music of "Gerontius," during that week in the spring of 1916, shone with a new significance and became *a symbol of intercession;* while in "The Spirit of England" was seen, transfigured, the face of human suffering, and there was as yet no sign of disillusion in that face—not yet had the broken songs of the soldier-poets been heard.[87]

Clara Butt's claim that death and the future life were among the most pressing issues thrown up by the war matched the perceptions of Anglican clergy, of whom "Is it well with the fallen?" had become one of the most frequently asked theological questions both by laity on the home front and among the troops at the western front.[88] For many, the attempts by the national Church to meet the complex spiritual needs of the people were found wanting. Despite individual acts of extraordinary heroism, Anglican chaplains were deemed to be less than fully prepared for their ministry at the front: it was the Roman Catholic padres who earned a reputation for supreme courage, risking their lives to administer extreme unction to the dying while the Anglican clergy, initially at least, were commanded to stay behind the lines and generally did as they were told, without demur. For at least one soldier, confession and absolution meant that "the Church of Rome sent a man into action mentally and spiritually cleansed," and thus prepared for death, whereas "the Church of England could only offer you a cigarette."[89] In almost two years of war, the violent and premature deaths of so many young men overseas, whose bodies and personal effects were often irrecoverable by their grieving families, rendered traditional mourning practices and rituals irrelevant, inadequate, or impossible. At home, ostentatious expressions of grief by relatives were discouraged as unpatriotic, as was the placing of memorial plaques in churches until after the war for fear of lowering morale. The result was widespread, chronic, and unresolved grief among those "left behind," for which release was craved no matter how temporary or what conventional or unconventional guise it might take.[90] In these extreme, highly charged times, the harder lines of British Protestantism gradually softened in a variety of directions—toward Catholicism, spiritualism, and an evolving ecumenism.[91] Public prayer for the departed, for example, still stigmatized by the abuses of the medieval chantry system, had not commonly been a part of Anglican worship in 1914, but by 1917 the demand for such orisons had persuaded the Archbishop of Canterbury to produce a new Form of Prayers, including a discretionary prayer for the dead; even then, one or two of his bishops protested that such prayers were contrary to scripture and Anglican teachings.[92] Anglo-Catholics welcomed this shift in the Church's position, openly offering requiems and issuing cards that bore the portraits of soldiers for whom the requiem was to be given.[93] In this context the early discussion of plans for a temporary monument to the dead in Whitehall is revealing: initially Lloyd George's idea was to build a "catafalque . . . past which the troops would march and salute the dead"; Lord Curzon, however, considered this "more essentially suitable to the Latin temperament." Lutyens was finally instructed to produce a nondenominational structure, and it was his suggestion that the name be changed from catafalque to cenotaph, meaning "empty tomb" and implying resurrection, but pointedly avoiding association with the Latin mass for the dead.[94]

For musically aware listeners of the time, references to the motifs from *Gerontius* associated with "Christ's Peace" and "Christ's Agony" that run through *The Spirit of England* articulated a further meaningful theme for those at the front and at home. A British soldier was called upon to sacrifice himself for the greater good (to be willing to kill and be killed), but also, for some, to atone for a sense of national sin—the selfish materialism, disunity, and moral dissipation of the older generations. Binyon hints at this in the second stanza, line 3, of "The Fourth of August." Similarly, the protagonist of H. G. Wells's wartime novel, *Mr. Britling Sees It Through* (1916), is haunted by the notion of "redemption by the shedding of blood" once war becomes a reality.[95] Wells describes Mr. Britling musing on a few such home truths—among them the complacency of the British government before the war—in the opening scenes of this semiautobiographical novel:

Not only was [Mr. Britling] a pampered, undisciplined sort of human being; he was living in a pampered, undisciplined sort of community. The two things went together. . . . This confounded Irish business, one could laugh at it in the daylight, but was it indeed a thing to laugh at? We were drifting lazily towards a real disaster. We had a government that seemed guided by the principles of Mr. Micawber, and adopted for its watchword "Wait and see." For months now this trouble had grown more threatening. Suppose presently that civil war broke out in Ireland! Suppose presently that these irritated, mishandled suffragettes did some desperate irreconcilable thing, assassinated for example! That bomb in Westminster Abbey the other day might have killed a dozen people. . . . Suppose the smouldering criticism of British rule in India and Egypt were fanned by administrative indiscretions into a flame.[96]

If the mass shedding of blood was a catharsis by which the nation would be united and cleansed, individual redemption and collective redemption were thus intertwined, inviting parallels between the heroism of the most low-born Tommy in the trenches and the atonement vouchsafed to Christians through the Blood of Christ. At the front British Protestants were brought into a relationship with Catholic imagery and culture such as most had probably never known. Fighting in a Catholic country and often along-side Catholic comrades, they came across roadside shrines in every village—crucifixes, calvaries, madonnas, and saints—that would sometimes assume a symbolic value according to the extent to which they had been spared or suffered shell damage.[97] Amid the carnage and desolation of the trenches, such symbolism encouraged a powerful identification with the sufferings of Christ, both for the soldier at the front—as a fellow sufferer probably more than as a savior—and for his relatives at home looking for consolation. The poetry of the trenches is full of references to Christ, as in "The Redeemer" from Siegfried Sassoon's *The Old Huntsman and Other Poems*. In the rain-sodden night, the speaker struggles along a ditch with his company; in the burst of a shell he looks back at his comrade and sees a vision of Christ laboring under the cross. The merging of the two images implies a connection of pain, endurance, and unprotesting self-sacrifice suffered by one extraordinary but ordinary man for the redemption of others: "But to the end, unjudging, he'll endure / Horror and pain, not uncontent to die / That Lancaster on Lune may stand secure."[98] After the war, this idea would also find expression in Stanley Spencer's canvas *The Resurrection of the Soldiers* at the Oratory of All Souls, Sandham Memorial Chapel (Burghclere, Hampshire), which drew on the artist's own experiences of action at Salonica. Here the viewer is literally overwhelmed by images of the cross, as soldiers emerge from the ground, dusting themselves down and shaking hands with resurrected comrades, and present their crosses to the figure of Jesus in the middle distance. Lying on the side of a collapsed wagon, a single soldier ponders the figure of Christ on a crucifix.[99]

Relatives of combatants found comfort in images of Christ on the battlefield, which not only seemed to confirm the nobility and holiness of the cause, but also, if death was to be the fate of their loved ones, the promise of redemption by self-sacrifice. One of the most popular images of consolation, one with strong Catholic overtones, was a colored print taken from an oil painting commissioned for the Christmas 1914 edition of *The Graphic*, titled *Duty* or *The Great Sacrifice* (see figure 3). The artist, James Clark, depicts a young soldier lying dead from a head wound on the battlefield ("sacrificed on the altar of duty to country"), his hand touching the feet of a spectral Christ, haloed by the sun, who seems to gaze down in recognition from the cross. This print was circulated across the country, endorsed by at least five of the nation's bishops, and further copies of this, dubbed

Figure 3. James Clark, *Duty*, also known as *The Great Sacrifice*, oil on canvas, 1914. Donated by Clark to the Royal Academy's War Relief Exhibition on January 8, 1915, it was bought by Queen Mary, who gave it to Princess Beatrice in memory of her son Prince Maurice Battenberg who had died at Ypres in 1914. Beatrice presented it to St. Mildred's Church, Whippingham, Isle of Wight, where it now hangs in the Battenberg Chapel. Photo Rachel Cowgill.

the "most inspired Picture of the War," were offered for sale in *The Graphic* of February 6, 1915.[100] It could be found hanging in churches, Sunday Schools, soldiers' institutes, public halls, classrooms, and private houses, and after the war it was used in several places as a design for stained-glass memorial windows.[101] The print was so ubiquitous it is difficult to imagine that Elgar and his associates were unaware of it, just as the mass rallies and jingoistic speeches of the charismatic Anglican bishop of London, Arthur Foley Winnington-Ingram (1858–1946)—born in Worcestershire, like Elgar—must also have entered their consciousness at some level. Christ was often in the bishop's sights, and he often spoke of the war as a struggle between "Christ and Odin," "Berlin against Bethlehem," or of "the Nailed Hand and the Iron Fist."[102] Sometimes delivered in his uniform as chaplain to the London rifle brigade, and from a truck swathed in Union Jacks or an altar of drums, his fervent, imperialist sermons did much to alienate his countrymen, particularly in the months following the Somme; but throughout the war years his message was simple and unswerving, as in this example, speaking of bereaved parents who had visited him for succor in Advent 1916:

> The precious blood of their dearest boy mingles with the Precious Blood which flowed in Calvary; again the world is being redeemed by precious blood. "CHRIST did what my boy did; my boy imitated what CHRIST did" they say.[103]

The presence of the motifs associated with Christ from *The Dream of Gerontius* in *The Spirit of England* does not imply that Elgar shared the bishop's starry-eyed jingoism. Daniel M. Grimley has noted how Elgar repeatedly undercuts even his most powerful and assertive moments of uplifting nobility in *The Spirit of England,* particularly in the final movement, "For the Fallen." The resulting atmosphere of uncertainty, melancholy reflection, and vulnerability is intensified by several striking features: the return to the opening material of "For the Fallen" in the closing moments; the movement's harmonic circularity, the putatively aspiring semitonal ascent in the overall tonal scheme of the trilogy (G, A-flat major/minor, and A minor); and particularly by the pensive rocking between A major and A minor in the final bars, marked *morendo*. With a passing reference to Catholic doctrine concerning the afterlife, Grimley observes:

> Elgar's music therefore suggests a state of musical, as well as spiritual purgatory. In Elgar's setting, Binyon's words "At the going down of the sun and in the morning / We will remember them" become

an anguished expression of longing for closure or death, and not merely a patriotic act of remembrance. Far from being a moment of consolation, it is the most troubled music in the whole work.[104]

It was this profound emotional complexity that made *The Spirit of England* such a powerful work expressing a righteous idealism tempered by grief and attrition as the war dragged on. H. G. Wells concludes his 1916 novel with an ambiguity that echoes Elgar's final measures. Adopting the persona of Mr. Britling, whose only son is killed in action, the author works through his emotional and rational responses to the war toward a declaration of faith in "our sons who have shown us God"; but the seemingly serene pastoral sunrise with which the novel concludes is tainted by the inevitability of further bloodshed, especially in the chilling final line ("From away towards the church came the sound of an early worker whetting a scythe").[105]

Elgar conducted the completed *Spirit of England* on October 31, 1917, (the eve of All Saints' Day), along with *The Dream of Gerontius*, in a Choral Union concert at Leeds Town Hall, and again on November 24 at a Royal Choral Society Concert at the Royal Albert Hall. For twenty years or so afterward, the composer continued to direct cathedral performances of "For the Fallen" at the Three Choirs Festival and, as previously noted, for Armistice Day services and concerts broadcast by the BBC.[106] In *The Spirit of England* Elgar reengaged with eschatological themes familiar from *The Dream of Gerontius* and his fraught oratorio project that culminated in the abandonment of *The Last Judgement*—namely, afterlife, purgatory, and redemption. This vein of Roman Catholic doctrine was combined with a reflective and consoling, though ultimately inconclusive message to his fellow countrymen and women tested to extremes in the worst excesses of the war that theirs was a divine cause, and their physical and spiritual suffering necessary for the emergence of a newly purified Europe: "redemption by the shedding of blood."[107] The Catholic elements discussed here are discernible but never brought conspicuously into the foreground, Elgar demonstrating again his ability to explore aspects of his own spirituality in music without disturbing Protestant sensibilities. Indeed, *The Spirit of England* seems in many ways to anticipate the more ecumenical and internationalist outlook that emerged among Anglicans in the years after the war—a step on the way to John Foulds's *World Requiem* (1919–21), dedicated to "the memory of the Dead—a message of consolation to the bereaved of all countries."[108] With its eclectic text, combining passages from the Latin Mass for the Dead, John Bunyan, and the fifteenth-century Hindu mystic Kabir among others, Foulds's score was certainly far removed from the traditions of English oratorio prevalent in the eighteenth and nineteenth centuries in which England, through metaphor, is depicted as a Protestant bastion in a sea of decadent and minatory Catholicism.

The contexts in which *The Spirit of England* were heard over the airwaves in the years after 1918 also seem to point to the future, although it is not always clear how far programming decisions were influenced by Elgar himself. On November 11, 1924, in a BBC concert broadcast from Birmingham, the cantata was heard in the midst of a miscellaneous sequence apparently assembled to create a narrative from mourning to jubilation: the hymn "O God Our Help in Ages Past"; Sullivan's Overture *In Memoriam;* Elgar's *The Spirit of England;* a "dramatic recital" of poetry by Rupert Brooke; "I Know that My Redeemer Liveth" from Handel's *Messiah;* Elgar's "The Immortal Legions" from his recent *Pageant of Empire* music; as well as the first *Pomp and Circumstance* march.[109] In 1925 Elgar conducted the London Wireless Orchestra in the introspective third movement of his First Symphony and the "Meditation" from his *Lux Christi* (an instrumental interlude from Elgar's first oratorio that is saturated with themes associated with Christ in that work) as a prelude to the commemoration service at Canterbury Cathedral; this was followed immediately by the complete *Spirit of England,* and later in the evening by the first and second *Pomp and Circumstance* marches.[110] And Elgar's *Enigma* Variations, op. 36, and "For the Fallen" concluded the radio program *In Memoriam 1914–1918: A Chronicle,* compiled by E. A. Harding and Val Gielgud, and broadcast from all BBC stations on Armistice Day evening in 1932. Poetry reading formed the main part of this program, which combined the voices of soldier and noncombatant poets alike, in a selection drawn from John Masefield, Rupert Brooke, Herbert Asquith, Laurence Binyon, Julian Grenfell, Alan Seeger, Wilfrid Gibson, William Noel Hodgson, Edward Shanks, Siegfried Sassoon, Robert Graves, Wilfred Owen, Richard Aldington, Lord Dunsany, and Thomas Hardy.[111] One can only wonder what sort of impact these events might have had on the young Benjamin Britten—then a schoolboy—and how much, if anything, he may have later recalled of such broadcasts as he began to interleave texts drawn from the requiem mass with poems by Wilfred Owen, preparing to commemorate the dead of another war in his *War Requiem* of 1961 for Coventry Cathedral.[112]

NOTES

My thanks to the Arts and Humanities Research Council (United Kingdom) for supporting part of this research, and to the staffs of the Elgar Birthplace Museum; Brotherton Library Special Collections (University of Leeds); British Library; BBC Written Archives; and St. Mildred's Church, Whippingham, Isle of Wight for their assistance. I am grateful to Byron Adams, Charles Edward McGuire, Derek Scott, and Aidan J. Thomson for generous suggestions and comments on an early version of this essay read as a paper at the Second Biennial Conference of the North American British Music Studies Association, August 2006, as well as to Julian Rushton for his thoughts at various stages of the project.

1. Epigraph: H. G. Wells, *The War That Will End War* (London: Frank & Cecil Palmer, 1914), repr. in W. Warren Wagar, ed., *H. G. Wells: Journalism and Prophecy, 1893–1946* (London: Bodley Head, 1965), 57.

2. Richards argues that *The Dream of Gerontius* "may not be a directly imperial work, but it contains something of the spirit of Elgar's Empire, the idea of Empire as a vehicle for struggle and sacrifice." Jeffrey Richards, *Imperialism and Music: Britain, 1876–1953* (Manchester and New York: Manchester University Press, 2001), 60–61.

3. W. H. Reed completely ruled out discussion of Elgar's faith in his memoir, *Elgar as I Knew Him* (London: Victor Gollancz, 1936). Though acknowledging the "very strong trait" of "mysticism" that "came out in all [Elgar] did, and of course found its way into his music," Reed declared this "is no place to discuss creeds or religions, or what he believed and what he did not." Citing the third movement of *Spirit of England* and a secular part-song of 1909, he continued, "[Elgar] has more of that quality which we call—for want of a better word—spirituality than perhaps any other composer. One can open the pages of almost any of his works—oratorios, symphonies, or short works like "For the Fallen" or "Go, Song of Mine" [op. 57]—to find this quality evident and unmistakable" (138–39).

4. See Byron Adams, "Elgar's Later Oratorios: Roman Catholicism, Decadence and the Wagnerian Dialectic of Shame and Grace," and John Butt, "Roman Catholicism and Being Musically English: Elgar's Church and Organ Music," in *The Cambridge Companion to Elgar*, ed. Daniel M. Grimley and Julian Rushton (Cambridge: Cambridge University Press, 2004), 81–105; 106–19.

5. Jerrold Northrop Moore, *Spirit of England: Edward Elgar in His World* (London: Heinemann, 1984), 56.

6. Ibid., 150.

7. Donald Mitchell, "Some Thoughts on Elgar," *An Elgar Companion*, ed. Christopher Redwood (Ashbourne: Sequoia Publishing, 1982), 284. Mitchell's perception has been reinforced through the recording history of the work: *The Spirit of England* is often paired with Elgar's *Coronation Ode* and packaged with cover art based on images of the British monarchy, billowing Union Jacks, etc. See, for example, the 1985 Chandos recording (CHAN 8430) that reproduces an image of "The King as He Will Appear in Coronation Robes" from a Colman's Starch trade card issued just before the coronation of Edward VII in 1902 (Mary Evans Picture Library, ref. 10083782).

8. See also Basil Maine's description of this section, in *Elgar: His Life and Works*, 2 vols. (London: G. Bell, 1933), 2:239. Maine makes a clear distinction, however, between the tone of *The Spirit of England* and that of other, imperialist Elgar works: "The conception is

grandiose, but not as the 'Pomp and Circumstance' Marches are. It moves along with no less splendour, but with a more austere deliberation."

9. See, for example, Bernard Porter's summary dismissal of *The Spirit of England* in "Elgar and Empire: Music, Nationalism and the War," in *Oh, My Horses! Elgar and the Great War,* ed. Lewis Foreman (Rickmansworth: Elgar Editions, 2001), 148–49. Porter does concede that the third movement ("For the Fallen,") "may be thought to compensate for the bitterness (but not the jingoism, still) of the rest." Porter, "Elgar and Empire: Music Nationalism and the War," 149.

10. For a detailed discussion of Elgar's early training as a Catholic, see Charles Edward McGuire's essay in this volume.

11. Letter from Elgar to Frank Schuster, 25 August 1914, in *Edward Elgar: Letters of a Lifetime,* ed. Jerrold Northrop Moore, (Oxford: Clarendon Press, 1990), 276–77.

12. On the fate of the horses at Mafeking, see Robert Baden-Powell, *Lessons from the 'Varsity' of Life* (London: C. A. Pearson, 1933), 207–9. Robert Anderson also reads Elgar's remark in the light of the mass mustering of horsepower undertaken by Britain, Russia, Germany, and Austria in the first weeks of August; see Robert Anderson, *Elgar and Chivalry* (Rickmansworth: Elgar Editions, 2002), 341.

13. Elgar to Schuster, 25 August 1914, Moore, *Letters of a Lifetime,* 276. Declaring his age (fifty-seven) on a "Householder's Return" for a Parliamentary Recruiting Committee, Elgar stated, "There is no person in this house qualified to enlist: I will do so if permitted"; quoted in Moore, *Letters of a Lifetime,* 283.

14. Cammaerts was a geographer by training (via the University of Brussels and Université Nouvelle) and something of "*un homme de lettres.*" Though Belgian by birth, he was a devout Anglican, and was deeply committed to the Anglo-Belgian Union. He had moved to England in 1908, married the Shakespearean actress Tita Brand, and in 1931 would become professor of Belgian Studies and Institutions at the University of London. *Carillon* was Elgar's contribution to an anthology assembled by the novelist Hall Caine to raise funds for the citizens of occupied Belgium, *King Albert's Book: A Tribute to the Belgian King and People from Representative Men and Women Throughout the World* (London: Daily Telegraph, Christmas 1914), 84–89. For a summary of Elgar's activities during the war years, including the periods in which he was working on *The Spirit of England,* see Andrew Neill, "Elgar's War: From the Diaries of Lady Elgar, 1914–1918"; and Martin Bird, "An Elgarian Wartime Chronology," in Foreman, *Elgar and the Great War,* 3–69; 389–455. On the revision of "Land of Hope and Glory," see Moore, *Letters of a Lifetime* (London: Elkin Matthews, 1914), 277–83.

15. According to Robert Anderson, the copy of Binyon's *The Winnowing-Fan: Poems on the Great War* (London: Elkin Matthews, 1914) which Elgar worked from and annotated is held at the library of the Elgar Birthplace Museum (hereafter EBM); see Robert Anderson, *Elgar in Manuscript* (London: British Library, 1990), 197. At present the copy cannot be traced. Elgar's work on *The Spirit of England* began in early February: Alice Elgar records an afternoon visit from Binyon and several other friends on February 7, 1915, two days after which she notes in her diary, "E. put off going to Tree's Dejeuné [*sic*] & composed violently." Bird, "An Elgarian Wartime Chronology," 397.

16. See Lewis Foreman, "The Winnowing-Fan: British Music in Wartime," in *Elgar and the Great War,* 125; and David Cannadine, "War and Death, Grief and Mourning in Modern Britain," in *Mirrors of Mortality: Studies in the Social History of Death,* ed. Joachim Whaley (London: Europa, 1981), 223–24. On *With Proud Thanksgiving,* see Robert Anderson and Jerrold Northrop Moore, foreword to *Elgar Complete Edition* 10:x–xi. This commission may have been prompted by Kipling's recommendation that the Whitehall Cenotaph be inscribed with Binyon's quatrain: Kipling had been deeply moved by the poem, which was sent to him by a soldier at the front on hearing that the author's only son, John, was

missing in action (in fact, killed) at Loos in 1915; see John Hatcher, *Laurence Binyon: Poet, Scholar of East and West* (Oxford: Clarendon Press, 1995), 210–11. Elgar produced the orchestral version of *With Proud Thanksgiving* for the jubilee of the Royal Choral Society and the Royal Albert Hall on May 7, 1921.

17. Ronald Taylor lists six live broadcast performances of *The Spirit of England* (and four partial performances, presumably of "For the Fallen" as a self-standing item) between 1922 and 1934; see his "Music in the Air: Elgar and the BBC," in *Edward Elgar: Music and Literature,* ed. Raymond Monk (Aldershot: Scolar Press, 1993), 336. See also Jenny Doctor, "Broadcasting's Ally: Elgar and the BBC," in *Cambridge Companion to Elgar,* 202–3.

18. Letter from Elgar to Alice Stuart-Wortley, 12 September 1923, in *Edward Elgar: The Windflower Letters. Correspondence with Alice Caroline Stuart Wortley and Her Family,* ed. Jerrold Northrop Moore (Oxford: Clarendon Press, 1989), 284. See also Maine, *Elgar* 2:240. Ultimately it would be "Nimrod" from the *Enigma* Variations that would be established as Elgar's contribution to the rites of war remembrance. On the music of Armistice Day and Remembrance Day, see Richards, *Imperialism and Music,* 152–64.

19. See James Morgan Read, *Atrocity Propaganda 1914–1919* (New Haven: Yale University Press, 1941), 7.

20. Colvin to Elgar, EBM L3453.

21. Quoted in S. Levy, letter to the editor, "'For the Fallen,'" *Times Literary Supplement,* 23 November 1946, 577.

22. Hatcher, *Laurence Binyon,* 190–91. On Binyon's own religious beliefs, see 129–34 passim.

23. Ibid., 195. For Binyon's published work, including his studies of Eastern art, Blake, and later studies of Christopher Smart, Dante, and others, see 299–310. Other composers were also drawn to "For the Fallen," including Cyril Rootham, whose setting slightly predated Elgar's and from whom Elgar encountered considerable obstruction during the composition of *The Spirit of England;* see John Norris, "The Spirit of Elgar: Crucible of Remembrance," in Foreman, *Elgar and the Great War,* 241–44. The composer and war poet Ivor Gurney toyed with setting the poem for baritone and piano while at the front; see letters from Gurney to Mrs. Voyrich, 16 September 1916, and to Marion Scott, 11 January 1917, in *Ivor Gurney: Collected Letters,* ed. R. K. R. Thornton (Ashington and Manchester: Mid-Northumberland Arts Group and Carcanet, 1991), 148–49,184.

24. Quoted in Hatcher, *Laurence Binyon,* 1. In their experiences of the war, David Cannadine stresses the difference between "those at the front, who saw and purveyed *death,* and those at home, who saw no death, no carnage and no corpses, but experienced *bereavement.*" Cannadine,"War and Death, Grief and Mourning in Modern Britain," 213. On this important distinction, see also Jay Winter, *Sites of Memory, Sites of Mourning: The Great War in European Cultural History* (Cambridge: Cambridge University Press, 1995), passim. From 1915 Binyon used his annual leave from the British Museum to work as a volunteer ambulance driver, hospital orderly, and medical reporter in France; see Hatcher, *Laurence Binyon,* 198–210. It is worth noting here that Binyon's long dramatic poem, *The Madness of Merlin* (London: Macmillan, 1947), based on Geoffrey of Monmouth's tale of a twelfth-century Welsh prince who waged war on the Picts but was horrified by the slaughter and fled the battlefield to roam the forests, had been offered by him to Elgar as the basis for an opera several years before work began on *The Spirit of England;* see letter from Binyon to Elgar, 11 July [1904/9], EBM L2312.

25. Sidney Colvin considered Ruskin the "idol of my boyhood": "I used to devour my Scott and Shakespeare, and *Faery Queene* and *Modern Painters* and *Stones of Venice . . .* and learn long screeds of them, both verse and prose, by heart." As a student at Cambridge he sought out and was befriended by the Ruskins, and aspired to become "something like a Ruskin and a Matthew Arnold rolled into one." Sidney Colvin, *Memories and Notes of Persons*

and Places, 1852–1912 (London: Edward Arnold, 1921); and retirement speech (1912), quoted in E. V. Lucas, *The Colvins and Their Friends* (London: Methuen, 1928), 5, 8.

26. John Ruskin, *Modern Painters*, vol. 3, last chapter, quoted in Sidney Colvin, letter to the editor, "1855 and 1915," *Times Literary Supplement*, 31 December 1914, 590.

27. Cannadine, "War and Death, Grief and Mourning in Modern Britain," 195.

28. Hatcher, *Laurence Binyon*, 192. Colvin was not the only one to push Elgar to write a "requiem." Later that year, on November 25, Percy Scholes wrote an "Appeal to Elgar" in the pages of the *Evening Standard* and *St. James's Gazette*, in which he lamented the over-reliance on Brahms's *German Requiem* at military funerals and called for Elgar to write a "British Requiem": "In 'Gerontius,' Elgar was able to take us into the chamber of death, and the places that lay beyond, to show us death and judgment, to stir us with dread and sooth us with comfort, to move us to sorrow and to final joy. In 'Carillon,' by certain means of the utmost simplicity, he has expressed the feelings of a nation mourning the woes of the present and rejoicing in the hopes of the happiness to come again, and has done so in a way that has given his work an appeal to audiences in this country such as no other work at present before us enjoys. Elgar is a sincere Catholic, as 'Gerontius' testifies; but he is a Briton, too. Cannot he write a choral piece which shall be wide enough in its verbal utterance to express the feelings of us all, whatever our faith, something vocally not too difficult for our choral societies . . . ? Something we would have that can be sung in Westminster Abbey and [the Roman Catholic] Westminster Cathedral, in church, in chapel and in concert-room, which can be sung here and in Canada and Australia and South Africa."

29. Paul Rodmell, *Charles Villiers Stanford* (Aldershot: Ashgate Press, 2002), 192–93. For Scholes, Stanford's "fine" Requiem did not meet the criteria for a "national death song" (see preceding note), because it represented "a ritual not understood by a majority of our countrymen" and the text was in Latin. Stanford had played through the whole of his new Requiem for Elgar while on a visit to Malvern. It is not known how Elgar responded to this performance. Jeremy Dibble, "Elgar and His British Contemporaries," in *Cambridge Companion to Elgar*, 20–21. On earlier attitudes to musical settings of Roman Catholic texts in England, see Rachel Cowgill, "'Hence, Base Intruder, Hence': Rejection and Assimilation in the Early English Reception of Mozart's Requiem," in *Europe, Empire, and Spectacle in Nineteenth-Century British Music*, ed. Rachel Cowgill and Julian Rushton (Aldershot: Ashgate Press, 2006), 9–27. On other British "requiems" from the war years, see Foreman, "The Winnowing-Fan: British Music in Wartime," 113–14.

30. For extensive investigation of the deep-seated divisions between Catholics and Protestants in nineteenth-century English culture, see D. G. Paz, *Popular Anti-Catholicism in Mid-Victorian England* (Stanford, Calif.: Stanford University Press, 1992), John Wolffe, *God & Greater Britain: Religion and National Life in Britain and Ireland 1843–1945* (London and New York: Routledge, 1994); and Michael Wheeler, *The Old Enemies: Catholic and Protestant in Nineteenth-Century English Culture* (Cambridge: Cambridge University Press, 2006). These divisions also extended to matters of musical style, as is apparent in Herbert Thompson's review of a Hull Harmonic Society performance of Gounod's *Messe solonnelle*, *Yorkshire Post* (23 March 1918): "One can understand its popularity as a concert piece, for it is highly attractive music, tuneful and effective, and expressive, in a rather superficial way, of its theme. But that it should have been accepted so much as it has been in the service of the English Church is more remarkable, for one would think its perfumed exotic quality strangely at variance with the Anglo-Saxon temperament, at least in matters of religious observance." Anglican music should be dignified and sober in comparison, he explains, but not dry or overly erudite. See press-cuttings collection, dated and annotated by Thompson himself, Leeds University, Brotherton Library Special Collections, MS 164.

31. Adams, "Elgar's Later Oratorios," 83.

32. Transcribed by Jerrold Northrop Moore from a conversation with Elgar's doctor, Arthur Thomson, in *Edward Elgar: A Creative Life* (Oxford: Oxford University Press, 1984), 818.

33. From conversations between Moore and members of the Leicester family in Moore, *Elgar: A Creative Life*, 823. See also Charles Edward McGuire's essay in this volume. Though legalized in 1902, cremation remained a controversial choice in British society until well after the First World War, mainly because of widespread belief in the resurrection of the material body. The Church of England officially accepted cremation in 1944, but it was not until 1965 that the Vatican Council reversed its 1886 ban on cremation for Catholics. See *Death in England: An Illustrated History*, ed. Peter C. Jupp and Clare Gittings (Manchester: Manchester University Press, 1999), 249–51, 264–66.

34. Butt, "Roman Catholicism and Being Musically English," 107; Philip Leicester, manuscript account of Elgar's visit, 2 June 1914, in Moore, *Letters of a Lifetime*, 269–74. For more on the Leicester family, see Charles Edward McGuire's essay in this volume, as well as that of Matthew Riley.

35. For accounts of Elgar's sacred music composition, see Butt, "Roman Catholicism and Being Musically English"; and John Allison, *Edward Elgar: Sacred Music* (Bridgend: Seren, 1994). Elgar turned down an invitation to compose a mass for the Leeds Festival in 1903–1904 in order to continue his work on the First Symphony and *The Apostles;* see letter from Frederick Spark to Elgar, cited in Cecil Bloom, "Elgar—The Leeds Connection, Part I," *Elgar Society Journal* 9 (1995): 75.

36. Quotation from Butt, "Roman Catholicism and Being Musically English," 117.

37. From 1906 Elgar's interest in *The Last Judgement* fluctuated, but the project was on his mind in the early years of the war: Atkins offered him a commission if he finished the trilogy for the Three Choirs Festival in 1914, and in 1915 Elgar told Henry Embleton of the Leeds Festival Committee that he might complete the projected oratorio after the war. He would continue to gather relevant reading matter until around 1923, including R. H. Charles, *Lectures on the Apocalypse* (1922) and other material on the Antichrist. See Charles Edward McGuire, *Elgar's Oratorios: The Creation of an Epic Narrative* (Aldershot: Ashgate Press, 2002), 293–301.

38. E. Wulstan Atkins, *The Elgar-Atkins Friendship* (Newton Abbot, London, and North Pomfret, Vt.: David & Charles, 1984), 165, 169–70.

39. Charles Edward McGuire, "One Story, Two Visions: Textual Differences between Elgar's and Newman's *The Dream of Gerontius*," in *The Best of Me: A Gerontius Centenary Companion*, ed. Geoffrey Hodgkins (Rickmansworth: Elgar Editions, 1999), 84–101.

40. The excised passage reads: "Now let the golden prison ope its gates, / Making sweet music, as each fold revolves / Upon its ready hinge. And ye great powers, / Angels of Purgatory, receive from me / My charge, a precious soul, until the day, / When, from all bond and forfeiture released, / I shall reclaim it for the courts of light." Elgar's deletions in Newman's poem are detailed in Hodgkins, *Best of Me*, 41–55.

41. Lewis Foreman, "Elgar and *Gerontius:* The Early Performances," in Hodgkins, *Best of Me*, 211–13.

42. Jerrold Northrop Moore, ed., *Elgar and His Publishers: Letters of a Creative Life*, Vol. I, *1885–1903* (Oxford: Clarendon Press, 1987), 351–52, 354–55. See also Atkins, *Elgar-Atkins Friendship*, 70–73.

43. Anthony Boden, *Gloucester, Hereford, Worcester—Three Choirs: A History of the Festival* (Stroud: Alan Sutton, 1992), 142–43, 148. At the 1910 Three Choirs performance of *Gerontius* in Gloucester Cathedral, Elgar's oratorio was preceded by the premiere of Vaughan Williams's *Fantasia on a Theme of Thomas Tallis*, which may have been an attempt to create a Protestant *cordon sanitaire* around the Roman Catholic oratorio. See Charles Edward McGuire, "Vaughan

Williams and the English Music Festival," in *Vaughan Williams Essays,* ed. Byron Adams and Robin Wells (Aldershot: Ashgate Press, 2003), 260–61.

44. Adams, "Elgar's Later Oratorios," 95.

45. Elgar may have intended to call this movement "England"; see "Performances of 'The Dream of Gerontius' and New Choral Work by Sir Edward Elgar: A Remarkable Scheme," *The Musical Times,* 1 April 1916.

46. Elgar repeats this stanza at the conclusion of the first movement.

47. A sketch of this passage carries the note "aeroplanes stanza III." See British Library Add. MS 47908, fol. 142.

48. Stanzas three, four, and six here were omitted when Elgar reworked "For the Fallen" two years after the war for the dedication of the Cenotaph in Whitehall, giving this the title *With Proud Thanksgiving.* See Robert Anderson, *Elgar* (New York: Schirmer, 1993), 205–6.

49. This and the following stanza formed part of the section marked *Marziale* in the manuscript vocal score (British Library, Add MS. 58040), described by Elgar in a letter to Ernest Newman of 15 April 1916, as "a sort of idealised (perhaps) Quick March,—the sort of thing which ran in my mind when the dear lads were swinging past so many, many times." See Moore, *Letters of a Lifetime,* 297.

50. Elgar altered this line to read: "They shall not grow old."

51. Robert Bridges, Preface, *The Spirit of Man: An Anthology in English & French from the Philosophers & Poets Made by the Poet Laureate in 1915* (London: Longmans Green, 1916); the month of publication is given in Alan Wilkinson, *The Church of England and the First World War* (London: SPCK), 171. The Binyon settings are not referred to as "The Spirit of England" in the Elgars' journals and correspondence until the later stages of composition: *The Musical Times* announced the projected title on April 1, 1916. Bridges' "preface" conveys much the same message as Binyon's "The Fourth of August," condemning Prussian aggression unequivocally, stating: "Common diversions divert us no longer; our habits and thoughts are searched by the glare of the conviction that man's life is not the ease that a peace-loving generation has found it or thought to make it; and it is in their abundant testimony to the good and beautiful that we find support for our faith, and distraction from a grief that is intolerable constantly to face, nay impossible to without that trust in God which makes all things possible. We may see that our national follies and sins have deserved punishment; and if in this revelation of rottenness we cannot ourselves appear wholly sound, we are still free and true at heart, and can take hope in contrition, and in the brave endurance of sufferings that should chasten our intention and conduct; we can even be grateful for the discipline: but beyond this it is offered us to take joy in the thought that our country is called of God to stand for the truth of man's hope, and that it has not shrunk from the call. Here we stand upright, and above reproach: and to show ourselves worthy will be more than consolation; for truly it is the hope of man's great desire, the desire for brotherhood and universal peace to men of good-will, that is at stake in this struggle. Britons have ever fought well for their country, and their country's Cause is the high Cause of Freedom and Honour. That fairest earthly fame, the fame of Freedom, is inseparable from the names of Albion, Britain, England: it has gone out to America and the Antipodes, hallowing the names of Canada, Australia, and New Zealand; it has found a new home in Africa: and this heritage is our glory and happiness. We can therefore be happy in our sorrows, happy even in the death of our beloved who fall in the fight; for they die nobly, as heroes and saints die, with hearts and hands unstained by hatred or wrong." Another prompt may have been the publication in 1915 of the R. Hon. George William Erskine Russell's *The Spirit of England,* in which Russell discussed the conduct of a nation in wartime: "I have often been accused of being unjust to the military spirit. In reply, I point to the spirit which animates the present conduct of Germany, and if that is

the military spirit, I am perfectly just to it, for it is, and I have called it, damnable. It has absolutely nothing in common with the spirit which fights for freedom and national existence, or sacrifices itself for the salvation of the weak." George William Erskine Russell, *The Spirit of England* (London: Smith, Elder & Co., 1915), 84–85, quoted in *The Bookman* 48 (August 1915): 142–43. As this was the same issue in which a wartime sonnet by Alice Elgar appeared, her husband may well have read the review that contained this quotation. See note 62 below.

52. Figures cited here are the rehearsal numbers printed in Novello's vocal scores and the full scores of these works in the *Elgar Complete Edition*. For discussion of the "Novissima hora est" motif and its significance for interpretations of *The Dream of Gerontius*, see Aidan Thomson, "Rereading Elgar: Hermeneutics, Criticism and Reception in England and Germany, 1900–1914," Ph.D. diss., Oxford University, 2002, 182–247, esp. 193. It should be noted that the tags for these motifs were supplied by Elgar's friend August Jaeger, with the composer's acquiescence. See Hodgkins, *Best of Me*, 86–87.

53. Moore, *Elgar: A Creative Life*, 303, 305.

54. Elgar points out this reuse of the passage from "The Fourth of August" in a letter to Ernest Newman, 17 June 1917, quoted in Moore, *Letters of a Lifetime*, 307.

55. Elgar drew Newman's attention to this thematic link between the movements, admitting to feeling "a certain connection in the spirit of the words 'BUT not to fail' and 'To the end they remain.'" See letter from Elgar to Newman, 15 April 1916, Moore, *Letters of a Lifetime*, 296–97. Newman communicated this in his article "'The Spirit of England': Edward Elgar's New Choral Work," *The Musical Times* (1 May 1916): 235–39.

56. Maine, *Elgar*, 2:240.

57. Moore, *Letters of a Lifetime*, 307. Elgar wrote to Binyon on April 17 to tell him that he had completed *The Spirit of England*, see EBM L3738.

58. See, for example, Andrew Neill, "Elgar's War," 45; John Norris, "Spirit of Elgar," 249; Anderson, *Elgar in Manuscript*, 149.

59. See British Library, Add. MS 47908, fols. 132–35; Anderson, "Sources," *Elgar Complete Edition* 10:xxi.

60. Theo Barker, "Speyer, Sir Edgar, Baronet," *Oxford Dictionary of National Biography Online*, accessed August 28, 2006. Binyon had met Elgar on at least one occasion courtesy of the Speyer household. See letter from Binyon to Elgar, 4 June 1909, EBM L2300 ("I hope you will not have forgotten, though it is a good long time ago now, meeting me at Mrs Speyer's"). See also Sophie Fuller's essay in this volume, 231.

61. Elgar Diaries (photostatic copies), 13:1914–15, EBM.

62. Letter from Streatfeild to Lady Elgar, enclosing a copy of her typewritten sonnet, 9 July 1915, EBM L6362; the sonnet was published in *The Bookman* 48 (August 1915): 121.

63. According to Trevor Wilson, this was "a special time of hate in Britain"; see his *The Myriad Faces of War: Britain and the Great War, 1914–1918* (Cambridge: Polity Press, 1986), 182. On the Bryce Report and its impact on the home front, see esp. 182–91; also Read, *Atrocity Propaganda*.

64. See also William Thompson Hill, *The Martyrdom of Nurse Cavell: The Life Story of the Victim of Germany's Most Barbarous Crime* (London: Hutchinson, 1915).

65. Elgar to Newman, 15 April 1916 in Moore, *Letters of a Lifetime*, 296–7.

66. *Musical Times* (1 June 1916): 235–9.

67. Stefan Zweig, *The World of Yesterday: An Autobiography*, trans. Cedar and Eden Paul (London: Cassell, 1987), 180. Ernst Lissauer, *Worte in die Zeit: Flugblätter 1914*, Blatt I (Göttingen, 1914). Exemplars of the following German editions of musical settings are held at the British Library: "Gott strafe England" (Munich: Simplicissimus Verlag, [n.d.]); and Guido Hassl, *"Gott strafe England!" Militär- und andere Humoresken* (Regensburg: Pustei,

1915). The third stanza was considered the most extreme, concluding with "Sie lieben vere-int, sie hassen vereint, / Sie haben aller nur einen Feind. / England." A passage from Lissauer's poem is read aloud in English to Mr. Britling, who listens in utter bewilderment, in H. G. Wells, *Mr. Britling Sees It Through* (London and New York: Cassell, 1916), 271–72.

68. Exemplars of these songs are held at the Bodleian Library, Oxford, and the British Library, and date from 1916 and 1917.

69. See the *Times*, 10 February 1917, for a report on the Royal College event; for the quoted passage concerning the military band burlesque, see the *Times*, 19 January 1918. I am grateful to Duncan Boutwood for drawing my attention to the Parry rendition.

70. Elgar to Newman, 17 June 1917 in Moore, *Letters of a Lifetime*, 307.

71. *The Musical Times* (1 July 1917): 295–97. See esp. 295 and 296.

72. Ibid., 296. The text here is of course "Low-born clods / of brute earth, / They aspire / to become gods."

73. Herbert Thompson, review of *The Dream of Gerontius* and *The Spirit of England* (complete), *Yorkshire Post*, 1 November 1917; and review of *The Dream of Gerontius*, *Yorkshire Post*, 5 March 1917. These observations were based on a long familiarity with *Gerontius:* by Thompson's own reckoning, the latter was the thirty-ninth performance he had attended. See Leeds University, Brotherton Library Special Collections, Diary of Herbert Thompson MS 80, and press cuttings collection MS 164.

74. Thompson, *Yorkshire Post*, 5 October 1917; press cuttings collection MS 164.

75. Goethe, who saw and who foretold
    A world revealed
    New-springing from its ashes old
    On Valmy field,

    When Prussia's sullen hosts retired
    Before the advance
    Of ragged, starved, but freedom-fired
    Soldiers of France;

    If still those clear, Olympian eyes
    Through smoke and rage
    Your ancient Europe scrutinize,
    What think you, Sage?

    Are these the armies of the Light
    That seek to drown
    The light of lands where freedom's fight
    Has won renown?

    Will they blot also out your name
    Because you praise
    All works of men that shrine the flame
    Of beauty's ways,

    Wherever men have proved them great,
    Nor, drunk with pride,
    Saw but a single swollen State
    And naught beside,

Nor dreamed of drilling Europe's mind
With threat and blow
The way professors have designed
Genius should go?

Or shall a people rise at length
And see and shake
The fetters from its giant strength,
And grandly break

This pedantry of feud and force
To man untrue
Thundering and blundering on its course
To death and rue?"

Hubert Parry, director of the Royal College of Music, shared Binyon's view and likened Germany's actions to the fall of Lucifer; see his speech to Royal College of Music students, September 1914, in *College Addresses*, ed. H. C. Colles (London: Macmillan Publishing, 1920), 215–29. Bridges also wrote of the willing connivance of German intellectuals "at the contradictory falsehoods officially imposed upon their assent" in his preface to *The Spirit of Man*.

76. See Matthew Riley's chapter in this volume for further connections between H. G. Wells's writings and Elgar.

77. Wells, *Journalism and Prophecy*, 56–57. In Wells's *God and the Invisible King* (London: Cassell, 1917) insanity is associated with extreme sin and disharmony arising from man's dark evolutionary past; see chapter on "Modern Ideas of Sin and Damnation." On Wells's religious beliefs, see Willis B. Glover, "Religious Orientations of H. G. Wells: A Case Study in Scientific Humanism," *Harvard Theological Review*, 65 (January 1972): 117–35.

78. The chorus comprises an alla marcia setting of the lines "Then loosen thy sword in the scabbard / and settle the helm on thine head. / For men betrayèd are mighty, / and great are the wrongfully dead." Elgar dedicated this score to Francis Edward Younghusband's Fight for Right movement, the foundation of which moved Robert Bridges to commission Parry's *Jerusalem* in March of the same year; see Jeremy Dibble, *C. Hubert H. Parry: His Life and Music* (Oxford: Clarendon, 1992), 483. Moore notes that Elgar's song was requested by the tenor Gervase Elwes; see Moore, *Elgar: A Creative Life*, 700.

79. Elgar Diaries, EBM; Atkins, *The Elgar-Atkins Friendship*, 267; Charles Mott would later be killed at the front; see Charles A. Hooey, "An Elgarian Tragedy: Remembering Charles Mott," in Foreman, *Elgar and the Great War*, 313.

80. Elgar Diaries, EBM.

81. Alice Elgar's diary, quoted in Bird, "An Elgarian Wartime Chronology," 411.

82. For Basil Maine's recollection of the impact of the war on musical life, see *Elgar*, 1:205. Choral performances were hampered by the scarcity of male voices. Other forms of concert life appear to have continued, however; see Foreman, "The Winnowing-Fan: British Music in Wartime," 91–92, 94–95. See also Christopher Fifield, *Ibbs and Tillett: The Rise and Fall of a Musical Empire* (Aldershot: Ashgate Press, 2005), 92–105.

83. *The Musical Times* (1 June 1916): 296, quoted in Hodgkins, *Best of Me*, 247–50. A program for this oratorio series is held at the Centre for Performance History, Royal College of Music.

84. Letter of R. A. Streatfeild to Alice Elgar, 14 May 1916, EBM L3732.

85. Winifred Ponder, *Clara Butt, Her Life-Story* [. . .] *with a Foreword by Dame Clara Butt* (London: George G. Harrap, 1928), 167–68.

86. Frances Colvin to Elgar, [8 May 1916], EBM L3460. On May 14, 1916, R. A. Streatfeild wrote to Lady Elgar calling for the first movement to be brought out at last: "I feel very strongly, & I wonder if you do too, that we ought to have 'The Fourth of August'

as soon as possible. 'To Women,' divinely beautiful as it is, is not in its place as a *beginning*. It is perfect as the slow movement of the trilogy, but is too intimate & personal in feeling to be the start of the whole. We want something dealing with broader and more general-ized emotions for that, & then 'To Women' will gain enormously by coming as a contrast"; see EBM L3732.

87. Maine, *Elgar,* 1:205. Emphasis added.

88. Wilkinson, *The Church of England in the First World War* (London: SPCK, 1978), 178.

89. Guy Chapman, *A Passionate Prodigality: Fragments of an Autobiography* (London: Nicholson & Watson, 1933), quoted in Wilkinson, *Church of England in the First World War,* 111. Wilkinson describes it as "tragic" that the chaplain-general from 1901 to 1925 was Bishop John Taylor Smith, "a pietistic Evangelical with no university theological training" (124). Furthermore, there were complaints that under Bishop Smith's jurisdiction Anglo-Catholics were discriminated against in the appointment of chaplains; see Wilkinson (126).

90. Pat Jalland, *Death in the Victorian Family* (Oxford: Oxford University Press, 1996), 358–81.

91. George W. E. Russell had anticipated that this would be the case: in his book *The Spirit of England* of 1915, he observed that "to several generations of Englishmen, a hatred of Roman Catholicism seemed a national virtue. They were apparently unable to discern even a trace of Christianity in the form of religion which we encounter when we travel in France or Italy or cross the Irish Channel. We long vaunted our resolve to 'knit the hearts of the Empire into one harmonious concord,' but (until the other day) we declined to let Irish Catholics have the schools or universities suited to them, because their religion was, as we gracefully put it, 'a lie and a heathenish superstition.' If the war has done nothing else for us, it has shown us scenes in France and Belgium before which this particular prejudice must, I should think, give way." Russell, *Spirit of England,* 282.

92. The explicit prayers for the dead contained in the 1549 Prayer Book had been almost entirely excised in the 1552 and 1662 revisions; see William Keiling, *Liturgiae Britannicae, or the Several Editions of the Book of Common Prayer of the Church of England, From Its Compilation to the Last Revision [...] Arranged to Show their Respective Variations,* 2nd ed. (London: William Pickering; Cambridge: J. Deighton, 1851). Wilkinson, *Church of England,* 176–77.

93. See, for example, Paul B. Bull's powerful sermon "Beyond the Veil," in *Peace and War: Notes of Sermons and Addresses* (London: Longmans, 1917), 86–92. Anglican support for the erection of street shrines (both to those serving and those lost in action overseas) can be seen as a similar moment of accommodation. Some Anglicans opposed the shrines because of their Catholic connotations—that is, their imagery, especially the use of the cross or crucifix and religious acts associated with them—but at least one clergyman who spoke out against them suffered physical assault, seemingly the reverse of the popular anti-Catholic violence seen during the mid-Victorian period. See Alex King, *Memorials of the Great War in Britain: The Symbolism and Politics of Remembrance* (Oxford and New York: Berg Publishers, Ltd., 1998), 47–60.

94. See Cannadine, "War and Death, Grief and Mourning in Modern Britain," 219–21, citing National Archives: Public Record Office (Kew), CAB 23/11, 1 July 1919.

95. For the phrase "redemption by the shedding of blood" see Wells, *Mr. Britling Sees It Through,* pp.283–84.

96. Ibid., 114–15, 284. See also Bridges, preface to *The Spirit of Man,* quoted in n. 51 above.

97. Wilkinson, *Church of England,* 190–91. This found an echo in the activities of the Society for Raising Wayside Crosses, which were probably encouraged by photographs and letters sent home from the front. On this organization, founded in 1916 with the Earl of Shaftesbury as its president, see King, *Memorials of the Great War,* 73–74; Rev. Sidney F. Smith, *Wayside Crosses and Holy Images* (London: Catholic Truth Society, 1917), 1–24; and

Rev. E. Hermitage Day, "Wayside Crosses and War Shrines," in *The Crucifix: An Outline Sketch of Its History,* ed. Katherine Kennedy (London: A. R. Mowbray, 1917), 77–84.

98. Siegfried Sassoon, *The Old Huntsman and Other Poems,* (London: William Heineman, 1917). The final stanza reads as follows: "He faced me, reeling in his weariness, / Shouldering his load of planks, so hard to bear. / I say that he was Christ, who wrought to bless / All groping things with freedom bright as air, / And with His mercy washed and made them fair. / Then the flame sank, and all grew black as pitch, / While we began to struggle along the ditch; / And someone flung his burden in the muck / Mumbling: 'O Christ Almighty, now I'm stuck!'"

99. Reproduced in Roy Strong, *The Spirit of Britain: A Narrative History of the Arts* (London: Pimlico, 1999), 603. See also *Art of the First World War,* item 104, http://www.art-ww1.com. The saturation of imagery associated with Christ helps to explain why rumors of German soldiers crucifying a Canadian officer with bayonets against a barn door at Ypres in 1915 aroused such a hysterical response across all levels of British society; see Read, *Atrocity Propaganda,* 41–42. For how this legend and others arose among the troops at the front, see also Paul Fussell, *The Great War and Modern Memory* (Oxford: Oxford University Press, 1975), 115–25. Due to centuries of Protestant suspicion of idolatry, the cross had only recently begun to be rehabilitated as a religious symbol and funerary monument in late nineteenth-century England (though it was often expressed in Celtic form to avoid Roman Catholic associations); see King, *Memorials of the Great War,* 129. On the battlefields, however, it was the preferred form for the hastily constructed markers of the graves of dead comrades, and after the war, there would be considerable popular resistance to the decision by the Imperial War Graves Commission not to use the cross as the template for the official war cemetery headstone. Cyril Winterbotham, who was killed in action on August 27, 1916, ended his poem "The Cross of Wood" with the words "Rest you content; more honourable far / Than all the Orders is the Cross of Wood, / The symbol of self-sacrifice that stood / Bearing the God whose brethren you are." E. B. Osborn, ed., *The Muse in Arms: A Collection of War Poems, for the Most Part Written in the Field of Action, by Seamen, Soldiers, and Flying Men Who Are Serving, or Have Served, in the Great War* (London: John Murray, 1917), 159–60. It falls beyond the scope of this current study to discuss *The Spirit of England* in relation to the images of the resurrection and Passion of Christ that recur in literary and artistic responses to the Great War elsewhere in Europe; for a relevant study, though one that mostly overlooks music, see Winter, *Sites of Memory, Sites of Mourning.* For more general insights into the relationship between religio-military identity and the story of Christ's Passion, see Jon Davies, "The Martial Uses of the Mass: War Remembrance as an Elementary Form of Religious Life," in *Ritual and Remembrance: Responses to Death in Human Societies,* ed. Jon Davies (Sheffield: Sheffield Academic Press, 1994), 152–64.

100. See reviews submitted to and published in *The Graphic,* 2 January 1915, by the Bishops of Bath & Wells, London, Hull, Stepney, Lichfield and Wakefield. The picture also inspired a range of poetic interpretations that appeared in subsequent issues of *The Graphic.*

101. See, for example, St. Mary Magdalene Church, Windmill Hill, Enfield, and St. John's Church, Windermere. St. John's was recently converted into assisted housing and the memorial window has been placed in storage by the Diocese of Carlisle. On the art and design of British war memorials in general, see the United Kingdom Inventory of War Memorials, http://www.uknim.org.uk.

102. Arthur Foley Winnington-Ingram, *A Day of God, Being Five Addresses on the Subject of the Present War* (London: Wells, Gardner, 1914), 10, 41, 42, 58; *Times Recruiting Supplement,* 3 November 1915; Arthur Foley Winnington-Ingram, *The Potter and the Clay* (London: Wells, Gardner, Darton, 1917), 11, 36.

103. Arthur Foley Winnington-Ingram, *Rays of Dawn* (London: Wells, Gardner, 1918), 66. On Winnington-Ingram's conduct during the war years, including his notorious sermon of hate in which he advocated the killing of Germans from the pulpit of Westminster Abbey, see Wilkinson, *Church of England,* 217–18, 251–54.

104. Daniel M. Grimley, "'Music in the Midst of Desolation': Structures of Mourning in Elgar's *The Spirit of England,*" in *Elgar Studies,* ed. J. P. E. Harper-Scott and Julian Rushton (Cambridge: Cambridge University Press, 2007). I am grateful to Daniel M. Grimley for making a draft of his essay available to me prior to publication. Ivor Atkins records how Elgar was "deeply moved" when he conducted a performance of "For the Fallen" followed immediately by the sounding of "The Last Post" from the Lady Chapel of Worcester Cathedral during a memorial service ("Recital of Solemn Music") given by the Worcester Festival Choral Society on March 15, 1917. The full "programme" was: Psalm 23 "The Lord Is My Shepherd"; "For the Fallen"; "The Last Post"; Russian Contakion of the Departed; Prelude, *The Dream of Gerontius;* J. S. Bach, Chorale "Jesu Meine Freude"; Handel, "I Know that My Redeemer Liveth," *Messiah;* hymn, "O God Our Help in Ages Past"; and the national anthem, "God Save the King." See Atkins, *Elgar-Atkins Friendship,* 281–84.

105. Wells, *Mr. Britling Sees It Through,* 432–33. Wells had three sons, the last of whom was born in 1914; none were lost in the First World War.

106. See Herbert Thompson's review in the *Yorkshire Post,* 1 November 1917; Charles A. Hooey, "Spirit Insights," *Elgar Society Journal* 9 (November 1996): 296–302. "The Fourth of August" had been premiered by Elgar three days earlier on October 28, 1917; see Atkins, *Elgar-Atkins Friendship,* 286. On the BBC broadcasts, see n. 17 above.

107. It is worth noting the extraordinary pressure placed on Elgar by Binyon, among others, when Elgar temporarily halted work on *The Spirit of England* over his dispute with Rootham (see n. 23 above): "Think of England, of the English-speaking peoples, in whom the common blood stirs now as it never did before; think of the awful casualty lists that are coming, & the losses in more & more homes; think of the thousands who will be craving to have this grief glorified & lifted up & transformed by an art like yours—and though I have little understanding of music, as you know, I understand that craving when words alone seem all too insufficient & inexpressive—think of what you are witholding [*sic*] from your countrymen & women. Surely it would be wrong to let them lose this help and consolation." Letter from Binyon to Elgar, 27 March 1915, EBM L6350.

108. John Foulds, *A World Requiem,* op. 60 (London: Paxton, 1923). Foulds's *World Requiem* was recommended for national performance by the British Music Society and adopted by the British Legion for its Festivals of Remembrance at the Royal Albert Hall, Armistice Days from 1923 to 1926. See Lewis Foreman, *From Parry to Britten: British Music in Letters, 1900–1945* (London: Batsford, 1987), 166–67 and Malcolm MacDonald, *John Foulds: His Life and Music* (Rickmansworth: Triad Press, 1975), 26–31. Inserted in the copy of the score housed in Special Collections at the Brotherton Library, University of Leeds, is a program for the first of these performances, featuring a white cross on a red background and pronouncing the requiem "A Cenotaph in Sound" (see Music E-2 FOU).

109. *Radio Times,* 7 November 1924, 296.

110. *Radio Times,* 6 November 1925, 300.

111. BBC, Programme-as-Broadcast, National Programme, 11 November 1932, BBC Written Archives.

112. Writing of "For the Fallen" in the 1969 Aldeburgh Festival program book, Britten recalled that Elgar's score "has always seemed to me to have in its opening bars a personal tenderness and grief, in the grotesque march an agony of distortion, and in the final sequences a ring of genuine splendour"; quoted in Michael Kennedy, *A Portrait of Elgar,* 2nd ed. (London: Oxford University Press, 1982), 181.

PART IV

SUMMATION

Transcending the Enigmas of Biography:

The Cultural Context of Sir Edward Elgar's Career

LEON BOTSTEIN

There has been a sustained and growing interest in Edward Elgar and his music since the late 1960s, notably beyond the borders of Britain.[1] In light of the wealth of distinguished English composers since Elgar's death, the historical question regarding the interplay between musical culture and national identity comes readily to mind. Why—before Elgar achieved international recognition—had England been viewed internally as well as on the Continent as "a land without music"?[2] This phrase, made popular in its German form as part of a derisive anti-English cultural chauvinism, sums up the nearly universal conceit that the English had not, by the late nineteenth century, nurtured a school of musical composition in which regional and local markers of national particularity—even invented ones—could win the affections of a transnational audience and public, much as other "national" traditions and schools (e.g., the Czech and Russian) had throughout the second half of the nineteenth century.[3]

Put another way, why had no composer of Elgar's stature emerged among the English since Henry Purcell, despite England's preeminence throughout the eighteenth and nineteenth centuries not only in politics and commerce, but also in literature, science, philosophy, architecture, and painting?[4] After all, in terms of concert life and amateurism, nineteenth-century Britain had one of Europe's most active musical cultures.[5] Given the rapid acknowledgment of Elgar as England's leading composer after 1900, this puzzling historical paradox leads to a further question: In what sense was Elgar a distinctly English original? What did he invent and bequeath as a lasting dimension of Englishness to his English successors? Or was Britain's sustained second "renaissance" in music in the twentieth century, after Elgar's death and extending at least through the career of Benjamin Britten, only marginally national (apart from those few composers who pursued an explicitly nationalist agenda)?[6] It can be argued that, after an eighteenth century when George Frederic Handel, Joseph Haydn, and Italian opera reigned supreme in public and domestic English musical culture, the revitalization of English music after 1900 was largely derivative of Continental trends, a replay of the pre-Elgar era when English musical life was dominated by Felix Mendelssohn and the music of Continental Romanticism.

In Elgar's music, as Vaughan Williams suggested in a 1935 short article, "What Have We Learnt from Elgar?," a rhetorical grandiosity coexists with a restrained but intense intimacy and lyricism.[7] Using the orchestra and an amalgam of influences, Elgar fashioned a late-Romantic idiom of expression (without resorting to so-called folk traditions that serve as obvious markers of national identity) that came to exemplify both an idealized attachment to the rural landscape and England's bold and confident, if not imperious, spirit. Elgar's melodic sensibility accomplished the former and his mastery of modern orchestral sonority and gesture the latter. One also hears in Elgar's music a moral severity, an approachable melodic clarity, and a restraint and calm that together manage to transform subjective emotion into a compelling didactic engagement with the listener. And the composer's presence, his personality and style, seems not so overwhelming and distinctive as, for example, Richard Wagner's.

Using the forms of both large-scale orchestral majesty and intimate string writing, Elgar gave voice to a proud but personal eloquence in which the musical rhetoric seemed to carry a public moral conceit that was also distinctly English. With self-awareness, Elgar lent carefully framed moments of musical beauty the aspect of ethical gravity. His musical phrases conveyed the personal and intimate but, presented in an elegant and refined manner, avoided the raw intensity of the confessional. Likewise, the dignity and grandeur of his large-scale works, even the most blatantly patriotic and national, while veering toward the pompous, always retained a sense of proportion. Elgar managed to lend imperial conceits not only a sense of propriety but also, through affecting beauty, justification. The composer thereby made it possible for his listeners to identify and appropriate sentiments, if not sentimentality, with an intensity of their own beyond mere admiration or enjoyment. Elgar's music suggested the appearance of accessible objectivity. He provided the room and opportunity for listeners to respond with empathy and identification without a sense of excess, emotional distance, or impersonality.

Elgar's music resonated with his public as both particularly English and attuned to the historical moment. His success depended in part on the disciplined detachment with which sentiment, sweetness, solidarity, community, and confidence took musical form within the practices and vocabulary of late-nineteenth-century musical rhetoric. Elgar helped fashion the markers and substance of the late-Victorian and early-modern English self-image without subordinating his own individuality.[8] His reception as a great composer remains intertwined with his significance and popularity as a representative voice of the spirit and pride of England. His music is understood as expressing something authentic about the modern English character, landscape, and self-image. Because the gesture, rhetoric, and sonority he fashioned have come to locate the unique power, intensity, confidence, and refinement of the English, Elgar's music has retained its role as an embodiment of Englishness, limiting his influence as a model for composers other than his English successors. The fabricated but lasting array of musical signs of a national sensibility, if not tradition, that continue to sound in the work of British composers and British culture is Elgar's distinct and unique legacy.[9]

Another reason for Elgar's sustained and increased popularity in the concert repertory is that, in the context of twentieth-century composition, Elgar wrote music that was clearly conservative in style, not unlike that of Richard Strauss (whom Elgar admired and who thought Elgar to be his finest English contemporary). Despite the complexity and adventuresome nature of *Falstaff*, Elgar remained committed to the rhetorical tradition of expressiveness that came under intense critical scrutiny by modernists after World War I and again after World War II. In the development of musical materials, Elgar, like Strauss, adapted Wagnerian harmonic practice and orchestral sonorities with a residual allegiance to classical and traditional technical means. Both Elgar and Strauss (like Brahms and in contrast to Wagner) acknowledged the weight of history and mirrored some degree of awe for the traditions of composition. This is persistently evident in the musical work of both composers. They reconcile in their orchestral music the seemingly competing strategies of so-called absolute music and program music. Despite recent efforts to construe Elgar as a modernist innovator, he remained within the framework of the ideas, conflicts, forms, and vocabulary of the late nineteenth century. A parallel to the case Arnold Schoenberg made in 1933 on behalf of Johannes Brahms as a "progressive" is difficult to make for Elgar.[10]

Was there a connection between Elgar's aesthetic conservatism and his Englishness? Since Elgar, why have so many prominent and successful English composers seemingly continued to resist dominant forms of modernism? Is this a prejudice of reception, where the public expects an Elgarian-invented "Englishness" from English composers the way it expects reductive signs of the Russian, the American, and the Mexican from composers of those nations? Although Elgar was influenced by Wagner and

Brahms as well as Robert Schumann and Strauss, his successors—including those who participated in the pastoral and folk revival of the midcentury, composers such as Ralph Vaughan Williams, Gustav Holst, Frank Bridge, George Butterworth, Arthur Bliss, and Gerald Finzi—were often inspired by the models of Claude Debussy and Igor Stravinsky. They appropriated Elgarian traits and pursued a synthesis between some English elements and a conservative adaptation of styles from outside of England. Unlike Béla Bartók, Stravinsky, or Debussy, neither Elgar nor his successors transformed national musical attributes as representing the universal (whether those national elements were invented in the nineteenth century or were authentically more historically remote, in the sense of "folk" music).

Precisely on account of its ingratiating character, Elgar's music has benefited from the decline and defeat of modernism after the mid-1970s. That collapse has led musicians and their audiences back to twentieth-century music that was once derided as old-fashioned. Strauss, as much as Stravinsky or Schoenberg, is now considered a major figure of the twentieth century, a prophetic voice of postmodernism. Ironically, the influence of figures such as Elgar, Dimitri Shostakovich, Aaron Copland, and Jean Sibelius (as opposed to Stravinsky and Schoenberg) on subsequent generations of composers has been limited to their relevant national spheres. Neither Strauss nor Alexander Zemlinsky (whose compositions, for all their variety and commanding quality, never cut free from the aesthetic premises of the later nineteenth century) had significant imitators. In Elgar's case, his musical gestures and rhetoric can be heard in most major English figures that followed him. Consider, for example, William Walton (despite Elgar's reservations concerning the younger composer's music), both in his early and late work. In Walton's 1929 Viola Concerto the first and last movements reveal debts to Elgarian rhetoric, and the 1939 Violin Concerto owes much to Elgar's. As late as the 1962 *Hindemith Variations*, one hears echoes of Elgarian lyricism, expressiveness, and particularly the techniques of variation, rhythmic ingenuity, orchestration, and humor.

Few composers have attracted and baffled critics and historians as Elgar has done. The composer is known for his plea on behalf of the primacy of music as "absolute," a mode of life and expression possessed of its own logic and in no need of narrative or symbolic meaning:

I hold that the Symphony without a programme is the highest development of art. *Views to the contrary we shall often find,* held by those to whom the joy of music came late in life or would deny to musicians that peculiar gift, which is their own, a musical ear, or an *ear for music. I use,* as you notice, a very old-fashioned expression *but we all know what* it conveys: a love of music for its own sake.[11]

Despite this pronouncement, much of Elgar's music, particularly for orchestra (including the symphonies), was either explicitly programmatic and narrative (including musical reflections of intimate feelings) or thinly veiled as such.[12] Elgar was required to explain his admiration of Strauss "as the greatest genius of our days" by suggesting, counterfactually, that "I am sure Richard Strauss could give us a symphony to rank among, or above the finest if he chose."[13]

This apparent contradiction mirrors an ongoing and unresolved uncertainty, if not conflict, in the attempt to link Elgar's music to his biography and his historical context. On the one hand, he is said to have been a composer motivated by personal intimacies. He was also a resentful outsider (as a Catholic born to a family of limited means, engaged in commercial trade) whose deep attachments were often secret. At the same time he appears to have been an adherent to a nostalgic, if not anti-urban, pastoral ideal of England. Although an autodidact in all arenas, including composition, he was possessed of overt literary and religious beliefs. The employment of both secret and explicit programs for instrumental music therefore fits both the man and the audience for whom he wrote.[14]

On the other hand, Elgar has been characterized as a callow, social-climbing boor, if not bore (someone who sold his Gagliano violin for a billiard table, disdained talk about music, and sported the image of the golf-playing squire); desperate to be accorded conventional external recognition (therefore eager for an inherited peerage); shrewd in his manipulation of the press; socially and politically conservative; enthusiastic about science (with a laboratory and patents to his name); a man who evinced deep religious feeling; and a booster of English imperial ambitions and conceits. His defensive and aggressive attitude to his privileged and academically trained contemporaries suggests at the same time an arrogant ambition to outshine all in his craft, popularity, international reputation, and aesthetic standards. Elgar's rhetoric on behalf of the formal and aesthetic autonomy of music parallels his self-image as the English heir to traditions exemplified by Mozart's Fortieth and Brahms's Third symphonies.

Elgar's music provides evidence for both the private and public aspects of his image and personality. Unlike Wagner and Schoenberg (and for that matter, Mendelssohn, Bartók, Schumann, and Stravinsky, the last by means of ghostwriters and an amanuensis), and his own contemporaries C. Hubert Parry and Vaughan Williams, Elgar did not write about music (the Peyton Lectures notwithstanding) in a fashion that assists the interpretation of his music; even his letters are unhelpful in this regard. We are therefore left with only the music.[15] On the one side are the well-known, small-scale intimate works (the music for strings such as the Elegy for Strings and the Introduction and Allegro) and the larger works with explicit, intimate content (the Cello Concerto, the *Wand of Youth* Suites, and *The Dream of Gerontius*). Explicit, symbolic, and indirect evocations of nature persist not only in the programmatic works, but in the symphonies as well.[16] On the other side are the extroverted *Pomp and Circumstance* marches, the *Coronation Ode*, *King Olaf*, *Caractacus*, and aspects of the two symphonies that suggest an ambitious, public, and patriotic personality. At the center of this interpretive divide is Elgar's most famous work, the *Enigma* Variations. If his "Land of Hope and Glory," extracted from the Trio of *Pomp and Circumstance* March no. 1, has become a second national anthem, the "Nimrod" variation, for all its overt origin as a personal portrait of a dear friend, has become just as powerful a public evocation of something distinctly English. That fact highlights the biographical enigma.

It has been alleged that in recent years devoted Elgarians have sought to downplay the patriotic gore in Elgar's music and character. The rise of an anticolonial and anti-imperialist historiography since the late 1960s has led to readings of Elgar as not a mirror but a leading creator of the cultural ethos of late-Victorian and Edwardian political and cultural conceits, a musical equivalent of Rudyard Kipling. In this context, the dominant critical stance of the present, one of praise and near-deification of Elgar, has encountered serious challenge.[17] This revisionism has in turn been challenged not merely by efforts to link Elgar with a benign English patriotism based in a pastoral nostalgia for premodernity.[18] Rather, Elgar's life has been scrutinized as possessed of a secret character, marked not only by successive attachments to two women apart from Lady Elgar (Alice Stuart-Wortley, whom the composer nicknamed "Windflower," and in later years Vera Hockman), but also to men. A homoerotic interior, particularly within the *Enigma* Variations, has been persuasively argued, much to the dismay of more conventionally admiring scholars, some of whom share some distaste for the public, patriotic Elgar.[19] That homoerotic dimension is clearly consonant with a powerful thread within late-nineteenth-century English culture, apparent in literature, cultural criticism, religion, and painting.

The irony in the pursuit of a homoerotic subtext is that its existence can be used to buttress arguments on both sides of the well-known, Janus-faced portrait of Elgar. The pressure to suppress homosexuality reflects massive changes in the attitudes to homosexuality and sexuality that took place in the second half of the nineteenth century, accelerated by the redefinition of English manliness required by the military requirements of an empire.[20] The trial of Oscar Wilde is the defining moment of that process. In his Peyton lectures, Elgar himself defined the task of modern music in England to assert a "healthy" robust manliness, set explicitly in opposition to an effeminate aestheticism. For English music, he wrote,

> there are many possible futures. But the one I want to see coming into being is something that shall grow out of our own soil, some-thing broad, noble, chivalrous, healthy and above all, an out-of-door sort of spirit. To arrive at this it will be necessary to throw over all imitation. It will be necessary to begin and look at things in a differ-ent spirit.[21]

These respectable public ambitions for musical art coincided with the celebration of sports in elite schools, the ideal of a healthy "out-of-door" sensibility, understood as compatible with manly adventure into the exotic and courage on the battlefield—all central experiences of the British Empire.[22] The Elgarian mode, even in the legendary passages marked *nobilmente*, allowed the composer to express through eloquence and grandeur a disciplined and aggressive manliness, while at the same time signaling an intimacy of feeling that may have contained contradictory secrets and suppressed feelings. Understood therefore as a man torn by inner conflict, the two sides of Elgar become reconciled as complemen-tary. There are miniatures of intimacy and calm evocations of landscape and solitude, but the primary ambition is neither one of mystical contem-plation nor explicitly subjective aestheticism. The ideals of nobility and chivalry suggest a commitment to music as a public, civic art tied to the *vita activa*. The mores of the age force the personal to survive as a coded subtext to a public art, not as a direct confessional. Since the deeply per-sonal demanded secrecy, the scale and public ambition of Elgar's music offered the ideal cloak and protection. The contradiction between the pompous, brash, and nearly militaristic Elgar of the *Crown of India* and the searingly expressive emotionalism of the second movement of the Cello Concerto are themselves evidence of the complex and competing claims of the private and the public spheres on English artists and intellectuals of Elgar's generation, particularly before 1914. The relative decline in Elgar's popularity in England after World War I and particularly in the 1930s (a claim that is itself in some dispute) can then be understood as reflecting the gradual collapse of late-Victorian hypocrisies.[23] Extreme sac-rifices and compromises became increasingly unnecessary, as Britten's rise to fame and fortune as England's representative composer from the 1940s on would suggest.[24]

There are, however, sources for understanding and interpreting Elgar and his music that are not contingent on debates concerning Elgar's intimate life and the issues of his sexuality and gender identity, sources that are at once historical and biographical and that recast these seemingly contradictory dimensions. Elgar's relationship to literature, religion, and painting offers important clues.

In literature, it is useful to consider Elgar's favorite author, and his mother's—Henry Wadsworth Longfellow. The novel *Hyperion* was a treasured inheritance from his mother, and it was *Hyperion* that Elgar gave as a gift late in life to his last close female friend. Longfellow was the source not only for Elgar's first successes, including *The Black Knight*, "Spanish Serenade," "Rondel," and most importantly, *King Olaf*, but also for his first large-scale oratorio, *The Apostles*.[25]

In the realm of religion, the importance to Elgar of John Henry Cardinal Newman's theological views and the cultural criticism of Matthew Arnold and John Ruskin demands reconsideration. Newman was not only the author of the text of what is perhaps Elgar's masterpiece, *Gerontius*, but also the leading force in late-Victorian Catholic thought. Elgar was attracted by the explicit theology in Newman's poem and also by the cardinal's articulation of the place of Catholicism in modernity and its relationship not to the liberalism and evangelicalism of the 1830s but to the world of science and learning of the century's last decades, when debates over papal infallibility and the cultural consequences of scientific progress were intense.[26] It was the Newman of the *Apologia Pro Vita Sua*, *The Idea of a University*, and *An Essay in Aid of a Grammar of Assent* who informs the intellectual context for Elgar. Though his traditional faith in God may have waned in later years, theology mattered to Elgar, even if indirectly through its consequences on the politics of culture. Basic constructs of meaning with regard to life and death and the human community influenced his version of the role that art, and therefore the musician, played in the public life to which he aspired.

Finally, Elgar's allegiance to Longfellow and his internalization of assumptions within Victorian English Catholic thought corresponded to a lifelong affection for the work of specific Pre-Raphaelite painters and other examples of imaginary and idealized realism, notably Ivan Kramskoi's 1872 painting, *Christ in the Wilderness*. These three sources—literary, religious, and visual—illuminate the tensions within Elgar the man as well as his powerful but eclectic amalgam of musical debts to the past, from Bach, Mozart, and Mendelssohn to Wagner and Brahms.

Arnold and Longfellow:
The Transcendence of the Philistine

The framework most pertinent to Edward Elgar's career was the intense debate in Britain during his formative years regarding the political, social, and moral place of art and culture—the public consequences of the cultivation of education, taste, and judgment in the face of the power of religion in a secular material culture. At the center of this discussion was Matthew Arnold, whose 1869 *Culture and Anarchy* did much to frame the discourse and establish its terms. Elgar certainly knew of Arnold as a poet, having studied his verse.[27] The terms Arnold made famous in his prose—the categories of "Barbarian" (the landed aristocracy), "Philistine" (the middle classes), and "Populace" (the working classes), as well as his opposition to Hebraism and Hellenism, were sufficiently well-known to enter the language of a 1915 review of Elgar's *The Starlight Express*.[28]

Elgar's personal position in Arnold's polemical social geography, the composer's resentments and ambitions notwithstanding, was clearly that of the Philistine. In Elgar's self-assessment, pride of achievement was mixed with defensiveness and shame. He never forgot that, unlike Parry (whom he liked and admired) and even Charles Villiers Stanford (whom he derided), he was without either aristocratic provenance or family means and therefore had made his career the hard way, in the provinces and without benefit of academic training or standing.[29] Arnold's plea was for the betterment of the Philistine, the transformation of the middle classes of Elgar's type through culture. The hope for the future of civilization was not in the all-too-common imitation of regressive Barbarian mores by the economically successful middle classes or, far worse, the descent into chaos, amorality, and violence characteristic of the Populace. Rather, the cultivation of "sweetness and light," of the Hellenic sensibility that "speaks of thinking clearly, seeing things in their essence and beauty, as a grand and precious feat for man to achieve," was necessary to transform the Philistines whom Arnold credited with making England economically great.[30] The Hellenic had failed in previous ages of history because it was "premature" in the development of humankind.[31] The historical moment was made imperative not only by the danger from the masses below but also by the material achievements of the middle classes.

The central role Arnold accorded culture as a social idea, as a means of civilizing modernity, was influenced by his awareness of the progress not only of industry and commerce but of science and reason as well. As Arnold's deep respect for Newman suggests, he believed that although religion, particularly in its Hebraic form, needed to be resisted and overcome, its contribution had not been trivial. The social, scientific, and economic progress of modernity was the result of mechanical and material efficiencies, and the primacy placed on work and labor all derived from religious doctrine. Hebraism's "wonderful strength" was its "strictness of conscience" that centered on the fear and avoidance of sin.[32] Whether in its Puritan or Jewish modes, Hebraism, like Hellenism, responded to real "wants of human nature."[33] It led to work and discipline, a taste for the practical and mechanical—what Max Weber in 1905 would term the "spirit of capitalism" that derived from the explicit sacred dictates and secular consequences of inner-worldly asceticism.[34]

In contrast, the Hellenic revealed the "spontaneity of consciousness" of human nature, by which ignorance is eradicated, clarity of sight developed, and with that clarity, a sense of beauty.[35] Hellenism invested human life with an "aërial ease, clearness, and radiancy," wrote Arnold, and was therefore the achievement of "sweetness and light" in humanity.[36] If the Hellenic highlighted the human as "a gentle and simple being, showing the traces of a noble and divine nature," then the Hebraic defined the human as "an unhappy chained captive, labouring with groanings that cannot be uttered to free himself from the body of this death."[37]

For Arnold the time had come, partly out of fear of the power and violence of the populace, for the Philistines to shed the Hebraic and embrace the Hellenic.[38] This was not a plea for aestheticism or for radical individuality. Quite the contrary. Hellenism "is the impulse to the development of the whole man, to connecting and harmonising all parts of him, perfecting all, leaving none to take their chance."[39] In place of the Hebraic insistence on strict morality, obedience, action, and therefore industry, Arnold called for a Hellenic movement that would allow all of mankind—not a few—to recognize the intelligible laws of nature that reveal that "many things are not seen in their true nature and as they really are, unless they are seen as beautiful."[40] That historical moment had arrived. Although the dominance of the Hebraic, with its unnatural stress on rigid rationality and its "defect of . . . feeling" had resulted in the material advances of modern life, the "loss of spiritual balance" had reached a critical point that challenged all order, authority, and, above all, beauty and culture.[41]

The disciplined Philistines, who were "particularly stiff-necked and perverse in the resistance to light and its children . . . who not only do not pursue sweetness and light, but who even prefer to them that sort of machinery of business, chapels, tea-meetings" and political speech making, needed to be weaned of what in the twentieth century came to be termed as cheap popular taste or middlebrow culture.[42] Basic utilitarian literacy and the work ethic, combined with a highly disciplined moral code sufficient for industry, could not erect the barriers against, nor defeat the onslaught of, mass vulgarity and immorality with its penchant for brutality and resistance to legitimate order and authority. That was the real danger, even though the optimistic utopian possibilities of a civilized modernity led by a transformed middle class pervade Arnold's text: he believed the spread of true culture and discernment could transform the values by which individuals and society lived.

Arnold's version of English historical evolution and its society was influential, but his sense of the necessity and propitious character of the historical moment was not exceptional. Indeed, within the arena of music, a field most certainly of "feeling" and "sweetness and light," the self-conscious realization among leading English figures that the time was ripe for an English return to a cultured aesthetic, and therefore a renaissance of English music, was common. By midcentury, calls within the Anglican Church for a renewal of the liturgical role of music through choral singing were well under way, inspired in part by the Oxford Movement and, after 1850, by the perceived threat of Catholicism.[43] The impetus for the so-called choral revival included an Arnold-like demand that the aesthetic dimension, and with it the community of feeling, needed to be disseminated to solidify not only faith and the place of the Church but also a larger social and cultural commitment on the part of the English to civilized order.[44]

The most prominent and popular of Elgar's predecessors, Sir Arthur Sullivan, adapted the historical narrative implicit in Arnold's *Culture and Anarchy* in an address he gave at Birmingham's town hall in 1888 titled "About Music." Sullivan told his audience—precisely the segment of the population in a city that embodied the achievements of English industrialization and on whom Arnold hoped to visit his project of secular cultural reformation—that

> I will not go into the causes which, for nearly 200 years, made us lose that high position, and threw us into the hands of illustrious foreigners, Handel, Haydn, Spohr, Mendelssohn (so long the favourite composers of the English), and of the Italian Opera, which exclusively occupied the attention of the fashionable classes, and, like a great car of Juggernaut, overrode and crushed all efforts on behalf of native music.[45]

Nonetheless, he offered this conclusion, which praised and pointed to his audience and distinguished them from Arnold's Barbarians—whom Sullivan termed the "fashionable classes" (and to whom, in Arnold's view, a legitimate historical debt needed to be acknowledged):

My belief is that this was largely due to the enthusiasm with which commerce was pursued, and to the extraordinary way in which religious and political struggles, and, later still, practical science, have absorbed our energies. We were content to *buy* our music, while we were *making* churches, steam-engines, railways, cotton-mills, constitutions, anti-Corn-Law Leagues, and Caucuses. Now, however, as I have already said, the condition of things is changing—it *has* changed. And yet I cannot but feel that we are only at the entry of the Promised Land. Habits of mind and modes of action are still to be found which show that we have much to do before we become the musical people that we were in the remoter ages of our history.[46]

The self-consciousness of the historical moment, an British national pride in the revival of a distinctly British musical culture and therefore, in the sense of Arnold, the salvation of order, culture, morality, and authority, helped shape Elgar's ambition. His persistent rehearsal of the presumed deficit of the circumstances of his birth noted by all his biographers and commentators—modest means, provincial origins, and low social station, marked by trade and commerce—was a calculated rhetorical use of facts. The highlighting of the extent that he, Elgar, was neither an aristocrat, nor an academic, nor a member, in Arnold's sense, of the Barbarian class, which despite its privileges seemed to have passed its prime and historical significance, was a sign of his recognition of a mission and opportunity to which he was uniquely suited. He, someone who was not born into the gentry, could achieve national fame and assume the leadership of a new generation.

Therefore Elgar willingly exploited the fact that he was self-taught, had no advantages, and was entirely responsible for his own success, owing nothing to institutions or patrons. He was the model of English achievement in a highly competitive world filled with residual social privileges and prejudices. He earned that stature through merit and hard work, measured not by popularity but by the judgment of the cultured public. Consequently he understood not only the genuine standards of culture, but the public Arnold sought to reach.

This conceit helped Elgar reach a large audience of discerning and cultivated listeners (not an "indiscriminating crowd") implied by the growing numbers of participants in the amateur instrumental and choral life of the country, much of it centered outside of London.[47] These participants resembled him more than they did Parry or the old aristocracy, Arnold's Barbarians. Elgar not only credited newspaper criticism (the quintessential medium of the Philistines) with a leading role and place in English musical life, but also assiduously, if not obsessively, cultivated them and shrewdly used the powerful medium of music journalism to advance his career and reputation.[48] Indeed, the symbolic and substantive importance of Elgar's modest social origins was not lost on George Bernard Shaw. They seemed for Shaw to prove Elgar's reputation as an innovator, a new Beethoven. Since he had no access to the conventional modes of training he could not be an imitator. In Shaw's view, Elgar's modesty led him to eschew fashion; his originality was superior to fashionable moderns (for Shaw, that meant Stravinsky and Debussy), free from pedantry, devoid of pretension. The irony evident in Elgar's personal style and manner was not lost on Shaw. Elgar came across as indistinguishable from any other "very typical English country gentleman who does not know a fugue from a fandango."[49] The cultured, self-made artist succeeded in passing for a Barbarian.

Notwithstanding his facade of aristocratic nonchalance with respect to matters of art when in the company of others, after his rise to prominence Elgar saw himself as a force for the improvement of the standards of amateur musical life among his countrymen.[50] His public, however, was not the "general POPULAR public."[51] Elgar wished to use music to emancipate the best of his fellow middle-class citizens from the "commonplace" with something distinctly English—inspired by "their own country, their own literature . . . their own climate," absent of "sentimentality or decadence."[52] Elgar called for a greater civic investment in musical institutions of high standards so that music could function as "ennobling."[53] In the place of *"frivolous and squalid"* music (that "we ourselves would avoid like a plague"), Elgar, like Sullivan, wished that *"we may once again* be a musical land and *produce a 'school'* . . . of serious English music which shall have a hold on the affections of the people, and SHALL be held in respect *abroad*."[54] Arnold's project from earlier decades is recalled and rehearsed, only strengthened by the more blatant chauvinism characteristic of the decades immediately preceding World War I. Elgar, like Arnold, distinguished the audience from the crowd, and emphasized institutions directed at the middle classes, those who respected professionalism, who realized that "hard work is apparently the only way to achieve success in art[,] business or politics."[55] For Elgar as for Arnold, Hebraic discipline was the necessary foundation for the triumph of the Hellenic in music. The mores of middle-class discipline could be turned to elevating the cultural standards of his own people, Arnold's Philistines.[56]

Elgar's ambition with respect to leading a school of music that could have a significant civic and cultural impact on England was mirrored in the manner and style of the music he sought to compose. He wished to craft music that was at once modern and up to date, capable of receiving international recognition, and yet neither decadent nor obscure. At the same time, he eschewed mere popularity as well as imitation. He wanted to reconcile wide-scale comprehensibility and immediate response with originality and qualities that garnered the praise of amateur, connoisseur, critic, and colleague alike. Elgar's preferred genres were those with large publics—choral music and orchestral music. The modern orchestra was a reflection of historical progress and modernity, and the proper vehicle for communicating on a grand scale, just as writing for the major choral festivals ensured fame and a following. Elgar's enthusiastic embrace of the BBC, radio broadcasting, and gramophone recording later in his career reveals a logical extension of his attachment not only to the civilizing dimension of music but to a conception of what serious modern music needed to be in its synthesis of historically validated high aesthetic norms and immediate but wide accessibility.[57]

The model for Elgar's particular compositional ideal came not from music but from literature. Much has been made of Elgar's early exposure to scores and performances and his process of self-teaching, particularly his discovery of Mozart and Beethoven.[58] What has been overlooked, despite the many seminal musical works of Elgar based on Longfellow's texts, is the powerful influence the poet exerted on the composer. Elgar closely identified Longfellow's *Hyperion* with his mother, who introduced Longfellow's novel to him in his childhood. (For a synopsis of *Hyperion*, see Byron Adams's essay in this volume.) As he wrote in 1899 to Hans Richter (to whom he sent a copy), it was through *Hyperion* that "I, as a child, received my first idea of the great German nations."[59] In fact, Elgar had visited Heidelberg in 1892 to see the place he had read about in Longfellow.[60] The Longfellow attachment lasted Elgar's entire life, as is suggested by his fleeting notion in 1923 of setting a Longfellow poem whose text he sent to his publisher.[61] And there is, of course, the gift in December 1931 of *Hyperion* to Vera Hockman with the comment "I am going to give you a little book— Longfellow's *Hyperion*—which for many years belonged to my mother; since then it has gone with me everywhere. I want you to have it because you are my mother, my child, my lover and my friend."[62]

Jerrold Northrop Moore's view is that Elgar's early encounter with Longfellow inspired the composer's pastoral and nostalgic side. "Actual" feminine attraction was "replaced by the feminine symbolism of Nature and season and countryside—of reality defeated by an ideal."[63] *Hyperion* was, writes Moore, an "exemplar for Edward."[64] The deep connection Elgar's mother and her son felt to Longfellow was hardly exceptional. For a musician of Elgar's generation, the link was not uncommon, as evidenced by Samuel Coleridge-Taylor's successful setting of "Song of Hiawatha" as well as the apparent link between the poem and Antonín Dvořák's Ninth Symphony.[65] Today Longfellow may be remembered, if at all, for his romantic characterization in verse of the Native American, particularly in "Hiawatha." But that memory, as Christoph Irmscher's fine book on Longfellow makes clear, is a distortion.[66]

Longfellow, as Irmscher writes, "invented poetry as a public idiom."[67] No poet or writer was so well-known or so widely read, in part owing to cheap editions, throughout the United States and even the rest of the world. Longfellow may have been the first American to earn a living by writing poetry. What was remarkable about his career was his ambition to objectify the poetic voice and use it to disseminate cultural literacy. The assumption of an overpowering authorial subjectivity, with which we often associate poetry, was absent. In its stead were two ambitions. First, Longfellow sought to incorporate and transmit, in an accessible form, the traditions of learning and history from the advent of Christianity and the age of Dante to German Romanticism. Hence the story of *Hyperion*, which incorporates a translation and adaptation of a poem by the German poet Ludwig Uhland. Though Edgar Allan Poe's searing criticism of Longfellow as an author who stole others' works may have been extreme, it was partially on point. Longfellow's project was one of democratic didacticism, not in Walt Whitman's sense of displaying invention, individualism, and modernity, but in the sense of connecting a community of readers with the history, traditions, and cultures of the world.[68]

Longfellow succeeded in North America as well as in Europe, and not merely as a voice of the exotic, as indicated by Franz Liszt's *The Bells of Strasbourg*, an influential setting of a passage drawn from Longfellow's "The Golden Legend."[69] Elgar's reliance in *The Apostles* on Longfellow's version of the story of Judas and Mary Magdalene in "The Divine Tragedy," as well as the poet's deep affinity with Catholicism and its heritage, had a European precedent in music, one that helped inspire Wagner's last foray into Christian legend, *Parsifal*.[70]

Second, Longfellow sought to break down the barriers of so-called high culture. The spread of musical culture during Elgar's lifetime, measured by the rise of publishing houses and sales of instruments and the growing popularity of musical instruction, followed quickly on the heels of the extension of literacy.[71] New simplified modes of choral notation helped spur membership in amateur societies, and concert life expanded throughout the country. Poetry, long regarded as a privileged form of expression requiring more than rudimentary literacy, had been, like music, an aristocratic pastime. Self-expression through cultural mediums such as poetry and musical composition had been limited to the gentry by mere virtue of the restriction of access to education. Longfellow understood that with the extension of literacy, the writing of poetry could become a widespread, middle-class hobby.

Longfellow managed to reach a mass audience by providing a model of poetic construction that could be imitated. As Alice Elgar's poetic efforts suggest, poetry became a pastime, much like the amateur music making Elgar experienced in his childhood.[72] Borrowing freely from the rich repository of Western culture, Longfellow, through his adaptations, found a way to submerge his own personality and encourage his readers to use poetry to express their sentiments. Longfellow's poetry, as viewed from the perspective of his many and diverse readers, generated what Irmscher aptly construes as a "sentimental collaboration" between reader and writer, not dissimilar to the emergent function of listening to music in public spaces, an event in which meaning is imagined and invented by the individual listener in response to a composer's work.[73] Longfellow inspired readers to empathize with profound emotions by writing poetry of their own. Through the utilization of tradition, ultimately realized by Longfellow in his translation of Dante, a new population of readers was introduced to a cultural world otherwise accessible only to those few privileged enough to attend university. Longfellow gave them confidence that they could command the poetic and aesthetic tools that could unlock if not unleash in themselves an imaginary and ideal world of feeling and thought ordinarily closed to them.[74]

Elgar and his mother, Ann, were exemplars of Longfellow's public. The paradoxical and perhaps unsettling fact is that Longfellow, somewhat like the composer Giacomo Meyerbeer, is at best now regarded as no more than a historical figure of passing interest, and at worst as a sentimentalist rejected with reason by the generations that followed. Yet it is no more possible to dismiss Longfellow as part of an ephemeral, noncanonical popular literature of the past than it is to reduce Meyerbeer's works to the status of kitsch or, in Elgar's terms, "frivolous and squalid music." Longfellow was taken seriously in his lifetime as a learned and serious writer, just as Meyerbeer, despite his detractors, was widely admired by discerning contemporaries, including Liszt. Both Longfellow and Meyerbeer possessed a nontrivial craft for which we have lost the emotional and critical capacity of appreciation.

Nonetheless, Longfellow's formal strategy—his creation of a public, poetic rhetoric through which ideas and feelings could be spread, creating a community of admirers, imitators, and readers, all of whom believed they had a personal relationship with the author—parallels Elgar's achievement. By using techniques adapted from Continental traditions ranging from Mendelssohn to Wagner, Elgar used the modern vehicle of orchestral and large-scale choral genres to craft a distinctly objective-sounding musical rhetoric that listeners found expressive of landscape, national pride, intimacy in the form of friendship, and religious sentiment, even in works without explicit programmatic meaning. By eschewing the extremes of musical practice, which he deemed decadent or imitatively academic, and by focusing on melodic and harmonic transparency, Elgar achieved a Longfellow-like accessibility without making cynical concessions to popular taste or sacrificing the highest cultural markers of craft and art. By adhering to recognized forms and musical vocabulary, he could reach a public like himself, one new to the practice of the arts, while avoiding for the most part the blatantly sentimental and crude. The public in question was none other than Arnold's Philistines. Elgar, like Longfellow, became a didactic if not prophetic figure in the process of improving the culture of the nation, reaching even the working classes.[75] As he opined in a 1905 interview:

> We Englishmen have in our naval and military history, in our religious struggles and traditions, in our national temper and qualities, in our literary and social achievements, and in our legends and tales, sufficient material to inspire and hearten the weakest and most cold-blooded of men. It is impossible for us Englishmen to do great work and have a school of music of our own, until we embody in it our national characteristics.[76]

His task was derivative of Arnold's: to use secular culture in the form of music to effect a national transformation, preserving the manly, industrial, and imperial discipline but elevating the citizenry to a Hellenic sensibility that in turn could fashion a sense of national community and tradition. Ironically, the key inspiration came from an American who successfully introduced, through poetry, the Hellenic values of a cultural tradition not only to his Philistine countrymen but Britain's as well.

Elgar transferred the unique and dominant contemporary impact of Longfellow into music, first by setting his poems and then by subsuming his works into purely instrumental music. The composer understood his public because it mirrored the cultural class to which he belonged, along with his mother and his wife (an amateur poet similar to Longfellow's many correspondents). And the public returned to Elgar the same sympathy and empathy Longfellow had inspired in his readers. This was no more apparent than during World War I when Elgar, initially reluctant to turn against German colleagues who had been so generous and important to him, found himself at the center of the expression of patriotism and nationalism through music.[77]

Ruskin, Newman, and the Construct of Community

Edward Elgar was at once proud and defensive about his status as an autodidact. Although on occasion he feigned a gentleman's disdain for serious conversation, at the same time he acted in a manner (including writing letters to editors) designed to display his erudition. Spurred by Brian Trowell's extensive 1993 essay, a scholarly debate concerning the degree and extent of Elgar's learning and reading has emerged.[78] Among the prominent English writers Elgar explicitly cited (but unlike Longfellow, never directly utilized as a framework for musical composition) was John Ruskin, whose words appear on the last page of the autograph score of *Gerontius*. Indeed, Ruskin was perhaps the most influential and prolific writer on the connections between art and society.[79] As in Arnold's case, Ruskin's many-sided and prodigious output—ranging from social reform to art and architecture—drew much of its inspiration from the intense religious debates of mid-nineteenth-century England. Dissatisfaction with what appeared to be a cold, emotionally bankrupt, and theologically compromised but politically vital Anglican establishment led to the Tractarians and the Oxford Movement. At the time of the birth of the Oxford Movement, the primary religious movements competing with the established church were, as Newman claimed, evangelicalism and a liberalism that heralded secularism (it was this latter enthusiasm that drew Matthew Arnold away from religion).[80] Anglo-Catholicism emerged at midcentury as well as a Catholic revival, both in response to the evangelicals and the liberals of the 1830s and 1840s.

By the mid-1870s, the renaissance in English Catholicism had two seemingly contradictory trends. The first was a mystical spiritualism associated with Catholic doctrine and liturgy, which would become closely allied with fin-de-siècle aestheticism and decadence. The deathbed conversion of Oscar Wilde can be taken as an example of this. The second trend was the development of a liberal Catholicism linked to the trajectory of Newman's thought after his conversion in 1845. Elgar's pronounced Tory political and social conservatism (he resigned in protest from the Athenaeum when Ramsey MacDonald was elected) and his ambitious patriotism suggest that his affinities to the Catholic religion into which he was born and to which his mother was devoted were not so much mystical as devotional; he was attracted to the authority and legitimacy of Catholicism and therefore its traditions and history. Likewise, Elgar's love of science would have made him sympathetic to Newman's later efforts to reconcile the more contemporary liberalism of the second half of the century with Catholicism. Newman encouraged within Catholicism the symbiosis of reason in science and reason in faith (in part through the positing of an "illative sense" that resided alongside an acceptance of the rules of evidence and methods of modern knowledge).[81]

Religion, in Elgar's lifetime, particularly in the years before World War I, was a serious concern among educated English men and women, as the cases of George Eliot and Christina Rossetti suggest. The issues were not only explicitly political, as suggested by the debate over the disestablishment of the Irish Church or revealed by the crisis surrounding the restoration of a Catholic hierarchy in England by the Pope. The issues mediated by religion were deeply personal and related to fundamental questions regarding life and death and the meaning of the individual's temporal existence. There is a tendency in contemporary scholarly literature to reduce the engagement with religion, particularly the Catholic revival and the rise of Anglo-Catholicism, with dimensions of the struggle within Victorian society to deal with shifting conceptions of gender and sexuality, particularly homoeroticism and homosexuality.[82] Elgar's choice of Newman's "The Dream of Gerontius" at a crucial juncture in his career reveals all the dimensions of the centrality of religion.[83] The author was notorious for his conversion and role as Tractarian. The political significance of the poem lay in the aura surrounding the death at Khartoum of General Charles Gordon, on whose corpse was found an annotated copy of the poem. Above all, the poem's subject matter is profoundly theological in its portrayal of a man's journey from life to death and his subsequent entrance into purgatory. At its core are theological claims regarding the divine judgment and eventual receipt of grace.

One clue to Elgar's personal reading of the poem, which he edited for use as a libretto for a work that is part opera, part cantata, and part oratorio, lies in his decision to attach a quotation from Ruskin at the end. As Trowell suggests, there is much in Ruskin with which Elgar would not have sympathized, notably his social radicalism. But they shared the notion that music possessed ethical significance, that it could help form a national community, and that it was in the national interest to do so. But apart from their shared enthusiasm for certain Pre-Raphaelite painters, the importance of Ruskin is the link between Ruskin and Elgar's conception of the religious significance of the public vocation of the artist.[84] *Gerontius* was one of the few Elgar works to achieve a real following on the Continent, particularly in German-speaking Europe, and then mostly in Catholic regions, such as Düsseldorf and Vienna.[85] The theology of the work was as much the object of critical debate as the music.

Elgar selected the passage from Ruskin's book *Sesame and Lilies*, which consisted of three lectures in the edition published in 1871.[86] As Ruskin made clear in the preface, the impetus for his lectures, directed at the young, was that they were "written in the hope of awakening the youth of England, so as far as my poor words might have any power with them, to take some thought of the purposes of life into which they are entering, and the nature of the world they have to conquer."[87] The influence of reading Ruskin on Elgar can be surmised as having two dimensions. The first is stylistic, by which the character of Ruskin's prose, not unlike the influence of Henry Thoreau or Ralph Waldo Emerson on Charles Ives, can be considered. Ruskin's form of eloquence is self-consciously aesthetic and the structure of his arguments in *Sesame and Lilies* intentionally tangential and elaborate, as elegantly designed as a complex garden. Ruskin's style transcended the conventions of prose as mere utilitarian instrument of logic and information, without conceding a veritable boundary between the language of argument and that of fiction. This prose style—elaborate, theatrical, and disarmingly engaging with overlong stretches of extended argument—has more than an incidental connection with the musical rhetoric in *Gerontius*. Elgar's encounter with Ruskin's use of language may well have encouraged the composer's adaptation of Wagnerian mannerisms into his own deeply personal and theological framework in which divine grace, truth, and salvation were at stake far more plausibly than in *Parsifal* (despite its Christian surface).

This hypothesis has its own, albeit unsympathetic, advocate in one of Elgar's contemporaries, the writer E. M. Forster. Although Forster had a deep interest in music, he seems to have had no contact with Elgar. But in his novel *Howards End*, published in 1910, the insurance clerk Leonard Bast, in a manner curiously reminiscent of Elgar's well-known biography, is an autodidact seeking to acquire culture in order to improve himself, much in the spirit of Arnold's transformation of the Philistine. Bast reads and goes to concerts. This is what Forster made of Bast's reading of Ruskin: "Leonard was trying to form his style on Ruskin: he understood him to be the greatest master of English prose. . . . He felt that he was being done good to, and that if he kept on with Ruskin, and the Queen's Hall Concerts, and some pictures by Watts, he would one day push his head out of the grey waters and see the universe."[88]

Forster appears not to have been a particular admirer of Elgar's. In the fifth chapter of *Howards End* a music concert is described in detail. Beethoven is held up as the unsurpassable model (a view that Elgar may have shared), but Brahms's "Four Serious Songs" come in for derision and Mendelssohn is dismissed. A discussion of English music ensues with a particularly sharp rejection of Elgar, which is then followed by the characters in the chapter beating a fast exit from *Pomp and Circumstance*. Forster expresses extreme skepticism regarding the self-consciously national element of

English music as involving too great a sacrifice of the apparent universality of the instrumental repertoire of Viennese classicism and early Romanticism, particularly Beethoven.[89]

Indeed, as his two essays on music from 1939 and 1941 indicate, Forster was a strong devotee of the idea that the best music is "untrammelled and untainted by reference."[90] His is a Ruskin-like position that music as a transcendent art cannot be captured by language. The difference is that Ruskin does not deny music meaning in the sense Forster wishes to. Elgar may have tried to balance programmatic with so-called absolute music, and may have expressed a preference for the latter, but his fame rested on music that he himself freely admitted had extramusical significance, whether personal, dramatic, or political. Therefore Forster's implicit disdain for Elgar is not surprising.

In his preface to the 1882 edition of *Sesame and Lilies*, Ruskin identified his readership as "chiefly . . . young people belonging to the upper, or undistressed middle, classes; who may be supposed to have choice of the objects and command of the industries of their life. It assumes that many of them will be called to occupy responsible positions in the world, and they have leisure, in preparation for these, to play tennis or to read Plato."[91] Ruskin's readers were Arnold's Philistines (with a smattering of Barbarians) and Longfellow's admirers. But the text, as the generous allusions and citations suggest (along with Ruskin's own apology that the third lecture, "The Mystery of Life and the Arts," might read like a sermon), is driven by an underlying religious and theological premise. In this regard it differs markedly from the surface secular character of Arnold's *Culture and Anarchy*.

Ruskin wished that his readers would not waste time with "books of the hour" but those of all time.[92] As with literature, art, too, needed to be of the highest character and quality. The exemplars were Milton and Dante. But the underlying criterion was the artist's motive with respect to the meaning of life and fact of death. "Nothing I have ever said," wrote Ruskin, "is more true or necessary . . . than my strong assertion that the arts can never be right in themselves, unless their motive is right."[93] For Ruskin, aesthetic criteria were tied inextricably to ethical criteria and social imperatives. This included, besides the necessities of life, providing the populace with proper books in aesthetically pleasing form. Such a synthesis of aesthetic judgment and moral claims derived from Ruskin's attachment to a view of life rooted in faith regarding the "ends of life."[94] The highest achievements of life, those that transcended speech and language and lay closest to its mystery, were in the realm of art. Ruskin's Christianity was a religion of charity and compassion in which the greatest and highest of gifts was the possibility of realizing the "strength of England" by turning a new generation's "intellect from dispute of words to discernment of things."[95] That power of discernment lay in the cultivation of an aesthetic sensibility.

Ruskin called not for aestheticism, but for using the moral character and formal properties of art on behalf of humanity. More specifically, the arts could prosper only "when they had true purpose, and were devoted to the proclamation of divine truth or law."[96] The enemies of moral progress were practical men, men of the present, practiced in business but tone deaf to the deeper essence of life and the imagination. Art, and notably music— forms of expression that transcended language—were for Ruskin the instruments of moral edification, and therefore a force for the creation of a more just social order, superior to politics and organized religion. The arts were needed to transform the everyday, from the use of time to the housing and clothing of the populace.

Perhaps the most compelling dimension of Ruskin's influence on Elgar is how the writer's transformation of Christian ideals into a program of aesthetic and moral transformation affected the composer's conception of how one confronts death, the very subject of *Gerontius*. How may one's virtue be judged and one's place in the hereafter determined? Ruskin challenged the individual, particularly the artist, to find hope not in the migration of the soul to heaven but in a Christian spirit here on earth. "Let us, for our lives," wrote Ruskin, "do the work of Men while we bear the form of them, if indeed those lives are *Not* as a vapour and do *Not* vanish away."

> The poets and prophets, the wise men, and the scribes, though they have told us nothing about a life to come, have told us much about the life that is now. . . . They have dreamed of mercy, and of justice; they have dreamed of peace and good-will; they have dreamed of labour undisappointed, and of rest undisturbed; they have dreamed of fullness in harvest, and overflowing in store; they have dreamed of wisdom in council, and of providence in law; of gladness of parents and strength of children, and glory of grey hairs.[97]

At first glance, this distinctly non-Catholic theology seems at odds with Elgar's devotion to Catholicism. But it provided precisely the framework by which the ambition of an artist could be reconciled with modern Catholicism, replete with more traditional notions of a divine obligation to act in the world with noble purpose, particularly in the service of one's community. Ruskin's text helps illuminate the attraction of Newman's poem to Catholic and Anglican readers alike, for the story of Gerontius is not one of a saint, and the reward in his dream is not heaven. Here, the quotation from Ruskin that Elgar used is telling:

This is the best of me; for the rest, I ate, and drank, and slept, loved, and hated, like another; my life was as the vapour, and is not; but *this* I saw and knew: this, if anything of mine, is worth your memory.[98]

Gerontius is an Everyman figure who, when faced with death, transcends his fear. The listeners to Elgar's version (in which, as one scholar has put it, "Elgar's relentless focus on Gerontius' humanity is clearly seen") develop sympathy for Gerontius's character and spirit as emblematic of an admirable but flawed mortal.[99] General Gordon's own devotion to the poem helped spread its fame. Newman admired Gordon and was moved by the importance the poem held for the general, who seemed to have lived his life for his nation, without fear, "always on his deathbed," acting as if each day would be his last.[100] In the dream, the fate of Gerontius's soul is not tragic. Purgatory is not timeless damnation, and hell is robbed of much of its terror.

Indeed, Elgar's setting of the poem is curiously subversive, for it leaves readers and listeners with a profound sense of admiration for the manner in which Gerontius understood and approached the prospect of death. The implicit theology is that the spirit of God is present in the living individual. That spirit lends the conduct of one's life, including courage in the face of death in full knowledge of one's imperfections, an aspect of the divine. The grace of God becomes linked to the manner in which God's presence has resided in one's spirit during life, a notion that for the artist implied the presence of a Ruskin-like moral motive behind the achievement of worldly ends on behalf of humankind. Elgar's version places the greatest weight on Gerontius's dream experience *prior* to death. As Elgar told his friend A. J. Jaeger, "I imagined Gerontius to be a man like us, not a Priest or a Saint, but a *sinner*, a repentant one of course but still no end of a *worldly man* in his life, & now brought to book."[101] The music, in the best sense of Ruskin's admonitions, was in Elgar's terms "a good, healthy full-blooded romantic, remembered worldliness, so to speak. It is, I imagine, much more difficult to tear one's self away from a well-to-do world than from a cloister."[102]

Although Elgar spent considerable time researching the sources for his oratorios *The Apostles* and *The Kingdom* and relied on both Anglican and Catholic experts and collaborators, his views were hardly idiosyncratic; rather, they mirrored the views and influence of Cardinal Newman. The allure of Catholicism for Newman rested in its fundamental objectivity. He had left the Anglican Church because he rejected the basic claim of the evangelicals. There was not, indeed, a justification by faith alone: an individual could not simply receive Christ through personal experience directly through Scripture and thus achieve a state of grace. There was, for Newman and other converts, an objectivity to the fundamental tenets of Christianity, an objectivity that had been tested by time and by the continuity of a community. The Catholic Church represented that historic, communal, and doctrinal legitimacy and authority.

Furthermore, the historic, organic development of Christ's presence on earth in the form of a universal body of the faithful placed the community, not the individual, in the center. The laws governing the expression of faith were shared. In that regard, the centrality of the Eucharist was contingent on the equally potent assumption that the community of the faithful, given its size and power, demanded and possessed legitimate leadership. The Protestant belief in a personal reading of Scripture was no adequate surrogate for the centrality of the clergy as the sole representatives of doctrine. To Newman, there was an objectivity inherent in the primacy of the clergy, an objectivity earned and proven by the traditions of ascetic discipline and monasticism.

The basic notions of authority, community, and the individual's place in it mirrored Elgar's own aesthetic. The nature of art was not merely about individual achievement but also about the successful dissemination of normative criteria. The implicit individualism associated with the evangelical cause did not appeal to a composer who believed that through his hard work and discipline he had become a legitimate heir to a great tradition whose aesthetic authority could not be challenged. Despite a virtual absence of formal training (with the exception of piano lessons early in his life and violin studies with Adolphe Pollitzer), Elgar owed his authority and station to ascetic discipline, loyalty to universalism, and the organic continuity of compositional practice. His legitimacy derived from the acceptance of a great tradition in the art of music that paralleled the objective doctrinal and communitarian continuity of the Catholic Church.

Although much has been written about the liability Elgar's Catholicism posed for his career, the fact is that despite his occasional protestations to the contrary it did not place an insurmountable barrier in his path. Although his oratorios stuck to the notion of a single Catholic Church, his texts consistently maintained a position that would not offend the Anglican majority. Furthermore, he never veered toward a glorification of Rome, instead placing the center of his credo in a patriotism not dissimilar to Newman's. His synthesis of modernity and loyalty to Catholicism agreed with the temper of his times.[103] In the wake of the debate over papal infallibility, a strain of Catholic thought developed in England that resisted the extreme authoritarian and mystical sides of the Catholic experience. It was this modernized, liberal Catholicism of the late nineteenth century with which Elgar felt most comfortable.

Amid all this lay the central theme of *Gerontius*: divine presence resides in the living human being and is expressed in the conduct of one's life. Though death offers liberation, the hope for grace rests in the extent to which the divine presence is revealed in one's life and character. This was not a Lutheran doctrine of good works but was distinct in requiring adherence to objective norms and doctrines validated by a community, not attained through the subjective experience of a personalized encounter with Christ. The making of art was one means for an individual to realize the ideal. Aesthetic norms suggested the possibility of divine sanction and required a resonant response from a universal community. In this regard, Elgar's musical achievement qualified. The implicit religious foundation of his compositional practice, rooted in history, authority, tradition, and measurable by the assent of the community, also explains Elgar's affinity for the Pre-Raphaelite painters.

Painting: The Realization of the Imagined Ideal

The movement known as Pre-Raphaelite burst on the English scene in 1849. The painters of the group, much like the members of the Oxford Movement and the Cambridge Apostles, constituted themselves as a brotherhood. As was the case with similar associations of intellectuals and artists of that generation, the group was held together by a spiritual and intellectual idealism critical of inherited eighteenth-century pieties. A cold rationalism, a disregard of the organic character of history, a resistance to acknowledging the limitations of human action, an arrogance toward tradition, and an all-too-radical individualism all came under scrutiny. Pre-Raphaelite ideology and the aesthetic consequences and reception of their art in Edward Elgar's lifetime make their work a key to understanding the composer.

It was not so much the brotherhood, the idealization of friendship, the use of religious imagery and symbolism from the pre-Reformation past, or the homoerotic underpinnings of the Pre-Raphaelite brotherhood that formed the basis of affinity for the adult Elgar. Rather, it was a close personal link. Alice Stuart-Wortley, Elgar's "Windflower," was John Everett Millais's daughter. In 1903, she gave Elgar an engraving of her father's portrait of Cardinal Newman (see figure 1).[104]

Like the Pre-Raphaelites, and consistent with Longfellow's didactic ambitions, Elgar was drawn to premodern subject matter ranging from Caractacus and King Olaf to Jean Froissart. In these contexts, the underpinnings of the music were idealized versions of history. Elgar's intent was not so

Figure 1. John Everett Millais, *Portrait of Cardinal Newman*, 1881.

much to regenerate myth (in the Wagnerian sense) as to create a symbiosis of realism and normative aesthetics. The compositional strategy, as
Jaeger's pamphlets on *The Apostles* and *The Kingdom* suggest, was to use
the Wagnerian leitmotif.[105] In this way Elgar could establish musical signifiers whose repetition and audible transformation within a complex fabric
helped the listener achieve a sense of representation and narration. Clearly

the musician, unlike the novelist or the painter, possessed no easy instrument of correspondence with reality. But Elgar's ambivalence about the effort to create parallels notwithstanding, he did adapt the model set by Wagner, who successfully reached a wide public—precisely Arnold's Philistines—with a musical drama that combined so-called normative aesthetic values with narrative accessibility.[106]

Painting more than music has a readily available capacity to manipulate the illusion of realism. But in the hands of the Pre-Raphaelites, as Ruskin argued on their behalf, aesthetic norms (of the sort argued in Germany by Johann Joachim Winckelmann) were applied to a reconstructed past and tradition, whether of antiquity or the Middle Ages. The choice of symbolic, mythic, and religious subject matter cast in a distinctly premodern manner stood in stark contrast to the genre painting and portraiture typical of eighteenth-century painting. Furthermore, the Pre-Raphaelites construed realism in a way that was strikingly historical, cultivating techniques that suggested the refined craftsmanship of the medieval masters, eschewing even the use of perspective and depth.

Elgar's pride in his command of form and his attention to detail, particularly in orchestration, mirrors the extreme attention to illustrative detail in the painting of the Pre-Raphaelites. A poignant example of this was Elgar's admiring comments and advice he sent to Parry concerning the latter's *The Vision of Life*. Parry responded that the struggle to achieve aesthetic perfection in the realization of a work of art reminded him of Millais's own struggles.[107]

At the core of the Pre-Raphaelite project was the idealization of reality. In Elgar's favorite, Millais's *Isabella*, from 1849 (figure 2), a representation of Keats's poem (later set to music in a brilliant tone poem by Frank Bridge in which musical gestures suggest and narrate the emotional intensity of the poem's story), the quite modern, almost hyperrealistic gestures, faces, and attitudes are striking.[108] So, too, is the idealized meticulousness with which the wallpaper and fabrics are realized. The idealization is communicated in a manner sharply divergent from eighteenth-century genre and landscape painting by the use of vivid color and the refinement of the delineation. Realism is not only transcended, but idealized: something in *Isabella* even approaches later painterly movements such as Magical Realism and Surrealism. This effort to transfigure realism through idealization and meticulous exaggeration is paralleled by Elgar's musical strategy, which employs complex norms of absolute musical form and technique to elevate both program and choral music, thereby edifying the broad public he wished to reach.

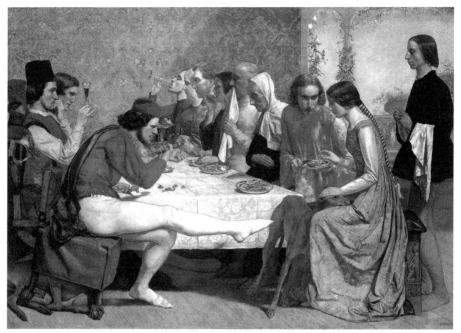

Figure 2. John Everett Millais, *Isabella,* 1849.

Millais and his fellow Pre-Raphaelites chose subject matter that was imaginary, symbolic, or religious rather than quotidian or patently historical. But the core of believability was required, as were the illusion of a direct contact between picture and viewer and the effacement of the painter's individuality. These goals are analogous to the immediate identification with and comprehensibility of musical communication, evident in the transparency and formal clarity of the leitmotifs so dear to Elgar. As William Michael Rossetti observed in 1903:

> A leading doctrine with the Pre-Raphaelites . . . was that it is highly inexpedient for a painter, occupied with an ideal or poetical subject, to portray his personages from the ordinary hired models; and that on the contrary he ought to look out for living people who, by refinement of character and aspect, may be supposed to have some affinity with those personages—and, when he has found such people to paint from, he ought, with substantial though not slavish fidelity, to represent them as they are.[109]

This helps explain Elgar's use of programs that implied an ideal or poetical subject for music—from Caractacus to Falstaff—and his transformation of them into music, by adapting, following Strauss's example, musically strategic evocations of realism, without slavish imitation but with contemporary, almost modern, authenticity. This connection between normative idealism and realism reconciles Elgar's avowed allegiance to absolute music and his consistent reliance on idealized nonmusical subject matter (whether that subject matter was religious or intimately personal) as a framework.

Religion was a key subject matter for the Pre-Raphaelites, as it was for Elgar. With his characterizations of Judas and Mary Magdalene in *The Apostles*, the mix of realism with aesthetic idealism shows his debt not only to Longfellow but also to the Pre-Raphaelites. The painterly equivalent of Elgar's *Apostles* is Millais's *Christ in the House of His Parents* (figure 3). In this painting, all the elements—realism, idealization, and normative aesthetic craftsmanship of a traditional manner taken to the most minute detail—can be seen. The connection to Elgar is also theological. *Christ in the House of His Parents* was linked to Anglo-Catholicism. Millais spent time at Oxford and was associated with the Tractarians, among them Newman. The narrative of *Christ in the House of His Parents* reveals the influence of Edward Bouverie Pusey as well as the Tractarian and Roman Catholic emphasis

Figure 3. John Everett Millais, *Christ in the House of His Parents*, 1849–50.

on the sacrament as reflective of the sacred memory of Christ's physical suffering, his bleeding. The necessity of infant baptism and the receipt of the sacrament from a priesthood separated from everyday life, in a monastic discipline descended from the apostles, is signaled by the wound in the hand of the young Jesus near the center of the canvas, suggestive of the wounds he would later receive on the cross, which is being washed away in the presence of his mother. This emphasis on sacrament and priestly authority, framed with a decisive role for Mary, transmitted through tradition by the historical continuity of Christ's followers, was central not only to the Tractarians but, as Newman observed, also led logically to Catholicism and stood in contrast to the doctrines of justification by faith alone and the subjective response to Scripture characteristic of Protestantism.[110]

Millais was not the only Pre-Raphaelite painter to interest Elgar and his wife. Alice Elgar, in a classic Longfellow-like response, was inspired by Edward Burne-Jones's *The Golden Stairs* (figure 4) to write a poem of her own.[111] Once again, the painting represents the real in the ideal: one of the women it depicts is the mother of Alice Stuart-Wortley.[112] Burne-Jones's *Ascension*, a stained-glass window at St. Philip's Cathedral in Birmingham (figure 5), was admired by Elgar, who conducted a performance of *The Apostles* there. Though Burne-Jones also came from Oxford and was influenced by the spirit of the Oxford Movement, what distinguishes him from Millais but suggests an affinity with Elgar's musical strategies is his emphasis on formal design. The focus in Millais is on a searing wealth of minute detail, with a stark realism in the psychological character of the figures, their posture, and faces, while in Burne-Jones the stress is on the compositional structure. His faces are strangely distant and formal, their gaze hypnotic and depersonalized within a commanding architectural design. Elgar's resistance to excessive subjectivity, his inclination to hide the personal beneath a compelling aesthetic framework, and his capacity to generate melody that permitted the listener to interject his or her own subjective meaning parallel Burne-Jones's removed and neutral representation of the human figure and face.

Both Millais and Burne-Jones sought their inspiration in pre-Renaissance painting, but in Burne-Jones's version the overall aesthetic structure was foregrounded as a vehicle for subjective appropriation rather than minute observation. In Millais's canvases, the detail is forcefully realized. In Elgar's music, the melodic material and rhetorical sweep have lent themselves to such disparate readings precisely because of their place in an overwhelming large-scale musical structure. The sections of *The Apostles* and *The Kingdom* that have attracted attention (the Virgin Mary's "The Sun goeth down" in *The Kingdom*, the scenes with Judas in *The Apostles*) are more like

Figure 4. Edward Burne-Jones, *The Golden Stairs*, 1880.

Figure 5. Edward Burne-Jones, *Ascension*, stained-glass window,
St. Philip's Cathedral, Birmingham.

Millais, while the Prelude to *The Apostles* and the setting of the Lord's Prayer in *The Kingdom* are suggestive of Burne-Jones. Indeed, the realism of Millais finds its analog in the manner in which the characters in Elgar's later oratorios assume a rich, psychologically powerful specificity and therefore a plausible contemporaneousness, often defined by Elgar's own autobiographical projections.[113]

This attempt to link Elgar with the strategies of the Pre-Raphaelites leads back to the centrality of Catholic culture in Elgar's aesthetic. The emphasis on authority and history, and on the community of the faithful, Newman's vision of the legitimacy of the Catholic Church as a singular and historic vehicle of doctrine, with its priests and emphasis on sacrament, reflect themselves in Elgar's efforts to create a community of listeners, forge solidarity through art, and use the time-honored historic practices and models of composition as the framework with which to express his personal voice.

It is ironic that, for all of his Englishness, the one painting Elgar used as a direct religious inspiration for his music was by the Russian painter

Figure 6. Ivan Kramskoi, *Christ in the Wilderness,* 1872.

Ivan Kramskoi. While visiting Charles Vincent Gorton, the Anglican canon who advised Elgar on the texts of *The Apostles* and *The Kingdom*, Elgar saw "my ideal picture of the Lonely Christ as I have *tried* (and tried hard) to realise . . . the Character" in Kramskoi's *Christ in the Wilderness* (figure 6).[114] Both Elgar's comments and the painting reveal the essence of the composer's Ruskin-like aesthetic transformation of a religious ideal, in a manner consistent with the ideology of the Pre-Raphaelites. Although Kramskoi does not affect a premodern painterly surface and color, as his English contemporaries did (the perspective is indebted to Renaissance and eighteenth-century practices), the rigorous attention to formal structure and detail is present. As with Millais, the figure is psychologically present as real and human. The face is contemporary. So, too, is the barren landscape. However, the pose of the figure and his gaze represent an aesthetic idealization of suffering, dignity, contemplation, and humility. Elgar recognized in Kramskoi his own usage of modern means—the orchestra, the harmonic practice, and the tradition of nineteenth-century symphonic and oratorio models, and yet the use of craft and structure, as in Longfellow, to distance the artist's subjectivity through the artifice of aesthetic tradition. Christ is real, but he seems to be an everyman, a real human figure whom we can personally identify as both human and divine. He is real and ideal, modern and timeless, particular and general. The viewer of the painting, like the listener and participant in Elgar's music, is elevated by identification, through art, all consonant with a noble, idealistic tradition.

In this manner, Arnold's project and Ruskin's aspirations found their medium in Elgar. If the ideology was the modern but loyal Catholicism of Newman, the technical strategy of composition was suggested by the example of Longfellow. In the end, Elgar's ambition was at one with his times. He believed that although a work of music would in some philosophical sense always be "great" if it remained buried and hidden from view, the justification for artistic "inspiration" and the hard work required to realize his plans was to find "its proper place educating, helping and improving mankind."[115] As a public art that demanded participation through composition, performance, listening, and critical debate, music possessed a power to do so. The need for music to join in the larger project of elevating the citizenry through aesthetic means seemed, to Elgar, particularly acute in Britain, where music had for so long ignored them. The object of cultural transformation was, for Elgar, "practical everyday life." The time had come not only for a musician to "discourse usefully on his time" but also to act as composer and advocate, bringing the authoritative and historic traditions and norms of musical art to bear on that imperative in a distinctively English manner.[116]

This synthesis of patriotic fervor, humanitarian idealism, and conceit in the civic power of great art music defined Elgar's personality and his pursuit of success and fame. But most important, his vision of the vocation of the composer as reformer of society and legislator of community through musical culture shaped the fundamental character of his works. Like Longfellow's poetry, Elgar's music (its suppressed autobiographical subtexts notwithstanding) drew his countrymen into a widespread, shared public expression of sentiment that continues to inform the composer's lasting appeal.

NOTES

1. This essay is indebted to the immense literature on Elgar, the history of English music from Elgar's time forward, and the voluminous scholarship on English history and culture in the nineteenth and early twentieth centuries. Therefore only a representative sample of the bibliography is possible. As is anyone who writes about Elgar, I am indebted to the scholarship of Jerrold Northrop Moore, particularly *Edward Elgar: A Creative Life* (New York: Oxford University Press, 1984); *Spirit of England: Edward Elgar in His World* (London: Heinemann, 1984); *Elgar: Child of Dreams* (London: Faber and Faber, 2004); *Letters of a Lifetime* (Oxford: Clarendon Press, 1990); and *Elgar and His Publishers: Letters of a Creative Life*, 2 vols. (Oxford: Clarendon Press, 1987). Robert Anderson's *Elgar* (New York: Schirmer Books, 1993); Michael Kennedy's *The Life of Elgar* (Cambridge: Cambridge University Press, 2004); and Diana M. McVeagh's *Edward Elgar, His Life and Music* (1955; repr., Westport, Conn.: Hyperion, 1979) were valuable, as was Stewart R. Craggs's *Edward Elgar: A Source Book* (Aldershot: Scolar Press, 1995). I also wish to thank the following individuals for their help: Byron Adams, Christopher Gibbs, Deirdre d'Albertis, Lynne Meloccaro, Paul De Angelis, Jane Smith, and Irene Zedlacher.

2. The phrase *"das Land ohne Musik"* appeared in the title of a book (not about music, ironically) by Oscar Schmitz published in Germany during World War I. Consider the condescending and perfunctory treatments of Elgar and English music in leading German histories of music written in the early decades of the twentieth century, particularly those by Walter Niemann, *Die Musik der Gegenwart* (Berlin: Schuster & Loeffler, 1913); Heinrich Köstlin, *Geschichte der Musik im Umriss*, ed. Wilibald Nagel (Liepzig: Breitkopf & Härtel, 1910); and Karl Storck, *Die Musik der Gegenwart* (Stuttgart: Muth'sche Verlagshandlung, 1919); all from the early decades of the twentieth century.

3. One facile explanation derives from England's economic and political prominence. The celebratory, self-congratulatory culture that requires public display (that is, the contrast between literature and musical composition and performance) may not lend itself to being seen by subordinate nations as exotic, attractive, or comforting. Furthermore, the position of power renders the imperial power a net consumer, a culture that borrows freely from others as a right without self-doubt.

4. Charles Villiers Stanford had an international career in the 1890s before Elgar burst on the scene at the end of the decade. See Jeremy Dibble, *Charles Villiers Stanford: Man and Musician* (Oxford: Oxford University Press, 2002).

5. On public music making in midcentury England, see Michael Musgrave, *The Musical Life of the Crystal Palace* (New York: Cambridge University Press, 1995). Perhaps the best source on the character of concert life from the very end of the nineteenth century through Elgar's lifetime and well into the late twentieth century is the exhaustive study of England's major artists management firm in Christopher Fifield, *Ibbs and Tillet: The Rise and Fall of a Musical Empire* (Aldershot: Ashgate, 2005).

6. See Ralph Vaughan Williams's early essays, first compiled in the early 1930s under the title *National Music*, particularly "Should Music Be National?" and "Some Conclusions," in which the composer squares a circle, so to speak, by arguing for the evolution of distinct national qualities through an analogy to the origin of California wine in French vines, and by claiming that universality in music (e.g., the case of Wagner's *Die Meistersinger*) can be achieved only by embracing the particular and inventing a persuasive voice for national sentiment. See Vaughan Williams, *National Music and Other Essays*, 2nd ed. (Oxford: Clarendon Press, 1996), 1–11, 62–73.

7. Ibid., 248–55.

8. See David Cannadine, "The Context, Performance and Meaning of Ritual: The English Monarchy and the 'Invention of Tradition', c. 1820–1977," in *The Invention of Tradition*, ed. Eric Hobsbawm and Terence Ranger (1983; repr., Cambridge: Cambridge University Press, 2006), 130, 136–37, 144. It can be argued that Elgar's eclectic appropriation of foreign influences reflected a particularly nineteenth-century English, imperial arrogance, the right of empire to use in a syncretic fashion the achievements of other cultures.

9. See John Caldwell, *The Oxford History of English Music*, vol. 2 (Oxford: Oxford University Press, 1999), 265–66, 291–94, 325–30, 556.

10. See the elaborate effort in J. P. E. Harper-Scott, *Edward Elgar, Modernist* (Cambridge: Cambridge University Press, 2006).

11. Edward Elgar, *A Future for English Music and Other Lectures*, ed. Percy M. Young (London: Dennis Dobson, 1968), 207. Young used italics to denote Elgar's handwritten insertions into the original typescript of the lectures he delivered at the University of Birmingham in 1905.

12. Elgar's symphonies need to be placed in the context of the quite astonishing output of English symphonic music, particularly in the early twentieth century. See Jürgen Schaarwächter, *Die britische Sinfonie, 1914–1945* (Cologne: Dohr, 1995).

13. Elgar, *A Future for English Music*, 207. Elgar probably did not realize that Strauss had tried his hand at symphonic form as a young man. It is not clear what he, writing in 1905, made of the *Symphonia Domestica* (1903) and might later think of *An Alpine Symphony*, completed in 1915.

14. Extensive research by historians and musicologists into the state of England's musical culture during Elgar's lifetime makes plain that, owing to the country's dynamic economic development both at home and throughout the empire, England could boast a middle-class public with levels of literacy and culture sufficient to constitute one of the most important in Europe. The evidence is visible as early as the 1790s when Haydn made his famous trips to London. From that point on, England became a major destination for European artists, performers, and composers. Furthermore, England was a major producer and consumer of musical instruments and during the nineteenth century developed a lively publishing industry for music. By the mid-nineteenth century, as English novels indicate, particularly those by Jane Austen and George Eliot, an admirable level of amateurism and engagement with music was widespread beyond London among both the gentry and the middle class. It is for that reason that Mendelssohn found such a congenial response in England. The English choral tradition, notably in Birmingham, resulted in significant commissions of music, including Mendelssohn's *Elijah* and Dvořák's Requiem. The extent of concert life and its attendant audience is what brought Hans Richter to

England and made England perhaps the most rewarding venue for a performer of Joseph Joachim's stature. In short, musical culture was part of the business of culture. For a significant population in England that was literate and had sufficient leisure, a taste for music was integrated into established norms of personal development and domestic life. See Cyril Ehrlich, *The Piano: A History*, rev. ed. (Oxford: Clarendon Press, 1990), chaps. 2, 5, 8, 9, 10; Donald Burrows, "Victorian England: An Age of Expansion," in *The Late Romantic Era: From the Mid-19th Century to World War I*, ed. Jim Samson (Englewood Cliffs, N.J.: Prentice Hall, 1991), 266–94; G. R. Searle, *A New England? Peace and War, 1886–1918* (Oxford: Clarendon Press, 2004), chap. 15; K. Theodore Hoppen, *The Mid-Victorian Generation, 1846–1886* (Oxford: Clarendon Press, 1998), chap. 11.

15. As the first Richard Peyton Professor of Music, Elgar delivered a course of lectures at the University of Birmingham during 1905–6. See Elgar, *A Future for English Music*.

16. See Matthew Riley, "Rustling Reeds and Lofty Pines: Elgar and the Music of Nature," *19th-Century Music* 26, no. 2 (Fall 2002): 155–77.

17. See Jeffrey Richards, *Imperialism and Music, England 1876–1953* (Manchester: Manchester University Press), chap. 3; Meirion Hughes, *The English Musical Renaissance and the Press, 1850–1914: Watchmen of Music* (Aldershot: Ashgate, 2002), chap. 7; Meirion Hughes and Robert Stradling, *The English Musical Renaissance, 1840–1940: Constructing a National Music*, 2nd ed. (Manchester: Manchester University Press, 2001); and Stephen Hinton's review of the 1993 first edition of Hughes and Stradling's book in *Journal of Modern History* 67, no. 3 (September 1995): 710–12. See also Cannadine, "Context, Performance and Meaning of Ritual," 101–64.

18. Given Elgar's energetic dabbling as a chemist and his enthusiasm for recording and broadcasting—let alone his evident patriotism for imperial England—the emphasis on the personal and rural still requires the "other" Elgar to be understood and not merely de-emphasized.

19. See Byron Adams, "The 'Dark Saying' of the Enigma: Homoeroticism and the Elgarian Paradox," *19th-Century Music* 23, no. 3 (Spring 2000): 218–35; and the prologue in Kennedy, *Life of Elgar*.

20. See Ronald Hyam, *Empire and Sexuality: The English Experience* (Manchester: Manchester University Press, 1992); Richard Dellamora, *Masculine Desire: The Sexual Politics of Victorian Aestheticism* (Chapel Hill: University of North Carolina Press, 1990); Karen Chase and Michael Levenson, *The Spectacle of Intimacy: A Public Life for the Victorian Family* (Princeton, N.J.: Princeton University Press, 2000); Martha Vicinus, ed., *Suffer and Be Still: Women in the Victorian Age* (Bloomington: Indiana University Press, 1972); Richard Dellamora, ed., *Victorian Sexual Dissidence* (Chicago: University of Chicago Press, 1999); Graham Robb, *Strangers: Homosexual Love in the Nineteenth Century* (New York: W. W. Norton, 2003); Thomas Laqueur, *Making Sex: Body and Gender from the Greeks to Freud* (Cambridge, Mass.: Harvard University Press, 1990), chaps. 5 and 6; and David Hilliard, "UnEnglish and Unmanly: Anglo-Catholicism and Homosexuality," *Victorian Studies* 25, no. 2 (Winter 1982): 181–210.

21. Elgar, *A Future for English Music*, 57.

22. See Nalini Ghuman Gwynne, "Elephants and Moghuls, Contraltos and G-Strings: How Elgar Got His Englishness," in "India in the English Musical Imagination, 1890–1940," Ph.D. diss., University of California, Berkeley, 2003, 109–86. In this context, one should also note the establishment of the Boy Scouts; see Michael Rosenthal, *The Character Factory: Baden-Powell's Boy Scouts and the Imperatives of Empire* (New York: Pantheon Books, 1986).

23. For a revision of the claims that Elgar's place in English music declined, see John Gardiner, "The Reception of Sir Edward Elgar 1918–c.1934: A Reassessment," *Twentieth-Century English History* 9, no. 3 (1998): 370–95.

24. Byron Adams has noted that for Britten the decade of the 1950s was not an easy time to be homosexual. The real improvement in England came in the mid-1960s. See

also chap. 1, "Carrying Music to the Masses," in Paul Kildea's *Selling Britten: Music and the Market Place* (New York: Oxford University Press, 2002), 9–41.

25. Craggs, *Elgar: A Source Book*, 58, 60, 61, 64.

26. For general accounts of the contested issues, see *The Mid-Victorian Generation*, chaps. 12–13; and Searle, *A New England?*, pt. 4. With particular respect to religious debates, see Duncan Forbes, *The Liberal Anglican Idea of History* (Cambridge: Cambridge University Press, 1952); and Michael Wheeler, *The Old Enemies: Catholic and Protestant in Nineteenth-Century English Culture* (Cambridge: Cambridge University Press, 2006). Several points need to be made regarding Elgar's status as a Catholic. First, as Wheeler's book makes clear, there was no shortage of anti-Catholic sentiment in late-nineteenth-century England. Nonetheless, it is safe to say that prejudice against Catholics did not prevent Elgar from achieving enormous success. That achievement may be due in part to the success of his oratorios, which at one and the same time celebrated the profoundly Catholic allegiance to the historic community of the body faithful and the traditions with which it was associated. Second, even though Elgar's career may not have been damaged by his status as a Catholic, he never tired of expressing the belief that his Catholicism was a disadvantage he had to battle constantly. Elgar's success in communicating with the broad spectrum of the English audience should not in any way minimize the importance of the ongoing tensions that confessional differences generated socially, politically, and culturally in England during his lifetime.

27. Elgar golfed with one of Arnold's sons and in 1905 worked on setting the poet's "Empedocles on Etna," returning to it briefly in 1927. Dedicated to Muriel Foster, a fragment called "Callicles" survives. See Moore, *Edward Elgar: A Creative Life*, 177; and Craggs, *Elgar: A Source Book*, 78.

28. Moore, *Edward Elgar: A Creative Life*, 693–94.

29. On Stanford and Parry and their relationship to Elgar, see Jeremy Dibble's *C. Hubert Parry, His Life and Music* (Oxford: Oxford University Press 1992), as well as his *Charles Villiers Stanford*.

30. Matthew Arnold, *Culture and Anarchy*, ed. R. H. Super (Ann Arbor: University of Michigan Press, 1980), 168. On the context of Arnold's views and his relationship to Newman, see David J. DeLaura, *Hebrew and Hellene in Victorian England: Newman, Arnold, and Pater* (Austin: University of Texas Press, 1969), chaps. 1–9.

31. Arnold, *Culture and Anarchy*, 169.

32. Ibid., 168, 165.

33. Ibid., 167.

34. See Max Weber, *The Protestant Ethic and the Spirit of Capitalism*, trans. Talcott Parsons (New York: Scribner, 1958).

35. Arnold, *Culture and Anarchy*, 165.

36. Ibid., 167.

37. Ibid., 169.

38. Ibid., 181. See also the account of Arnold in Martin J. Weiner, *English Culture and the Decline of the Industrial Spirit, 1850–1860* (New York: Cambridge University Press, 1981), 35–37.

39. Arnold, *Culture and Anarchy*, 184.

40. Ibid.

41. Ibid., 173.

42. Ibid., 140.

43. On the Oxford Movement, see Peter B. Nockles, *The Oxford Movement in Context: Anglican High Churchmanship, 1760–1857* (Cambridge: Cambridge University Press, 1994).

44. See Bernarr Rainbow, *The Choral Revival in the Anglican Church, 1839–1872* (New York: Oxford University Press, 1970).

45. Arthur Sullivan, "About Music," in *Sir Arthur Sullivan: Life Story, Letters and Reminiscences*, ed. Arthur Lawrence (New York: Herbert S. Stone, 1899), 271.

46. Sullivan, "About Music," 271–72.

47. Elgar, *A Future for English Music*, 163.

48. In this sense Elgar exploited the residues of an eighteenth-century notion of the naive artist, whose gift and artistry were somehow superior by being spontaneous and bereft of culture and cultivation. By the mid-nineteenth century this sympathy had largely vanished, rendering that judgment either condescending or derogatory. See Hughes, *The English Musical Renaissance and the Press*, 162–89.

49. Bernard Shaw, "Sir Edward Elgar," in *Shaw's Music*, vol. 3 (New York: Dodd, Mead & Company, 1981), 727. The essay was originally published in 1920.

50. As Anderson points out, Elgar consciously crafted the first 1896 oratorio, *The Light of Life*, to appeal to the established tastes of the audience. At the same time, in the spirit of Arnold, he used fashion to edify. A fugue was required and Elgar produced one that was "not a 'barn-door' fugue, but one with an independent accompaniment. There's a bit of a canon, too, and in short, I hope there's enough counterpoint to give the real English religious respectability!" Quoted in Anderson, *Elgar*, 207–8. See also the extensive discussion of the oratorio culture, narrative structures, and Elgar's approach, from *The Light of Life* onward, in Charles Edward McGuire, *Elgar's Oratorios: The Creation of an Epic Narrative* (Aldershot: Ashgate, 2002), particularly the first three chapters.

51. Elgar, *A Future for English Music*, 33.

52. Ibid., 49, 51.

53. Consider Elgar's lavish praise for the leaders and citizens of Düsseldorf in contrast to their English counterparts. "Our public men" he wrote, "are unmusical" whereas in Düsseldorf, an orchestra is viewed as an "asset," and the "annual loss" is not minded since music "is a feature of the town life." Ibid., 257.

54. Ibid., 211, 225.

55. Ibid., 223.

56. Ibid., 133–43.

57. On Elgar's relationship to the BBC and recording, see Ronald Taylor, "Music in the Air: Elgar and the BBC," in *Edward Elgar: Music and Literature*, ed. Raymond Monk (Aldershot: Scolar Press, 1993), 327–55. See also Timothy Day, "Elgar and Recording," 184–94; and Jenny Doctor, "Broadcasting's Ally: Elgar and the BBC," 195–203, both in *The Cambridge Companion to Elgar*, ed. Daniel Grimley and Julian Rushton (Cambridge: Cambridge University Press, 2004).

58. See Moore, *Elgar: Child of Dreams*, 10–11; Moore, *Edward Elgar: A Creative Life*, 43, 45, 57, 60–62, 64, 70–72; Kennedy, *Life of Elgar*, 13–17; Anderson, *Elgar*, 4–13; and Shaw, "Sir Edward Elgar," 725–28.

59. Elgar, *Letters of a Lifetime*, 81. Elgar's Germanophilism was pronounced, as was his debt to Richter. Both sentiments suffered during World War I. On the Elgar–Richter relationship, see Christopher Fifield, *True Artist and True Friend: A Biography of Hans Richter* (New York: Oxford University Press, 1993).

60. Elgar, *Letters of a Lifetime*, 39.

61. Elgar, *Elgar and His Publishers: Letters of a Creative Life*, 2:828–29.

62. Quoted in Moore, *Edward Elgar: A Creative Life*, 795.

63. Ibid., 65.

64. Ibid.

65. See Michael Beckerman's "Dvořák's 'New World' Largo and 'The Song of Hiawatha,'" *19th-Century Music* 16, no. 1 (Summer 1992): 35–48; and his *New Worlds of Dvořák: Searching in America for the Composer's Inner Life* (New York: W. W. Norton, 2003).

66. Christoph Irmscher, *Longfellow Redux* (Urbana and Chicago: University of Illinois Press, 2006).

67. Ibid., 3.

68. Ibid., 50.

69. Interestingly, Longfellow had a portrait of Liszt and parts of Dante's coffin in his study in Cambridge.

70. On Longfellow's connection to Catholicism, see Horace Scudder, ed., *The Complete Poetical Works of Henry Wadsworth Longfellow* (1922; repr., Cutchogue, N.Y.: Buccaneer Books, 1993), 361–62.

71. See Burrows, "Victorian England: An Age of Expansion"; and Musgrave, *Musical Life of the Crystal Palace*.

72. Much of Alice's poetry was written before she became Lady Elgar. See Moore, *Edward Elgar: A Creative Life*, 124–27, 141, 181–82, 185, 190, 205, 222, 277–81, 522.

73. Mary Louise Kete, quoted in Irmscher, *Longfellow Redux*, 26.

74. It bears repeating, as an encomium, that this account is indebted to Irmscher's brilliant book.

75. See the similar argument made by Michael Pope in *"King Olaf* and the English Choral Tradition," in *Elgar Studies*, ed. Raymond Monk (Aldershot: Scolar Press, 1990), 58–60.

76. Quoted in Brian Trowell, "Elgar's Use of Literature," in *Edward Elgar: Music and Literature*, 197.

77. See Glenn Watkins, *Proof Through the Night: Music and the Great War* (Berkeley: University of California Press, 2003), 42–45. Although Elgar wrote a considerable body of patriotic work before World War I, one thinks of "Carillon" (1914), *Polonia* (1915), *The Spirit of England* (1916), and the Kipling settings, *The Fringes of the Fleet* (1917).

78. Trowell, "Elgar's Use of Literature," 182–326.

79. For a discussion of Ruskin with respect to issues of the redefinition of masculinity and the aesthetic in Elgar's generation, see Dellamora, *Masculine Desire*, chap. 6.

80. See Frank M. Turner, *John Henry Newman: The Challenge to Evangelical Religion* (New Haven, Conn.: Yale University Press, 2002); and John Henry Newman, *Apologia Pro Vita Sua*, ed. David J. DeLaura (New York: W. W. Norton, 1968).

81. See John Henry Newman's *Grammar of Assent*," pt. 2, chap. 9, "The Illative Sense," 270–99; and his *The Idea of University* (Notre Dame, Ind.: University of Notre Dame Press, 1982), esp. 161–81. See also Ian Ker, *John Henry Newman* (New York: Oxford University Press, 1988), 122.

82. See, for example, Hilliard, "UnEnglish and Unmanly: Anglo-Catholicism and Homosexuality."

83. The doctrinal implications of the poem were the subject of lively debate, including the necessity of concessions regarding changes to permit performances in Anglican contexts. See Moore, *Edward Elgar: A Creative Life*, 316–37; Esther R. B. Pese, "A Suggested Background for Newman's 'Dream of Gerontius'," *Modern Philology* 47, no. 2 (November 1949): 108–16; and Mrs. Richard Powell, "The First Performance of 'Gerontius,'" *The Musical Times* 100, no. 1392 (February 1959): 78–80. On *Gerontius*, see also Percy M. Young, *Elgar, Newman, and the Dream of Gerontius: In the Tradition of English Catholicism* (Aldershot: Scolar Press, 1995).

84. Trowell, "Elgar's Use of Literature," 229–32.

85. *Gerontius* had perhaps it greatest Continental success in Düsseldorf, where in 1890, out of a population of 144,000 thousand people, 105,000 were Catholics. On Viennese critical reaction to *Gerontius*, see Sandra McColl, "*Gerontius* in the City of Dreams: Newman, Elgar, and the Viennese Critics," *International Review of the Aesthetics and Sociology of Music* 32, no. 1 (June 2001): 47–64.

86. The quotation comes from the first of these lectures, "Of Kings' Treasuries."

87. John Ruskin, *The Complete Works of John Ruskin*, vol. 18 (London: George Allen, 1905), 34.

88. E. M. Forster, *Howards End* (New York: W. W. Norton, 1997), 38. I want to thank my Bard College colleague, Deirdre d'Albertis, a specialist in Victorian literature, for bringing this passage to my attention in response to an oral presentation of this essay given at a Bard Faculty Seminar in February 2007.

89. See Forster's *Howards End* and his music essays, "The C Minor of That Life" and "Not Listening to Music," in *Two Cheers for Democracy* (London: Edward Arnold, 1951).

90. Forster, "Not Listening to Music," 138.

91. Ruskin, *Complete Works*, 51.

92. Ibid., 60.

93. Ibid., 152.

94. Ibid., 153.

95. Ibid., 186.

96. Ibid., 153.

97. Ibid., 178–79.

98. Ibid., 61.

99. McGuire, *Elgar's Oratorios*, 136.

100. Sheridan Gilley, *Newman and His Age*, 2nd ed. (London: Darton, Longman and Todd, 2003), 430–31.

101. Elgar, *Letters to Publishers*, 1:228.

102. Ibid.

103. Newman was also avid in his interest in music. He played the violin and was particularly devoted to the quartets of Beethoven. See Ian Ker, *John Henry Newman*, 573–74, 610.

104. Anderson, *Elgar*, 65.

105. See A. J. Jaeger's *The Apostles: Analytical and Descriptive Notes* (London: Novello, n.d.); and his *The Kingdom: Analytical and Descriptive Notes* (Borough Green: Novello, n.d.).

106. On the issue of realism as a concept in nineteenth-century music, see Carl Dahlhaus, *Realism in Nineteenth-Century Music*, trans. Mary Whittall (New York: Cambridge University Press, 1985). Even beyond Wagner, rhetorical correspondences in musical practice could form the basis of an analogy to realism if, as in Liszt's tone poems, the structure followed either a literary or pictorial framework.

107. Anderson, *Elgar*, 80.

108. Ibid., 99, 115.

109. Quoted in Elizabeth Prettejohn, *The Art of the Pre-Raphaelites* (Princeton, N.J.: Princeton University Press, 2000), 191.

110. Ibid., 243.

111. Percy M. Young, *Alice Elgar: Enigma of a Victorian Lady* (London: Dobson, 1978), 65.

112. Anderson, *Elgar*, 17–18.

113. See Byron Adams's "Elgar's Later Oratorios. Roman Catholicism, Decadence, and the Wagnerian Dialectic of Shame and Grace," in Grimley and Rushton, *Cambridge Companion to Elgar*, 92–93.

114. Quoted in Moore, *Edward Elgar: A Creative Life*, 401. Kramskoi (1837–87) was a leading St. Petersburg painter and art critic. *Christ in the Wilderness* was bought in 1872 by Pawel Tretyakov and now resides in the Tretyakov Gallery in Moscow. The painting is reproduced in *The Tretyakov Gallery: A Panorama of Russian and Soviet Art* (Leningrad: Aurora Art Publishers, 1983), plate no. 57; see also 335. Anderson refers to this painting (*Elgar*, 59) and gives its proper date but mistakenly identifies it as *The Temptation of Christ*.

115. Elgar, *A Future for English Music*, 33.

116. Ibid., 201.

INDEX

Index

Subject and Name Index

Note: EE stands for Edward Elgar throughout the index

Notes on the Contributors

Byron Adams, professor of composition and musicology at the University of California, Riverside, has been published widely on English music and has broadcast over the BBC. He is co-editor of *Vaughan Williams Essays*, and contributed entries on William Walton and Sylvia Townsend Warner to the second edition of the revised *New Grove Dictionary of Music and Musicians*. His articles, reviews, and essays have appeared in journals such as *19th-Century Music*, *Music and Letters*, and the *John Donne Journal* and have been included in volumes such as *Queer Episodes in Music and Modern Identity* (University of Illinois Press, 2002), *The Cambridge Companion to Elgar* (2004), and *Walt Whitman and Modern Music* (Garland, 2000). In 2000, he was presented with the Philip Brett Award by the American Musicological Society.

Leon Botstein is president and Leon Levy Professor in the Arts and Humanities at Bard College. He is the author of *Judentum und Modernität* (1991) and *Jefferson's Children: Education and the Promise of American Culture* (1997). He is the editor of *The Compleat Brahms* (1999) and *The Musical Quarterly*, as well as coeditor, with Werner Hanak, of *Vienna: Jews and the City of Music, 1870–1938* (2004). The music director of the American and the Jerusalem symphony orchestras, he has recorded works by, among others, Szymanowski, Hartmann, Bruch, Toch, Dohnányi, Bruckner, Chausson, Richard Strauss, Mendelssohn, Popov, Shostakovich, and Liszt for Telarc, CRI, Koch, Arabesque, and New World Records.

Rachel Cowgill is senior lecturer in music and deputy director of the Centre for English Music (LUCEM) at the University of Leeds. Her research focuses on British musical cultures; Mozart reception; Italian opera; and gender, music, and performativity. Her work has been published in the *Journal of the Royal Musical Association*, *Early Music*, *Cambridge Opera Journal*, *Musical Times*, as well as in edited volumes from Ashgate, Berlin Verlag, and Oxford University Press. With Julian Rushton, she co-edited the collection *Europe, Empire, and Spectacle in Nineteenth-Century British Music* (Ashgate, 2006) and, with Peter Holman, *Music in the British Provinces 1690–1914* (Ashgate, forthcoming). With Holman, Cowgill co-edits the book series, Music in Britain, 1600–1900. Cowgill has recently been appointed editor of the *Journal of the Royal Musical Association* and completed a book entitled *Redeeming the Requiem: The Early English Reception of Mozart's Last Work* (Boydell & Brewer, forthcoming).

Sophie Fuller studied music at King's College, London University, where she completed her doctoral thesis, "Women Composers during the British Musical Renaissance, 1880–1918." For ten years she was a lecturer in music at the University of Reading and is the author of *The Pandora Guide to Women Composers: Britain and the United States, 1629–Present* (1994) and co-editor of two collections of essays: with Lloyd Whitesell, *Queer Episodes in Music and Modern Identity* (University of Illinois Press, 2002); and with Nicky Losseff, *The Idea of Music in Victorian Fiction* (Ashgate, 2004). She currently teaches at Trinity College of Music, London, and serves on the editorial board of the journal *twentieth-century music*.

Nalini Ghuman is an assistant professor of music at Mills College. She was awarded a Ph.D. in musicology from the University of California, Berkeley, where she was a Fellow of the Townsend Center for the Humanities. Ghuman was honored with an AMS 50 Alvin Johnson Dissertation Fellowship by the American Musicological Society. She is currently working on a book titled *India in the English Musical Imagination, 1890–1940* and has a chapter in *Western Music and Race* edited by Julie Brown (Cambridge University Press, 2007).

Daniel M. Grimley is senior lecturer/associate professor in music at the University of Nottingham, and has published widely on Scandinavian music, Finnish music, the music of Edward Elgar, and music and landscape. He is editor of the *Cambridge Companion to Sibelius* (2004), and co-editor with Julian Rushton of the *Cambridge Companion to Elgar* (2004). Grimley recently completed a volume titled *Grieg: Music, Landscape and Norwegian Identity* (Boydell & Brewer, 2006). He was one of the organizers of the Elgar conference at Surrey University in April 2002. Future projects include a book on Nielsen and a study of music and landscape in Nordic music, 1890–1930.

Deborah Heckert was awarded a Ph.D. in musicology from Stony Brook University, where her dissertation explored the British revival of the masque in the nineteenth and early twentieth centuries. Her current research focuses on the Victorian music hall, on which subject Heckert has given papers at such conferences as the Annual Meeting of the American

Musicological Society and the Conference of Music in Nineteenth-Century Britain. She has been a recipient of the Ralph Vaughan Williams Fellowship and of a fellowship from the Yale Center for British Art.

Charles Edward McGuire is associate professor of musicology at the Oberlin College Conservatory of Music. His research interests include the music of Edward Elgar and Ralph Vaughn Williams; the oratorio; sight-singing in the nineteenth century (especially the Tonic Sol-fa method); the links between music and politics and philanthropy; music and narrative; and film music. His has published articles in the journals *19th-Century Music* and *The Elgar Society Journal*. McGuire has contributed extended essays to several volumes, including *Vaughan Williams Essays* (Ashgate, 2003), *A Special Flame: The Music of Elgar and Vaughan Williams* (Elgar Editions, 2004), *The Cambridge Companion to Elgar* (2004), *Chorus and Community* (University of Illinois Press, 2006), and *Elgar Studies* (Cambridge University Press, 2007). He is the author of *Elgar's Oratorios: The Creation of an Epic Narrative* (Ashgate, 2000) and *The People's Music: The Curwens, Tonic Sol-fa and Victorian Moral Philanthropy*.

Matthew Riley is lecturer in music at the University of Birmingham, where in 2005 he organized the centenary celebrations of Elgar's appointment as the University's first Professor of Music. He is author of *Edward Elgar and the Nostalgic Imagination* (Cambridge University Press, 2007) and various articles on the composer. His other research interests include music theory and analysis and musical thought in the decades around 1800.

Alison I. Shiel has a degree in music from the University of Aberdeen, Scotland, and a particular interest in the church music of Salzburg in the eighteenth century. She has produced several performing editions of the sacred music of Michael Haydn, and, as research assistant for the celebrated Haydn scholar H. C. Robbins Landon, worked on a complete edition of the Haydn string quartets. In 1996, Shiel's scholarly investigations of the history of the Aberdeen Bach Choir awakened her interest in Charles Sanford Terry and Terry's close friendship with Edward Elgar.

Aidan J. Thomson completed his Ph.D. thesis (a study of English and German reception of Elgar's music before 1914) at Magdalen College, Oxford University, in 2002. He taught at the universities of both Oxford and Leeds before being appointed Lecturer in Music at Queen's University, Belfast, in 2003. He has published articles and book chapters in

19th-Century Music, *The Cambridge Companion to Elgar*, and *Elgar Studies*, and is currently completing a monograph titled *Demythologizing Elgar*. Besides Elgar, his research interests include the Internationale Musikgesellschaft before 1914 and the music of Arnold Bax.